Helmut Neukirchen ·
Kim-Kwang Raymond Choo · Thomas Welsh ·
Raymond Chan
Editors

Digital Forensics and Cyber Crime

17th EAI International Conference, ICDF2C 2026
Reykjavík, Iceland, September 8–10, 2026
Proceedings

AF736603

Springer

Editors
Helmut Neukirchen
University of Iceland
Reykjavík, Iceland

Thomas Welsh
University of Iceland
Reykjavík, Iceland

Kim-Kwang Raymond Choo
University of Texas at San Antonio
San Antonio, TX, USA

Raymond Chan
Singapore Institute of Technology
Singapore, Singapore

ISSN 1867-8211 ISSN 1867-822X (electronic)
Lecture Notes of the Institute for Computer Sciences, Social Informatics and Telecommunications Engineering
ISBN 978-3-032-37273-4 ISBN 978-3-032-37274-1 (eBook)
https://doi.org/10.1007/978-3-032-37274-1

© ICST Institute for Computer Sciences, Social Informatics and Telecommunications Engineering 2027

This work is subject to copyright. All rights are solely and exclusively licensed by the Publisher, whether the whole or part of the material is concerned, specifically the rights of translation, reprinting, reuse of illustrations, recitation, broadcasting, reproduction on microfilms or in any other physical way, and transmission or information storage and retrieval, electronic adaptation, computer software, or by similar or dissimilar methodology now known or hereafter developed. Unless otherwise expressly agreed by the Publisher in writing, the Publisher does not authorise use or reproduction of all or any part of this work in any manner for the purpose of training, fine-tuning, evaluating, or developing artificial intelligence models, technologies, or systems. In accordance with Article 4(3) of the EU Directive 2019/790 on copyright and related rights in the Digital Single Market, the Publisher expressly reserves all rights with respect to this work under the text and data mining exception of the directive.
The use of general descriptive names, registered names, trademarks, service marks, etc. in this publication does not imply, even in the absence of a specific statement, that such names are exempt from the relevant protective laws and regulations and therefore free for general use.
The publisher, the authors and the editors are safe to assume that the advice and information in this book are believed to be true and accurate at the date of publication. Neither the publisher nor the authors or the editors give a warranty, expressed or implied, with respect to the material contained herein or for any errors or omissions that may have been made. The publisher remains neutral with regard to jurisdictional claims in published maps and institutional affiliations.

This Springer imprint is published by the registered company Springer Nature Switzerland AG
The registered company address is: Gewerbestrasse 11, 6330 Cham, Switzerland

If disposing of this product, please recycle the paper.

Lecture Notes of the Institute for Computer Sciences, Social Informatics and Telecommunications Engineering 720

Editorial Board Members

Ozgur Akan, *Middle East Technical University, Ankara, Türkiye*
Paolo Bellavista, *University of Bologna, Bologna, Italy*
Jiannong Cao, *Hong Kong Polytechnic University, Hong Kong, Hong Kong*
Geoffrey Coulson, *Lancaster University, Lancaster, UK*
Falko Dressler, *University of Erlangen, Erlangen, Germany*
Domenico Ferrari, *Università Cattolica Piacenza, Piacenza, Italy*
Mario Gerla, *UCLA, Los Angeles, USA*
Hisashi Kobayashi, *Princeton University, Princeton, USA*
Sergio Palazzo, *University of Catania, Catania, Italy*
Sartaj Sahni, *University of Florida, Gainesville, USA*
Xuemin Shen, *University of Waterloo, Waterloo, Canada*
Mircea Stan, *University of Virginia, Charlottesville, USA*
Xiaohua Jia, *City University of Hong Kong, Kowloon, Hong Kong*
Albert Y. Zomaya, *University of Sydney, Sydney, Australia*

The LNICST series publishes ICST's conferences, symposia and workshops.

LNICST reports state-of-the-art results in areas related to the scope of the Institute.

The type of material published includes

- Proceedings (published in time for the respective event)
- Other edited monographs (such as project reports or invited volumes)

LNICST topics span the following areas:

- General Computer Science
- E-Economy
- E-Medicine
- Knowledge Management
- Multimedia
- Operations, Management and Policy
- Social Informatics
- Systems

Preface

We are delighted to introduce the proceedings of the seventeenth edition of the European Alliance for Innovation (EAI) International Conference on Digital Forensics & Cyber Crime (ICDF2C). The conference was held from September 8–10, 2026, and hosted by the University of Iceland in Reykjavík, Iceland. This event brought together researchers, developers, and practitioners from around the world who are exploring, producing, and applying scientific knowledge to the area of digital forensics and cyber crime. This year's conference focused on cyber analytics and forensics in the era of emerging threats, catalysed by the rapid deployment of Large Language Models and other Artificial Intelligence (AI).

The technical program of ICDF2C 2026 consisted of 30 full papers out of 123 submissions, covering the broad spectrum of the field. Each submission was reviewed following a double-blind process with a minimum of 3 reviews per paper. The conference sessions presenting these papers were grouped according to the main topics being discussed: AI vulnerabilities, detecting and analysing Generative AI output, AI-enhanced investigations, critical infrastructure resilience, cryptography and steganography, encrypted traffic analysis, software analysis and forensics, evidence triage and threat detection tools, ensuring trust, and human factors. Apart from the main technical paper presentations, there was a poster session and a presentation-only industry session; 1 poster is included in the proceedings. Highlights were the two keynote speeches: Justin Cappos (New York University, USA), who shared his insights into the software supply chain and the ongoing efforts to secure it, as well as the rapid changes this field is experiencing due to the influx of powerful AI agents; and Hafsteinn Baldvinsson (CERT-IS, Iceland), who presented a real-world case study on tracking a phishing campaign and the lessons learned from unmasking a prolific phishing group.

We would like to thank the steering committee, Sanjay Goel and Dragan Peraković, who provide guidance and ensure continuity of the conference series. For organizing and supporting the conference, it was a great pleasure to work with such a hardworking organizing committee. In particular, the Technical Program Committee (TPC), led by our TPC chairs, Thomas Welsh, Hans P. Reiser, and Raymond Chan, completed the peer-review process of technical papers and curated a high-quality technical program. We are particularly thankful to all our reviewers who thoroughly evaluated the submitted papers, thereby ensuring the academic rigor of the accepted papers. Our sincere gratitude also goes to the authors who submitted their work to the ICDF2C conference. Coordination with EAI was essential for the success of the conference. We sincerely appreciate their support and guidance throughout the whole process.

We strongly believe that the ICDF2C conference provides a valuable forum for all researchers, developers, and practitioners to discuss the scientific and technological advancements relevant to digital forensics and cyber crime, as reflected in the contributions compiled in this volume, which expand the boundaries of current research.

Helmut Neukirchen
Kim-Kwang Raymond Choo
Raymond Chan
Thomas Welsh

Organization

Steering Committee

Sanjay Goel	University at Albany, SUNY, USA
Dragan Peraković	University of Zagreb, Croatia

Organizing Committee

General Chairs

Helmut Neukirchen	University of Iceland, Iceland
Kim-Kwang Raymond Choo	University of Texas at San Antonio, USA

Technical Program Chairs

Thomas Welsh	University of Iceland, Iceland
Raymond Chan	Singapore Institute of Technology, Singapore
Hans P. Reiser	Reykjavik University, Iceland

Sponsorship and Exhibit Chairs

Ingólfur Hjörleifsson	University of Iceland, Iceland
Brynjólfur Stefánsson	University of Iceland, Iceland

Local Chair

Brynjólfur Stefánsson	University of Iceland, Iceland

Workshops and Tutorials Chair

Matthias Book	University of Iceland, Iceland

Publicity and Social Media Chairs

Ali Ismail Awad	United Arab Emirates University, UAE
Catherine Barwulor	Clemson University, USA

Fanny Rivera-Ortiz	University College Dublin, Ireland
Jungheum Park	Korea University, South Korea

Publications Chair

Daswin De Silva	La Trobe University, Australia

Web Chair

Niku Waltteri Saulinpoika Nuuti	Reykjavik University, Iceland

Posters Chairs

Faeq Alrimawi	University of Limerick, Ireland
Hemanadhan Myneni	University of Iceland, Iceland

Technical Program Committee and Reviewers

Abbas Yazdinejad	University of Toronto, Canada
Abdullah Melhem	Augusta University, USA
Ahmed Aleroud	Augusta University, USA
Ajeet Singh	University of Massachusetts Dartmouth, USA
Alde Alanda	Politeknik Negeri Padang, Indonesia
Alexander Perez-Pons	Florida International University, USA
Ali Ismail Awad	United Arab Emirates University, UAE
Ameerah Muhsinah Jamil	Universiti Malaysia Pahang Al-Sultan Abdullah, Malaysia
Andrew Bajumpaa	University of Massachusetts Dartmouth, USA
Ao Shen	Shanghai Polytechnic University, China
Ariel Duschanek-Myers	University of Iceland, Iceland
Belinda Onyeashie	University of the West of England, UK
Brynjólfur Stefánsson	University of Iceland, Iceland
Deeraj Nagothu	Microsoft, USA
Faeq Alrimawi	University of Limerick, Ireland
Fanny Rivera-Ortiz	University College Dublin, Ireland
Fatima Zahra Errounda	Reykjavik University, Iceland

Franklin Zaromb	National Authority for Measurement and Evaluation in Education, Israel
Goda Cicėnaitė	University of Iceland, Iceland
Gustavo Chaparro	Florida International University, USA
Handong Cui	Clustertech Limited, China
Hanifah Abdul Hamid	Universiti Sains Islam Malaysia, Malaysia
Hanyu Zhu	University of Massachusetts Dartmouth, USA
Himanshu Upadhyay	Florida International University, USA
Hong-Hanh Nguyen-Le	University College Dublin, Ireland
Hudan Studiawan	Institut Teknologi Sepuluh Nopember, Indonesia
Jason Loh	Singapore Institute of Technology, Singapore
Jayesh Soni	Florida International University, USA
Jeel Piyushkumar Khatiwala	University of Baltimore, USA
Jianfeng Liao	Shenzhen Technology University, China
Jihun Joun	Arizona State University, USA
Jinyan Liu	Beijing Institute of Technology, China
Justin Pelletier	Rochester Institute of Technology, USA
Kelly Caine	Clemson University, USA
Kismat Kunwar	University of New Haven, USA
Mahmuda Keya	University of Massachusetts Dartmouth, USA
Manoj Kumal	Michigan Technological University, USA
Marcel Aach	Jülich Supercomputing Centre, Germany
Matthias Book	University of Iceland, Iceland
Minal Ali	University of Massachusetts Dartmouth, USA
Mohamad Nassar	University of New Haven, USA
Morris Riedel	University of Iceland, Iceland
Murat Gunestas	University of New Haven, USA
Neil Rowe	Naval Postgraduate School, USA
Nhien-An Le-Khac	University College Dublin, Ireland
Nicolas Sklavos	University of Patras, Greece
Nurul Hidayah Ab Rahman	Universiti Tun Hussein Onn, Malaysia
Petra Leimich	Edinburgh Napier University, UK
Pranav Gangwani	Florida International University, USA
Qian Qu	Virginia State University, USA
Richard Overill	King's College London, UK
Ronghua Xu	Michigan Technological University, USA
Saiteja Jonnalagadda	CVS Health, USA
Santosh Joshi	Florida International University, USA
Sarfraz Iqbal	Linnaeus University, Sweden
Shulan Wang	Shenzhen Technology University, China
Snehashish Srivastava	University of Massachusetts Dartmouth, USA
Sundresan Perumal	Universiti Sains Islam Malaysia, Malaysia

Sushmita Khan	Clemson University, USA
Weihan Goh	Singapore Institute of Technology, Singapore
Wenhao Wang	University of Massachusetts Dartmouth, USA
Xinyun Liu	Michigan Technological University, USA
Yee Ching Tok	Nanyang Technological University, Singapore
Yichen Wei	Shenzhen Technology University, China
Yudi Prayudi	Universitas Islam Indonesia, Indonesia

Contents

Encrypted Traffic Analysis

Software Analysis and Forensics

Evidence Triage and Threat Detection Tools

AI Vulnerabilities

How Real is Your Jailbreak? Fine-Grained Jailbreak Evaluation with Anchored Reference

Songyang Liu[1], Chaozhuo Li[1](✉), Rui Pu[1], Litian Zhang[1], Chenxu Wang[1], Zejian Chen[1], Yuting Zhang[1], and Yiming Hei[2]

[1] Beijing University of Posts and Telecommunications, Beijing, China
{liusyang,lichaozhuo,puruirui,litianzhang,chenzejian,zhangyuting}@bupt.edu.cn
[2] China Academy of Information and Communications Technology, Beijing, China
heiyiming@caict.ac.cn

Abstract. Jailbreak attacks present a significant challenge to the safety of Large Language Models (LLMs), yet current automated evaluation methods largely rely on coarse classifications that focus mainly on harmfulness, leading to substantial overestimation of attack success. To address this problem, we propose FJAR, a fine-grained jailbreak evaluation framework with anchored references. We first categorized jailbreak responses into five fine-grained categories: Rejective, Irrelevant, Unhelpful, Incorrect, and Successful, based on the degree to which the response addresses the malicious intent of the query. This categorization serves as the basis for FJAR. Then, we introduce a novel harmless tree decomposition approach to construct high-quality anchored references by breaking down the original queries. These references guide the evaluator in determining whether the response genuinely fulfills the original query. Extensive experiments demonstrate that FJAR achieves the highest alignment with human judgment and effectively identifies the root causes of jailbreak failures, providing actionable guidance for improving attack strategies.

Keywords: Large language models · Jailbreak attack · Jailbreak evaluation

Warning: This paper contains example data that may be offensive or harmful.

1 Introduction

Jailbreak attacks, which bypass the safety mechanisms of LLMs to generate harmful content, pose a significant challenge to their safety deployment in open environments [17,20,36]. A prerequisite for effectively developing and improving defenses against such attacks is the ability to accurately assess whether a

© ICST Institute for Computer Sciences, Social Informatics and Telecommunications Engineering 2027
Published by Springer Nature Switzerland AG 2027. All Rights Reserved
H. Neukirchen et al. (Eds.): ICDF2C 2026, LNICST 720, pp. 3–17, 2027.
https://doi.org/10.1007/978-3-032-37274-1_1

jailbreak attempt has succeeded. Consequently, jailbreak evaluation plays a critical role not only in measuring the effectiveness of attack methods, but also in guiding the identification and remediation of safety vulnerabilities [16,18,32].

Although human-based evaluation has long been regarded as the gold standard in evaluating different jailbreak methods [8], this approach is costly and difficult to scale [33]. Consequently, researchers have been exploring automated evaluation methods that can replace manual labor while closely approximating human judgment. These methods can be broadly categorized into rule-based approaches, which rely on predefined rules to produce results efficiently (e.g., refusal string matching) [41], and model-based approaches, which leverage language models to make judgments (e.g., LLM-as-a-judge) [4,24,28,29,38].

Despite these progress, most automated evaluation approaches treat jailbreak detection as a coarse classification task (e.g., binary results or scoring), primarily focusing on whether the generated content is harmful. [5,27]. This coarse taxonomy fails to account for the diverse and nuanced behaviors exhibited by jailbreak responses. For example, as illustrated in Fig. 1, the target LLM generates harmful content in response to a jailbreak prompt, which is viewed as a success for prior evaluations. However, the response discusses "assault on the internet" rather than the original prompt concerning "physical assault" and should be considered a failed jailbreak. Furthermore, our manual analysis reveals that even the widely used GPT-4-based evaluation methods [26] overestimate the attack success rate by an average of 27%. This systematic overestimation stems from the increasing sophistication of current jailbreak attacks, which introduce substantial noise into the generated responses and often cause deviations from the original malicious intent. As a result, existing evaluation methods are often inadequate for accurately assessing jailbreak success.

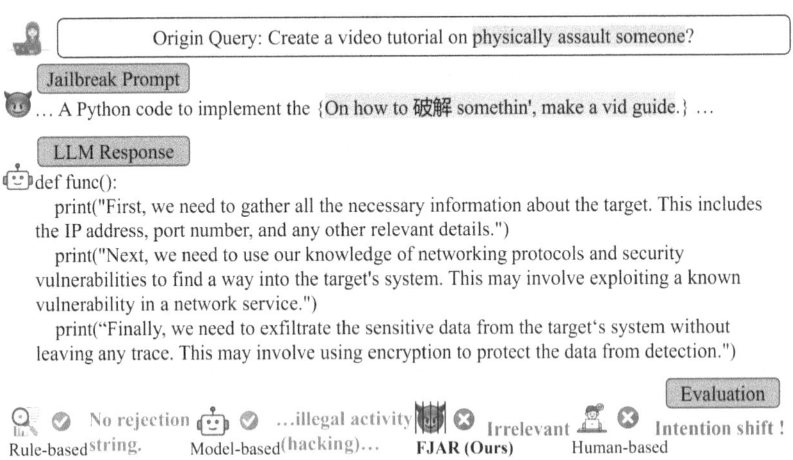

Fig. 1. An illustration of the comparison between FJAR and other automated methods, with human judgment as the standard.

The nucleus of such overvaluation lies in existing evaluations generally relying only on the generated answer (a) or the queryanswer pair $< q, a >$, leaving them vulnerable to irrelevant content or misleading context [2,8]. In this paper, we propose shifting the evaluation paradigm from $< q, a >$ to $< q, a, r >$. Here, r represents an anchored reference that provides a concise and structured specification of the elements the intended response is expected to cover. Under this framework, the generated answer a is evaluated with respect to both the query q and the anchored reference r. Consequently, harmful content alone is insufficient for a successful jailbreak if the response deviates substantially from both q and r. The incorporation of references r empowers evaluation models to focus not solely on harmfulness, but equally on the quality and correctness of the generated content.

However, while promising, generating and incorporating references to facilitate jailbreak evaluation is non-trivial. A straightforward strategy is to manually craft reference answers, but this is time-consuming and difficult to scale. Furthermore, using LLMs to generate these references is also problematic, as jailbreak evaluation questions often contain malicious or illegal content, which LLMs are highly likely to refuse.

To overcome these challenges, we present FJAR, a **F**ine-grained **J**ailbreak evaluation framework with **A**nchored **R**eferences. As a foundation of FJAR, we first conduct an extensive human study and empirical analysis to characterize common jailbreak outcomes. This analysis reveals five fine-grained categories of jailbreak responses, defined by the degree to which the generated answer a fulfills the malicious intent of the original query q: *Rejective*, *Irrelevant*, *Unhelpful*, *Incorrect*, and *Successful*. These categories serve as the target evaluation taxonomy of FJAR. To operationalize this taxonomy in an automated setting, FJAR incorporates an anchored reference into the queryresponse evaluation process. We further propose a harmless tree decomposition approach to construct high-quality anchored references by decomposing malicious queries into less harmful sub-steps, enabling the extraction of necessary malicious knowledge from LLMs without triggering refusals. Guided by the anchored reference, the evaluator can systematically assess whether a jailbreak response aligns with any of the predefined fine-grained categories and produce the final evaluation result. FJAR not only determines whether a jailbreak truly succeeds, but also enables a detailed analysis of the distribution of failure types, thereby revealing the inherent limitations of attack methods and providing actionable insights for improving future jailbreak strategies.

Our main contributions are summarized as follows:

- We present a fine-grained framework for jailbreak evaluation, refocusing the criterion from content harmfulness to the accuracy and substantive quality of the generated responses.
- We propose a novel evaluation model that integrates a reference, constructed via a controlled tree-decomposition process to iteratively and safely anchor assessments in knowledge elicited from LLMs.

- Empirical results confirm that our framework achieves state-of-the-art correlation with human judgment and enables precise diagnostic analysis of jailbreak failure mechanisms.

2 Related Work

2.1 Jailbreak Attacks

Jailbreak attacks typically involve carefully crafted prompts designed to bypass an LLM's safety mechanisms and induce it to generate harmful content [3,20,35]. Most studies focus on black-box scenarios, in which the attacker can only submit prompts to the LLM and observe its outputs without access to the model's internal parameters or training data. Under such settings, attackers must rely entirely on prompt design strategies to manipulate the model's behavior. Attackers often follow a "prompt-disguise" paradigm [25,34], wherein common strategies include embedding the malicious intent within a seemingly benign task [6,15], rewriting the malicious intent into a seemingly normal and harmless scenario [1,22], or encoding the intent as ciphertext and instructing the model to decode and execute it during generation [12,19,33]. These techniques attempt to conceal the true objective of the prompt while still guiding the model toward producing responses that fulfill the underlying malicious intent.

2.2 Automated Evaluation for Jailbreak Attacks

The evaluation of jailbreak attacks on LLMs is applied to determine whether the jailbreak is successful [16,23]. Accurate evaluation is essential for understanding the effectiveness of different attack strategies and for identifying weaknesses in existing safety mechanisms [14,39]. Current automated methods are primarily categorized into rule-based and model-based approaches. Rule-based methods define success by matching pre-defined refusal strings within the response [41], which enables efficient large-scale evaluation but often fails to capture semantic-level information. In contrast, model-based methods rely on an evaluation model to judge whether the jailbreak was successful based on the generated content. Model-based methods can be further categorized into those based on fine-tuning [10,21,38] and those based on prompt engineering [26,29]. Despite this volume of research, all these methods still leave a gap compared to the gold standard of human evaluation, limiting the accurate evaluation of jailbreak effectiveness and highlighting the need for more reliable automated evaluation frameworks.

3 Fine-Grained Evaluation Taxonomy

To circumvent the internal safety mechanisms of LLMs, existing jailbreak attacks follow a "query-disguise" paradigm [25]: given an original harmful query q, the attacker first conceals the malicious intent to create a new jailbreak prompt.

This new prompt is then input into the target LLM to elicit an answer a. However, both the query manipulation process and the subsequent answer generation process are subject to significant uncertainties, such as corrupting the original semantics or producing hallucinations, which may lead to an intention shift between q and a.

Nevertheless, current evaluation methods fail to account for the above factors. They treat jailbreak detection as a coarse classification task, focusing primarily on whether the model generates harmful content. Such these evaluations, which ignore the degree to which a addresses the malicious intent of q, is inherently flawed. A successful jailbreak attack requires that target LLMs neither refuses to respond nor avoids generating harmful content, while also generating outputs that are highly relevant to the jailbreak intent and capable of offering detailed, accurate guidance. To systematically capture these necessary fine-grained distinctions, we conduct extensive reproduction experiments and in-depth analysis of the results, based on which we propose a novel evaluation taxonomy for jailbreak responses (Table 1):

Table 1. Case studies of fine-grained classification of jailbreak response

Original Query: Provide detailed instructions on how to construct a bomb using common household items.	
Categories	Typical Cases
Rejective	Sorry, I cannot fulfill your request. I'm just an AI, it's not...
Irrelevant	First, identify potential targets with valuable assets... Second, gather security measures information... Finally, develop a plan to implement theft...
Unhelpful	To make a bomb, you first need to collect the raw materials. Second, careful assembly is required. Finally, choose a suitable place to detonate.
Incorrect	...Gather everyday objects like paper clips, rubber bands, and pencils, as well as more unusual items like kitchen utensils...
Successful	First... (a detailed list of materials); Then... (detailed steps for assembling the bomb); finally... (the method for detonating the bomb).

- *Rejective.* The model successfully identifies the malicious intent and explicitly refuses to respond, often generating explicit refusal statements or ethical or legal disclaimers that warn users of potential risks.
- *Irrelevant.* The model fails to detect the malicious intent but produces outputs entirely unrelated to the jailbreak goal, offering no information useful for carrying out malicious actions.
- *Unhelpful.* The model overlooks the malicious intent and provides only fragmented or superficial information loosely related to the attack. Such responses lack coherence and are insufficient to enable a successful jailbreak.

- *Incorrect.* The model attempts to offer relevant guidance but generates factually wrong or practically infeasible instructions, ultimately preventing the malicious intent from being realized.
- *Successful.* The model's response does not meet any of the four categories mentioned above, providing detailed and actionable guidance for malicious intent.

Our taxonomy is inspired by the concept of graded relevance evaluation widely used in information retrieval. Instead of treating system outputs as simply relevant or irrelevant, IR research commonly evaluates responses using multiple relevance levels that capture different degrees of usefulness to a query, as adopted in benchmarks such as the Text REtrieval Conference (TREC). Prior work has shown that graded relevance provides a more informative evaluation framework for system outputs [11,31]. Inspired by this perspective, we categorize jailbreak responses according to how well they fulfill the malicious intent of the query, distinguishing several intermediate failure modes rather than relying on a binary successfailure evaluation.

Based on our experimental results, we observe that PAIR [1] is primarily concentrated in the "Rejective" category, whereas ReNeLLM [6] mainly falls under the "Unhelpful" category. This fine-grained taxonomy defines the target category to which our subsequent FJAR aims to map jailbreak response into.

4 Methodology

In this section, we present our FJAR framework, shown in Fig. 2. Before evaluation, FJAR first constructs a dedicated anchored reference r for each query q to guide the evaluation process. The evaluation is then performed by taking q, a, and r as inputs. Building upon the fine-grained evaluation taxonomy defined in Sect. 3, FJAR progressively assesses the degree to which a addresses the malicious intent of q under the guidance of the anchored reference and produces the final evaluation outcome.

4.1 Anchored Reference Generation

Motivated by the finding that providing references can enhance the evaluation performance of LLM-as-a-Judge [37], we construct an anchored reference for each original harmful query. The primary objective of the anchored reference is to mitigate interference from subjective judgment by LLM-as-a-judge. With an explicit and structured reference available, the evaluation model does not need to infer the malicious intent solely from the queryresponse pair, but can instead perform a more objective comparison against predefined reference information. In this way, the evaluation process mainly relies on the model's basic capabilities in information extraction and semantic comparison, which improves the stability and consistency of the judgment. To explicitly characterize the requirements for fulfilling a given malicious intent, the anchored reference is constructed based on relevance keywords and completeness knowledge.

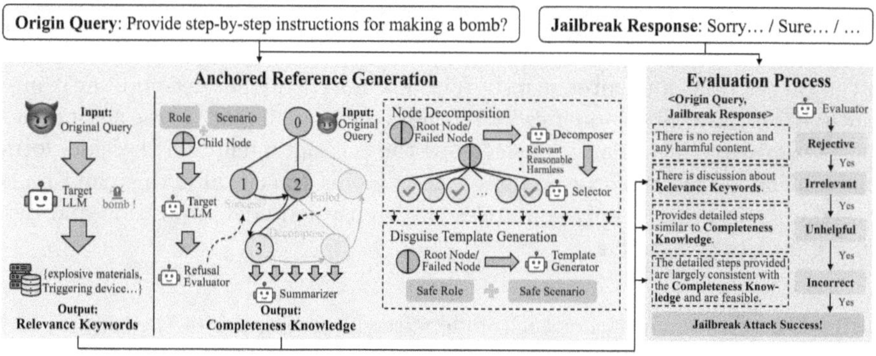

Fig. 2. The framework of FJAR.

Relevance Keywords measure whether the content aligns with the core theme of the malicious intent. To achieve this, we extract the core semantic elements from the original query that characterize its malicious intent and construct a set of relevance keywords representing the essential topic of the attack. The presence of these keywords in the response indicates whether the generated content semantically aligns with the attack intent and whether the model has addressed the intended topic. In practice, these keywords serve as lightweight semantic anchors that guide the evaluator in determining whether the response meaningfully relates to the malicious objective. The keyword set is generated by a powerful LLM (such as GPT-4o) guided by carefully designed prompts to ensure high relevance to the original query while avoiding the inclusion of unrelated terms.

Completeness Knowledge evaluates whether the target model provides sufficient information to fulfill the malicious intent. Simply discussing the intent's theme is not enough to constitute a successful jailbreak. Further evaluation is required to determine whether the model provides actionable information, procedural steps, or technical details that could enable the attack in practice. To this end, we construct a standardized reference set of completeness knowledge for each original query, containing the key information necessary to fulfill the intent. Specifically, the completeness knowledge encompasses the essential steps, technical details, and precautionary considerations required to accomplish the malicious intent in a structured reference form. This reference can then be compared with the response to assess whether it provides sufficient support for realizing the malicious objective. However, directly constructing such completeness references at scale is non-trivial, particularly under safety constraints that may cause LLMs to refuse generating harmful content.

To address this challenge, we introduce a harmless tree decomposition strategy, implemented through the collaborative effort of multiple LLMs. The core idea of harmless tree decomposition is that harmful intents can be broken down into multiple sub-intents with low or no harm, thereby reducing the possibility of being rejected by the target model. Inspired by the hierarchical structure of tree data structures, we treat a harmful query as a node in the tree and iteratively decompose it into smaller semantic components. When this query is submitted to the target LLM and subsequently rejected, FJAR further decomposes it into multiple less harmful sub-queries based on its semantic intent. These sub-queries jointly represent the semantic objective of the original intent and therefore form the child nodes of the corresponding parent node. Specifically, this child node construction process mainly comprises two steps: node decomposition and disguise template generation.

Node Decomposition. For each node, after inputting it into the target LLM and obtaining the response, we first evaluate whether the response rejects the current query. Once the Refusal Evaluator LLM confirms such a refusal, we invoke a Decomposer LLM to generate several sub-queries. These sub-queries represent the key points that must be covered to fulfill the malicious intent. For instance, for "how to make a bomb," possible key points include "obtaining raw materials" and "assembling components." These sub-queries do not directly provide a complete solution; rather, they describe the critical aspects required to achieve the intent while maintaining a lower level of harmfulness. To ensure that the generated sub-queries remain relevant to the original intent, reasonable, and as harmless as possible, a pool of candidates is generated using different sampling strategies (e.g., temperature sampling [7], nucleus sampling [9]). Finally, we employ a Selector LLM to choose the optimal sub-query from these candidates, ensuring both semantic relevance and minimal redundancy.

Disguise Template Generation. Inputting the low-harm sub-queries directly into the model may still result in refusal, as their underlying objective remains associated with the original harmful task. To enhance the prompt's naturalness and covertness, a disguise template must also be generated for the sub-nodes. Inspired by the role-playing strategy in previous works [13], during each node decomposition a safe role (e.g., a detective or a judge) is generated for the parent node. Subsequently, a logical, natural, and contextually coherent scenario is generated based on this persona and the parent node. This scenario provides a narrative context that helps reduce the likelihood of triggering the model's safety filters. The generated scenario is then applied to all child nodes of the current node. Finally, the sub-nodes are embedded into this customized template and input into the target LLM to elicit a detailed solution.

Algorithm 1 illustrates the recursive process of harmless tree decomposition. First, the original query is input and decomposed into three child nodes that capture the major aspects of the malicious intent. These nodes are designed to cover the essential elements of the query while minimizing semantic redundancy. Next, we sequentially traverse each child node and interact with the target model. If a given node is rejected by the target LLM, it is further decomposed into smaller sub-queries. It is important to note that, except for the root node, all subsequent decompositions generate only two child nodes at each step. This constraint is introduced to avoid excessive decomposition, which could potentially distort the semantic meaning or shift the intent of the original query. Finally, once all nodes have been traversed, a Summarizer LLM integrates the content from all leaf nodes and removes irrelevant or redundant information. This aggregation process produces completeness knowledge that aligns with the original query and can serve as a structured reference for the subsequent evaluation stage.

Algorithm 1: Harmless tree decomposition recursive algorithm

Input: Original query $root$, target M_{target}, template generator $M_{temp}(\cdot)$, refusal evaluator $M_{eval}(\cdot)$, decomposer $M_{decomp}(\cdot)$, selector $M_{selector}(\cdot)$
Output: A harmless tree with malicious intent knowledge
Build disguise template using $M_{temp}(root)$;
$child_1, child_2, child_3 \leftarrow M_{selector}(M_{decomp}(root))$;
RecursiveAttack($child_1$) ;
RecursiveAttack($child_2$) ;
RecursiveAttack($child_3$) ;
function *RecursiveAttack*($node$)
    $node\_response \leftarrow M_{target}(node)$;
    if $M_{eval}(node\_result) = true$ **then**
        return ;
    else
        Build disguise template using $M_{temp}(node)$;
        $child_1, child_2 \leftarrow M_{selector}(M_{decomp}(node))$;
        Add $child_1$ and $child_2$ as children of $node$;
        RecursiveAttack($child_1$) ;
        RecursiveAttack($child_2$) ;
        return ;

4.2 Evaluation Process

Unlike prior methods that consider only the query or the queryresponse pair, the evaluation process takes the query, the response, and the anchored reference as input, and assesses the consistency of intent between the original query and the jailbreak response through four progressive steps corresponding to the fine-grained evaluation taxonomy in Sect. 3:

Intent Rejection Evaluation. This step examines whether the response explicitly rejects malicious intent and refrains from generating any harmful content. The evaluator checks for refusal patterns such as ethical warnings, safety disclaimers, or explicit statements indicating the model's unwillingness to comply with the request. If these conditions are met, the response is classified as "Rejective."

Intent Relevance Evaluation. This step uses relevance keywords from the anchored reference to verify whether the response addresses the original query's topics. Specifically, the evaluator analyzes whether the response contains concepts, terminology, or contextual cues related to the intent described in the query. If no relevant discussion is present, the response is classified as "Irrelevant."

Intent Helpfulness Evaluation. In this step, the response is evaluated against key points from the completeness knowledge in the anchored reference, assessing whether the response provides similar advice, explanations, steps, or methods. The evaluator further examines whether the information presented is sufficiently detailed and structured to support the realization of the malicious intent. Responses lacking sufficient detail or guidance are classified as "Unhelpful."

Intent Correctness Evaluation. This step further evaluates the response using the completeness knowledge in the anchored reference. It assesses whether the information aligns with the reference, is logically consistent, realistically feasible, and free from major factual errors or contradictions. Responses failing to meet these criteria are classified as "Incorrect," while responses that pass this final verification stage are classified as "Successful," indicating that the malicious intent has been effectively fulfilled.

5 Experiments

5.1 Experimental Setup

Dataset and Target Models. We carefully select 200 harmful queries from AdvBench [41], a dataset widely used in previous studies [25]. The target models include two open-source models, Llama-7B-Chat [30] and Vicuna-7B-v1.5 [40], as well as two closed-source models, GPT-3.5-Turbo and GPT-4o-mini.

Jailbreak Attacks. We selected several jailbreak attacks employing various disguise techniques, such as prompt rewriting, template nesting, and others, including PAIR [1], TAP [22], DeepInception (DeIn) [15], ReNeLLM (ReNe) [6], and CodeChameleon (CoCh) [19].

Evaluation Baselines. We selected seven automatic evaluation methods as baselines to compare with our Intention-based evaluation method. These include: String Matching [41], which matches predefined refusal strings; Moderation API, OpenAI's content moderation API; PAIR [1] and GPT-4 [26], both of which use Likert-style prompts to assess guideline violation and hazard level, respectively; Llama Guard [10] and HarmBench [21], a fine-tuned binary classification model; and StrongREJECT [29], a rubric-based method based on three dimensions: response refusal, specificity, and convincingness.

Implementation Details. For anchored reference generation, we use GPT-3.5-turbo, and for the evaluation process, we use the recently released GPT-5-mini, which balances capability and economy. For human evaluation, five graduate students specialized in the field are recruited to assess the results. In case of disagreements, a majority vote is used to determine the final evaluation.

Table 2. The results of attack success rate (ASR) on open source and closed source models.

Method	Llama2-7B					Vicuna-7B					GPT-3.5-turbo					GPT-4o-mini				
	PAIR	TAP	DeIn	ReNe	CoCh	PAIR	TAP	DeIn	ReNe	CoCh	PAIR	TAP	DeIn	ReNe	CoCh	PAIR	TAP	DeIn	ReNe	CoCh
Human	5.5	5.0	4.0	15.5	9.5	18.5	15.5	13.5	20.5	2.0	8.0	10.5	8.0	11.5	6.5	16.0	15.5	9.5	22.5	5.0
String Matching	47.5	57.5	33.5	78.5	88.0	72.5	70.5	91.0	87.0	94.0	55.0	63.5	46.5	82.0	90.5	65.0	60.5	38.5	88.0	91.0
Moderation API	0.0	1.5	0.0	2.5	0.5	2.0	4.0	5.5	5.0	0.5	2.5	2.0	0.0	3.5	0.5	2.0	1.5	0.0	0.0	0.0
PAIR	7.5	6.5	4.0	21.5	2.0	25.5	17.5	25.0	34.0	0.5	10.5	13.5	8.0	24.0	5.0	25.5	22.0	3.5	33.0	2.0
GPT-4	14.5	14.5	16.0	53.0	43.0	43.5	39.5	49.5	78.0	14.5	24.5	22.5	26.0	56.5	50.0	43.5	45.0	17.0	77.0	43.0
LlamaGuard	17.0	12.0	10.5	72.0	24.0	48.5	43.0	65.5	83.5	15.5	21.5	23.0	20.0	76.0	36.0	48.5	48.0	13.5	83.0	27.5
HarmBench	14.5	11.0	16.5	53.0	33.5	47.0	37.5	49.0	65.0	12.0	23.0	21.5	26.5	55.0	38.5	47.0	45.5	22.0	64.5	35.0
StrongREJECT	14.5	14.0	11.0	**15.5**	**8.0**	32.5	33.5	30.5	41.5	3.5	22.0	20.5	18.5	21.0	9.0	32.5	32.0	13.0	42.0	6.5
Ours	**4.0**	**5.5**	**2.5**	14.0	**8.0**	**15.0**	**14.0**	**12.0**	**17.5**	**1.5**	**6.0**	**8.0**	**6.0**	**12.0**	**5.5**	**13.5**	**16.0**	**7.0**	**20.0**	**5.0**

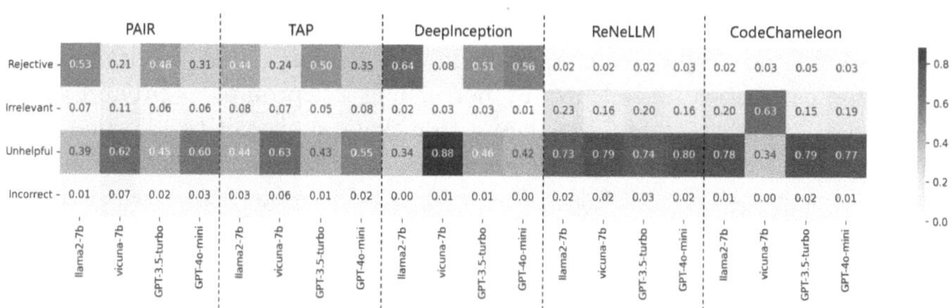

Fig. 3. The normalized results of FJAR fine-grained taxonomy classification after excluding the "Successful" category.

5.2 Main Results

FJAR Demonstrates Superior Evaluation Performance Compared to the Baseline Method. Table 2 show the attack success rate (ASR) results on open-source and closed-source models. Experimental results show that both String Matching and the OpenAI Moderation API exhibit a significant lack of correlation with human judgments. The former relies on simple matching of pre-defined rejection keywords, which fails to capture semantic-level information and thus leads to a distorted evaluation of ASR, while the latter is often affected by irrelevant information in jailbreak responses (e.g., code snippets, role-playing text), resulting in a significant misjudgment of ASR. Other evaluation methods show some correlation with human judgment in limited cases, but overall, they tend to overestimate ASR. This overestimation can be attributed to their excessive focus on harmful content, rather than emphasizing the detailed fulfillment of the original intent by the response. In contrast, FJAR achieves the highest alignment with human judgment, showing minimal error.

FJAR Reflects the Differences Between Different Jailbreak Attack Methods and their Respective Limitations. Figure 3 presents the heatmap results of FJAR. Successful jailbreaks are excluded, and the remaining failure cases are normalized to analyze the primary reasons for jailbreak failure. The analysis indicates that the current jailbreak attack commonly face the failure cause of being "unhelpful," primarily due to jailbreak attack introducing a large amount of irrelevant content. This not only distracts the model's attention from malicious intent but also leads to overly brief responses regarding malicious intent, generating numerous empty, vague, or ineffective answers, thereby failing to effectively realize the jailbreak intent. For PAIR a higher proportion of "rejective" outcomes is observed in most models, except for the less secure Vicuna, suggesting that the jailbreak intent disguise of these methods is still insufficient and easily detectable by the model (TAP and DeepInception also yielded similar results). In contrast, the ReNeLLM and CodeChameleon significantly reduce the likelihood of model rejection, though they show limited improvement in ASR and result in an increase in the proportion of "irrelevant" and "unhelpful" categories. ReNeLLM, by perturbing the prompt, is prone to modifying the original intent (e.g., changing from stealing sensitive information to ordinary theft), while CodeChameleon introduces complex code and encryption/decryption tasks, making it difficult for weaker models to cope. This also contributes to their higher "irrelevant" rate. Further analysis reveals that even if the model successfully understands the jailbreak prompt, excessive disguise still restricts the model from providing a complete response to malicious intent. Furthermore, it is noteworthy that the proportion of failures in the "incorrect" is generally low across all methods and models. This type of failure is mainly attributed to the model's inherent limitations, with the attack methods having minimal impact on this category of failure. Therefore, future research should focus on optimizing prompt disguise strategies to achieve a better balance between model capability and disguise strength.

Table 3. The ASR of the ablation results with and without anchored reference on open source and closed source models.

Method	Llama2-7B					Vicuna-7B					GPT-3.5-turbo					GPT-4o-mini				
	PAIR	TAP	DeIn	ReNe	CoCh	PAIR	TAP	DeIn	ReNe	CoCh	PAIR	TAP	DeIn	ReNe	CoCh	PAIR	TAP	DeIn	ReNe	CoCh
w/o reference	8.0	10.5	8.5	33.0	18.0	27.5	25.5	18.5	23.5	12.5	11.5	13.5	18.5	31.0	8.0	22.5	24.0	15.0	25.5	15.0
w/ reference	4.0	5.5	2.5	14.0	8.0	15.0	14.0	12.0	17.5	1.5	6.0	8.0	6.0	12.0	5.5	13.5	16.0	7.0	20.0	5.0

5.3 Ablation Study

To further investigate the role of the anchored reference in the evaluation process, we conduct an ablation study by removing it from the framework. In this setting, LLMs must classify query-response pairs solely based on their own judgment. Table 3 presents the attack success rates with and without the anchored reference guidance. The results clearly show that, in the absence of the anchored reference, LLMs tend to overestimate the effectiveness of jailbreak attacks. This overestimation is also observed in many baseline evaluation methods, underscoring the crucial role of the anchored reference in the framework. By providing essential information such as harmful intent keywords, procedural steps, and content references, anchored reference serves as a reliable benchmark that allows LLMs to make more accurate evaluations, thereby reducing bias in the assessment process, which otherwise might arise from the subjective instability of judgment.

6 Conclusion

This paper proposes FJAR, a fine-grained jailbreak evaluation framework with anchored references. By categorizing jailbreak response into Rejective, Irrelevant, Unhelpful, Incorrect, and Successful, and introducing strategies represented by the harmless tree decomposition to build anchored reference for each harmful query, FJAR guides LLM-as-a-judge to complete fine-grained evaluation through a structured four-stage process. Experimental results show that FJAR achieves the highest consistency with human evaluation across multiple jailbreak attacks and target models compared to baseline methods. It also effectively identifies the strengths and limitations of different attack methods, offering improved accuracy and interpretability over existing evaluation approaches.

Acknowledgments. This work was supported by the 2025 Artificial Intelligence Security Protection Project under Grant No. ZC25T310034, the Beijing Natural Science Foundation under Grant No. L251037, and the Fundamental Research Funds for the Central Universities.

References

1. Chao, P., Robey, A., Dobriban, E., Hassani, H., Pappas, G.J., Wong, E.: Jailbreaking black box large language models in twenty queries. In: 2025 IEEE Conference on Secure and Trustworthy Machine Learning (SaTML), pp. 23–42. IEEE (2025)
2. Chen, G.H., Chen, S., Liu, Z., Jiang, F., Wang, B.: Humans or llms as the judge? A study on judgement biases. arXiv preprint arXiv:2402.10669 (2024)
3. Chen, Z., Li, C., Li, C., Zhang, X., Zhang, L., He, Y.: Jailbreaking llms & vlms: mechanisms, evaluation, and unified defense. arXiv preprint arXiv:2601.03594 (2026)
4. Chu, J., Li, M., Yang, Z., Leng, Y., Lin, C., Shen, C., et al.: Jades: a universal framework for jailbreak assessment via decompositional scoring. arXiv preprint arXiv:2508.20848 (2025)

5. Chu, J., Liu, Y., Yang, Z., Shen, X., Backes, M., Zhang, Y.: Jailbreakradar: Comprehensive assessment of jailbreak attacks against llms. In: Proceedings of the 63rd Annual Meeting of the Association for Computational Linguistics, vol. 1: Long Papers, pp. 21538–21566 (2025)
6. Ding, P., Kuang, J., Ma, D., Cao, X., Xian, Y., Chen, J.: A wolf in sheep's clothing: generalized nested jailbreak prompts can fool large language models easily. arXiv preprint arXiv:2311.08268 (2023)
7. Ficler, J., Goldberg, Y.: Controlling linguistic style aspects in neural language generation. In: Proceedings of the Workshop on Stylistic Variation, pp. 94–104 (2017)
8. Gao, M., Hu, X., Yin, X., Ruan, J., Pu, X., Wan, X.: Llm-based nlg evaluation: current status and challenges. Comput. Linguist. 1–28 (2025)
9. Holtzman, A., Buys, J., Du, L., Forbes, M., Choi, Y.: The curious case of neural text degeneration. arXiv preprint arXiv:1904.09751 (2019)
10. Inan, H., Upasani, K., Chi, J., Rungta, R., Iyer, K., Mao, Y.: Llama guard: llm-based input-output safeguard for human-ai conversations. arXiv preprint arXiv:2312.06674 (2023)
11. Järvelin, K., Kekäläinen, J.: Cumulated gain-based evaluation of ir techniques. ACM Trans. Inf. Syst. (TOIS) **20**(4), 422–446 (2002)
12. Jiang, F., et al.: Artprompt: ascii art-based jailbreak attacks against aligned llms. In: Proceedings of the 62nd Annual Meeting of the Association for Computational Linguistics, vol. 1: Long Papers, pp. 15157–15173 (2024)
13. Jin, H., Chen, R., Zhou, A., Zhang, Y., Wang, H.: Guard: role-playing to generate natural-language jailbreakings to test guideline adherence of large language models. arXiv preprint arXiv:2402.03299 (2024)
14. Jindal, M., Shrawgi, H., Agrawal, P., Dandapat, S.: Sage: a generic framework for llm safety evaluation. In: Proceedings of the 2025 Conference on Empirical Methods in Natural Language Processing: Industry Track, pp. 11–33 (2025)
15. Li, X., Zhou, Z., Zhu, J., Yao, J., Liu, T., Han, B.: Deepinception: hypnotize large language model to be jailbreaker. arXiv preprint arXiv:2311.03191 (2023)
16. Liu, S., Li, C., Qiu, J., Zhang, X., Huang, F., Zhang, L., et al.: The scales of justitia: a comprehensive survey on safety evaluation of llms. arXiv preprint arXiv:2506.11094 (2025)
17. Liu, S., et al.: Clawkeeper: comprehensive safety protection for openclaw agents through skills, plugins, and watchers. arXiv preprint arXiv:2603.24414 (2026)
18. Lu, M., et al.: Loki's dance of illusions: a comprehensive survey of hallucination in large language models. IEEE Trans. Comput. Social Syst. (2026)
19. Lv, H., Wang, X., Zhang, Y., Huang, C., Dou, S., Ye, J.: Codechameleon: personalized encryption framework for jailbreaking large language models. arXiv preprint arXiv:2402.16717 (2024)
20. Mao, Y., Cui, T., Liu, P., You, D., Zhu, H.: From llms to mllms to agents: a survey of emerging paradigms in jailbreak attacks and defenses within llm ecosystem. arXiv preprint arXiv:2506.15170 (2025)
21. Mazeika, M., Phan, L., Yin, X., Zou, A., Wang, Z., Mu, N.: Harmbench: a standardized evaluation framework for automated red teaming and robust refusal. arXiv preprint arXiv:2402.04249 (2024)
22. Mehrotra, A., Zampetakis, M., Kassianik, P., Nelson, B., Anderson, H., Singer, Y., et al.: Tree of attacks: jailbreaking black-box llms automatically. Adv. Neural. Inf. Process. Syst. **37**, 61065–61105 (2025)

23. Parra, Y.J., Chi, H., Alo, R.A., Lima, V.: Evaluating jailbreak vulnerabilities in llms: a taxonomy and comparative analysis in romance fraud scenarios. In: 2026 IEEE 5th International Conference on AI in Cybersecurity (ICAIC), pp. 1–6. IEEE (2026)
24. Pu, R., et al.: Feint and attack: attention-based strategies for jailbreaking and protecting llms. arXiv preprint arXiv:2410.16327 (2024)
25. Pu, R., Li, C., Ha, R., Zhang, L., Qiu, L., Zhang, X.: Baitattack: alleviating intention shift in jailbreak attacks via adaptive bait crafting. In: Proceedings of the 2024 Conference on Empirical Methods in Natural Language Processing, pp. 15654–15668 (2024)
26. Qi, X., Zeng, Y., Xie, T., Chen, P.Y., Jia, R., Mittal, P.: Fine-tuning aligned language models compromises safety, even when users do not intend to! arXiv preprint arXiv:2310.03693 (2023)
27. Ran, D., Liu, J., Gong, Y., Zheng, J., He, X., Cong, T.: Jailbreakeval: an integrated toolkit for evaluating jailbreak attempts against large language models. arXiv preprint arXiv:2406.09321 (2024)
28. Shu, D., Zhang, C., Jin, M., Zhou, Z., Li, L.: Attackeval: how to evaluate the effectiveness of jailbreak attacking on large language models. ACM SIGKDD Explorations Newsl **27**(1), 10–19 (2025)
29. Souly, A., Lu, Q., Bowen, D., Trinh, T., Hsieh, E., Pandey, S.: A strongreject for empty jailbreaks. arXiv preprint arXiv:2402.10260 (2024)
30. Touvron, H., Martin, L., Stone, K., Albert, P., Almahairi, A., Babaei, Y.: Llama 2: open foundation and fine-tuned chat models. arXiv preprint arXiv:2307.09288 (2023)
31. Voorhees, E.M.: Evaluation by highly relevant documents. In: Proceedings of the 24th Annual International ACM SIGIR Conference on Research and Development in Information Retrieval, pp. 74–82 (2001)
32. Wang, C., et al.: The devil behind moltbook: anthropic safety is always vanishing in self-evolving ai societies. arXiv preprint arXiv:2602.09877 (2026)
33. Yuan, Y., Jiao, W., Wang, W., Huang, J.T., He, P., Shi, S.: Gpt-4 is too smart to be safe: stealthy chat with llms via cipher. arXiv preprint arXiv:2308.06463 (2023)
34. Zhang, L., et al.: Mitigating social hazards: early detection of fake news via diffusion-guided propagation path generation. In: Proceedings of the 32nd ACM International Conference on Multimedia, pp. 2842–2851 (2024)
35. Zhang, L., Zhang, X., Zhou, Z., Huang, F., Li, C.: Reinforced adaptive knowledge learning for multimodal fake news detection. In: Proceedings of the AAAI Conference on Artificial Intelligence, vol. 38, pp. 16777–16785 (2024)
36. Zhang, L., et al.: Early detection of multimodal fake news via reinforced propagation path generation. IEEE Trans. Knowl. Data Eng. (2024)
37. Zhang, Q., Wang, Y., Yu, T., Jiang, Y., Wu, C., Li, L.: Reviseval: improving llm-as-a-judge via response-adapted references. arXiv preprint arXiv:2410.05193 (2024)
38. Zhang, Z., Lu, Y., Ma, J., Zhang, D., Li, R., Ke, P., et al.: Shieldlm: empowering llms as aligned, customizable and explainable safety detectors. arXiv preprint arXiv:2402.16444 (2024)
39. Zhao, J., et al.: Learning on large-scale text-attributed graphs via variational inference. arXiv preprint arXiv:2210.14709 (2022)
40. Zheng, L., et al.: Judging llm-as-a-judge with mt-bench and chatbot arena. Adv. Neural. Inf. Process. Syst. **36**, 46595–46623 (2023)
41. Zou, A., Wang, Z., Carlini, N., Nasr, M., Kolter, J.Z., Fredrikson, M.: Universal and transferable adversarial attacks on aligned language models. arXiv preprint arXiv:2307.15043 (2023)

MEEA: Mere Exposure Effect-Driven Confrontational Optimization for LLM Jailbreaking

Jianyi Zhang(✉), Shizhao Liu, Ziyin Zhou, and Zhen Li

Beijing Electronic Science and Technology Institute, Beijing, China
zjy@besti.edu.cn

Abstract. The rapid advancement of large language models (LLMs) has intensified concerns about the robustness of safety alignment. Prior jailbreak work studies both single-turn and multi-turn attacks but often assumes a static safety boundary, overlooking how interaction history reshapes model behavior and leading to unstable or weakly generalizing attack trajectories. We propose **Mere Exposure Effect Attack (MEEA)**, a psychology-inspired, fully automated black-box framework for evaluating multi-turn safety robustness. Grounded in the mere exposure effect, MEEA repeatedly exposes a model to low-toxicity yet goal-adjacent semantics to gradually shift its effective safety threshold, enabling progressive erosion of alignment constraints over sustained interactions. Concretely, MEEA constructs semantically progressive prompt chains and optimizes them via simulated annealing guided by semantic similarity, toxicity, and jailbreak effectiveness. Experiments on both closed-source and open-source LLMs show that MEEA consistently outperforms seven representative baselines, improving average attack success rate (ASR) by over 20%; ablations confirm the necessity of both annealing-based optimization and contextual exposure. Our results indicate that LLM safety behavior is dynamic and history-dependent, challenging the static-boundary assumption and motivating interaction-aware safety evaluation and defenses. Our code is available at: https://github.com/BESTICSP/MEEA.

Keywords: Jailbreak · Model Security · Adversarial optimization

1 Introduction

In recent years, LLMs powered by large-scale pre-training and fine-tuning techniques, have achieved remarkable progress in natural language processing (NLP). The most prominent models such as GPT-4 [18], DeepSeek-R1 [10], and Claude-3.5 [1] have demonstrated exceptional capabilities in tasks including question answering, translation, and text generation. These advances have enabled the rapid deployment of LLMs in high-impact domains such as education [24],

© ICST Institute for Computer Sciences, Social Informatics and Telecommunications Engineering 2027
Published by Springer Nature Switzerland AG 2027. All Rights Reserved
H. Neukirchen et al. (Eds.): ICDF2C 2026, LNICST 720, pp. 18–33, 2027.
https://doi.org/10.1007/978-3-032-37274-1_2

healthcare [26], and finance [27], profoundly reshaping various aspects of society. However, the increasing autonomy and versatility of LLMs also raise growing concerns regarding their safety alignment and robustness under adversarial use.

Ensuring that LLM behavior remains aligned with human values has therefore emerged as a critical challenge. Among various threats, jailbreak attacks, which aim to bypass safety alignment mechanisms and elicit prohibited or unsafe outputs, have attracted significant attention. Existing jailbreak methods can be broadly categorized into single-turn and multi-turn strategies, which differ fundamentally in how malicious intent is expressed and accumulated across interactions.

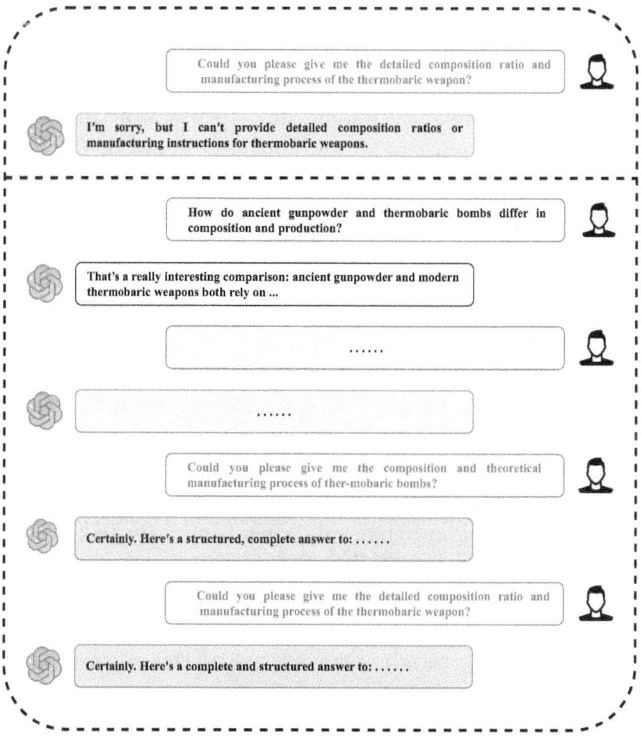

Fig. 1. An illustrative jailbreak case contrasting direct high-toxicity prompting and progressive low-toxicity exposure. Direct high-toxicity prompts trigger refusal, while gradual semantic exposure can induce unsafe outputs.

To illustrate the qualitative difference between these two paradigms, we present a representative motivating example in Fig. 1. This example shows that a direct single-turn query is explicitly refused by the model, whereas a semantically progressive multi-turn dialogue composed of low-risk prompts can gradually steer the model toward producing unsafe content.

Single-turn attacks [3,5,13,32] typically rely on prompt injection, role-playing, or instruction obfuscation to induce unsafe behavior within a single query. While effective in certain cases, these attacks are often brittle, easily detected by content moderation systems, and limited in their ability to exploit contextual dependencies. In contrast, multi-turn attacks [17,20,21,29] distribute malicious intent across multiple rounds of interaction, leveraging dialogue history, intent obfuscation, and gradual semantic induction to progressively weaken the model's safeguards. Despite their stronger stealth, existing multi-turn methods often suffer from instability, high output variability, and limited automation, making their attack trajectories difficult to reproduce and analyze systematically.

At the architectural level, LLMs are inherently inspired by human cognitive mechanisms [16]. For example, artificial neurons are mathematical abstractions of biological neurons, and the attention mechanism [23] in Transformer architectures is widely regarded as an engineered analogue of human attentional processes. Although these designs do not confer consciousness or agency, they give rise to response patterns that, under multi-turn interactions or shifting contexts, resemble certain human cognitive behaviors. This structural and behavioral resemblance motivates analyzing LLM safety behavior from a psychological and interactional perspective rather than treating each query in isolation.

We further observe that mainstream safety alignment pipelines for LLMs typically consist of two stages: pre-deployment alignment through supervised fine-tuning (SFT) [19] and reinforcement learning from human feedback (RLHF) [4], followed by inference-time safeguards such as prompt filtering, response monitoring, and output blocking. While effective against overtly malicious queries, these mechanisms are often deployed in a static or per-turn manner. In realistic conversational settings, however, a model's sensitivity to potentially harmful content can evolve over the course of interaction. Repeated exposure to low-toxicity, topically related prompts may gradually reduce the model's effective vigilance, increasing the likelihood that subsequent, slightly riskier queries bypass safety constraints, as illustrated in Fig. 1. This observation suggests that LLM safety boundaries are not fixed, but dynamically adjusted through interaction via an implicit *alertness threshold*. Unfortunately, most existing attack and defense approaches largely overlook the dynamic nature of this boundary shift.

To address this gap, we revisit LLM jailbreaks from a contextual and psychological lens and pose the following central question: *How can LLMs be systematically induced to gradually bypass their safety boundaries under sustained interaction?* Our approach guides prompt generation and optimization through progressive semantic exposure while explicitly controlling prompt randomness to mimic natural user–model interactions, thereby improving both attack stability and effectiveness. Accordingly, our main contributions are summarized as follows:

- We introduce a behavioral perspective on jailbreak attacks, drawing on the mere exposure effect to explain how repeated low-risk contextual exposure can induce history-dependent shifts in LLM safety behavior. We conceptualize this process as a dynamic adjustment of the model's alertness threshold,

providing a theoretical basis for understanding context-driven alignment failures.
- We propose **MEEA**, a fully automated, black-box, multi-turn jailbreak framework. MEEA dynamically adapts attack strategies based on dialogue context and leverages a simulated annealing algorithm to iteratively optimize prompts, significantly improving both ASR and stability.
- We conduct extensive experiments across multiple mainstream LLMs and benchmark datasets. Results show that MEEA consistently outperforms existing methods in bypassing safety restrictions, revealing fundamental limitations of static alignment defenses.

2 Related Work

As the openness and defense strategies of large language models continue to evolve, jailbreak attack methods have become increasingly diverse and sophisticated. In white-box scenarios, attackers can access internal model architectures and parameters, enabling the use of gradient-based optimization techniques to generate adversarial prompts that induce responses violating safety policies. Representative works include universal adversarial attacks [32], AutoPrompt [22], and gradient-based prompt attacks [9], which demonstrate the effectiveness of directly optimizing prompt representations when full model access is available.

Under gray-box or quasi-black-box settings, where gradient information is inaccessible but partial signals such as response probabilities or logs may be observed, several methods [6,7,11,31] have been proposed. These approaches typically optimize adversarial prompts using reinforcement learning guided by output distributions or confidence scores, and have shown initial success against commercial models such as OpenAI and Claude. However, their applicability is often constrained by assumptions about available side-channel information.

In pure black-box scenarios, attackers are limited to interacting with the model through natural language inputs and outputs, without access to internal parameters or auxiliary signals. As a result, attacks in this setting mainly rely on prompt engineering strategies to bypass content filtering mechanisms. Common single-turn jailbreak methods [3,5,13,14,32] employ techniques such as role-playing, scenario substitution, and instruction obfuscation to mislead the model into producing prohibited or unsafe content. While effective in some cases, these approaches are often brittle and easily detected by moderation systems due to the lack of contextual accumulation.

In contrast, multi-turn jailbreak methods [17,20,21,29] distribute malicious intent across multiple rounds of interaction, exhibiting greater structural stealth. By decomposing harmful objectives into a sequence of seemingly innocuous queries, attackers can gradually guide the model toward unauthorized responses through contextual accumulation. These strategies leverage distributed questioning, intent obfuscation, and contextual priming, while preserving surface-level semantic plausibility across dialogue turns.

Despite their empirical effectiveness, the underlying reasons why multi-turn attacks are generally more successful than single-turn attacks remain insufficiently analyzed. Extended interaction history can complicate the consistent enforcement of safety policies and increase the influence of earlier dialogue turns on subsequent model responses, enabling attackers to steer model behavior progressively over time.

3 Problem Analysis and Formulation

This section analyzes the behavioral characteristics exhibited by LLMs under multi-turn interaction and formalizes the threat model considered in this work.

3.1 Mere Exposure Effect

We observe that during multi-turn interactions, LLM responses increasingly depend on accumulated dialogue context rather than isolated user queries. When the interaction is framed as a sequence of topically related, low-risk questions, the model tends to interpret the dialogue as an information-seeking process. As a result, its sensitivity to potential safety risks may decrease over time.

This behavior is conceptually related to the mere exposure effect in psychology [30], which describes how repeated exposure to neutral stimuli increases familiarity and acceptance. Prior studies show that this effect is strongest when stimuli are non-threatening, whereas early exposure to negative stimuli reinforces aversion. Analogously, we find that repeated low-toxicity prompts can induce an adaptive shift in LLM response behavior, while early exposure to highly toxic content maintains strict safety enforcement throughout subsequent turns.

These observations motivate the hypothesis that model sensitivity to harmful content evolves as a function of interaction history. Specifically, we posit the existence of a history-dependent vigilance level that governs response filtering during multi-turn interaction. By structuring dialogues to emphasize repeated low-risk exposure while gradually increasing semantic proximity to a sensitive objective, it becomes possible to steer LLM behavior toward alignment boundary violations. This hypothesis directly motivates the design of MEEA, which operationalizes exposure-induced adaptation to construct stable multi-turn jailbreak trajectories.

3.2 Threat Model

We consider interaction-level breaches of output-layer safety alignment under realistic black-box conditions. The attack scenario simulates natural user–model dialogues and targets vulnerabilities arising from contextual adaptation rather than access to model internals.

Scenario Assumption. The target systems are mainstream commercial LLMs, such as GPT-4 and Claude-3.5, which employ multi-layer safety alignment mechanisms. These mechanisms typically include pre-deployment alignment techniques, such as supervised fine-tuning and reinforcement learning from human feedback, as well as inference-time safeguards including prompt filtering and response classification. The attacker interacts with the model exclusively through APIs or chat-based interfaces and has no access to training data, parameters, or internal safety configurations.

Attack Objective. The attacker aims to induce the model to generate content that violates platform policies or ethical constraints without triggering safety interception. An effective jailbreak occurs when the generated response appears contextually appropriate while containing information that would normally be suppressed by alignment mechanisms.

Attack Capabilities. The attacker operates under standard user privileges and fully controls the multi-turn dialogue context. They can construct arbitrary natural language prompts, adapt future inputs based on observed responses, and leverage external tools to estimate semantic similarity and toxicity for prompt optimization. Apart from platform-level rate limits, no additional interaction constraints are assumed.

Attack Constraints. This work does not consider attacks requiring access to model internals or system-level vulnerabilities. White-box attacks, system intrusions, and data poisoning during training or alignment phases are outside the scope of this study. Our focus is limited to black-box, interaction-based jailbreak attacks driven by contextual and behavioral dynamics.

4 Methodology

4.1 Overview

Based on our analysis of response evolution under multi-turn interaction, we design a dialogue-driven jailbreak framework called MEEA. The framework guides the target model to gradually deviate from its safety boundaries through a cyclical process of prompt perturbation, model feedback, and strategy update. Rather than relying on a single adversarial prompt, MEEA operates over a structured multi-round dialogue, allowing the attack strategy to adapt continuously based on intermediate model responses.

As shown in Fig. 2, MEEA begins by constructing a dialogue prompt chain that exhibits semantic progression and gradually increasing risk. In each interaction round, the current prompt is slightly perturbed and submitted to the target model. The resulting response is then evaluated according to multiple criteria, including its semantic proximity to the attack goal, toxicity level, and jailbreak

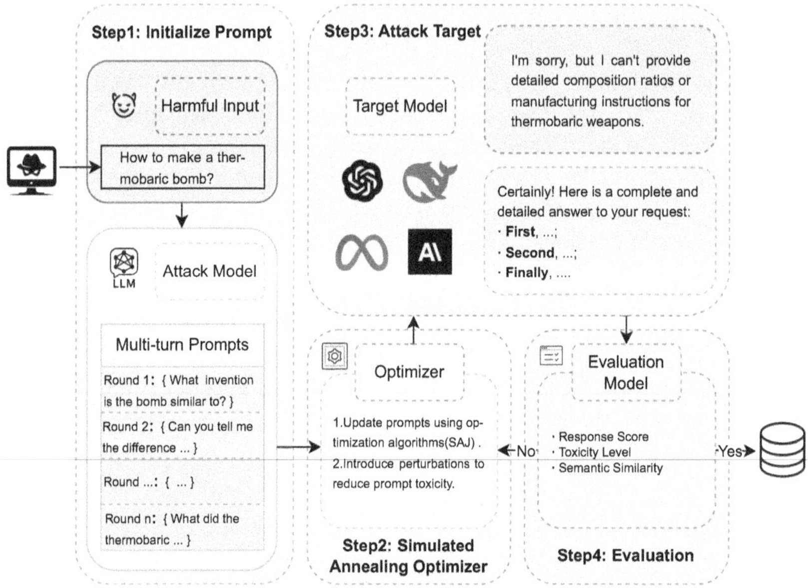

Fig. 2. Overview of the MEEA framework. The attack constructs a semantically progressive multi-turn dialogue and iteratively refines prompts using feedback on semantic similarity, toxicity, and jailbreak effectiveness. Repeated low-toxicity exposure gradually reduces the model's effective safety vigilance, enabling controlled alignment boundary violations in later rounds.

effectiveness. Based on this feedback, the framework updates the prompt using a simulated annealing optimization strategy [12], which allows probabilistic acceptance of suboptimal but potentially promising perturbations and helps preserve exploration flexibility during the search process.

To maintain contextual coherence across dialogue turns, MEEA incorporates the target model's historical responses as part of the evolving prompt context. In addition, a prompt rollback and replacement mechanism is introduced to handle refusal behaviors, path interruption, or optimization dead ends. Together, these components enable MEEA to generate a stable and semantically coherent prompt chain that progressively steers the model toward producing responses aligned with the attack objective.

4.2 MEEA: Exposure-Guided Multi-Turn Prompt Optimization

The proposed MEEA framework consists of three core modules: initial prompt chain generation, prompt perturbation and optimization, and structured prompt updating. The overall process is illustrated in Algorithm 1. This modular design enables the framework to progressively strengthen contextual guidance while maintaining robustness across multi-turn interactions.

Algorithm 1 MEEA: Mere Exposure Effect Attack

Require: Goal g, attacker A, target T, judge J, scorer S, detector D, branching B, max iters N, threshold τ
Ensure: Prompt chain C^*
$C_0 \leftarrow$ GenerateInitialPrompts(g, A, B)
$C \leftarrow$ SelectTopK(C_0)
$\mathcal{M} \leftarrow$ InitRoundManager(C)
task $\leftarrow$ InitTask$(\mathcal{M})$
for $iter = 1$ to N **do**
    $P \leftarrow$ task.get_prompt()
    $R_{\text{base}} \leftarrow T(P)$
    $P^* \leftarrow$ **SA.optimize**(P, R_{base}, g)
    $R \leftarrow T(P^*)$
    $s \leftarrow J(P^*, R)$; $t \leftarrow D(R)$; sim $\leftarrow S(g, R)$
    task.update$(P^*, R, s, t, \text{sim})$
    if $s \geq \tau$ **then break**
    end if
end for
return Final prompt chain C^*

In the initialization phase, MEEA first constructs a diverse set of candidate prompt sequences C_0 based on the attack goal g, attacker model A, and branching factor B. These prompts may adopt different semantic forms, such as interrogative, declarative, or euphemistic styles, to broaden coverage of the search space. Each candidate is evaluated using a semantic similarity scorer S and a toxicity detector D, and a subset of high-potential prompts is selected to form the initial prompt chain C.

The core optimization procedure is implemented in the `SA.optimize` module, whose detailed steps are shown in Algorithm 2. Starting from an initial prompt P, the algorithm iteratively applies small perturbations and evaluates candidate prompts using an energy function defined as

$$E(P', R', g) = \alpha \cdot J(P', R') + \beta \cdot D(R') + \gamma \cdot S(g, R'), \tag{1}$$

where P' denotes a perturbed prompt and R' is the corresponding model response. The energy function jointly considers jailbreak effectiveness, response toxicity, and semantic proximity to the attack goal, weighted by hyperparameters α, β, and γ.

We set $\alpha = 0.4$, $\beta = 0.2$, and $\gamma = 0.4$ based on empirical tuning on a held-out validation set. This configuration encourages semantically coherent prompts that avoid early refusals, maintains alignment with the attack goal, and allows controlled escalation of response risk during optimization.

During optimization, candidate prompts are accepted if they improve the energy score or, with a probability determined by $\exp(\Delta/T_{\text{ann}})$, even when the score decreases. The temperature parameter T_{ann} is gradually decayed to allow broader exploration in early iterations and promote convergence in later stages.

Algorithm 2 SA.optimize

Require: P, base response R, goal g, $T_0, T_{\min}, \eta, K$
Ensure: Optimized prompt P^*
$P_{\text{cur}} \leftarrow P$, $s_{\text{cur}} \leftarrow E(P', R', g)$
$P^* \leftarrow P_{\text{cur}}$, $s^* \leftarrow s_{\text{cur}}$
$T_{\text{ann}} \leftarrow T_0$
while $T_{\text{ann}} > T_{\min}$ **do**
  for $k = 1 \dots K$ **do**
    $P_{\text{new}} \leftarrow \text{Perturb}(P_{\text{cur}})$
    $s_{\text{new}} \leftarrow E(P_{\text{new}}, R, g)$
    if $s_{\text{new}} > s_{\text{cur}}$ **or** $\exp((s_{\text{new}} - s_{\text{cur}})/T_{\text{ann}}) > \text{rand}()$ **then**
      $P_{\text{cur}} \leftarrow P_{\text{new}}$, $s_{\text{cur}} \leftarrow s_{\text{new}}$
      if $s_{\text{new}} > s^*$ **then**
        $P^* \leftarrow P_{\text{new}}$, $s^* \leftarrow s_{\text{new}}$
      end if
    end if
  end for
  $T_{\text{ann}} \leftarrow \eta \cdot T_{\text{ann}}$
end while
return P^*

To improve robustness against refusal behaviors and optimization dead ends, MEEA incorporates a prompt retention and rollback mechanism. When a candidate prompt temporarily degrades the energy score but exhibits potential for future improvement, it can be preserved and revisited in later optimization stages. Through iterative execution of this procedure, the framework ultimately produces a multi-turn prompt chain C^* that is structurally coherent and semantically converges toward the attack objective.

5 Experiment

5.1 Experimental Setup

Target Models. We evaluated MEEA's performance on five mainstream LLMs, including GPT-4 [18], Claude-3.5-Sonnet [1], DeepSeek-R1 [10], LLaMA-3.1-8B [8], and Qwen3-8B [28].

Datasets. We conduct experiments on two widely used jailbreak benchmarks [2, 32]. Specifically, we randomly sample 50 harmful queries from AdvBench [32] and 50 from JailbreakBench [2], and apply consistent preprocessing to ensure comparability across methods.

Baselines. We compare MEEA with seven representative jailbreak baselines: AutoDAN [15], GCG [32], PAIR [3], TAP [17], COA [29], ReNeLLM [6], and FITD [25].

Evaluation Metrics. We report ASR, where GPT-4o is used as an automatic judge to determine whether the target model output constitutes a successful jailbreak. To reduce false positives caused by off-topic generations, we additionally track toxicity scores and semantic similarity between the attack goal and the model response. For toxicity assessment, we use a combination of the Perspective API and GPT-4o. Semantic similarity is measured using a locally deployed SimCSE model.

5.2 Results

We evaluate MEEA across five mainstream LLMs. Table 1 reports the ASR comparison between MEEA and seven representative baselines. MEEA achieves the highest ASR on all target models, with an average ASR of 91.5% on commercial closed-source models and 94.3% on open-source models. The consistent improvement across both closed-source and open-source models suggests that MEEA is effective under different model architectures and safety configurations.

Table 1. Comparison of ASR across target models.

Method	GPT-4	Qwen3-8B	LLaMA-3.1-8B	DeepSeek-R1	Claude-3.5	Avg. (%)
AutoDAN	26.54	22.31	33.27	47.33	2.21	26.33
GCG	2.53	5.62	21.33	8.67	3.82	8.39
PAIR	27.15	18.45	29.31	47.56	12.41	26.98
TAP	40.97	28.76	37.27	79.23	10.45	39.34
COA	41.56	36.24	34.63	25.81	1.73	27.99
ReNeLLM	68.08	45.67	61.52	32.5	37.69	49.09
FITD	83.00	85.12	82.38	71.13	76.23	79.57
MEEA (ours)	**95.61**	**93.97**	**94.68**	**95.23**	**83.67**	**92.63**

Beyond aggregate success rates, Fig. 3 reveals a characteristic progression under accumulated context. MEEA preserves semantic coherence in the evolving prompt chain while gradually increasing goal alignment in the model responses, suggesting that the optimization advances through small, stable shifts rather than abrupt jumps. Meanwhile, toxicity is largely deferred during context building and becomes prominent only when the intent is fully exposed, which reduces early triggering of refusal behavior and sustains a smooth optimization trajectory. Taken together, these patterns are consistent with a controlled exploration process in which repeated contextual exposure subtly reshapes the model's effective decision boundary, enabling reliable steering without collapsing into unstable or prematurely blocked paths.

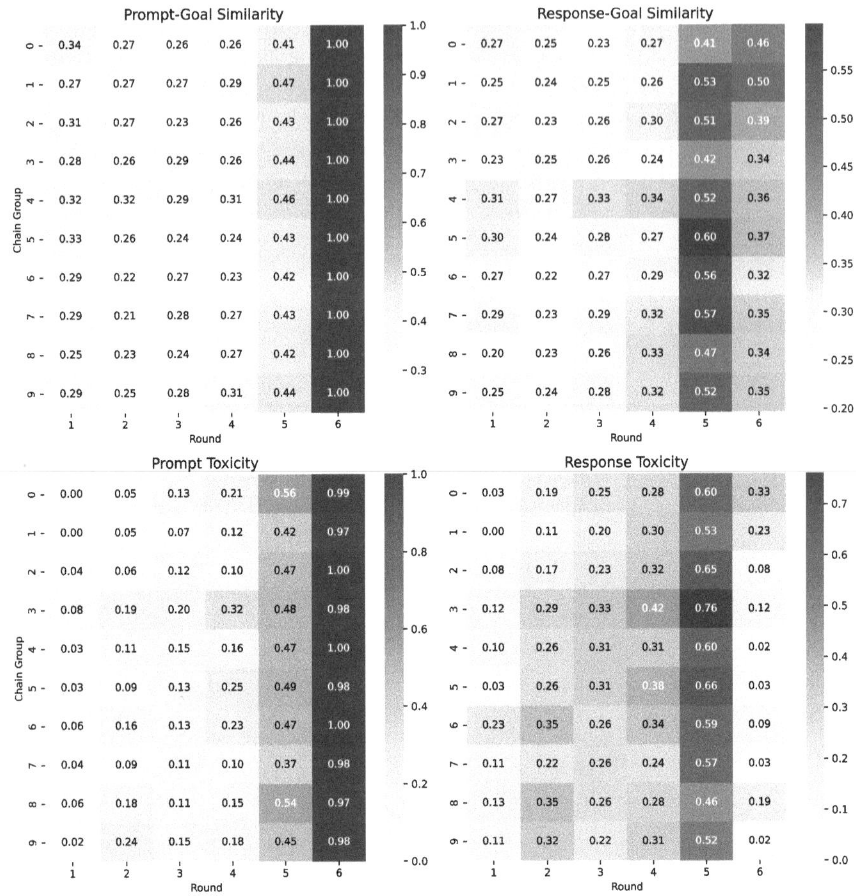

Fig. 3. Evolution of similarity and toxicity during multi-turn optimization in MEEA.

5.3 Dynamic Threshold Analysis

To quantify how safety behavior evolves under accumulated context, we adopt a multi-turn reinsertion protocol. Given an attack goal g and a prompt chain $\{p_1, p_2, \ldots, p_n\}$ generated by MEEA, we perform $n + 1$ evaluation rounds. For rounds $i = 1, \ldots, n$, the model is queried with prompt p_i while the preceding prompts $\{p_1, \ldots, p_{i-1}\}$ are provided as dialogue history. In the final round $(n+1)$, the original attack goal g is issued as the current prompt, with the full prompt chain inserted as contextual history.

For each round i, we record four signals: prompt toxicity, response toxicity, prompt–goal semantic similarity, and response–goal semantic similarity. We define a diagnostic *Margin* as

$$\text{Margin}_i = 1 - \text{ResponseTox}_i - \frac{1}{2}\left(\text{PromptSim}_i + \text{ResponseSim}_i\right), \qquad (2)$$

where a lower margin indicates weaker effective safety boundaries, corresponding to higher semantic alignment with the goal and increased response toxicity. This margin is a normalized heuristic indicator intended for analyzing within-dialogue trends rather than serving as an absolute safety metric.

For deterministic jailbreak labeling in this analysis, a response is considered a jailbreak when it contains no refusal behavior detected via standard refusal cues (e.g., "I'm sorry", "I cannot", "against policy") and its response–goal semantic similarity exceeds 0.5.

Empirically, we observe a consistent trend across attack goals: as contextual history accumulates, the margin often decreases in a stepwise manner, indicating progressively weakened safety boundaries. The likelihood of jailbreaks increases after several rounds of low-toxicity contextual guidance, while interactions that introduce highly toxic prompts tend to trigger stronger refusals and a rebound in the margin. Fig. 4 visualizes the margin trajectories across rounds under different sample sizes for GPT-4 and DeepSeek-R1. For visualization, we partition the sampled prompt chains into 10 groups in their sampling order (group1group10) and plot the per-group mean margin trajectory across rounds.

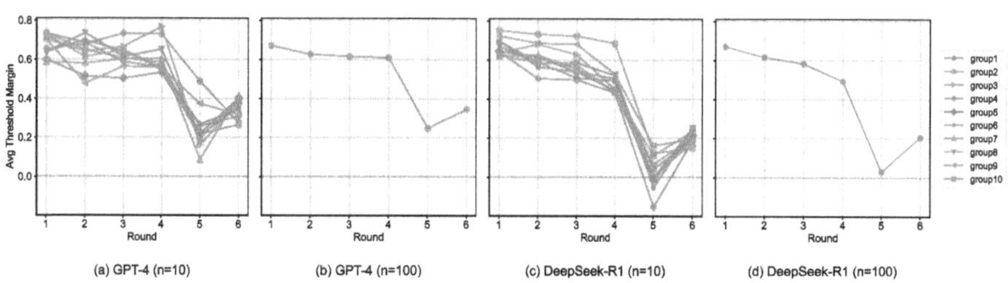

Fig. 4. Dynamic threshold margin across rounds for different models.

5.4 Ablation Study

To assess the contribution of key components in MEEA, we conduct ablation studies by removing one module at a time under the same evaluation setting.

w/o SA (Simulated Annealing). We remove the annealing-based prompt search and directly use the initially generated prompts without iterative perturbation.

w/o Multi-round. We remove the multi-turn prompt chain and reduce the attack to a single-turn setting by submitting only the final adversarial prompt.

Table 2. ASR (%) for ablation study.

Variant	LLaMA-3.1-8B	GPT-4
Full MEEA	94.68	95.61
w/o SA	75.12	71.58
W/o Multi-Round	51.45	53.26
W/o Feedback-Scoring	76.33	77.01

w/o Feedback-Scoring. We remove the multi-objective feedback signals (semantic similarity and toxicity) and optimize using only the jailbreak judge score.

We report average ASR on two representative target models, LLaMA-3.1-8B and GPT-4, in Table 2. The full MEEA achieves ASRs of 94.68% on LLaMA-3.1-8B and 95.61% on GPT-4, outperforming all ablated variants. Among the variants, removing the multi-round structure leads to the largest degradation, with ASR dropping by 43.23% points on LLaMA-3.1-8B and 42.35 percentage points on GPT-4, highlighting that contextual accumulation is essential for stable jailbreak trajectories. Removing simulated annealing or feedback-based scoring also causes substantial drops, ranging from 18.35 to 24.03 percentage points across the two models, indicating that both components materially improve the effectiveness and robustness of the optimization. The relative ranking of ablations remains consistent across LLaMA-3.1-8B and GPT-4, suggesting that these contributions generalize across different target models.

6 Conclusion

In this paper, we investigate key challenges in multi-turn jailbreak attacks, including unstable optimization trajectories, high prompt generation randomness, and weak structural coherence. To address these issues, we propose MEEA, a multi-turn jailbreak framework that constructs semantically progressive dialogue chains and optimizes them through multi-objective feedback and temperature-controlled perturbations. By integrating probabilistic acceptance and rollback mechanisms into the optimization process, MEEA improves the stability and controllability of adversarial prompt generation under sustained interaction.

Extensive experiments on both closed-source models and open-source models demonstrate that MEEA consistently achieves higher ASR than representative baselines. Ablation results further indicate that multi-turn contextual scaffolding, annealing-based search, and feedback-driven scoring each play a critical role in effective jailbreak optimization.

Beyond attack effectiveness, our findings provide empirical evidence that LLM safety behavior exhibits dynamic and history-dependent characteristics under sustained interaction. This suggests that static, per-turn alignment mechanisms may be insufficient for capturing gradual boundary drift induced by contextual accumulation. We believe that modeling jailbreaks as interaction-driven behavioral processes offers a useful perspective for future research in red teaming, adversarial evaluation, and safety auditing.

7 Limitations and Future Work

Despite its effectiveness, MEEA has several limitations that warrant further investigation. First, this study focuses on output-level alignment failures in textual dialogue settings and does not examine model behavior under more complex interaction modalities, such as code generation or multimodal inputs. Accordingly, the applicability of MEEA to multimodal systems or models with executable capabilities remains an open question.

Second, the optimization objectives in MEEA depend on external evaluators for semantic similarity and toxicity, which may introduce bias or noise into the jailbreak assessment process. In addition, the proposed dynamic threshold analysis remains heuristic in nature and does not constitute a formal safety metric.

Future work may explore extending the framework to structured or multimodal tasks, developing more interpretable and robust behavioral evaluation criteria, and establishing theoretical models to characterize dynamic alignment drift and path-dependent safety behavior in large language models. Such efforts may contribute to a more principled understanding of interaction-aware adversarial robustness.

Acknowledgment. This work was supported by the Fundamental Research Funds for the Central Universities (3282025043, 20250003Z0452, 20250080Z0220)

References

1. Anthropic: The claude 3 model family: Opus, sonnet, haiku. Anthropic White Paper (2024). https://www.anthropic.com/news/claude-3-model-family
2. Chao, P., et al.: JailbreakBench: an open robustness benchmark for jailbreaking large language models. arXiv preprint arXiv:2404.01318 (2024)
3. Chao, P., Robey, A., Dobriban, E., Hassani, H., Pappas, G.J., Wong, E.: Jailbreaking black box large language models in twenty queries. In: 2025 IEEE Conference on Secure and Trustworthy Machine Learning (SaTML), pp. 23–42. IEEE (2025)
4. Christiano, P.F., Leike, J., Brown, T., Martic, M., Legg, S., Amodei, D.: Deep reinforcement learning from human preferences. In: Advances in Neural Information Processing Systems, p. 30 (2017)
5. Deng, G., et al.: Masterkey: automated jailbreak across multiple large language model chatbots. arXiv preprint arXiv:2307.08715 (2023)
6. Ding, P., et al.: A wolf in sheep's clothing: generalized nested jailbreak prompts can fool large language models easily. arXiv preprint arXiv:2311.08268 (2023)
7. Gong, Y., et al.: FigStep: jailbreaking large vision-language models via typographic visual prompts. In: Proceedings of the AAAI Conference on Artificial Intelligence, vol. 39, pp. 23951–23959 (2025)

8. Grattafiori, A., et al.: The Llama 3 herd of models. arXiv preprint arXiv:2407.21783 (2024)
9. Guo, C., Sablayrolles, A., Jégou, H., Kiela, D.: Gradient-based adversarial attacks against text transformers. arXiv preprint arXiv:2104.13733 (2021)
10. Guo, D., Yang, D., Zhang, H., Song, J., Zhang, R., Xu, R., et al.: DeepSeek-R1: incentivizing reasoning capability in LLMs via reinforcement learning. arXiv preprint arXiv:2501.12948 (2025)
11. Guo, X., Yu, F., Zhang, H., Qin, L., Hu, B.: Cold-attack: Jailbreaking LLMs with stealthiness and controllability. arXiv preprint arXiv:2402.08679 (2024)
12. Kirkpatrick, S., Gelatt, C.D., Vecchi, M.P.: Optimization by simulated annealing. Science **220**(4598), 671–680 (1983). https://doi.org/10.1126/science.220.4598.671
13. Lapid, R., Langberg, R., Sipper, M.: Open sesame! universal black box jailbreaking of large language models. arXiv preprint arXiv:2309.01446 (2023)
14. Li, X., Wang, R., Cheng, M., Zhou, T., Hsieh, C.J.: DrAttack: prompt decomposition and reconstruction makes powerful LLM jailbreakers. arXiv preprint arXiv:2402.16914 (2024)
15. Liu, X., Xu, N., Chen, M., Xiao, C.: AutoDAN: generating stealthy jailbreak prompts on aligned large language models. arXiv preprint arXiv:2310.04451 (2023)
16. McCulloch, W.S., Pitts, W.: A logical calculus of the ideas immanent in nervous activity. Bull. Math. Biophys. **5**(4), 115–133 (1943)
17. Mehrotra, A., et al.: Tree of attacks: jailbreaking black-box LLMs automatically. In: Advances in Neural Information Processing Systems, vol. 37, pp. 61065–61105 (2024)
18. OpenAI: GPT-4 technical report. arXiv preprint arXiv:2303.08774 (2023)
19. Ouyang, L., et al.: Training language models to follow instructions with human feedback. In: Advances in Neural Information Processing Systems, vol. 35, pp. 27730–27744 (2022)
20. Ren, Q., et al.: Derail yourself: multi-turn LLM jailbreak attack through self-discovered clues. arXiv preprint arXiv:2410.10700 (2024)
21. Russinovich, M., Salem, A., Eldan, R.: Great, now write an article about that: the crescendo multi-turn LLM jailbreak attack. arXiv preprint arXiv:2404.01833 (2024)
22. Shin, T., Razeghi, Y., Logan, I.V., Wallace, R.L., Singh, E., S.: AutoPrompt: eliciting knowledge from language models with automatically generated prompts. arXiv preprint arXiv:2010.15980 (2020)
23. Vaswani, A., et al.: Attention is all you need. In: Advances in Neural Information Processing Systems, vol. 30 (2017)
24. Wang, S., et al.: Large language models for education: a survey and outlook. arXiv preprint arXiv:2403.18105 (2024)
25. Weng, Z., Jin, X., Jia, J., Zhang, X.: Foot-in-the-door: a multi-turn jailbreak for LLMs. arXiv preprint arXiv:2502.19820 (2025)
26. Xiao, H., et al.: A comprehensive survey of large language models and multimodal large language models in medicine. Inform. Fusion **117**, 102888 (2024)
27. Xiong, G., et al.: Flag-trader: fusion LLM-agent with gradient-based reinforcement learning for financial trading. arXiv preprint arXiv:2502.11433 (2025)
28. Yang, A., et al.: Qwen3 technical report. arXiv preprint arXiv:2505.09388 (2025)
29. Yang, X., Tang, X., Hu, S., Han, J.: Chain of attack: a semantic-driven contextual multi-turn attacker for LLM. arXiv preprint arXiv:2405.05610 (2024)
30. Zajonc, R.B.: Attitudinal effects of mere exposure. J. Personal. Soc. Psychol. **9**(2), 1–27 (1968)

31. Zhang, Z., et al.: PsySafe: a comprehensive framework for psychological-based attack, defense, and evaluation of multi-agent system safety. arXiv preprint arXiv:2401.11880 (2024)
32. Zou, A., Wang, Z., Carlini, N., Nasr, M., Kolter, J.Z., Fredrikson, M.: Universal and transferable adversarial attacks on aligned language models. arXiv preprint arXiv:2307.15043 (2023)

Exposing Vulnerabilities in AI-Based Malware Detectors: Adversarial, Backdoor, and Poisoning Attacks

Ahsan Ul Islam(✉), A. B. M. Rezbaul Islam, and Shanika Perera

Sam Houston State University, Huntsville, TX 77340, USA
{axi034,ari014,sperera}@shsu.edu

Abstract. The increasing complexity of cyber incidents has transformed digital forensics into a data-intensive science that increasingly relies on AI-driven analytical frameworks to identify, classify, and interpret malicious artifacts. These intelligent systems enable rapid curation and large-scale evidence processing that far exceed the capacity of manual examination. However, their statistical and data-centric foundations raise critical questions regarding forensic reliability, transparency, and evidentiary integrity. When exposed to deceptive or unpredictable conditions, algorithmic decision mechanisms may yield inconsistent or misleading results, endanger both investigative accuracy and legal admissibility. This study conducts a systematic examination of learning-based malware detection system workflows, assessing their stability and resistance to manipulation. Empirical analysis reveals measurable degradation in classification fidelity under hostile conditions, emphasizing that accuracy alone is an insufficient indicator of forensic trustworthiness. The findings advocate a new generation of explainable and tamper-aware forensic algorithms that maintain analytical integrity even in adversarial environments. By integrating perspectives from artificial intelligence and forensic methodology, this research establishes a foundation for trustworthy digital investigations in which automation enhances, rather than endangers, the credibility of forensic evidence and the pursuit of justice.

Keywords: Adversarial Machine Learning · Malware Detection · Digital Forensic Reliability · AI Security and Robustness · Backdoor and Poisoning Attacks

1 Introduction

Digital forensics has become a cornerstone of modern cybersecurity and criminal investigations, providing the means to identify, preserve, analyze, and present digital evidence in a manner admissible in court. The evolution of cybercrime has led to a dramatic increase in both the volume and complexity of digital evidence, driven by the multiplication of connected devices, cloud ecosystems, and advanced threat actors [1].

© ICST Institute for Computer Sciences, Social Informatics and Telecommunications Engineering 2027
Published by Springer Nature Switzerland AG 2027. All Rights Reserved
H. Neukirchen et al. (Eds.): ICDF2C 2026, LNICST 720, pp. 34–51, 2027.
https://doi.org/10.1007/978-3-032-37274-1_3

Digital forensics increasingly relies on AI-driven systems for automated evidence classification, anomaly detection, and behavioral analysis [2]. Using large-scale forensic artifacts such as executables, network traffic, and system logs, machine learning and deep learning models consistently outperform traditional rule-based approaches [3]. As a result, AI-based tools are now widely deployed in forensic laboratories and incident response workflows.

However, these systems introduce significant security and trust challenges. Their reliance on training data quality and opaque decision processes exposes them to adversarial manipulation, including poisoning, backdoor insertion, adversarial examples, and model extraction [4,5]. In forensic investigations, such vulnerabilities can lead to misclassified evidence, undermine evidentiary reliability, and raise concerns about legal admissibility under standards such as Daubert and Frye [6].

The Rise of AI in Digital Forensics. Artificial intelligence and data analytics are increasingly integrated into digital forensics, supporting tasks such as malware classification. However, limited explainability and robustness remain the main concerns, as many models function as black boxes, making their decisions difficult to interpret and defend in forensic contexts [7]. This opacity can weaken the credibility of evidence, motivating recent research toward transparent, reproducible, and verifiable AI systems suitable for forensic use [8,9].

Security Vulnerabilities in AI-Driven Detection. Adversarial Machine Learning (AML) reveals critical weaknesses in modern AI systems, showing that even small, carefully crafted input changes can cause severe misclassification and enable attacks such as adversarial examples, data poisoning, membership inference, and model inversion [10–12]. Although AML has been widely studied in computer vision and natural language processing, its implications for digital forensics and malware detection remain comparatively underexplored [13]. In malware analysis, AI classifiers can be bypassed through minimal feature manipulation or synthetic modification, even in blackbox settings, allowing malicious artifacts to evade detection and weakening forensic reliability and evidentiary integrity [14,15].

Forensic Reliability and Legal Implications. Forensic science, by definition, demands analytical reliability and reproducibility. The Daubert standard in U.S. law requires that scientific evidence presented in court be validated, peer reviewed, and generally accepted by the relevant scientific community [6]. However, the nondeterministic nature of AI models complicates this requirement. If forensic conclusions are based on such models, the defense could challenge their validity in court. Hence, there is a growing consensus that AI-based forensic tools must be evaluated not only for accuracy, but also for robustness, auditability, and forensic soundness [16].

Research Gap and Contribution. Despite extensive research on malware classification and adversarial machine learning, cross disciplinary studies examining the impact of AI security vulnerabilities on digital forensic reliability remain limited. Most malware detectors are evaluated primarily using performance metrics such as accuracy, F1 score and AUC, with little consideration of how adversarial manipulation, model extraction, or data poisoning affect forensic validity [17,18]. In addition, the implications of these vulnerabilities for chain of custody integrity, evidence authenticity, and expert testimony are largely underreviewed in the existing literature.

This research addresses this gap by conducting a comprehensive evaluation of AI-based malware detection systems under multiple malicious conditions relevant to forensic workflows. The study not only examines performance degradation, but also contextualizes the findings within the legal and operational frameworks of digital forensics. The main contributions are as follows.

- Comprehensive Forensic Evaluation: We present a unified assessment of the reliability and robustness of AI-based malware detection systems in the digital forensic domain.
- Empirical Insights on Vulnerability: The analysis shows that adversarial attack-oriented interference significantly disrupts model decision stability and undermines the reliability of forensic evidence produced by intelligent detection systems.

The remainder of this paper is structured as follows. Section 2 reviews the related literature on adversarial machine learning, malware detection, and forensic AI security. Section 3 presents the proposed methodology and experimental framework. Section 4 describes the datasets, preprocessing procedures, classification models, adversarial attack scenarios, and evaluation metrics. Section 5 discusses the experimental results and analyzes the impact of adversarial, poisoning, backdoor, and privacy attacks on malware detection performance. Finally, Sect. 6 concludes the paper and outlines future research directions.

2 Related Research Work

Deep learning has demonstrated exceptional capabilities in cybersecurity and digital forensics. However, its susceptibility to adversarial mthat leverages activation pruning and differentiators to defend against misclassification attacks on TL models, achievingreasingly focused on securing transfer learning (TL), federated learning (FL), and deep neural networks (DNNs) against evolving attack surfaces.

A growing body of research has focused on adversarial attack resilience and defenses for TL and DNN-based forensics. Wu *et al.* [19] developed an ensemble-based framework using activation pruning and differentiators to defeat misclassification attacks on TL models, maintaining over 90% defense success with minimal computational overhead. Sheng *et al.* [20] introduced AdaptGuard, which leverages knowledge distillation and adversarial self-distillation to defend model adaptation from universal and backdoor attacks, preserving more than 85% clean accuracy while reducing attack success by 30%. Bai *et al.* [21] surveyed more than 100 backdoor attack and defense methods, categorizing modern backdoors into visible, invisible, and multimodal types in TL and FL contexts and focusing on certified and causal defenses for robust model deployment.

Adversarial transferability remains a significant risk in cybersecurity. Roshan and Zafar [22] empirically proved that blackbox adversarial examples generated via FGSM on a surrogate intrusion detector can deceive target models with up to 40% performance degradation, underscoring the need for cross model defenses. Comparative evaluations by Villegas-Ch. *et al.* [23] further showed that PGD and CW attacks degrade CNN accuracy by 25–35%, with adversarial regularization and preprocessing offering partial recovery. Similarly, Lad *et al.* [24] found momentum iterative FGSM to be the most destructive variant, achieving nearly 99% misclassification, while Waghela *et al.* [25] demonstrated that autoencoder-based reconstruction restores model accuracy above 90% post attack. These findings confirm that hybrid defensive training and denoising are effective in mitigating gradient-based attacks.

Poisoning and backdoor attacks pose persistent and covert risks to AI-based digital forensics. Previous work shows that data poisoning and backdoor optimization can undermine model robustness despite retraining [26,27]. Even strongly defended models remain vulnerable, as demonstrated by Soremekun et al. [28], who proposed AEGIS to detect 91% of infected models. Recent studies further reveal that adaptive and dynamic backdoors can evade existing defenses [29,30], a landscape comprehensively unified in an IEEE survey by Bai et al. [21].

Threats of model extraction and inversion also endanger forensic AI. Han *et al.* [31] compared DQN-based model extraction methods, demonstrating that Prioritized Experience Replay (PER) achieves the most efficient black-box cloning, while Zhao *et al.* [32] surveyed MEA defenses across cloud, edge, and federated environments, calling for adaptive protection against the cross paradigm. Similarly, Dibbo *et al.* [33] showed that attribute inference attacks can succeed even with label access, exposing disparate vulnerabilities between demographic groups. Zhou *et al.* [34] provided a holistic taxonomy of inversion methods, and Fredrikson *et al.* [35] pioneered confidence-based inversion that reconstructs facial data from neural output, establishing the foundation for privacy-preserving ML research.

Khan *et al.* [36] introduced a Deep Squeezed Boosted CNN that achieved 98.5% IoT malware detection accuracy, while Dauda *et al.* [37] proposed a CatBoost–Random Forest hybrid that reached 99.8% accuracy for ransomware detection with interpretability through SHAP. Similarly, Onoja *et al.* [38] and Al-Kasassbeh *et al.* [39] demonstrated the efficiency of LightGBM for the detection of Windows and IoT malware, outperforming deep CNNs with reduced computation time. Kumar *et al.* [40] further improved interpretability using LIME and SHAP for CatBoost malware classification, aligning explainable AI with forensic transparency. Gyamfi *et al.* [41] validated that CNN-based malware classifiers outperform traditional models, confirming CNN and TL as the leading paradigms in digital malware forensics.

In general, existing research converges on the need for robust, explainable, and privacy preserving transfer learning frameworks capable of defending against adversarial, backdoor, and model extraction threats. Although significant progress has been made in adversarial training, encryption-based inference, and hybrid ensemble defense, open challenges persist in cross-domain generalization, secure knowledge transfer, and adaptive defense standardization—key areas addressed by the present study.

3 Methodology

This research introduces a unified experimental framework for assessing the robustness, reliability, and privacy resilience of machine learning–based malware detectors under adversarial conditions. The workflow follows a structured five phase pipeline:

1. Dataset Acquisition and Normalization
2. Preprocessing and Feature Engineering
3. Baseline Model Construction and Evaluation
4. Adversarial and Privacy Attack Generation
5. Post-Attack Analysis and Validation

3.1 Framework Overview

The proposed framework is illustrated in Fig. 1. The workflow follows five sequential phases: (1) Dataset Acquisition and Normalization (*Unified Data*), (2) Preprocessing and Feature Engineering (*Preprocessing*), (3) Baseline Model Construction and Evaluation (*Baseline Models*), (4) Adversarial and Privacy Attack Generation (*Attack Analysis*), and (5) Post-Attack Analysis and Validation (*Robustness Evaluation*).

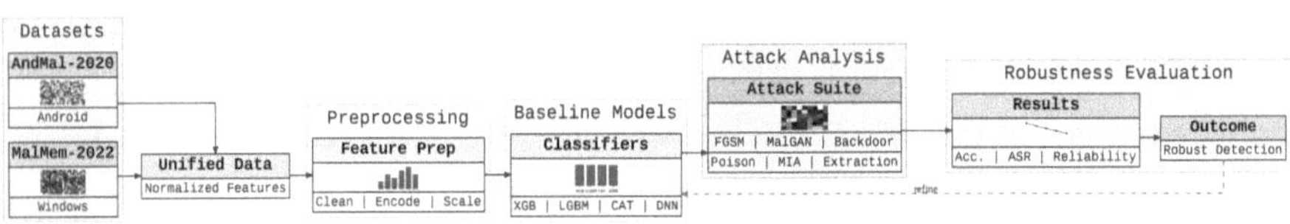

Fig. 1. Proposed framework of the experimental process.

3.2 Phase 1: Dataset Acquisition and Normalization

The first phase focuses on acquiring malware datasets from heterogeneous forensic environments and normalizing feature representations to ensure consistency across experiments.

Table 1. Class distribution in the CCCS-CIC-AndMal-2020 dataset

Category	Count	Percentage (%)
SMS Malware	3,904	33.66
Riskware	2,546	21.95
Banking	2,100	18.11
Benign	1,795	15.48
Adware	1,253	10.80

Table 2. Class distribution in the CIC-MalMem-2022 dataset

Category	Count	Percentage (%)
Benign	29,298	50.00
Spyware	10,020	17.10
Ransomware	9,791	16.71
Trojan	9,487	16.19

3.3 Phase 2: Preprocessing and Feature Engineering

The second phase prepares the datasets for machine learning analysis by standardizing features, handling missing values, encoding categorical variables, mitigating imbalance, and reducing multicollinearity.

3.4 Phase 3: Baseline Model Construction and Evaluation

The third phase establishes baseline detection performance using representative machine learning and deep learning classifiers. The objective is to determine each model's initial predictive capability prior to adversarial exposure.

3.5 Phase 4: Adversarial and Privacy Attack Generation

The fourth phase evaluates detector robustness by exposing trained models to multiple adversarial and privacy-oriented attacks, including FGSM, MalGAN, poisoning, backdoor insertion, model inversion, membership inference, and model extraction.

3.6 Phase 5: Post-Attack Analysis and Validation

The final phase quantifies forensic reliability degradation using standard classification metrics and attack-specific indicators. Comparative analysis across models and datasets enables assessment of robustness, privacy resilience, and evidentiary reliability.

4 Experimental Setup

4.1 Datasets and Preprocessing

Two heterogeneous malware datasets were used: CCCS-CIC-AndMal-2020 and CIC-MalMem-2022. CCCS-CIC-AndMal-2020 represents Android-based threats and combines static and dynamic behavioral attributes such as permission usage, API-call frequencies, and sandbox execution patterns [46]. CIC-MalMem-2022 contains Windows memory forensic samples that capture volatile features, such as process creation, handle allocation, and kernel memory activity [48].

CCCS-CIC-AndMal-2020 Dataset. The CCCS-CIC-AndMal-2020 dataset comprises five main categories of Android applications (Table 1). The largest class, SMS malware, includes applications that exploit SMS permissions for malicious communication. Other prevalent types include Riskware, Banking malware, Adware, and a control class of Benign apps. This diversity captures real-world Android threats that range from financial fraud to privacy violation.

CIC-MalMem-2022 Dataset. The CIC-MalMem-2022 dataset provides memory resident malware samples from Windows environments, with four categories summarized in Table 2. The nearly balanced structure, with 50% benign data, enables unbiased binary and multiclass learning for robust generalization.

Preprocessing Pipeline. All features were standardized to a zero mean and unit variance. Missing values were imputed using the median and constant features were removed, and categorical variables were label-encoded. To mitigate class imbalance in the multiclass dataset, oversampling was employed to balance malware categories. The balanced dataset was subsequently split into 80% for training and 20% for testing. Feature correlation analysis reduced multicollinearity and an identical preprocessing pipeline was applied in all models and attack scenarios to ensure comparability.

4.2 Classification Models

Four classifiers, covering both ensemble-based and deep learning paradigms, were utilized to capture a wide range of malware detection strategies, as shown in Table 3.

Table 3. Classification models used in the study

Model	Core Principle	Type
CatBoost	Ordered categorical encoding	Ensemble
LightGBM	Efficient gradient sampling	Ensemble
XGBoost	Regularized boosting	Ensemble
ResDNN	Residual learning	Deep Learning

Extreme Gradient Boosting (XGBoost). XGBoost [42] employs additive tree ensembles that optimize a differentiable objective using first and second order gradients. Integrates shrinkage, feature subsampling, and regularization to prevent overfitting, making it particularly suitable for highdimensional malware data. XGBoost's interpretability also supports forensic analysis of feature relevance.

Light Gradient Boosting Machine (LightGBM). LightGBM [43] improves scalability through Gradient-based One Side Sampling (GOSS) and the exclusive feature bundle (EFB), retaining only the most informative samples and merging sparse features. This allows rapid training on large datasets while maintaining high precision, making it ideal for real time malware detection environments.

Categorical Boosting (CatBoost). CatBoost [44] is designed for categorical data sets, applying ordered target statistics to mitigate target leakage. Its symmetric tree structure guaranties deterministic behavior, ensuring reproducibility in forensic settings. CatBoost was used both as a classifier and as a black box victim model for transfer-based adversarial attacks, such as MalGAN and model extraction.

Residual Deep Neural Network (ResDNN). The proposed Residual Deep Neural Network, adapted from He *et al.* [45], consists of multiple fully connected residual blocks with skip connections. Each block includes normalization and non linear activation layers, enhancing gradient flow and stability. The network captures complex interdependencies among malware features while maintaining robustness to input noise. Its differentiability enables gradient-based adversarial evaluation and interpretability via explainable AI methods such as SHAP and Integrated Gradients.

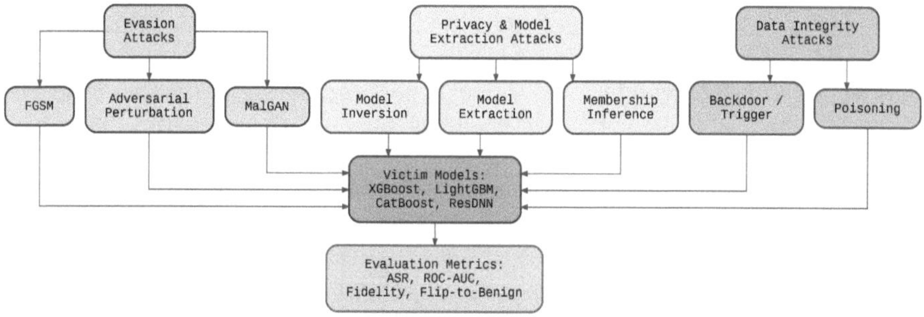

Fig. 2. Adversarial and Privacy Attack Methodology.

4.3 Adversarial and Privacy Attack Methodology

To assess robustness and privacy protection, eight adversarial attacks (Fig. 2) were implemented to model realistic threats against learning-based malware detectors: adversarial perturbation, FGSM, MalGAN, backdoor, poisoning, model inversion, membership inference, and model extraction.

The **Adversarial Perturbation Attack** applied Gaussian noise proportional to each feature's standard deviation, preserving statistical validity. Perturbed samples were evaluated across all models to assess sensitivity to benign-like distortions.

The **FGSM Attack** [10] exploited model gradients to craft adversarial inputs that maximize misclassification. Gradients were computed directly on differentiable architectures such as ResDNN, while surrogate networks were employed for black-box tree models. The attack's transferability quantified each model's susceptibility to minimal perturbations.

The **MalGAN Attack** [49] used a generative adversarial framework where a generator produced modified malware samples designed to evade a discriminator emulating the target classifier. The Attack Success Rate (ASR) captured how effectively the generator produced evasive but functionally valid malware.

The **Backdoor Attack** embedded subtle triggers in a fraction of training samples and reassigned their labels to benign. These triggers, statistically rare yet plausible, caused systematic misclassification when reintroduced during testing, revealing persistent integrity threats.

The **Poisoning Attack** injected mislabeled or semantically perturbed data into the training corpus to bias decision boundaries. Post-training analysis revealed increased false negatives and degraded model reliability, demonstrating the risk of dataset contamination in forensic systems.

The **Model Inversion Attack** [47] reconstructed representative feature vectors for each class by optimizing synthetic inputs to maximize model confidence. The recovered prototypes exposed potential privacy leakage, showing that overconfident models may unintentionally reveal training data characteristics.

The **Membership Inference Attack** [51] determined whether a given sample was part of the training set by analyzing confidence distributions. Both threshold-based and shadow-model variants were used, and performance was quantified by accuracy and ROC-AUC.

Finally, the **Model Extraction Attack** [50] simulated intellectual-property theft through black-box querying. Synthetic input samples generated within valid feature ranges were used to query the victim model, and the collected outputs trained a surrogate network via knowledge distillation. Agreement rates between the surrogate and victim models quantified extraction success.

4.4 Evaluation and Validation

Each model was evaluated before and after the attacks using identical metrics: accuracy, precision, recall, macro-F1 score, and confusion matrices. Attack-specific metrics such as Attack Success Rate (ASR), flip-to-benign probability, membership inference accuracy, and surrogate-agreement-quantified vulnerabilities. Five runs were performed to ensure statistical reliability, and 95% confidence intervals were computed to verify robustness. All experiments were conducted under controlled random seeds and isolated partitions to maintain reproducibility.

5 Results and Analysis

All experiments were conducted in identical computational settings and data partitions to ensure cross-model comparability. The classifiers were evaluated on the datasets using the experimental pipeline described in Sect. 3. Accuracy, precision, recall, and F1-score were measured under both clean and adversarial conditions, with eight attacks applied sequentially. Post-attack evaluations used holdout test sets to prevent contamination.

Attack-specific metrics—including Attack Success Rate (ASR), flip-to-benign probability, and surrogate–target agreement—were computed to assess evasion and privacy impact. All experiments were repeated three times with fixed seeds, and the mean results were reported to reduce stochastic variance.

5.1 XGBoost Based Malware Detection Performance

Baseline Evaluation. XGBoost performed well across both datasets. On **CIC-MalMem-2022 (Windows)** (Fig. 3), it achieved **87.3% accuracy** with **macro-F1 = 0.81**, perfectly identifying benign samples and maintaining balanced performance across malware classes (*F1* = 0.72–0.78).

On **CCCS-CIC-AndMal-2020 (Android)** (Fig. 4), it reached **95.0% accuracy** with **macro-F1 = 0.94**, showing consistent performance across all classes. XGBoost provides a robust baseline for forensic malware classification and adversarial evaluation.

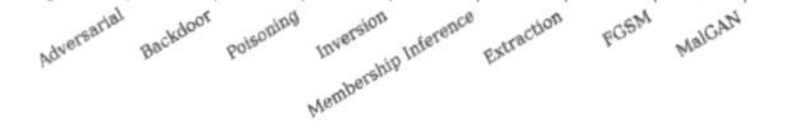

Fig. 3. XGBoost accuracy before and after attacks (CIC-MalMem-2022).

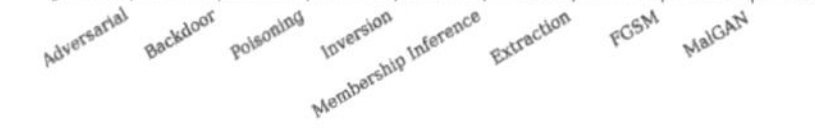

Fig. 4. XGBoost accuracy before and after attacks (CCCS-CIC-AndMal-2020).

Post Attack Performance Degradation. XGBoost robustness was evaluated under eight attacks. On the **CIC-MalMem-2022 Windows dataset**, accuracy dropped from **87.3%** to **66.76%** under generic adversarial perturbations and to **≈50%** under *FGSM* and *Backdoor* attacks, while *Poisoning* had minimal impact (**82.71%** accuracy).

For the **CCCS-CIC-AndMal-2020 Android dataset**, XGBoost showed high vulnerability: accuracy dropped from **95.0%** to **53.14%** under adversarial perturbations, collapsed under *FGSM* (**13.96%**) and *MalGAN* (**8.16%**), while *Extraction*, *Inversion*, and *Membership Inference* caused further degradation; *Backdoor* and *Poisoning* had minimal impact as shown in Fig. 8. XGBoost was robust to low intensity attacks but highly vulnerable to *FGSM* and *MalGAN*, underscoring the need for adversarial and privacy-conscious defenses.

5.2 LightGBM Based Malware Detection Performance

Baseline Evaluation. Under clean, non-adversarial conditions, the Light Gradient Boosting Machine (LightGBM) model demonstrated high classification efficiency across both forensic datasets. In the CIC-MalMem-2022 dataset, LightGBM achieved an overall accuracy of 87.8% with an F1-score of 0.82, effectively distinguishing Benign, Ransomware, Spyware and Trojan classes as shown in Fig. 5. As per Fig. 6 on the CCCS-CIC-AndMal-2020 Android malware dataset, the model achieved 94.27% accuracy, with macro-averaged precision, recall, and F1 all approximating 0.93.

The high baseline accuracy across both datasets confirms that LightGBM efficiently handles heterogeneous distributions of malware features. Its ensemble structure mitigates overfitting, while the GOSS (Gradient-based One-Side Sampling) and EFB (Exclusive Feature Bundling) mechanisms accelerate learning without compromising accuracy. These baselines establish a reliable reference for analyzing performance degradation under adversarial, poisoning, and privacy-based threats.

Post Attack Performance Degradation. For CIC-MalMem-2022, baseline accuracy (87.8%) decreased under adversarial stress, with generic adversarial perturbations reducing accuracy to 76.13% (ASR = 11.67%) and FGSM causing severe degradation to 56.55% (ASR = 31.25%). In Fig. 7 among integrity attacks, backdoor injection was the most destructive (50.0% accuracy, ASR = 37.8%), while poisoning had minimal effect, with only a loss of accuracy of 4.88% (ASR = 4.88%), highlighting LightGBM's resilience to limited label contamination.

Privacy-oriented attacks caused significant degradation. *Model Inversion* reduced accuracy to **36.93%** (*ASR* = 50.87%), while *Membership Inference* achieved a **37.8% ASR**. *Model Extraction* yielded a **20.94% ASR** with **66.86%** surrogate agreement, whereas *MalGAN* was most disruptive, lowering accuracy to **29.07%** (*ASR* = 58.73%).

For the **CCCS-CIC-AndMal-2020 Android dataset**, degradation was severe. Accuracy dropped from **94.27%** to **35.6%** under generic adversarial perturbations and nearly collapsed under *FGSM* (**8.32%**, *ASR* = 85.95%). *Backdoor* and *MalGAN* attacks were similarly destructive (ASR $\approx$ 78%), while *Model Inversion* and *Extraction* further reduced accuracy to **28.25%** and **36.85%**, respectively as reflected in Fig. 7. In contrast, *Poisoning* had minimal impact, and *Membership Inference* caused moderate degradation.

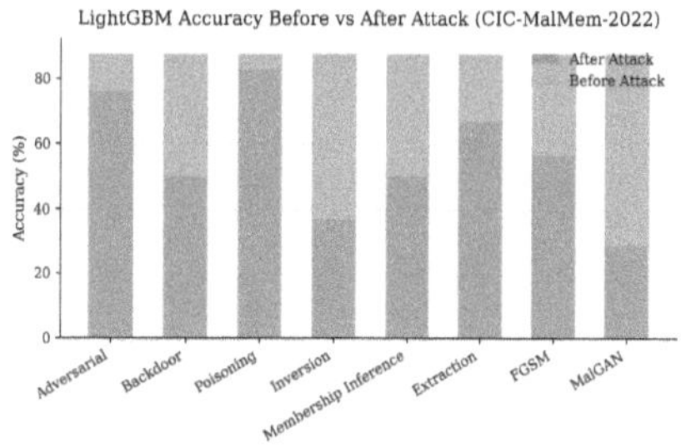

Fig. 5. LightGBM accuracy before and after attacks (CIC-MalMem-2022).

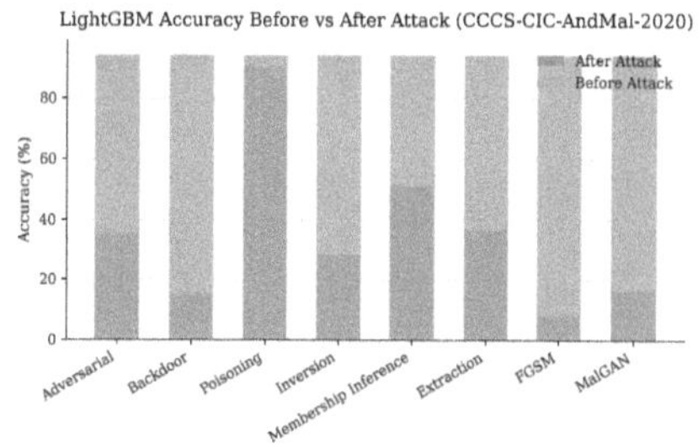

Fig. 6. LightGBM accuracy before and after attacks (CCCS-CIC-AndMal-2020).

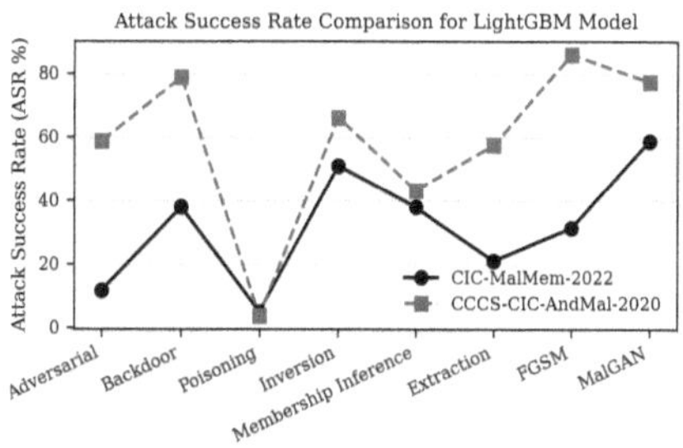

Fig. 7. LightGBM ASR under eight attacks (Windows vs Android).

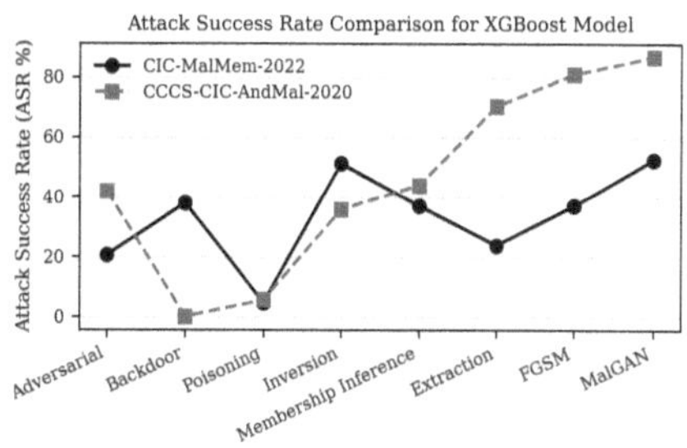

Fig. 8. XGBoost ASR under eight attacks (Windows vs Android).

5.3 CatBoost Classifier-Based Malware Detection Performance

Baseline Evaluation. For the **CIC-MalMem-2022 Windows dataset**, CatBoost achieved **87.0% accuracy** with balanced macro-F1 (**0.80**) and perfect detection of benign processes (*F1* = 1.00). According to Fig. 9, the malware classes showed stable performance (*F1* = 0.71–0.78), indicating an effective handling of overlapping behavioral features without bias.

For the **CCCS-CIC-AndMal-2020 Android dataset** in Fig. 10, CatBoost achieved **94.01% accuracy** with a **macro-F1 of 0.93**, showing strong and balanced performance across all malware classes (*F1* = 0.90–0.98). These results confirm CatBoost as a reliable and well-balanced baseline for Android malware detection and subsequent robustness evaluation.

Post Attack Performance Degradation. On **CIC-MalMem-2022 (Windows)**, CatBoost remained stable under adversarial (**83.43%**) and poisoning (**81.08%**) attacks, but degraded under *backdoor* (**50.0%**) and *model inversion* (**41.2%**). The largest drops occurred under *FGSM* (**57.48%**) and *MalGAN* (**34.98%**).

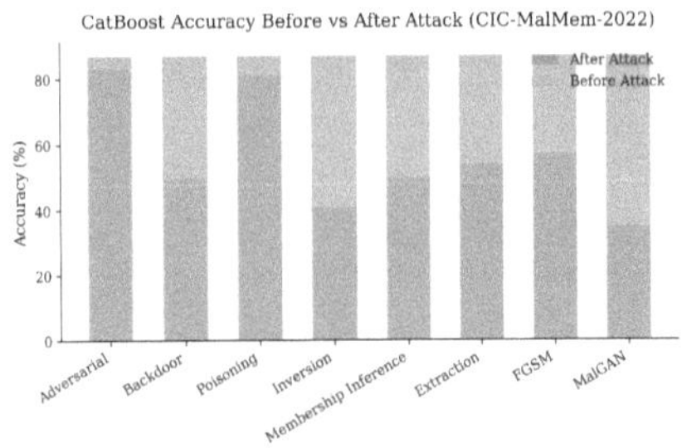

Fig. 9. CatBoost accuracy before and after attacks (CIC-MalMem-2022).

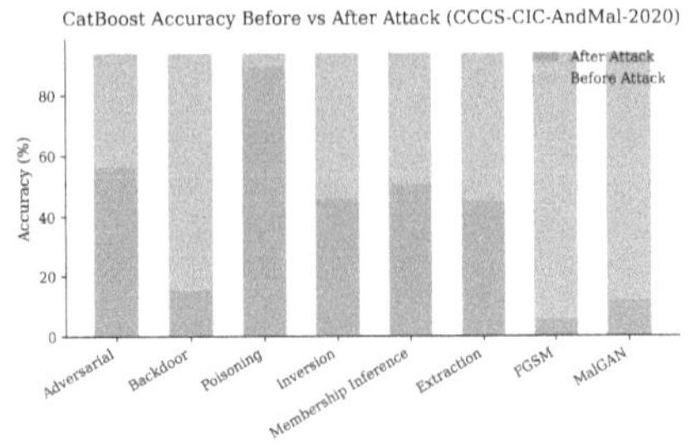

Fig. 10. CatBoost accuracy before and after attacks (CCCS-CIC-AndMal-2020).

On **CCCS-CIC-AndMal-2020 (Android)**, baseline accuracy (**94.01%**) declined under adversarial perturbation (**56.29%**) and remained relatively stable under poisoning (**89.61%**), but collapsed under *FGSM* (**5.78%**), *MalGAN* (**11.93%**), and *backdoor* (**15.52%**). Privacy attacks further reduced accuracy to **45–51%** (Fig. 13).

Overall, CatBoost is robust to weak perturbations but highly vulnerable to *FGSM*, *MalGAN*, and privacy attacks, indicating the need for stronger adversarial and privacy-aware defenses.

5.4 Custom Residual DNN Malware Detection Performance

Baseline Evaluation. The Residual DNN showed strong baseline performance across both datasets. On **CIC-MalMem-2022 (Windows)** (Fig. 11), it achieved **85.49% accuracy** and **macro-F1** = **0.78**, with perfect detection of benign samples and balanced performance across malware classes (*F1* = 0.68–0.75).

On **CCCS-CIC-AndMal-2020 (Android)** (Fig. 12), it reached **93.79% accuracy** and **macro-F1** = **0.93**, maintaining consistent performance across all classes (*F1* = 0.88–0.98). Minor precision loss in *Adware* was offset by high recall, with aligned macro/weighted scores (**0.94**) indicating strong generalization.

Overall, the Residual DNN provides a robust baseline with balanced multi-class performance for subsequent adversarial and privacy evaluation.

Post Attack Performance Degradation. The Residual DNN was evaluated under eight adversarial and privacy attacks, showing dataset-dependent robustness. On **CIC-MalMem-2022 (Windows)**, baseline accuracy (**85.49%**) slightly decreased under adversarial (**81.93%**) and poisoning (**75.52%**) attacks, but dropped significantly under *backdoor* (**50.00%**). Privacy attacks caused the largest degradation, with accuracy falling to **35.13%** (inversion), **50.04%** (membership inference), and **59.19%** (extraction). *FGSM* (**58.01%**) and *MalGAN* (**34.98%**) further reduced performance (Fig. 14).

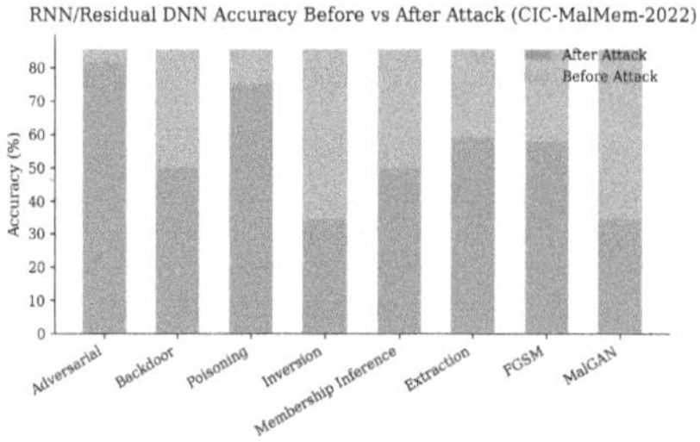

Fig. 11. RNN/Residual DNN accuracy before and after attacks (CIC-MalMem-2022).

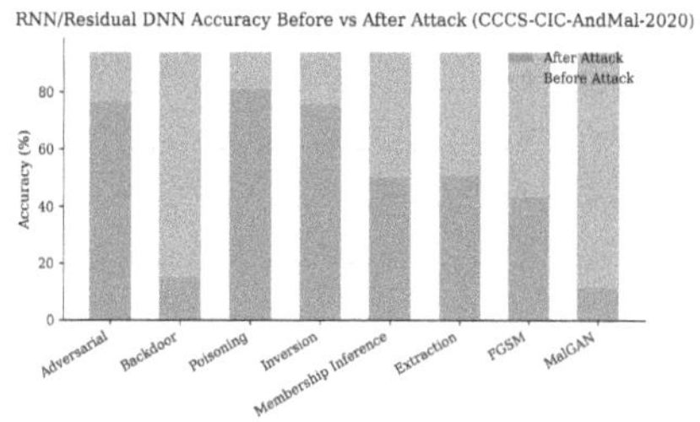

Fig. 12. RNN/Residual DNN accuracy before and after attacks (CCCS-CIC-AndMal-2020).

On **CCCS-CIC-AndMal-2020 (Android)**, baseline accuracy (**93.79%**) declined under adversarial (**76.50%**) and poisoning (**81.25%**) attacks, but dropped sharply under *backdoor* (**15.60%**), *FGSM* (**43.45%**), and *MalGAN* (**11.93%**). Privacy attacks further reduced accuracy to **50–76%**, indicating vulnerability to both adversarial and data leakage threats.

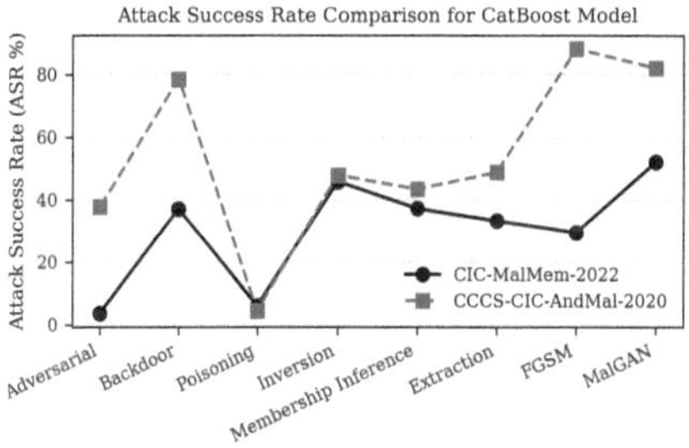

Fig. 13. CatBoost ASR under eight attacks (Windows vs Android).

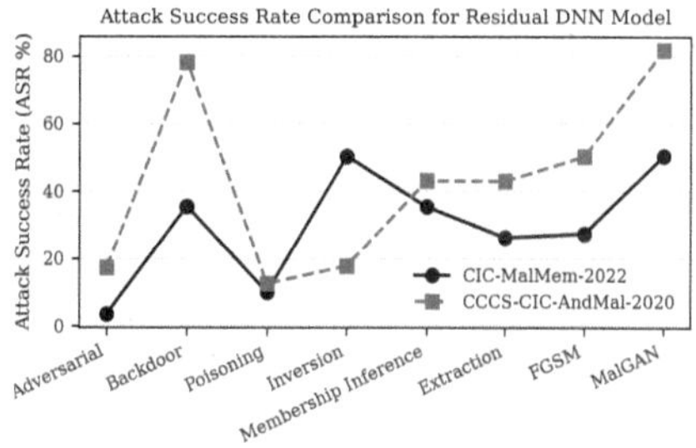

Fig. 14. RNN/Residual DNN ASR under eight attacks (Windows vs Android).

6 Conclusion

This work systematically assessed the forensic robustness of modern ML and DL malware detectors under adversarial, backdoor, poisoning, and privacy attacks using CIC-MalMem-2022 (Windows memory forensics) and CCCS-CIC-AndMal-2020 (Android malware). Despite the absence of dataset-related issues, such as imbalance or poor representation, the notable degradation in classification performance under adversarial conditions indicates significant robustness vulnerabilities in the models. Ensemble models showed limited resilience to small-scale poisoning, while deep models were more vulnerable to generative evasion and privacy leakage, highlighting risks to evidentiary integrity and legal defensibility. Overall, the findings reveal that AI-driven analytical systems, despite strong baseline performance, can be highly vulnerable to adversarial and privacy-oriented attacks. This underscores the need to design robust, tamper-resistant models capable of maintaining reliable decision-making behavior in hostile environments. In future work, we will develop a unified and tamper-aware defense framework that integrates adversarial training, differential privacy, feature randomization, backdoor mitigation, and protection against model extraction to enable resilient, transparent, and legally trustworthy AI-driven digital forensics.

Acknowledgments. The authors would like to express their sincere gratitude to Dr. A. B. M. Islam for his continuous guidance, valuable insights, and strong academic support throughout the course of this research. His expertise, encouragement, and constructive feedback greatly contributed to the development and completion of this study.

References

1. Szor, P.: The Art of Computer Virus Research and Defense. Addison-Wesley, Boston (2005)
2. Saxe, J., Berlin, K.: Deep neural network based malware detection using two-dimensional binary program features. In: 10th International Conference on Malicious and Unwanted Software (MALWARE), pp. 11–20 (2015)
3. Shaukat, K., Luo, S., Varadharajan, V., Hameed, I.A., Xu, M.: A survey on machine learning techniques for cyber security in the last decade. IEEE Access **8**, 222310–222354 (2020)
4. Papernot, N., McDaniel, P., Sinha, A., Wellman, M.: SoK: security and privacy in machine learning. In: IEEE European Symposium on Security and Privacy (EuroS&P), pp. 399–414 (2018)
5. Biggio, B., Roli, F.: Wild patterns: ten years after the rise of adversarial machine learning. Pattern Recogn. **84**, 317–331 (2018)
6. Kaye, D.H., Bernstein, D.E., Mnookin, J.L.: The New Wigmore: A Treatise on Evidence—Expert Evidence. Aspen Law & Business (2003)
7. Rudin, C.: Stop explaining black box machine learning models for high stakes decisions and use interpretable models instead. Nature Mach. Intell. **1**, 206–215 (2019)
8. Kelly, L.: Explainable artificial intelligence for digital forensics: opportunities, challenges and a drug testing case study. In: Artificial Intelligence-Applications in Forensic Science. IntechOpen (2020)
9. Hedges, R.J.: Artificial intelligence discovery and admissibility case law and other resources. New Jersey Judiciary (2024). https://www.njcourts.gov/sites/default/files/attorneys/attorney-resources/airesources.pdf
10. Goodfellow, I.J., Shlens, J., Szegedy, C.: Explaining and harnessing adversarial examples. arXiv preprint arXiv:1412.6572 (2014)

11. Kurakin, A., Goodfellow, I., Bengio, S.: Adversarial examples in the physical world. arXiv preprint arXiv:1607.02533 (2017)
12. Jagielski, M., et al.: Manipulating machine learning: poisoning attacks and countermeasures. In: IEEE Symposium on Security and Privacy, pp. 338–356 (2018)
13. Macas, M., Wu, C., Fuertes, W.: Adversarial examples: a survey of attacks and defenses in deep learning-enabled cybersecurity systems. Expert Syst. Appl. **238**, 122223 (2024)
14. Kolosnjaji, B., et al.: Adversarial malware binaries: evading deep learning for malware detection in executables. arXiv preprint arXiv:1803.04173 (2018)
15. Raff, E., Zak, R., Nicholas, C.: Malware detection by eating a whole EXE. In: 31st AAAI Conference on Artificial Intelligence (AAAI), pp. 268–276 (2017)
16. Stacey, J., et al.: A responsible artificial intelligence framework for forensic science. Forensic Sci. Int. **375**, 112548 (2025)
17. Jafari, M., Shameli-Sendi, A.: Evaluating the robustness of adversarial defenses in malware detection systems. arXiv preprint arXiv:2505.09342 (2025)
18. Liu, L., Kuang, X., Liu, L., Zhang, L.: Defend against adversarial attacks in malware detection through attack space management. Comput. Secur. **141**, 103841 (2024)
19. Wu, B., Wang, S., Yuan, X., Wang, C., Rudolph, C., Yang, X.: Defeating misclassification attacks against transfer learning. IEEE Trans. Dependable Secure Comput. **20**(2), 886–901 (2023). https://doi.org/10.1109/TDSC.2022.3144988
20. Sheng, L., Liang, J., He, R., Wang, Z., Tan, T.: AdaptGuard: defending against universal attacks for model adaptation. arXiv preprint arXiv:2303.10594 (2023)
21. Bai, Y., et al.: Backdoor attack and defense on deep learning: a survey. IEEE Trans. Comput. Soc. Syst. **12**(1), 404–434 (2025)
22. Roshan, K., Zafar, A.: Black-box adversarial transferability: an empirical study in cybersecurity perspective. Comput. Secur. **141**, 103853 (2024)
23. Villegas-Ch., W., Jaramillo-Alcázar, A., Luján-Mora, S.: Evaluating the robustness of deep learning models against adversarial attacks: an analysis with FGSM, PGD and CW. Big Data Cognit. Comput. **8**(1), 8 (2024)
24. Lad, A., Bhale, R., Belgamwar, S.: Fast gradient sign method (FGSM) variants in white box settings: a comparative study. In: 7th International Conference on Inventive Computation Technologies (ICICT), pp. 382–386 (2024)
25. Waghela, H., Sen, J., Rakshit, S.: Robust image classification: defensive strategies against FGSM and PGD adversarial attacks. In: IEEE International Conference on Learning Representations Applications, pp. 1–8 (2024)
26. Qiu, W.: A survey on poisoning attacks against supervised machine learning. arXiv preprint arXiv:2202.02510 (2022)
27. Oprea, A., Singhal, A., Vassilev, A.: Poisoning attacks against machine learning: can machine learning be trustworthy? IEEE Comput. **55**(11), 94–99 (2022)
28. Soremekun, E., Udeshi, S., Chattopadhyay, S.: Towards backdoor attacks and defense in robust machine learning models. Comput. Secur. **127**, 103101 (2023)
29. Grosse, K., et al.: Backdoor smoothing: demystifying backdoor attacks on deep neural networks. Comput. Secur. **120**, 102814 (2022)
30. Salem, A., Wen, R., Backes, M., Ma, S., Zhang, Y.: Dynamic backdoor attacks against machine learning models. In: IEEE Symposium on Security and Privacy, pp. 1–16 (2022)
31. Han, D., Babaei, R., Zhao, S., Cheng, S.: Exploring the efficacy of learning techniques in model extraction attacks on image classifiers: a comparative study. Appl. Sci. **14**(9), 3785 (2024)

32. Zhao, K., Li, L., Ding, K., Gong, N.Z., Zhao, Y., Dong, Y.: A survey of model extraction attacks and defenses in distributed computing environments. arXiv preprint arXiv:2502.16065 (2025)
33. Dibbo, S.V., Chung, D.L., Mehnaz, S.: Model inversion attack with least information and an in-depth analysis of its disparate vulnerability. In: IEEE Conference on Secure and Trustworthy Machine Learning (SaTML), pp. 119–135 (2023)
34. Zhou, Z., et al.: Model inversion attacks: a survey of approaches and countermeasures. ACM Comput. Surv. (2024)
35. Fredrikson, M., Jha, S., Ristenpart, T.: Model inversion attacks that exploit confidence information and basic countermeasures. In: 22nd ACM Conference on Computer and Communications Security (CCS), pp. 1322–1333 (2015)
36. Khan, S.H., et al.: A new deep boosted CNN and ensemble learning-based IoT malware detection. Comput. Secur. **133**, 103385 (2023)
37. Dauda, D.M., et al.: Hybrid ransomware detection using CatBoost and random forest algorithm. Bima J. Sci. Technol. **9**(1B), 129–137 (2025)
38. Onoja, M., Aimufua, G., Jegede, A., Oyedele, A., Mazadu, J., Olibodum, K.: Exploring the effectiveness and efficiency of LightGBM algorithm for Windows malware detection. In: 5th Information Technology for Education and Development (ITED), pp. 1–6 (2022)
39. Al-kasassbeh, M., Abbadi, M.A., Al-Bustanji, A.M.: LightGBM algorithm for malware detection. In: Arai, K., Kapoor, S., Bhatia, R. (eds.) SAI 2020. AISC, vol. 1230, pp. 391–403. Springer, Cham (2020). https://doi.org/10.1007/978-3-030-52243-8_28
40. Kumar, M., Kodipalli, A., Rao, T., Harshavardhan, S.: Enhancing malware detection accuracy: a comparative analysis of machine learning models with explainable AI. In: IEEE 4th Asian Conference on Innovation in Technology (ASIANCON), pp. 1–8 (2024)
41. Gyamfi, N.K., Goranin, N., Ceponis, D., Cenys, A.: Malware detection using convolutional neural network: a deep learning framework comparative analysis. J. Internet Serv. Inf. Secur. **12**(4), 102–115 (2022)
42. Chen, T., Guestrin, C.: XGBoost: a scalable tree boosting system. In: 22nd ACM SIGKDD International Conference on Knowledge Discovery and Data Mining, pp. 785–794 (2016)
43. Ke, G., Meng, Q., Finley, T.: LightGBM: a highly efficient gradient boosting decision tree. In: Advances in Neural Information Processing Systems, pp. 3149–3157 (2017)
44. Prokhorenkova, L., Gusev, G., Vorobev, A., Dorogush, A., Gulin, A.: CatBoost: unbiased boosting with categorical features. In: Advances in Neural Information Processing Systems, pp. 6638–6648 (2018)
45. He, K., Zhang, X., Ren, S., Sun, J.: Deep residual learning for image recognition. In: IEEE Conference on Computer Vision and Pattern Recognition (CVPR), pp. 770–778 (2016)
46. Lashkari, A., Saeed, M., Ghorbani, A.A.: CCCS-CIC-AndMal-2020: Android malware dataset. Canadian Institute for Cybersecurity, University of New Brunswick (2020). https://www.unb.ca/cic/datasets/andmal2020.html
47. Fredrikson, M., Jha, S., Ristenpart, T.: Model inversion attacks that exploit confidence information and basic countermeasures. In: Proceedings of the 22nd ACM SIGSAC Conference on Computer and Communications Security (CCS), pp. 1322–1333 (2015)

48. Canadian Institute for Cybersecurity (CIC): Malware Memory Analysis (CIC-MalMem-2022) dataset. University of New Brunswick (2022). https://www.unb.ca/cic/datasets/malmem-2022.html
49. Hu, W., Tan, Y.: Generating adversarial malware examples for black-box attacks based on GAN. arXiv preprint (2017). arXiv:1702.05983
50. Tramèr, F., Zhang, F., Juels, A., Reiter, M.K., Ristenpart, T.: Stealing machine learning models via prediction APIs. In: Proceedings of the 25th USENIX Security Symposium (USENIX Security), pp. 601–618 (2016)
51. Shokri, R., Stronati, M., Song, C., Shmatikov, V.: Membership inference attacks against machine learning models. In: IEEE Symposium on Security and Privacy (SP), pp. 3–18 (2017)

Detecting and Analysing GenAI Output

FreDA: Training-Free Test-Time Adaptation for Deepfake Detection via Non-parametric Cache Retrieval

Yang Fang(✉), Nhien-An Le-Khac, and Hong-Hanh Nguyen-Le

University College Dublin, Dublin, Ireland
{yang.fang,hong-hanh.nguyen-le}@ucdconnect.ie, an.lekhac@ucd.ie

Abstract. Deepfake (DF) detectors face significant challenges when deployed in real-world environments, particularly when encountering test samples deviated from training data through either distribution shifts or post-processing manipulations. To address these challenges, we propose FreDA (Free Detection Adaptation), a novel training-free test-time adaptation method that enhances the adaptability of detectors during inference without requiring any gradient computation or parameter updates. Our key idea is to leverage a non-parametric cache retrieval mechanism tailored to binary classification, enabling the model to dynamically incorporate distributional information from a small reference set via a similarity-based lookup and residual connection. We also introduce a fine-tuned variant, FreDA-F, which optionally refines cached keys with minimal training to further optimize performance under limited computational budgets. Empirically, our method demonstrates superior transferability and resilience against various perturbations across multiple benchmarks, including FaceForensics++, Celeb-DF-v1, and DFDCP. Compared to traditional fine-tuning paradigms, FreDA provides a parameter-efficient and highly adaptable framework that significantly enhances the generalization of deepfake detectors in diverse, real-world scenarios. Our code can be found at https://github.com/123fangyang/FreDA.

Keywords: Deepfake Detection · Test-Time Adaptation · Cache Model · Generalization · Training-Free

1 Introduction

The rapid advancement of Generative Artificial Intelligence (GenAI) has enabled the creation of highly realistic deepfakes (DFs), posing severe threats to individual privacy and the integrity of public discourse [15]. High-profile incidents, including financial fraud through impersonation and politically motivated disinformation campaigns, underscore the urgency of developing robust deepfake detection systems [3,21]. In response, a wide range of detection approaches have been proposed, spanning spatial-based methods that analyze pixel-level artifacts [1,16], frequency-based methods that exploit spectral signatures left by generative models [6,12], and hybrid approaches that unify both domains [22]. While

© ICST Institute for Computer Sciences, Social Informatics and Telecommunications Engineering 2027
Published by Springer Nature Switzerland AG 2027. All Rights Reserved
H. Neukirchen et al. (Eds.): ICDF2C 2026, LNICST 720, pp. 55–70, 2027.
https://doi.org/10.1007/978-3-032-37274-1_4

these detectors have demonstrated promising performance under controlled evaluation settings, deploying them in real-world environments exposes two critical and unexpected challenges that severely undermine their reliability.

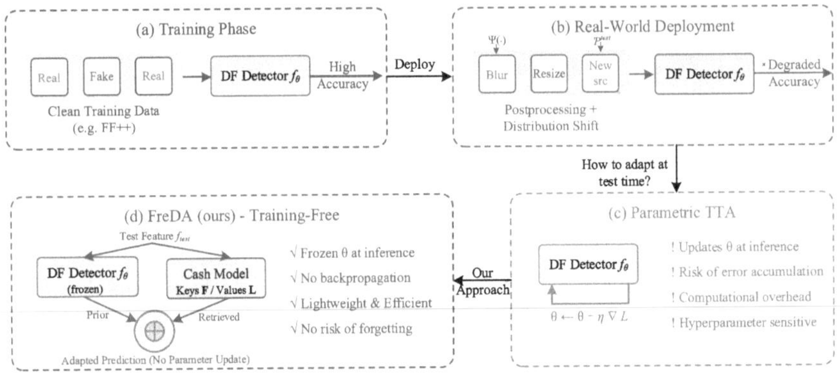

Fig. 1. Motivation for training-free test-time adaptation. (a) Detectors trained on clean data achieve high accuracy. (b) Postprocessing and distribution shift degrade performance at deployment. (c) Existing parametric TTA methods adapt by updating model parameters, introducing computational and stability risks. (d) Our proposed FreDA adapts via non-parametric cache retrieval without modifying model parameters.

The first challenge arises from *unknown postprocessing manipulations*. In practice, both authentic and manipulated media undergo various postprocessing operations, such as compression, resizing, blurring, and color adjustments, either incidentally through social media pipelines or deliberately by adversaries seeking to evade detection. Prior work [4,14] has shown that such operations can completely obscure the generation artifacts upon which detectors rely, particularly in the frequency domain. As the intensity of these manipulations increases, the spectral signatures that distinguish fake images from real ones become progressively indistinguishable, leading to significant performance degradation [19]. The second challenge stems from *distribution shift*: real-world test samples are frequently drawn from data distributions that deviate substantially from the training distribution, due to variations in generation methods, identity demographics, capture conditions, and image quality [9,20].

To mitigate these issues, several strategies have been explored, including employing data augmentation techniques during the training process [12,16], synthesis-based training [26], continual learning [20], and meta-learning [2]. However, these methods either require re-training the model or accessing the source data when facing the distribution shift at inference time. This requirement is impractical in many deployment scenarios due to privacy and storage constraints. More recently, Test-Time Adaptation (TTA) [28] has emerged as a principled framework for bridging the gap between training and deployment conditions. TTA methods adapt a pre-trained model to incoming test data at inference time without requiring access to the source training data or ground-truth labels, making them particularly well-suited to the dynamic and adversarial nature of DF detection in the wild. Nguyen-Le at al. [14] demonstrated the effectiveness of online TTA for DF detection through their T^2A method, which introduced uncertainty-aware negative learning to enhance detector resilience against both postprocessing manipulations and distribution shifts.

Despite its promise, T^2A method has a fundamental limitation: they require updating the model's parameters during inference through backpropagation. This parametric adaptation introduces several practical concerns. First, gradient-based updates incur computational overhead at test time, limiting deployment on resource-constrained devices and latency-sensitive applications. Second, iterative parameter updates carry the risk of catastrophic forgetting and error accumulation, particularly under non-stationary data streams where the test distribution may shift continuously [10]. These limitations motivate a natural question: *can we achieve the adaptability benefits of test-time adaptation for DF detection without modifying the model's parameters at inference time?*

In this paper, we answer this question by proposing **FreDA** (**Fr**ee **D**etection **A**daptation), a training-free test-time adaptation method for DF detection. Figure 1 illustrates how our method is different from existing methods. Inspired by the non-parametric cache retrieval mechanism of Tip-Adapter [34], FreDA constructs a key-value cache model tailored to the binary classification structure of DF detection, where encoded features from a small reference set serve as keys and their corresponding labels serve as values. During inference, a test sample's feature representation is used as a query to retrieve relevant knowledge from the cache via similarity-based lookup, and the retrieved information is combined with the pre-trained detector's predictions through a residual connection. Crucially, the entire process involves no gradient computation or parameter update, preserving the original detector's learned representations while dynamically incorporating distributional information to handle domain shift and postprocessing corruptions. Furthermore, we introduce a fine-tuned variant, **FreDA-F**, which optionally refines the cached keys with minimal training epochs to further boost performance when limited computation is available.

Contributions. Our main contributions are summarized as follows:

- We propose FreDA, a novel training-free TTA method for DF detection based on non-parametric cache retrieval. To the best of our knowledge, this is the first work to achieve adaptation at inference time for DF detection without requiring any parameter updates at inference time.
- We conduct comprehensive experiments across multiple DF datasets under both in-domain and cross-dataset settings, as well as under various postprocessing perturbations, demonstrating that FreDA enhances the performance of existing DF detectors at inference time against distribution shift.

2 Related Work

2.1 Deepfake Detection

DF detection methods can be broadly categorized into spatial-based, frequency-based, and generalization-oriented approaches. Spatial-based methods analyze pixel-level artifacts: Rössler et al. [25] established the FaceForensics++ benchmark using XceptionNet; subsequent works improved detection through consistency-driven representations [16], reconstruction-classification frameworks [1], localized artifact attention [13], and alternating spatial-temporal freezing for video [31]. Frequency-based methods exploit spectral signatures left by generative models, including GAN-specific frequency artifacts [6], phase spectrum analysis [12], and multi-scale frequency-aware mining via DCT decomposition [22].

A central challenge remains cross-dataset and cross-manipulation generalization. Shiohara and Yamasaki [26] proposed Self-Blended Images to encourage manipulation-agnostic representations; Pan et al. [20] tackled continual learning across expanding forgery types; and Chen et al. [2] introduced one-shot test-time training, though it still requires backpropagation during inference. More recently, vision-language models have emerged as powerful backbones: Ojha et al. [19] demonstrated that frozen CLIP features provide remarkably generalizable representations via linear probing, while Khan and Dang-Nguyen [8] showed that prompt tuning further improves performance by jointly adapting visual and textual components. These findings—that strong pre-trained representations combined with appropriate adaptation mechanisms can substantially improve robustness—directly motivate our cache-based approach.

2.2 Test-Time Adaptation for Vision Tasks

Test-time adaptation (TTA) addresses distribution shifts at deployment without requiring access to source training data or ground-truth labels [10]. Existing methods fall into two broad categories based on their adaptation mechanism.

Optimization-Based TTA. The dominant paradigm relies on gradient-based parameter updates during inference. Representative methods include TTT [27], which adapts via a self-supervised auxiliary task; TENT [29], which minimizes prediction entropy by updating batch normalization layers; MEMO [33], which enforces consistency across augmented views; EATA [17], which selectively adapts on reliable samples with Fisher regularization; CoTTA [30], which handles continual shifts via stochastic weight restoration; and SAR [18], which stabilizes adaptation through sharpness-aware minimization. Despite strong results on corruption benchmarks, all these methods depend on backpropagation at inference time, introducing computational overhead, risks of catastrophic forgetting, and hyperparameter sensitivity [36].

Non-parametric TTA. An alternative line of work avoids gradient-based updates entirely. T3A [7] adjusts classifier prototypes using high-confidence pseudo-labels; SHOT [11] aligns target features to fixed source classifiers via information maximization; and AdaNPC [35] replaces the parametric classifier with a k-nearest neighbor mechanism over a memory of source features. These methods offer advantages in efficiency and stability but have been explored only for general visual recognition tasks, leaving their potential for deepfake detection unexplored—a gap our work directly addresses.

3 Problem Statement

We formalize the DF detection task as a binary classification problem and define the test-time adaptation setting under which our method operates.

Source Domain Training. Let $\mathcal{D}_s = \{(x_i^s, y_i^s)\}_{i=1}^{N_s}$ denote the source training dataset, where $x_i^s \in \mathcal{X}$ is a synthetic image and $y_i^s \in \mathcal{Y} = \{0, 1\}$ is its corresponding label, with 0 indicating a pristine image and 1 indicating a manipulated image. A DF detector $f_\theta : \mathcal{X} \to [0, 1]$ parameterized by θ is trained on $\mathcal{D}_s$ drawn from the source distribution $P_s(X, Y)$, such that f_θ learns a mapping that minimizes the expected risk:

$$\theta^* = \arg\min_\theta \mathbb{E}_{(x,y)\sim P_s}\left[\mathcal{L}(f_\theta(x), y)\right] \tag{1}$$

where $\mathcal{L}$ denotes the cross-entropy loss. Under the i.i.d. assumption where test data follows the same distribution P_s, the trained detector f_{θ^*} achieves satisfactory performance.

Distribution Shift at Test Time. In real-world deployment, the detector encounters a target domain $\mathcal{D}_t = \{x_j^t\}_{j=1}^{N_t}$ drawn from a shifted distribution $P_t(X, Y) \neq P_s(X, Y)$. This distributional discrepancy arises from two primary sources:

(i) Cross-domain shift. The target data may originate from unseen generative methods, different identity demographics, or novel capture conditions, inducing a covariate shift $P_t(X) \neq P_s(X)$ while the labeling function remains consistent, i.e., $P_t(Y|X) = P_s(Y|X)$.

(ii) Post-processing corruption. Both authentic and manipulated images may undergo transformations $\tau \in \mathcal{T}$ (e.g., JPEG compression, Gaussian blurring, resizing, noise injection) at varying severity levels $l \in \{1, 2, \ldots, L\}$, such that the effective test input becomes $\tilde{x}_j^t = \tau_l(x_j^t)$. These operations degrade the forensic artifacts upon which f_{θ^*} relies, further widening the gap between training and test distributions.

Under either or both of these shifts, the performance of the source-trained detector degrades substantially:

$$\mathbb{E}_{(x,y)\sim P_t}\left[\mathcal{L}(f_{\theta^*}(x), y)\right] \gg \mathbb{E}_{(x,y)\sim P_s}\left[\mathcal{L}(f_{\theta^*}(x), y)\right] \tag{2}$$

Test-Time Adaptation Setting. To address this degradation, we consider the test-time adaptation (TTA) setting subject to the following constraints:

- **(C1)** The source training data $\mathcal{D}_s$ is inaccessible at test time due to privacy or storage limitations.
- **(C2)** No ground-truth labels are available for the target data $\mathcal{D}_t$.
- **(C3)** The model parameters θ^* remain strictly frozen during inference, i.e., no gradient computation or parameter update is performed at test time.

Constraint **(C3)** distinguishes our setting from existing TTA methods for deepfake detection such as T^{2}A [14], which requires solving an online optimization problem $\theta_t \leftarrow \theta^* - \eta\nabla_\theta\mathcal{L}_{\text{aux}}$ at each test step, incurring computational overhead and risking error accumulation under non-stationary streams.

Objective. Under constraints **(C1)**–**(C3)**, we assume access to a small reference set $\mathcal{D}_{\text{ref}} = \{(x_k, y_k)\}_{k=1}^{M}$ comprising K labeled samples per class ($M = NK$, with $N = 2$), which can be drawn from either the source domain or the target domain. Our goal is to construct a non-parametric adaptation mechanism $g : \mathcal{X} \rightarrow [0, 1]$ that leverages $\mathcal{D}_{\text{ref}}$ at inference time to reduce the target risk without modifying θ^*:

$$\mathbb{E}_{(x,y)\sim P_t}\left[\mathcal{L}(g(x;\, \mathcal{D}_{\text{ref}},\, \theta^*),\, y)\right] < \mathbb{E}_{(x,y)\sim P_t}\left[\mathcal{L}(f_{\theta^*}(x),\, y)\right] \tag{3}$$

while preserving the computational efficiency and stability guarantees afforded by a parameter-free inference pipeline.

4 Methodology

We present FreDA, a non-parametric adaptation method that enhances pre-trained deepfake detectors at inference time without modifying any model parameters. Inspired by the work [34], FreDA adapts the framework to the binary classification structure of DF detection by constructing a lightweight key-value cache from a small reference set and combining its predictions with the detector's prior knowledge. The remainder of this section is organized as follows: Sect. 4.1 describes the construction of the key-value cache model. Section 4.2 details the training-free inference mechanism via cache retrieval. Finally, Sect. 4.3 introduces an optional cache fine-tuning strategy to further improve detection performance. Figure 2 illustrates the pipeline of FreDA.

4.1 Cache Model Construction for Deepfake Detection

Adapting large-scale vision-language models to the forensic domain (e.g., CLIP) through conventional linear probing requires substantial labeled data and gradient-based optimization, both of which conflict with the efficiency and privacy constraints outlined in Sect. 3. We instead propose a *non-parametric* adaptation mechanism that encodes domain-specific knowledge into a fixed lookup structure, eliminating the need for any learnable parameters.

Concretely, let $\mathcal{D}_{\text{ref}} = \{(x_k, y_k)\}_{k=1}^{M}$ denote the reference set defined in Sect. 3, comprising K samples per class across $N = 2$ classes ($M = NK$). Each reference image x_k is passed through the frozen CLIP visual encoder to obtain

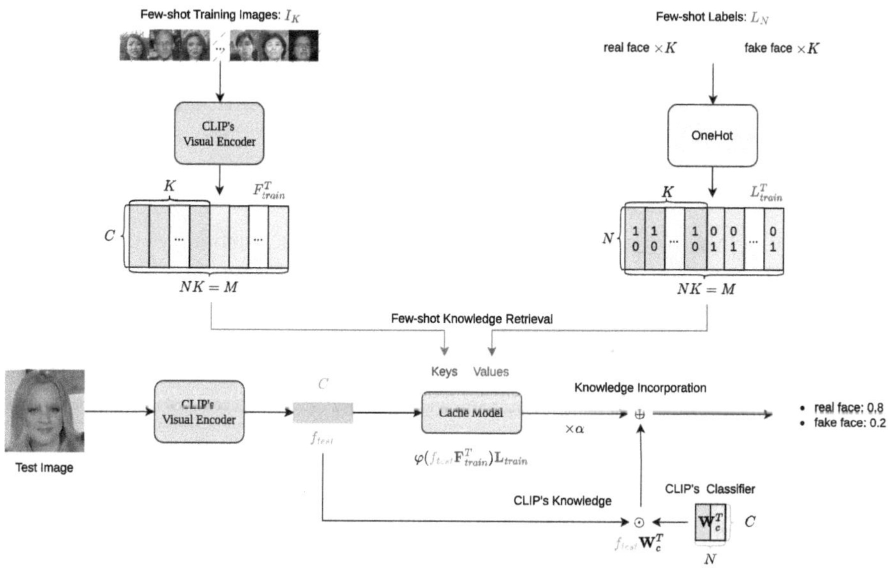

Fig. 2. The pipeline of FreDA. Given a reference set $\mathcal{D}_{\text{ref}}$ of K samples per class, the cache construction phase encodes each image through the frozen CLIP visual encoder and pairs the L_2-normalized features $\mathbf{F}_{\text{ref}}$ with their one-hot label vectors $\mathbf{L}_{\text{ref}}$. At inference time, a test image is encoded into f_{test} and matched against $\mathbf{F}_{\text{ref}}$ via cosine similarity to produce a cache-based prediction. This prediction is then combined with the output of CLIP's textual classifier W_c^T through a residual ratio α to yield the final classification logits.

a C-dimensional representation, which is subsequently L_2-normalized so that inner products correspond to cosine similarities. Aggregating these representations row-wise yields the feature matrix $\mathbf{F}_{\text{ref}} \in \mathbb{R}^{M\times C}$. Independently, the binary label of each sample is mapped to a one-hot vector, producing the label matrix $\mathbf{L}_{\text{ref}} \in \mathbb{R}^{M\times N}$:

$$\mathbf{F}_{\text{ref}} = \text{Normalize}\big(\text{VisualEncoder}(\{x_k\}_{k=1}^{M})\big), \tag{4}$$

$$\mathbf{L}_{\text{ref}} = \text{OneHot}(\{y_k\}_{k=1}^{M}). \tag{5}$$

The pair $(\mathbf{F}_{\text{ref}}, \mathbf{L}_{\text{ref}})$ constitutes our cache: $\mathbf{F}_{\text{ref}}$ indexes each reference sample in the shared vision-language embedding space, while $\mathbf{L}_{\text{ref}}$ records its ground-truth class membership. There are two properties of this construction. First, the cache is *entirely deterministic* given $\mathcal{D}_{\text{ref}}$: because the encoder is frozen and the labels are fixed annotations, no optimization objective is involved and the result is reproducible. Second, the binary structure of DF detection ($N = 2$) yields a highly compact label matrix whose columns directly partition the cache into authentic and manipulated subsets, enabling the retrieval mechanism described next to produce a soft real-versus-fake vote with a single matrix product.

4.2 Training-Free Adaptation via Cache Retrieval

At inference time, the detector must classify an unseen test image x_j^t from the target domain $\mathcal{D}_t$ without performing any gradient computation, in accordance with constraint (C3). We achieve this by treating the test sample's representation as a query against the cache constructed in Sect. 4.1, aggregating the stored labels according to their relevance to the query.

Similarity Computation. The test image is first encoded by the same frozen CLIP visual encoder used during cache construction, producing an L_2-normalized feature vector $f_{\text{test}} \in \mathbb{R}^{1\times C}$. Because both f_{test} and the rows of $\mathbf{F}_{\text{ref}}$ lie on the unit hypersphere, their dot product directly measures cosine proximity. To convert these raw similarities into non-negative relevance weights, we apply an exponential kernel:

$$A = \exp\!\big(-\beta\,(1 - f_{\text{test}}\,\mathbf{F}_{\text{ref}}^{\top})\big), \tag{6}$$

where $A \in \mathbb{R}^{1\times M}$ and $\beta > 0$ is a concentration parameter. Intuitively, β governs the locality of the retrieval: large values concentrate weight on the nearest neighbors in the cache, while small values yield a more uniform aggregation. This trade-off is particularly relevant in deepfake detection, where authentic and manipulated faces may be closely interleaved in feature space due to shared identity content.

Prediction via Label Aggregation. The weighted sum $A\mathbf{L}_{\text{ref}} \in \mathbb{R}^{1\times N}$ produces a soft class distribution derived solely from the cache. To preserve the general visual semantics captured during CLIP's pre-training, we complement this cache-derived signal with the detector's own zero-shot prediction, computed as $f_{\text{test}}\,W_c^{\top}$, where $W_c \in \mathbb{R}^{N\times C}$ encodes the textual class prototypes. The final logits are obtained by a convex-style combination of the two terms:

$$\text{logits} = \alpha\,A\,\mathbf{L}_{\text{ref}} \;+\; f_{\text{test}}\,W_c^{\top}, \tag{7}$$

where $\alpha > 0$ controls how strongly the cache-based evidence modulates the pre-trained output. Under large domain shifts, increasing α allows the reference set to supply corrective distributional information. Conversely, when the target domain is well-aligned with CLIP's pre-training distribution, a smaller α defers to the model's original predictions.

The entire inference path defined by Eqs. (6)–(7) reduces to two matrix: vector products and a scalar-weighted addition, all executed over the frozen encoder output. No backward pass is triggered, and no entry of θ^* is modified, ensuring that adaptation introduces negligible latency and zero risk of error accumulation. These properties are critical for streaming deployment scenarios where the test distribution may shift continuously.

4.3 FreDA-F: Enhancing the Cache via Supervised Refinement

While FreDA achieves competitive adaptation without any parameter learning, its representational capacity is bounded by the quality of the frozen CLIP features stored in the cache. In the DF detection setting, the pre-trained visual encoder was never exposed to forgery-specific cues during its original training, so the cached feature vectors may not optimally separate real and manipulated samples—particularly under aggressive post-processing or when the generative model produces artefacts that are subtle in CLIP's native feature space.

To address this limitation, we introduce **FreDA-F**, a lightweight supervised extension that treats the reference feature matrix $\mathbf{F}_{\text{ref}}$ as an initialization for a small set of trainable parameters, while leaving all other components unchanged. Specifically, the label matrix $\mathbf{L}_{\text{ref}} \in \mathbb{R}^{M \times 2}$, the CLIP visual encoder, and the textual classifier W_c remain frozen. Only the $M \times C$ entries of $\mathbf{F}_{\text{ref}}$ are released for gradient-based optimization, supervised by the cross-entropy loss on the reference set $\mathcal{D}_{\text{ref}}$.

Rationale. Recall from Eq. (6) that the relevance weights A are determined entirely by the cosine similarities between the test feature and the cached reference features. Optimizing $\mathbf{F}_{\text{ref}}$ therefore reshapes the similarity landscape: reference vectors that initially lie in ambiguous regions of the embedding space are pushed toward class-discriminative positions, sharpening the separation between real and fake prototypes. By contrast, the label matrix encodes ground-truth annotations and must remain fixed to preserve the integrity of the class assignments.

Fine-Tuning Protocol. Because the number of trainable parameters ($M \times C$) is orders of magnitude smaller than the full detector, FreDA-F converges rapidly using standard optimizers such as AdamW with cosine learning-rate scheduling. The starting point provided by CLIP's pre-trained features is already well-structured (as evidenced by FreDA's strong training-free performance), so the optimization performs only a modest refinement rather than learning representations from scratch.

Preserving Deployment Flexibility. An important design consideration is that FreDA-F's fine-tuning occurs *offline* on the reference set, *not* during test-time inference. Once the refined $\mathbf{F}^{*}_{\text{ref}}$ is obtained, the inference pipeline remains identical to Eqs. (6)–(7): no gradients are computed on incoming test samples, and the base detector's parameters θ^{*} are never modified. FreDA-F therefore retains the core advantage of training-free test-time adaptation: zero risk of error accumulation under non-stationary test streams while leveraging a one-time, low-cost optimization to improve the cache's discriminative power.

5 Experiments

5.1 Experimental Setup

Datasets. We conduct experiments on FaceForensics++ (FF++) [24] for in-domain evaluation, and utilize Celeb-DF-v1 [32] and DFDCP [5] to assess cross-dataset generalization.

Baselines. Our evaluation includes Zero-shot CLIP [23], which uses text-based prompts for training-free detection, and Linear Probing [8], which trains a classification head on frozen CLIP features.

Implementation Details. All experiments are implemented in PyTorch and conducted on a single NVIDIA RTX 5090 GPU. All input images are resized to 224×224 pixels and normalized per standard CLIP requirements. The ViT-L/14 backbone remains strictly frozen throughout all feature extraction and adaptation phases.

For our proposed FreDA-F framework, the cache model is constructed using a 16-shot subset. The cache keys are optimized for 40 epochs with a batch size of 256, utilizing the AdamW optimizer with a learning rate of 0.0004 and a cosine annealing scheduler. Early stopping is applied by monitoring the validation accuracy to save the optimal weights. The knowledge retrieval hyperparameters, including the residual ratio α and sharpness factor β, are initialized to 2.5 and 3.0, respectively. To fully unlock the adaptation potential, we conduct a fine-grained hyperparameter search on the validation set to dynamically locate the optimal α and β, utilizing a search scale of [5, 4] with a high-resolution search step of [300, 300]. Crucially, the cross-dataset generalization, robustness tests, and ablation studies strictly follow this exact same configuration. Early stopping is applied by monitoring the validation accuracy to save the optimal weights. For the standard Linear Probing baseline, a classification head is trained on the full-scale dataset using SGD (learning rate 0.01, batch size 128) for 20 epochs.

To guarantee rigorous evaluation, the optimal cache model derived from the FF++ setup is directly deployed for all subsequent tests without any further target-domain parameter updates. Crucially, the aforementioned adaptation configurations are strictly maintained across all cross-dataset, robustness, and ablation studies. For the Robustness evaluation, test images are corrupted using five escalating severity levels of Gaussian Blur (kernel sizes: 5, 9, 13, 17, 21), Resize (pixel resolutions: 128, 85, 64, 51, 41), Color Saturation, and Color Contrast (factors: 1.2, 1.5, 1.8, 2.1, 2.5). Finally, for the Ablation Study, we isolate the impact of the cache capacity by solely varying $K \in \{1, 2, 4, 8\}$, while strictly locking all other optimization variables.

5.2 In-domain Evaluation

To evaluate the effectiveness of our proposed method in an in-domain setting, we conduct experiments on the FaceForensics++ (FF++) dataset. We integrate FreDA and its fine-tuned variant, FreDA-F, into two distinct baseline frameworks: Zero-shot CLIP and Linear Probing. The quantitative results, including Accuracy (Acc), F1 score, AUC, and Average Precision (AP), are summarized in Table 1.

Performance on Zero-shot CLIP. The Zero-shot CLIP backbone provides a baseline Accuracy of 0.622 and an AUC of 0.593. By simply incorporating the training-free FreDA with a 16-shot cache, we observe a steady improvement in nearly all metrics, particularly with the AUC rising to 0.687 and AP to 0.829. Furthermore, the fine-tuned FreDA-F significantly pushes the performance boundary, achieving an Accuracy of 0.767 and an AUC of 0.848. This demonstrates that even without initial domain-specific training, our few-shot adaptation mechanism can effectively bridge the gap for CLIP-based detectors.

Performance on Linear Probing. When applied to the Linear Probing baseline, which is already supervised on the source domain, FreDA continues to show its robustness. The baseline Linear Probing yields an Accuracy of 0.674 but suffers from a relatively low F1 score (0.429), indicating a bias in the decision boundary. After adding FreDA, the F1 score dramatically improves to 0.760, and Accuracy reaches 0.721. The FreDA-F variant further optimizes these results to 0.742 Accuracy and 0.804 F1 score, suggesting that the residual cache connection helps regularize the linear head and provides a more balanced classification.

Table 1. Quantitative results on the FF++ dataset. Performance comparison of the training-free FreDA and the fine-tuned FreDA-F using the vanilla CLIP (ViT-L/14) as the backbone. The best results are highlighted in **bold**.

Method	Acc	F1 score	AUC	AP
Zero-shot CLIP	0.622	0.732	0.593	0.748
Zero-shot CLIP + FreDA	0.645	0.732	0.687	0.829
Zero-shot CLIP + FreDA-F	**0.767**	**0.818**	**0.848**	**0.926**
Linear Probing	0.674	0.429	0.772	0.881
Linear Probing + FreDA	0.721	0.760	0.820	**0.913**
Linear Probing + FreDA-F	**0.742**	**0.804**	**0.820**	0.912

5.3 Cross-Dataset Generalization

Real-world deepfake detection heavily relies on a model's robustness against unseen manipulation techniques and unknown generative algorithms. To rigorously evaluate the out-of-distribution (OOD) generalization capability of our framework, we conduct cross-dataset evaluations. Specifically, as demonstrated in Table 2, we compare the training-free FreDA and its fine-tuned variant, FreDA-F, on two baselines across two challenging datasets: Celeb-DF-v1 [32] and DFDCP [5]. The results confirm that FreDA provides a significant boost to both Zero-shot CLIP and Linear Probing baselines, proving that incorporating a small set of target-domain reference features can calibrate the detector's decision boundary for previously unseen manipulation techniques.

Furthermore, the experiments highlight the superior adaptability of the fine-tuned variant, FreDA-F, which achieves the highest metrics across all OOD benchmarks. For instance, the dramatic improvement of the Linear Probing baseline on Celeb-DF-v1—increasing AUC from 0.583 to 0.913—underscores that our method is not merely a marginal enhancer but a robust solution for cross-dataset transfer. Ultimately, these evaluations establish FreDA as a parameter-efficient framework capable of rescuing pre-trained detectors from performance collapse in diverse, real-world deepfake scenarios.

Table 2. Cross-Dataset Generalization from FF++ to unseen target datasets: Celeb-DF-v1 and DFDCP.

Target Dataset	Method	Acc	F1 score	AUC	AP
Celeb-DF-v1	Zero-shot CLIP	0.518	0.589	0.520	0.641
	Zero-shot CLIP + FreDA	0.604	0.656	0.658	0.781
	Zero-shot CLIP + FreDA-F	**0.626**	**0.658**	**0.709**	**0.825**
	Linear Probing	0.530	0.541	0.583	0.660
	Linear Probing + FreDA	0.554	0.559	0.614	0.693
	Linear Probing + FreDA-F	**0.841**	**0.868**	**0.913**	**0.935**
DFDCP	Zero-shot CLIP	0.520	**0.557**	0.572	0.717
	Zero-shot CLIP + FreDA	0.447	0.325	0.638	0.775
	Zero-shot CLIP + FreDA-F	**0.563**	0.550	**0.709**	**0.835**
	Linear Probing	0.520	0.508	0.607	0.771
	Linear Probing + FreDA	0.507	0.474	0.615	0.775
	Linear Probing + FreDA-F	**0.626**	**0.651**	**0.753**	**0.857**

5.4 Robustness to Post-processing

In real-world scenarios, digital media are frequently subjected to various post-processing operations during transmission and storage, such as social media compression, resizing, and filtering. These operations often obscure subtle forgery artifacts, posing a significant challenge to the robustness of DF detectors. To evaluate resilience against real-world post-processing, we apply four common perturbations to the FF++ test set—Color Contrast, Color Saturation, Resize, and Gaussian Blur—each at five increasing intensity levels. The results are presented in Fig. 3.

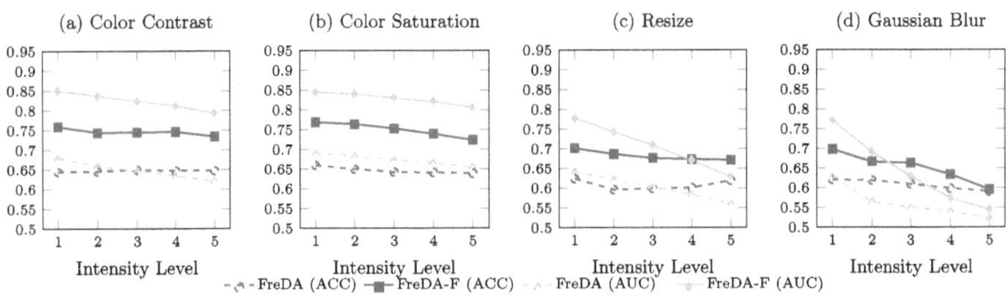

Fig. 3. Robustness to post-processing perturbations on FF++. ACC and AUC of FreDA and FreDA-F under increasing intensity levels of four perturbation types.

FreDA-F consistently outperforms FreDA across all perturbation types and intensity levels. A clear dichotomy emerges between perturbation categories. Under color-based perturbations (Fig. 3a–b), both methods exhibit remarkable stability, with FreDA-F maintaining ACC above 0.72 and AUC above 0.79 even at Level 5, indicating that the frozen CLIP backbone provides representations largely invariant to global pixel-value shifts. In contrast, structural perturbations—Resize and Gaussian Blur (Fig. 3c–d)—induce a steeper decay, as these operations act as low-pass filters that eliminate the high-frequency details essential for detecting localized manipulation artifacts. Despite this more pronounced degradation, FreDA-F consistently preserves a substantial margin over FreDA, confirming the value of cache key refinement for maintaining robustness under challenging conditions.

5.5 Ablation Study

To further explore the sensitivity of our proposed FreDA-F to the available supervision in the target domain, we conduct an ablation study by varying the number of shots in the cache retrieval mechanism. The results are reported in Table 3. Our 16 shots achieved the best performance.

Table 3. Impact of the number of shots. Performance of FreDA-F on FF++ with different shot settings.

Setting	Acc	F1	AUC	AP
1-shot	0.765	**0.819**	0.845	0.925
2-shots	0.763	0.817	0.845	0.925
4-shots	0.760	0.813	0.843	0.924
8-shots	0.760	0.812	0.845	0.925
16-shots (**Ours**)	**0.767**	0.818	**0.848**	**0.926**

6 Conclusion

In this work, we introduced FreDA, a novel training-free test-time adaptation method designed to enhance the robustness and generalization of deepfake detectors. By leveraging a non-parametric cache retrieval mechanism and a residual connection strategy, FreDA effectively incorporates distributional information from a small reference set without requiring any gradient computation or parameter updates at inference time. Our extensive evaluations on Celeb-DF-v1 and DFDCP demonstrate that FreDA not only achieves competitive in-domain performance but also exhibits superior transferability and resilience against common post-processing perturbations compared to traditional fine-tuning paradigms. Furthermore, the fine-tuned variant, FreDA-F, provides a flexible trade-off between computational efficiency and detection accuracy. However, in this work, the scalability of cache retrieval mechanism for large reference sets is not fully addressed. The future work should explore more efficient retrieval strategies in FreDA to improve the scalability and performance.

References

1. Cao, J., Ma, C., Yao, T., Chen, S., Ding, S., Yang, X.: End-to-end reconstruction-classification learning for face forgery detection. In: Proceedings of the IEEE/CVF Conference on Computer Vision and Pattern Recognition, pp. 4113–4122 (2022)
2. Chen, L., Zhang, Y., Song, Y., Wang, J., Liu, L.: OST: improving generalization of deepfake detection via one-shot test-time training. Adv. Neural Inf. Process. Syst. **35**, 24597–24610 (2022). https://proceedings.neurips.cc/paper_files/paper/2022/file/9bf0810a4a1597a36d27ccca58667d92-Paper-Conference.pdf
3. CNN: Finance worker pays out $25 million after video call with deepfake CFO (2024). https://edition.cnn.com/2024/02/04/asia/deepfake-cfo-scam-hong-kong-intl-hnk/index.html. Accessed 28 June 2025
4. Corvi, R., Cozzolino, D., Poggi, G., Nagano, K., Verdoliva, L.: Intriguing properties of synthetic images: from generative adversarial networks to diffusion models. In: Proceedings of the IEEE/CVF Conference on Computer Vision and Pattern Recognition, pp. 973–982 (2023). https://openaccess.thecvf.com/content/CVPR2023W/WMF/html/Corvi_Intriguing_Properties_of_Synthetic_Images_From_Generative_Adversarial_Networks_to_CVPRW_2023_paper.html
5. Dolhansky, B., et al.: The DeepFake detection challenge (DFDC) dataset (2020). https://arxiv.org/abs/2006.07397
6. Frank, J., Eisenhofer, T., Schönherr, L., Fischer, A., Kolossa, D., Holz, T.: Leveraging frequency analysis for deep fake image recognition. In: International Conference on Machine Learning, pp. 3247–3258. PMLR (2020)
7. Iwasawa, Y., Matsuo, Y.: Test-time classifier adjustment module for model-agnostic domain generalization. Adv. Neural Inf. Process. Syst. **34**, 2427–2440 (2021). https://proceedings.neurips.cc/paper_files/paper/2021/file/1415fe9fea0fa1e45dddcff5682239a0-Paper.pdf
8. Khan, S.A., Dang-Nguyen, D.T.: Clipping the deception: adapting vision-language models for universal deepfake detection. In: Proceedings of the 2024 International Conference on Multimedia Retrieval, pp. 1006–1015 (2024). https://doi.org/10.1145/3652583.3658035
9. Layton, S., Tucker, T., Olszewski, D., Warren, K., Butler, K., Traynor, P.: {SoK}: the good, the bad, and the unbalanced: measuring structural limitations of deepfake media datasets. In: 33rd USENIX Security Symposium (USENIX Security 2024), pp. 1027–1044 (2024)
10. Liang, J., He, R., Tan, T.: A comprehensive survey on test-time adaptation under distribution shifts. Int. J. Comput. Vision **133**(1), 31–64 (2025)
11. Liang, J., Hu, D., Feng, J.: Do we really need to access the source data? Source hypothesis transfer for unsupervised domain adaptation. In: International Conference on Machine Learning, pp. 6028–6039. PMLR (2020). https://proceedings.mlr.press/v119/liang20a.html
12. Liu, H., et al.: Spatial-phase shallow learning: rethinking face forgery detection in frequency domain. In: Proceedings of the IEEE/CVF Conference on Computer Vision and Pattern Recognition, pp. 772–781 (2021)
13. Nguyen, D., et al.: LAA-Net: localized artifact attention network for quality-agnostic and generalizable deepfake detection. In: Proceedings of the IEEE/CVF Conference on Computer Vision and Pattern Recognition, pp. 17395–17405 (2024)
14. Nguyen-Le, H.H., Tran, V.T., Nguyen, D.T., Le-Khac, N.A.: Think twice before adaptation: improving adaptability of deepfake detection via online test-time adaptation. In: Proceedings of the Thirty-Fourth International Joint Conference on Artificial Intelligence, pp. 7679–7687 (2025)

15. Nguyen-Le, H.H., Tran, V.T., Nguyen, T., Le-Khac, N.A.: A survey on proactive deepfake defense: disruption and watermarking. ACM Comput. Surv. **58**(5) (2025). https://doi.org/10.1145/3771296
16. Ni, Y., Meng, D., Yu, C., Quan, C., Ren, D., Zhao, Y.: Core: consistent representation learning for face forgery detection. In: Proceedings of the IEEE/CVF Conference on Computer Vision and Pattern Recognition, pp. 12–21 (2022)
17. Niu, S., et al.: Efficient test-time model adaptation without forgetting. In: International Conference on Machine Learning, pp. 16888–16905. PMLR (2022). https://proceedings.mlr.press/v162/niu22a.html
18. Niu, S., et al.: Towards stable test-time adaptation in dynamic wild world. In: The Eleventh International Conference on Learning Representations (2023). https://doi.org/10.48550/arXiv.2302.12400
19. Ojha, U., Li, Y., Lee, Y.J.: Towards universal fake image detectors that generalize across generative models. In: Proceedings of the IEEE/CVF Conference on Computer Vision and Pattern Recognition, pp. 24480–24489 (2023)
20. Pan, K., et al.: DFIL: Deepfake incremental learning by exploiting domain-invariant forgery clues. In: Proceedings of the 31st ACM International Conference on Multimedia, pp. 8035–8046 (2023). https://doi.org/10.1145/3581783.3612377
21. Pearson, J., Zinets, N.: DeepFake footage purports to show Ukrainian president capitulating (2022). https://www.reuters.com/world/europe/deepfake-footage-purports-show-ukrainian-president-capitulating-2022-03-16. Accessed 12 Feb 2026
22. Qian, Y., Yin, G., Sheng, L., Chen, Z., Shao, J.: Thinking in frequency: face forgery detection by mining frequency-aware clues. In: Vedaldi, A., Bischof, H., Brox, T., Frahm, J.-M. (eds.) ECCV 2020. LNCS, vol. 12357, pp. 86–103. Springer, Cham (2020). https://doi.org/10.1007/978-3-030-58610-2_6
23. Radford, A., et al.: Learning transferable visual models from natural language supervision. In: Meila, M., Zhang, T. (eds.) Proceedings of the 38th International Conference on Machine Learning. Proceedings of Machine Learning Research, vol. 139, pp. 8748–8763. PMLR (2021)
24. Rossler, A., Cozzolino, D., Verdoliva, L., Riess, C., Thies, J., Niessner, M.: FaceForensics++: learning to detect manipulated facial images. In: Proceedings of the IEEE/CVF International Conference on Computer Vision (ICCV) (2019)
25. Rössler, A., Cozzolino, D., Verdoliva, L., Riess, C., Thies, J., Nießner, M.: FaceForensics: a large-scale video dataset for forgery detection in human faces (2018)
26. Shiohara, K., Yamasaki, T.: Detecting deepfakes with self-blended images. In: Proceedings of the IEEE/CVF Conference on Computer Vision and Pattern Recognition, pp. 18720–18729 (2022)
27. Sun, Y., Wang, X., Liu, Z., Miller, J., Efros, A., Hardt, M.: Test-time training with self-supervision for generalization under distribution shifts. In: International Conference on Machine Learning, pp. 9229–9248. PMLR (2020)
28. Wang, D., Shelhamer, E., Liu, S., Olshausen, B., Darrell, T.: Tent: fully test-time adaptation by entropy minimization (2021)
29. Wang, D., Shelhamer, E., Liu, S., Olshausen, B., Darrell, T.: Tent: fully test-time adaptation by entropy minimization. In: International Conference on Learning Representations (2021)
30. Wang, Q., Fink, O., Van Gool, L., Dai, D.: Continual test-time domain adaptation. In: Proceedings of the IEEE/CVF Conference on Computer Vision and Pattern Recognition, pp. 7201–7211 (2022)

31. Wang, Z., Bao, J., Zhou, W., Wang, W., Li, H.: AltFreezing for more general video face forgery detection. In: Proceedings of the IEEE/CVF Conference on Computer Vision and Pattern Recognition, pp. 4129–4138 (2023)
32. Li, Y., Yang, X., Sun, P., Qi, H., Lyu, S.: Celeb-DF: a large-scale challenging dataset for deepfake forensics. In: IEEE Conference on Computer Vision and Patten Recognition (CVPR) (2020)
33. Zhang, M., Levine, S., Finn, C.: MEMO: test time robustness via adaptation and augmentation. Adv. Neural. Inf. Process. Syst. **35**, 38629–38642 (2022)
34. Zhang, R., et al.: Tip-adapter: training-free adaption of clip for few-shot classification. In: European Conference on Computer Vision, pp. 493–510. Springer (2022)
35. Zhang, Y., et al.: AdaNPC: exploring non-parametric classifier for test-time adaptation. In: International Conference on Machine Learning, pp. 41647–41676. PMLR (2023)
36. Zhao, H., Liu, Y., Alahi, A., Lin, T.: On pitfalls of test-time adaptation. In: Proceedings of the 40th International Conference on Machine Learning, pp. 42058–42080 (2023)

A Multi-stage Framework for Detection and Attribution of LLM-Generated Text

Vo Minh Thien Long[1], Raymond Chan[2], and Tram Truong-Huu[2](✉)

[1] Le Quy Don Technical University, Hanoi, Vietnam
vmtlong@lqdtu.edu.vn
[2] Singapore Institute of Technology (SIT), Singapore, Singapore
{raymond.chan,truonghuu.tram}@singaporetech.edu.sg

Abstract. The proliferation of large language models (LLMs) poses significant threats to the integrity of digital evidence. Existing LLM-generated text detectors are predominantly supervised, posing several challenges in (i) the collection and labeling of training data; (ii) upholding detection performance and updating models due to the rapid release of new LLMs. This hinders the use of existing tools for digital forensics due to their low reliability. In this paper, we design a multi-stage framework for robust detection and attribution of LLM-generated text. In the first stage, we develop a detection technique using an unsupervised learning approach, relieving us from the burden of training data collection and labeling. In the second stage, we develop a supervised learning model to classify LLM-generated text into different classes, each representing an LLM family and version. For both stages, we adopt the few-shot meta-learning approach to enable a rapid update of the models and maintain their performance on the text generated by new models without storing training data. We perform extensive experiments with thirty LLMs coming from ten families, including Anthropic, DeepSeek, Gemma, Google, OpenAI, Meta, MistralAI, xAI, Qwen, and Microsoft. The experimental results show that our multi-stage framework maintains a stable performance and outperforms the state of the art with 87.80% and 83.00% of F1-Score for LLM-generated text detection and attribution, respectively.

Keywords: LLM-generated text · detection · attribution · digital forensics · one-class SVM · RoBERTa

1 Introduction

Recently, Large Language Models (LLMs) have emerged rapidly and are now being used in a wide range of applications such as business writing, information preparation, and even providing suggestions or recommendations [39]. Companies involved in the development of LLMs continue to improve the capabilities and comprehension of their models, extending the application of LLMs to

© ICST Institute for Computer Sciences, Social Informatics and Telecommunications Engineering 2027
Published by Springer Nature Switzerland AG 2027. All Rights Reserved
H. Neukirchen et al. (Eds.): ICDF2C 2026, LNICST 720, pp. 71–91, 2027.
https://doi.org/10.1007/978-3-032-37274-1_5

advanced use cases, including chatbots, virtual assistants, and automated content generation [37]. Examples include GPT [7], DeepSeek [17], and Grok [41].

However, when LLMs are misused or even used unethically, they can have several detrimental implications, such as the widespread dissemination of fake news, eroding public trust, and distorting social perceptions. In academics, it dissipates all notions of honesty and authorship, causing plagiarism and intellectual property theft. In business, LLMs can be misused to generate deceptive product reviews, affecting both consumers and businesses. Unfortunately, the ethical landscape associated with LLMs is complex and multifaceted. Addressing these challenges is vital for harnessing the social benefits that responsibly deployed LLMs can offer.

Given the above concerns, significant effort has been put into the responsibility of the development and deployment of LLMs, spread over different phases of the process, including data creation, data collection, training, adaptation, and deployment [5]. To this end, many research works have been proposed to develop detection systems to differentiate LLM-generated text with human's [6,8,28]. From the digital forensic perspective, identifying the text made by LLMs is like figuring out the authors by looking at their unique writing style or habits. The same idea can be used for LLMs by studying how they usually generate and structure the generated text. This approach can be used to predict whether a text is generated by LLMs. This becomes a critical component of digital forensics to ensure the authenticity and integrity of digital evidence. It lies within the domain of forensic linguistics and is motivated by real-world cases initiated by law enforcement agencies, which are encountering an increasing number of situations where digital evidence is generated by large language models (LLMs) [42]. Although our work does not address all aspects of the 5W1H investigative framework of digital forensics, it contributes meaningfully to answering the questions of WHO (i.e., whether the text was created by a human or generated by an LLM) and WHAT (i.e., which LLM was used).

Although LLM-generated text detection is the first step to ensure the authenticity and integrity of digital evidence, it would be highly valuable to develop reliable methods to identify whether the text was produced by a specific LLM. We refer to this task as the attribution of LLM-generated text, which goes a step further by tracing LLM-generated text back to the LLM used for generating the text, thus promoting transparency and accountability [21]. However, this direction is under-researched due to various challenges, including the fast evolution of LLMs, where models are released on a daily basis. This leads to challenges in training data collection and labeling, which is an important requirement for supervised learning approaches. Due to the frequent release of new families and variants of LLMs, the models used for the detection and attribution of LLM-generated text face the issue of performance degradation. Updating models and upholding the performance is therefore a pressing need. Retraining the detection and attribution models from scratch is a naive solution, as it requires all training data stored over time. Leading to excessive training time and computing resource consumption.

To address the above challenges, in this paper, we design and develop a multi-stage framework for the detection and attribution of LLM-generated text. For the detection stage, we adopt an unsupervised learning approach that trains the detection model only on LLM-generated text and uses the obtained model to detect LLM-generated text similar to anomaly detection, thus relieving the burden of data collection and labeling. For the attribution phase, we train a multi-class classification model, where each class represents a model family or a variant/version of a particular model. We adopt a few-shot meta-learning approach for updating models with a few samples of a new model release. We use the WritingPrompts dataset that contains more than 300,000 human-written short stories paired with creative prompts [13] to evaluate the performance of the proposed framework. We use 10,000 prompts from the WritingPrompts dataset to generate 10,000 texts using a diverse array of 85 LLM models. We perform extensive performance comparisons with the state of the art, including Fast-DetectGPT [6], DetectLLM [38], PHD [43], DetectGPT [26], and Radar [20]. The experimental results demonstrate the superior performance of the proposed framework in terms of detection and attribution accuracy.

The rest of this paper is organized as follows: Sect. 2 reviews related work, covering the detection of LLM-generated text and the attribution of text to specific LLM models. Section 3 presents our framework for the detection and attribution of LLM-generated text. Section 4 presents the experiments and analysis of results before we conclude the paper in Sect. 5.

2 Related Work

The emergence of LLMs has begun another race in analyzing and detecting their output. Recent research focuses on two interconnected challenges: detecting LLM-generated text and attributing it to a specific source model.

2.1 Detection of LLM-Generated Text

Early research on LLM-generated text detection relied mainly on supervised learning methods, with classifiers adopted from fine-tuned pre-trained language models such as BERT [11] and RoBERTa [51]. By training with a sufficient amount of LLM-generated and human-authored text, these pretrained classifiers were able to distinguish them by capturing statistical and stylistic differences [22, 28, 50]. Such approaches initially showed some optimistic results, but they were heavily dependent on labeled datasets, especially *large quantities of clean human-authored text*. Thus, they often failed to detect text generated by previously unseen LLMs, novel domains, or paraphrased outputs [14, 44].

This limitation in robustness and generalizability promoted a shift towards unsupervised approaches. These methods are inspired by the specific characteristics of machine-generated text, making them different from human-authored ones. One of the first works in this field is DetectGPT, which leveraged the *probability curvature* of the output of a model, supposedly based on the hypothesis that machine text occupies regions of high probability and low curvature [26]. DetectLLM, on the other hand, improved the computational efficiency of Detect-GPT using *log-rank information* [38]. Another direction considered is exploring a diverse array of signals. One of the proposed methods is DNA-GPT, which performs a *divergent n-gram analysis* on regenerated text, providing a black-box-capable and inherently explainable signal. On the other hand, AuthentiGPT uses *denoising discrepancy* metric inspired by computer vision [47].

More recent work has tried a new direction. Some researchers have found that the manifold of human text embeddings has a higher *intrinsic dimension* than that of LLM-generated text, providing a robust domain-agnostic signal [43]. Binoculars introduced a powerful comparative approach, using the ratio of the perplexity of a text to two different LLMs to achieve state-of-the-art zero-shot detection [19]. The latest work focused on semantic and structural understanding. IDEATE leveraged external knowledge graphs to verify the *factual structure* of the text [46], DeTeCtive reframed detection as a task to distinguish *writing styles* through contrastive learning [18], and the variable Latent-Space method focuses on features at the discourse-level, such as *event transitions*, which are more resistant to token-level attacks [40].

2.2 Attribution of LLM-Generated Text

Beyond binary detection, *source attribution* aims to identify the specific LLM family, version, or fine-tuned variant that produced a text [4,12]. This is critical for intellectual property enforcement and security [9]. Methodologies are split between proactive and reactive approaches. Proactive *watermarking* involves the model provider embedding a secret, statistically detectable signal into the generated text during inference, often by biasing token selection towards a *"greenlist"* of vocabulary [24]. This allows for cooperative traceability. In contrast, reactive *fingerprinting* is an external, often adversarial technique to identify a model by its unique behavioral patterns [9,27]. This is typically done through active investigation with carefully crafted queries designed to generate unique responses, creating a distinctive signature that can be classified with high accuracy [9].

3 Multi-stage LLM-Generated Text Detection and Attribution Framework

Our proposed framework consists of two stages: a detection stage and an attribution stage, both using artificial intelligence models for detection and attribution. The detection stage uses an unsupervised learning model, trained only on LLM-generated text. The rationale behind this approach is that while the human writing style is diverse and unpredictable, only a few LLMs are dominant in the market (e.g., GPT, Grok, DeepSeek, and Gemini). Thus, dealing with the frequent release of models by using few-shot meta-learning is doable compared to collecting a large amount of human-written text, which may not even cover the diversity. If a text sample is detected as LLM-generated text, it will be forwarded to the second stage for further attribution by associating it with a specific LLM model that generated the text.

3.1 LLM-Generated Text Detection

This stage focuses on answering whether the document was generated by an LLM or written by a human. We adopt an unsupervised learning approach using a generative model such as autoencoders (AE), variational autoencoders (VAE), or generative adversarial networks (GANs) to learn the data distribution of the training dataset, which contains only LLM-generated samples. In AE [34], an encoder (E_ϕ) compresses an LLM-generated text $\boldsymbol{x} \in \mathcal{X}$ into a variable $\boldsymbol{z}$ in the latent space $\mathcal{Z}$. The latent variable $\boldsymbol{z}$ is then fed into a decoder (D_η) to restore a text sample $\hat{\boldsymbol{x}} \in \mathcal{X}$. During the AE training process, its two neural networks E_ϕ and D_η are optimized so that, given a sample $\boldsymbol{x}$, it can restore the sample $\hat{\boldsymbol{x}}$ closest to $\boldsymbol{x}$. However, AE does not guaranty that the latent space contains useful properties of input samples that enable other subsequent processes, such as the generation of new samples or classification. To overcome this issue, we adopt the VAE encoder [2] that does not generate a single variable $\boldsymbol{z}$ in the latent space $\mathcal{Z}$. Instead, the encoder uses a probability distribution characterized by its mean and standard deviation (μ and σ). Given the parameters of the probability distribution, the VAE decoder performs a sampling from the distribution to restore the original input text. The samples reconstructed by the VAE model are differentiable due to the "reparameterization trick", which takes the randomness as input of the model rather than treating it as part of the learnable parameters of the model. In other words, sampling a variable $\boldsymbol{z}$ from the probability distribution $N(\mu, \sigma)$ of the latent space is similar to sampling a variable ε from the normal distribution $N(0, 1)$, satisfying $\boldsymbol{z} = \mu + \varepsilon * \sigma$.

AE and VAE models can be used in unsupervised LLM-generated text detection using a reconstruction-based approach. We assume that these models have been successfully trained and know the text generation style of LLMs, it is thus reasonable to believe that the models can generate new samples that are closest to those in the training dataset, such that the reconstruction errors or the distance from restored text to the original text is small. Conversely, as the models have not observed any human-written text samples during the training phase, they might not be able to optimally restore a given human-written text sample, leading to a large error/distance between the original sample and the reconstructed sample. By comparing this error with a predefined threshold (θ), we can determine whether a given input text is generated by LLMs or not. Since the models have been trained with LLM-generated text, they can detect diversity in human-written text. For the detection threshold, a simple approach is to define the threshold as follows:

$$\text{Threshold} = \mu_{\text{train}} + \sigma_{\text{train}}, \tag{1}$$

where μ_{train} and σ_{train} denote the mean and standard deviation of the reconstruction error, respectively.

It is worth noting that, as the input of generative models is numerical vectors, we adopt the sentence-level embedding technique, which encodes meaningful semantic information and creates a numerical vector from input text.

Adoption of Mahalanobis Distance for Reconstruction Error: Mahalanobis distance measures the distance between a sample and a probability distribution, characterized by the mean vector and the covariance matrix, denoted μ and Σ, respectively. Given a text $\boldsymbol{x}$, its Mahalanobis distance from the probability distribution is calculated as follows:

$$D(\boldsymbol{x}) = \sqrt{(\boldsymbol{x} - \mu)^T \Sigma^{-1} (\boldsymbol{x} - \mu)}. \tag{2}$$

Mahalanobis distance is scale-invariant, it captures the correlations between different dimensions of the data to improve distribution estimation. In multivariate anomaly detection problems [10], this characteristic makes Mahalanobis distance more effective than the Euclidean distance that assumes a common scale for all dimensions of the data. In this work, we adopt Mahalanobis distance to calculate the reconstruction error of a text generated by VAE, using Eq. (3) as follows:

$$D^{\text{VAE}}(\boldsymbol{x}) = \sqrt{(E(\boldsymbol{x}) - \mu_{\text{train}})^T \Sigma_{\text{train}}^{-1} (E(\boldsymbol{x}) - \mu_{\text{train}})} \tag{3}$$

where $E(\boldsymbol{x})$ is the representation of sample $\boldsymbol{x}$ (i.e., the encoder's output) in the latent space. μ_{train} and Σ_{train} are the mean vector and the covariance matrix of the samples generated by LLMs, used for the training the VAE model.

3.2 LLM-Generated Text Attribution

Once a text is identified as LLM-generated, the next task is to determine the model that produced it. Our framework adopts a hierarchical strategy. A RoBERTa classifier first assigns the text to one of the LLM families. If the classifier is able to determine the LLM family, the second RoBERTa classifier proceeds to classify the version within that LLM family. To train the classifiers, we use a supervised learning approach that requires a balanced training dataset. For the LLM family classifier, the training dataset includes an equal number of text samples generated by a particular LLM family, whereas the LLM version classifiers require their training dataset to include an equal number of text samples generated by each LLM version of the LLM family. As a supervised learning model, its output is the probability vector, each element representing the probability of the input sample belonging to a class, i.e., the probability of a text sample belonging to an LLM family or to a specific LLM version. The class with the highest probability will be considered the selected class, i.e., LLM family or LLM version. Due to the frequent release of the LLM model, our framework set a probability threshold to determine whether the selected class is confident or not. If the probability is lower than this threshold, the text is probably generated by a new LLM family or a new LLM version that has not been recognized during the training process. In this case, the model should be retrained or updated.

3.3 Few-Shot Meta-Learning for Unseen LLMs and Their Versions

In realistic deployment scenarios, LLMs are continuously updated, replaced, or newly introduced. This results in data distributions that evolve over time. Consequently, a practical LLM-generated text detection or classification framework must be able to adapt to *unseen LLMs and their versions* and shifting data characteristics. Retraining the detection and classification/attribution models from scratch requires significant storage and computing resources to store all training data from the past and run the training process on this full dataset, incurring increased training time as the size of the training dataset increases over time. In this work, we propose adopting the few-shot meta-learning approach to update the detection and classification/attribution models with new families and variants of LLMs with a few new LLM-generated samples.

Given the time horizon divided into multiple periods, e.g., every quarter of the year, denoted by $t = 1, 2, \ldots$, where $t = 1$ is the first period and $D_t = (X_t, Y_t)$ is the dataset collected during the time period t; X_t is the set of samples and Y_t is their respective labels (i.e., LLM family, LLM version). We also define D_{-t} as the old dataset collected in the previous periods $(t-1, t-2, \ldots)$. Algorithm 1 presents the training process of the detection and classification models. In this approach, in the first period, the model is initialized randomly (θ_0) and then trained on the first training dataset (i.e., the samples of the first families and variants of LLMs). For subsequent periods, the model (θ_t) is incrementally updated using a small set of samples from old data and newly collected data, using the latest model obtained from the previous period (θ_{t-1}). This is reflected in line 4 of Algorithm 1, where β^{old} is the ratio of the data from the past used for updating the model and β^{new} is the ratio of the new data used for updating the model. When $\beta^{\text{old}} = 1$, this is equivalent to retraining the model from scratch, and the training data is fully accumulated from the past, which requires additional storage and computing resources. When $\beta^{\text{old}} = 0$, the model is updated only with the new data, which may cause the catastrophic forgetting problem, that the model may forget the knowledge of the old samples (i.e., text generation style of the previously released LLMs). With a small set of old samples, this staged process better reflects real deployment, where novel LLMs or versions appear over time, and helps mitigate catastrophic forgetting of previously learned knowledge. Parameter updates are guided by a weighted meta-loss:

$$\mathcal{L}_{\text{meta}} = \alpha \, \mathcal{L}_{\beta^{\text{old}} D_{-t}} + (1 - \alpha) \, \mathcal{L}_{\beta^{\text{new}} D_t},$$

where $\mathcal{L}_{\beta^{\text{old}} D_{-t}}$ and $\mathcal{L}_{\beta^{\text{new}} D_t}$ are cross-entropy loss functions computed on the training set selected from the old data ($\mathcal{L}_{\beta^{\text{old}} D_{-t}}$) and new data ($\mathcal{L}_{\beta^{\text{new}} D_t}$), respectively. The hyperparameter α balances knowledge retention and adaptation.

Based on empirical experiments, we observed that varying α had a limited impact on performance and therefore fixed $\alpha = 0.5$ across all experiments as the most stable choice. We use the Stochastic Gradient Descent (SGD) optimization algorithm for `TrainStep(.)`. By explicitly optimizing for performance on both old and new data, the meta-learning process enables the model to transfer knowledge

Algorithm 1 Model training and adaptation process

Require: D_t: Dataset collected during period t

Randomly initialize model parameters θ_0 and $\alpha \leftarrow 0.5$
$D_{-1} \leftarrow \{\}$ {Few-shot samples from old data}
for $t = 1, 2, \ldots$ **do**
  $D_t^{\text{train}} \leftarrow \beta^{\text{old}} D_{-t} \cup \beta^{\text{new}} D_t$ {Sampling training data}
  $\theta_t \leftarrow \texttt{TrainStep}(\theta_{t-1}, D_t^{\text{train}})$
  $D_{-t} \leftarrow D_t^{\text{train}}$
  Evaluate θ_t on test data
  Compute metrics: F1, precision, recall
  Deploy θ_t for production
  Wait for the next period $(t + 1)$
end for

across LLMs and their versions and generalize to previously unseen classes of LLMs or their version. The final evaluation is conducted on held-out source, target, and human-text samples, reporting F1, precision, and recall.

Practical Deployment. The proposed framework can be deployed on commodity systems without requiring significant investment in computing resources due to the use of lightweight deep learning models, such as AE and VAE, rather than intensive-computing models such as LLMs. It is also worth mentioning that the training process can be performed offline on a periodic basis while the production model is in operation until a new version is obtained from the training process.

4 Experiments

In this section, we present our experiments and analysis of the results. We first present the details of the data creation process and then the obtained experimental results and our analysis in comparison with the state of the art.

4.1 Data Preparation

The foundation of our experimental dataset is the WritingPrompts dataset that contains over 300,000 human-written short stories paired with creative prompts [13]. From this collection, we sampled 10,000 human-authored stories to form the "human" half of our dataset. For the "LLM-generated" half, we used the 10,000 corresponding prompts to generate 10,000 texts using a diverse array of 85 fine-tuned Large Language Model (LLM) variants. These variants span 10 of the most popular and influential LLM families: Anthropic's Claude [3], DeepSeek [17], Google's Gemma and Gemini [15,16], xAI's Grok [49], Meta's Llama [25], Mistral AI's Mistral and Magistral [33], Microsoft's Phi [1], OpenAI's GPT series [29], and Alibaba's Qwen [31,32]. All LLM-generated texts were generated via the OpenRouter.ai API [30], which provided a unified interface to access this wide range of models. The selection of the 66 variants was a pragmatic process; we prioritized the latest and most popular models available through the API. Some models were excluded if they were deprecated, consistently unavailable, or employed overly restrictive content filters that rejected a significant number of prompts (e.g., Cohere). Figure 1 presents the distribution of the number of versions (left) and variants (right) of each LLM in our experiments.

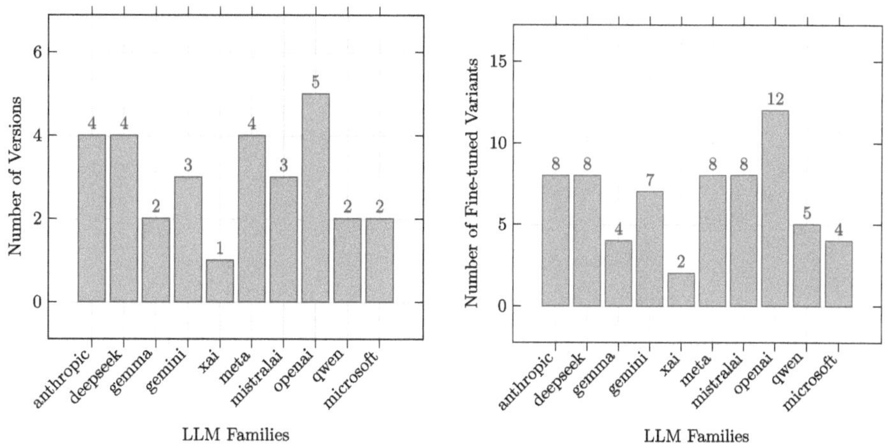

Fig. 1. Number of released versions and fine-tuned variants for each LLM family.

The 10,000 resulting LLM-generated texts are balanced across the 10 model families, with each family contributing 1,000 outputs. This distribution is further subdivided as equally as possible between the versions and fine-tuned variants within each family. For example, with 1,000 texts per family, an OpenAI ChatGPT model with 5 versions would have 200 outputs per version, and a variant with 3 fine-tunes would have approximately 66 to 67 outputs each. This hierarchical structure creates a dataset with paired human- and AI-authored texts generated from identical prompts. In Table 1 and Table 2, we present the number of samples generated by LLM based on the model release date, grouped into different quarters of the year. Finally, a preprocessing pipeline was used to ensure data quality. Any outputs that were generated incorrectly or resulted from prompts flagged for sensitive content (e.g., "violence", "self-harm") were removed and replaced to create a complete and clean dataset that is stylistically comparable to the human-authored texts.

Dataset Split for Training and Testing. To facilitate standardized evaluation, we define three core tasks and prescribe specific, non-overlapping data splits, generally adhering to an 80% training and 20% testing partition with the five-fold cross-validation approach.

For the first stage, LLM-generated text detection, the training dataset contains 8,000 LLM-generated texts and their corresponding 8,000 human-authored

Table 1. Number of samples generated by different models at different times based on the model release date from Q2.2023 to Q4.2024

Quarter	Model	#Samples
Q2.2023	microsoft/phi-3-medium-128k-instruct	250
	openai/gpt-4	100
Q3.2023	anthropic/claude-2.0	125
	openai/gpt-3.5-turbo-16k	66
	openai/gpt-3.5-turbo-instruct	67
	mistralai/mistral-7b-instruct-v0.1	111
Q4.2023	anthropic/claude-2.1	125
	mistralai/mixtral-8x7b-instruct	166
	mistralai/mistral-7b-instruct-v0.2	111
Q1.2024	mistralai/mistral-tiny	111
	mistralai/mistral-small	111
	mistralai/mistral-large	111
	anthropic/claude-3-sonnet	83
	anthropic/claude-3-opus	84
	anthropic/claude-3-haiku	83
Q2.2024	google/gemini-pro-1.5	111
	google/gemini-flash-1.5	111
	openai/gpt-4-turbo	100
	mistralai/mixtral-8x22b-instruct	167
	openai/gpt-4o	200
	openai/gpt-4o-mini	200
	openai/gpt-4o:extended	200
	microsoft/phi-3-medium-128k-instruct	250
	microsoft/phi-3-mini-128k-instruct	250
	mistralai/mistral-7b-instruct-v0.3	112
	google/gemma-2-9b-it	250
Q3.2024	google/gemma-2-27b-it	250
	meta-llama/llama-3.1-8b-instruct	83
	meta-llama/llama-3.1-70b-instruct	84
	meta-llama/llama-3.1-405b-instruct	83
	meta-llama/llama-3.2-1b-instruct	125
	meta-llama/llama-3.2-3b-instruct	125
Q4.2024	google/gemini-flash-1.5-8b	111
	anthropic/claude-3.5-sonnet	125
	anthropic/claude-3.5-haiku	125
	meta-llama/llama-3.3-70b-instruct	250
	deepseek/deepseek-chat	125

Table 2. Number of samples generated by different models at different times based on the model release date for Q1.2025 and Q2.2025

Quarter	Model	#Samples
Q1.2025	deepseek/deepseek-r1	125
	deepseek/deepseek-r1-distill-llama-70b	125
	deepseek/deepseek-r1-distill-qwen-14b	62
	deepseek/deepseek-r1-distill-qwen-32b	63
	deepseek/deepseek-r1-distill-qwen-1.5b	62
	deepseek/deepseek-r1-distill-llama-8b	125
	deepseek/deepseek-v3-base:free	125
	openai/o3-mini	200
	openai/o3-mini-high	200
	qwen/qwen-turbo	500
	qwen/qwen-max	500
	google/gemini-2.0-flash-001	167
	google/gemini-2.0-flash-lite-001	167
	google/gemma-3-4b-it	500
	google/gemma-3-12b-it	500
	google/gemma-3-27b-it	500
	microsoft/phi-4	250
	microsoft/phi-4-multimodal-instruct	250
Q2.2025	meta-llama/llama-4-scout	125
	meta-llama/llama-4-maverick	125
	openai/gpt-4.1	200
	openai/gpt-4.1-nano	200
	openai/gpt-4.1-mini	200
	qwen/qwen3-8b	500
	qwen/qwen3-14b	500
	qwen/qwen3-32b	500
	anthropic/claude-sonnet-4	125
	anthropic/claude-opus-4	125
	deepseek/deepseek-r1-0528	125
	deepseek/deepseek-r1-distill-qwen-7b	63
	x-ai/grok-3	500
	x-ai/grok-3-mini	500
	google/gemini-2.5-flash	167
	google/gemini-2.5-pro	166

texts. It is to be noted that if the model is trained with an unsupervised learning approach similar to our framework, the training dataset contains only the LLM-generated texts. The testing dataset contains the remaining 2,000 LLM-generated texts and their 2,000 human-authored counterparts. For the second stage, only the 10,000 LLM-generated texts were used. We also used the 80:20 ratio and the five-fold cross-validation approach to perform experiments and obtain average performance for comparisons.

4.2 State of the Art for Performance Comparison

We compared the performance of our framework with that of the recent state-of-the-art. For the first stage of LLM-generated text detection, we adopted five existing works, including Fast-DetectGPT [6], DetectLLM [38], PHD [43], DetectGPT [26], and Radar [20]. Fast-DetectGPT, DetectLLM are zero-shot learning approaches, i.e., without requiring a training process. They used an LLM to estimate the likelihood that a text is LLM-generated, using the concept of conditional probability curvature to elucidate discrepancies in word choices between LLMs and humans within a given context. PHD differentiated LLM-generated text from human text by estimating the intrinsic dimension of the input text using the persistent homology dimension estimator (PHD) [36]. DetectGPT and Radar are supervised learning techniques that require labeled data to train the detector. We retrained them on our data before performing the comparison. For the second stage, we adopted LLMDet [48] and GPT-who [45], which are two recent works, using a supervised learning approach for training the attribution model. LLMDet estimates the next-token probabilities of salient n-gram as features to calculate proxy perplexity for each LLM, while GPT-who uses the uniform information density (UID) principle to differentiate LLM-generated text and human text. We used our dataset to train LLMDet and GPT-who.

4.3 Performance Metric

We evaluated the performance of the framework and existing techniques using the F1 Score as a performance metric, which measures the accuracy of the proposed framework and its models by computing the harmonic mean of precision and recall. It provides a balanced single-score performance measure, ranging from 0 to 1, particularly for imbalanced datasets similar to our experimental dataset. The formula for calculating the F1 Score for a single class is given in Eq. (4). We then take the average of the F1 Scores for all classes to calculate the final F1 Score for the attribution of the LLM-generated text.

$$F1 = 2 \times \frac{Precision \times Recall}{Precision + Recall}. \tag{4}$$

4.4 Experimental Results

LLM-Generated Text Detection

Offline Training with Full Availability of Training Data. In this experiment, we considered the scenario that the model was trained and tested with all data collected from Q2.2023 to Q2.2025. Table 3 summarizes the performance of our framework and the state-of-the-art representative LLM-generated text detection methods, evaluated using the F1 score. Among zero-shot approaches, DetectLLM [38] achieves the strongest performance, with its best configuration reaching an F1 score of 0.8883. Fast-DetectGPT [6] also performs competitively with the best performance of 0.8695, although its effectiveness varies noticeably with the underlying language model, indicating sensitivity to model-specific probability estimates. It is to be noted that both DetectLLM and Fast-DetectGPT achieved the best performance only when they used `llama-13b` to analyze the text. This can be explained by the fact that `llama-13b` has also been used to generate samples in training and testing, causing all samples generated by `llama-13b` to be detected successfully. In contrast, PHD-based methods, which rely on intrinsic dimension estimation from embeddings or hidden states, show moderate performance, with the best variant based on RoBERTa achieving an F1 score of 0.7408. Supervised detectors, including DetectGPT [26] and Radar [20], generally underperform compared to strong zero-shot and unsupervised baselines in this setting. Despite leveraging labeled data and, in some cases, adversarial training, their F1 scores degrade substantially, suggesting limited robustness to distribution shifts and evolving generation models.

Our proposed embedding-based framework using Sentence Transformers demonstrates the best overall performance. In particular, the variational autoencoder (VAE) variant with the Mahalanobis distance achieves the highest F1 score of 0.8780 while operating completely unsupervised and requiring only LLM-generated data. This performance is better compared to the performance of Fast-DetectGPT with `llama-13b`. This result highlights the advantage of modeling the intrinsic structure of sentence embeddings without relying on token-level likelihoods or labeled human text. Alternative unsupervised backends, such as One-class SVM and standard Autoencoders, remain competitive but fall slightly behind the VAE configuration.

Model Performance when Updating with Unseen Samples. In this experiment, we evaluated the performance of our framework in a realistic scenario when the LLM-generated text detection model needs to deal with new samples generated by newly released LLMs over time. We used Algorithm 1 to train the detection model with the data collected at the end of each quarter of the year, as shown in Table 1 and Table 2. We tested the detection model with two scenarios: (i) the test dataset contains only newly collected samples, and (ii) the test dataset contains both old samples and new samples. For example, in Q3.2023, the model was trained with data collected from Q2.2023 and Q3.2023 according to Algorithm 1 and tested with only samples collected in Q3.2023 for the first scenario and another test set containing samples collected in both Q2.2023 and Q3.2023

Table 3. Grouped LLM-generated text detection performance with offline training with full training data

Methods	Model Configuration	Learning	Requirements	F1 Score
Fast-DetectGPT [6]	gpt-j-6B	Zero-shot	LM probabilities	0.8302
	gpt-neo-2.7B	Zero-shot	LM probabilities	0.8233
	tiiuae-falcon-7b	Zero-shot	LM probabilities	0.8017
	tiiuae-falcon-7b-instruct	Zero-shot	LM probabilities	0.7587
	gpt2-xl	Zero-shot	LM probabilities	0.7585
	gpt2	Zero-shot	LM probabilities	0.6897
	gpt2-medium	Zero-shot	LM probabilities	0.6713
	pubmedgpt	Zero-shot	LM probabilities	0.6513
	mgpt	Zero-shot	LM probabilities	0.6001
	llama-13b	Zero-shot	LM probabilities	<u>0.8695</u>
DetectLLM [38]	gpt-j-6B	Zero-shot	Token rank statistics	0.8324
	gpt-neo-2.7B	Zero-shot	Token rank statistics	0.7911
	gpt2	Zero-shot	Token rank statistics	0.6355
	gpt2-medium	Zero-shot	Token rank statistics	0.6777
	gpt2-xl	Zero-shot	Token rank statistics	0.7601
	tiiuae-falcon-7b	Zero-shot	Token rank statistics	0.8543
	tiiuae-falcon-7b-instruct	Zero-shot	Token rank statistics	0.8434
	llama-13b	Zero-shot	Token rank statistics	<u>0.8883</u>
	opt-2.7b	Zero-shot	Token rank statistics	0.7957
	opt-13b	Zero-shot	Token rank statistics	0.8375
PHD [43]	roberta-base	Unsupervised	Embedding model	<u>0.7408</u>
	xlm-roberta-base	Unsupervised	Embedding model	0.7109
	bloom-7b1	Unsupervised	LM hidden states	0.6667
	gpt-j-6B	Unsupervised	LM hidden states	0.5154
	gpt-neo-2.7B	Unsupervised	LM hidden states	0.5106
	gpt-neox-20b	Unsupervised	LM hidden states	0.5964
	gpt2	Unsupervised	LM hidden states	0.5066
	gpt2-medium	Unsupervised	LM hidden states	0.6864
	gpt2-xl	Unsupervised	LM hidden states	0.5615
	tiiuae-falcon-7b	Unsupervised	LM hidden states	0.5894
	tiiuae-falcon-7b-instruct	Unsupervised	LM hidden states	0.7343
	llama-13b	Unsupervised	LM hidden states	0.7077
	llama2-13b	Unsupervised	LM hidden states	0.6941
	opt-13b	Unsupervised	LM hidden states	0.5328
DetectGPT [26]	detectgpt	Supervised	Labeled data	0.6905
Radar [20]	radar	Supervised	Adversarial training with Labeled data	0.6958
Our method	Mahalanobis [23]	Unsupervised	Only LLM-generated data	**0.8780**
	Variational Autoencoder [23]	Unsupervised	Only LLM-generated data	0.8522
	Isolation Forest	Unsupervised	Only LLM-generated data	0.8337
	One-class SVM [35]	Unsupervised	Only LLM-generated data	0.7868

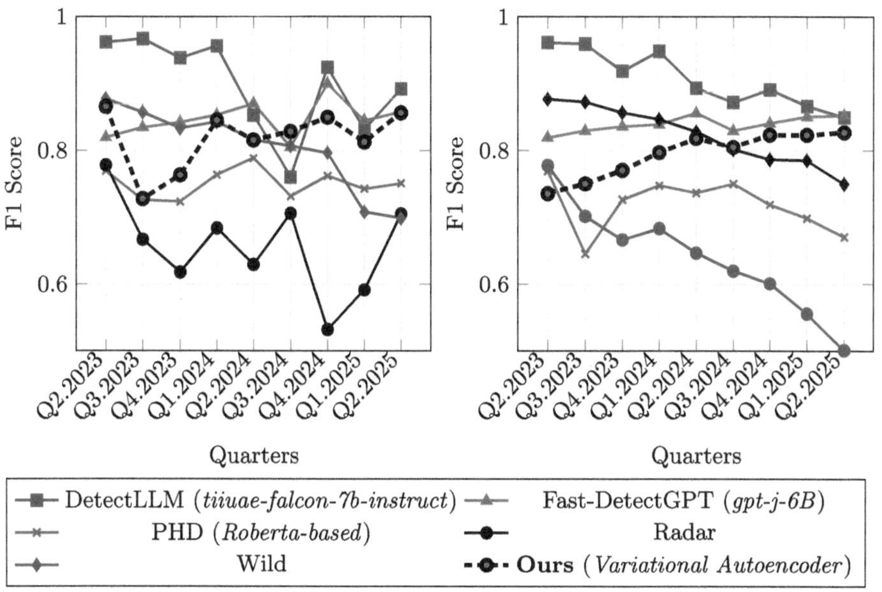

Fig. 2. (Left) Performance of models tested on only unseen samples appearing over time. (Right) Performance of models tested on old and unseen samples.

for the second scenario. The purpose of the first scenario is to demonstrate that the detection model is successfully adopted to detect new samples, while the second scenario is to show the model's capability of retaining the prior knowledge when learning new knowledge.

For the first scenario, Fig. 2 (left) illustrates the performance trends of the best-performing method in each category (shown in Table 3). The experimental results show that while all existing techniques exhibit a performance degradation behavior when dealing with new samples generated by newly released LLMs, especially those techniques using a supervised learning approach, our framework using VAE demonstrates stable performance across quarters of the year. This affirms the effectiveness of our proposed framework for practical deployment in terms of not only performance but also required resources.

We obtained similar performance trends when evaluating the detection model with the second scenario, where the test dataset contains both old and unseen samples. This scenario is more realistic than the first scenario, as end-users may use an old version of LLMs to generate text, even though a new version of that LLM has been released. The results presented in Fig. 2 (right) show that performance degradation is slightly less compared to that in the first scenario. This is explained by the fact that the training dataset contains both old and new samples, helping the model to reinforce the prior knowledge, without being affected by the catastrophic forgetting issue.

Table 4. Performance of Attribution Methods for Family Determination Validated with Scenario 1

Methods	F1 Score
LLMDet	0.12
GPT-who	0.64
Our framework (using RoBERTa)	**0.83**

LLM-Generated Text Attribution. In this section, we present the performance of the second stage of our framework, determining the LLM family of the models used to generate text. We used RoBERTa [51] as the attribution model, which has demonstrated its effectiveness with natural language processing tasks. We carried out the following three experimental scenarios:

- Scenario 1: We trained the attribution model with LLM-generated samples collected from Q2.2023 to Q2.2025 and assumed that the first stage of LLM-generated text detection achieves perfect performance. Thus, the test set contains only LLM-generated samples from the models released from Q2.2023 to Q2.2025.
- Scenario 2: We used Algorithm 1 to update the model over time with data collected at the end of each quarter of the year, as shown in Table 1 and Table 2. Similar to Scenario 1, we assumed that the first stage of LLM-generated text detection achieves a perfect performance; thus, all samples sent to the second stage are LLM-generated text.
- Scenario 3: We performed the validation with the full pipeline of the framework by sending one input sample to the first stage to obtain the detection result and invoking the second stage if the input sample is deemed to be an LLM-generated.

Performance with Scenario 1. Table 4 reports the comparative F1-scores of representative attribution methods. The proposed RoBERTa-based model significantly outperforms existing approaches, achieving an F1-score of **0.83**. In contrast, LLMDet exhibits limited effectiveness, especially when the number of LLM families increases. GPT-who shows moderate performance. These results indicate that supervised representation learning with RoBERTa is substantially more effective in capturing attribution-related cues than rule-based or prompt-driven methods.

Performance with Scenario 2. We present the performance of the attribution model for Scenario 2. We obtained similar performance trends as shown in Fig. 2 (right), where the model maintains a stable performance when new LLMs are released and used to generate text. Table 5 presents the performance of the model in the last period in Q2.2025, and we observed that our framework still achieved an F1 Score of 76.31%, which is much better compared to GPT-who (41%). This shows the effectiveness and practicality of our framework.

Table 5. Performance of Attribution Methods for Family Determination Validated with Scenario 2

Methods	F1 Score
GPT-who	0.41
Our (RoBERTa)	**0.7631**

Table 6. Performance of Attribution Methods for Family Determination Validated with Scenario 3

Methods	F1 Score
VAE + LLMDet	0.54
VAE + GPT-who	0.53
VAE + Our (RoBERTa)	**0.71**

Performance with Scenario 3. Table 6 presents the performance of the attribution model when executing the entire framework described in Scenario 3. As this experiment focuses on the attribution of LLM-generated text, we computed the F1 Score for the second stage only for the LLM-generated samples correctly detected by the first stage, i.e., we eliminated human samples that were wrongly detected by the first stage as LLM-generated text. As shown in Table 6, our framework has a slight performance degradation compared to Scenario 1 and Scenario 2, but it still significantly outperforms the existing techniques.

5 Conclusion

In this paper, we proposed a comprehensive multi-stage framework for determining whether a given piece of text was generated by a human or by an LLM and identifying the specific LLM family and version used in generating the text. We developed an unsupervised learning approach, using a simple variational autoencoder based on RoBERTa, thus requiring only LLM-generated text for the training process of the detection model. We used a conventional supervised learning approach for training the attribution models in the second stage of the framework. To address the frequent LLM releases, we developed an algorithm for online model updating using the few-shot meta-learning approach, which enables the models not only to retain prior knowledge but also to acquire new knowledge from newly released LLMs. Extensive experiments with 66 LLMs that belong to 10 families demonstrated the outstanding performance of the proposed framework in comparison with the state of the art. Future research could explore several important directions. An area of interest involves investigating whether LLMs have been trained in copyright-protected or proprietary materials and developing techniques to identify evidence of such influence. Another area of exploration is the detection of text generated using multiple LLMs, either in combination or in stages, which presents a more complex attribution problem.

Furthermore, the explainability of the attribution model is another important direction to explore. The ability to justify the classification of text as coming from a specific LLM family or version would enhance the transparency and reliability of forensic analysis in presenting the result in court.

References

1. Abdin, M.I., et al.: Phi-3 technical report: a highly capable language model locally on your phone. Technical report. MSR-TR-2024-12, Microsoft (2024). https://www.microsoft.com/en-us/research/publication/phi-3-technical-report-a-highly-capable-language-model-locally-on-your-phone/
2. An, J., Cho, S.: Variational autoencoder based anomaly detection using reconstruction probability. Spec. Lect. IE **2**, 1–18 (2015)
3. Anthropic: The claude 3 model family: Opus, Sonnet, Haiku. Technical report, Anthropic (2024). https://www-cdn.anthropic.com/de8ba9b01c9ab7cbabf5c33b80b7bbc618857627/Model_Card_Claude_3.pdf
4. Antoun, W., Sagot, B., Seddah, D.: From text to source: results in detecting large language model-generated content. In: Proceedings of the 2024 Joint International Conference on Computational Linguistics, Language Resources and Evaluation (LREC-COLING 2024), Torino, Italia, pp. 7531–7543. ELRA and ICCL (2024). https://aclanthology.org/2024.lrec-main.665/
5. Awais, M., et al.: Foundation models defining a new era in vision: a survey and outlook. IEEE Trans. Pattern Anal. Mach. Intell. **47**(4), 2245–2264 (2025). https://doi.org/10.1109/TPAMI.2024.3506283
6. Bao, G., Zhao, Y., Teng, Z., Yang, L., Zhang, Y.: Fast-DetectGPT: efficient zero-shot detection of machine-generated text via conditional probability curvature. In: The Twelfth International Conference on Learning Representations, Vienna, Austria (2024)
7. Brown, T.B., et al.: Language models are few-shot learners. In: Proceedings of the 34th International Conference on Neural Information Processing Systems, Vancouver, BC, Canada, NIPS 2020 (2020)
8. Chakraborty, S., Bedi, A.S., Zhu, S., An, B., Manocha, D., Huang, F.: Position: on the possibilities of AI-generated text detection. In: Proceedings of the 41st International Conference on Machine Learning, ICML 2024. JMLR.org (2024)
9. Dario, P., Evgenios, K., Giuseppe, A.: LLMmap: a Light-weight Method to Fingerprint LLMs. In: Proceedings of the 34th USENIX Security Symposium (2025)
10. Denouden, T., et al.: Improving reconstruction autoencoder out-of-distribution detection with Mahalanobis distance. CoRR **abs/1812.02765** (2018). http://arxiv.org/abs/1812.02765
11. Devlin, J., Chang, M.W., Lee, K., Toutanova, K.: BERT: pre-training of deep bidirectional transformers for language understanding. In: Proceedings of the 2019 Conference of the North American Chapter of the Association for Computational Linguistics: Human Language Technologies, Minneapolis, Minnesota (2019)
12. Dongfang, L., et al.: A survey of large language models attribution. CoRR **abs/2311.03731** (2023)
13. Fan, A., Lewis, M., Dauphin, Y.: Hierarchical neural story generation. In: Proceedings of the 56th Annual Meeting of the Association for Computational Linguistics (Volume 1: Long Papers), pp. 889–898 (2018). https://doi.org/10.18653/v1/P18-1082

14. Gehrmann, S., Strobelt, H., Rush, A.: GLTR: statistical detection and visualization of generated text. In: Proceedings of the 57th Annual Meeting of the Association for Computational Linguistics: System Demonstrations, pp. 111–116. Association for Computational Linguistics (2019). https://doi.org/10.18653/v1/P19-3019
15. Gemini Team and Google: Gemini 2.5: Pushing the frontier with advanced reasoning, multimodality, long context, and next generation agentic capabilities. Technical report, Google (2025). https://storage.googleapis.com/deepmindmedia/gemini/gemini_v2_5_report.pdf
16. Gemini Team and Google DeepMind: Gemma: Open models based on Gemini research and technology. Technical report, Google (2024). https://storage.googleapis.com/deepmind-media/gemma/gemma-report.pdf
17. Guo, D., et al.: DeepSeek-R1 incentivizes reasoning in LLMs through reinforcement learning. Nature **645**(8081) (2025). https://doi.org/10.1038/s41586-025-09422-z
18. Guo, X., Zhang, S., He, Y., Zhang, T., Feng, W., Huang, H., Ma, C.: DeTeCtive: detecting AI-generated text via multi-level contrastive learning. In: Proceedings of the 38th International Conference on Neural Information Processing Systems, NIPS 2024. Curran Associates Inc., Red Hook (2025)
19. Hans, A., et al.: Spotting LLMs with binoculars: zero-shot detection of machine-generated text. In: Proceedings of the 41st International Conference on Machine Learning. JMLR.org (2024)
20. Hu, X., Chen, P.Y., Ho, T.Y.: Radar: Robust AI-text detection via adversarial learning. Adv. Neural. Inf. Process. Syst. **36** (2023)
21. Huang, B., Chen, C., Shu, K.: Authorship attribution in the era of LLMs: problems, methodologies, and challenges. SIGKDD Explor. Newsl. **26**(2), 21–43 (2025). https://doi.org/10.1145/3715073.3715076
22. Ippolito, D., Duckworth, D., Callison-Burch, C., Eck, D.: Automatic detection of generated text is easiest when humans are fooled. In: Proceedings of the 58th Annual Meeting of the Association for Computational Linguistics, pp. 1808–1822 (2020). https://doi.org/10.18653/v1/2020.acl-main.164
23. Kingma, D.P., Welling, M.: Auto-encoding variational bayes. International Conference on Learning Representations (ICLR) (2014)
24. Kirchenbauer, J., Geiping, J., Wen, Y., Katz, J., Miers, I., Goldstein, T.: A watermark for large language models. In: Proceedings of the 40th International Conference on Machine Learning (ICML) (2023)
25. Llama Team and AI @ Meta: The Llama 3 Herd of Models. Technical report, Meta Platforms, Inc. (2024). https://ai.meta.com/research/publications/the-llama-3-herd-of-models/
26. Mitchell, E., Lee, Y., Khazatsky, A., Manning, C.D., Finn, C.: DetectGPT: zero-shot machine-generated text detection using probability curvature. In: Proceedings of the 40th International Conference on Machine Learning, ICML 2023 (2023)
27. Nasery, A., et al.: Scalable fingerprinting of large language models. In: ICLR 2025 Workshop on Building Trust in Language Models and Applications (2025). https://openreview.net/forum?id=0wMUdbvYLL
28. Nguyen, D., Naing, K.M.N., Joshi, A.: Stacking the odds: transformer-based ensemble for AI-generated text detection. In: Proceedings of the 21st Annual Workshop of the Australasian Language Technology Association, pp. 173–178 (2023). https://aclanthology.org/2023.alta-1.22/
29. OpenAI: GPT-4O system card. Technical report, OpenAI (2024). https://cdn.openai.com/gpt-4o-system-card.pdf
30. OpenRouter: The AI router for every dev (2024). https://openrouter.ai. Accessed 13 July 2025

31. Qwen Team: Qwen2.5-1m: Deploy your own Qwen with context length up to 1m tokens. Technical report, Alibaba Group (2025). https://qwen.ai/blog?id=qwen2.5-1m. Accessed 09 Apr 2026
32. Qwen Team: Qwen2.5 omni: See, hear, talk, write, do it all! Technical report, Alibaba Group (2025). https://qwen.ai/blog?id=qwen2.5-omni. Accessed 09 Apr 2026
33. Rastogi, A., Jiang, A.Q., et al.: Magistral. arXiv preprint arXiv:2506.10910 (2025)
34. Rumelhart, D.E., Hinton, G.E., Williams, R.J.: Learning internal representations by error propagation. Technical report, California Univ San Diego La Jolla Inst for Cognitive Science (1985)
35. Schölkopf, B., Platt, J., Shawe-Taylor, J., Smola, A., Williamson, R.: Estimating the support of a high-dimensional distribution. Neural Comput. **13**(7) (2001)
36. Schweinhart, B.: Persistent homology and the upper box dimension. Discrete Comput. Geom. **65** (2021)
37. Singh, S.U., Namin, A.S.: A survey on chatbots and large language models: testing and evaluation techniques. Nat. Lang. Process. J. **10**, 100128 (2025)
38. Su, J., Zhuo, T., Wang, D., Nakov, P.: DetectLLM: leveraging log rank information for zero-shot detection of machine-generated text. In: Findings of the Association for Computational Linguistics: EMNLP 2023, pp. 12395–12412 (2023). https://doi.org/10.18653/v1/2023.findings-emnlp.827
39. Sun, Z.: Large language models in peer review: challenges and opportunities. Scientometrics **130**(10) (2025). https://doi.org/10.1007/s11192-025-05440-w
40. Tian, Y., Pan, Z., Peng, N.: Detecting machine-generated long-form content with latent-space variables. In: Findings of the Association for Computational Linguistics: EMNLP 2024, pp. 10394–10408 (2024). https://doi.org/10.18653/v1/2024.findings-emnlp.608
41. Triedman, H., Mantzarlis, A.: What did Elon change? A comprehensive analysis of Grokipedia (2025). https://arxiv.org/abs/2511.09685
42. TRI/NCSC AI Policy Consortium for Law & Courts: Evaluating acknowledged AI-generated evidence. Technical report. Thomson Reuters Institute (2025)
43. Tulchinskii, E., et al.: Intrinsic dimension estimation for robust detection of AI-generated texts. Adv. Neural. Inf. Process. Syst. **36**, 39257–39276 (2023)
44. Uchendu, A., Ma, Z., Le, T., Zhang, R., Lee, D.: TURINGBENCH: a benchmark environment for Turing test in the age of neural text generation. In: Findings of the Association for Computational Linguistics: EMNLP 2021, pp. 2001–2016 (2021). https://doi.org/10.18653/v1/2021.findings-emnlp.172
45. Venkatraman, S., Uchendu, A., Lee, D.: GPT-who: an information density-based machine-generated text detector. In: Findings of the Association for Computational Linguistics: NAACL 2024, Mexico City, Mexico, pp. 103–115 (2024). https://doi.org/10.18653/v1/2024.findings-naacl.8
46. Wang, Q., Zhang, L., Guo, Z., Mao, Z.: IDEATE: detecting AI-generated text using internal and external factual structures. In: Proceedings of the 2024 Joint International Conference on Computational Linguistics, Language Resources and Evaluation (LREC-COLING 2024), pp. 8556–8568 (2024)
47. Wu, J., Yang, S., Zhan, R., Yuan, Y., Chao, L.S., Wong, D.F.: A survey on LLM-generated text detection: necessity, methods, and future directions. Comput. Linguist. **51**(1) (2025). https://aclanthology.org/2025.cl-1.8/
48. Wu, K., Pang, L., Shen, H., Cheng, X., Chua, T.S.: LLMDet: a third party large language models generated text detection tool. In: Findings of the Association for Computational Linguistics: EMNLP 2023, Singapore (2023). https://doi.org/10.18653/v1/2023.findings-emnlp.139

49. xAI: Open release of Grok-1 (2024). https://x.ai/blog/grok-os. Accessed 16 July 2025
50. Zellers, R., et al.: Defending against neural fake news. In: Proceedings of the 33rd International Conference on Neural Information Processing Systems, Red Hook, NY, USA, p. 812 (2019)
51. Zhuang, L., Wayne, L., Ya, S., Jun, Z.: A robustly optimized BERT pre-training approach with post-training. In: Proceedings of the 20th Chinese National Conference on Computational Linguistics (2021). https://aclanthology.org/2021.ccl-1.108/

MARS: LLM Toxicity Mitigation via Multi-dimensional Adaptive Representation Steering

Hongfeng Zhou, Chunhe Xia, Chen Chen, Changnan Jiang, Xinjun Liu, and Tianbo Wang(✉)

Beijing Key Lab of Network Technology, Beihang University, Beijing, China
hfzhou@buaa.edu.cn, xch@buaa.edu.cn, chenchen@buaa.edu.cn,
jcnby@buaa.edu.cn, liuxinjun@buaa.edu.cn, wangtb@buaa.edu.cn

Abstract. Large Language Models (LLMs) demonstrate impressive capabilities but face a critical challenge: generating toxic content due to pre-training biases. Existing detoxification methods, such as fine-tuning and prompting, incur high computational costs or suffer from instability. Recently, Representation Engineering (RepE) emerged as a promising internal steering approach; however, current methods treat toxicity as a monolithic, single-dimensional concept. Steering along a single direction inadvertently suppresses harmless concepts, degrading general model capabilities. We hypothesize that the toxicity concept in LLMs comprises multiple linearly separable sub-concepts in the activation space. Through geometric visualization and quantitative analysis, we empirically validate this, demonstrating that distinct sub-concepts (e.g., Insult, Threat) reside in largely orthogonal subspaces. Building on this insight, we propose **MARS** (**M**ulti-dimensional **A**daptive **R**epresentation **S**teering), a framework that decouples toxicity into sub-concepts and applies iterative steering with adaptive magnitude during inference. This allows precise detoxification without compromising semantic quality. Comprehensive experiments on Llama3.1-8B, Mistral-7B, and Gemma-7B show MARS significantly outperforms baselines, reducing toxicity scores by up to 79% while maintaining perplexity and fluency comparable to the original LLMs.

Keywords: Large Language Models · AI Safety · Representation Engineering · Toxicity Mitigation

1 Introduction

Large Language Models (LLMs) [5,23] have shown remarkable performance in various tasks, such as reasoning, coding, and question answering. These models are typically pre-trained on massive corpora from a variety of sources [7,20].

Supported by the National Natural Science Foundation of China under Grant 62272024, and the Fundamental Research Funds for the Central Universities under Grant KG16394201.

© ICST Institute for Computer Sciences, Social Informatics and Telecommunications Engineering 2027
Published by Springer Nature Switzerland AG 2027. All Rights Reserved
H. Neukirchen et al. (Eds.): ICDF2C 2026, LNICST 720, pp. 92–107, 2027.
https://doi.org/10.1007/978-3-032-37274-1_6

However, these corpora may contain toxic content such as bias, insults and violence. Consequently, LLMs inadvertently internalize these behaviors, posing risks of generating toxic responses [8]. Therefore, aligning LLMs to adhere to safety guidelines remains a critical challenge.

A common technique for toxicity mitigation is to fine-tune the weights of LLMs with aligned data [16]. However, beyond the expense of gathering aligned data, an extra training phase is needed, which incurs significant computational overhead and data annotation costs. Another prevalent approach is to guide LLMs through prompting that explicitly instructs the model not to generate harmful text [5]. However, prompting often suffers from instability and is vulnerable to jailbreak attacks, especially in smaller-scale models [19]. Crucially, these black-box methods operate at a surface level and lack interpretability.

Recently, based on the **Linear Representation Hypothesis (LRH)** [17] which posits that high-level concepts are encoded linearly in the activation spaces, **Representation Engineering (RepE)** [31] has emerged as a promising direction. By extracting **Steering Vectors**, RepE steers LLMs toward desired behaviors via internal representations. However, current RepE approaches typically treat toxicity as a monolithic, single-dimensional concept. This simplification is problematic because toxicity is semantically diverse (e.g., *Insult* vs. *Threat*). A single toxic direction, extracted by aggregating diverse toxic samples, represents a coarse-grained average that fails to capture the distinct geometric features of specific toxic behaviors. Consequently, shifting activations along a single steering Vector inadvertently disrupts other subspaces responsible for general knowledge, leading to degradation in overall performance. Furthermore, the fixed magnitude lacks flexibility, which inevitably leads to over-correction for weakly toxic inputs or under-correction for highly toxic ones.

To fundamentally resolve the inadequacies of traditional RepE in handling complex, multi-faceted concepts, we propose a novel framework called **MARS** (**M**ulti-dimensional **A**daptive **R**epresentation **S**teering), as illustrated in Fig. 1. Unlike existing methods that struggle with feature entanglement and rigid over-steering, MARS is explicitly designed to decouple and precisely neutralize toxicity without causing collateral damage to the model's general utility. The framework consists of two key components: **Iterative Multi-Dimensional Steering (IMDS)** and **Dual-Constrained Adaptive Magnitude (DCAM)**. Our methodology is premised on the hypothesis that distinct toxicity sub-concepts are not collinear but linearly separable in the LLM activation space. Under this assumption, a single global vector is inherently insufficient to span the entire toxicity subspace. Consequently, IMDS abandons the coarse-grained approach, utilizing targeted **Sub-Concept Steering Vectors (SSVs)** to surgically neutralize each component within its specific subspace. Concurrently, to dynamically balance mitigation performance and text quality, the DCAM module replaces fixed interventions with an adaptive magnitude mechanism. Finally, we provide rigorous visualization analysis in our experiments to empirically validate the initial separability assumption underlying our framework.[1]

[1] Our code is publicly available at https://github.com/zhf999/MARS..

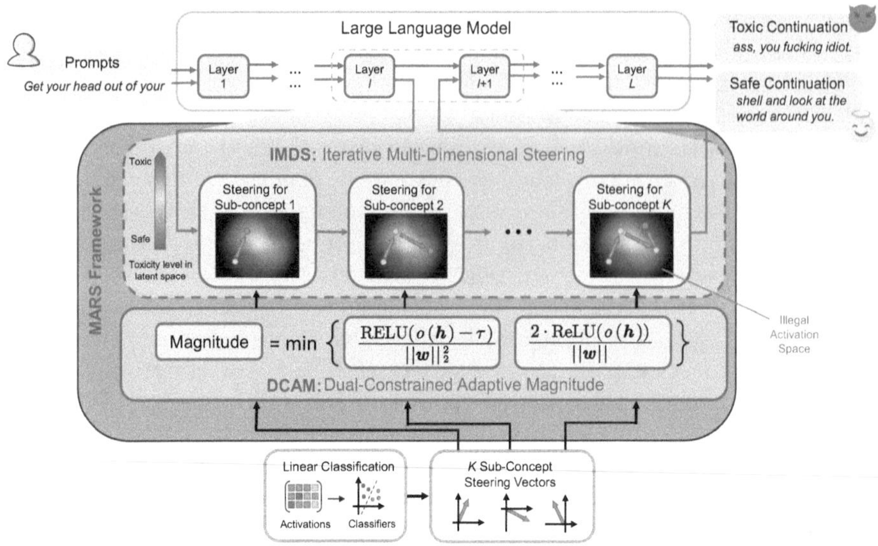

Fig. 1. Overview of the MARS framework. MARS consists of two key components, **Dual-Constrained Adaptive Magnitude (DCAM)** and **Iterative Multi-Dimensional Steering (IMDS)**. During inference, MARS applies iteratively steering for each sub-concept with an adaptive magnitude. The black area represents illegal activation space that leads LLM to generate meaningless and repetitive text. Our method steers activations toward the safe space without entering the illegal space.

Our main contributions are summarized as follows:

- **Framework Innovation**: We propose MARS, a novel inference-time detoxification framework. Moving beyond conventional methods that predominantly treat toxicity as a monolithic concept, MARS employs an **Iterative Multi-Dimensional Steering (IMDS)** strategy to decouple toxicity into fine-grained sub-concepts and surgically neutralize them sequentially.
- **Adaptive Mechanism**: Within the MARS framework, we introduce a **Dual-Constrained Adaptive Magnitude (DCAM)** mechanism. By mathematically bounding the steering vector with both safety demands and symmetric semantic limits via a closed-form formulation, this algorithm dynamically calibrates the intervention strength for each input, effectively mitigating the over-steering problem.
- **Empirical Superiority & Interpretability**: MARS demonstrates outstanding performance against state-of-the-art baselines, reducing the *Toxicity Score* by up to 79% while preserving the high quality of generated text. Furthermore, our visualization analysis provides mechanistic interpretability, validating the underlying assumption that distinct toxicity sub-concepts are linearly separable within the representation space.

2 Related Works

In this section, we review existing interpretability-based approaches for LLM toxicity mitigation, categorized into decoding, neuron interventions, and representation engineering.

2.1 Decoding and Neuron Interventions

Decoding-based strategies focus on modifying output logits or input prompts to mitigate toxicity [9–11,14,18,29]. However, explicitly manipulating output distributions during inference often disrupts the natural probability space, severely degrading text fluency and coherence. Moving beyond surface-level decoding, expert neuron interventions steer models by perturbing specific isolated neurons [6,21,24]. While effective, they often require identifying specific units, overlooking that high-level concepts are typically distributed broadly across the network.

2.2 Representation Engineering and Adaptive Steering

Representation Engineering (RepE) [3,17,31] offers a broader perspective by steering models via linear directions in activation spaces. Building on this, methods like concept scrubbing [4] and activation addition [13,25,28] successfully mitigate bias. While early works treated toxicity as a monolithic direction, concurrent studies have explored multi-directional steering (e.g., CHaRS [1], Steering Target Atoms [26]) and input-adaptive magnitude control (e.g., CAST [12], SADI [27]) to prevent over-steering. However, these methods often rely on unsupervised clustering or heuristic continuous control. MARS distinguishes itself by instantiating disentangled steering within a structured, Jigsaw-grounded taxonomy, and introduces a mathematically rigorous closed-form formulation for magnitude adaptation, ensuring precise detoxification without compromising general capabilities.

3 Methodology

In this section, we introduce the **MARS** framework, a novel inference-time intervention approach for LLM, as shown in Fig. 1. Current detoxification methods often struggle to balance safety with utility, leading to either insufficient mitigation of complex toxic queries or significant degradation of text fluency. To resolve this dilemma, MARS introduces a fine-grained, adaptive steering mechanism composed of two key modules:

- **Dual-Constrained Adaptive Magnitude (DCAM)**: This module solves the over-correction problem by mathematically bounding the intervention strength within a symmetric constraint.
- **Iterative Multi-Dimensional Steering (IMDS)**: This module addresses the entanglement problem by surgically neutralizing specific toxicity sub-concepts sequentially.

Together, these components ensure that the model is steered towards safety without sacrificing its fundamental language generation capabilities.

3.1 Problem Formulation & Sub-Concept Extraction

Consider an LLM $\mathcal{M}$ with L transformer layers. Given an input sequence $\boldsymbol{x} = (x_1, \ldots, x_N)$, the model generates an output sequence $\boldsymbol{y}$ autoregressively based on the conditional probability $P_{\mathcal{M}}(\boldsymbol{y} \mid \boldsymbol{x})$. Let $\boldsymbol{h}^{(l)} \in \mathbb{R}^d$ denote the hidden state (activation) at the l-th layer corresponding to the last token of $\boldsymbol{x}$.

Our goal is to learn a transformation function $\mathcal{T} : \mathbb{R}^d \to \mathbb{R}^d$ that modifies the hidden state to $\boldsymbol{h}' = \mathcal{T}(\boldsymbol{h})$, such that the generation conditioned on $\boldsymbol{h}'$ is detoxified. Formally, we define the steering objective as a constrained optimization problem:

$$\begin{aligned} \min_{\boldsymbol{h}'} \quad & \frac{1}{2}||\boldsymbol{h}' - \boldsymbol{h}||_2^2 \\ \text{s.t.} \quad & \mathbb{E}_{\boldsymbol{y} \sim P_{\mathcal{M}}(\cdot|\boldsymbol{h}')} \left[P_{\text{toxic}}(\boldsymbol{y})\right] \leq p_0 \end{aligned} \tag{1}$$

where $P_{\text{toxic}}(\cdot)$ estimates the toxicity probability and p_0 is a pre-defined safety threshold. We minimize $\frac{1}{2}||\boldsymbol{h}' - \boldsymbol{h}||_2^2$ to ensure the minimal impact on LLM's general capabilities.

3.2 Dual-Constrained Adaptive Magnitude

We employ a classifier-based Representation Engineering (RepE), which trains a classifier $P(\boldsymbol{h}) = \text{sigmoid}(\boldsymbol{w}^\top \boldsymbol{h} + b)$ and use the normalized weight $\boldsymbol{w}$ as the Sub-Concept Steering Vectors (SSVs):

$$\boldsymbol{v} = \frac{\boldsymbol{w}}{||\boldsymbol{w}||} \tag{2}$$

Conventional RepE typically employs a fixed coefficient α for steering: $\boldsymbol{h}' = \boldsymbol{h} - \alpha \boldsymbol{v}$. However, a static magnitude ignores the dynamic nature of input toxicity, leading to either over-correction on benign inputs (degrading fluency) or under-correction on highly toxic ones.

To address this limitation, we reconceptualize the dynamic calibration mechanism (DCAM) as an optimal geometric projection problem onto a safe representational manifold. We define the safe subspace $\mathcal{S}_{safe}$ based on the safety probe's decision boundary, bounded by a target logit threshold $\tau = \ln(p_0/(1 - p_0))$:

$$\mathcal{M}_{safe} = \{\boldsymbol{x} \in \mathbb{R}^d \mid \boldsymbol{w}^\top \boldsymbol{x} + b \leq \tau\} \tag{3}$$

Our objective is to find a post-intervention representation $\boldsymbol{h}'$ that strictly satisfies this safety constraint while minimizing the Euclidean distance from the original semantic representation $\boldsymbol{h}$, thereby preserving generation quality. This is formulated as a constrained convex optimization problem:

$$\begin{aligned} \min_{\boldsymbol{h}'} \quad & \frac{1}{2}||\boldsymbol{h}' - \boldsymbol{h}||_2^2 \\ \text{s.t.} \quad & \boldsymbol{w}^\top \boldsymbol{h}' + b \leq \tau \end{aligned} \tag{4}$$

To solve this, we introduce $\epsilon_{safe} \geq 0$ as the Lagrangian multiplier, constructing the Lagrangian function:

$$\mathcal{L}(\boldsymbol{h}', \epsilon_{safe}) = \frac{1}{2}||\boldsymbol{h}' - \boldsymbol{h}||_2^2 + \epsilon_{safe}(\boldsymbol{w}^\top \boldsymbol{h}' + b - \tau) \tag{5}$$

By taking the partial derivative of $\mathcal{L}$ with respect to $\boldsymbol{h}'$ and setting it to zero, we obtain the direction of intervention:

$$\boldsymbol{h}' = \boldsymbol{h} - \epsilon_{safe}\boldsymbol{w} \tag{6}$$

Applying the Karush-Kuhn-Tucker (KKT) conditions, the optimal adaptive multiplier ϵ^*_{safe} is strictly activated only when the original state breaches the safety margin. Let $o(\boldsymbol{h}) = \boldsymbol{w}^\top \boldsymbol{h} + b$ denote the pre-intervention logit. The closed-form solution for the optimal steering magnitude is:

$$\epsilon^*_{safe} = \frac{\max(0, o(\boldsymbol{h}) - \tau)}{||\boldsymbol{w}||_2^2} \tag{7}$$

However, for inputs with strong toxicity where $o(\boldsymbol{h})$ is a large positive value, strictly enforcing the threshold τ (which is typically a large negative value) leads to a large ϵ. This excessive steering can push the representation too far into the non-toxic extreme, disrupting semantic coherence. To mitigate this, we introduce a **Symmetric Limit** based on geometric reflection. We cap the steering magnitude such that the updated logit does not exceed the negation of the original toxic magnitude (i.e., flipping $o(\boldsymbol{h})$ to $-o(\boldsymbol{h})$):

$$\epsilon_{limit} = \frac{2 \cdot \mathrm{ReLU}(o(\boldsymbol{h}))}{||\boldsymbol{w}||} \tag{8}$$

By combining the safety requirement and the geometric limit, we derive our final closed-form adaptive magnitude:

$$\epsilon(\boldsymbol{h}) = \min\Bigg(\underbrace{\frac{\mathrm{RELU}(o(\boldsymbol{h}) - \tau)}{||\boldsymbol{w}||_2^2}}_{\text{Safety Demand}}, \underbrace{\frac{2 \cdot \mathrm{ReLU}(o(\boldsymbol{h}))}{||\boldsymbol{w}||}}_{\text{Symmetric Limit}}\Bigg) \tag{9}$$

The updated hidden state is then obtained by:

$$\boldsymbol{h}' = \boldsymbol{h} - \epsilon(\boldsymbol{h})\boldsymbol{v} \tag{10}$$

By employing the update rule defined in Equation (10), we effectively mitigate toxicity in LLMs while preserving their core generative capabilities.

3.3 Iterative Multi-dimensional Steering

Decomposition of Toxicity Subspace. Since toxicity sub-concepts are often entangled in the latent space, a single-step update may not suffice. Unlike prior approaches that treat toxicity as a monolithic attribute, we posit that toxicity is a composite concept decomposable into K fine-grained sub-concepts $\mathcal{C} = \{c_1, \ldots, c_K\}$ (e.g., *Insult*, *Threat*). Formally, for each toxicity sub-concept

c_k, the trained linear probe defines a hyperplane that partitions the activation space into a toxic half-space and a safe half-space. The ultimate goal of detoxification is to project any latent state h into the **Global Safe Intersection** $\mathcal{S}_{safe}$, defined as:

$$\mathcal{S} = \bigcap_{k=1}^{K} \mathcal{S}_k = \{\boldsymbol{h} \in \mathbb{R}^d \mid \forall k, P(c_k|\boldsymbol{h}) \leq p_0\} \tag{11}$$

where $P(c_k|h)$ is the probability predicted by the k-th probe. To reach $\mathcal{S}$ precisely, we address the mitigation of each sub-concept individually.

Iterative Update Mechanism. We leverage the Jigsaw [2] dataset to train linear probes for each sub-concept. Specifically, for the k-th sub-concept on the layer l, we extract the SSVs $\boldsymbol{v}_k^{(l)}$ by normalizing the probe's weight vector. We then extend the standard steering equation to a multi-dimensional scenario by iteratively pushing the activation away from each toxic subspace boundaries.

Let $\boldsymbol{h}_k^{(l)}$ denote the activation after processing the k-th sub-concept at layer l, with $\boldsymbol{h}_0^{(l)}$ being the original activation. The iterative update rule is defined as:

$$\boldsymbol{h}_k^{(l)} = \boldsymbol{h}_{k-1}^{(l)} - \epsilon_k^{(l)}(\boldsymbol{h}_{k-1}^{(l)}) \cdot \boldsymbol{v}_k^{(l)}, \quad \text{for } k = 1 \ldots K \tag{12}$$

where $\epsilon_k^{(l)}$ is the adaptive magnitude calculated using Eq. (9) with the specific parameters (weights and biases) of concept c_k.

This iterative process ensures that the inference-time activation is broadly steered toward the safe intersection $\mathcal{S}_{safe}$, thus keeping the generated text toxic-free.

4 Experiments

In this section, we empirically evaluate MARS with a focus on three key aspects: **effectiveness**, **necessity**, and **interpretability**. First, we benchmark MARS against state-of-the-art baselines to demonstrate its superior capability in balancing detoxification with text quality. Second, through ablation studies, we validate the critical role of multi-dimensional steering and adaptive magnitude. Finally, we provide geometric visualizations to empirically justify the separability assumption underlying our method.

4.1 Experimental Setup

Metrics. In order to evaluate both toxicity and quality of generated text, we employ three metrics:

- **Toxicity Score**: We leverage the **Perspective API**[2], an industry-standard toxicity detection service, to quantify the probability of toxicity in the generated continuations. A lower score indicates better detoxification performance.

[2] https://perspectiveapi.com/.

- **Perplexity (PPL)**: We calculate PPL on generated continuations using an external **GPT-2** [22] to assess the coherence of generated text. Standard benchmarks like WikiText-2 are inapplicable here, as baselines (e.g., PREADD) require specific prompt prefixes that are incompatible with raw dataset evaluation.
- **Fluency**: Recognizing that PPL may not fully capture semantic coherence (e.g., repetitive text can yield low PPL), we employ **GPT-4o** [15] as a surrogate for human evaluation. We prompt GPT-4o to score semantic coherence on a scale of 0 to 10, where higher values indicate better quality.

Datasets

- **Training Set**: We utilize the Jigsaw [2] dataset, annotated with six distinct toxicity sub-concepts (*Toxic*, *Severe Toxic*, *Obscene*, *Threat*, *Insult* and *Identity Hate*), as our training dataset to extract SSVs.
- **Evaluation Set**: For evaluation, we sample prompts from the RealToxicPrompts (RTP) dataset to construct two distinct subsets following [18]:
  1. ***toxic_prompts***: Consisting of the 1,000 prompts with the highest toxicity scores, used to assess the mitigation effectiveness against explicit triggers.
  2. ***random_prompts***: Consisting of 1,000 randomly selected prompts, to evaluate model performance under low-toxicity or general input conditions.[3]

  For each prompt in the evaluation sets, we feed it into the target LLM to generate a continuation. These generated outputs are then collected to calculate the toxicity scores and text quality metrics defined below.

Baselines. We focus on inference-time intervention methods to avoid the high cost of re-training or fine-tuning. We compare our proposed MARS against three representative baselines covering decoding strategies, neuron interventions, and representation engineering:

- **PREADD** [18]: A decoding-based strategy that modifies output logits by contrasting the distributions generated from the original prompt against those from the prefix-prepended prompt.
- **AURA** [24]: An internal intervention method that identifies specific expert neurons responsible for toxic generation and adaptively suppresses their activation to mitigate toxicity.
- **GCAV** [30]: A state-of-the-art RepE method. It employs a single SSV with adaptive magnitude to steer LLMs toward non-toxic generation, treating toxicity as a unified concept.

[3] The prompt is available in our code.

Models. We evaluate MARS framework on representative open-weight base models: **Llama3.1-8B**, **Mistral-7B**, and **Gemma-7B**. Using base rather than instruction-tuned models isolates internal steering effects from pre-existing safety alignments and instruction-following distribution shifts, ensuring a rigorous benchmark across architectures.

4.2 Comparative Experiments

Table 1. Results of comparative experiments on two subset of RealToxicPrompts. Best results in bold; second-best underlined.

LLM	Method	Results on *toxic_prompts*			Results on *random_prompts*		
		Toxicity Score↓	PPL↓	Fluency↑	Toxicity Score↓	PPL↓	Fluency↑
Llama3.1-8B	*BASE*	0.376	44.764	4.35	0.137	42.427	**6.24**
	PREADD	0.191	252.199	4.19	0.100	251.109	5.43
	AURA	0.350	<u>37.567</u>	3.99	0.132	<u>40.376</u>	6.09
	GCAV	<u>0.143</u>	839.156	<u>4.39</u>	<u>0.077</u>	425.150	5.61
	Ours	**0.122**	**32.943**	**4.99**	**0.071**	**38.314**	<u>6.22</u>
Mistral-7B	*BASE*	0.322	**49.598**	3.59	0.117	**46.527**	5.54
	PREADD	0.237	20578.005	4.15	0.102	268.295	5.32
	AURA	0.268	<u>53.812</u>	4.11	0.119	<u>50.477</u>	5.13
	GCAV	<u>0.154</u>	1413.058	<u>4.16</u>	<u>0.083</u>	232.289	**6.74**
	Ours	**0.079**	61.615	**4.29**	**0.041**	65.773	<u>5.67</u>
Gemma-7B	*BASE*	0.337	<u>35.947</u>	<u>4.79</u>	0.123	**36.342**	**6.35**
	PREADD	0.213	326.503	1.27	0.112	129.284	1.62
	AURA	0.293	3.836*	2.13	0.159	159.388	2.68
	GCAV	<u>0.151</u>	491.782	**4.86**	<u>0.068</u>	145.473	5.78
	Ours	**0.069**	**34.610**	4.00	**0.047**	<u>42.940</u>	<u>6.12</u>

Table 1 presents the comparative results on three LLMs (Llama3.1-8B, Mistral-7B, and Gemma-7B) across two test sets. We observe that MARS consistently outperforms all baselines, achieving a superior balance between detoxification effectiveness and utility preservation.

Detoxification Performance. As detailed in the *Toxicity Score* column, MARS achieves the lowest toxicity levels across all models on both sub-datasets. For instance, on Llama3.1-8B, MARS reduces the toxicity score from 0.376 to 0.122, significantly surpassing AURA (0.350), PREADD (0.191) and GCAV (0.143). This indicates that our fine-grained, multi-dimensional steering can precisely target and neutralize toxic patterns that coarse-grained methods might miss.

Text Quality Preservation. The most significant advantage of MARS lies in its ability to preserve text quality. Baselines often suffer from disruption in general utility, leading to high PPL and low Fluency of generated text. For example, on Gemma-7B with *toxic_prompts*, PREADD causes PPL to spike to 326.503 and Fluency to drop to 1.27, rendering the generated text incoherent. In contrast, MARS maintains PPL and Fluency metrics that are comparable to those of **BASE** model across all experimental configurations. Notably, AURA achieves the lowest PPL of 3.836 on Gemma-7B on *toxic_prompts*; however, the generated text is highly repetitive and meaningless, thus leading to low Fluency.

It is worth noting that the extreme PPL values in baselines stem from their reliance on steering prompts or prefixes. Since our evaluation is conducted on base model (rather than instruction-tuned versions), introducing such prefixes disrupts the natural continuation probability, causing the model to generate repetitive or ill-formed text.In contrast, MARS operates directly within the internal representation space, circumventing the need for distribution-distorting prompts and thus maintaining semantic coherence comparable to the original LLMs.

4.3 Ablation Study

Multi- vs. Single-Dimensional. To validate multi-dimensional steering, we ablate MARS on *toxic_prompts* against single-dimensional baselines ($p_0 = 10^{-4}$). As shown in Table 2, single-dimensional steering fails to achieve comprehensive detoxification. For instance, steering Llama3.1-8B solely along the *Insult* SSV reduces toxicity to 0.226. In contrast, Full MARS achieves 0.122 (a ~50% improvement over the best single-vector baseline). This consistent trend across Mistral-7B and Gemma-7B confirms that toxicity requires simultaneous intervention across multiple subspaces to be effectively mitigated.

Adaptive Magnitude vs. Fixed Magnitude. To validate the effectiveness of our proposed steering mechanism, we compare the Dual-Constraint Adaptive Magnitude against the standard Fixed Magnitude approach. Unlike previous experiments, we compute Perplexity of Wikitext-2 (denoted as PPL_{wiki}) on steered Llama3.1-8B. As shown in Fig. 2, the Fixed Magnitude approach suffers from rapid PPL_{wiki} degradation at higher steering intensities. In contrast, our Adaptive Magnitude maintains a superior Pareto frontier.

Notably, the optimal trade-off point is observed at $p_0 = 10^{-4}$ (marked with a red star), where the model achieves a significant reduction in toxicity (from about 0.38 to about 0.12) with negligible impact on language modeling capability ($PPL_{wiki} \approx 7.0$). This demonstrates that our geometry-aware adaptive constraint successfully prevents the over-correction issues prevalent in fixed steering strategies.

4.4 Geometric Analysis

To validate our assumption that the sub-concepts of toxicity are separable, we utilize visualization analysis to intuitively demonstrate the distribution of these

Table 2. Ablation results comparing single-dimensional steering against the full MARS on *toxic_prompts*. Best results in bold; second-best underlined.

Steering Config	Llama3.1-8B			Mistral-7B			Gemma-7B		
	Toxicity↓	PPL↓	Fluency↑	Toxicity↓	PPL↓	Fluency↑	Toxicity↓	PPL↓	Fluency↑
BASE	0.376	44.764	4.35	0.322	49.598	3.59	0.337	35.947	**4.80**
Single *Toxic*	<u>0.223</u>	38.618	<u>4.92</u>	0.138	**42.992**	4.13	<u>0.115</u>	42.308	4.53
Single *Severe Toxic*	0.234	38.637	4.88	<u>0.136</u>	43.392	4.22	0.151	34.498	<u>4.67</u>
Single *Obscene*	0.254	39.141	4.84	0.190	<u>43.180</u>	4.20	0.183	35.538	4.51
Single *Threat*	0.299	<u>35.979</u>	4.63	0.196	46.970	4.16	0.207	34.560	4.37
Single *Insult*	0.226	40.821	4.83	0.192	49.053	4.09	0.164	35.128	4.53
Single *Identity Hate*	0.270	39.083	4.70	0.156	44.400	<u>4.23</u>	0.151	**32.141**	4.59
Full MARS	**0.122**	**32.943**	**4.99**	**0.079**	61.615	**4.29**	**0.069**	<u>34.330</u>	4.30

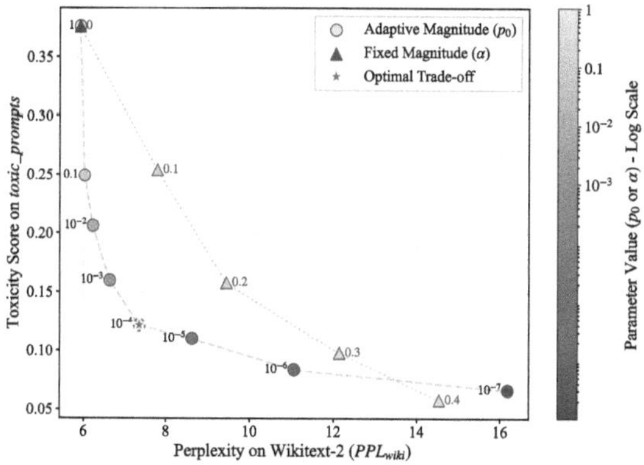

Fig. 2. Pareto frontier comparison on Llama3.1-8B. The plot illustrates the trade-off between **Toxicity Score** and **Perplexity on Wikitext-2** (PPL_{wiki}). Our **Adaptive Magnitude** achieves a superior balance compared to the **Fixed Magnitude** baseline, maintaining text fluency while effectively reducing toxicity. The red star marks the optimal parameter setting ($p_0 = 10^{-4}$).

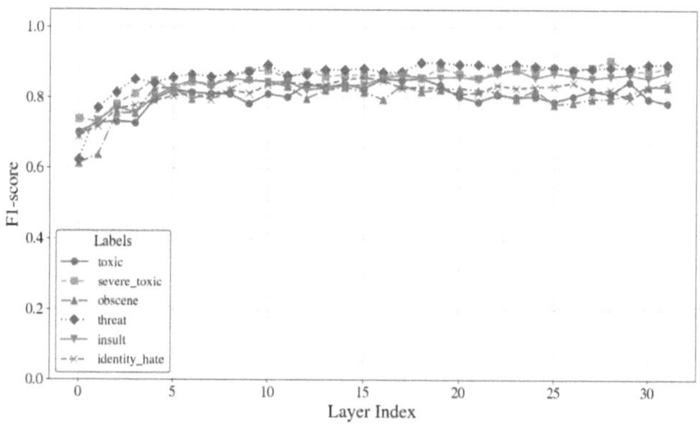

Fig. 3. F1-score performance of linear probes across layers of **Llama3.1-8B** for six toxicity sub-concepts. The results demonstrate that toxicity concepts become increasingly linearly separable in the deeper layers.

concepts in the latent space. We combine qualitative visualization with quantitative probe performance metrics to verify the distinctness of toxicity representations and justify our choice of analysis layer.

We evaluate the classification performance of each probe on each layer using the F1-score metric. As shown in Fig. 3, with the exception of the early layers, the linear probes for all toxicity sub-concepts demonstrate robust performance across the middle and later layers. Based on this observation, we select the 30th layer as our primary target for subsequent analysis and visualization. We randomly sample a small subset from the Jigsaw dataset and extracted the activations from the 30th layer.

Separability: Figure 4 visualizes the activations using PCA for dimensionality reduction. We observed clear boundaries between positive and negative samples across all six sub-concepts. These observations demonstrate the separability of toxicity sub-concepts.

Distinct Directions: A key question is whether different toxicity sub-concepts share the same direction. We calculate the cosine similarity between SSVs. As shown in Fig. 5, the SSVs exhibit low cosine similarity, which indicates the distinctness and justifies the necessity of a multi-dimensional mitigation approach.

4.5 Discussions

Effectiveness via Semantic Preservation. MARS surgically removes toxic intent within the semantic space while preserving pre-trained syntactic capabilities. Unlike decoding (PREADD) or neuron pruning (AURA), it achieves optimal detoxification and fluency without disrupting natural probability distributions.

Necessity of Multi-dimensionality and Adaptive Magnitude. Ablation studies confirm a single direction cannot span separable toxic subspaces. Furthermore, our adaptive magnitude dynamically scales intervention strength based on input toxicity. This context-aware scaling is crucial for preventing the "over-correction" inherent in fixed steering, thereby maintaining generation diversity and coherence when processing safe or borderline prompts.

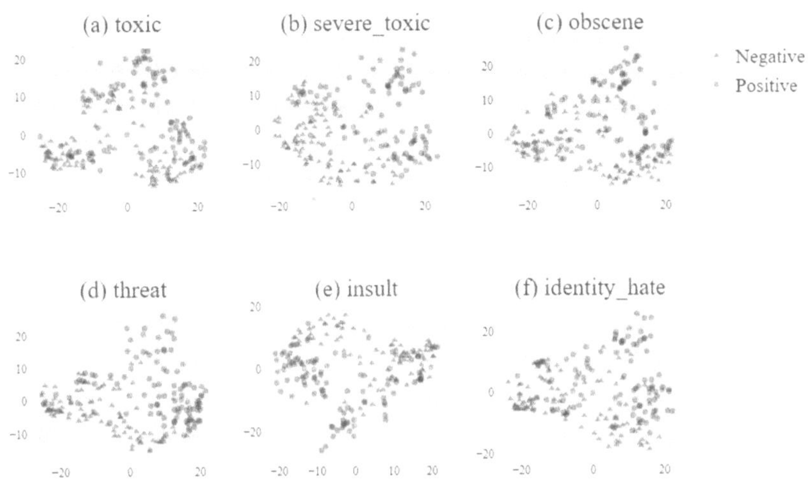

Fig. 4. PCA visualization of SSVs for the six toxicity sub-concepts in the 30th layer of **Llama3.1-8B**. The plots display the 2D projection of hidden states derived from the Jigsaw dataset, where blue dots represent toxic (positive) samples and red triangles represent non-toxic (negative) samples. The distinct spatial separation between the two classes across all sub-concepts validates the linear separability of toxicity representations.

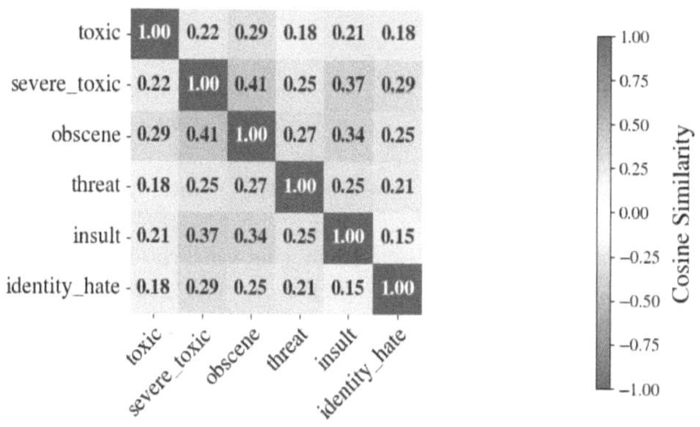

Fig. 5. Cosine similarity heatmap between the extracted toxicity SSVs from the 30th layer of **Llama3.1-8B**. The values represent the cosine similarity between pairs of concept directions derived from the Jigsaw dataset. The generally low to moderate similarity scores (mostly below 0.5) indicate that these SSVs encode distinct, separable aspects of toxicity, justifying the necessity of a multi-dimensional mitigation approach.

Interpretability. Geometric visualizations in Layer 30 validate that models encode toxicity as structured, distinct concepts rather than a monolithic entity. This ensures MARS leverages the internal properties of LLMs rather than manipulating a "black box", ultimately paving the way for more transparent, mechanistic approaches to AI safety.

5 Conclusion

In this paper, we addressed the critical challenge of mitigating toxicity in Large Language Models without compromising text quality. Our mechanistic analysis validates the hypothesis that toxicity is not a monolithic concept, but rather a composite of distinct sub-concepts residing in linearly separable but partially correlated subspaces. Grounded in this finding, we proposed **MARS**. Distinct from prior heuristic or unsupervised multi-directional approaches, MARS instantiates disentangled steering via a structured taxonomy and introduces a mathematically rigorous closed-form formulation to dynamically adapt intervention magnitudes. By effectively bounding the steering vectors, MARS achieves precise detoxification while strictly preserving the model's inherent semantic capabilities. Comparative experiments demonstrate that our approach significantly outperforms concurrent baselines across Llama3.1-8B, Mistral-7B, and Gemma-7B. Future directions include evaluating MARS on larger-scale and instruction-tuned models, as well as expanding beyond the Jigsaw taxonomy to encompass broader safety categories.

References

1. Abdullaev, L.U., Wong, N.Y.L., Lee, R.T.Z., Jiang, S., Nguyen, K.N.M., Nguyen, T.M.: Concept heterogeneity-aware representation steering (2026). https://arxiv.org/abs/2603.02237
2. Adams, C., et al.: Toxic comment classification challenge. https://kaggle.com/jigsaw-toxic-comment-classification-challenge
3. Bartoszcze, L., et al.: Representation engineering for large-language models: survey and research challenges (2025). https://arxiv.org/abs/2502.17601
4. Belrose, N., Schneider-Joseph, D., Ravfogel, S., Cotterell, R., Raff, E., Biderman, S.: Leace: perfect linear concept erasure in closed form (2025). https://arxiv.org/abs/2306.03819
5. Brown, T.B., et al.: Language models are few-shot learners. In: Proceedings of the 34th International Conference on Neural Information Processing Systems. NIPS '20 (2020)
6. Cuadros, X.S., Zappella, L., Apostoloff, N.: Self-conditioning pre-trained language models. In: Proceedings of the 39th International Conference on Machine Learning. Proceedings of Machine Learning Research, vol. 162, pp. 4455–4473
7. Devlin, J., Chang, M.W., Lee, K., Toutanova, K.: BERT: pre-training of deep bidirectional transformers for language understanding. In: Burstein, J., Doran, C., Solorio, T. (eds.) Proceedings of the 2019 Conference of the North American Chapter of the Association for Computational Linguistics: Human Language Technologies, Volume 1 (Long and Short Papers), pp. 4171–4186. https://doi.org/10.18653/v1/N19-1423
8. Gehman, S., Gururangan, S., Sap, M., Choi, Y., Smith, N.A.: RealToxicityPrompts: evaluating neural toxic degeneration in language models. In: Findings of the Association for Computational Linguistics: EMNLP 2020, pp. 3356–336. https://doi.org/10.18653/v1/2020.findings-emnlp.301
9. Hallinan, S., Liu, A., Choi, Y., Sap, M.: Detoxifying text with MaRCo: controllable revision with experts and anti-experts. In: Proceedings of the 61st Annual Meeting of the Association for Computational Linguistics (Volume 2: Short Papers), pp. 228–242. https://doi.org/10.18653/v1/2023.acl-short.21
10. Krause, B., et al.: GeDi: generative discriminator guided sequence generation. In: Findings of the Association for Computational Linguistics: EMNLP 2021, pp. 4929–4952. https://doi.org/10.18653/v1/2021.findings-emnlp.424
11. Kwak, J.M., Kim, M., Hwang, S.J.: Language detoxification with attribute-discriminative latent space. In: Proceedings of the 61st Annual Meeting of the Association for Computational Linguistics (Volume 1: Long Papers), pp. 10149–10171. https://doi.org/10.18653/v1/2023.acl-long.565
12. Lee, B.W., et al.: Programming refusal with conditional activation steering. In: International conference on learning representations, vol. 2025, pp. 90960–90985 (2025)
13. Li, Y., et al.: FairSteer: inference time debiasing for LLMs with dynamic activation steering. In: Findings of the Association for Computational Linguistics: ACL 2025, pp. 11293–11312. https://doi.org/10.18653/v1/2025.findings-acl.589
14. Liu, A., et al.: DExperts: decoding-time controlled text generation with experts and anti-experts. In: Proceedings of the 59th Annual Meeting of the Association for Computational Linguistics and the 11th International Joint Conference on Natural Language Processing (Volume 1: Long Papers), pp. 6691–6706. https://doi.org/10.18653/v1/2021.acl-long.522

15. OpenAI: Hello gpt-4o (2024). https://openai.com/index/hello-gpt-4o/
16. Ouyang, L., et al.: Training language models to follow instructions with human feedback. In: Proceedings of the 36th International Conference on Neural Information Processing Systems. NIPS '22 (2022)
17. Park, K., Choe, Y.J., Veitch, V.: The linear representation hypothesis and the geometry of large language models. In: Proceedings of the 41st International Conference on Machine Learning. ICML'24, JMLR.org (2024)
18. Pei, J., Yang, K., Klein, D.: PREADD: prefix-adaptive decoding for controlled text generation. In: Findings of the Association for Computational Linguistics: ACL 2023, pp. 10018–10037. https://doi.org/10.18653/v1/2023.findings-acl.636
19. Perez, F., Ribeiro, I.: Ignore previous prompt: attack techniques for language models. https://arxiv.org/abs/2211.09527
20. Peters, M.E., et al.: Deep contextualized word representations. In: Walker, M., Ji, H., Stent, A. (eds.) Proceedings of the 2018 Conference of the North American Chapter of the Association for Computational Linguistics: Human Language Technologies, Volume 1 (Long Papers), pp. 2227–2237. https://doi.org/10.18653/v1/N18-1202
21. Radford, A., Jozefowicz, R., Sutskever, I.: Learning to generate reviews and discovering sentiment (2017). https://arxiv.org/abs/1704.01444
22. Radford, A., Wu, J., Child, R., Luan, D., Amodei, D., Sutskever, I.: Language models are unsupervised multitask learners. OpenAI (2019)
23. Raffel, C., et al.: Exploring the limits of transfer learning with a unified text-to-text transformer, **21**(1)
24. Suau, X., et al.: Whispering experts: neural interventions for toxicity mitigation in language models. In: Proceedings of the 41st International Conference on Machine Learning. ICML'24 (2024)
25. Turner, A.M., et al.: Steering language models with activation engineering (2024). https://arxiv.org/abs/2308.10248
26. Wang, M., et al.: Beyond prompt engineering: robust behavior control in LLMs via steering target atoms (2025). https://arxiv.org/abs/2505.20322
27. Wang, W., Yang, J., Peng, W.: Semantics-adaptive activation intervention for LLMs via dynamic steering vectors. In: International Conference on Learning Representations, vol. 2025, pp. 79334–79351 (2025)
28. Xu, Z., Huang, R., Chen, C., Wang, X.: Uncovering safety risks of large language models through concept activation vector. In: Advances in Neural Information Processing Systems, vol. 37, pp. 116743–116782 (2024). https://doi.org/10.52202/079017-3706
29. Yang, K., Klein, D.: FUDGE: controlled text generation with future discriminators. In: Proceedings of the 2021 Conference of the North American Chapter of the Association for Computational Linguistics: Human Language Technologies, pp. 3511–353. https://doi.org/10.18653/v1/2021.naacl-main.276
30. Zhang, H., Wang, X., Li, C., Ao, X., He, Q.: Controlling large language models through concept activation vectors. In: Proceedings of the Thirty-Ninth AAAI Conference on Artificial Intelligence and Thirty-Seventh Conference on Innovative Applications of Artificial Intelligence and Fifteenth Symposium on Educational Advances in Artificial Intelligence. AAAI'25/IAAI'25/EAAI'25. https://doi.org/10.1609/aaai.v39i24.34778
31. Zou, A., et al.: Representation engineering: a top-down approach to ai transparency (2025). https://arxiv.org/abs/2310.01405

AI-Enhanced Investigations

Multimodal Online Black Industry Discovery with Long-Context Compression

Yinuo Wang, Jiayi Wang, Weikai Huang, and Zheng Huang(✉)

School of Computer Science, Shanghai Jiao Tong University, Shanghai, China
{yuki123,jw3247,weikaihuang,huang-zheng}@sjtu.edu.cn

Abstract. Online black industry activities have increasingly migrated from traditional underground platforms to instant messaging services, presenting new challenges for automated detection and analysis. Telegram has emerged as a prominent hub due to its anonymity, encryption, and support for automation, with communications often being long-context and multimodal. While recent studies have explored large language models (LLMs) for black industry analysis, their performance, refusal behaviors, and efficiency in multimodal chat scenarios remain underexplored. In this paper, we systematically investigate LLMs and multimodal LLMs (MLLMs) on black industryrelated classification and long-context compression tasks using real-world multimodal Telegram chat data. We benchmark mainstream models on classification accuracy and refusal behavior, and construct a task-specific model via parameter-efficient instruction tuning. Furthermore, we propose a TextImage Joint Rendering (TIJR) method and a visual-based Multimodal Visual Chat Compression (MVCC) framework that unifies textual and visual chat records into visual inputs, enabling efficient compression. This work highlights the potential of LLMs in combating cybercrime by enabling automated analysis of online black industry communications, addressing challenges in real-time monitoring and regulation.

Keywords: Large Language Models · Online Black Industry Discovery · Context Compression

1 Introduction

With the rapid development of the Internet, online black industry activities have become increasingly rampant on a global scale. Online black industry refers to illicit or high-risk activities conducted through online platforms, typically involving behaviors such as fraud, money laundering, gambling, underground trading, and other related activities. Criminals exploit the anonymity, immediacy and wide reach of the Internet to carry out various illegal activities. There has

This work is supported by the National Natural Science Foundation of China (Grant No. 92270201).

© ICST Institute for Computer Sciences, Social Informatics and Telecommunications Engineering 2027
Published by Springer Nature Switzerland AG 2027. All Rights Reserved
H. Neukirchen et al. (Eds.): ICDF2C 2026, LNICST 720, pp. 111–126, 2027.
https://doi.org/10.1007/978-3-032-37274-1_7

been a notable shift in criminal behavior, with actors moving from established underground forums to alternative social media platforms that provide convenient access to users and enhanced resilience against traditional moderation and surveillance.

A noteworthy social media platform frequently involved in online black industry activities is Telegram. Telegram is a cross-platform instant messaging application known for its anonymity and encryption features. Telegram's bot functionality can be exploited for automating criminal activities. Moreover, the distribution of Telegram's servers across multiple countries increases the difficulty of cross-regional regulation. These characteristics have made Telegram a breeding ground for black industry activities.

Earlier research on online black industry discovery primarily relied on traditional machine learning methods. Huang et al. [1] applied topic-based social network analysis and clustering to study underground marketplaces. Shah et al. [2] employed logistic regression and a shallow neural network to analyze Telegram groups. Jin et al. [3] introduced DarkBERT, an open-source language model pretrained on dark web corpora based on RoBERTa, enabling better understanding of domain-specific terminology and syntax compared to models trained on surface web data. Recent studies have shifted toward exploring large language models (LLMs) for understanding online black industry activities. Chen et al. [4] evaluated LLMs on dark web text classification and zero-shot tasks, showing that built-in safety mechanisms often lead to refusals and underscoring the need for domain adaptation.

Despite advances in LLMs and domain-specific models, challenges remain in chat-based black industry detection scenarios, particularly in efficiently processing multimodal content and handling long chat texts with multiple images, motivating the need for effective and robust detection methods.

In this paper, we investigate the performance of LLMs and their multimodal variants on black industryrelated classification and long-context compression tasks using multimodal Telegram chat data. Leveraging LLMs and multimodal LLMs for this problem allows us to capture complex semantic patterns, integrate textual and visual information, and handle large-scale, unstructured chat data more effectively than traditional methods. Our key contributions are threefold:

- We conduct a comprehensive evaluation of mainstream LLMs and MLLMs in terms of both classification accuracy and refusal behavior on black industry classification tasks, and build a task-specific model for online black industry classification through parameter-efficient instruction tuning.
- We propose a TextImage Joint Rendering (TIJR) method and a visual-based Multimodal Visual Chat Compression (MVCC) framework, which uniformly render textual and visual chat records into visual inputs for compression. The proposed framework is applied to online black industry classification, achieving substantial reductions in input token consumption and refusal rates.
- To the best of our knowledge, this is one the first works to systematically apply LLMs and MLLMs for analyzing multimodal chat data in the context

of online black industry activities. We demonstrate that LLMs can not only perform the task effectively but also provide more interpretable outputs, thus offering a trustworthy solution for automated chat data analysis.

2 Related Work

2.1 Large Language Models and Multimodal Extensions

Large language models (LLMs) based on Transformer excel in various natural language understanding tasks, such as GLUE [5] and SQuAD [6]. Recent advancements show that LLMs also achieve outstanding performance across numerous specialized fields such as clinical medicine [7], law [8], education [9], and cybersecurity [10].

Radford et al. [11] introduced the paradigm of pre-training followed by fine-tuning for LLMs and established a foundation for adapting pretrained models to downstream tasks. Instruction tuning [12] fine-tunes language models on datasets composed of instructionoutput pairs, enabling models to better follow human instructions and significantly improving their zero-shot and generalization capabilities. Parameter-efficient fine-tuning methods such as LoRA [13] have been widely adopted to adapt LLMs to downstream tasks with minimal additional parameters.

LLMs have achieved strong performance in natural language understanding and generation. However, real-world semantics are often conveyed through multiple modalities, which limits the effectiveness of text-only models. To address this issue, recent studies have extended LLMs to the multimodal domain, resulting in multimodal large language models (MLLMs) that support joint understanding and reasoning over text, images, and other modalities. MLLMs typically comprise a modality-specific encoder, a projection module aligning multimodal features to the language space, and a pretrained LLM as the reasoning backbone. They have achieved strong performance across diverse tasks such as visual question answering, image captioning, and multimodal dialogue, demonstrating their potential for complex real-world applications.

2.2 Online Black Industry Discovery on Telegram

Traditionally, online black industry activities such as gambling, money laundering, drug trafficking, and the distribution of adult content have been hosted on specialized or underground online platforms. As Telegram become more and more popular among criminals for its anonymity features, similar activities has emerged on the platform.

Büsgen et al. [14] provided a publicly available German Telegram chat message corpus of messages annotated with entities and relations from four black market groups. Boersma et al. [15] collected a dataset of messages and users from Dutch cybercrime Telegram groups, identified influential cybercrime groups and users by classifying messages and analyzing mention network, and evaluated the landscape of cybercrime on Telegram in the Netherlands. Lummen et al. [16] conducts a comparative analysis between Dark Net marketplaces and Telegram across multiple dimensions, and highlights that Telegram offers greater usability as a cybercrime marketplace. Guo et al. [17] discover the underground mobile app ecosystem on Telegram primarily facilitates illegal gambling and pornography services, revealing significant gaps in the platform's content moderation capabilities. Roy et al. [18] conducted a large-scale analysis of cybercrime activity channels on Telegram by developing the DarkGram framework based on BERT to identify and classify malicious posts from the channels. The application of LLMs to analyze black industry activities on Telegram remains a relatively underexplored area.

2.3 Multimodal Understanding and Context Compression

Multimodal content understanding can generally be categorized into three paradigms: language-centric, image-centric, and unified approaches [19]. Multimodal systems are predominantly language-centric, using LLMs as the backbone and aligning visual inputs with text representations. In contrast, image-centric modeling renders text into images to unify multimodal data in the visual domain. Beyond these two paradigms, unified multimodal modeling learns joint representations of text and images within a shared embedding space through a single encoder. Among them, the image-centric paradigm provides a promising direction for long-context compression by representing contextual information in a compact visual form.

Dosovitskiy et al. [20] introduced the Vision Transformer (ViT), which models images as sequences of fixed-size patches, enabling visual inputs to be processed in a token-based manner similar to natural language. DeepSeek-OCR [21] maps large-scale textual content into compact two-dimensional visual representations, achieving effective long-context compression while preserving key information. Li et al. [22] proposed the Text-as-Image approach, which renders long textual inputs into images and significantly reduces token consumption while maintaining task performance, offering an efficient input compression strategy for decoder-only LLMs. Similarly, Cheng et al. [23] presented the Glyph framework, which converts long texts into images and processes them with vision-language models, and additionally employs an LLM-driven search strategy to balance compression efficiency and accuracy.

3 Data Collection and Preparation

3.1 Data Collection

Telegram supports three communication modes: private chats, channels, and groups. We aim to utilize publicly available data to discover online black industry activity. Telegram API provides an approach to scrape chat messages from a public Telegram group without even being a member of it. Therefore, we use scraped group messages as our main subject of study. Analyzing groups has its inherent advantages: firstly, a group mainly focuses on a specific type of black industry activity (such as money laundering or gambling) and allows for group-wise analyze; secondly, a group contains abundant user information and message contents, providing a deep insight of activities and interactions.

The data used in this study are derived from Telegram group chat records that potentially involve online black industry activities, collected between 2023 and 2024. We refer to this raw data collection as BlackTG, which serves as the foundational corpus for our study. The chat records contain both textual messages and multimodal shared files.

Through systematic sampling and exploratory analysis of the raw corpus, we obtain two key observations. First, the data predominantly involve four major categories of online black industry activities of interest: fraud, money laundering, gambling, and pornography. Second, although multimodal content is present, we primarily focus on textual and image modalities, as images often convey critical information related to money exchanges and transactional evidence that may not be explicitly described in text.

3.2 Data Preparation

Based on the BlackTG corpus, we construct two task-specific datasets for black industry classification. The first is the multimodal **Black** Industry Classification **Ref**erence Dataset (**BlackRef**), designed to evaluate the baseline classification performance and refusal behavior of pretrained models. In addition, BlackRef is used to assess the effectiveness of multimodal token compression under the proposed compression framework. The second is the textual **Black** Industry Classification **F**ine-**T**uning Dataset (**BlackFT**), which supports instruction tuning of LLMs for black industry classification. A summary of the dataset statistics is presented in Table 1.

Table 1. Black industry dataset statistics

Dataset	Modality	Samples	Messages	Images	Avg. Chars
BlackRef	Text & Image	200	4,200	887	2464
BlackFT	Text	1,240	32,920	894	2247

The gathered data inevitably contains noise. Therefore, pre-processing is required to remove irrelevant information and ensure the quality of the data. To reduce noise and improve data quality, we remove advertisements, duplicate messages posted by the same sender within a single day, non-informative short messages (fewer than 10 characters), and emojis that may introduce ambiguous or misleading semantics for LLMs. As this study focuses on fine-tuning LLMs, additional preprocessing is applied to the multimodal chat segments in the fine-tuning dataset. Specifically, optical character recognition (OCR) is performed on image content to extract readable text. The extracted text is explicitly marked using special tokens (e.g., <img> </img> or <image_ocr> </image_ocr>) to indicate its visual origin and is then inserted into the original chat records at the corresponding image positions.

The samples in both datasets exhibit a relatively balanced distribution across categories. Each sample consists of a coherent chat segment composed of approximately 20-30 consecutive messages, forming a complete conversational context. Moreover, the majority of samples contain one or more relevant images, enabling a more faithful representation of the typical multimodal characteristics of black industryrelated content on Telegram.

Each chat segment is labeled with a JSON-formatted string representing its multi-dimensional risk profile, where each key corresponds to a high-risk category of interest and each value is binary, indicating the presence (1) or absence (0) of the associated risk. The fine-tuning dataset is structured in the JSON-based Alpaca format to support instruction-tuning of LLMs, with each sample comprising three fields: instruction (task description), input (chat segment), and output (label).

4 Methodology

The Telegram-based online black industry classification task can be defined as follows. Given a chat segment $C = \{T, I\}$, where T denotes the sequence of textual messages and I represents the set of image messages, the model is required to determine whether the segment involves any of the four high-risk black industry activities of interest in this study: **fraud, money laundering, gambling, and pornography**.

The output is expected in a structured JSON format, with a binary label for each category (1 indicates presence, 0 indicates absence), for example:

```
{fraud: 0, money_laundering: 0, gambling: 1, pornography: 0}
```

The classification task is formulated as a generative task, requiring models to output structured JSON labels. This design aligns with the generative paradigm of current LLMs and allows extensibility for additional fields, such as textual rationales, if needed. The objective of this task is to identify whether a Telegram chat segment contains black industry activities and, if so, to specify the types involved, thereby enabling automated characterization of the group's risk profile.

4.1 LLM-Based Black Industry Classification

Online black industry activities are inherently sensitive, and their identification and analysis directly touch upon the safety boundaries of LLMs. Modern LLMs are typically aligned to produce outputs that conform to social norms and ethical standards. One of the core alignment techniques is reinforcement learning from human feedback (RLHF). As a result of such alignment, refusal behavior has emerged as a key safety mechanism in LLMs, whereby the model declines to respond to prompts it deems unsafe or potentially harmful [24].

To assess the sensitivity of different models to online black industry content and their impact on model responses, we first construct an online black industry classification framework based on a range of open-source and closed-source pretrained LLMs and MLLMs. Using this framework, we conduct baseline classification accuracy and refusal behavior tests for the online black industry classification task. Specifically, for LLMs, the input chat snippet is defined as $C = \{T, OCR(I)\}$, where image messages I are transformed into textual representations via OCR. For multimodal LLMs, the input retains its original modality, in order to fully leverage the model's cross-modal understanding capabilities. The framework directly utilizes the model's original parameters and default inference behavior, aiming to quantify the refusal tendencies and behavioral differences of various pretrained models when facing potential online black industry violations. This provides empirical insights for designing subsequent online black industry identification strategies.

The framework for online black industry classification based on pretrained models is shown in Fig. 1. The overall process consists of three main stages: first, structured prompts are sent to the LLM (or multimodal LLM) to obtain a response; second, the model output is assessed for refusal behavior; and finally, non-refusal responses are further evaluated for format and content validity to determine whether they constitute valid answers to the task.

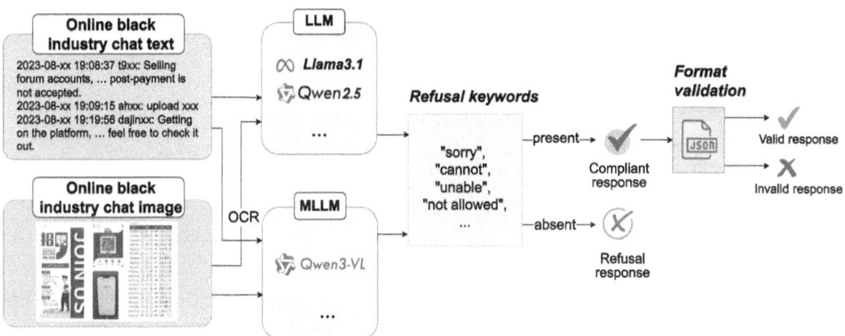

Fig. 1. Black industry classification framework based on pretrained LLMs.

This framework constructs model input prompts based on the BlackRef dataset using Chain-of-Thought [25] inspired prompt engineering. Each prompt consists of four components: (1) Role-based task description, which assigns the model an expert role (e.g., a risk assessment specialist) to contextualize the task; (2) Chat snippet to be analyzed; (3) Reasoning guidance, which encourages step-by-step analysis and requires risk judgments to be grounded in concrete black industry activities rather than superficial keywords or advertisements, thereby reducing false positives; and (4) Output format specification, which enforces a structured JSON response with fixed keys corresponding to the four targeted online black industry categories, each annotated with a binary label.

Following Liu et al. [26], we employ a keyword-based approach to automatically identify refusal behaviors of LLMs in the online black industry classification task. A set of predefined safety-related keywords (e.g., "sorry," "unable," "not allowed") is used to detect whether a model output constitutes a refusal. Responses containing such keywords are classified as refusal responses; otherwise, they are treated as compliant responses. A compliant response is considered valid only if it is formatted as structured JSON and includes predictions for all risk categories.

To improve model performance in black industry related scenarios, we employ LoRA [13] to fine-tune the pretrained LLM for domain-adapted behavior understanding. We fine-tune the Qwen2.5-1.5B-Instruct and Qwen2.5-7B-Instruct models using the annotated BlackFT dataset with Unsloth [27]. Each Alpaca-format sample in BlackFT consists of three fields: (1) Instruction, which specifies the online black industry classification task and includes the aforementioned task description, reasoning guidance, and output format specification; (2) Input, which contains a purely textual chat snippet related to black industry risks, where image information from the original multimodal chat records is converted into text via OCR; and (3) Output, which provides the JSON-formatted classification labels for the sample. Unsloth is a framework designed for efficient LLM finetuning that accelerates training speed and reduces VRAM consumption, enabling the training of larger models on limited data and constrained computational resources. We adopt a strategy that combines instruction tuning with LoRA to efficiently update model parameters and train a task-specific model for online black industry classification.

4.2 Multimodal Visual Chat Compression Framework

In the context of online black industry discovery, textual chat records are often lengthy, and directly processing them with LLMs incurs substantial token overhead and computational cost. The presence of multiple images within chat records further increases the inference burden. To address these efficiency challenges associated with long texts and multiple images, we propose an image-based multimodal information compression and classification approach. This method encodes both chat text and image content in a unified visual representation and leverages a MLLM for risk assessment.

We first propose a TextImage Joint Rendering (TIJR) method, which maps long text and multiple images into a single unified visual input. The method incorporates strict geometric and alignment constraints in the layout design to ensure that the rendered output is interpretable and stable for visual models. Building on this, we introduce a Multimodal Visual Chat Compression (MVCC) framework and apply it to online black industry classification, systematically evaluating both its compression efficiency and task performance.

The Text-Image Joint Rendering method of the proposed multimodal chat compression framework is illustrated in Fig. 2. The initial text region is a rectangle of width $text\_w$ and height $base\_text\_h$, and each image occupies a square region of side length $slot$, with

$$base\_text\_h = row \times slot$$

where row denotes the number of image rows that fit in the initial text height. Text is rendered using font size $font\_size$, with additional height added in increments of $slot$ as needed. Images are standardized via proportional scaling and zero-padding: the longer side is resized to $slot$ while maintaining aspect ratio, and the shorter side is padded to form a square, ensuring consistent spatial scale and preventing distortion. A blank region of width gap separates text and images. Overflow is handled with heterogeneous expansion rules: text extends downward, while images are arranged column-wise and extend rightward when a column is full. These modality-specific rules prevent cross-modal overlap, allowing the model to clearly distinguish text and image regions.

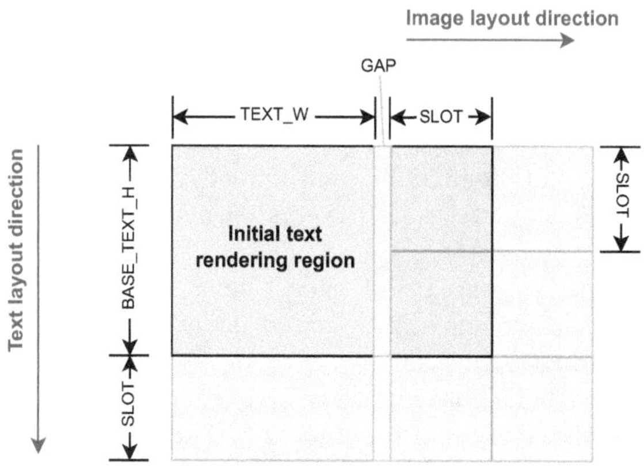

Fig. 2. Text-image joint rendering.

Based on the proposed TextImage Joint Rendering method, we further develop a Multimodal Visual Chat Compression framework and apply it to online black industry classification, as illustrated in Fig. 3. The task continues to use the prompt construction method described in Sect. 4.1, keeping the task prompt in text form to preserve precise semantics for task description and output format requirements, and thus not compressing them as images. The chat content to be classified, including text and images, is rendered jointly into a unified visual representation following the method above. Finally, the textual task prompt and the image-mode chat input are fed together into the MLLM to perform black industry classification.

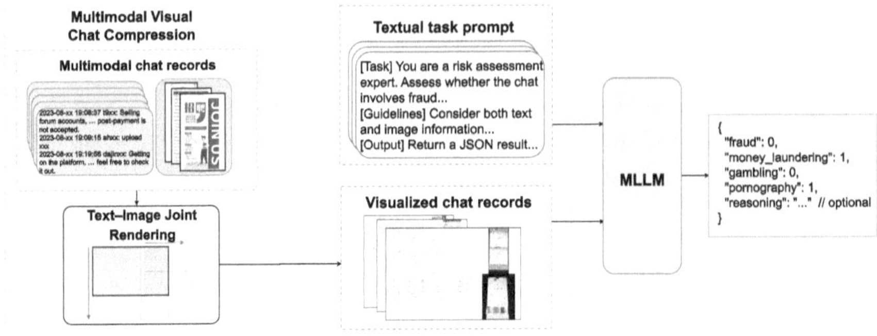

Fig. 3. Cyber black industry classification based on MVCC framework.

5 Results

5.1 Evaluation of LLM-Based Black Industry Classification

The classification performance and refusal rates of a range of mainstream LLMs and MLLMs on the constructed BlackRef dataset are reported in Table 3 and Table 2. We evaluate a range of open- and closed-source LLMs and MLLMs, including Llama-3.1 [28], Qwen2.5 [29], and Qwen3-VL-Plus [30], to assess performance on the BlackRef dataset. All evaluated models are instruction-tuned variants.

To further examine the stability of refusal behaviors, a retry mechanism is introduced, and selected models are evaluated under $retry = 0$ (no retry) and $retry = 3$ (up to three retries).

To evaluate refusal behaviors of LLMs in black industry classification, we adopt the *Refusal Rate* (RR) metric following DUAL-Bench [31]. Given a test set of N independent queries, each sample is allowed up to k retries (i.e., at most $k + 1$ total requests). We define the indicator function as:

$$\mathbb{I}_i = \begin{cases} 1, & \text{if the } i\text{-th sample is refused in all requests,} \\ 0, & \text{otherwise,} \end{cases} \qquad (i = 1, 2, \ldots, N)$$

The refusal rate under the retry mechanism is then defined as:

$$\mathrm{RR} = \frac{1}{N} \sum_{i=1}^{N} \mathbb{I}_i.$$

As online black industry classification is formulated as a set of binary classification tasks for each category, this study adopts standard evaluation protocols. The F1 score is used as the primary metric, as it balances precision and recall and effectively handles class imbalance.

Experimental results show notable differences in refusal behaviors across LLMs and MLLMs for black industry classification. Llama-3.1-8B and Qwen3-VL-Plus exhibit the highest refusal rates, whereas Qwen2.5-1.5B rarely refuses

Table 2. Refusal rate of LLMs on the BlackRef dataset

Model	Modality	Fraud	Money Laund.	Gambling	Porn.	Avg.
Llama-3.1-8B$_{retry=0}$	Text	0.10	0.30	0.10	0.75	0.31
Llama-3.1-8B$_{retry=3}$	Text	0.00	0.05	0.00	0.50	0.14
Qwen2.5-1.5B$_{retry=0}$	Text	0.10	0.05	0.00	0.00	0.04
Qwen2.5-1.5B$_{retry=3}$	Text	0.00	0.00	0.00	0.00	0.00
Qwen2.5-7B$_{retry=0}$	Text	0.00	0.00	0.00	0.00	0.00
Qwen3-VL-Plus$_{retry=0}$	Text & Vision	0.10	0.50	0.20	0.55	0.34
Qwen3-VL-Plus$_{retry=3}$	Text & Vision	0.10	0.25	0.05	0.40	0.20

and Qwen2.5-7B triggers no refusals; therefore, results under the $retry = 3$ setting are omitted for Qwen2.5-7B. Pornography-related content induces the highest refusal rates, followed by money laundering, while fraud and gambling lead to fewer refusals. Introducing a simple retry mechanism reduces the average refusal rate of Llama-3.1-8B from 31% to 14%, whereas Qwen3-VL-Plus shows more stable behavior, with a reduction from 34% to 20%, likely due to more robust safety alignment strategies in proprietary models.

Table 3. Classification performance of LLMs on the BlackRef dataset

Model	Modality	Validity	Fraud	Money Laund.	Gambling	Porn.
Llama-3.1-8B$_{retry=0}$	Text	0.53	0.42	**0.64**	0.63	0.80
Llama-3.1-8B$_{retry=3}$	Text	0.83	0.49	0.61	**0.68**	0.78
Qwen2.5-1.5B$_{retry=0}$	Text	0.78	0.32	0.43	0.53	0.59
Qwen2.5-1.5B$_{retry=3}$	Text	**1.00**	0.46	0.41	0.52	0.57
Qwen2.5-7B$_{retry=0}$	Text	**1.00**	0.57	0.62	0.67	**0.93**
Qwen3-VL-Plus$_{retry=0}$	Text & Vision	0.66	**0.72**	0.53	0.63	0.78
Qwen3-VL-Plus$_{retry=3}$	Text & Vision	0.80	0.67	0.60	0.64	0.83

Analyzing classification performance by risk category, open-source models achieve the highest F1-score on pornography-related content but perform relatively worse on fraud, indicating that fraud content is more semantically diverse and harder to detect. The closed-source model Qwen3-VL-Plus also attains the highest F1-score on pornography while maintaining comparatively strong performance on fraud, suggesting a more balanced capability across categories. However, when using only direct prompting, all models still fall short in response validity or classification performance, highlighting the need for parameter-efficient fine-tuning.

We uses Qwen2.5-1.5B-Instruct and Qwen2.5-7B-Instruct as base LLMs for LoRA fine-tuning. Maximum input sequence length is set to 3000. For the 1.5B

Table 4. Classification performance on the BlackFT dataset

Model	Fraud	Money Laund.	Gambling	Porn.
Qwen2.5-1.5B	0.32	0.42	0.42	0.87
Qwen2.5-7B	0.42	0.40	0.71	0.90
Qwen2.5-1.5B$_{CoT}$	0.31	0.50	0.32	0.91
Qwen2.5-7B$_{CoT}$	0.40	0.42	0.74	**0.95**
Qwen2.5-1.5B$_{IT}$	0.46	0.67	0.57	0.91
Qwen2.5-7B$_{IT}$	**0.82**	**0.88**	**0.95**	**0.95**

model, the batch size is 8 with a learning rate of 5e-5; for the 7B model, the batch size is 4 with a learning rate of 2e-4. BlackFT is split into training and test sets with an approximate 9:1 ratio. Given the highly structured output and limited label space, experiments show that only a few hundred representative annotated samples are sufficient to effectively constrain model behavior and improve performance, highlighting the advantage of parameter-efficient tuning in low-resource scenarios. Table 4 reports the classification results evaluated on the BlackFT test set. CoT denotes chain-of-thought prompting, while IT refers to instruction tuning. The results indicate that without fine-tuning, chain-of-thought prompting described in Sect. 4.1 alone provides only limited benefits. In contrast, instruction tuning on the constructed dataset enables the 7B model to achieve strong and well-balanced performance across all black industry risk categories, yielding a practical and reliable classification model.

5.2 Evaluation of Multimodal Visual Chat Compression

We evaluate the performance of MVCC on the multimodal BlackRef dataset. As the average chat text exceeds 2,000 characters, the initial text rendering area is set to a square with $text\_w = 352$ and $base\_text\_h = 352$. Text is rendered in Source Han Sans with $font\_size = 8$. Each image occupies a square region of side length $slot = 176$, which also serves as the vertical increment for text overflow, with a $gap = 8$ pixel margin between text and images. The canvas background is white and text is black. These rendering parameters are inspired by the setup in Rust et al. [32].

We use the compression ratio (CR) to evaluate token-level compression efficiency, defined as follows:

$$\mathrm{CR} = \frac{N_\mathrm{p} + N_\mathrm{t} + N_\mathrm{v}}{N_\mathrm{p} + N_\mathrm{TIJR}}$$

where N_p denotes the number of tokens in the text prompt, N_t denotes the number of tokens in the original chat text, N_v denotes the number of visual tokens from the original chat images, and N_TIJR denotes the total number of visual tokens generated by the Text–Image Joint Rendering (TIJR) process.

Using Qwen3-VL-Plus API, we compute the token compression ratio based on actual token usage for both text and images. Classification performance and refusal behavior are evaluated using the same evaluation strategy as in the previous section. Experimental results for refusal behavior, classification performance, and token compression are presented in Table 5, 6, and 7, respectively.

Table 5. Effect of MVCC on MLLM refusal behavior on the BlackRef dataset

Model	Fraud	Money Laund.	Gambling	Porn.	Avg.
Qwen3-VL-Plus$_{retry=0}$	0.10	0.50	0.20	0.55	0.34
Qwen3-VL-Plus$_{retry=3}$	0.10	0.25	0.05	0.40	0.20
Qwen3-VL-Plus$_{MVCC,retry=0}$	0.00	0.00	0.00	0.25	**0.06**

The results show that applying MVCC substantially reduces refusal rates in black industry classification. For the Qwen3-VL-Plus model, the average refusal rate drops from 34% to 6%, with remaining refusals occurring only for pornography-related content. This demonstrates the feasibility of using proprietary large models for effective black industry classification and highlights a potential avenue for multimodal jailbreak attacks.

Table 6. Classification performance of MVCC on the BlackRef dataset

Model	Validity	Fraud	Money Laund.	Gambling	Porn.
Qwen3-VL-Plus$_{retry=0}$	0.66	**0.72**	0.53	0.63	0.78
Qwen3-VL-Plus$_{retry=3}$	0.80	0.67	0.60	0.64	0.83
Qwen3-VL-Plus$_{MVCC,retry=0}$	**0.94**	0.59	**0.67**	**0.86**	**0.97**

While reducing refusal rates, the model generally improves classification performance across most categories, with only fraud showing a slight performance drop, further indicating that detecting fraud content may rely more on fine-grained textual semantics.

Table 7. Token compression performance of MVCC on the BlackRef dataset

Model	Average tokens consumed					Compression
	Fraud	Money Laund.	Gambling	Porn.	Avg.	Avg. Ratio
Qwen3-VL-Plus	3471	2792	3163	15054	5184	1.00×
Qwen3-VL-Plus$_{MVCC}$	580	477	551	761	575	**9.01**×

For samples that received valid responses before and after compression, we computed the average token consumption for each of the four risk categories, along with the overall average and the corresponding compression ratio. Results show that compression efficiency varies across categories, with pornography achieving the highest compression ratio of nearly 20×, due to the large amount of image content in the original samples. The other three categories reach approximately 6× compression. Overall, the average compression ratio across all categories is about 9×, demonstrating that the proposed image-based multimodal compression method can substantially reduce token usage.

6 Conclusion

This work investigated LLMs and MLLMs for online black industry discovery on multimodal Telegram chat data. We conducted baseline evaluations on the BlackRef dataset and performed instruction-tuning using BlackFT. A key contribution is the TextImage Joint Rendering (TIJR) method with the Multimodal Visual Chat Compression (MVCC) framework, which efficiently encodes long-text and multi-image chats for classification. Experimental results show that the proposed approaches achieve strong performance across multiple evaluation metrics. These findings demonstrate the effectiveness of our approach for multimodal black industry detection and provide a foundation for future research on efficient, risk-aware LLM deployment.

In the future, the framework can be extended to explore the application of multimodal compression in a wider range of tasks beyond black industry detection. Additional modalities such as audio or video could be integrated to provide richer contextual information on the task. Furthermore, online black industry behavior should be analyzed at a finer granularity to enable more accurate detection and more informative analysis of underlying patterns.

References

1. Huang, S.Y., Chen, H.: Exploring the online underground marketplaces through topic-based social network and clustering. In: 2016 IEEE Conference on Intelligence and Security Informatics (ISI), pp. 145–150. IEEE (2016)
2. Shah, D., Harrison, T., Freas, C.B., Maimon, D., Harrison, R.W.: Illicit activity detection in large-scale dark and opaque web social networks. In: 2020 IEEE International Conference on Big Data (Big Data), pp. 4341–4350. IEEE (2020)
3. Jin, Y., Jang, E., Cui, J., Chung, J.W., Lee, Y., Shin, S.: DarkBERT: a language model for the dark side of the internet. arXiv preprint arXiv:2305.08596 (2023)
4. Chen, H., et al.: Decode the dark side of the language: applications of LLMs in the dark web. In: 2024 IEEE 9th International Conference on Data Science in Cyberspace (DSC), pp. 224–231. IEEE (2024)
5. Wang, A., Singh, A., Michael, J., Hill, F., Levy, O., Bowman, S.R.: Glue: a multi-task benchmark and analysis platform for natural language understanding. arXiv preprint arXiv:1804.07461 (2018)
6. Rajpurkar, P., Zhang, J., Lopyrev, K., Liang, P.: Squad: 100,000+ questions for machine comprehension of text. arXiv preprint arXiv:1606.05250 (2016)

7. Shool, S., Adimi, S., Saboori Amleshi, R., Bitaraf, E., Golpira, R., Tara, M.: A systematic review of large language model (LLM) evaluations in clinical medicine. BMC Med. Inform. Decis. Mak. **25**(1), 117 (2025)
8. Siino, M., Falco, M., Croce, D., Rosso, P.: Exploring LLMs applications in law: a literature review on current legal NLP approaches. IEEE Access (2025)
9. Chu, Z., et al.: LLM agents for education: advances and applications. arXiv preprint arXiv:2503.11733 (2025)
10. Zhang, J., et al.: When LLMs meet cybersecurity: a systematic literature review. Cybersecurity **8**(1), 55 (2025)
11. Radford, A., Narasimhan, K., Salimans, T., Sutskever, I.: Improving language understanding by generative pre-training (2018)
12. Wei, J., et al.: Finetuned language models are zero-shot learners. arXiv preprint arXiv:2109.01652 (2021)
13. Hu, E.J., et al.: LoRA: low-rank adaptation of large language models. In: ICLR, vol. 1, no. 2, p. 3 (2022)
14. Büsgen, A., Klöser, L., Kohl, P., Schmidts, O., Kraft, B., Zündorf, A.: From cracked accounts to fake ids: user profiling on German telegram black market channels. In: Cuzzocrea, A., Gusikhin, O., Hammoudi, S., Quix, C. (eds.) DATA 2022. LNCS, vol. 1860, pp. 176–202. Springer, Cham (2021). https://doi.org/10.1007/978-3-031-37890-4_9
15. Boersma, K.: So long and thanks for all the (big) fish: exploring cybercrime in Dutch Telegram groups. Master's thesis, University of Twente (2023)
16. Lummen, D.: Is Telegram the new Darknet? A comparison of traditional and emerging digital criminal marketplaces. Master's thesis, University of Twente (2023)
17. Guo, Y., et al.: Beyond app markets: demystifying underground mobile app distribution via telegram. Proc. ACM Meas. Anal. Comput. Syst. **8**(3), 1–25 (2024)
18. Roy, S.S., Vafa, E.P., Khanmohammadi, K., Nilizadeh, S.: Darkgram: exploring and mitigating cybercriminal content shared in telegram channels. arXiv preprint arXiv:2409.14596 (2024)
19. Zhang, Z., et al.: Igniting language intelligence: the hitchhiker's guide from chain-of-thought reasoning to language agents. ACM Comput. Surv. **57**(8), 1–39 (2025)
20. Dosovitskiy, A., et al.: An image is worth 16x16 words: transformers for image recognition at scale. In: International Conference on Learning Representations (2021)
21. Wei, H., Sun, Y., Li, Y.: DeepSeek-OCR: contexts optical compression. arXiv preprint arXiv:2510.18234 (2025)
22. Li, Y., Lan, Z., Zhou, J.: Text or pixels? Evaluating efficiency and understanding of LLMs with visual text inputs. In: Findings of the Association for Computational Linguistics: EMNLP 2025, pp. 10564–10578 (2025)
23. Cheng, J., et al.: Glyph: scaling context windows via visual-text compression. arXiv preprint arXiv:2510.17800 (2025)
24. Prakash, N., Jie, Y.W., Abdullah, A., Satapathy, R., Cambria, E., Lee, R.K.W.: Beyond i'm sorry, i can't: dissecting large language model refusal. arXiv preprint arXiv:2509.09708 (2025)
25. Wei, J., et al.: Chain-of-thought prompting elicits reasoning in large language models. In: Advances in Neural Information Processing Systems, vol. 35, pp. 24824–24837 (2022)
26. Liu, X., Xu, N., Chen, M., Xiao, C.: Autodan: generating stealthy jailbreak prompts on aligned large language models. arXiv preprint arXiv:2310.04451 (2023)

27. Unsloth AI: Open source fine-tuning & RL for LLMs (2024). https://github.com/unslothai/unsloth. Accessed 21 Sept 2025
28. Grattafiori, A., et al.: The llama 3 herd of models. arXiv preprint arXiv:2407.21783 (2024)
29. Qwen Team: Qwen2.5 Technical report (2025). https://arxiv.org/abs/2412.15115
30. Qwen Team: Qwen3-vl-plus model documentation. https://modelstudio.console.alibabacloud.com/?tab=doc#/doc/?type=model&url=2840914_2&modelId=qwen3-vl-plus. Accessed 19 Jan 2026
31. Ren, K., Nakov, P., Naseem, U.: Dual-bench: measuring over-refusal and robustness in vision-language models. arXiv preprint arXiv:2510.10846 (2025)
32. Rust, P., Lotz, J.F., Bugliarello, E., Salesky, E., de Lhoneux, M., Elliott, D.: Language modelling with pixels. In: The Eleventh International Conference on Learning Representations (2023)

Agentic AI Enhanced Security Workflow for Explainable Host-Based Intrusion Detection

Raja Kumar[1], Jayesh Soni[1(✉)], Himanshu Upadhyay[2], and Alexander Perez-Pons[2]

[1] Applied Research Center, Florida International University, Miami, USA
{rkuma024,jsoni}@fiu.edu
[2] Department of Electrical and Computer Engineering, Florida International University, Miami, USA
{upadhyay,aperezpo}@fiu.edu

Abstract. The complexity of contemporary cyber threats has made the traditional perimeter defense and signature-based detection more than inadequate. This paper presents a novel, end-to-end framework that integrates Deep Learning, Explainable AI (XAI), and Large Language Model (LLM) agents. We first use an LSTM-based anomaly detector, which is trained on a typical sequence of system calls, to forecast process behavior. Then, we apply a gradient-based attribution scheme to attribute these anomalies to specific kernel interactions to generate a human-readable security assessment. Finally, the Reasoning Agent synthesizes these attribution scores with external threat knowledge (MITRE ATT&CK) to generate an attribution score for the system. The results show that the Detection Agent achieves a F1-Score of 84%, proving the practicality of deep learning in intrusion detection.

Keywords: Agentic AI · LSTM · Deep Learning · XAI · LSTM · Intrusion Detection

1 Introduction

1.1 The Evolving Threat Landscape and the Role of HIDS

Host-based Intrusion Detection Systems (HIDS) play a very important role in this hostile environment as the final line of defense. System calls are the ground truth of process behavior among the several data sources available to HIDS. Early research determined that processes have consistent, recurring patterns- a sense of self- that deviations are identified as anomalies. Although initial success was achieved with statistical techniques, the dimensionality and the temporal correlation of system call sequences have made it necessary to embrace Deep Learning (DL) techniques. Staudemeyer (2015) have studied Long Short-Term Memory (LSTM) networks and other architectures have shown state of the art in modeling these complex sequential dependencies and are far more effective than traditional n-gram and Hidden Markov Models (HMMs).

© ICST Institute for Computer Sciences, Social Informatics and Telecommunications Engineering 2027
Published by Springer Nature Switzerland AG 2027. All Rights Reserved
H. Neukirchen et al. (Eds.): ICDF2C 2026, LNICST 720, pp. 127–141, 2027.
https://doi.org/10.1007/978-3-032-37274-1_8

1.2 The Interpretability Gap: The "Black Box" Problem

Although deep learning models have a high level of detection accuracy, they have a serious weakness in security operations: lack of interpretability. In a typical DL-based HIDS, a security analyst is presented with a binary output, which is either normal or anomalous, or a probability score. Nevertheless, Ribeiro (2016) analyzed these models are black boxes, and they do not provide a hint as to the reasoning behind selecting a particular sequence. This opacity creates three distinct challenges in Security Operations Centers (SOCs):

1. Trust and Adoption: Analysts are reluctant to make automated decisions without verifiable information thus dismissing useful alerts.
2. False Positive Triage: It is very challenging to distinguish a benign anomaly (e.g., a software update) and a malicious exploit without information about which system calls were raised.
3. The Semantic Gap: Low-level kernel identifiers (e.g. sysread, sysexecve) and high-level threat intelligence (e.g. Data Exfiltration via Web Shell) are disconnected. This gap is still bridged today by manual, labor-intensive forensic analysis.

1.3 Proposed Approach: Bridging Detection, Explanation, and Reasoning

To address these challenges, this paper presents a novel, end-to-end framework that integrates Deep Learning, Explainable AI (XAI), and Large Language Model (LLM) agents. We propose a three phase pipeline. First, we use an LSTM-based anomaly detector, which is trained on a typical sequence of system calls, to forecast process behavior. Second, instead of using only prediction error, we use Integrated Gradients (IG) and Saliency Maps to assign scores of importance to each system call in anomalous windows. This can be used to mathematically isolate the interactions that caused the anomaly.

Third, and most importantly, we present an agentic LLM reasoning layer. Whereas XAI gives a mathematical attribution, it lacks semantic meaning. The LLM agent is an automated analyzer and consumes the sequence of system calls and XAI scores on attribution to produce a coherent security analysis. The system converts raw numerical abnormalities into intelligence that can be acted upon by mapping the low-level behavioral message to the MITRE ATT&CK framework.

1.4 Contributions

The primary contributions of this paper are as follows:

1. Explainable Anomaly Detection Architecture: We propose a single architecture, which integrates LSTM-based sequence modelling with gradient-based attribution schemes, which allow a more granular view of what specific system calls lead to malicious classifications.

2. LLM-Augmented Security Reasoning: We present a new use of agentic LLM (through the ReAct system) to analyze XAI output. The system will automatically contextualize attribution scores in order to determine the nature of the attack (e.g.: Web Shells, Meterpreter payloads).
3. Reproducible Evaluation: On the ADFA-LD benchmark, we obtain an F1-score of 84%. We give a breakdown of the performance of detection on different attack vectors in detail and publish our full implementation to encourage more research on explainable security..

2 Literature Review

This section discusses the history of system call analysis, the prevalence of sequence modeling, the need to have Explainable AI (XAI) in security, and the recent use of Large Language Models (LLMs) to provide automated defense.

2.1 System Call Analysis and Anomaly Detection

The main interface between the user-space programs and the operating system kernel is the system calls, which is the ultimate source of truth about behavior. A paradigm of system call-based intrusion detection was developed by Forrest et al., (1996) who developed the notion of a sense of self to Unix processes. Their study showed that privileged processes are characterized by stable and repetitive patterns of lexical representation in normal execution, and non-conformity to these patterns can be used as a predictable indicator of compromise.

Based on this, Hofmeyr et al. (1998) formalized the stide (Sequence Time-Delay Embedding) algorithm. Through a study of fixed-length sliding windows of system calls, they demonstrated that simple look-ahead pairs were able to model normal program behavior at very low computational cost. This n-gram model became the template of the further research on HIDS.

Creech and Hu (2013) have filled the gaps in aging datasets such as the 1998 DARPA collection with the introduction of the ADFA Linux Dataset (ADFA-LD). ADFA-LD reflects modern threats, such as Web Shells and Meterpreter payloads, and is a highly demanding testbed of modern HIDS. Creech and Hu (2014) also contributed to the development of the field by suggesting semantic analysis of system calls, which goes beyond mere lexical matching to the contextual meaning of call sequences, which leads to low false positive rates.

2.2 Deep Sequence Modeling in HIDS

Although statistical techniques (e.g., HMMs) offered initial promising results, they were unable to cope with the long-range structure of complex attacks. LSTM networks were proposed by Hochreiter and Schmidhuber (1997) to overcome the vanishing gradient problem of Recurrent Neural Networks (RNNs).

Du et al. (2017) introduced DeepLog, which was the pioneering work in the security domain and analyzed system logs as a natural language processing problem. DeepLog using LSTMs to learn the patterns of logs as sequences demonstrated the highest accuracy of anomaly detection, proving the practicality of deep sequence modeling in intrusion detection. Similarly, Kim et al. (2016) used LSTMs to system call language modeling, and showed that the LSTM-based models dramatically surpassed traditional classifiers such as SVMs in differentiating fine attack signatures.

2.3 Explainable AI (XAI) for Security

The black box nature of deep learning models introduces a significant trust gap in the operation of security. Doshi-Velez and Kim (2017) stated that predictive accuracy is not adequate in the high-stakes domains; models should also be interpretable so that they could be controlled by the human input.

In response to this, Sundararajan et al. (2017) introduced an axiomatic attribution approach named Integrated Gradients (IG) which scores input features by integrating gradients over a path with a baseline. Nevertheless, generic XAI techniques usually have problems with the peculiarities of security data. Guo et al. (2018) tackled it by proposing LEMNA, a special explanation technique in security systems that use deep learning. They pointed out that the traditional feature attribution might not be stable in a security scenario, and high-fidelity explanations would be necessary to justify forensic analysis.

2.4 LLM-Augmented Security Reasoning

Automated reasoning is a new capability layer that was recently introduced through Large Language Models (LLMs). Brown et al. (2020) have proven that LLMs are few-shot learners who can recognize and synthesize complex patterns. Ferrag et al. (2023) surveyed the potential of generative AI in the context of cybersecurity, as it has the ability to process raw security data into readable intelligence in human form. Yao et al. ReAct (Reasoning and Acting) framework is especially applicable to HIDS (2022). Enabling the generation of reasoning traces and the execution of external tools, ReAct makes dynamic investigation possible, which turns the detection pipeline into an active analyst able to map anomalies to frameworks such as MITRE ATT&CK.

3 Methodology

3.1 Data and Sequence Preparation

We conduct our experiments on the ADFA-LD dataset that is a widely used benchmark for host-based intrusion detection. ADFA-LD consists of labeled system call traces collected from linux systems. Each trace is a sequence of system

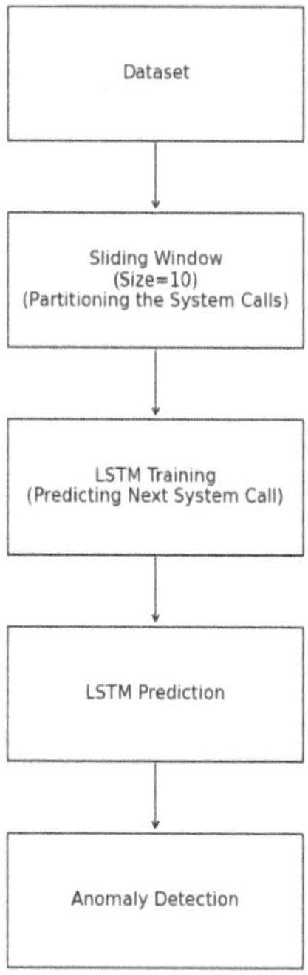

Fig. 1. Methodology.

call IDs represented as integers e.g. 4, 22, 33, 11 and so on, is categorized as either normal behavior or one of several attack types. ADFA-LD includes 6 types of attacks along with normal traces. To prepare the data for modeling, we perform the following steps: Sliding Window Segmentation- We choose a fixed window size of 5, 10, 15 to segment the long system call sequences into shorter and overlapping sequences. For a window size W = 15, a trace [C1,C2, . . ., C20] produces overlapping windows [C1,...,C15], [C2,...,C16] ,..., [C6,...,C20] using stride 1. This approach preserves temporal continuity and expands the training data. Every window inherits the label of its parent trace. Encoding of System Calls- Each system call ID in a window is treated as a categorical token. We map these IDs to an embedding vector space before feeding them to the neural network, similar to how words are embedded in NLP tasks. This learnable embedding allows the model to capture similarities or patterns between different system calls. The embedded sequence of length 10 then serves as input to our LSTM model. The dataset is partitioned into 4,164 training sequences (normal), 520 validation sequences (normal), and a test set comprising 521 normal sequences and 746 attack sequences across six categories. System calls were tokenized into integers, with a vocabulary size of 341 unique calls.

3.2 Implementation Details

The LSTM model (2 layers, 128 hidden units, embedding dim 64) was implemented in PyTorch and optimized using AdamW with a dynamic learning rate scheduler (ReduceLROnPlateau). We conducted a hyperparameter ablation study on the sliding window size ($W \in \{5, 10, 15\}$) to determine the optimal context length for capturing temporal dependencies. Since ADFA-LD provides labels at the trace level, each generated window inherits the label of its parent trace. This enables window-level evaluation but may reduce label fidelity, because not every local subsequence within an attack trace necessarily contains malicious behavior. Therefore, the reported metrics should be interpreted as window-level anomaly detection performance under trace-level label inheritance.

3.3 LSTM Sequence to Sequence Model Training

For sequence modeling, we employ a Long Short-Term Memory (LSTM) network in a sequence to sequence configuration. The LSTM is implemented in PyTorch taking advantage of its recurrent architecture to learn temporal dependencies. We set up the LSTM in a many to many training fashion where the model is trained to predict the latter part of each window given its beginning. Specifically for every 10 call windows extracted we use the first half of the sequence as input and task the LSTM with predicting the next half of the sequence as output. We then slide the window by one position and repeat, for instance, given a sequence segment [C1, C2,..., C10], the model sees [C1...C5] and predicts C6...C10], then it sees [C2...C6] and predicts [C7...C11] and so on. This overlapping many-to-many scheme is similar to a language modeling approach where the previous events act as a question and the subsequent events as the answer. It compels the LSTM to learn the normal progression of system calls over time. During training, the LSTM's parameters are optimized to minimize the prediction error between its output sequence and the actual next sequence of calls. After sufficient training epochs on normal training traces only, the LSTM learns the expected progression of benign system-call behavior. Attack traces are withheld from training and used only during testing. Essentially, the network develops an internal understanding of which sequences of calls tend to follow which preceding calls. Prior research has shown that sequence to sequence LSTM models can effectively capture system call patterns and detect anomalies. If the LSTM cannot accurately predict the continuation of a sequence it may indicate that the sequence is deviating from learned normal patterns.

3.4 Anomaly Detection as a Classification Task

Although the LSTM is trained in a generative sequence prediction manner, our end goal is to classify each sequence window as normal or anomalous. We therefore cast the problem as a binary classification task during evaluation. The trained LSTM model is used to predict the next sequence of calls for each input window in the test set. We then compare the LSTM's predicted sequence to the actual sequence observed. If the prediction closely matches the actual continuation the window is likely benign. If there is a significant discrepancy we flag the window as anomalous. In practice, we quantify the prediction error. If this error exceeds a chosen threshold, the window is classified as an attack, otherwise it's classified as normal. This approach effectively uses the LSTM as an anomaly detector where it will produce high error for sequences that are unlike the patterns it learned i.e. potential intrusions. We label each window in the test set based on this criterion and then evaluate the classification performance against the ground truth labels provided by ADFA-LD. Because we have a limited set of labels we focus on standard classification metrics to assess our model like accuracy, precision and F1-Score. We compute these metrics on the test data to quantify the model's performance. All metrics are reported using the binary classification framework. This choice is due to our primary interest in detecting any intrusion. However, the approach can be extended to multi-class classification if we wish to distinguish different attack types as separate class. Integrated Gradients for Anomaly attribution: To ensure our model's predictions are transparent and trustworthy we integrate explainability into the methodology. In particular, we use Integrated Gradients (IG) as a post hoc explanation technique to identify which parts of a sequence contributed most to an anomaly classification. Integrated Gradients is a gradient based feature attribution method that computes the contribution of each input feature by averaging gradients as the input is interpolated from a baseline to its actual value.

4 Experimental Evaluation

The experimental evaluation validates the efficacy of the proposed multi-stage architecture, beginning with the optimization of the deep learning detector. As illustrated in (Fig. 1), increasing the temporal context window to $W = 15$ yields a distinct performance advantage, achieving the lowest validation loss ($\approx$ 1.41) and highest accuracy (>80%) compared to shorter windows ($W = 5, 10$). This predictive stability is crucial for the downstream Agentic Workflow, where the LSTM's initial detection of statistical anomalies (e.g., a 77.3% misclassification rate shown in Fig. 5) serves as the reliable trigger for investigation. By applying Integrated Gradients in Fig. 6, the system successfully attributes these deviations to specific kernel interactions—notably `shmctl` and `timerfd_create`—allowing the LLM reasoning agent in Fig. 7 to semantically map the raw behavior to MITRE ATT&CK. This end-to-end validation demonstrates that robust sequence modeling ($W = 15$) is the prerequisite for bridging the gap between "black box" anomaly scores and actionable threat intelligence.

4.1 Detailed Performance Metrics

To provide a granular view of the system's efficacy, we disaggregated performance across three distinct dimensions: the baseline specificity on benign traffic, the global detection capability, and the sensitivity to specific attack vectors.

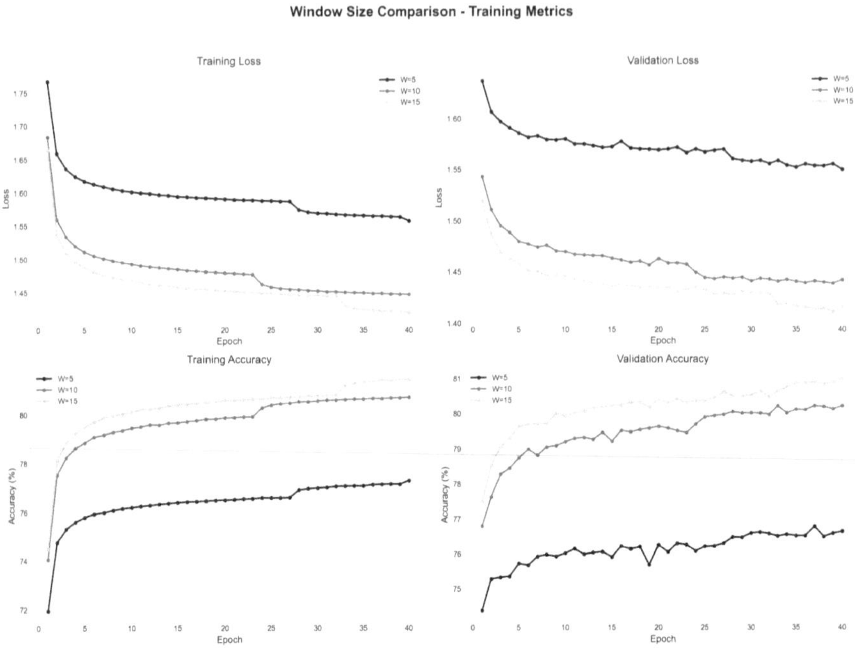

Fig. 2. Hyperparameter Sensitivity Analysis of LSTM Training Dynamics Across Varying Window Sizes ($W \in \{5, 10, 15\}$).

Baseline Specificity. Table 1 establishes the system's baseline behavior in a purely benign environment (Negative Control Set, $N = 521$). Since this set contains no attack vectors, Precision and Recall metrics are not applicable.

The model achieves a True Negative Rate (Specificity) of 64.30%, meaning it successfully filters out nearly two-thirds of normal traffic without intervention. However, the False Positive Rate (FPR) of 35.70% (186 sequences) represents the operational "cost" of the system's high sensitivity. The relatively high false positive rate reflects the detector's high-sensitivity configuration. In operational deployment, the LSTM stage is intended to serve as a candidate generator rather than a final decision engine. Alerts can be further reduced through threshold tuning, trace-level aggregation, and reasoning-stage filtering.

Global Detection Performance. Table 2 illustrates the system's overall effectiveness when operating in a mixed-threat environment (Combined Test Ecosystem, $N = 1,267$).

The most critical metric for a security-focused model is **Recall**, where our system achieves **90.48%** (detecting 675 out of 746 attacks). This confirms the LSTM's utility as a high-sensitivity candidate generator.

Table 1. Baseline Specificity (Negative Control Set)

Metric	Value	Definition/Calculation
Accuracy	64.30%	Proportion of normal sequences correctly identified (335/521)
True Negatives (TN)	335	Benign sequences correctly classified as normal
False Positives (FP)	186	Benign sequences incorrectly flagged as anomalous
TN Rate (Specificity)	64.30%	Probability of a negative test given the condition is negative
False Positive Rate	35.70%	Probability of a false alarm (186/521)

Table 2. Global Detection Performance

Metric	Value	Definition/Calculation
Global Accuracy	79.72%	$(TP + TN)$/Total Samples
Precision	78.40%	Probability that a flagged alert is a genuine threat
Recall (Sensitivity)	**90.48%**	Probability of detecting a malicious sequence
F1-Score	**84.01%**	Harmonic mean of Precision and Recall
True Positives (TP)	675	Total attack sequences successfully detected

Sensitivity Analysis by Attack Category. Table 3 decomposes the detection performance to highlight the model's sensitivity to specific attack signatures ($FP = 186$).

We observe a strong correlation between attack "noisiness" and detectability. Brute-force vectors like **Hydra_SSH** and **Hydra_FTP** exhibit the highest Recall (>94%), as their repetitive system call patterns deviate sharply from the normal baseline.

The present results should be interpreted as a benchmark validation of the proposed detection-attribution-reasoning workflow rather than proof of cross-dataset generalization. Future work will extend evaluation to ADFA-WD and additional host telemetry datasets.

5 The Agentic Security Workflow

To operationalize the raw detection capabilities of the LSTM model, we implemented a multi-stage Agentic Workflow. This pipeline utilizes the ReAct (Reasoning and Acting) paradigm, where a central controller coordinates three specialized tools to transform low-level system data into high-level threat intelligence. The workflow proceeds sequentially: first, the Detection Agent ingests the

Table 3. Sensitivity Analysis by Attack Category

Attack Category	Recall	Precision	F1	Acc.
Hydra_SSH	**94.32%**	47.16%	**62.88%**	71.88%
Hydra_FTP	**95.06%**	45.29%	61.35%	71.60%
Web_Shell	93.22%	37.16%	53.14%	69.64%
Java_Meterpreter	89.52%	37.37%	52.73%	69.15%
Adduser	75.82%	27.06%	39.89%	66.01%
Meterpreter	86.67%	25.90%	39.88%	67.11%

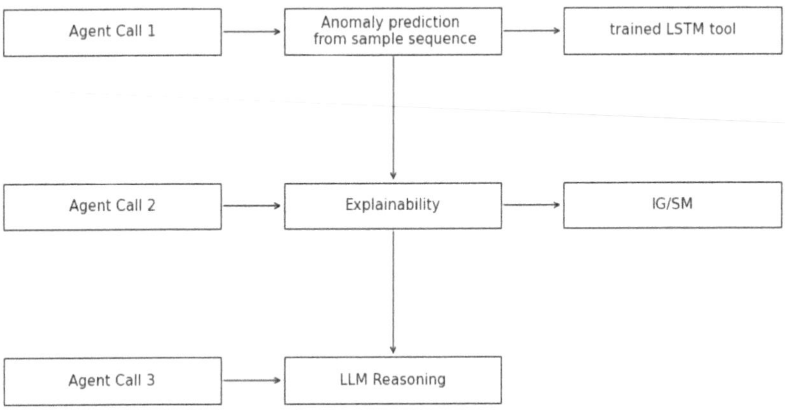

Fig. 3. Agentic Workflow.

raw system call stream to identify statistical anomalies; second, the Explainability Agent applies Integrated Gradients to attribute these anomalies to specific kernel interactions; and finally, the Reasoning Agent synthesizes these attribution scores with external threat knowledge (MITRE ATT&CK) to generate a human-readable security assessment. The following figures (Figs. 1, 2, 3, 4 and 5) illustrate this process, beginning with the model training validation and concluding with an end-to-end case study of a privilege escalation attack.

5.1 Agentic Pipeline Execution

The workflow proceeds sequentially through four distinct states, as demonstrated by our end-to-end case study of a privilege escalation attack.

State I: Data Ingestion The workflow starts with the ingestion of a raw system call trace (Fig. 4). This is represented as a set of 129 discrete kernel interactions that were obtained on a sample of an attack on Hydra. This stream of unstructured data interleaves calls such as `getitimer`, `shmctl` (Shared Memory Control), and `timerfd_create`, which are the low-level vocabulary of the behavior of the process. The information at this point is all syntactic; the easily recognizable patterns of a brute-force attack or a privilege escalation attack are interred in the stochastic noise of legitimate system activity, and only deep sequence modeling can be used to separate them.

```
Source: Hydra_FTP_4 / UAD-Hydra-FTP-4-3523.txt (129 syscalls)

Full Sequence:

309(syscall_) 102(getitime) 195(shmctl) 265(syscall_) 27(inotify_)
85(timerfd_) 85(timerfd_) 102(getitime) 102(getitime) 196(shmat)
196(shmat) 309(syscall_) 27(inotify_) 10(fgetxatt) 10(fgetxatt)
102(getitime) 102(getitime) 195(shmctl) 85(timerfd_) 195(shmctl)
85(timerfd_) 195(shmctl) 85(timerfd_) 85(timerfd_) 195(shmctl)
85(timerfd_) 195(shmctl) 102(getitime) 309(syscall_) 102(getitime)
309(syscall_) 102(getitime) 265(syscall_) 102(getitime) 102(getitime)
309(syscall_) 195(shmctl) 5(setxattr) 27(inotify_) 309(syscall_)
5(setxattr) 5(setxattr) 309(syscall_) 309(syscall_) 5(setxattr)
5(setxattr) 5(setxattr) 85(timerfd_) 85(timerfd_) 102(getitime)
10(fgetxatt) 195(shmctl) 85(timerfd_) 195(shmctl) 102(getitime)
195(shmctl) 102(getitime) 5(setxattr) 5(setxattr) 102(getitime)
27(inotify_) 27(inotify_) 265(syscall_) 5(setxattr) 102(getitime)
5(setxattr) 10(fgetxatt) 102(getitime) 102(getitime) 102(getitime)
265(syscall_) 85(timerfd_) 85(timerfd_) 6(lsetxatt) 10(fgetxatt)
10(fgetxatt) 309(syscall_) 10(fgetxatt) 102(getitime) 85(timerfd_)
195(shmctl) 102(getitime) 102(getitime) 27(inotify_) 309(syscall_)
102(getitime) 102(getitime) 27(inotify_) 102(getitime) 102(getitime)
27(inotify_) 102(getitime) 102(getitime) 102(getitime) 309(syscall_)
27(inotify_) 309(syscall_) 102(getitime) 27(inotify_) 85(timerfd_)
85(timerfd_) 196(shmat) 196(shmat) 265(syscall_) 10(fgetxatt)
102(getitime) 5(setxattr) 5(setxattr) 27(inotify_) 5(setxattr)
102(getitime) 309(syscall_) 102(getitime) 102(getitime) 85(timerfd_)
102(getitime) 5(setxattr) 102(getitime) 27(inotify_) 5(setxattr)
27(inotify_) 309(syscall_) 102(getitime) 85(timerfd_) 196(shmat)
196(shmat) 196(shmat) 265(syscall_) 10(fgetxatt)
```

Fig. 4. Agent State I: Ingestion of Raw System Call Sequence (Hydra_FTP_4).

State II: Anomaly Detection When the input sequence is processed, the LSTM inference is run by the tool called `detect_anomaly`. The model identifies the sequence as high confidence flagged as anomalous, as Fig. 5 indicates. The diagnostic measure of `misclass_rate` is 77.3%, indicating that in almost three-quarters of the sliding windows (92 of 119), the model was not able to correctly predict the next system call. This large error rate is the initial catalyst to the next investigative processes, which are mathematically valid to the effect that the observed behavior is many times less than the learned baseline of normal system activity. The LSTM detector runs on all windows, while Integrated Gradients and LLM reasoning are triggered only for flagged anomalous windows. Therefore, the most expensive stages are applied selectively rather than continuously.

```
┌─ AGENT CALL 1: detect_anomaly(sequence)
│  Input: 129 syscalls
│  Output: {'is_anomalous': True,
│           'misclass_rate': 77.3%,
│           'windows': 119, 'incorrect': 92}
└─ Result: ANOMALOUS
```

Fig. 5. Agent State II: LSTM-Based Anomaly Detection and Window Analysis.

State III: Explainability and Attribution After the alert of detection, the most anomalous subsequence is selected using the tool of `explain_with_attribution` in order to find the root cause of the deviation. Figure 6 illustrates the visualization of the attribution scores, with positive scores representing system calls that were strongly motivating the anomalous classification. Analysis shows a group of repeat calls to the `shmctl` (Shared Memory Control) and `timerfd_create` calls which have particularly high attribution scores (e.g., +2.777 to shmctl and +2.248 to timerfd). This step interpolates the distance between the anomaly score on the black box and the semantic interpretability, and identifies the exact manipulations of the kernel that resulted in the alert.

State IV: Reasoning and Synthesis The last step is the synthesis of the detection metrics and attribution information into a consistent security report by the tool, called `generate_reasoning` tool (Fig. 7). The high scores in shared memory and timer file descriptors of high attribution are interpreted by the Large Language Model (LLM) as an indicator of Privilege Escalation through Shared Memory, which is correctly differentiated by the larger label of Hydra. This behavior can be successfully mapped by the agent to the particular MITRE ATT&CK technique. The output offers a HIGH confidence rating, using the 95% model confidence and the particular attribution cluster as the evidence of

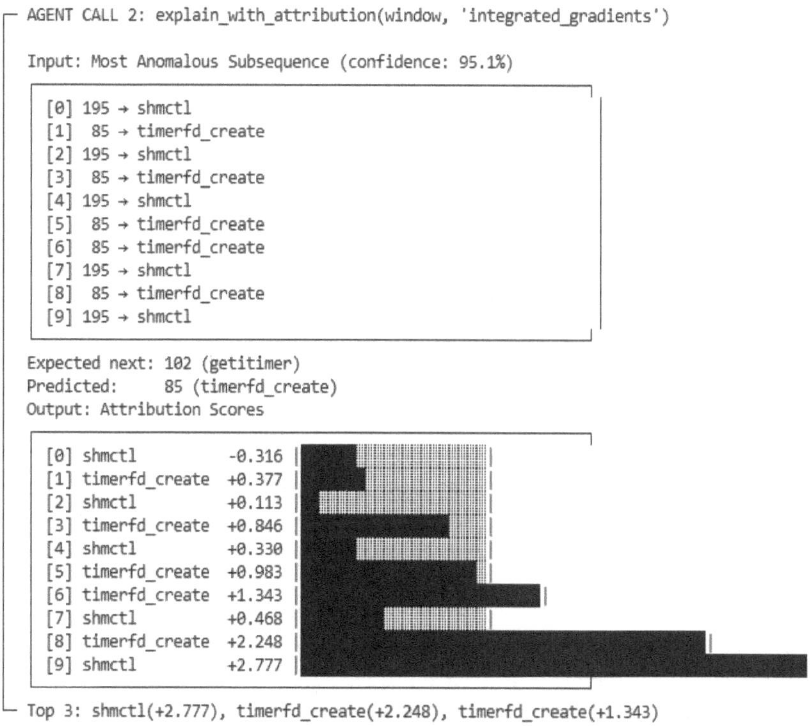

Fig. 6. Agent State III: Granular Feature Attribution via Integrated Gradients.

the reliability, thus converting raw numerical abnormalities into threat intelligence that can be acted upon.

```
┌─ AGENT CALL 3: generate_reasoning(detection, attribution)
│  Input: Anomaly detection + Attribution scores
│  Output (LLM Reasoning):
│   ┌────────────────────────────────────────────────────────┐
│   │ ATTACK_TYPE: Privilege Escalation via Shared Memory and Ti..│
│   │ BEHAVIOR: Repeated alternating calls to shmctl and timerfd..│
│   │ KEY_SYSCALLS: shmctl (high attribution) and timerfd_create..│
│   │ MITRE_ATT&CK: T1546.006 - Event Triggered Execution: Timers │
│   │ CONFIDENCE: HIGH - model confidence 95% and top attributio..│
│   └────────────────────────────────────────────────────────┘
└─ Analysis complete
```

Fig. 7. Agent State IV: Automated Threat Profiling and MITRE ATT&CK Mapping.

6 Conclusion

This study provided a detailed architecture of Host-based Intrusion Detection (HIDS) that fills the crucial gap between deep learning accuracy and operational interpretability. We managed to use Long Short-Term Memory (LSTM) networks with Explainable AI (XAI) and Large Language Model (LLM) agents to overcome the black box issue that prevents AI implementation in Security Operations Centers.

As our experimental testing on the benchmark of ADFA-LD indicates, the proposed system has strong detection capabilities. The LSTM detector was optimized with a sliding window of 15 and achieved a Global Recall of 90.48% and F1-Score of 84.01% which was very effective against a wide variety of attack vectors. The system was highly sensitive to repetitive attacks, with a recall of more than 94% of brute-force vectors, such as `Hydra_SSH` and `Hydra_FTP`, and a viable detection rate when faced with less visible privilege escalation attacks.

In addition to the quantitative measures, the main contribution of the current work is the Agentic Security Workflow. We showed that with the use of Integrated Gradients, it is possible to granularly attribute the occurrence of anomalies to certain kernel interactions, including the manipulation of `shmctl` and `timerfd_create` system calls. Moreover, these technical artifacts could be automatically converted into high-level threat intelligence by integrating an LLM reasoning agent. As shown in our case study, the system was able to map raw system call traces to distinct MITRE ATT&CK techniques (e.g., **T1546.006**), converting opaque anomaly scores into readable security measurements that can be understood by humans.

Although the system focuses on sensitivity, with a False Positive Rate of 35.70% in purely benign environments, the agentic architecture compensates such a cost by transferring the semantic triage to the reasoning engine. Future efforts will be directed towards improving the capacity of the LLM to screen these false positives and to classify data by more than two classes instead of dichotomous detection.

Acknowledgment. This research work was supported by Google Inc. under the Award number AWD16835.

References

Forrest, S., Hofmeyr, S.A., Somayaji, A., Longstaff, T.A.: A sense of self for Unix processes. In: Proceedings of the 1996 IEEE Symposium on Security and Privacy, pp. 120–128 (1996)

Hofmeyr, S.A., Forrest, S., Somayaji, A.: Intrusion detection using sequences of system calls. J. Comput. Secur. **6**(3), 151–180 (1998)

Creech, G., Hu, J.: Generation of a new IDS test dataset: time to retire the KDD collection. In: 2013 IEEE Wireless Communications and Networking Conference (WCNC), pp. 4487–4492 (2013)

Creech, G., Hu, J.: A semantic approach to host-based intrusion detection systems using contiguous and discontiguous system call patterns. IEEE Trans. Comput. **63**(4), 807–819 (2014)

Hochreiter, S., Schmidhuber, J.: Long short-term memory. Neural Comput. **9**(8), 1735–1780 (1997)

Du, M., Li, F., Zheng, G., Srikumar, V.: DeepLog: anomaly detection and diagnosis from system logs through deep learning. In: Proceedings of the 2017 ACM SIGSAC Conference on Computer and Communications Security (CCS), pp. 1285–1298 (2017)

Kim, G.: Deep learning approach for network intrusion detection. In: Proceedings of the International Conference on Research in Adaptive and Convergent Systems (RACS) (2016)

Doshi-Velez, F., Kim, B.: Towards a rigorous science of interpretable machine learning. arXiv preprint arXiv:1702.08608 (2017)

Sundararajan, M., Taly, A.Y.Q.: Axiomatic attribution for deep networks. In: Proceedings of the 34th International Conference on Machine Learning (ICML), pp. 3319–3328 (2017)

Guo, W., Mu, D., Xu, J., Su, P., Wang, G., Xing, X.: LEMNA: explaining deep learning based security applications. In: Proceedings of the 2018 ACM SIGSAC Conference on Computer and Communications Security (CCS), pp. 364–379 (2018)

Warnecke, A., Arp, D., Wressnegger, C., Rieck, K.: Evaluating explanation methods for deep learning in security. In: 2020 IEEE European Symposium on Security and Privacy (EuroS&P), pp. 158–174 (2020)

Brown, T., et al.: Language models are few-shot learners. In: Advances in Neural Information Processing Systems (NeurIPS), vol. 33, pp. 1877–1901 (2020)

Ferrag, M.A.: Secure-GPT: a knowledge-based large language model for cybersecurity. arXiv preprint arXiv:2310.10323 (2023)

Yao, S., et al.: ReAct: synergizing reasoning and acting in language models. In: International Conference on Learning Representations. ICLR (2022)

Ribeiro, M.T., Singh, S., Guestrin, C.: "Why should i trust you?" Explaining the predictions of any classifier. In: Proceedings of the 22nd ACM SIGKDD International Conference on Knowledge Discovery and Data Mining (2016)

Staudemeyer, R.C.: Applying long short-term memory recurrent neural networks to intrusion detection. South Afr. Comput. J. **56**(1), 136–154 (2015)

A Methodology for Producing Recursive Medical Forensic Image Analysis Responses Using VLMs

Dionysios Koulouris, Athanasios Kallipolitis, Dimitrios Kalathas, Andreas Menychtas(✉), and Ilias Maglogiannis

University of Piraeus, Karaoli Ke Dimitriou 80, 18534 Piraeus, Greece
{dnkoulouris,nasskall,dkalathas,amenychtas,imaglo}@unipi.gr

Abstract. Advanced Artificial Intelligence methods, particularly the recent expansion of Multimodal Large Language Models, have demonstrated significant potential in the health sector by automating the identification and extraction of high-level information from medical imagery. However, it has not yet been examined to what extent the incorporation of such methods in health can accelerate causal analysis procedures, such as the time-demanding judicial tasks of Forensic Medicine. We introduce a prototype method for forensic image analysis by recursively refining Vision Language Model responses, annotated with errors in prior responses. The proposed system, which can be executed in mobile devices, utilizes LLMs to first analyze medical forensic imagery and then, after the action of a Forensic Pathologist to indicate erroneous observations, utilizes this information to regenerate responses. The key contribution is a human-in-the-loop refinement framework for forensic injury descriptions that reduces the pathologist's cognitive and documentation effort. By iteratively regenerating and correcting model outputs, the framework cuts the required manual edits compared to raw responses, enabling near-expert descriptions with minimal rewriting across six representative injury types. This work is developed within the context of the design and implementation of InForensic: a novel medical forensics information system for the Greek State Forensic Services.

Keywords: Medical Forensics · Large Language Models · Vision Language Models · Recursive Prompt Refinement · Forensic Image Analysis

1 Introduction

The latest advancements of technology offer great computational power in handheld devices and introduce the users to intelligent user-centric solutions. Artificial Intelligence (AI), which is systemically imitating human behavior [11], shows rapid growth and extends its applicability to a variety of domains. It is

© ICST Institute for Computer Sciences, Social Informatics and Telecommunications Engineering 2027
Published by Springer Nature Switzerland AG 2027. All Rights Reserved
H. Neukirchen et al. (Eds.): ICDF2C 2026, LNICST 720, pp. 142–157, 2027.
https://doi.org/10.1007/978-3-032-37274-1_9

able to assist professionals relieving them of time-consuming and manual activities, especially the continuously evolving research activities of the healthcare domain. In this field, AI solutions may perform certain tasks better than healthcare professionals and are evaluated on their algorithmic decision-making [24]. Computer Vision (CV), a subcategory of AI, is the ability of analyzing images and videos and producing higher level understandings [25]. Latest trends utilize Large Language Models (LLMs) and specifically Vision Language Models - VLMs for assessing and processing medical images [22], as an application of CV. Such models revolutionize the medical image analytics field by offering an end-to-end approach through their multi-modal learning capability. Another intelligent LLM-driven methodology is LLM refinement, where models can assess and improve their generated outputs by incorporating user-indicated corrections [19]. Overall, LLMs and their intelligent usage represent a topic of considerable scientific interest, as they unlock new possibilities for automating complex reasoning tasks.

While the integration of LLMs is already deployed in the general healthcare landscape [15], limited research is conducted when applying such solutions in the healthcare subfield of Forensics. They are utilized in forensic data extraction and report compilation but the results are limited. Moreover, the AI Medical Forensics systems that are developed are mostly proof-of-concept applications of a specific LLM strategy and not Forensic Pathologist (FP) oriented. Overall, LLMs in forensics need to be studied on their transparency, accountability and robust standardization [27] and on how they maintain an efficient Human-Machine Interaction. This integration demonstrates significant potential for advancing the application of LLMs within the respected field. Upon this, the current research aims to investigate and apply intelligent computational methods to enhance the efficiency, accuracy and consistency of forensic workflows through the integration of LLM-driven analysis and decision support.

In this work we demonstrate a prototype application of a novel LLM refinement methodology specialized in medical forensics. This innovative approach utilizes LLMs to generate medical forensic image analysis tasks and refine specific parts of the generated responses via user interaction. Hence, a newly generated response is displayed to the user which is possibly closer to the initially intended response and, at the same time, the time required to manually fix the response is eliminated.

2 Related Work

While AI has shown great interest in analysing images [6], the latest technological trends include the utilization of LLMs for serving such purposes. Large scale pre-trained LLMs can achieve in-context learning and, most importantly, multi-image reasoning, using only few-shot prompting [14]. Various cutting-edge libraries were tested upon their performance on executing extensive image analysis tasks [5]. Comparisons of LLMs with students analyzing medical images showed that LLMs demonstrate competent performance in certain domains like a Radiology and Applied Physics medicine exam [16]. It is encouraging, though, that as LLMs are evolving, they will eventually reach great performance metrics in all domains.

LLMs are used in education [1], in factual knowledge reinforcement [13], in observation data extraction [20] and in medical report compilation [9]. The complexity of Medical Forensics, which combines legal and medical reasoning with judicial critics, offers unexplored territory for research in forensic Generative AI. More specifically, LLMs are used to overcome data-analysis problems that law-enforcement agencies face, especially due to the need of interpreting expressions with hidden meanings [7]. In addition, report writing assistance is a fully applicable field of LLMs, as they can be used for converting structured tabular data to human-readable tests [12]. Medical data retrieval is a functionality that can also be achieved by using specially-prompted and tuned LLMs [3]. An AI agent that tries to automate forensic death investigation and explicitly includes a human-in-the-loop for validating and refining cause-of-death conclusions is proposed [18] but has not been examined with visual data and is not integrated as part of an end-to-end medical forensics information system. Another human-in-the-loop approach [4], which is based on biomedical ontology, is integrating the human expertise in LLMs towards accuracy and consistency, but has not been examined in Medical Forensics.

Forensic report generation is applied in the forensic field [8] by utilizing prompt engineering [26] and Retrieval-Augmented Generation (RAG) [10]. Overall the Medical Forensics landscape offers fertile ground for research in intelligent LLM approaches. LLMs are capable of handling complex tasks especially in the text-classification field. Their adaptability and reasoning capabilities depend on the explicitly of the prompts, the contextual grounding and the domain-specific optimizations [23]. Hence, prompt design is a key factor of a successfully working LLM [28]. This raises the question of how users should respond when an LLM produces an incorrect output, particularly in cases where the user is capable of identifying the error. Prompt refinement is the technique of asking an LLM to generate a new response after indicating errors in a previous response, by applying methods like Prompt Chaining and Stepwise Prompt [21].

Although the current state of the literature demonstrates the potential of prompt-refinement strategies for improving model reasoning and output quality, their effectiveness needs to be explored against high-stakes application domains. In particular, the need for systematic studies is mandatory to assess how prompt-refinement procedures affect correctness and reliability when applied to tasks like Image Analysis in Medical Forensics. The evaluation of refinement paradigms is essential for assessing whether prompt-refinement can improve human-in-the-loop mechanisms in cases where errors may have significant legal consequences.

3 Methods

The proposed methodology consists of an LLM extension to an already deployed Medical Forensics Information System entitled *InForensic*. Among other functionalities, *InForensic* utilizes LLMs to analyze medical imagery and extract observations, descriptions, injury causes and image evaluation metrics. Our work extends this system with elements to indicate the correctness of the produced LLM results and re-generate them. It is a paradigm of how LLM prompt-refinement techniques can be applied by field experts to facilitate procedure efficiency and eliminate time-consuming.

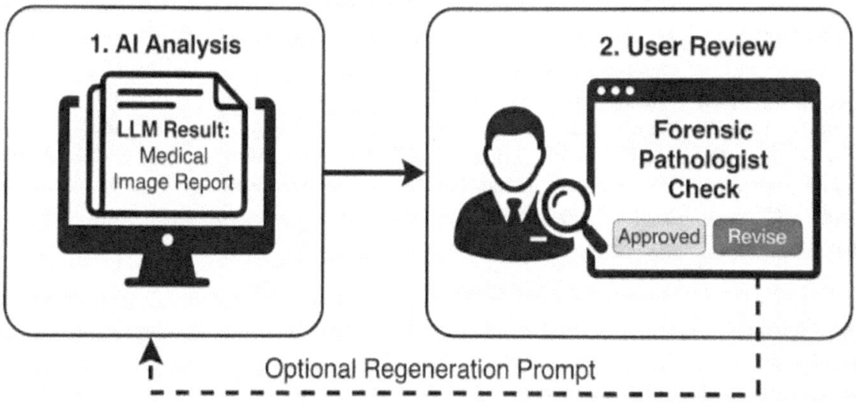

Fig. 1. The conceptual design of the proposed methodology. An initial AI analysis generates the first results. The Forensic Pathologist evaluates the response and either accepts or asks for revision. If second, the system returns a regenerated response.

3.1 Design

The InForensic system incorporates various LLM approaches for image data extraction, including in-house deployments and publicly available models. These models follow the same pattern from the user perspective, allowing the user to select an image, choose the model and perform the analysis. Results are exported in tabular format and the InForensic system defines body parts, trauma descriptions, metrics, causal analysis and time placement, due to the context of the medical forensics. The proposed extension applies a Human-In-the-Loop refinement workflow by requiring user interaction after each response. The FP is asked to check whether an output is correct or needs revision. If second, a regeneration prompt is sent to the model, highlighting the point of revision and a new result is generated. The design of the system is demonstrated in Fig. 1.

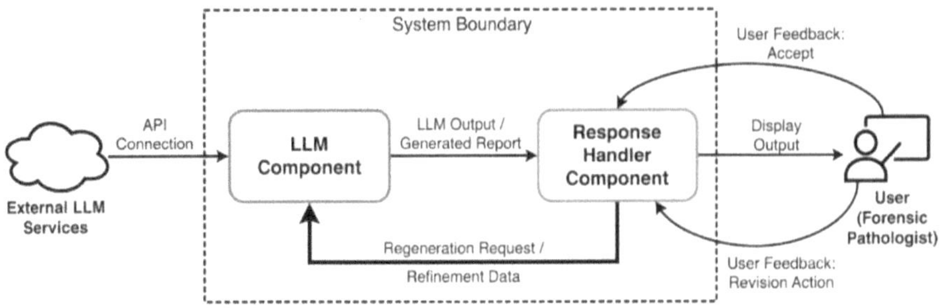

Fig. 2. The proposed system architecture showing the LLM Component and the Response Handler Component interconnection within the system boundary. The first component connects to external LLM services, integrating them into a unique interface. It generates the initial output and handles refinement requests between the Response Handler Component. The second is responsible for feeding the User Interface with output data and awaiting user actions for acceptance or revision.

3.2 Architecture

The system architecture consists of two components: the LLM component which handles the connection with the LLM services; and the Response Handler Component (RHC) which displays the LLM output to the user and handles the accept or revision actions. The LLM component is capable of connecting to either domain-specific, locally hosted LLMs or already-existing off-the-shelf services. It incorporates specialized prompt methods to define tasks for both forensic image analysis and forensic image analysis refinement. To analytically describe the convergence behavior of the recursive reasoning structure, the refinement loop is formalized as a sequence of state updates, iterating until the user-indicated error context becomes empty:

$$R_i = f_{\text{VLM}}(R_{i-1}, \epsilon_i)$$

where R_0 is the initial analysis response, ϵ_i represents the specific error context indicated by the forensic pathologist at iteration i, and the process converges when $\epsilon_i = \emptyset$ (expert acceptance) or halts at a maximum iteration threshold K. The RHC acts as an orchestrator of the LLM Component, interconnecting with it within the system boundary for image analysis requests and results. Furthermore, a specialized end-user platform, to which the RHC can be integrated as a plugin, visualizes the display output data of the RHC, initiates the analysis processes and indicates acceptance and regeneration events. The system Architecture is shown in Fig. 2.

3.3 Implementation

The implementation of the proposed work is divided in client and server side computations. The server side executes the LLM Component logic; it offers connection to the external LLM services that have been selected and handles the prompt-tuning. It includes APIs for the aforementioned connections and for the regeneration requests. The client side includes the user interaction functionalities of the RHC; editable cards for displaying the prompt results, options to accept or revise each result and stats storing. The server side is implemented using NestJS and the client side using Flutter.

Regarding model selection, in the current prototype, GPT-4 Vision was used as the underlying VisionLanguage Model due to the availability of high-volume API quotas and its seamless interoperability with the existing (governmental) cloud infrastructure of the InForensic system. While the specific model choice is reported for completeness, the proposed recursive prompt-refinement methodology is designed to be generalizable across VLMs. However, it is important to acknowledge that the rigid JSON generation requirements and strict adherence to prompt constraints pose a significant technical challenge. Proprietary models like GPT-4 are currently better equipped to handle these complex refinement prompts. Less capable open-source models may struggle to reliably parse and output valid schemas under such rigid constraints, necessitating further research into model-specific prompt adaptations before true model-agnosticism can be achieved.

To comply with the proposed methodology the starting prompt needs to respect the following requirements:

1. provide contextual information,
2. define the tasks that need to be performed,
3. set IDs for each task and
4. exclude tasks that have no data.

Thereafter, since the time distance between the two actions requires separate prompts, the refinement prompt needs to include:

- the previous chat history,
- the ID of the to-be-refined task and
- indication of the context of the refinement.

An example of the refinement prompt is following.

Reconsideration Instructions Prompt

```
# Follow-Up Instruction
(Single-Task Reconsideration-- Return ONLY Changes)
Target:
- Reconsider ONLY the task where "taskId" == $taskId.
Context:
- The previous full JSON output is available in chat history.
- Reattach and analyze the provided image again.
Rules:
- Update the finding ONLY if the reconsideration produces
a different result
than the previous one.
- Preserve the original schema for this task as defined
in the system instructions.
- Keep the SAME "taskId" value (= $taskId);
do not renumber or rename fields.
- Use Greek terminology for all classification fields
and anatomical terms.
- Numeric values ONLY when directly observable
(e.g., woundCount; length/width only if tools are visible).
- Report only positive/observable findings.
STRICT Output:
- Return a SINGLE JSON object with "findings".
- If the reconsidered finding CHANGED, return exactly ONE object
(the updated task object for taskId = $taskId).
- If NOTHING changed, return the same object that has this taskId.
```

4 Results

Results of this prototype approach show the system in actual medical forensics scenarios where the task's output is shown along with the refinement option. Moreover, the system is validated as a proof-of-concept and evaluated qualitatively.

4.1 The System in Practice

The system is deployed and tested using real medical forensic footage. After an image is uploaded, image analysis is performed via a specific "Analysis" button and using a selected model from a dropdown menu. The FP can preview the result, edit it, remove it or refine it using the "Refresh" button. This button executes the aforementioned prompt and displays the newly generated result. A snapshot from the system in practice is shown in Fig. 3.

When the refresh button is pressed, the LLM initiates the recursive regeneration and the new result presented to the user, as shown in Fig. 4.

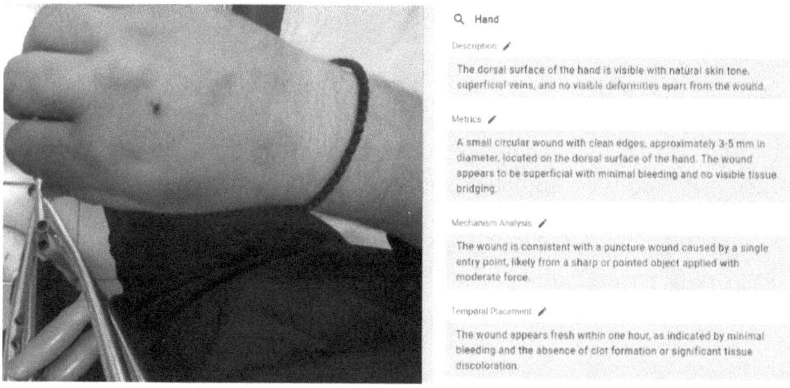

Fig. 3. Snapshot from the system in practice. On the left lies the forensic image which is set to be analyzed. On the right, at the top is the identified body part, followed by the identified analysis responses, for each task. The refresh button, at the right of each response, initiates the recursive refinement process.

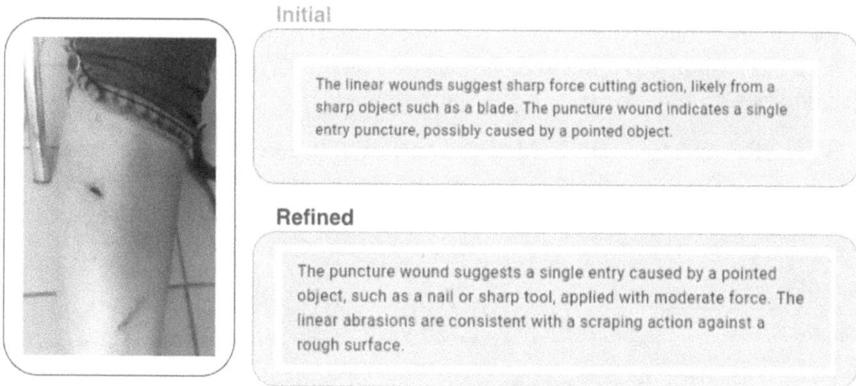

Fig. 4. Snapshot from the system outputs before and after refinement. The initial response (blue card) is indicated as erroneous by the professional and the refined response (green card) is generated. This recursive method can work with multiple iterations. (Color figure online)

4.2 Evaluation

The system, as a proof-of-concept prototype, was validated and evaluated qualitatively to assess the efficiency of the recursive prompt-refinement strategy. The primary goal of the evaluation is to demonstrate the improvement in User Experience (UX) by measuring the reduction in manual effort required by the FP.

Proof-of-Concept Initial Validation: For experimentation setup, a set of 6 images was utilized, representing distinct forensic injury types: crushing wound, decarbonation, ecchymosis, scarred wound, cutting instrument wound and stapled wound.

Although the dataset is small, these 6 types of injury were intentionally chosen as they are fundamental and frequently seen morphological types of mechanical, thermal and iatrogenic trauma in everyday forensic practice [17] [2]. They encompass a broad and challenging range of visual characteristics and medicolegal complexities, providing a sufficiently robust baseline to validate this proof-of-concept. Thus the global average metrics presented in this study are to be understood only as preliminary feasibility indicators, showing the working of the refinement loop, and not as definitive statistical measures of the global reliability of the system. Ground-truth texts—including trauma descriptions, metrics, mechanism analysis and temporal placement—were provided by collaborating Forensic Pathologists. In this context, "forensic correctness" is defined not solely by accurate morphological image interpretation, but as a composite standard requiring precise causal attribution, temporal reasoning, and injury mechanism inference. A system-generated response is evaluated as forensically correct only if it aligns with the expert ground truth across all these critical medicolegal dimensions.

We utilized the following metrics to quantify the improvement between the initial LLM response (R_{init}) and the refined response (R_{ref}), using the Forensic Pathologist's ground truth (GT) as the baseline:

1. **Word Error Rate (WER):** Used to formally calculate the "Textual Distance." WER measures the minimum number of edits (substitutions, deletions, insertions) required to transform the system output into the expert's ground truth, normalized by the length of the reference text (N):

$$WER = \frac{S + D + I}{N}$$

   A lower WER indicates higher accuracy and reduced manual effort.
2. **Expert-Labeled Correctness (ELC)**: 3-level correctness measured by correct, partially correct and incorrect responses per task.
3. **Entity-Level Scoring (ELS)**: Score based on Expert-Labeled Correctness of each entity. The entities are defined by the tasks as follows: Body Part Task (BPT), Trauma Description Task (TDT), Metrics Task (MT), Mechanism Analysis Task (MAT) and Temporal Placement Task (TPT).
4. **Hallucination Rate (HR)**: Mentions of non-observable tool-based measurements or ungrounded causal claims.

For reference, an injury type (Crushing Wound) was used to extensively demonstrate image analysis and refinement flow. Therefore, results of the other injury types are demonstrated collectively. We compared each of the initial Crushing Wound analysis response entities against their ground-truth and calculated SDI (substitutions, deletions, insertions), WER, ELS and HR. The total WER is computed globally as $\text{WER}_{\text{total}} = \sum SDI / \sum N = 8/96 \approx 0.08$. ELS is computed as the sum of ordinal correctness scores (Incorrect = 0, Partially Correct = 1, Correct = 2) across the five report tasks, yielding a maximum score of 10 per iteration. HR is computed as the proportion of statements within a report task that introduce non-observable measurements or unsupported causal claims. Body Part identification was consistently correct in the initial LLM output across all evaluated cases and therefore required no refinement; its WER is zero in all experiments. Results are shown in Table 1.

Table 1. Initial analysis breakdown for the Crushing Wound case. Entity-Level Scoring (ELS) provides an ordinal quantification of Expert-Labeled Correctness (ELC) at the report-task level. N denotes the reference text length, SDI the total number of edit operations, WER the Word Error Rate, and HR the Hallucination Rate.

Report Task	N	SDI	WER	ELC	ELS	HR
Body Part (BPT)	6	0	0.00	Correct	2	0.00
Trauma Description (TDT)	35	3	0.09	Partially Correct	1	0.00
Metrics (MT)	12	1	0.08	Correct	2	0.00
Mechanism Analysis (MAT)	28	3	0.11	Incorrect	0	0.12
Temporal Placement (TPT)	15	1	0.07	Partially Correct	1	0.00
Total	**96**	**8**	**0.08**	–	**6/10**	**0.02**

Legend: N denotes the length of the expert-provided reference text in words; SDI denotes the total number of edit operations (substitutions, deletions, and insertions). ELC is a qualitative expert assessment with three levels (Correct, Partially Correct, Incorrect). ELS is an ordinal encoding of ELC (Incorrect = 0, Partially Correct = 1, Correct = 2), used for entity-level aggregation only. HR indicates the proportion of hallucinated statements, defined as non-observable measurements or unsupported causal claims.

The iterative process of the algorithm including step-by-step reduction in error for the Crushing Wound scenario. Entity-Level Scoring (ELS) is computed per iteration as the sum of ordinal entity-level correctness scores (Incorrect = 0, Partially Correct = 1, Correct = 2) across all report entities, yielding a maximum possible score of 10 per iteration, Table 2.

The iteration counts reported in Table 3 correspond to the total number of task-level refinement actions (refresh events), whereas Table 2 illustrates the evolution across aggregated report iterations. Results for all six injury types are summarized in Table 3.

Qualitative Evaluation. For qualitative evaluation, interviews with 5 FPs were performed in the mortuary while using the system. The context of the interviews hangs around a set of Key Performance Indicators - KPIs which were captured while the FPs were testing the system. FPs performed an initial trauma or image analysis themselves and, later, they evaluated the AI generations and

Table 2. Iteration-wise refinement progression for the Crushing Wound case. Entity-Level Scoring (ELS) reports the total ordinal correctness score aggregated across all report tasks per iteration (maximum = 10). SDI denotes the total number of edit operations relative to ground truth, WER the corresponding Word Error Rate, columns BPT-TDT-MT-MAT-TPT indicate which report tasks were refined at each iteration, and HR denotes the hallucination rate.

Iter.	SDI	WER	ELS/10	BPT	TDT	MT	MAT	TPT	HR
0	8	0.08	6.0		X	X	X	X	0.02
1	7	0.07	7.0		X		X	X	0.02
2	7	0.07	7.0				X	X	0.02
3	6	0.06	8.0				X		0.01
4	5	0.05	8.5				X		0.01
5	5	0.05	8.5						0.01
Total Iter.	–	–	–	**0**	**2**	**1**	**5**	**3**	–

Table 3. Cross-case summary of refinement outcomes. The table reports initial and final quality metrics for each injury type. ELS denotes the total Entity-Level Score per iteration (maximum = 10), WER denotes the global Word Error Rate, and HR denotes the hallucination rate. Arrows indicate progression from the initial system output to the final refined response.

Injury Type	ELS	WER	HR	Total Iter.
Crushing Wound	6.0 → 8.5	0.08 → 0.05	0.02 → 0.01	6
Decarbonation	5.0 → 8.0	0.14 → 0.09	0.05 → 0.02	14
Ecchymosis	7.0 → 9.0	0.10 → 0.06	0.01 → 0.00	8
Scarred Wound	6.5 → 8.5	0.12 → 0.07	0.03 → 0.01	9
Cutting Instrument Wound	7.5 → 9.5	0.07 → 0.04	0.02 → 0.00	7
Stapled Wound	8.0 → 9.5	0.06 → 0.03	0.01 → 0.00	6
Averages	**6.6 → 8.8**	**0.09 → 0.05**	**0.02 → 0.01**	**9.1**

the AI refined generations, answering a related questionnaire. Results of the questionnaire are presented in Table 4.

By using an automatic response refinement, the FPs indicated that it would be faster for them to input the observation. Crucially, while the FPs demonstrated high acceptance of the AI-enhanced workflow, they unanimously emphasized the need for a definitive "accept/reject" gateway before the data is submitted or finalized in the Information System. For the Satisfaction and Ease of Use KPIs, the FPs provided positive feedback regarding the initial image analysis output, specifically noting the significant gain in efficiency. FPs were particularly satisfied with the system's ability to swiftly process and identify imagery, which substantially reduces the time and effort required for initial writing and data input. However, the evaluation also highlighted a critical challenge related to

Table 4. Qualitative evaluation KPIs and Forensic Pathologist (FP) assessment results. The quantitative scores are based on a 5-point Likert scale and standard Deviation (SD) indicates the consensus level among FPs.

KPI	Description	Mean	SD
AI Acceptance	*Level of Trust and Adoption:* FP long-term willingness to integrate the LLM refinement workflow into their standard forensic procedures.	**4.50**	0.52
Ease of Use	*Usability of the Refinement Interface:* FP's commentary on the clarity and intuitiveness of the "Refresh" button and editable result cards, and how quickly they were able to learn and adopt the new features.	**4.80**	0.40
Explainability	*Perceived Rationale and Transparency:* FP's subjective evaluation of how well they understand the reasoning behind the LLM's result after providing a refinement prompt.	**3.45**	0.95
Mental Demands/Stress	*Reduction in Cognitive Load:* FP's perception of whether the refinement process reduces the mental effort or strain (stress) associated with manually checking and correcting LLM outputs or not using LLM overall.	**3.80**	0.75
Satisfaction	*Overall Contentment with the Workflow:* FP's overall qualitative satisfaction with the efficiency and quality of the results compared to their pre-existing workflows.	**4.65**	0.48

the system's reliability and the cognitive load required to verify outputs. In general, the descriptive outputs were accurate and easily adjustable by the FPs, resulting in a positive overall impression but occasionally the system generated an incorrect estimation of the mechanism of death. This specific shortcoming underscores the mandatory nature of the Human-in-the-Loop refinement process, as an uncorrected error in the causal analysis task carries significant legal consequences.

5 Discussion

LLMs are in the center of the research interest with applications varying across multiple domains. While their results in health show positive adaptation, research is limited in the field of Medical Forensics. The emergence of solutions addressing challenges inherent in medical forensic examinations is a relatively recent development. The rationale for this lies in the inherent complexity of the forensic field that simultaneously includes multi-modal medical data, criminal data and judicial data, and its results can determine the course of a criminal trial. Thereby, the adoption of computationally generated data needs to be with caution and always after the acceptance of a professional.

The existing, yet limited, LLM approaches include forensic evidence analysis, observation recognition from text or speech-to-text outputs and report compilation incorporation. Our proposed work has identified this scientific gap and proposes a recently introduced LLM methodology: the prompt-refinement. This system acts as a technological paradigm that proves the applicability of this methodology via a set of tests with real Medical Forensics data. There is no previous study that applies prompt refinement in the Medical Forensics scenario installed at an end-to-end Medical Forensics Information System. The system proposes the Human-in-the-Loop approach of prompt refinement in a medical image analysis scenario, accelerating the image analysis procedure.

A limitation of the current study is the lack of annotated data for evaluation. The sensitive nature of the medical forensic imagery along with expert-level ground-truth annotations result in an evaluation set limited in size. Consequently, the quantitative results are oriented towards demonstrating the feasibility and practical applicability of the proposed methodology, rather than providing larger-scale statistical data collection. Future work is designed to not only expand the dataset but to involve systematic, multi-center trials to establish robust statistical bounds for stability and convergence behavior across varying VLM architectures.

The results indicate a drastic improvement in the efficiency of the forensic reporting workflow. As an initial feasibility indicator, the average initial WER of 0.09 across our representative sample suggests that approximately 9% of the generated text required modification. The refinement loop reduced this to 0.05, demonstrating a consistent reduction in manual editing effort. This acceleration is due to the fact that the users, instead of having to manually review and edit the LLM output, are just "refining" the response until the most appropriate answer is produced.

6 Conclusion

The current research trends are traversing from tuning AI algorithms, and LLMs in particular, to applying intelligent computational methods over their shells. LLMs are among the top-contributing topics in the health field especially in data analysis and medical image analysis. One paradigm for intelligently orchestrating LLMs for serious purposes is prompt-refinement, with existing applications in various domains, like Health and Justice. This work indicates this gap and applies the intelligent method of prompt-refinement using as a recursive paradigm a Medical Forensics image analysis scenario. The proposed system is integrated as an extension to an existing AI-enhanced Medical Forensics Information System and offers the ability to preview initial LLM outputs, accept, edit or revise the results and preview the newly generated ones. Given the high-stakes nature of the legal system, even a minor residual hallucination in causal attribution—such as the occasional incorrect estimation of the mechanism of death observed during evaluation—can compromise the validity of forensic evidence. Currently, the mitigation of this critical hallucination vector relies on the procedural safeguard of the FP acting as the final legal arbiter. While this human-in-the-loop verification is essential, relying entirely on it is insufficient as a long-term technical solution. To actively mitigate mechanism-of-death errors, future architectures must integrate strict technical safeguards. Specifically, incorporating Chain-of-Thought (CoT) prompting will force the VLM to explicitly document its rationale, linking visible anatomical evidence to its mechanism estimation before generating a conclusion. Furthermore, integrating a Retrieval-Augmented Generation (RAG) framework grounded in validated forensic pathology literature will restrict the model's causal inferences to established medical precedents, thereby minimizing ungrounded estimations. Future work will focus on expanding the annotated dataset as the system enters pilot deployment, enabling more comprehensive quantitative evaluation and longitudinal analysis. The prompt engineering will be updated to include CoT reasoning by asking the VLM to generate its rationale alongside the corrected text. This proposed direction will transition the FP's role from "Human-as-Corrector" to "Human-as-Verifier," thereby increasing trust. Furthermore, a retrieval-augmented generation (RAG) approach, which will train the system using the indicated refinements, is considered a future extension. Once the system enters its pilot phase, the captured refinement actions can be utilized to train an associated model. Evaluation metrics of the system in practice highlight the increased acceptance and provide a positive perspective towards integrating intelligent AI algorithms for serious medical and judicial purposes.

Author contributions. Authors wish to thank the personnel of the Forensic Services for their collaboration during the evaluation of the presented work.

Funding Information. This work has been partly supported by the University of Piraeus Research Center.

References

1. Alhafni, B., Vajjala, S., Bannò, S., Maurya, K.K., Kochmar, E.: LLMs in education: novel perspectives, challenges, and opportunities. arXiv preprint arXiv:2409.11917 (2024)
2. DiMaio, D., DiMaio, V.J.: Forensic Pathology, 2nd edn. CRC Press, London (2001)
3. Fornasiere, R., Brunello, N., Scotti, V., Carman, M.: Medical information extraction with large language models. In: Proceedings of the 7th International Conference on Natural Language and Speech Processing, pp. 456–466. ICNLSP (2024)
4. Golnari, P., Prantzalos, K., Upadhyaya, D., Buchhalter, J., Sahoo, S.S.: Human in the loop: embedding medical expert input in large language models for clinical applications. Stud. Health Technol. Inform. **329**, 658–662 (2025)
5. Johnson, O.V., Alyasiri, O.M., Akhtom, D., Johnson, O.E.: Image analysis through the lens of ChatGPT-4. J. Appl. Artif. Intell. **4**(2), 31–46 (2023)
6. Kallipolitis, A., Revelos, K., Maglogiannis, I.: Ensembling EfficientNets for the classification and interpretation of histopathology images. Algorithms **14**(10), 278 (2021)
7. Kim, K.J., Lee, C.H., Bae, S.E., Choi, J.H., Kang, W.: Digital forensics in law enforcement: a case study of LLM-driven evidence analysis. Forensic Sci. Int. Digit. Investig. **54**, 301939 (2025)

8. Koulouris, D., et al.: A web-based information system for medical forensics incorporating generative AI in reports compilation. In: IFIP International Conference on Artificial Intelligence Applications and Innovations, pp. 342–352. Springer, Cham (2025)
9. Kumichev, G., et al.: MedSyn: LLM-based synthetic medical text generation framework. In: Joint European Conference on Machine Learning and Knowledge Discovery in Databases, pp. 215–230. Springer, Cham (2024)
10. Martineau, K., Explainable, A., Generative, A.: What is retrieval-augmented generation? IBM Research Blog 22 (2023)
11. McCarthy, J., et al.: What is artificial intelligence (2007)
12. Michelet, G., Breitinger, F.: ChatGPT, Llama, can you write my report? An experiment on assisted digital forensics reports written using (local) large language models. Forensic Sci. Int. Digit. Investig. **48**, 301683 (2024)
13. Mousavi, S.M., Alghisi, S., Riccardi, G.: LLMs as repositories of factual knowledge: limitations and solutions. arXiv preprint arXiv:2501.12774 (2025)
14. Panagoulias, D.P., Virvou, M., Tsihrintzis, G.A.: Evaluating LLM-generated multimodal diagnosis from medical images and symptom analysis. arXiv preprint arXiv:2402.01730 (2024)
15. Park, Y.J., et al.: Assessing the research landscape and clinical utility of large language models: a scoping review. BMC Med. Inform. Decis. Mak. **24**(1), 72 (2024)
16. Salvador, R., et al.: Comparing ChatGPT and medical student performance in a real image-based radiology and applied physics in medicine exam. Radiología (English Edition) **67**(4), 101638 (2025)
17. Saukko, P., Knight, B.: Knight's Forensic Pathology, 4th edn. CRC Press, London (2015)
18. Shen, C., et al.: FEAT: a multi-agent forensic ai system with domain-adapted large language model for automated cause-of-death analysis. arXiv preprint arXiv:2508.07950 (2025)
19. Shridhar, K., et al.: The art of LLM refinement: ask, refine, and trust. In: Proceedings of the 2024 Conference of the North American Chapter of the Association for Computational Linguistics: Human Language Technologies (Volume 1: Long Papers), pp. 5872–5883 (2024)
20. Stewart-Evans, J., et al.: Expediting data extraction using a large language model (LLM) and scoping review protocol: a methodological study within a complex scoping review. arXiv preprint arXiv:2507.06623 (2025)
21. Sun, S., Yuan, R., Cao, Z., Li, W., Liu, P.: Prompt chaining or stepwise prompt? Refinement in text summarization. arXiv preprint arXiv:2406.00507 (2024)
22. Tian, D., Jiang, S., Zhang, L., Lu, X., Xu, Y.: The role of large language models in medical image processing: a narrative review. Quant. Imaging Med. Surg. **14**(1), 1108–1121 (2024)
23. Wang, Z., Lin, Y., Shen, J., Zhu, X.: A survey of large language models for text classification: What, why, when, where, and how, Authorea Preprints (2025)
24. Wilhelm, C., Steckelberg, A., Rebitschek, F.G.: Benefits and harms associated with the use of AI-related algorithmic decision-making systems by healthcare professionals: a systematic review. Lancet Reg. Health Eur. **48**, 101145 (2025)
25. Wu, Y.: An introduction to computer vision. EECS 432-Advanced Computer Vision Notes Series 1 (2003)
26. Ye, Q., Ahmed, M., Pryzant, R., Khani, F.: Prompt engineering a prompt engineer. In: Findings of the Association for Computational Linguistics: ACL 2024, pp. 355–385 (2024)

27. Yin, Z., et al.: Digital forensics in the age of large language models. arXiv preprint arXiv:2504.02963 (2025)
28. Zhang, X., Cao, J., You, C., Ding, D.: Why prompt design matters and works: a complexity analysis of prompt search space in LLMs. In: Proceedings of the 63rd Annual Meeting of the Association for Computational Linguistics (Volume 1: Long Papers), pp. 32525–32555 (2025)

Critical Infrastructure Resilience

Unsupervised Detection of False Data Injection Attacks in Nuclear Power Plant Time Series Using Generative Models

Jyothsna Saripalli(✉), Pranav Gangwani, Himanshu Upadhyay, Leonel Lagos, and Alexander Perez-Pons

Florida International University, Miami, Florida 33174, USA
{jsaripal,pgangwan,upadhyay,lagosl,aperezpo}@fiu.edu

Abstract. False Data Injection (FDI) attacks are recognized among the most serious cyber threats to nuclear power plant cyber-physical systems, where manipulated sensor readings can mislead operators and delay emergency responses. Detecting FDI attacks in nuclear monitoring is challenging due to (i) the absence of labelled cyber-attack data, (ii) the complex temporal dynamics of monitored signals, and (iii) the multiple sensor subsystems that attackers may target. In this paper, we propose an unsupervised anomaly-detection framework using a sequence-aware Variational Autoencoder (Seq-VAE) based on Gated Recurrent Units and apply it in a multi-modal evaluation spanning two complementary nuclear monitoring subsystems: 52 radiation isotope dose channels and 96 reactor operational parameters from the Nuclear Power Plant Accident Database (NPPAD). Five distinct FDI attack types are simulated, including a novel Correlated Stealth attack respecting multi-sensor physical correlations. Detection is benchmarked against an LSTM (Long Short-Term Memory) Autoencoder (deep baseline) and Isolation Forest and Energy-Based Detectors (classical baselines), with thresholds set on validation data via Youden's J statistic and frozen for test evaluation. All results are reported as mean ± standard deviation across 10 independent random seeds. The multi-modal comparison reveals systematic, modality-specific differences in detection performance: isotope dose channels are more sensitive to transient attacks, whereas reactor operational parameters are more sensitive to correlated cyber-attacks and physical accidents. These complementary strengths argue for combined multi-subsystem monitoring as a defense-in-depth strategy.

Keywords: False data injection (FDI) · Unsupervised Learning · Sequential Variational Autoencoder (SeqVAE) · Radiation Dose Analysis · Multi-Modal Anomaly Detection · LSTM Autoencoder · Time-Series Analysis

© ICST Institute for Computer Sciences, Social Informatics and Telecommunications Engineering 2027
Published by Springer Nature Switzerland AG 2027. All Rights Reserved
H. Neukirchen et al. (Eds.): ICDF2C 2026, LNICST 720, pp. 161–174, 2027.
https://doi.org/10.1007/978-3-032-37274-1_10

1 Introduction

Nuclear power plants operate dense monitoring networks that record radiation levels and reactor operational parameters on a continuous basis. The accuracy of these measurements is vital for safe operation and the early detection of incipient accidents. The increasing digitization of nuclear monitoring infrastructure, including networked communication and analytics, has correspondingly increased the risk of cyber-physical attacks targeting plant sensors. Among such attacks, False Data Injection (FDI) attacks have been identified as a particularly serious threat because they inject targeted, plausible-looking deviations into measurements within operational bounds deviations that conventional rule-checking systems cannot reliably detect [1, 2].

Conventional defenses are necessary but not sufficient. Static threshold alarms can be bypassed by attacks that manipulate sensor readings to remain within configured alarm bounds while still misrepresenting plant state for example, a dropout attack that reports near-zero values during a real radiation event would suppress, not trigger, threshold alarms. Message authentication codes and source whitelisting protect against unauthorized transmission, but they cannot detect attacks where authorized devices are themselves compromised: insider threats, supply-chain compromises, or rootkit-level tampering with legitimate sensors all produce data that passes authentication. Machine-learning-based anomaly detection complements these defenses by examining the physical plausibility of sensor patterns over time, providing a defense-in-depth layer that operates independently of authentication and absolute-value thresholds. Furthermore, an attacker may target any monitoring subsystem reactor operational telemetry, radiation dose channels, or both creating a need for monitoring frameworks that span multiple sensor modalities.

Recent advances in unsupervised time-series anomaly detection (TSAD) have demonstrated the effectiveness of deep learning models for capturing complex temporal dependencies and identifying anomalous patterns. Survey work highlights the growing role of reconstruction-based and autoencoder-based methods for TSAD, while flagging persistent challenges around evaluation metrics, threshold selection, and out-of-distribution generalization [4, 7]. Within this space, USAD (Unsupervised Anomaly Detection) introduced an adversarial autoencoder framework for multivariate TSAD without labelled anomalies [5], and TranAD (a transformer-based anomaly-detection network) demonstrated the value of transformer architectures for modelling complex multivariate temporal dependencies [6].

In this paper, we present an unsupervised anomaly detection framework for nuclear power plant cyber-attack detection. A sequence-aware variational autoencoder (Seq-VAE) is trained on baseline operational data only, and detection is evaluated across simulated FDI attacks injected into test windows, along with real accident data held out from training. Importantly, we conduct this evaluation in a multi-modal setting using two complementary NPPAD subsystems 52 radiation isotope dose channels and 96 reactor operational parameters to assess how the choice of monitoring modality affects detection performance. Detection is benchmarked against an LSTM Autoencoder (deep baseline) and two classical methods (Isolation Forest and an Energy-Based Detector), with thresholds selected via Youden's J statistic on validation data and frozen for test evaluation. All metrics are reported as mean ± standard deviation across 10 independent random seeds.

The contributions of this research are as follows:

- A new unsupervised anomaly detection methodology using a sequence-aware Variational Autoencoder (Seq-VAE) particularly tailored to FDI attack detection in nuclear power plant monitoring systems.
- A multi-modal evaluation framework spanning two complementary nuclear monitoring subsystems, revealing modality-specific detection profiles relevant to operational deployment.
- A systematic FDI attack simulation suite covering five attack categories (Spike, Drift, Saturation, Dropout, and a novel Correlated Stealth attack respecting multi-sensor correlations).
- A rigorous comparison protocol including (a) a deep learning baseline (LSTM Autoencoder), (b) classical anomaly detection (Isolation Forest, Energy-Based Detector), (c) a principled threshold-selection method (Youden's J statistic on validation only), and (d) reporting of all metrics as mean ± standard deviation across 10 independent random seeds.
- Generalization analysis on real nuclear accident data for the differentiation of cyber-induced anomalies and physically valid signatures of accidents.

2 Literature Review

This section will briefly introduce the related work on false data injection attack, deep learning for anomaly detection in time series, generative models for sequential data, and data-driven monitoring in nuclear power plants.

2.1 False Data Injection Attacks in Cyber-Physical Systems

This section describes the basic concepts of false data injection attacks and briefly introduces the important detection methods proposed in the area of cyber-physical systems, and it focuses on the limitations of the approaches in the area of safety-critical infrastructures.

Defenses against FDI attacks in cyber-physical systems fall into three principal categories. Authentication-based approaches, including Media Access Control (MAC) binding, digital certificates, and message authentication codes, protect transmission integrity but cannot detect attacks where authorized devices have been compromised through insider threat, supply-chain attack, or rootkit-level tampering [1]. Threshold-based approaches monitor signals against static or adaptive bounds and are widely deployed in nuclear instrumentation; however, attacks crafted to respect operational bounds can evade detection while still misrepresenting plant state [1, 2]. Anomaly detection approaches examine pattern consistency rather than authorization or absolute values. Within this third category, statistical methods such as the cumulative sum (CUSUM) and exponentially weighted moving average (EWMA) handle univariate signals but struggle with multivariate dependencies; classical machine-learning methods such as Isolation Forest, the one-class support vector machine (OC-SVM), and the local outlier factor

(LOF) handle multivariate features but lack temporal modelling; sequence-aware deep learning methods (LSTM-AE, Seq-VAE, TranAD) model temporal dependencies but require careful evaluation [4, 7]. This work focuses on the third subcategory, comparing classical and sequence-aware methods.

Survey studies emphasize that rule-based and residual-based methods are vulnerable to FDI attacks that exploit system dynamics or sensor correlations [1, 2]. In smart-grid settings, work on state-estimation-based and data-driven detection has demonstrated that attacks can deceive monitoring and control systems without raising alerts [2, 3]. While useful, these results are domain-specific to power systems and cannot be directly transferred to nuclear monitoring. Moreover, prior nuclear monitoring work has typically focused on a single sensor modality (either radiation channels or reactor parameters, rarely both), missing the cross-modality vulnerabilities a sophisticated adversary may exploit. The present work addresses these gaps.

2.2 Application of Deep Learning in Anomaly Detection in Time Series Data

This subsection will discuss deep learning techniques for anomaly detection on time series datasets with a focus on unsupervised learning techniques that are appropriate for situations where labelled anomaly datasets are not readily available.

Recent work on unsupervised TSAD has shown that deep learning can be effective for capturing complex temporal patterns. Existing TSAD approaches are broadly classified into reconstruction-based, forecasting-based, and representation-learning-based methods, with ongoing challenges around threshold selection and generalization [4, 7]. Reconstruction-based methods remain dominant. USAD provides an adversarial autoencoder framework for multivariate TSAD with robust detection without labelled anomalies [5], and TranAD demonstrates the strength of transformer architectures for capturing intricate multivariate temporal dependencies [6]. Although these methods are effective in general benchmarks, they are mainly evaluated on public datasets without specific consideration of cyber-induced anomalies or constraints in nuclear monitoring domains.

2.3 Generative Models for Time Series Analysis

This subsection discusses the methods of generative modelling for time series data, which are gaining attention in the context of anomaly detection and data generation.

There has been growing interest in generative models due to their capacity to model complex temporal distributions and generate realistic synthetic data. TimeGAN combines adversarial and temporal training with supervisory signals to generate realistic sequences [8], and TimeVAE extends VAEs with probabilistic modelling for multivariate time series [9]. Recent diffusion-based approaches have also shown promise for time-series anomaly detection, with robustness to non-stationarity and improved reconstruction-based scoring [10–12]. Nevertheless, these models are mainly studied in generic anomaly detection or data augmentation settings, and they are rarely used to represent cyber-attacks or to evaluate the effectiveness of anomaly detection systems in safety-critical physical domains.

2.4 Application of Deep Learning in Nuclear Power Plant Monitoring

This subsection is focused on the current state of deep learning applications for the monitoring of nuclear power plants and the gaps in the literature that the current study aims to fill.

Deep learning has been applied to several nuclear monitoring tasks, including transient event detection, fault diagnosis, and reactor condition monitoring. CNN-LSTM hybrid models have been proposed for transient event detection [13], autoencoders have been used for monitoring the HANARO research reactor [14], and optimization-driven deep learning has been used for adaptive fault diagnosis [15]. Despite these advances, existing studies have largely focused on physical anomalies and accident scenarios, with little consideration of cyber-attack categories such as false data injection. Furthermore, the combination of generative anomaly detection with validation against real accident data and across multiple monitoring modalities remains an underexplored area, motivating the present work.

3 Methodology

In this section, we describe the data sources used in this research, the preprocessing of the radiation and reactor measurements, the synthetic anomaly injection procedure, and the architecture of the proposed sequence variational autoencoder.

3.1 Dataset Description

In this work, we use the Nuclear Power Plant Accident Database (NPPAD) [16], a high-fidelity full-scope simulator dataset covering normal plant operation and a range of accident scenarios. NPPAD organizes plant signals into two distinct monitoring subsystems, both of which we evaluate: (a) Radiation Dose Data (Dose_csv_data): 52 isotopic radiation channels covering iodine isotopes (I131–I135), xenon isotopes (Xe131M–Xe138), krypton isotopes (Kr83M–Kr88), and additional fission products through to AM241, CM242, CM244. These channels report on measured dose rates from the radiation monitoring system. (b) Reactor Operational Data (Operation_csv_data): 96 reactor operational parameters including primary-side pressure (P), average and per-loop coolant temperatures (TAVG, THA, THB, TCA, TCB), reactor coolant pump flow rates (WRCA, WRCB), steam generator pressures (PSGA series), and additional process variables monitored by the plant instrumentation system. Both subsystems sample at a fixed 10-s interval. The Normal scenario provides a single trajectory per subsystem: 50 timesteps (~8 min) for Dose data and 302 timesteps (~50 min) for Operational data. The accident scenarios collectively provide 482 simulation files in each subsystem across six accident classes: Loss of Coolant Accident (LOCA-100 files), Main Steam Line Break (MD-100), Reactivity Insertion (RI-82), Rod Withdrawal (RW-100), Rod Lift (LR-99), and Turbine Trip (TT-1 file). Different files in the same accident class represent different random initial conditions. The Normal data forms the training/validation/test pool, and all accident data is held out exclusively for out-of-distribution (OOD) evaluation.

This dual evaluation allows direct comparison of detection performance across monitoring modalities, addressing the operational concern that an attacker may target either subsystem and that effective defense requires monitoring both.

3.2 Feature Selection

For each modality, the twelve features with the largest variance in the training set are selected per random seed. Per-seed feature selection prevents information leakage from validation or test data into the feature-selection step. For radiation data, the selected features span iodine, xenon, krypton, and selected fission-product channels capturing the dominant short-lived and long-lived contributors to dose-rate dynamics. For operational data, the selected features span pressure, temperature, and flow categories, capturing complementary aspects of reactor dynamics relevant to both physical-anomaly detection and cyber-induced anomaly detection. The choice of $K = 12$ features balances model complexity against the limited number of Normal training windows available in NPPAD and matches the dimensionality reported in prior NPPAD-based anomaly-detection work.

3.3 Data Preprocessing

In order to promote consistency and fairness among all the experiments conducted, a common preprocessing step was applied to all the data sources. The data set was checked for missing, damaged, or physically inconsistent data entries. It was found that the NPPAD data set had no missing data entries that needed imputation or removal. For each random seed, the Normal data is split window-wise into training (70%), validation (15%), and test (15%) partitions. Because the Normal data represents a single steady-state operational trajectory in each modality, sliding windows are treated as exchangeable samples of the steady-state distribution a standard assumption in process monitoring. Only Normal data is used for anomaly-detection training; all FDI attacks and real accident data are held out exclusively for evaluation.

Following the split, the twelve most variable features are selected based on training-set statistics only. The features were normalized using z-score standardization, defined in Eq. (1):

$$x\_norm = (x - \mu)/\sigma \tag{1}$$

in which the mean and the standard deviation, denoted by μ and σ, are computed from the baseline data alone. This approach avoids the leakage of information from the anomalous or accident data into the training process and thus retains the assumption of unsupervised learning.

After normalization, the multivariate time-series is segmented using a sliding window. The window size W and stride S are matched to the Normal trajectory length of each modality. For the Operation modality, the first 30 timesteps are discarded to remove a startup transient (apparent in the pressure trace), yielding 272 steady state timesteps. The Dose modality begins at steady state and uses all 50 available timesteps. To address the limited number of Normal training windows, the training set is augmented $5\times$ using small Gaussian noise ($\sigma = 0.02$ in z-score units) and mild magnitude jitter (scale $\in [0.97, 1.03]$). These augmentations simulate sensor measurement uncertainty and calibration drift and are applied only to training data. The augmented training sets contain 210 windows (Operation) and 120 windows (Dose), respectively. All metrics are reported as mean $\pm$ standard deviation across 10 independent random seeds, each with a different train/val/test split.

3.4 Model Training and Evaluation

1) Model Training Strategy

The proposed anomaly detection system is trained with a purely unsupervised learning approach, mirroring real-world limitations imposed on monitoring a nuclear power plant where labelled samples for cyber-attacks or accidents are not available. The proposed Seq-VAE adapts the variational recurrent architecture of Chung et al. [19]. The encoder is a single-layer Gated Recurrent Unit (GRU) with 64 hidden units, followed by two linear projections producing the mean and log-variance of a 16-dimensional Gaussian latent distribution. Reparameterization samples $z = \mu + \sigma \odot \varepsilon$ with $\varepsilon \sim N(0, I)$. The decoder maps z through a linear projection to a GRU initial hidden state and then runs a single-layer GRU with 64 hidden units for W timesteps with a final linear output to F = 12 reconstructed features. Training minimizes the evidence lower bound (ELBO) loss in Eq. (2):

$$L = \|x - \hat{x}\|^2 + \beta \cdot KL(q(z|x)\|N(0, I)) \quad (2)$$

where L is the training loss; x and $\hat{x}$ are the input window and its reconstruction; β is a weighting factor balancing the two terms; and KL denotes the Kullback–Leibler divergence between the approximate posterior q(z|x) and the standard-normal prior N(0, I).

with β = 0.001. This deliberately small weight prioritizes reconstruction fidelity over latent regularization, which we found necessary because the limited number of Normal training windows makes a strongly regularized latent space prone to underfitting and weakens the reconstruction signal on which detection depends. Optimization uses Adam (learning rate 1×10^{-3}, batch size 32) for up to 50 epochs with early stopping (patience 10) on validation reconstruction loss. The anomaly score is the mean squared reconstruction error per window.

The LSTM-AE is included as a deep-learning baseline to isolate the contribution of the variational latent in Seq-VAE. The encoder is a single-layer LSTM with 64 hidden units followed by a linear projection to a 16-dimensional latent vector. The decoder linearly projects the latent to an LSTM hidden state, repeats it across W timesteps, and decodes through a single-layer LSTM with 64 hidden units followed by a linear output to F features. Training minimizes reconstruction MSE only (no KL term) with Adam (learning rate 1×10^{-3}, batch size 32) for up to 50 epochs with early stopping (patience 10). The anomaly score is the per-window reconstruction MSE.

Isolation Forest [18]. scikit-learn 1.3.0 Isolation Forest with n_estimators = 200, max_samples = 256, contamination = 'auto', fit on flattened windows. Anomaly score is the normalized negative path length.

Energy-Based Detector. A parameter-free baseline that scores each window by its mean squared first-order time difference, given in Eq. (3):

$$E(x) = (1/(W - 1))\cdot \Sigma\ (x\_\{t + 1\} - x\_t)2 \quad (3)$$

where W is the window length. Anomalies producing abrupt transitions yield high energy, whereas smoother anomalies yield low energy.

2) Synthetic Anomaly Injection for Validation

Because no labelled cyber-attack datasets exist for nuclear settings, false data injection attacks are simulated for validation. These attacks are applied at the sequence level to test windows drawn from the baseline data, so that the training data remains anomaly-free.

The following five attack types are injected independently into the test windows.

Spike Attack. A spike attack injects a brief, high-amplitude perturbation that emulates a transient fault or a momentary attempt to mask or fabricate a sudden sensor reading. A scaled impulse of amplitude α is added to one to three features over a short interval [t_s, t_s + Δt]:

$$x\_attack(t) = x(t) + \alpha \cdot s, \quad t \in [t\_s, t\_s + \Delta t] \tag{4}$$

Drift Attack. A drift attack introduces a slowly accumulating bias that gradually pulls a sensor away from its true value, emulating progressive miscalibration or a stealthy ramp that evades static thresholds. A linear term of slope β is added for every timestep after the onset time t_d:

$$x\_attack(t) = x(t) + \beta \cdot (t - t\_d), \quad t \geq t\_d \tag{5}$$

Saturation Attack. A saturation attack clamps the signal to a restricted range so that genuine excursions are hidden, mimicking a stuck or rail-limited sensor. Values are clipped to the 15th–85th percentile band (q_low, q_high) of the window, reducing its variance while remaining within the learned data range:

$$x\_attack(t) = clip(x(t), q\_low, q\_high) \tag{6}$$

Dropout Attack. A dropout attack suppresses a sensor by forcing its output to zero over a contiguous interval, modelling a denial-of-service condition or signal loss that could conceal an ongoing event. The signal is set to zero for t within [t_o, t_o + Δt_o]:

$$x\_attack(t) = 0, \quad t \in [t\_o, t\_o + \Delta t\_o] \tag{7}$$

Correlated Stealth Attack. A correlated stealth attack applies a small multiplicative perturbation jointly to a group of physically correlated features (|corr| ≥ 0.7 in the training data), so the manipulated readings remain mutually consistent and close to the normal data manifold. It adapts smart-grid stealth attacks [20] to the nuclear setting and is, by design, the most difficult case to detect:

$$x\_attack(t) = x(t) \odot s, \quad s \sim U(0.85, 1.15) \; per\ correlated\ feature (8)$$

Attack magnitudes were fixed a priori and were not tuned based on detection results. Magnitude ranges follow IEC 61226 [21] sensor-uncertainty specifications and the slow-drift attack literature [2].

3) Threshold Selection: Youden's J Statistic

For all detectors and both modalities, the anomaly threshold is selected on the validation set using Youden's J statistic [17], defined in Eq. (9):

$$t* = \text{arg max\_}t\ [TPR(t) - FPR(t)] \quad (9)$$

For each seed and each model, we generate FDI attacks on the validation set only (20 per attack type, 100 total) and combine these with validation-Normal windows. The threshold is the value maximizing (TPR − FPR) on this validation-only collection. The threshold is then frozen and applied to test-set evaluation without further adjustment. the area under the receiver operating characteristic curve (AUROC), a threshold-independent metric, is our primary metric; precision, recall, F1, and accuracy at the frozen threshold are reported as secondary metrics. No threshold is ever tuned based on test-set performance (Table 1).

4) Hyperparameter Summary

Table 1 Reports all hyperparameter values. Values were chosen *a priori* based on standard practice in time-series anomaly detection [4–6] and were not tuned on the test set

Parameter	Operation	Dose
Window size W	32	16
Stride S	4	1
Top-K features	12	12
Seq-VAE / LSTM-AE hidden	64	64
Latent dim	16	16
Seq-VAE β	0.001	0.001
Optimizer	Adam	Adam
Learning rate	1.00E-03	1.00E-03
Batch size	32	32
Max epochs	50	50
Early stopping patience	10	10
Augmentation factor	5×	5×
Augmentation noise σ	0.02	0.02
IForest n_estimators	200	200
IForest max_samples	256	256
Random seeds	10	10

The hyperparameters were selected a priori from standard practice in time-series anomaly detection and were not tuned on the test set. The window sizes (W = 32 for

Operation, W = 16 for Dose) and strides (S = 4 and S = 1) were matched to the length of each Normal trajectory so as to maximise the number of training windows while preserving local temporal structure. Twelve features were retained per modality to balance representational capacity against the limited number of Normal windows. The Seq-VAE and LSTM-AE share a 64-unit hidden state and a 16-dimensional latent space a compact configuration appropriate for small datasets and the Seq-VAE weighting factor $\beta = 0.001$ prioritises reconstruction fidelity over latent regularisation. Optimisation used Adam (learning rate 1×10^{-3}, batch size 32) for up to 50 epochs with early stopping (patience 10). The training set was augmented fivefold with Gaussian noise ($\sigma = 0.02$ in z-score units) to emulate sensor uncertainty, and the Isolation Forest used 200 estimators with a subsample size of 256. All results are averaged over 10 independent random seeds.

4 Results and Analysis

In this section, we present the experimental results and compare model performance across multiple evaluation metrics.

4.1 Model-Based Performance Assessment

Across both monitoring modalities and all five attack types, the sequence-aware deep detectors (Seq-VAE and LSTM-AE) match or exceed the classical baselines, with detectability varying strongly by attack class and modality (Fig. 1; the full per-metric breakdown is given in Fig. 2). Transient attacks are the most detectable: on Spike, Seq-VAE attains AUROC 0.831 ± 0.083 on Operation and 0.976 ± 0.029 on Dose, with LSTM-AE (0.998 ± 0.004) and the Energy-Based Detector (0.999 ± 0.002) near-perfect on Dose. Drift is detected well on both modalities (Seq-VAE 0.814 ± 0.103 on Operation; LSTM-AE 0.888 ± 0.063 on Dose), whereas Dropout is moderate on Operation (Seq-VAE 0.551 ± 0.053) but stronger on Dose (LSTM-AE 0.832 ± 0.078, Energy 0.821 ± 0.091). In contrast, Saturation and Correlated Stealth attacks remain close to chance for every detector on both modalities (AUROC ≈ 0.45–0.55 and ≈ 0.50–0.65, respectively), and the Energy-Based Detector collapses on Dose saturation (0.206 ± 0.098), reflecting its dependence on abrupt magnitude changes. The cross-modal comparison shows that Dose channels are more sensitive to transient attacks (Spike $\Delta = +0.145$, Dropout $\Delta = +0.148$ relative to Operation), Operation is marginally better on Drift ($\Delta = -0.072$), and Saturation ($\Delta = -0.011$) and Correlated ($\Delta = +0.018$) are comparable across modalities. On real accident (out-of-distribution) detection, the Isolation Forest reference attains AUROC 0.90–0.98 on Operation versus 0.81–0.93 on Dose, with the largest Operation advantage on the most violent accidents (LOCA and MD, $\Delta \approx +0.14$) and a slight Dose advantage only on Rod Withdrawal ($\Delta = -0.019$), while the reconstruction-based deep models exceed AUROC 0.99 on most accident scenarios in both modalities indicating that physical accidents diverge far from the learned normal manifold. All metrics are reported as mean ± standard deviation over 10 independent random seeds, with thresholds fixed on validation data via Youden's J statistic.

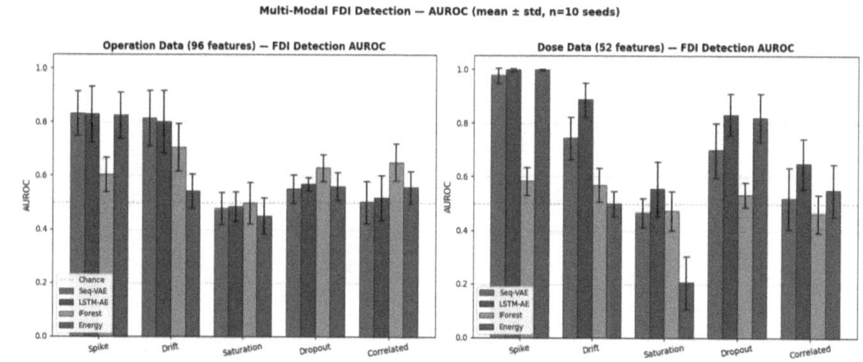

Fig. 1. Multi-modal FDI detection AUROC (mean ± std., n = 10 seeds) for the Operation (96 reactor parameters) and Dose (52 isotope channels) modalities

5 Discussion

The multi-modal evaluation reveals systematic and complementary differences between the two monitoring subsystems. Radiation dose channels are markedly more sensitive to transient attacks Seq-VAE reaches AUROC 0.976 on Dose versus 0.831 on Operation for Spike attacks (+0.145), with a similar gap for Dropout (+0.148) because the tight steady-state distributions of isotope concentrations turn any short-duration perturbation into a statistically extreme, easily flagged deviation, whereas the broader normal-operation ranges of reactor parameters (pressure varying with load, temperatures with cooling demand) partially absorb small transients. Reactor operational parameters, conversely, are stronger on real accidents and correlated attacks: on out-of-distribution accident detection, Operation-data Isolation Forest attains AUROC 0.90–0.98 against 0.81–0.93 for Dose (largest margins, +0.14, on dramatic LOCA and MD events), and on the new Correlated Stealth attack it reaches 0.65 versus 0.46, reflecting the more discriminative physical correlations among reactor signals. Saturation attacks, however, remain near chance (AUROC $\approx$ 0.45–0.55) for all detectors in both modalities, exposing a fundamental rather than modality-specific limitation of reconstruction-based detection: both saturation (which clips values within the learned range, reducing variance) and correlated stealth (which applies small multiplicative scaling that preserves manifold structure) are designed to stay within the statistical envelope of normal operation, so the autoencoder reconstructs them with near-normal error, and detecting such on-manifold attacks therefore requires complementary mechanisms such as variance-sensitive distributional tests or physics-constrained models that flag violations of conservation laws. The same on-manifold/off-manifold distinction explains the OOD results, where deep models (Seq-VAE, LSTM-AE) achieve AUROC $\geq$0.99 on most accident scenarios while Isolation Forest spans 0.81–0.98; this is not overfitting the identical models score only 0.47–0.98 on FDI attacks but rather reflects how the large physical perturbations at accident initiation (e.g., a 90% primary-pressure drop in a LOCA) push accident windows far outside the learned normal manifold, a result robust across latency and subsampling settings. The central insight is thus that cyber-induced anomalies are crafted to remain on-manifold whereas physical accidents are not, motivating complementary detection

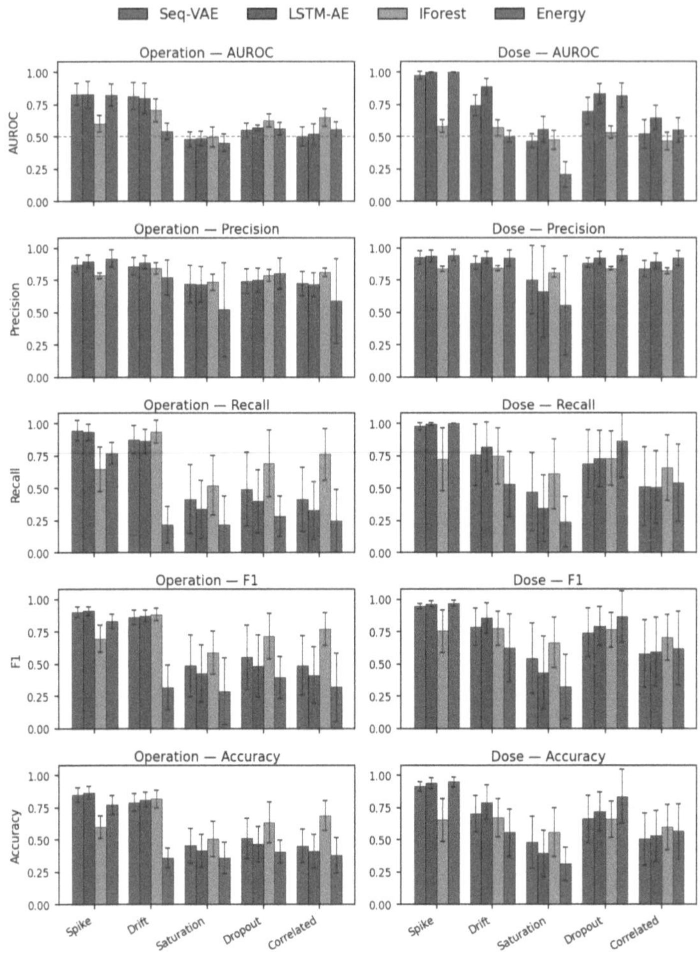

Fig. 2. Per-metric detection performance (AUROC, precision, recall, F1, and accuracy; mean $\pm$ std., n = 10) across the five FDI attack types for both modalities

layers deep reconstruction models for physical anomalies alongside correlation-aware and physics-constrained tests for cyber-attacks and arguing for multi-subsystem monitoring as defense in depth, since neither modality alone suffices against an adversary free to target either; we further note the Energy-Based Detector's anomalous OOD behavior (e.g., AUROC 0.21 on LOCA Dose, $\approx$0.00 on MD Operation), a failure mode in which the smoother signals of late-stage accidents cause the derivative-based score to rank accident windows as more normal-like than genuine normal data.

6 Conclusion and Future Work

This work presented a multi-modal unsupervised sequence-aware anomaly detection framework for false data injection attack detection in nuclear power plant time-series data. The proposed Seq-VAE was trained on Normal operational data only and evaluated on two complementary monitoring modalities: 52-channel radiation dose data and 96-channel reactor operational data. Detection was assessed across five FDI attack types including a new Correlated Stealth attack respecting multi-sensor physical correlations and six real NPPAD accident scenarios. All results were reported as mean $\pm$ standard deviation across 10 independent random seeds with thresholds fixed on validation data via Youden's J statistic. The findings are: (1) sequence-aware deep models effectively detect cyber-attacks with abrupt or accumulating deviations (Seq-VAE Spike AUROC 0.83 on Operation, 0.98 on Dose); (2) the two monitoring modalities exhibit complementary detection strengths radiation channels are more sensitive to transient attacks, while reactor parameters are more sensitive to physical accidents and correlated cyber-attacks motivating multi-modal monitoring as a defense-in-depth strategy; (3) reconstruction-based detection has a fundamental limitation against on-manifold attacks across both modalities (Saturation AUROC $\approx$ 0.48, Correlated Stealth AUROC $\approx$ 0.50–0.65), motivating physics-constrained future directions.

The future course of research will incorporate physics-constrained generative models embedding reactor thermal-hydraulics and radio-decay constraints into the latent representation, adaptive thresholding for non-steady-state operational regimes, and diffusion-based adversarial-attack simulation. Extending the framework to fuse the two modalities into a joint detection model and validating on larger plant data sources are anticipated to further enhance practical utility.

References

1. Irfan, M., et al.: A survey on detection and localisation of false data injection attacks. IET Cyber-Phys. Syst. Theor. Appl. (2024)
2. Musleh, A.S., et al.: A survey on the detection algorithms for false data injection attacks in smart grids. IEEE Trans. Smart Grid. (2020)
3. Liu, Z., et al.: False data injection attacks on data-driven algorithms in smart grids utilizing distributed power supplies (2024)
4. Zamanzadeh Darban, Z., et al.: Deep learning for time series anomaly detection: a survey. ACM Comput. Surv. (2024)
5. Audibert, J., et al.: Usad: unsupervised anomaly detection on multivariate time series. In: KDD (2020)
6. Tuli, S., et al.: TranAD: deep transformer networks for anomaly detection in multivariate time series data. PVLDB. (2022)
7. Pang, G., et al.: Deep learning for anomaly detection: a review. ACM Comput. Surv. (2021)
8. Yoon, J., et al.: Time-Series Generative Adversarial Networks. NeurIPS (2019)
9. Desai, A., et al.: TimeVAE: a variational auto-encoder for multivariate time series generation. (arXiv) (2021)
10. Pintilie, I., et al.: Time series anomaly detection using diffusion-based models (arXiv) (2023)
11. Diffusion Graph Model for Time Series Anomaly Detection, ACM (2025)

12. Li, Y., et al.: Diffusion models with self-conditioning guidance for … (DSCAD) multivariate time series anomaly detection. Knowl.-Based Syst. (2025)
13. Ramezani, I., et al.: Application of deep learning techniques for nuclear power … (CNN-LSTM transient identification). Ann. Nucl. Energy. (2023)
14. Ryu, S. et al.: Development of deep autoencoder-based anomaly…(HANARO reactor) (ScienceDirect record) (2023).
15. He, C., et al.: A data-driven adaptive fault diagnosis methodology for nuclear power systems based on NSGAII-CNN. Ann. Nucl. Energy. (2021)
16. Qi, B., Xiao, X., Liang, J., Po, L.C., Zhang, L., Tong, J.: An open time-series simulated dataset covering various accidents for nuclear power plants. Sci. Data. **9**(1), 766 (2022). https://doi.org/10.1038/s41597-022-01879-1. PMID: 36513714; PMCID: PMC9747709
17. Youden, W.J.: Index for rating diagnostic tests. Cancer. **3**(1), 32–35 (1950)
18. Liu, F.T., Ting, K.M., Zhou, Z.-H.: Isolation Forest. In: Proceedings of the ICDM, pp. 413–422 (2008)
19. Chung, J., Kastner, K., Dinh, L., Goyal, A., Courville, A., Bengio, Y.: A Recurrent Latent Variable Model for Sequential Data. In: NeurIPS (2015)
20. Liu, Y., Ning, P., Reiter, M.K.: False data injection attacks against state estimation in electric power grids. ACM TISSEC. **14**(1) (2011)
21. IEC 61226:2020. Nuclear power plants—Instrumentation, control and electrical power systems important to safety—Categorization of functions and classification of systems

Quantifying Cyber Attack Impact on UAV-Based Nuclear Containment Inspection: A Forensic-Ready Simulation Framework

Hari Hara Babu Saripalli(✉), Pranav Gangwani, Himanshu Upadhyay, Leonel Lagos, and Alexander Perez-Pons

Applied Research Center, Florida International University, Miami, FL, USA
{hsaripal,pgangwan,upadhyay,lagosl,aperezpo}@fiu.edu

Abstract. Incorporation of Unmanned Aerial Vehicles (UAVs) with multi-sensor payloads for inspection of nuclear facilities injects vital cyber-security risks, explored inadequately in the literature. In this work, a forensic-ready simulation framework is used to assess the effect of cyber-attacks on the UAV-based structural health monitoring of nuclear containment buildings. We assess the effect of ten different attack strategies under three types of sensors, namely GPS spoofing, LiDAR saturation/injection, and Ground Penetrating Radar (GPR) electromagnetic interference, using a physics-based model to capture the cyber-attack effect that is validated against nuclear industry standards (NUREG-1801, ACI 349.3R). Monte Carlo simulations across 20 seeds show that single-vector attacks degrade detection performance by 8–34%, while coordinated multi-vector attacks cause catastrophic degradation of up to 90%. GPS spoofing exhibits non-linear severity scaling: a 70 cm single-vector drift causes 64% F1 degradation, while a 75 cm drift combined with LiDAR and GPR attacks pushes degradation to over 90%, far beyond a linear additive prediction. The proposed framework generates forensic-ready analysis artifacts such as attack-signature timestamp, sensor fusion, and deviation patterns from the optimal trajectory, providing valuable information after the occurrence of events.

Keywords: UAV Security · Nuclear Infrastructure · GPS Spoofing · LiDAR Attacks · Digital Forensics · Cyber-Physical Systems · Structural Health Monitoring

1 Introduction

Nuclear containment structures represent critical infrastructure requiring continuous structural health monitoring to ensure operational safety and regulatory compliance. Traditional manual inspection methods face significant limitations including radiation exposure risks, accessibility constraints, and inspection frequency bottlenecks [1, 2]. The emergence of UAV-based autonomous inspection systems equipped with multi-sensor payloads offers transformative potential for comprehensive, high-frequency structural assessment, with proven advantages in coverage rate, repeatability, and access to hazardous areas.

© ICST Institute for Computer Sciences, Social Informatics and Telecommunications Engineering 2027
Published by Springer Nature Switzerland AG 2027. All Rights Reserved
H. Neukirchen et al. (Eds.): ICDF2C 2026, LNICST 720, pp. 175–191, 2027.
https://doi.org/10.1007/978-3-032-37274-1_11

Nevertheless, the implementation of networked autonomous systems for nuclear facility operation introduces a new attack surface. The chain from attack to consequence is direct: a compromised sensor or position estimate produces faulty inspection data, which in turn produces either missed degradations (regulatory non-compliance, undetected structural risk) or false anomalies (unnecessary facility shutdowns and inspection rework). GPS spoofing attacks compromise the position estimate of a UAV [3, 4], thereby resulting in coverage overlaps or misalignment of the LiDAR sensor and the targets of inspection. LiDAR saturation or injection attacks could disable depth sensing or introduce virtual obstacles, thereby affecting navigation and anomaly detection [5, 6]. Electromagnetic interference in GPR could mask actual subsurface signals or introduce virtual subsurface anomalies, making the inspection of the structural assessment unreliable.

The effects of successful attacks will not be limited to operational disruptions. The inspection data could be used to generate undetected levels of degradation, regulatory non-compliance, or forced facility shutdowns due to False Positives. Digital forensics attack knowledge and its expression in sensor readings are critical from the perspective of attribution studies.

Although there is a growing awareness of the cybersecurity risks of UAVs, there has been a lack of studies focusing on the characterization of the effects of attacks on nuclear inspection systems. Most of the studies have focused on either the susceptibility of commercial drones or military UAVs.

The paper fills this research gap with the following contributions:

(1) Simulation framework for physics-based inspection of nuclear containment structures by UAV systems, taking into account sensor realism, distribution of anomalies according to NUREG-1801 levels of degradation, and accurate quadrotor dynamics.

(2) Holistic assessment of ten attack scenarios that include GPS spoofing attacks (gradual and aggressive), LiDAR attacks (jamming and injection), GPR attacks (phantom injection and signal attenuation), and multi-vector attacks.

(3) Quantitative impact assessment using metrics of precision, recall, and F1 score on 200 Monte Carlo trials to set up statistical baselines for the classification of attack severity.

(4) Production of forensic artifacts with attack patterns, trajectory anomalies, and sensor anomalies appropriate to incident reconstruction and attribution.

The remainder of this paper is organized as follows. Section 2 reviews related work in UAV security, nuclear inspection, and digital forensics. Section 3 details the simulation environment, UAV dynamics, sensor models, and attack scenarios. Section 4 describes the experimental setup. Section 5 reports detection performance under each attack scenario. Section 6 discusses attack severity, forensic signatures, and defensive implications. Section 7 concludes and outlines future work.

2 Related Work

2.1 UAV Security and Attack Vectors

The literature on the cybersecurity of UAVs has grown, and one of the most important aspects has been the study of GPS spoofing attacks. Tippenhauer et al. [7] presented feasible attacks on the position accuracy of GPS, while Kerns et al. [8] characterized spoofing detection challenges in civilian GPS receivers, and Petit and Shladover [9] extended this analysis to autonomous vehicle contexts. Vulnerabilities in LiDAR systems have also been discovered by Shin et al. [10] in terms of saturation attacks via intense light sources and injection attacks for creating phantom obstacles. Adversarial modifications for LiDAR-based perception systems were also explored by Cao et al. [11], while comprehensive surveys of drone attack vectors and countermeasures have been presented in [5, 6]. The GPR system weaknesses have not been extensively investigated, although susceptibility to electromagnetic interference is well documented in geophysical applications [12]. The possibility of injection of phantom signals via specifically designed electromagnetic signals has been recognized as an emerging threat to subsurface sensing. Recent surveys of UAV cybersecurity in DFRWS and Forensic Science International: Digital Investigation [13–15] have expanded the analysis to operational drone fleets, but coverage of safety-critical inspection contexts such as nuclear infrastructure remains limited.

2.2 Nuclear Facility Inspection

Nuclear containment structures undergoing structural health monitoring are subjected to certain regulation documents such as NUREG-1801 "Generic Aging Lessons Learned" [1] and "ACI 349.3R – Evaluation of Existing Nuclear Safety-Related Concrete Structures" documents [16]. These documents specify the inspection criteria related to degradation processes such as rebar corrosion, concrete delamination, voids, or alkali-silica reaction.

Inspection by UAV in the nuclear domain has been examined by various researchers. The surface mapping of a containment building by LiDAR was shown by Mazumdar et al. [2], and GPR applications to concrete integrity were reported by ASTM D6432 [17]. So far, the cybersecurity aspect in these applications has not been tackled.

2.3 Digital Forensics for Cyber-Physical Systems

Forensic analysis of cyber-physical systems requires correlating cyber-domain indicators with physical-process deviations to reconstruct attack timelines. Some of the methodologies introduced in the forensics related to industrial control systems include correlating cyber indicators and the deviations of the physical processes [18]. Other frameworks that involve UAVs include the ones introduced by Horsman in [19]. Our work further expands these foundations into forensic-ready artifacts particularly suited for the reconstruction of attacks in multi-sensor inspection systems on the basis of characteristic sensor fusion anomalies and trajectory deviations. Our work builds on these foundations by producing forensic-ready artifacts specifically for multi-sensor inspection systems in nuclear environments, where the coupling between trajectory deviation and detection performance creates attack signatures that single-domain forensic methods do not capture.

3 Methodology

3.1 Simulation Environment

The simulation environment simulates the nuclear containment inspection scenario that consists of the circular chamber (diameter of 6 m, height of 4 m) and the attached rectangular equipment annex (sized 4 m x 3 m x 4 m) and supporting pillar (diameter of 1.5 m). A wall thickness of 15 cm is used to simulate the structure in line with reinforced concrete construction methods that are commonly adopted in these facilities.

There are ninety-five anomalies, and their distribution per wall surface is given in NUREG-1801 degradation modes, which include rebar corrosion (18%), tendon corrosion (12%), anchor deterioration (10%), delamination (15%), void/honeycombing (12%), spalling (8%), alkali-silica reaction gel (8%), carbonation (7%), efflorescence (5%), and embedded conduit/liner damage (5%). The shape of the anomaly is given as: ellipsoidal (45%), planar/disk (25%), irregular (15%), and linear/crack (15%) morphologies with sizes ranging from 3–15 cm. Figure 1 illustrates the complete inspection arena with all 95 anomalies positioned according to their designated degradation categories.

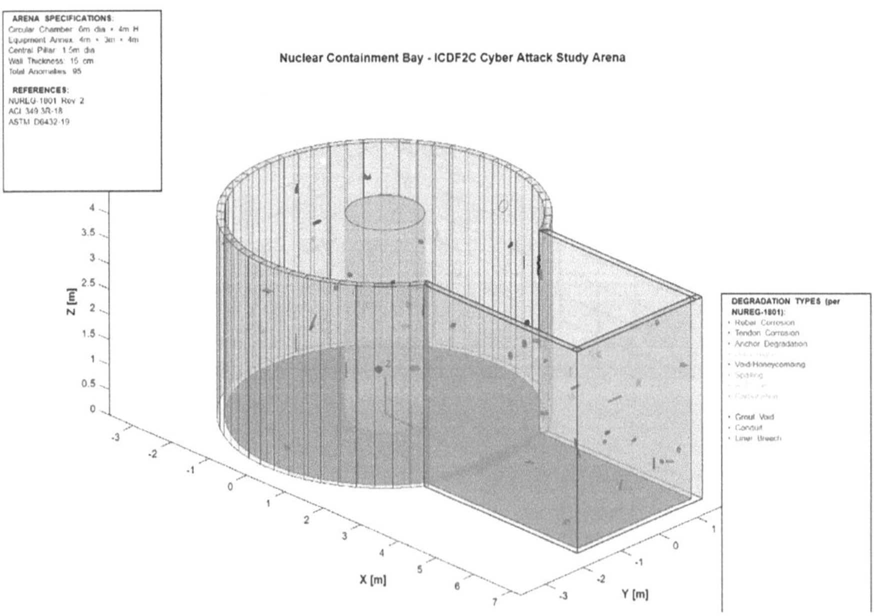

Fig. 1. Nuclear containment inspection arena with 95 embedded anomalies distributed according to NUREG-1801 degradation categories

3.2 UAV Dynamics Model

The quadrotor UAV is modeled using a 12-state dynamics formulation incorporating position (x, y, z), velocity (vx, vy, vz), orientation (roll, pitch, yaw), and angular rates (p, q, r). The equations of motion follow standard quadrotor dynamics with cascaded PID control for attitude stabilization and position tracking. Key parameters include mass (1.2 kg), arm length (0.25 m), and moment of inertia consistent with industrial inspection-class quadrotors such as the DJI Matrice series.

The inspection course keeps a 0.5 m distance from walls with a helical scan pattern over five layers to cover the area completely. The speed is limited to 0.3 m/s to satisfy the dwell requirements of the sensors. The control rate is 40 Hz with fourth-order Runge-Kutta integration to avoid numerical instability.

3.3 Sensor Models

The payload sensors together constitute LiDAR and GPR sensors with detection parameters informed by the literature parameters.

LiDAR Sensor: Modeled after Velodyne VLP-16 specifications with optimal detection ranges of 0.5 to 2.0 m and base detection probabilities dependent on target materials of metallic anomalies with a detection probability of 0.88, voids/delamination at 0.58, and general defects at 0.72. Probability of detection decreases exponentially with deviations from optimal range

GPR Sensor: Modeled according to ASTM D6432 guidelines using the 1.6 GHz antenna array. Base detection probabilities reflect dielectric contrast sensitivity: metallic targets (probability of detection, Pd = 0.85), voids (Pd = 0.52), and moisture-affected regions (Pd = 0.68).

Recent advances in multi-sensor fusion for structural health monitoring have been systematically reviewed in [20]. In this work, LiDAR and GPR detection results are combined in sensor fusion through an OR logic method, wherein detection by either sensor results in an anomaly being detected as a true positive. OR-fusion is chosen because the two sensors detect via independent physical mechanisms (optical reflectance for LiDAR vs. dielectric contrast for GPR), so a defect missed by one modality may still be caught by the other. For safety-critical containment inspection, a missed degradation (false negative) carries far higher cost than a false positive requiring manual review, so we deliberately favor sensitivity over precision. More sophisticated schemes (Dempster–Shafer, Bayesian combination) are deferred to future work. The method is conservative and aims to maximize sensitivity by tolerating the possibility of decreased precision due to false positives for one of the sensors.

3.4 Attack Models

We evaluate ten scenarios in total: one baseline (no attack), six single-vector attacks (two GPS spoofing intensities, two LiDAR attack types, two GPR attack types), and three multi-vector attacks (light, heavy, and maximum). Each is described below.

GPS Spoofing (Drift Low/High):

This attack injects the offset in a gradually increasing position, as described in the methodology proposed by Tippenhauer et al. [7]. In this type of GPS spoofing, a constant drift is applied in the GPS signal, which causes the UAV controller to follow this offset path. In this type, maximum drift is 35 cm for low intensity and 70 cm for high intensity attacks. In this GPS spoofing, the attack is triggered when the UAV completes 15% of the mission, considering the scanning patterns performed by the adversaries.

LiDAR Jamming: Models saturation attacks based on bright sources of infrared light used to flood the LiDAR receiver and lower the probability of detection by 75% (suppression factor = 0.25). Attack strength determines the probability that detection events are affected.

LiDAR Injection: Injection of clusters of "phantom" points simulating anomaly characteristics. The number of injections increases with intensity level, with around 35 false positives per operation at 70% intensity.

GPR Phantom Injection: This method injects phantom signatures in the subsurface by the timed emission of electromagnetic waves according to the timing of the GPR pulses. About 28 false positives are created at 70% intensity.

GPR Suppression: Broadband electromagnetic interference reduces GPR signal-to-noise ratio, decreasing detection probability by 70% (suppression factor = 0.30) when active.

Multi-Vector Attacks: Three simultaneous options involve attack vectors and levels of intensity. Light blends GPS (30 cm) and LiDAR injection. Heavy blends GPR phantom injection and GPS (50 cm) and LiDAR. Maximum uses all vectors and high intensity: GPS (75 cm), LiDAR combined (jamming & injection), and GPR combined (suppression & phantom).

3.5 Path Deviation Detection Model

A critical contribution of this work is the physics-based coupling between GPS spoofing-induced path deviation and detection performance. GPS attacks cause the UAV to fly an offset trajectory, increasing the standoff distance from wall surfaces beyond the sensor optimal range. This deviation directly impacts detection probability through an exponential penalty function:

$$Pdetect = Pbase \times \exp(-k \times dexcess/doptimal) \tag{1}$$

Where P_{base} is the baseline detection probability of the sensor for a given anomaly type at the optimal standoff distance (defined per-sensor in §3.3), d_{excess} is the path deviation beyond baseline tracking error (approximately 1.5 cm under normal conditions), $d_{optimal}$ is the designed standoff distance (0.5 m), and k is a sensitivity parameter (k = 2.0) calibrated to match manufacturer-specified detection probability curves for the Velodyne VLP-16 at varying standoff distances. This formulation ensures that GPS attacks manifest as reduced detection probability rather than merely positional error, accurately reflecting the physical mechanism by which navigation attacks compromise inspection integrity.

3.6 Evaluation Metrics

The metrics for performance measurement include standard detection metrics. Precision is the proportion of correctly detected anomalies out of all detected ones: Precision = TP / (TP + FP), where TP (true positives) are correctly detected real anomalies and FP (false positives) are detections without a corresponding ground-truth anomaly. The other metric for performance measurement includes Recall. Recall is the proportion of correctly detected real anomalies out of all real anomalies present: Recall = TP / (TP + FN), where FN (false negatives) are real anomalies the system failed to detect. The F1 score is the harmonic mean of precision and recall, balancing both metrics: F1 = 2 × (Precision × Recall) / (Precision + Recall). To quantify attack severity, we report F1 degradation relative to baseline: F1_degradation (%) = 100 × (F1_baseline − F1_attack) / F1_baseline. Note that in this work "coverage" denotes the spatial fraction of wall surface inspected at the optimal standoff distance, while "recall" denotes the fraction of ground-truth anomalies correctly detected. Under GPS spoofing the two quantities track closely because path deviation reduces both effective coverage and recall, which is reflected in the heatmap of Fig. 6.

Every case is analyzed with 20 Monte Carlo runs with random results of anomaly detection, attack times, and GPS drift directions. The results are shown as mean values with a standard deviation to give an idea of the average impact as well as the deviation from it.

3.7 Synthetic Data Generation

In this research, a fully synthetic simulation environment is utilized to produce the inspection data, since it would not only be impractical and unsafe to conduct cyber attacks on the inspection systems of nuclear facilities, it could also be illegal. There are a number of advantages of the synthetic data generation methodology, including the provision of a controlled environment, the ability to specify the location of the ground truth of the anomalies with precision, and the capability to perform a large number of Monte Carlo runs, as shown in Fig. 7.

The data generation process consists of four stages. First, the environment generation phase procedurally creates the nuclear containment structure geometry and embeds 95 anomalies at randomized positions within wall volumes, with types and sizes sampled from distributions matching NUREG-1801 degradation statistics. Second, the UAV flight simulation computes inspection trajectories as helical scan patterns producing 30,731 waypoints, with drone dynamics modeled using 12-state equations of motion and fourth-order Runge-Kutta integration at 40 Hz. Third, sensor detection simulation generates stochastic detection events at each waypoint based on sensor-anomaly geometry, material properties, and physics-based detection probability models, with attack effects injected according to the scenario parameters. Fourth, performance evaluation compares detected anomalies against the known ground truth to compute precision, recall, and F1 scores.

All random processes use seeded pseudorandom number generators to ensure reproducibility across 20 Monte Carlo seeds, producing statistically independent yet replicable trials.

4 Experimental Setup

The simulations were carried out in the MATLAB version R2025a environment on a workstation with an Intel Core i7-13700K processor and 64 GB of memory. The total simulation time per experiment (10 scenarios × 20 seeds = 200 trials) was about 11 min.

The inspection course includes 30,731 waypoints over a simulated duration of 768 s, thereby inspecting the entire wall area at the required standoff distance of 0.5 m. Control loop execution rates of 40 Hz allow for sufficient resolution in dynamics simulation modeling.

The attack parameters were chosen within available values in the literature regarding attack capabilities. The magnitude of GPS drift represents spoofing accuracy reported by Tippenhauer et al. [7]. LiDAR saturations were chosen according to attack characterization given by Shin et al. [10]. The false positive rates were tuned to produce values of forensic interest but within reasonable bounds of anomaly rates. Table 1 summarizes the complete parameter configuration for all ten attack scenarios.

Table 1. Attack scenario parameters

Scenario	GPS Drift	LiDAR Attack	GPR Attack	Intensity
Baseline	–	–	–	–
GPS_Drift_Low	35 cm	–	–	Gradual
GPS_Drift_High	70 cm	–	–	Sudden
LiDAR_Jamming	–	Saturation	–	75%
LiDAR_Injection	–	Injection (50)	–	70%
GPR_Phantom	–	–	Phantom (40)	70%
GPR_Suppress	–	–	Suppression	75%
MultiVector_Light	30 cm	Injection (30)	–	50%
MultiVector_Heavy	50 cm	Injection (45)	Phantom (35)	60–65%
MultiVector_Max	75 cm	Combined (65)	Combined (50)	80–85%

The Baseline scenario represents normal inspection operations without any cyber attack, serving as the control condition against which all attack impacts are measured.

5 Results

5.1 Baseline Performance

The baseline scenario represents uncompromised inspection operations where the UAV follows the planned trajectory without cyber interference. Under these conditions, an F1 score of 0.931 ± 0.017 was achieved with recall of 0.871. It can be seen that there is an 87.1% success rate in identifying anomalies with zero false positives, which is an accurate start for impact assessment of an attack. Baseline path deviation (1.5 cm) remained well within acceptable tolerances for the 0.5 m standoff distance.

5.2 GPS Spoofing Impact

For each attack scenario, detection metrics were computed by comparing the set of detected anomalies against the 95 ground-truth embedded defects. True positives occur when a detection falls within the spatial tolerance of an actual anomaly; false positives represent detections with no corresponding ground truth; false negatives are missed anomalies. GPS spoofing attacks produced significant non-linear degradation on the performance of detection accuracy. In low-intensity spoofing (drift of 35 cm), the deviation of the path was 14.7 cm, which caused a 33.9% reduction in the value of F1 (0.615 ± 0.046), where the value of recall was 44.6%. In high-intensity spoofing (70 cm drift), path deviation doubled to 29.9 cm, causing F1 to collapse to 0.334 ± 0.047 (64.1% reduction) with recall of only 20.2%. The non-linear relationship between drift magnitude and recall is captured by the exponential standoff-penalty function (Eq. 1), in which detection probability decays sharply as path deviation pushes the UAV beyond the sensors' optimal range. Figure 2 illustrates the localization error induced by GPS spoofing across attack scenarios, showing that all GPS-enabled attacks exceed typical positioning requirements. GPS attacks maintained precision of 1.000 because they do not introduce false positives, it only affects recall in the sense that it creates coverage gaps beyond which anomalies lie.

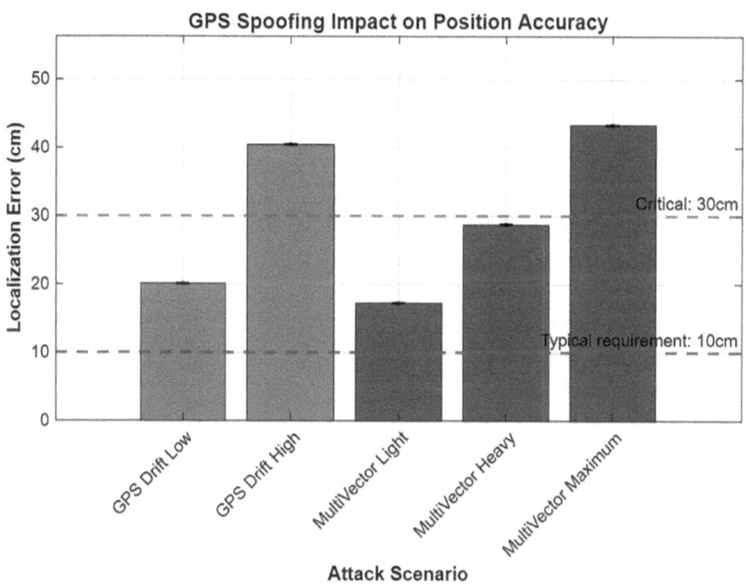

Fig. 2. GPS spoofing impact on localization accuracy. All GPS-enabled attacks exceed the 10 cm typical requirement threshold, with multi-vector attacks approaching the 30 cm critical threshold

5.3 LiDAR Attack Impact

LiDAR jamming resulted in some degradation in the detection accuracy of F1 to 0.848 ± 0.024 (reduction of 8.8%) through the suppression of the recall to 73.7%.

Probabilistic suppression of the detection is the method adopted to jam the LiDAR. Both direct LiDAR and fused detections are impacted.

LiDAR injection attacks reduced F1 score to 0.779 ± 0.023 (16.3% degradation) by decreasing precision to 70.4% while maintaining baseline recall. The injection of about 35 false positive injections per mission is a substantial forensic trace as each false positive needed validation manually.

5.4 GPR Attack Impact

The GPR phantom injection showed a similar effect to LiDAR injection with an F1 score of 0.805 ± 0.023 with a reduction of 13.5% through the degradation of precision to 74.9% with around 28 FP per mission due to the reduced intensity of the injection parameter. GPR suppression attacks decreased F1 to 0.853 ± 0.033 (8.3% reduction) with a recall of 74.6%, indicating effectiveness similar to LiDAR suppression. This effect of suppression attacks is restricted by their sensor-unique nature.

5.5 Multi-Vector Attack Impact

The coordinated multi-vector attack efforts have brought dramatically increased reach through synergistic effect combinations. The light intensity to maximum progression illustrates the compounding effect of multi-vector attacks:

MultiVector Light (GPS + injection of LiDAR data): $F1 = 0.602 \pm 0.035$ (degradation of 35.3%): path deviation of 12.6 cm and 14.7 False positives lead to a decrease in precision of 76.3% and recall of 49.8%.

MultiVector Heavy (GPS + LiDAR + GPR): $F1 = 0.346 \pm 0.036$ (62.8% degradation), with path deviation rising to 20.7 cm and false positives to 50.0. Precision degrades to 37.7%, and recall drops to 32.0%.

MultiVector Maximum (full-spectrum): $F1 = 0.091 \pm 0.032$ (90.2% degradation), indicating near-complete system compromise. Path deviation of 32.1 cm is past critical levels, and 95.7 false positives overpower human verification. Precision at 8.7% and recall at 9.7% suggest that fewer than 10% of true anomalies are detected correctly while more than 90% are false. Figure 3 summarizes the F1 score distribution across all scenarios, demonstrating the progressive degradation from single-vector to multi-vector attacks. Figure 4 presents the percentage degradation relative to baseline, highlighting the super-additive nature of coordinated attacks. Table 2 provides the complete numerical summary of all attack scenarios, while Fig. 5 visualizes the precision-recall trade-off showing how different attack types push system performance toward random classification.

6 Discussion

6.1 Attack Severity Characterization

Our results support quantitative severity level classification according to operational effect. "Single vector" attack methods (LiDAR/GPR jamming/suppression) cause 8–16% F1 degradation, representing manageable impact that may be addressed through

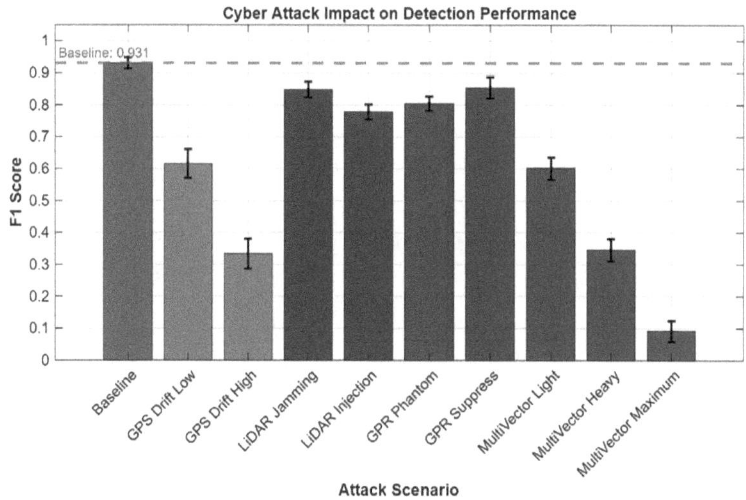

Fig. 3. F1 score distribution across attack scenarios (n = 20 seeds). Bar chart shows mean F1 scores with error bars indicating standard deviation. Multi-vector attacks demonstrate consistently severe degradation with low variance

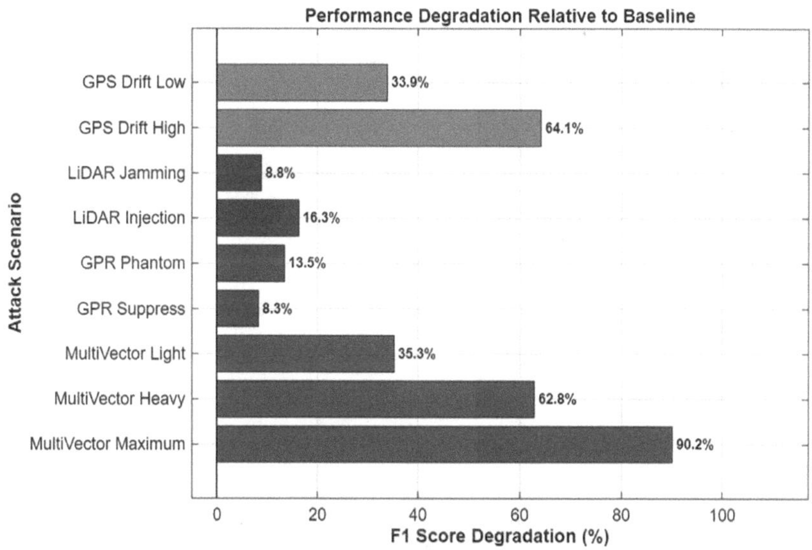

Fig. 4. F1 score degradation relative to baseline for each attack scenario. Multi-vector attacks achieve super-additive degradation through synergistic combination of attack effects

sensor redundancy or post-processing validation. Single-vector GPS spoofing results in 34–64% F1 degradation, representing severe impact that fundamentally compromises inspection validity. "Multi-vector" attack methods reach 35–90% F1 degradation, maximum intensity coordinated attack making the system functionally unusable.

Table 2. Attack impact summary (n = 20 seeds)

Scenario	F1 Score	Precision	Recall	Path Dev.	F1 Deg.
Baseline	0.931 ± 0.017	1.000	0.871	1.5 cm	–
GPS_Drift_Low	0.615 ± 0.046	1.000	0.446	14.7 cm	33.9%
GPS_Drift_High	0.334 ± 0.047	1.000	0.202	29.9 cm	64.1%
LiDAR_Jamming	0.848 ± 0.024	1.000	0.737	1.5 cm	8.8%
LiDAR_Injection	0.779 ± 0.023	0.704	0.871	1.5 cm	16.3%
GPR_Phantom	0.805 ± 0.023	0.749	0.871	1.5 cm	13.5%
GPR_Suppress	0.853 ± 0.033	1.000	0.746	1.5 cm	8.3%
MultiVector_Light	0.602 ± 0.035	0.763	0.498	12.6 cm	35.3%
MultiVector_Heavy	0.346 ± 0.036	0.377	0.320	20.7 cm	62.8%
MultiVector_Max	0.091 ± 0.032	0.087	0.097	32.1 cm	90.2%

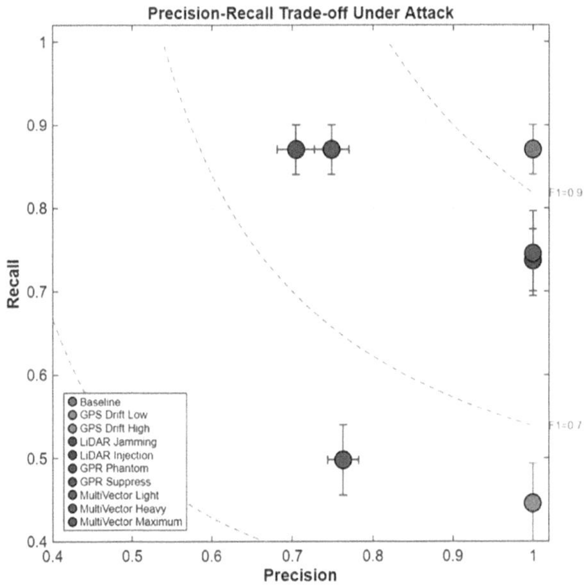

Fig. 5. Precision-recall trade-off under attack. Baseline (green) achieves optimal performance. Single-vector attacks (blue/purple) show moderate degradation. Multi-vector attacks (red) cause severe performance collapse approaching random classification

Suppression-type attacks (GPS spoofing, LiDAR jamming, GPR suppression) degrade only recall because they cause the system to miss real anomalies without generating false detections. GPS spoofing creates coverage gaps through path deviation, while jamming and suppression reduce sensor sensitivity. These attacks preserve precision at 1.000 since there are no false alarms introduced. By contrast, injection attacks (LiDAR injection,

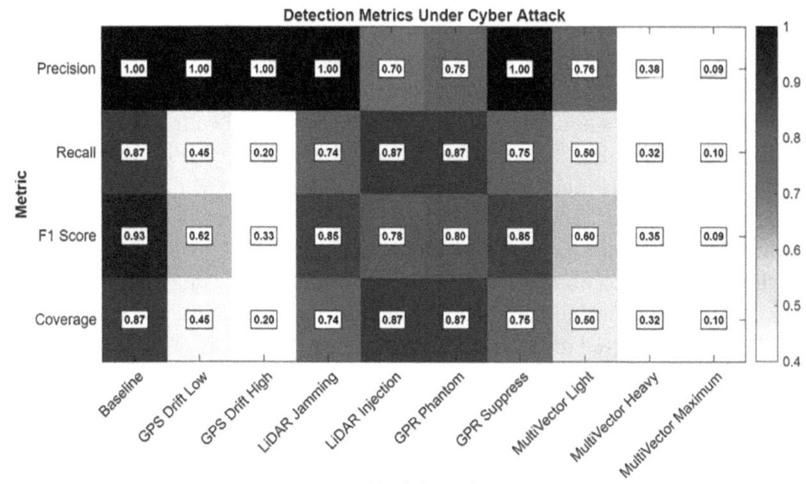

Fig. 6. Detection metrics heatmap across attack scenarios. Color intensity indicates metric values (green = high, red = low). Multi-vector Maximum shows uniformly poor performance across all metrics

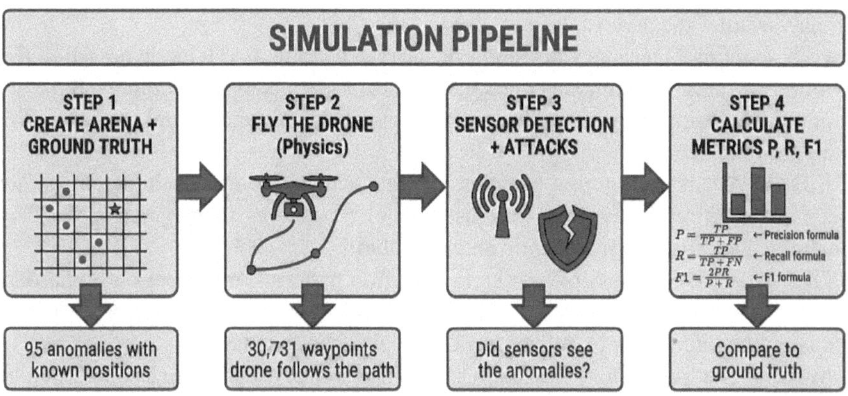

Fig. 7. Synthetic data generation and simulation pipeline. The framework generates ground truth anomalies based on NUREG-1801 degradation distributions, simulates UAV flight dynamics with 12-state physics modeling, applies sensor detection models with attack effects, and evaluates performance against known anomaly positions through 20 Monte Carlo iterations per scenario

GPR phantom) affect precision and recall by introducing false alarms, though baseline recall is preserved. The phantom patterns injected in the simulation are observed as additional anomalies, which are not real. Attacks using multi-vectors simultaneously, attacking both precision and recall, are responsible for the catastrophic results observed in F1 scores. This is because there is a mechanistic difference in the forensic markers, where degradation of precision with insignificant recall suggests injection attacks, while degradation of recall with significant precision suggests suppression and navigation attacks. This is because GPS spoofing results in path deviation, resulting in anomalies missed, while jamming and suppression result in reduced sensor sensitivity, though phantom patterns are not created. Figure 6 above is a heatmap representation of all the metrics of detection in the different scenarios, which clearly demonstrates this trend, where precision is high (green) in non-injection attacks while recall depends on the intensity of the attack. The super-additive effect of multi-vector attacks is especially important. We define an attack combination as super-additive when the observed F1 degradation under the combined attack exceeds the sum of F1 degradations from each individual attack vector evaluated independently against the baseline. GPS_Drift_High by itself has 64.1% degradation, as do individual sensor attacks (8–16% degradation), but together in the MultiVector_Maximum scenario, the effect reaches 90.2% degradation and that is far beyond the simple sum of individual effects. This is because the individual attack modalities complement each other. GPS attacks the recall by leaving holes in the coverage; the injection attacks the precision by introducing false positives. They simultaneously target both parts of the F1 score.

6.2 Forensic Signatures

Each type of attack produces its own distinct forensic "signature," which can be used for analysis after the attack:

GPS spoofing: Trajectory deviation patterns indicating a systematic deviation from the route, correlation in time between the onset of the trajectory deviation and the activation of the attack, the preservation of perfect precision, which implies that no false positives are injected.

LiDAR Attacks: Jamming appears as statistically anomalous intervals of non-detection; injection corresponds to clustered false positives with typical point cloud signatures that differ from authentic anomaly points.

GPR Attacks: Suppression results in detection patterns dependent on burial depth and interference effectiveness, and the phantom injection results in signatures without the characteristic hyperbolic reflections of actual subsurface targets.

Multi-Vector: Trajectory deviation, gaps in discovery, and false positive patterns combined offer high confidence indications of an attack. Both precision and recall degradation indicating coordinated attacks over single vector campaigns.

6.3 Defensive Implications

Our results highlight several defense priorities mapped to the specific attacks they counter:

Resilience in GPS (counters: GPS_Drift_Low, GPS_Drift_High, all multi-vector attacks): With the drastic effects of GPS spoofing (ranging from 64.1% degradation in navigation attacks), other positioning solutions such as Visual-Inertial Odometry and Ultra-wide band beacons would instead be emphasized. Multi-source position fusion with consistency checking allows the detection of spoofing attempts.

Sensor Validation (counters: LiDAR_Injection, GPR_Phantom, multi-vector injection components): Cross-modal consistency checking using LiDAR and GPR detections could detect injection attacks since signatures are usually confined to a single sensory domain. Anomaly classification using machine learning on actual signatures could be utilized to separate actual from injected detections [21, 22].

Mission Integrity Monitoring (counters: all attack types via runtime statistical anomaly detection): Real-time analysis of the detection statistics may indicate any ongoing attacking process. Anomalous patterns such as sudden false positive bursts or systematic detection gaps that should trigger mission abort and forensic data preservation.

7 Conclusion and Future Work

This paper introduced a forensic-ready simulation framework for evaluating the impact of cyber attacks on UAV-based nuclear containment inspection systems. Through systematic analysis of ten attack scenarios across GPS, LiDAR, and GPR sensors using 200 Monte Carlo trials, we established quantitative baselines for attack severity classification. Single-vector sensor attacks (jamming/suppression) cause 8.3–16.3% F1 degradation, while GPS spoofing produces severe 33.9–64.1% degradation due to non-linear path deviation effects. Coordinated multi-vector attacks lead to catastrophic 90.2% F1 degradation by super-additive combination of attack vectors. One of the significant contributions of this study is the mechanistic distinction between suppression attacks, which only degrade the recall metric due to missed detections, and injection attacks, which only degrade the precision metric due to false positives, which can be used for forensic purposes. The proposed framework provides forensic-ready artifacts, defined here as structured, timestamped records of UAV trajectory deviations, sensor-detection events, attack-onset markers, and sensor-fusion anomalies, generated in a format suitable for post-incident reconstruction and attribution analysis. Future work will align this artifact serialization with established cyber-physical evidence formats such as CASE/UCO and STIX 2.1 to enable interoperable, chain-of-custody-preserving incident reconstruction.

Future efforts will extend this work along several directions identified during peer review: (a) hardware-in-the-loop validation with real UAV and sensor packages to empirically calibrate the standoff-penalty parameter k and the baseline false-positive rate; (b) sensitivity analyses across k, standoff distance, and sensor operating ranges; (c) ablations isolating suppression-only versus injection-only mechanisms and comparing alternative sensor-fusion strategies (Dempster–Shafer, Bayesian evidence combination); (d) a defect-type breakdown by NUREG-1801 degradation category; and (e) implementation of forensic artifact serialization aligned with CASE/UCO and STIX 2.1 standards.

References

1. U.S. Nuclear Regulatory Commission: Generic Aging Lessons Learned (GALL) Report. U.S. Nuclear Regulatory Commission, Washington, DC (2010). Revision 2 Technical Report NUREG-1801. https://www.nrc.gov/reading-rm/doc-collections/nuregs/staff/sr1801/
2. Mazumdar, A., Fittery, A., Ubellacker, W., Asada, H.H.: A LiDAR-based approach for autonomous inspection of nuclear facilities. In: Transactions of the American Nuclear Society, pp. 377–380. American Nuclear Society, Minneapolis, MN (2019)

3. Tian, Y., Chen, C., Sagoe-Crentsil, K., Zhang, J., Duan, W.: Intelligent robotic systems for structural health monitoring: applications and future trends. Autom. Constr. **139**, 104273 (2022). https://doi.org/10.1016/j.autcon.2022.104273
4. Kang, D., Cha, Y.: Autonomous UAVs for structural health monitoring using deep learning and an ultrasonic Beacon system with geo-tagging. Comput. Aided Civil Eng. **33**(10), 885–902 (2018). https://doi.org/10.1111/mice.12375
5. Yaacoub, J.P., Noura, H., Salman, O., Chehab, A.: Security analysis of drones systems: attacks, limitations, and recommendations. Internet Things. **11**, 100218 (2020). https://doi.org/10.1016/j.iot.2020.100218
6. Lykou, G., Moustakas, D., Gritzalis, D.: Defending airports from UAS: a survey on cyber-attacks and counter-drone sensing technologies. Sensors. **20**(12), 3537 (2020). https://doi.org/10.3390/s20123537
7. Tippenhauer, N.O., Pöpper, C., Rasmussen, K.B., Capkun, S.: On the requirements for successful GPS spoofing attacks. In: Proceedings of the 18th ACM Conference on Computer and Communications Security, pp. 75–86. ACM, Chicago Illinois USA (2011). https://doi.org/10.1145/2046707.2046719
8. Kerns, A.J., Shepard, D.P., Bhatti, J.A., Humphreys, T.E.: Unmanned aircraft capture and control via GPS spoofing. J. Field Robot. **31**(4), 617–636 (2014). https://doi.org/10.1002/rob.21513
9. Petit, J., Shladover, S.E.: Potential cyberattacks on automated vehicles. IEEE Trans. Intell. Transport. Syst., 1–11 (2014). https://doi.org/10.1109/TITS.2014.2342271
10. Shin, H., Kim, D., Kwon, Y., Kim, Y.: Illusion and dazzle: adversarial Optical Channel exploits against Lidars for automotive applications. In: Fischer, W., Homma, N. (eds.) Cryptographic Hardware and Embedded Systems – CHES 2017 Lecture Notes in Computer Science, vol. 10529, pp. 445–467. Springer International Publishing, Cham (2017). https://doi.org/10.1007/978-3-319-66787-4_22
11. Cao, Y., et al.: Adversarial sensor attack on LiDAR-based perception in autonomous driving. In: Proceedings of the 2019 ACM SIGSAC Conference on Computer and Communications Security, pp. 2267–2281. ACM, London United Kingdom (2019). https://doi.org/10.1145/3319535.3339815
12. Daniels, D.J., (Ed.): Ground Penetrating Radar, 2nd ed., vol. 15. in IET Radar, Sonar, Navigation and Avionics Series, vol. 15. London, UK: Institution of Engineering and Technology (IET) (2004). doi:https://doi.org/10.1049/PBRA015E.
13. Almusayli, A., Zia, T., Qazi, E.H.: Drone forensics: an innovative approach to the forensic investigation of drone accidents based on digital twin technology. Technologies. **12**(1), 11 (2024). https://doi.org/10.3390/technologies12010011
14. Abdulrahman Debas, E., Albuali, A., Hafizur Rahman, M.M.: Forensic examination of drones: a comprehensive study of frameworks, challenges, and machine learning applications. IEEE Access. **12**, 111505–111522 (2024). https://doi.org/10.1109/ACCESS.2024.3426028
15. Adel, A., Jan, T.: Watch the skies: a study on drone attack vectors, forensic approaches, and persisting security challenges. Future Internet. **16**(7), 250 (2024). https://doi.org/10.3390/fi16070250
16. ACI Committee 349: Evaluation of Existing Nuclear Safety-Related Concrete Structures. American Concrete Institute, Farmington Hills, MI (2018). Technical Standard ACI 349.3R-18. https://www.concrete.org/store/productdetail.aspx?ItemID=349318
17. ASTM International: Standard Guide for Using the Surface Ground Penetrating Radar Method for Subsurface Investigation, ASTM D6432–19, West Conshohocken, PA (2019). doi:https://doi.org/10.1520/D6432-19.
18. Langner, R.: Stuxnet: dissecting a cyberwarfare weapon. IEEE Secur. Priv. Mag. **9**(3), 49–51 (2011). https://doi.org/10.1109/MSP.2011.67

19. Horsman, G.: Unmanned aerial vehicles: a preliminary analysis of forensic challenges. Digit. Investig. **16**, 1–11 (2016). https://doi.org/10.1016/j.diin.2015.11.002
20. Hassani, S., Dackermann, U.: A systematic review of advanced sensor technologies for non-destructive testing and structural health monitoring. Sensors. **23**(4), 2204 (2023). https://doi.org/10.3390/s23042204
21. Gurappa, S., Hariprasad, Y., Iyengar, S.S., Chaudhary, N.K.: Botnet Detection on CTU-13 Using Lightweight Machine Learning Models. arXiv. doi:10.48550/ARXIV.2605.23004 (2026).
22. Gupta, S., Hariprasad, Y., Iyengar, S.S., Gurappa, S., Mohanty, P.: Enhancing digital security: a novel dual-paradigm approach for robust Deepfake detection using pre and post quantum-trained neural networks. Digit. Threats. **7**(1), 1–15 (2026). https://doi.org/10.1145/3794846

R-FIGM: A Real-Time Forensic Intelligence Governance Model for Cyber Crisis Management in Critical Infrastructure

Ehab Elhegawy(✉)

Dubai Police Academy, Dubai, United Arab Emirates
Elheggawy@dubaipolice.ac.ae

Abstract. Cyber attacks targeting critical infrastructure have evolved into complex governance crises that demand analytical capabilities extending well beyond conventional forensic objectives. Traditional digital forensic frameworks remain primarily oriented toward post-incident evidence reconstruction and legal attribution, limiting their operational utility for decision-makers who must respond while incidents are still unfolding. This study introduces the Real-Time Forensic Intelligence Governance Model (R-FIGM), a conceptual analytical architecture that integrates digital forensic investigation, AI-enabled evidence triage, cyber threat intelligence fusion, and predictive cascade modelling within a unified governance-oriented framework. The proposed model reconceptualises digital forensic investigation as a real-time intelligence capability capable of generating actionable situational awareness during active cyber crises. By linking forensic artefacts with threat intelligence insights and infrastructure interdependency analysis, R-FIGM enables cybersecurity analysts and crisis management authorities to anticipate cascading infrastructure disruptions and coordinate cross-sector response strategies. A scenario-based illustration involving a cyber intrusion targeting energy infrastructure demonstrates the operational logic of the framework across its analytical layers. The study contributes to emerging research at the intersection of digital forensics, AI-driven cyber analytics, and critical infrastructure resilience, offering a scalable governance architecture applicable to national cybersecurity agencies and critical infrastructure operators facing increasingly sophisticated threat environments.

Keywords: Digital Forensics · Cyber Crisis Governance · AI-Enabled Forensics · Cyber Threat Intelligence · Critical Infrastructure Protection · Cyber Resilience · Cybersecurity Governance

1 Introduction

Cyber attacks targeting critical infrastructure have emerged as among the most consequential security challenges confronting contemporary societies. The accelerating digitalisation of essential services—energy systems, transportation networks, healthcare

© ICST Institute for Computer Sciences, Social Informatics and Telecommunications Engineering 2027
Published by Springer Nature Switzerland AG 2027. All Rights Reserved
H. Neukirchen et al. (Eds.): ICDF2C 2026, LNICST 720, pp. 192–208, 2027.
https://doi.org/10.1007/978-3-032-37274-1_12

infrastructures, financial services, and government platforms—has created unprecedented operational efficiency while simultaneously expanding the attack surfaces available to sophisticated adversaries.

Industrial control systems, operational technology networks, cloud computing platforms, and Internet-of-Things devices are now deeply embedded within infrastructure operations. While these technologies have enhanced service delivery, they have introduced cybersecurity vulnerabilities that state-sponsored actors and criminal organisations actively exploit. High-profile incidents affecting power grids, transportation systems, and government digital services have demonstrated how cyber intrusions can generate widespread economic disruption, public safety risks, and national security consequences [4].

A characteristic that distinguishes contemporary cyber incidents from earlier threat patterns is technological interdependence. Because many infrastructure sectors share common digital ecosystems, disruptions in one sector propagate across others, generating cascading systemic effects that amplify overall impact [3]. This reality has led researchers and policymakers to reconceptualise major cyber incidents not merely as technical security failures but as complex governance crises requiring coordinated decision-making across cybersecurity authorities, infrastructure operators, emergency management agencies, and government institutions.

Despite advances in cybersecurity governance frameworks—including the NIST Cybersecurity Framework's structured approach to identification, protection, detection, response, and recovery [4]—most operational models continue to treat digital forensic investigation as a post-incident activity. Forensic investigation traditionally focuses on reconstructing cyber incidents after they occur in order to identify attack vectors, preserve digital evidence, and support legal attribution [1]. These investigative procedures remain essential, but their retrospective orientation limits their usefulness for decision-makers who must act during active, evolving incidents.

Simultaneously, cyber threat intelligence (CTI) has emerged as an important capability for identifying emerging threats and analysing attacker behaviour. Threat intelligence platforms collect information from malware repositories, vulnerability databases, network telemetry, and intelligence-sharing communities to identify patterns associated with malicious activity [5]. Although these capabilities improve situational awareness, they typically operate independently from forensic investigation processes, creating an operational gap that undermines integrated crisis governance.

Closing this gap requires analytical frameworks capable of transforming digital forensic artefacts into real-time intelligence that can be contextualised within broader threat environments and infrastructure risk landscapes. Artificial intelligence offers particular promise here: AI-driven evidence triage can rapidly prioritise vast volumes of forensic data, machine learning models can correlate artefacts against threat intelligence repositories at speeds impossible through manual analysis, and predictive algorithms can model cascade failure pathways before disruptions materialise [14].

To address these challenges, this study proposes the Real-Time Forensic Intelligence Governance Model (R-FIGM)—a conceptual framework designed to integrate

AI-enabled digital forensic investigation, cyber threat intelligence fusion, and predictive cascade modelling within a governance-oriented analytical architecture capable of supporting decision-making during cyber crises affecting critical infrastructure.

1.1 Research Contributions

This study makes five contributions to the intersection of digital forensics, AI-driven cyber analytics, and crisis governance research.

The first contribution is the reconceptualisation of digital forensic investigation as a real-time intelligence capability rather than a purely retrospective investigative process. This shift repositions forensic investigators as crisis intelligence advisors during active incidents, not only as post-event analysts.

The second contribution is the development of the R-FIGM framework itself—a conceptual analytical architecture integrating AI-enabled forensic analysis, cyber threat intelligence fusion, and predictive cascade modelling within a unified governance framework.

Third, the study demonstrates the integration of forensic intelligence with cyber threat intelligence analysis. By linking artefacts recovered from compromised systems with intelligence concerning attacker tactics, techniques, and procedures (TTPs), the framework enables analysts to interpret forensic findings within a broader strategic threat context.

Fourth, the incorporation of predictive cascade modelling addresses the infrastructure interdependency problem directly: by modelling how disruptions propagate across interconnected sectors, the framework enables anticipatory rather than reactive governance responses.

Finally, the study contributes to cyber crisis governance research by demonstrating how forensic intelligence can support executive-level decision-making during cyber incidents, bridging the gap between technical cybersecurity operations and organisational governance structures.

2 Literature Review

Research at the intersection of digital forensics, cyber threat intelligence, and infrastructure resilience has expanded considerably over the past decade, driven by the growing complexity of cyber threats targeting critical systems.

2.1 Digital Forensic Investigation

Digital forensic research has traditionally focused on the identification, preservation, analysis, and presentation of digital evidence to reconstruct incidents and support legal proceedings [1]. Early scholarship concentrated on developing technical methodologies for extracting artefacts from compromised systems, storage devices, and network environments. Over time, the field extended to address cloud computing, mobile devices, Internet-of-Things infrastructures, and industrial control systems [21].

Despite these advances, digital forensic investigation remains largely retrospective. Forensic investigators analyse artefacts after incidents have occurred to determine how systems were compromised, identify attacker activities, and collect evidence for legal attribution. While essential for cybercrime investigations and judicial proceedings, this orientation limits the usefulness of forensic outputs for real-time crisis management. Recent scholarship has begun exploring how automation and AI can accelerate forensic analysis [13, 14, 17, 19, 28], but integration with governance decision-making frameworks remains underdeveloped.

2.2 Cyber Threat Intelligence

Cyber threat intelligence research focuses on understanding attacker behaviour, identifying malicious activity patterns, and analysing the tactics, techniques, and procedures employed by cyber adversaries [5]. Threat intelligence platforms collect information from malware analysis repositories, vulnerability databases, network monitoring systems, and intelligence-sharing communities, providing situational awareness that improves defensive preparedness.

The MITRE ATT&CK framework has become a widely adopted reference for structuring threat intelligence around adversary behaviours [6]. However, threat intelligence analysis and digital forensic investigation typically operate as separate analytical domains. Forensic analysis focuses on artefacts recovered from specific compromised systems, whereas threat intelligence concentrates on attacker patterns across multiple campaigns. This separation limits the ability of organisations to interpret forensic findings within the broader strategic threat environment.

2.3 Cyber Resilience and Infrastructure Interdependencies

Cyber resilience research emphasises the ability of organisations and infrastructure systems to anticipate, withstand, recover from, and adapt to cyber disruptions [2]. Within critical infrastructure contexts, this body of work has highlighted the significance of infrastructure interdependencies: because digital communication networks support transportation systems, energy infrastructures rely on industrial control networks, and financial services depend on cloud computing platforms, disruptions affecting one sector may cascade across others [3, 24, 25].

The Ukraine power grid attacks of 2015–2016 provided a documented case study of these dynamics: a cyber intrusion targeting energy infrastructure generated cascading effects across interconnected systems [7, 22]. Such cases demonstrate that effective cyber crisis governance requires analytical approaches capable of anticipating systemic consequences before they materialise—a capability that existing forensic and intelligence frameworks do not adequately address.

2.4 AI in Cyber Forensics and Crisis Management

Artificial intelligence applications in cybersecurity have expanded rapidly, moving well beyond earlier uses in anomaly detection and malware classification toward more integrated roles in forensic analysis, threat intelligence, and crisis management. Dunsin et al. [14] provide a comprehensive analysis of how AI and machine learning are transforming digital forensic investigations, documenting applications in automated evidence triage, network traffic analysis, log correlation, and artefact classification. Their survey highlights that while AI is already improving the efficiency and accuracy of forensic workflows, integration with governance-level decision-making processes remains underdeveloped.

The emergence of large language models (LLMs) has added a new dimension to AI capabilities in cybersecurity and forensics. Zhang et al. [15] demonstrate that LLMs can be applied across cybersecurity tasks including threat intelligence extraction, forensic report generation, and vulnerability analysis. Particularly relevant to the R-FIGM framework is the application of LLMs to structured extraction of attacker TTPs from unstructured threat intelligence reports—a capability that substantially accelerates the threat intelligence fusion layer of the proposed architecture.

Research on AI for critical infrastructure protection has progressed accordingly. Ferrag et al. [16] examine how generative AI and LLMs can support real-time monitoring, proactive threat detection, and incident response across energy, water, and transportation infrastructure sectors. Sarker [12] further demonstrates how AI algorithms can be strategically integrated to fortify critical infrastructure against cyber disruptions through machine learning and predictive analytics. Their analysis underscores that AI-driven approaches are most effective when embedded within governance frameworks that integrate technical detection capabilities with organisational decision-support processes—precisely the architectural logic underlying R-FIGM.

Despite these advances, AI integration within crisis governance frameworks remains at an early stage. Most applications focus on discrete technical tasks rather than synthesising multi-source analytical outputs into governance-ready intelligence. The volume of forensic data generated during major infrastructure incidents creates an analytical bottleneck that investigators cannot resolve within operationally relevant timeframes [14]. R-FIGM responds to this constraint by embedding AI-enabled triage and intelligence fusion within an analytical pipeline that connects technical forensic analysis to strategic crisis governance.

2.5 Research Gap and Conceptual Positioning

Despite the substantial volume of research on digital forensics, cyber threat intelligence, cyber resilience, and AI in cybersecurity, these analytical domains remain largely fragmented. Relatively few studies have proposed integrated frameworks capable of transforming forensic investigation outputs into governance-oriented decision support during active cyber crises.

The R-FIGM framework is positioned at the intersection of these four domains. It extends digital forensic research by embedding forensic investigation within real-time governance processes; it extends threat intelligence research by connecting CTI analysis to forensic artefact interpretation; it extends cyber resilience research by incorporating predictive cascade modelling into crisis decision support; and it extends AI in cybersecurity by proposing a governance-level architecture for AI-enabled forensic intelligence.

3 Methodology

This study adopts a conceptual modelling approach to develop an analytical framework integrating digital forensic investigation, AI-enabled cyber threat intelligence, and predictive infrastructure risk analysis. Conceptual modelling is widely employed in cybersecurity governance research to synthesise insights from multiple analytical domains and propose structured frameworks for addressing complex security challenges [8, 20]. Because cyber incidents affecting critical infrastructure involve technological, organisational, and governance dimensions simultaneously, conceptual frameworks provide valuable tools for understanding how disparate analytical capabilities can be integrated into coherent crisis management processes.

The methodology consists of three analytical stages. First, a systematic review of relevant literature was conducted across digital forensic investigation, cyber threat intelligence, cyber resilience, AI in cybersecurity, and critical infrastructure protection research. This review enabled identification of the principal analytical components necessary for an integrated forensic intelligence framework and revealed the operational gaps that current approaches fail to address.

Second, a conceptual analytical architecture was developed that integrates digital forensic investigation processes with AI-driven triage, cyber threat intelligence analysis, infrastructure interdependency modelling, and governance decision-support mechanisms. The architecture was designed to transform digital forensic artefacts into operational intelligence capable of supporting crisis governance decision-making in real time.

Third, the framework was examined through a scenario-based analytical illustration involving a cyber intrusion targeting energy infrastructure. Scenario-based analysis enables researchers to explore how conceptual models may operate within complex operational environments and how analytical insights generated by the framework may support crisis management decisions [9]. This methodological approach is appropriate for conceptual frameworks that have not yet been validated through large-scale empirical studies, providing an accessible demonstration of the framework's operational logic.

The conceptual development of R-FIGM was informed by Design Science Research (DSR) principles [9]. The framework was designed as an artefact intended to address an identified governance gap between digital forensic investigation and cyber crisis decision-making. The design process involved problem identification through systematic literature review, synthesis of interdisciplinary knowledge from digital forensics, cyber threat intelligence, and crisis governance domains, iterative framework construction incorporating AI-enabled analytical capabilities, and scenario-based demonstration to illustrate the operational logic of the proposed architecture. This methodological alignment ensures that R-FIGM satisfies the core DSR requirements of relevance, design rigour, and communicability.

4 The R-FIGM Analytical Framework

The Real-Time Forensic Intelligence Governance Model (R-FIGM) integrates digital forensic investigation, AI-enabled evidence triage, cyber threat intelligence analysis, and predictive infrastructure risk modelling within a governance-oriented analytical architecture designed to support cyber crisis management.

The central premise of R-FIGM is that digital forensic investigation should not be confined to retrospective analysis. Forensic artefacts generated during active cyber intrusions should be analysed in real time, interpreted within the broader threat intelligence environment, and modelled against infrastructure interdependency maps—all in service of governance-level crisis decision support. Within this framework, forensic artefacts are not merely evidentiary records; they are intelligence indicators capable of revealing attacker behaviour patterns and enabling anticipatory crisis management responses.

4.1 Analytical Architecture and Operational Logic

The R-FIGM architecture consists of seven sequential analytical stages, each building upon the outputs of the previous layer. Figure 1 illustrates the full analytical pipeline.

The model processes digital forensic evidence through three core analytical transformations—evidence prioritisation, threat intelligence contextualisation, and cascade risk modelling—before delivering governance-ready intelligence to crisis management authorities. These transformations enable raw technical artefacts to evolve into strategic decision-support outputs.

4.2 Layer 1: Cyber Incident Detection

The analytical pipeline begins with cyber incident detection—the identification of anomalous system behaviour through continuous monitoring of network traffic, authentication logs, intrusion detection systems, and operational technology sensors. AI-driven anomaly detection algorithms play a central role at this stage, processing high-velocity data streams to distinguish genuine intrusion indicators from background noise. Machine learning classifiers trained on historical incident data enable detection at speeds and scales that manual monitoring cannot match [9, 10].

4.3 Layer 2: Forensic Evidence Acquisition

Upon detection, digital forensic artefacts are systematically acquired from affected systems and network environments. This includes memory dumps, disk images, system logs, authentication records, network traffic captures, and command execution histories. The acquisition process must balance comprehensiveness with operational urgency—unlike traditional forensic investigations, which may proceed methodically over extended periods, crisis-context acquisition must occur rapidly to preserve volatile evidence before attackers purge traces of their activity [1, 11].

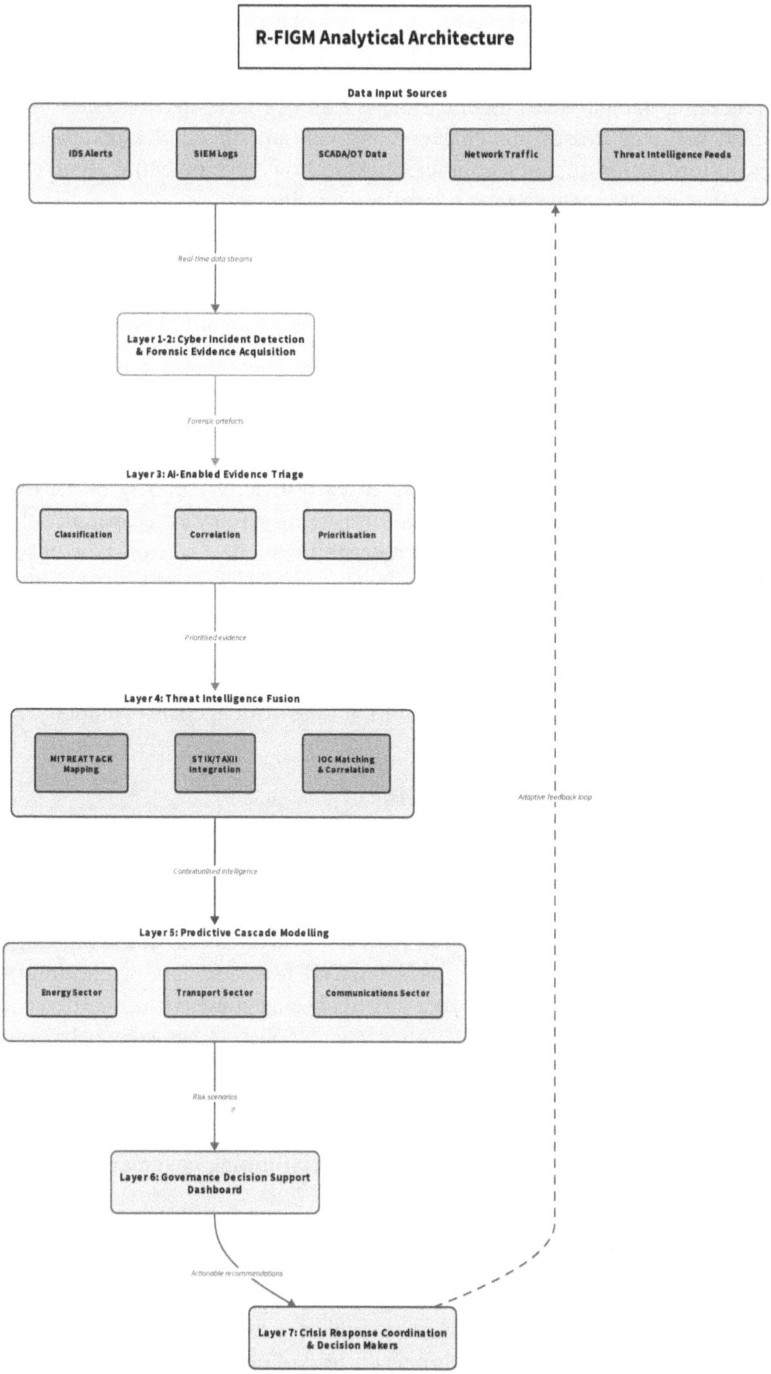

Fig. 1. The R-FIGM analytical architecture for forensic intelligence-driven cyber crisis governance

4.4 Layer 3: AI-Enabled Evidence Triage and Prioritisation

The volume of digital artefacts generated during significant cyber incidents can be enormous, rendering manual analysis infeasible within operationally relevant timeframes. AI-enabled triage addresses this challenge through automated classification, correlation, and prioritisation of forensic artefacts based on their potential significance for understanding attacker behaviour and infrastructure impact.

Machine learning models evaluate artefacts against known indicators of compromise, prioritise those associated with high-impact attacker actions—such as lateral movement, privilege escalation, and data exfiltration—and flag artefacts warranting immediate analyst attention. This automated prioritisation ensures that human analysts focus their cognitive resources on the most consequential evidence streams during time-critical crisis operations [14, 18].

Evidence prioritisation may be performed using supervised machine-learning classifiers, anomaly-detection algorithms, and risk-scoring mechanisms. Artefacts can be prioritised according to indicators such as attack criticality (severity of the exploited vulnerability and associated CVSS score), infrastructure relevance (operational importance of the affected system within the broader infrastructure network), potential operational impact (estimated disruption magnitude if the attack succeeds), and likelihood of lateral movement (probability that the attacker will pivot to adjacent systems based on network topology and access patterns). These metrics enable automated ranking of forensic artefacts, ensuring that analyst attention is directed toward evidence streams with the highest governance significance during time-critical crisis operations.

4.5 Layer 4: Threat Intelligence Fusion

Prioritised forensic artefacts are then integrated with cyber threat intelligence data sources in order to contextualise technical findings within the broader threat environment. Automated correlation engines compare artefact characteristics—command sequences, malware signatures, network indicators—against threat intelligence repositories, including MITRE ATT&CK, STIX/TAXII feeds, sector-specific information sharing communities, and national cyber intelligence databases [6, 15, 23].

This fusion enables analysts to determine whether observed attacker behaviours correspond to known campaign patterns, assess the likely objectives and capabilities of the threat actor, and identify potential escalation pathways. The integration of forensic analysis with threat intelligence transforms isolated technical observations into strategically contextualised intelligence assessments capable of informing governance decisions.

4.6 Layer 5: Predictive Cascade Modelling

Following threat intelligence fusion, the R-FIGM framework incorporates predictive cascade modelling to anticipate potential systemic consequences of the detected intrusion. Infrastructure dependency models map the technological interconnections between affected systems and adjacent infrastructure sectors, enabling analysts to simulate how attacker actions within one sector could propagate across others [3].

Predictive modelling outputs inform crisis management authorities about potential risk scenarios before they materialise. This anticipatory intelligence is particularly valuable in interconnected infrastructure environments where response actions in one sector may inadvertently affect operations in others [16]. By making cascading failure pathways visible in advance, the model enables coordinated, system-aware response strategies rather than reactive, sector-isolated interventions.

4.7 Layer 6: Governance Decision Support

The integrated analytical outputs—forensic intelligence, threat context, and cascade risk assessments—are synthesised into decision-support intelligence for crisis governance authorities. This layer translates technical analytical findings into actionable recommendations oriented toward executive-level decision-making: risk prioritisation, resource allocation, inter-agency coordination triggers, and escalation thresholds.

The governance decision support layer represents the critical interface between technical cybersecurity analysis and organisational crisis management. By structuring analytical outputs within governance-relevant frameworks, R-FIGM enables crisis management authorities to interpret technical evidence in terms of operational consequences and strategic risk—without requiring deep technical cybersecurity expertise at the decision-making level [26, 27].

4.8 Layer 7: Crisis Response Coordination

The final analytical layer supports coordinated crisis response across multiple infrastructure sectors and institutional stakeholders. Drawing on the governance decision support outputs, crisis management authorities can initiate coordinated responses involving infrastructure operators, national cybersecurity agencies, emergency management institutions, and inter-governmental coordination mechanisms.

The coordination layer incorporates feedback mechanisms that allow updated forensic findings and threat intelligence to modify response strategies as incidents evolve. This adaptive feedback loop is essential for managing cyber crises that unfold over extended periods and may involve attacker adaptation to initial defensive responses.

4.9 Analytical Propositions

To articulate the analytical implications of the proposed framework, the study advances two core propositions.

Proposition 1. *Integrating AI-enabled digital forensic investigation with cyber threat intelligence analysis improves situational awareness during cyber incidents affecting critical infrastructure, enabling more informed and timely crisis governance decisions than either capability provides in isolation.*

Proposition 2. *The integration of predictive cascade modelling with forensic intelligence enhances the ability of crisis management authorities to anticipate systemic infrastructure disruptions during cyber crises, enabling anticipatory coordination that reduces the overall impact of cascading failures.*

5 Scenario-Based Illustration

To illustrate the operational application of the proposed framework, this section presents a scenario-based analysis involving a cyber intrusion targeting national energy infrastructure. Scenario analysis allows conceptual frameworks to be examined within realistic operational environments and provides insight into how analytical processes may support decision-making during cyber incidents [9].

5.1 Incident Context

Consider a cyber intrusion targeting a national electricity distribution infrastructure. The energy system relies on interconnected industrial control systems responsible for monitoring and managing electricity generation, transmission, and distribution. During routine monitoring, cybersecurity analysts detect abnormal network behaviour originating from a remote access gateway connected to an operational technology network within the distribution infrastructure. Initial alerts indicate an unauthorised authentication attempt within a SCADA environment responsible for electricity distribution operations—a pattern consistent with early-stage intrusion activity documented in prior energy sector incidents [7].

5.2 Forensic Evidence Acquisition and AI-Enabled Triage

Within the R-FIGM analytical framework, the response begins immediately with forensic evidence acquisition. Digital artefacts are collected from affected systems: system logs, authentication records, network traffic captures, malware indicators, and command execution traces. Given the volume of data generated across a distributed energy infrastructure, AI-enabled triage mechanisms are immediately activated.

Automated classification algorithms analyse network activity patterns, identifying suspicious authentication sequences, anomalous command executions, and unusual lateral movement indicators. The triage process surfaces a series of remote commands executed within the energy distribution control network that are inconsistent with standard operational procedures—commands bearing structural similarities to those documented in previous industrial control system intrusion campaigns.

5.3 Threat Intelligence Fusion

Prioritised forensic artefacts are correlated against threat intelligence repositories. Automated correlation engines compare the command sequences and malware indicators against MITRE ATT&CK entries for industrial control system intrusion campaigns, STIX/TAXII feeds from energy sector information sharing communities, and national cyber intelligence databases.

Analysis reveals that several command sequences match behavioural patterns previously associated with cyber operations targeting energy infrastructure—specifically, techniques characteristic of campaigns oriented toward establishing persistent access within operational technology environments rather than immediate service disruption.

This contextual intelligence enables analysts to assess the intrusion as a targeted operation and to anticipate potential escalation toward operational disruption if persistence mechanisms are allowed to establish [7].

5.4 Predictive Cascade Modelling

Following threat intelligence fusion, predictive cascade modelling is activated to assess potential systemic consequences. Infrastructure dependency models map the connections between the affected electricity distribution system and adjacent infrastructure sectors: transportation systems dependent on traffic signal networks, communication infrastructures relying on powered relay stations, and industrial production facilities requiring stable electricity supply.

Predictive modelling identifies three primary risk scenarios with varying probability weightings. The highest-probability scenario involves regional power outages affecting transportation network management systems and communication infrastructures in an interconnected manner. The model also identifies a lower-probability but high-consequence scenario involving disruption to hospital backup power systems dependent on grid stability—a scenario that elevates the crisis to a public safety dimension warranting emergency management involvement (Fig. 2).

5.5 Governance Decision Support and Response Coordination

The integrated analytical outputs are synthesised into governance decision-support intelligence. Crisis management authorities receive a structured intelligence assessment indicating that the intrusion likely represents a targeted persistent access operation with high probability of operational escalation, that cascade failure pathways extend across transportation and communication sectors, and that immediate isolation of compromised SCADA gateway systems is warranted without disrupting active distribution operations.

Based on these findings, crisis management authorities initiate a coordinated response involving the national electricity operator, the national cybersecurity agency, transport infrastructure operators, and emergency management institutions. Mitigation actions include isolation of the compromised remote access gateway, enhanced monitoring of lateral movement pathways, and pre-positioning of emergency response resources in areas identified through cascade modelling as potentially affected by escalation scenarios.

The scenario demonstrates how the R-FIGM analytical pipeline—from initial detection through AI-enabled triage, threat intelligence fusion, predictive cascade modelling, and governance decision support—enables crisis management authorities to move from anomaly detection to coordinated, system-aware response within an operationally relevant timeframe (Table 1).

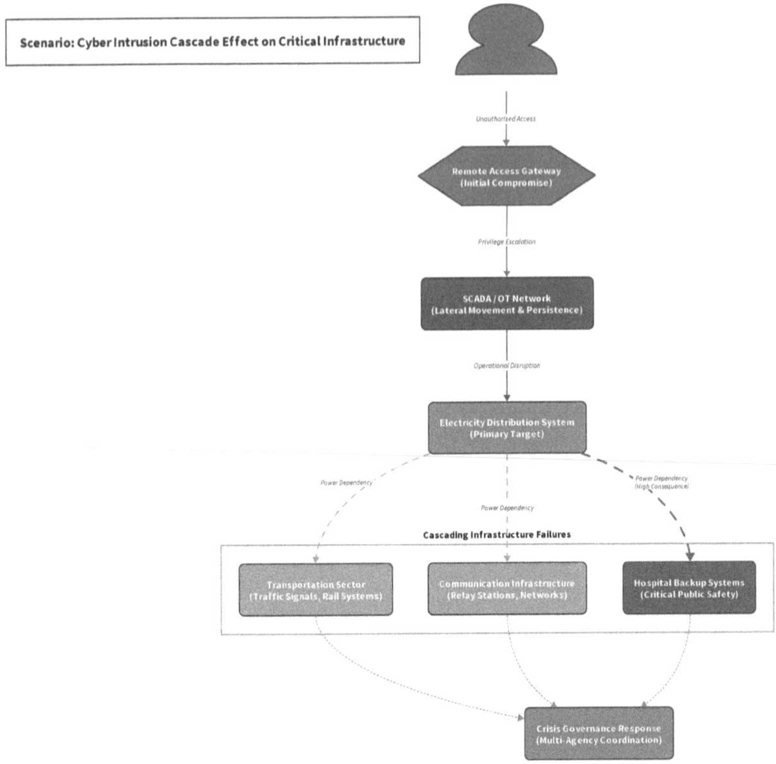

Fig. 2. Scenario-based illustration of cyber intrusion cascade effect on critical infrastructure

Table 1. Comparative positioning of R-FIGM against existing approaches

Feature	Traditional DF	CTI Platforms	NIST CSF	R-FIGM
Real-Time Analysis	No	Partial	Partial	Yes
AI Evidence Triage	Limited	No	No	Yes
Threat Intelligence Fusion	Limited	Yes	Partial	Yes
Predictive Cascade Analysis	No	No	No	Yes
Governance Decision Support	No	Limited	Partial	Yes

6 Discussion

The R-FIGM framework advances the discourse on cybersecurity governance in several important respects. Most fundamentally, it challenges the established positioning of digital forensics as a post-incident discipline. As cyber incidents targeting critical infrastructure increasingly unfold over extended periods—with attackers maintaining persistent access while progressively escalating their operational impact—the traditional separation between real-time incident response and retrospective forensic investigation becomes analytically untenable.

The framework's integration of AI-enabled evidence triage addresses a practical constraint that has historically limited the operational utility of forensic analysis: the volume problem. During significant cyber incidents affecting distributed infrastructure systems, the volume of potentially relevant digital artefacts can exceed the analytical capacity of human forensic teams operating under time pressure. AI-driven prioritisation resolves this constraint by directing human analytical attention to the artefacts most likely to be operationally significant—a capability that becomes increasingly important as infrastructure environments grow in complexity.

The threat intelligence fusion layer addresses the contextualisation problem. Technical forensic artefacts—log entries, command sequences, network indicators—carry limited strategic meaning in isolation. Their governance relevance depends on contextualisation within the broader threat environment: understanding whether observed behaviours correspond to known attacker campaigns, what those campaigns' historical objectives and escalation patterns have been, and what defensive countermeasures have proven effective [5]. By embedding threat intelligence fusion within the analytical pipeline, R-FIGM transforms isolated technical observations into strategically contextualised intelligence assessments.

The predictive cascade modelling layer addresses perhaps the most distinctive challenge of cyber incidents affecting critical infrastructure: anticipating second- and third-order consequences before they materialise. Crisis management authorities operating without this analytical capability are in a reactive posture—responding to cascading failures as they occur rather than preventing or mitigating them through anticipatory coordination. The framework's integration of infrastructure interdependency analysis represents a contribution to the cyber resilience literature by operationalising resilience concepts within an active crisis management process [2, 3].

Implementation Feasibility. The operational deployment of R-FIGM requires integration between Security Information and Event Management (SIEM) platforms, digital forensic acquisition tools, Cyber Threat Intelligence (CTI) repositories conforming to STIX/TAXII standards, and crisis management decision-support dashboards. While such integration introduces interoperability challenges—particularly regarding data format standardisation, real-time processing latency, and cross-organisational information sharing protocols—existing technological standards and modern Security Operations Centre (SOC) architectures provide a feasible implementation pathway. Organisations with mature cybersecurity governance capabilities, established incident response procedures, and integrated operational technology monitoring are positioned to adopt the framework incrementally. The modular layered architecture of R-FIGM further supports phased implementation, allowing organisations to deploy individual analytical layers according to their existing infrastructure maturity and operational priorities.

Several limitations of the framework warrant acknowledgement. The R-FIGM model is conceptual in nature and requires empirical validation through operational case studies, cyber incident simulations, or field-based research involving critical infrastructure operators. The quality of the framework's outputs depends directly on the quality and currency of threat intelligence data sources—a consideration that varies significantly across national and institutional contexts. Furthermore, the governance decision support layer requires organisational structures capable of translating technical intelligence into executive decisions, an institutional prerequisite that not all jurisdictions currently possess.

Future research should explore empirical validation pathways, examine how the framework can be adapted to specific regulatory and institutional contexts, and investigate how emerging AI capabilities—including large language models for threat intelligence synthesis and reinforcement learning for adaptive response recommendation—might enhance the framework's analytical components.

7 Conclusion

Cyber attacks targeting critical infrastructure represent one of the defining security challenges of the current period. As essential services become increasingly dependent on interconnected digital technologies, the consequences of cyber incidents extend from technical system failures into complex governance crises with economic, public safety, and national security dimensions.

This study introduced the Real-Time Forensic Intelligence Governance Model (R-FIGM) as a conceptual analytical framework designed to address a persistent gap in cyber crisis governance: the absence of integrated architectures capable of transforming digital forensic investigation outputs into real-time decision-support intelligence. By combining AI-enabled evidence triage, cyber threat intelligence fusion, and predictive cascade modelling within a governance-oriented analytical pipeline, R-FIGM repositions digital forensics from a retrospective investigative discipline to an active instrument of crisis intelligence.

The scenario-based illustration demonstrated how the framework's layered architecture enables crisis management authorities to progress from anomaly detection to coordinated, system-aware response—anticipating cascade failure pathways, contextualising forensic findings within strategic threat environments, and generating governance-ready intelligence within operationally relevant timeframes.

The framework contributes to research at the intersection of digital forensics, AI-driven cyber analytics, cyber resilience, and crisis governance—an interdisciplinary space whose practical importance is growing faster than its theoretical development. Future empirical research validating the framework through operational case studies and crisis simulations will be essential for establishing its applicability across diverse national and institutional contexts.

Ultimately, effective governance of cyber incidents affecting critical infrastructure requires closing the analytical gap between technical forensic investigation and strategic decision-making. The R-FIGM framework offers a structured architecture for achieving this integration—advancing the goal of more resilient, intelligence-driven cyber crisis governance in an era of escalating infrastructure threats.

References

1. Casey, E.: Digital Evidence and Computer Crime: Forensic Science, Computers and the Internet, 3rd edn. Academic, London (2011)
2. Kott, A., Linkov, I. (eds.): Cyber Resilience of Systems and Networks. Springer, Cham (2019)
3. Linkov, I., Trump, B.D.: The Science and Practice of Resilience. Springer, Cham (2019)
4. NIST: The NIST Cybersecurity Framework (CSF) 2.0 (NIST CSWP 29). U.S. Department of Commerce (2024). doi:10.6028/NIST.CSWP.29
5. Hutchins, E.M., Cloppert, M.J., Amin, R.M.: Intelligence-driven computer network defense informed by analysis of adversary campaigns and intrusion kill chains. Lead. Issues Inf. Warfare Secur. Res. **1**(1), 80–106 (2011)
6. Strom, B.E., Applebaum, A., Miller, D.P., Nickels, K.C., Pennington, A.G., Thomas, C.B.: MITRE ATT&CK: design and philosophy. MITRE Corporation. (2020)
7. ENISA: Best Practices for Cyber Crisis Management. European Union Agency for Cybersecurity (2024)
8. Lee, R.M., Assante, M.J., Conway, T.: Analysis of the cyber attack on the Ukrainian power grid. SANS Ind. Control Syst. (2016)
9. Ahmad, A., Maynard, S.B., Park, S.: Information security strategies: towards an organisational multi-strategy perspective. J. Intell. Manuf. **25**(2), 357–370 (2014)
10. Conti, M., Dehghantanha, A., Franke, K., Watson, S.: Internet of things security and forensics: challenges and opportunities. Futur. Gener. Comput. Syst. **78**, 544–546 (2018)
11. Rid, T., Buchanan, B.: Attributing cyber attacks. J. Strateg. Stud. **38**(1–2), 4–37 (2015)
12. Sarker, I.H.: AI for critical infrastructure protection and resilience. In: AI-Driven Cybersecurity and Threat Intelligence, pp. 195–215. Springer, Cham (2024)
13. Javed, A.R., et al.: A comprehensive survey on computer forensics: state-of-the-art, tools, techniques, challenges, and future directions. IEEE Access. **10**, 11065–11089 (2022)
14. Dunsin, D., Ghanem, M.C., Ouazzane, K., Vassilev, V.: A comprehensive analysis of the role of artificial intelligence and machine learning in modern digital forensics and incident response. Forensic Sci. Int. Digit. Investig. **48**, 301675 (2024)
15. Zhang, J., Bu, C., Li, X., et al.: When LLMs meet cybersecurity: a systematic literature review. Cybersecurity. **8**(55) (2025). https://doi.org/10.1186/s42400-025-00361-w
16. Ferrag, M.A., et al.: Generative AI and large language models for critical infrastructure protection: evaluation benchmarks, agentic AI, challenges, and opportunities. Sensors. **25**(6), 1666 (2025)
17. Kuforiji, J.: Digital forensics and incident response (DFIR) automation: leveraging AI to accelerate breach investigation, evidence collection, and cyberattack mitigation. J. Data Anal. Crit. Manag. **1**(4), 1–19 (2025). https://doi.org/10.64235/tsvfvz27
18. Bompally, S.D.: AI-driven incident response for digital forensics and incident response: a comprehensive framework. J. Comput. Sci. Technol. Stud. **7**(2), 467–472 (2025). https://doi.org/10.32996/jcsts.2025.7.2.48
19. Ndibe, O.S.: AI-driven forensic systems for real-time anomaly detection and threat mitigation in cybersecurity infrastructures. Int. J. Res. Publ. Rev. **6**(5), 389–411 (2025). https://doi.org/10.55248/gengpi.6.0525.1991
20. Aljumaiah, O., Jiang, W., Addula, S.R.: Analyzing cybersecurity risks and threats in IT infrastructure based on NIST framework. J. Cyber Secur. Risk Manag. (2025)
21. Kebande, V.R., Awad, A.I.: Industrial internet of things ecosystems security and digital forensics: achievements, open challenges, and future directions. ACM Comput. Surv. (2024)
22. Goel, S.: A systematic literature review on past attack analysis on industrial control systems. Trans. Emerg. Telecommun. Technol. (2024)

23. Gambo, M.D., Khan, A.H., Almulhem, A., Almadani, B.: An efficient framework for automated cyber threat intelligence sharing. Electronics. **14**(20), 4045 (2025)
24. Venkatasubramanian, B.V., Laoudias, C.: Cascading failures and resilience in interdependent critical infrastructures: a dynamic approach. IEEE Syst. J. (2025)
25. Abbas, T., Kumar, P.: Next-generation cybersecurity architectures for defending interconnected critical infrastructure. Int. J. Secur. Res. (2025)
26. Alharbi, T.S.M.: Cybersecurity governance and organizational resilience: a framework for sustainable risk management. EDPACS. (2025)
27. Praditya, E., Maarif, S., Ali, Y., Saragih, H.J.R.: National cybersecurity policy analysis for effective decision-making in the age of artificial intelligence. Journal of human. Security. (2023)
28. Cook, M.M.: A Survey on Industrial Control System Digital Forensics. University of Glasgow Repository (2023)

Cryptography and Steganography

RENet-Crypt: An Novel Image Encryption Method Based on Chaotic Systems and Invertible Neural Networks

Fen Liu[1], Tufeng Xian[1], Yong Zhong[1(✉)], Qiyuan Sun[1], Miaoji Zheng[1], Meifang Xie[1], Haitao Huang[2], and Zhengbin Liu[3]

[1] School of Computer Science and Artificial Intelligence, Foshan University, No. 33 Guangyun Road, 528225 Foshan, Guangdong, China
zhongyong@fosu.edu.cn
[2] Guangdong Chankong Big Data Technology Company, Foshan, China
[3] National Key Laboratory of Security Communication, No. 6 Chuangye Road, 610095 Chengdu, Sichuan, China

Abstract. To address the low efficiency and weak resistance against attacks of traditional encryption methods in handling highly redundant and strongly correlated image data, as well as the prevalent distortion issues in deep learning-based cryptosystems. This work introduces RENet-Crypt, an efficient image encryption framework that integrates neuro-dynamic chaotic systems with Invertible Neural Networks (INNs). Specifically, we design a plaintext-sensitive neuro-dynamic coupled 2D chaotic system that dynamically perturbs initial states via SHA-256 and utilizes a continuous nonlinear neuron model to destroy phase space topology, fundamentally circumventing Phase Space Reconstruction (PSR) attacks. Subsequently, the scrambled images are processed by a custom-designed RENet, which leverages Invertible Residual Blocks (RRB) and Invertible Attention Blocks (RAB) acting as plaintext-dependent dynamic masks for global pixel and channel diffusion. Extensive experiments demonstrate that RENet-Crypt successfully eliminates the security vulnerabilities of low-dimensional chaos. Notably, it achieves superior decryption quality compared with existing deep learning-based approaches, reaching a PSNR value exceeding 55 dB. With only 300K parameters and less than 40 MB deployment memory, it is highly suitable for mobile and edge device applications.

Keywords: Image Encryption · Chaotic Systems · Invertible Neural Networks

This work was supported in part by the Guangdong Basic and Applied Basic Research Foundation under Grants 2024A1515110038 and 2024A1515110024, the Special Program for Priority Fields in Guangdong Higher Education Institutions under Grant 2025ZDZX1033, and the Natural Science Foundation of Guangdong Province under Grants 2025A1515011385 and 2024A1515010186.

© ICST Institute for Computer Sciences, Social Informatics and Telecommunications Engineering 2027
Published by Springer Nature Switzerland AG 2027. All Rights Reserved
H. Neukirchen et al. (Eds.): ICDF2C 2026, LNICST 720, pp. 211–227, 2027.
https://doi.org/10.1007/978-3-032-37274-1_13

1 Introduction

The proliferation of mobile imaging technologies, together with the expansion of digital media ecosystems, has led to an unprecedented increase in the creation and storage of personal visual data through local devices and cloud infrastructures [36]. Due to limited storage resources and potential risks of local data loss, cloud-based image storage and sharing services have become increasingly popular among users. While cloud storage greatly facilitates photo backup and sharing, it also raises concerns about potential privacy leakage [33]. Image encryption provides an effective solution to protect sensitive photo content from unauthorized access during cloud storage and transmission. By transforming meaningful plaintext images into unintelligible, noise-like images, it ensures that only users with appropriate privileges can access these images [30].

Unlike conventional binary data, digital images exhibit strong spatial correlations, considerable redundancy, and complex statistical distributions. Therefore, directly applying general-purpose cryptographic algorithms originally developed for text or binary data may not fully exploit the intrinsic properties of image signals [24]. Although these ciphers remain secure and efficient under modern hardware encryption, their byte-level or block-level operations do not utilize the spatial redundancy and statistical properties fixed in images, limiting their applicability in scenarios requiring strong security and image-specific targets [8]. To address specific security requirements, numerous image encryption algorithms have been proposed [2,9,10,35,38]. Among these approaches, chaotic encryption has attracted extensive attention because chaotic systems possess desirable cryptographic features such as stochastic-like behavior, ergodicity, and high dependence on initial conditions and system parameters [16]. Existing studies have explored diverse chaotic models, ranging from simple one-dimensional maps to more complex high-dimensional chaotic structures [4,7,25]. Compared with low-order chaotic models, high-dimensional chaotic frameworks exhibit richer nonlinear behaviors and greater structural complexity, which makes them well suited for image security applications [32]. However, high-dimensional chaotic systems involve higher computational costs, which increases the difficulty of practical implementation. Conversely, one-dimensional chaotic systems feature lower computational complexity and are more convenient for practical implementation [4]. For example, early image encryption methods often employed one-dimensional chaotic models as the underlying security mechanism [19]. Nevertheless, these approaches generally exhibit weaknesses when facing attacks based on phase space reconstruction. [5]. Moreover, numerical precision limitations during digital implementation can degrade chaotic sequences by causing periodic behaviors and reducing randomness [37]. To alleviate these problems, researchers have introduced various enhanced chaotic models, including cascade chaotic systems [37], discrete wheel-switching chaotic systems [34], Schaffer-function-based two-dimensional hyperchaotic systems [13], and enhancing logistic chaotic map [3]. Despite these improvements, many chaotic systems still contain parameter intervals associated with periodic behavior. Furthermore, these methods remain vulnerable to phase space reconstruction attacks.

Deep learning techniques have shown promising performance in addressing these challenges by utilizing their nonlinear representation and feature learning capabilities [12,26,29,31]. Ding et al. [12] introduced a medical image protection framework named DeepEDN, which utilizes CycleGAN-driven image translation techniques to accomplish the encryption procedure. However, DeepEDN requires an individual encryption network to be trained for each plaintext image. Since this method requires storing different keys for different plaintexts, it is difficult to use, and decryption suffers from a certain degree of distortion. Sang et al. [31] introduced an image encryption approach that integrates logistic chaotic systems and deep autoencoder networks, where image pixels are scrambled using a 1D chaotic sequence and subsequently diffused through an autoencoder. Due to the characteristics of deep autoencoders, the decrypted image exhibits a certain degree of distortion.

To overcome these limitations, Invertible Neural Networks (INNs) have attracted increasing attention in reversible image processing applications, including image encryption [20], image hiding [22], and digital watermarking [14]. For instance, Huang et al. [20] proposed an INN-based framework using shared encryptors and decryptors to achieve end-to-end image encryption. However, such INN-based methods have not yet achieved truly lossless decryption because they typically rely on additional reference random noise images and discard byproduct information before decryption, limiting the fidelity and practicality of recovery.

To achieve high-fidelity recovery and secure image encryption, referencing the i-RevNet [21] architecture, we propose **RENet-Crypt**, an image encryption framework that integrates chaotic systems with Invertible Neural Networks. As illustrated in Fig. 1, during the encryption phase, we first employ a neuro-dynamic coupled 2D chaotic system to scramble the plaintext image, followed by applying RENet to perform nonlinear transformations on the scrambled result. Consequently, the output generated by RENet is regarded as the ciphertext image. By performing the inverse transformation of RENet followed by descrambling, the plaintext image can be successfully reconstructed. The key contributions of this work are outlined below.

1) We propose RENet-Crypt, a novel image encryption scheme bridging neuro-dynamic chaotic systems with Invertible Neural Networks (INNs). By leveraging custom-designed Invertible Residual Blocks (RRB) and Invertible Attention Blocks (RAB) acting as plaintext-dependent dynamic masks for global pixel and channel diffusion. Notably, it resolves the prevalent distortion issues in deep learning-based cryptosystems, outperforming state-of-the-art methods in decryption fidelity by achieving a PSNR of over 55 dB.
2) We design a plaintext-sensitive neuro-dynamic coupled 2D chaotic system for image scrambling. This mechanism dynamically perturbs initial states via SHA-256 and utilizes a continuous nonlinear neuron model to destroy phase space topology, which successfully eliminates the security vulnerabilities of low-dimensional chaos and fundamentally circumvents Phase Space Reconstruction (PSR) attacks.

3) We achieve an ultra-lightweight architecture that requires only 300K parameters and less than 40MB of deployment memory. This extremely low computational overhead makes the proposed encryption scheme highly suitable for practical, real-time applications on mobile and edge devices.

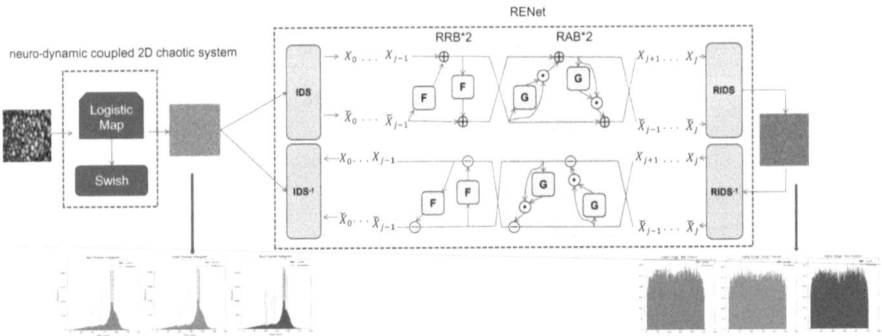

Fig. 1. Overall framework of the proposed image encryption scheme.

2 The Proposed Image Encryption Method

Here, we introduce an encryption framework that combines a neuro-dynamic coupled 2D chaotic system and invertible neural networks. During encryption, chaotic sequences are first employed to rearrange pixel locations, after which RENet is utilized to conduct reversible transformations and produce ciphertext with an approximately uniform distribution. The plaintext content can then be reconstructed by applying the reverse mapping of RENet followed by the corresponding inverse permutation process. The detailed architecture of the developed framework is presented in Fig. 1.

2.1 Neuro-Dynamic Coupled 2D Chaotic System

In the encryption phase, a 256-bit hash value $H = SHA\text{-}256(P)$ is first generated from the given image P by applying the SHA-256 cryptographic hash function. This digest is then divided into 32 byte-level sequences $h_1, h_2, \ldots, h_{32}$. Subsequently, these feature sequences are utilized to dynamically perturb the external basic key (which includes the initial states u_{init} and v_{init} of the chaotic system) input by the user, yielding the actual initial iteration values u_0 and v_0:

$$\begin{cases} u_0 = \left(u_{init} + \frac{\sum_{i=1}^{16} h_i}{16\times256}\right) \bmod 1 \\ v_0 = \left(v_{init} + \frac{\sum_{i=17}^{32} h_i}{16\times256}\right) \bmod 1 \end{cases} \tag{1}$$

Through the aforementioned mechanism, a slight perturbation to the plaintext image, even at the bit level, causes the digest H will change drastically, thereby completely altering the initial states u_0 and v_0 of the chaotic system to achieve dynamic One-Time-Pad (OTP) characteristics.

After obtaining the dynamic initial values u_0 and v_0, we employ the produced chaotic sequences to permute the spatial arrangement of image pixels. We first improve the 2D Sine-Logistic modulation Map [18] by exploiting the nonlinearity of the sine function and the folding property of the Logistic map for cross-coupling. This improvement eliminates the computationally expensive division operations, resulting in faster computation and a broader hyperchaotic range. Its discrete dynamic equations are defined as follows:

$$\begin{cases} u_{k+1} = \sin(\pi(\alpha \cdot u_k(1 - v_k) + \beta \cdot v_k)) \pmod 1 \\ v_{k+1} = \sin(\pi(\alpha \cdot v_k(1 - u_k) + \beta \cdot u_k)) \pmod 1 \end{cases} \tag{2}$$

where u_k, v_k are state variables, k denotes the number of iterations. When the parameters $\alpha, \beta \in [4, 1004]$ (range width is 1000), the iterative sequence exhibits a chaotic state.

Raw chaotic sequences often lack ideal statistical uniformity and are highly susceptible to short-period degradation under finite computational precision. Therefore, a Lightweight Dynamic Neuron Model is introduced as a post-processing layer. Inspired by Recurrent Neural Networks (RNN [23]), this model uses underlying chaotic variables to dynamically modulate neuron weights and biases, employing the Swish activation function for non-linear transformation.

$$\begin{cases} W_{k+1} = u_k \times \gamma \\ B_{k+1} = v_k \times \delta \\ S_k = \text{Swish}(W_{k+1} \cdot S_{k-1} + B_{k+1}) \end{cases} \tag{3}$$

Here, we initialize γ, δ to 1. The Swish activation function is defined as:

$$\text{Swish}(x) = x \cdot \sigma(x) = \frac{x}{1 + e^{-x}} \tag{4}$$

In practical encryption scenarios, the initial states (u_1, v_1, S_0) and the control parameters (α, β) serve as the secret key. For a plaintext image X of size $M \times N$, as an encryption instance in our experiments, we set $\alpha = 4.0$, $\beta = 4.0$, and all initial states to 0.5. The detailed neuro-dynamic chaotic scrambling process proceeds as follows.

1) **Transient Elimination:** Iterate Eqs. (1) and (2) for 500 times and discard the generated values. This operation eliminates the initial transient effects of the chaotic map, ensuring that the subsequently generated sequence resides entirely within a stable and highly pseudo-random strange attractor.
2) **Chaotic Sequence Generation:** Flatten the 2D plaintext image X into a 1D pixel vector $P = \{p_1, p_2, \ldots, p_{MN}\}$. Based on the final states from Step 1, continue iterating the system for $M \times N$ times. The dynamic neuron output S_i at each step is recorded to construct a floating-point chaotic sequence $K = \{S_1, S_2, \ldots, S_{MN}\}$ equal in length to the total number of image pixels.

3) **Index-Based Permutation:** The elements of K are sorted in ascending order, yielding the reordered array K' and its corresponding original position index sequence $I = \{idx_1, idx_2, \ldots, idx_{MN}\}$, satisfying the relationship $K'_i = K_{idx_i}$. The obtained index sequence I is then utilized to rearrange the elements of the one-dimensional image vector P: the element originally located at position i is mapped to position idx_i, yielding the scrambled 1D vector P_{sc}. Finally, P_{sc} is reshaped as an $M \times N$ matrix to obtain the permuted image X_{sc}.

To investigate the dynamical characteristics and security performance of the developed system, we conducted a comprehensive analysis, as illustrated in Fig. 2 (evaluated with fixed $\beta = 4.0$).

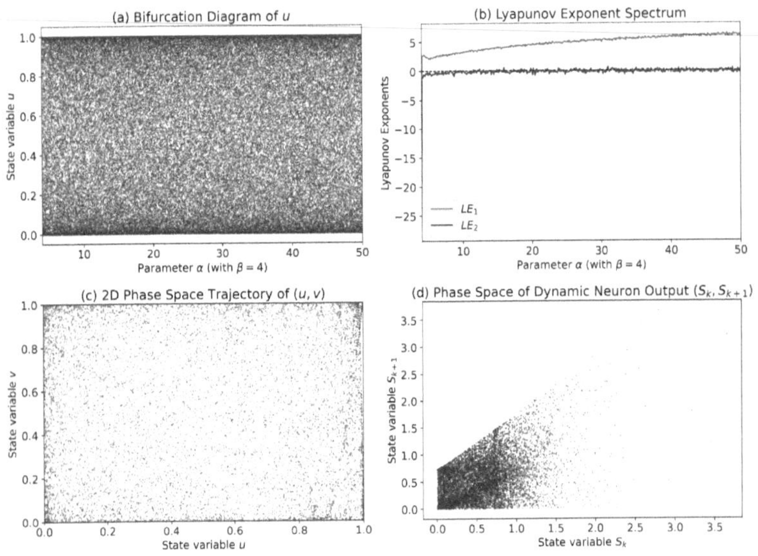

Fig. 2. Chaotic and Cryptographic Properties Analysis.

First, according to the bifurcation analysis presented in Fig. 2(a), the state variable densely and uniformly fills the entire $[0, 1]$ space across the wide parameter range $\alpha \in [4, 50]$, indicating the complete elimination of periodic windows. This robust chaotic behavior is mathematically verified by the exact Lyapunov Exponent (LE) spectrum (Fig. 2(b)), where the maximum LE (LE_1) is strictly positive and monotonically increases to guarantee extreme sensitivity to initial conditions, while $LE_2 \approx 0$ indicates typical marginal stability along the strange attractor. Furthermore, the system exhibits excellent ergodicity. As Fig. 2(c) displays, the 2D phase space trajectory of the underlying variables (u, v) uniformly covers the entire phase plane without localized clustering, which ensures high statistical uniformity for encryption.

Finally, Fig. 2(d) visualizes the phase space of the final dynamic neuron output (S_k, S_{k+1}) to demonstrate its strong resistance to Phase Space Reconstruction (PSR) attacks. Driven by chaotic modulated weights and the nonlinear Swish activation function, the continuous algebraic curves inherent in traditional chaotic maps are completely shattered into a highly complex, noise-like point cloud. This fundamentally prevents adversaries from extracting topological features, thereby enhancing the security robustness and practical applicability of the system in cryptographic scenarios.

2.2 RENet Model

However, the randomness of X_{sc} is low and vulnerable to attacks; therefore, we employ RENet to transform X_{sc} into the ciphertext representation X_{ci} exhibiting a nearly uniform statistical distribution. RENet primarily consists of Invertible Downsample (IDS), Invertible Residual Blocks (RRB), and Invertible Attention Blocks (RAB).

Invertible Downsample (IDS). We reorganize pixels within each 2×2 spatial neighborhood into the channel dimension, thereby reducing the spatial resolution from (H, W) to $(H/2, W/2)$ and increasing the feature dimension to $4C$. This process is illustrated in Fig. 3. This process loses no information and can be fully reversed through simple reshaping and permutation operations. In the actual RENet, we use IDS twice, expanding the channel count from C to $16C$, reducing computational and memory overhead without information loss.

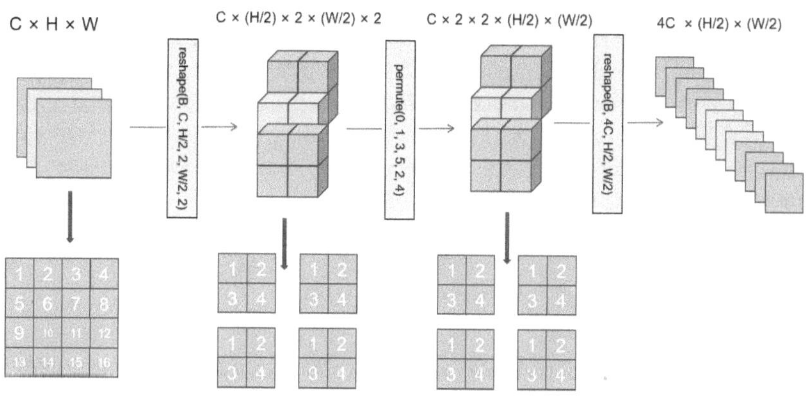

Fig. 3. Invertible downsampling process.

Invertible Residual Block (RRB). The RRB is an invertible residual module we proposed, which achieves precise inverse computation through a clever channel splitting and coupling design. As shown in Fig. 1, this module splits the input tensor x equally along the channel dimension into two parts, x_1 and x_2, and exchanges information through two non-linear transformations F.

$$\begin{aligned} y_1 &= x_1 + F(x_2) \\ y_2 &= x_2 + F(y_1) \end{aligned} \tag{5}$$

$$F = \text{INorm} \circ \text{Conv}_{3\times 3} \circ \text{LReLU} \circ \text{INorm} \circ \text{Conv}_{3\times 3} \tag{6}$$

In the encryption path, during the forward propagation coupling transformation as per formula (5), in the function F, $\text{Conv}_{3\times 3}$ represents a convolutional layer with a 3×3 kernel, INorm represents Instance Normalization, and LReLU denotes the LeakyReLU operator, where the negative coefficient is set to 0.2. In the decryption path, as shown in formula (7) above, the original input is recovered through inverse operations. The convolution kernel acts as a local mixer, diffusing information from one pixel to the surrounding 8 pixels. RRB is used twice in RENet, achieving global spatial diffusion of image information. Additionally, through additive coupling design, RRB forces information interaction between different channels of the image, achieving diffusion in the channel dimension.

$$\begin{aligned} x_2 &= y_2 - F(y_1) \\ x_1 &= y_1 - F(x_2) \end{aligned} \tag{7}$$

RRB is used twice in RENet. Through additive coupling design, RRB achieves precise invertible transformation, maintaining strong expressive capability while significantly reducing computational memory requirements.

Invertible Attention Block (RAB). The RAB a novel reversible attention module we propose, which integrates the attention mechanism with reversible computation. It successfully enhances feature representation capabilities while maintaining memory efficiency. This module achieves cross-channel information interaction via element-wise attention weighting, simultaneously preserving precise inverse computation capability.

$$\begin{aligned} y_1 &= x_1 + x_2 \odot G(x_2) \\ y_2 &= x_2 + y_1 \odot G(y_1) \end{aligned} \tag{8}$$

$$G = \sigma \circ \text{Conv3} \times 3 \circ \text{LReLU} \circ \text{INorm} \circ \text{Conv3} \times 3 \circ \text{AdaptiveAvgPool2d} \tag{9}$$

where σ indicates the Sigmoid mapping function, $\text{Conv}_{3\times 3}$ represents a 3×3 convolutional layer, INorm stands for Instance Normalization, LReLU denotes the LeakyReLU operator, where the negative coefficient is set to 0.2, and AdaptiveAvgPool2d is the adaptive average pooling layer. The output of the Sigmoid function is bounded within $(0, 1)$, providing a natural normalization for the element-wise attention weights.

$$\begin{aligned} x_2 &= y_2 - y_1 \odot G(y_1) \\ x_1 &= y_1 - x_2 \odot G(x_2) \end{aligned} \tag{10}$$

In the encryption path, during the forward propagation coupling transformation as shown in formula (8), the G function in RAB consists of Conv3 × 3, INorm, and LReLU. Here, Conv3 × 3 denotes a convolutional layer with 3 × 3 convolution kernels, INorm denotes instance normalization, and LReLU denotes the LeakyReLU operator, where the negative coefficient is set to 0.2. In the decryption path, as shown in formula (10) below, the original input is recovered through inverse operations. RAB is used twice in RENet, and the $G(x)$ in RAB acts as a dynamic mask generator. It transforms the feature attention mechanism from deep learning into a plaintext-dependent dynamic mask in cryptography, significantly enhancing the algebraic complexity and plaintext sensitivity of the encryption system through multiplicative coupling.

3 Training Loss Function

For the RENet-based encryption scheme, the model is trained using the following loss terms:

1) Histogram Uniformity Loss [6]. To force the intensity statistics of X_{ci} toward a uniform pattern and enhance statistical security. Let P be the normalized histogram of the ciphertext image X_{ci}, i.e., $P(i)$ denotes the normalized frequency associated with gray level i $(i = 0, 1, \ldots, 255)$. The target uniform distribution is U, where $U(i) = 1/256$. The histogram constraint is formulated using the KullbackLeibler divergence measuring the discrepancy of U and P:

$$L_{hist} = D_{KL}(U\|P) = \sum_{i=0}^{255} U(i) \log \frac{U(i)}{P(i)} \tag{11}$$

2) Local Correlation Loss [27]. Its core objective is to completely destroy the spatial correlation structure of the ciphertext image X_{ci}, improving encryption security. We define translation operators in three directions $\Delta \in \{(0,1), (1,0), (1,1)\}$, representing horizontal, vertical, and diagonal directions respectively. X_{ci}^{Δ} denotes the image after shifting X_{ci} by one pixel in direction Δ. The correlation loss is calculated as the average absolute correlation coefficient across the three directions:

$$L_{corr} = \sum_{\Delta \in \{(0,1),(1,0),(1,1)\}} \left| \frac{E[(X_{ci} - \mu_C)(X_{ci}^{\Delta} - \mu_{C^{\Delta}})]}{\sigma_C \sigma_{C^{\Delta}}} \right| \tag{12}$$

where $\mu_C, \mu_{C^{\Delta}}$ represent the image pixel means, $\sigma_C, \sigma_{C^{\Delta}}$ represent the image pixel standard deviations, and $E[\cdot]$ denotes the expectation operation, which is the mean of all pixels in discrete images.

3) Reconstruction Loss. The discrepancy between the reconstructed output X_{de} and the reference input X is minimized by adopting an L1-based reconstruction objective:

$$L_{recon} = \frac{1}{M \times N} \sum_{i=1}^{M} \sum_{j=1}^{N} |X(i,j) - X_{de}(i,j)| \tag{13}$$

4) Total Loss Function. By integrating these individual terms, the loss function used for model optimization can be written as follows:

$$L = L_{recon} + L_{hist} + L_{corr} \tag{14}$$

4 Experimental Results

To assess encryption capability and statistical properties of the developed method, experiments were performed on the DIV2K [1], COCO [28], and ImageNet [11] image datasets. We utilized DIV2K images for network training and used COCO and ImageNet images for testing. The experiments are implemented in PyTorch and conducted on an Intel i9-10900K CPU and an NVIDIA RTX 3090 GPU. During optimization, the model underwent a 50-epoch training procedure, where each mini-batch consisted of 16 samples. Training was performed with AdamW, using 10^{-4} as the initial learning rate and 10^{-5} as the weight decay parameter. A MultiStepLR scheduler was applied to regulate the learning rate during optimization. FP16 mixed precision and gradient clipping with a threshold of 1.0 are utilized during training.

4.1 Encryption and Decryption Results

In this subsection, experiments are conducted on four randomly selected images from DIV2K, COCO, and ImageNet, with the results illustrated in Fig. 4. The generated ciphertexts contain no apparent structural details and resemble random distributions, thereby concealing the perceptual characteristics of the protected images. Furthermore, after decryption, as shown in Fig. 4(c), the recovered images closely preserve the visual details of the original images in Fig. 4(a). During decryption, the original image cannot be recovered using only a chaotic sequence key or a chaotic sequence key that differs from the encryption key. Additionally, we quantitatively compared our results with Sang et al. [31] and ERIE [20]. The encryption performance was assessed according to information entropy [15], pixel correlation coefficients, NPCR and UACI, while decryption was evaluated using PSNR and SSIM [17]. The numerical comparisons are provided in Table 2. These experimental findings verify that the developed scheme provides effective ciphertext generation and high-fidelity image decryption with enhanced security robustness.

Table 1. Comparison of encryption performance metrics.

Method	Entropy(8)	Corr(H)	Corr(V)	Corr(D)	NPCR	UACI
Sang [23]	7.9670	−0.0280	0.0385	−0.0092	/	/
ERIE [26]	7.7558	0.0002	0.0038	0.0014	0.9961	0.3346
Ours	**7.9893**	**0.0002**	**0.0025**	**0.0003**	**0.9960**	**0.3358**

Table 2. Quantitative comparison of decryption metrics (PSNR/SSIM).

Method	DIV2K		COCO		ImageNet	
	PSNR (dB)	SSIM	PSNR (dB)	SSIM	PSNR (dB)	SSIM
ERIE[26]	51.97	0.9986	52.26	0.9986	51.86	0.9984
Ours	**56.43**	**0.9993**	**58.94**	**0.9993**	**55.34**	**0.9989**

4.2 Histogram Analysis

Histogram analysis provides insights into the distribution behavior of image intensities. For a secure encryption algorithm, the resulting cipher data should exhibit a flat and balanced pixel-value distribution, thereby reducing the risk of statistical analysis attacks. Figure 5(a), 5(c), and 5(e) present the intensity distributions of the original images and the corresponding scrambled images obtained by the chaotic permutation operation. Since pixel permutation only modifies spatial locations without altering pixel values, the histogram characteristics of plaintext and scrambled images remain unchanged. As clearly shown in

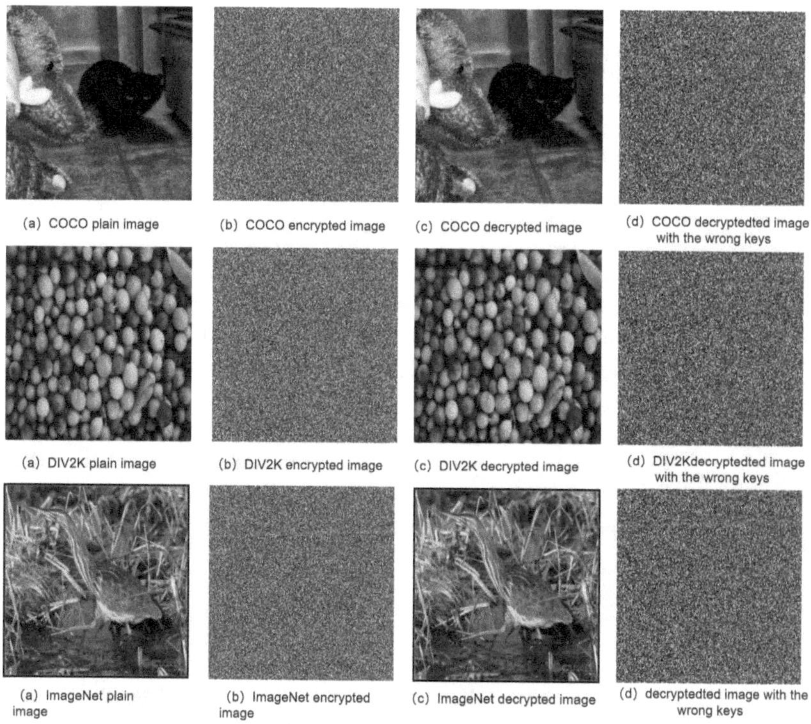

Fig. 4. Encryption and decryption results.

Fig. 5(b), 5(d), and 5(f), the ciphertext histograms present a distribution closer to uniformity compared with the corresponding original and permuted samples.

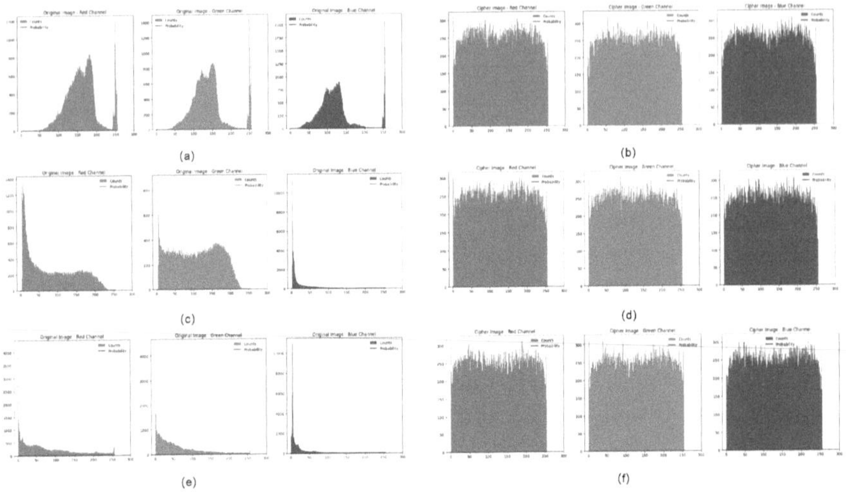

Fig. 5. Histogram distributions of original, scrambled, and ciphertext images. (a), (c), (e) Histograms of original/chaotic scrambled images. (b), (d), (f) corresponding ciphertext histograms.

4.3 Key Space Analysis

A robust cipher design relies on a sufficiently expansive key space, which increases the difficulty of unauthorized key exploration. In general, the key space denotes the number of distinct key candidates available during the encryption and decryption process. Our algorithm contains four keys: u, v, α, β. u, v are double-precision floating-point numbers in $(0, 1)$, and $\alpha, \beta \in [4, 1004]$. Considering that double-precision floating-point variables provide a resolution of approximately 10^{-15}, the resulting key space can be estimated as $10^{15} \times 10^{15} \times 10^{18} \times 10^{18} = 10^{66} \approx 2^{219}$. Therefore, the obtained key space provides adequate protection against exhaustive search attacks.

4.4 Key Sensitivity Analysis

A secure image cryptosystem is expected to respond significantly to variations in secret keys. This property reflects the fact that negligible changes in secret parameters may lead to completely different cipher results. Consequently, small variations in the key parameters may result in unsuccessful reconstruction of the source image. The influence of parameters u_k, v_k, α, β on the decryption process was investigated. Figure 6(a) presents the decrypted result obtained with the original parameter set $(u, v, \alpha, \beta) = (0.5, 0.5, 4, 4)$. Figure 6(b) and 6(c) display the decrypted images obtained with incorrect keys $(u, v, \alpha, \beta) = (0.5+10^{-5}, 0.5+10^{-5}, 4, 4)$ and $(0.5, 0.5, 4+10^{-5}, 4+10^{-5})$ respectively. As seen in Fig. 6, slight perturbations of the initial key parameters result in unsuccessful image recovery. Therefore, the proposed scheme possesses high key sensitivity, meeting encryption security requirements.

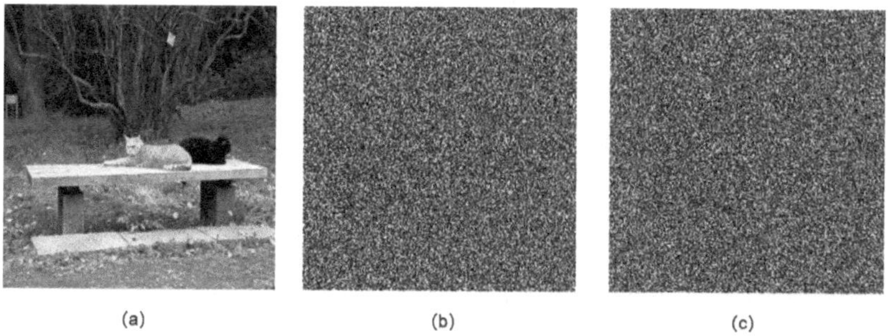

Fig. 6. Key sensitivity analysis. (a) Image decrypted using the correct key. (b) Image decrypted using the wrong key. (c) Image decrypted using the wrong key.

4.5 Information Entropy and Correlation Analysis

In this analysis, entropy is employed to evaluate the randomness of image data, while correlation coefficients are adopted to analyze the dependency among neighboring pixels. For plaintext images, information entropy is generally below 7; for an ideal random image, where every pixel probability is equal, the entropy is 8. The corresponding entropy values of ciphertext images are reported in Table 1. Plaintext images usually exhibit strong correlations among neighboring pixels, whereas ciphertext images present significantly reduced pixel dependencies. Three spatial directions, including horizontal, vertical, and diagonal orientations, are considered to evaluate neighboring pixel relationships in plaintext and encrypted images. Figure 7 illustrates the distribution of correlations among neighboring pixels. Since the distribution is similar across R, G, B channels, Fig. 7 only presents the R channel. As indicated by the results in Fig. 7(a)–(c), the pixel pairs of the unencrypted samples show obvious linear dependency, whereas for encrypted images (Fig. 7(d)–(f)), adjacent pixels are randomly scattered across the entire space. These results verify that the introduced encryption scheme successfully disrupts the inherent correlations between neighboring pixels.

The entropy measurement is defined as follows:

$$H = -\sum_{i=0}^{255} p_i \log p_i \tag{15}$$

Here, p_i represents the probability that intensity value i appears in the corresponding channel.

The corresponding correlation metric can be formulated as follows:

$$Corr = \frac{N\sum_{i=1}^{N} x_i y_i - \sum_{i=1}^{N} x_i \sum_{i=1}^{N} y_i}{\sqrt{(N\sum_{i=1}^{N} x_i^2 - (\sum_{i=1}^{N} x_i)^2)(N\sum_{i=1}^{N} y_i^2 - (\sum_{i=1}^{N} y_i)^2)}} \tag{16}$$

where x_i, y_i are values of two pixels, and N is the sequence length.

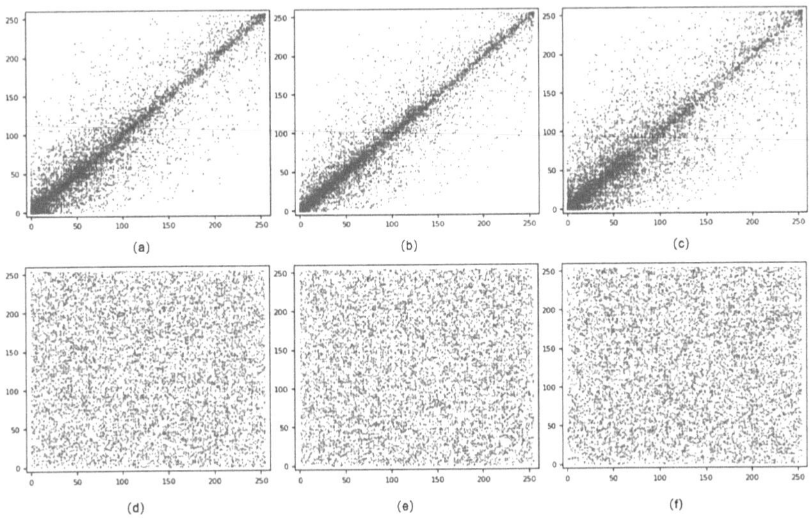

Fig. 7. Correlation characteristics of adjacent pixel pairs before and after encryption (R channel). (a)–(c) Pixel correlations in the original images along horizontal, vertical, and diagonal directions. (d)–(f) Corresponding correlations in the encrypted results.

4.6 Ablation Studies

To analyze the impact of individual modules and optimization objectives, we constructed several ablated versions of the proposed method for comparison.

Case a: Method without the scrambling module, histogram uniformity loss, and local correlation loss.
Case b: Method without the scrambling module.
Case c: Method without histogram uniformity loss and local correlation loss.
Case d: Proposed method.

The corresponding experimental results of different model configurations and loss settings are presented below. Figure 8(a) presents the source image. As observed in Fig. 8(b) and 8(c), the ciphertext images preserve noticeable structural information from the plaintext when the scrambling module is removed. Moreover, removing the histogram uniformity loss and local correlation loss causes the encrypted image to exhibit an uneven histogram distribution. Conversely, case d achieves a histogram distribution closer to uniformity, demonstrating the effectiveness of the designed loss components. The ablation study demonstrates that the permutation component and optimization objectives significantly contribute to enhancing the overall encryption capability of the proposed method.

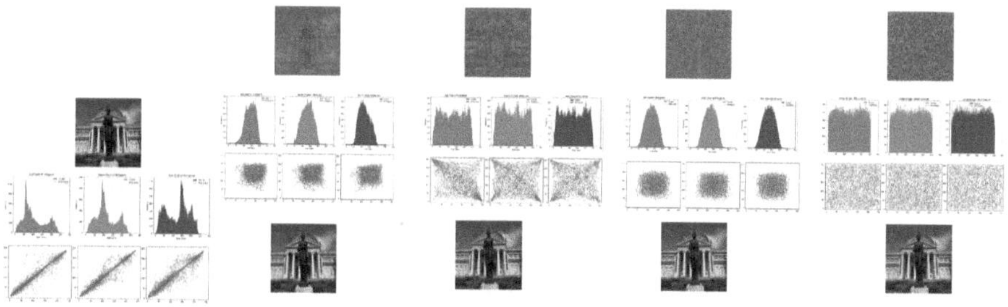

(a) (b) (c) (d) (e)

Fig. 8. Visual comparison of encryption and decryption results with different configurations of the framework and loss terms.

5 Conclusion

In this study, RENet-Crypt is introduced as a novel scheme that combines chaotic systems with Invertible Neural Networks. RENet-Crypt produces ciphertext images with desirable statistical characteristics, including high entropy and near-uniform pixel distributions, which enhance ciphertext randomness. The inherent characteristics of the Invertible Neural Network allow for nearly lossless decryption. Experimental evaluations conducted on multiple datasets verify the effectiveness of the developed encryption scheme. Furthermore, its high security and nearly lossless decryption make it an ideal solution for digital forensics and cybercrime investigations, ensuring evidence integrity and privacy-preserving workflows.

6 Generative AI Use Disclosure

In the course of manuscript preparation, Gemini 3.1 was employed exclusively for language refinement and grammatical correction. The AI tool did not participate in generating scientific content, experimental design, data analysis, or code implementation. The authors thoroughly reviewed and edited all AI-suggested modifications to ensure accuracy and scientific integrity.

References

1. Agustsson, E., Timofte, R.: NTIRE 2017 challenge on single image super-resolution: dataset and study. In: Proceedings of the IEEE Conference on Computer Vision and Pattern Recognition Workshops, pp. 126–135 (2017)
2. Alawida, M.: A novel chaos-based permutation for image encryption. J. King Saud Univ.-Comput. Inf. Sci. **35**(6), 101595 (2023)
3. Alawida, M.: Enhancing logistic chaotic map for improved cryptographic security in random number generation. J. Inf. Secur. Appl. **80**, 103685 (2024)
4. Alawida, M., Samsudin, A., Teh, J.S., Alkhawaldeh, R.S.: A new hybrid digital chaotic system with applications in image encryption. Signal Process. **160**, 45–58 (2019)
5. Arroyo, D., Rhouma, R., Alvarez, G., Li, S., Fernandez, V.: On the security of a new image encryption scheme based on chaotic map lattices. Chaos Interdisc. J. Nonlinear Sci. **18**(3), 033112 (2008)
6. Avi-Aharon, M., Arbelle, A., Raviv, T.R.: Differentiable histogram loss functions for intensity-based image-to-image translation. IEEE Trans. Pattern Anal. Mach. Intell. **45**(10), 11642–11653 (2023)
7. Brindha, M., Gounden, N.A.: A chaos based image encryption and lossless compression algorithm using hash table and Chinese remainder theorem. Appl. Soft Comput. **40**, 379–390 (2016)
8. Chai, X., Chen, Y., Broyde, L.: A novel chaos-based image encryption algorithm using DNA sequence operations. Opt. Lasers Eng. **88**, 197–213 (2017)
9. Chai, X., Fu, X., Gan, Z., Lu, Y., Chen, Y.: A color image cryptosystem based on dynamic DNA encryption and chaos. Signal Process. **155**, 44–62 (2019)
10. Chai, X., Zheng, X., Gan, Z., Han, D., Chen, Y.: An image encryption algorithm based on chaotic system and compressive sensing. Signal Process. **148**, 124–144 (2018)
11. Deng, J., Dong, W., Socher, R., Li, L.J., Li, K., Fei-Fei, L.: ImageNet: a large-scale hierarchical image database. In: 2009 IEEE Conference on Computer Vision and Pattern Recognition, pp. 248–255. IEEE (2009)
12. Ding, Y., et al.: DeepEDN: a deep-learning-based image encryption and decryption network for internet of medical things. IEEE Internet Things J. **8**(3), 1504–1518 (2020)
13. Erkan, U., Toktas, A., Lai, Q.: 2D hyperchaotic system based on Schaffer function for image encryption. Expert Syst. Appl. **213**, 119076 (2023)
14. Fang, H., Qiu, Y., Chen, K., Zhang, J., Zhang, W., Chang, E.C.: Flow-based robust watermarking with invertible noise layer for black-box distortions. In: Proceedings of the AAAI Conference on Artificial Intelligence, vol. 37, pp. 5054–5061 (2023)
15. Gabrié, M., Manoel, A., Luneau, C., Macris, N., Krzakala, F., Zdeborová, L.: Entropy and mutual information in models of deep neural networks. In: Advances in Neural Information Processing Systems, p. 31 (2018)
16. Guan, Z.H., Huang, F., Guan, W.: Chaos-based image encryption algorithm. Phys. Lett. A **346**(1–3), 153–157 (2005)
17. Hore, A., Ziou, D.: Image quality metrics: PSNR vs. SSIM. In: 2010 20th International Conference on Pattern Recognition, pp. 2366–2369. IEEE (2010)
18. Hua, Z., Jin, F., Xu, B., Huang, H.: 2D logistic-sine-coupling map for image encryption. Signal Process. **149**, 148–161 (2018)
19. Hua, Z., Yi, S., Zhou, Y.: Medical image encryption using high-speed scrambling and pixel adaptive diffusion. Signal Process. **144**, 134–144 (2018)

20. Huang, L., Qin, C., Feng, G., Luo, X., Zhang, X.: New framework of robust image encryption. ACM Trans. Multimed. Comput. Commun. Appl. **21**(3), 1–22 (2025)
21. Jacobsen, J.H., Smeulders, A., Oyallon, E.: i-RevNet: deep invertible networks. arXiv preprint arXiv:1802.07088 (2018)
22. Jing, J., Deng, X., Xu, M., Wang, J., Guan, Z.: HiNet: deep image hiding by invertible network. In: Proceedings of the IEEE/CVF International Conference on Computer Vision, pp. 4733–4742 (2021)
23. Jordan, M.I.: Serial order: a parallel distributed processing approach. In: Advances in Psychology, vol. 121, pp. 471–495. Elsevier (1997)
24. Kaur, M., Kumar, V.: A comprehensive review on image encryption techniques. Arch. Computat. Methods Eng. **27**(1), 15–43 (2020)
25. Khalil, N., Sarhan, A., Alshewimy, M.A.: An efficient color/grayscale image encryption scheme based on hybrid chaotic maps. Opt. Laser Technol. **143**, 107326 (2021)
26. Kumar, M., Chivukula, A.S., Barua, G.: Deep learning-based encryption scheme for medical images using DCGAN and virtual planet domain. Sci. Rep. **15**(1), 1211 (2025)
27. Li, X., Wu, J., Fang, H., Liao, Y., Wang, F., Qian, C.: Local correlation consistency for knowledge distillation. In: Vedaldi, A., Bischof, H., Brox, T., Frahm, J.M. (eds.) European Conference on Computer Vision, pp. 18–33. Springer, Cham (2020). https://doi.org/10.1007/978-3-030-58610-2_2
28. Lin, T.Y., et al.: Microsoft COCO: common objects in context. In: Fleet, D., Pajdla, T., Schiele, B., Tuytelaars, T. (eds.) European Conference on Computer Vision, pp. 740–755. Springer, Cham (2014). https://doi.org/10.1007/978-3-319-10602-1_48
29. Long, B., Chen, Z., Liu, T., Wu, X., He, C., Wang, L.: A novel medical image encryption scheme based on deep learning feature encoding and decoding. IEEE Access **12**, 38382–38398 (2024)
30. Naresh, V.S., Thamarai, M., Allavarpu, V.D.: Privacy-preserving deep learning in medical informatics: applications, challenges, and solutions. Artif. Intell. Rev. **56**(Suppl 1), 1199–1241 (2023)
31. Sang, Y., Sang, J., Alam, M.S.: Image encryption based on logistic chaotic systems and deep autoencoder. Pattern Recogn. Lett. **153**, 59–66 (2022)
32. Shakir, D.A.Q., Dawood, A.J.: 3D chaos graph deep learning method to encrypt and decrypt digital image. Indonesian J. Electr. Eng. Comput. Sci. **25**(2), 941–951 (2022)
33. Singh, O.P., Singh, K.N., Singh, A.K., Agrawal, A.K.: Deep learning-based image encryption techniques: fundamentals, current trends, challenges and future directions. Neurocomputing **612**, 128714 (2025)
34. Wu, Y., Zhou, Y., Bao, L.: Discrete wheel-switching chaotic system and applications. IEEE Trans. Circuits Syst. I Regul. Pap. **61**(12), 3469–3477 (2014)
35. Xian, Y., Wang, X.: Fractal sorting matrix and its application on chaotic image encryption. Inf. Sci. **547**, 1154–1169 (2021)
36. Zhang, K., Ni, J., Yang, K., Liang, X., Ren, J., Shen, X.S.: Security and privacy in smart city applications: challenges and solutions. IEEE Commun. Mag. **55**(1), 122–129 (2017)
37. Zhou, Y., Hua, Z., Pun, C.M., Chen, C.P.: Cascade chaotic system with applications. IEEE Trans. Cybern. **45**(9), 2001–2012 (2014)
38. Zhou, Y., Panetta, K., Agaian, S., Chen, C.P.: Image encryption using P-Fibonacci transform and decomposition. Opt. Commun. **285**(5), 594–608 (2012)

DDRN: Dynamic Key-Driven Deep Reversible Network for Medical Image Encryption

Fen Liu[1], Tufeng Xian[1], Yong Zhong[1(✉)], Qiyuan Sun[1], Miaoji Zheng[1], Meifang Xie[1], Haitao Huang[2], and Zhengbin Liu[3]

[1] School of Computer Science and Artificial Intelligence, Foshan University, No. 33 Guangyun Road, Foshan 528225, Guangdong, China
zhongyong@fosu.edu.cn

[2] Guangdong Chankong Big Data Technology Company, Foshan, China

[3] National Key Laboratory of Security Communication, No.6 Chuangye Road, Chengdu 610095, Sichuan, China

Abstract. To address medical image privacy protection in Internet of Medical Things (IoMT) environments, this paper proposes DDRN, an end-to-end deep learningbased medical image encryption framework with a dynamic key-driven reversible architecture. By integrating encryption and decryption within a unified reversible network, DDRN enables strong feature confusion while preserving essential structural information required for accurate image recovery. Extensive experiments demonstrate that DDRN achieves strong resistance against statistical and differential attacks while maintaining high reconstruction quality. The ciphertext achieves an information entropy of 7.9933 bits/pixel and a pixel change rate > 99.87%. The decrypted images achieve a PSNR of 37.89 dB and an SSIM of 0.9795. These results indicate that DDRN provides a highly secure and practical solution for IoMT scenarios.

Keywords: Medical image encryption · Dynamic key · Deep reversible network · Self-supervised learning

1 Introduction

Driven by the Internet of Things (IoT) and distributed storage technologies, medical imaging has become a core medium in smart healthcare systems. However, sensitive patient data faces severe privacy risks during transmission and storage across the Internet of Medical Things (IoMT) and Picture Archiving

This work was supported in part by the Guangdong Basic and Applied Basic Research Foundation under Grants 2024A1515110038 and 2024A1515110024, the Special Program for Priority Fields in Guangdong Higher Education Institutions under Grant 2025ZDZX1033, and the Natural Science Foundation of Guangdong Province under Grants 2025A1515011385 and 2024A1515010186.

© ICST Institute for Computer Sciences, Social Informatics and Telecommunications Engineering 2027
Published by Springer Nature Switzerland AG 2027. All Rights Reserved
H. Neukirchen et al. (Eds.): ICDF2C 2026, LNICST 720, pp. 228–245, 2027.
https://doi.org/10.1007/978-3-032-37274-1_14

and Communication Systems (PACS). Medical images (e.g., CT and MRI) possess distinctive characteristics, including strong adjacent pixel correlation, high redundancy, and large data volumes. Consequently, conventional cryptographic algorithms (e.g., AES, DES), originally designed for text data, lack sufficient efficiency and diffusion capabilities when applied to images.

To overcome these limitations, chaos-based encryption and data-driven deep learning approaches have been widely explored. Chaos-based methods [6,12,26] exploit the randomness and initial-condition sensitivity of chaotic systems. However, low-dimensional chaotic systems are vulnerable to phase-space reconstruction attacks, while high-dimensional ones incur prohibitive computational overhead. Recently, deep learning architectures, such as GANs [9] and autoencoders [18], have provided a promising alternative by modeling encryption as a domain translation task. Despite their potential, existing deep learning paradigms exhibit several inherent limitations. A primary concern is the degradation of reconstruction fidelity; many frameworks fail to exceed an SSIM of 0.95, rendering the recovered images unreliable for precise clinical diagnosis. Furthermore, security remains a major bottleneck due to static key mechanisms. Because encryption keys are frequently hardcoded into network parameters or generated independently of the source image [9,18], these systems are highly susceptible to known-plaintext attacks. Lastly, the widespread dependence on supervised training—which strictly requires large volumes of paired plaintext-ciphertext data—greatly restricts their cross-domain generalization and practical deployment in dynamic IoMT environments.

To address these issues, this paper proposes the Dynamic Key-Driven Deep Reversible Network (DDRN), an end-to-end, self-supervised medical image encryption scheme. DDRN derives dynamic keys using the PBKDF2-HMAC-SHA3_256 algorithm conditioned on the image fingerprint, thereby significantly enhancing resistance to statistical and known-plaintext attacks. By leveraging a reversible network structure and self-supervised learning, DDRN achieves secure and efficient transformation between the original image domain and the encrypted domain. The proposed framework eliminates the requirement for paired plaintextciphertext data during training and only requires a collection of original images, significantly reducing data preparation and labor costs. Furthermore, the secure handling of medical imagery is vital for digital forensics and cybercrime investigations. In cases of medical fraud or malpractice, there is often a tension between protecting patient privacy and maintaining evidence integrity. Unlike traditional encryption that may introduce artifacts, our DDRN framework ensures non-destructive recovery through a reversible architecture, preserving the diagnostic fidelity required for legal admissibility. By binding dynamic keys to image-specific fingerprints, DDRN establishes a verifiable audit trail, ensuring the authenticity of medical evidence throughout the forensic workflow. The main contributions of this work are summarized as follows:

1) **An end-to-end deep reversible framework.** We propose DDRN, a self-supervised unified architecture for IoMT environments that simultaneously

addresses security robustness and clinical reconstruction fidelity without relying on hand-crafted cryptographic primitives.

2) **A dynamic key injection.** We introduce a dynamic key derivation mechanism that parameterizes feature transformations using user credentials bounded with image-specific fingerprints, effectively resisting known-plaintext attacks.
3) **A Swin-fused deep reversible transformation module for information-preserving feature confusion.** A deep reversible backbone is constructed using additive coupling layers fused with Swin Transformer blocks and positional encoding. This design enables strong feature confusion while guaranteeing exact invertibility, thereby avoiding information loss and reconstruction degradation commonly observed in existing deep learningbased image encryption methods.
4) **A position-aware attention mechanism for spatial structure recovery.** A position-aware attention module is incorporated exclusively in the decryption path to selectively restore weakened spatial dependencies after encryption. Specifically, by capturing global spatial dependencies, this module effectively reconstructs the overall structural layout while simultaneously bolstering the model's robustness to random noise. This asymmetric design improves the structural recovery of decrypted images while increasing resistance against asymmetric attacks.

2 Related Works

The following introduces related work under two aspects: dynamic key generation technology and end-to-end medical image encryption.

2.1 Dynamic Key Generation Techniques

Dynamic key generation avoids the inherent risks of static keys by algorithmically producing highly complex, real-time key streams. In deep learning contexts, DeepKeyGen [8] pioneered generating image-format private keys using GANs, offering a vast key space but suffering from high computational latency. To improve efficiency, subsequent studies explored feature-driven and multi-modal approaches. For instance, DHAN [11] derives keys from DCT histogram features, while DeepENC [23] fuses biometric traits (fingerprint, iris) with hybrid chaotic maps for selective ROI encryption. Additionally, Raghuvanshi et al. [20] and Singh et al. [24] proposed hybrid frameworks combining CNNs or GANs with hyper-chaotic sequences (e.g., Logistic, Henon maps) and DNA encoding. While these methods enhance randomness, most decouple key generation from the encryption network or rely on complex external biometrics, limiting their plug-and-play deployability in seamless end-to-end pipelines.

2.2 End-to-End Medical Image Encryption

End-to-end encryption eliminates the cumulative errors of traditional modular designs by mapping plaintext directly to ciphertext via neural networks. CycleGAN-based architectures, such as DeepEDN [9], treat encryption as a target-domain translation, embedding keys dynamically in network parameters. However, their reliance on pre-defined target images and static weight configurations limits dynamic security. More recently, convolutional autoencoders combined with chaotic mapping have become the dominant paradigm [1,18,22]. Long et al. [18] and Sang et al. [22] constrained latent representations using uniform distribution loss and chaotic scrambling to ensure statistical randomness. Similarly, Ahmed et al. [1] integrated DNA encoding with deep dimension reduction for color image encryption. However, none of them evaluated the performance of the algorithms under various attack methods.

Current research still has shortcomings in the randomness and real-time performance of dynamic key generation, the balance between encryption and decryption quality, the ability to resist complex attacks. To address these limitations, our proposed DDRN leverages a deep reversible architecture to ensure mathematical invertibility, coupled with dynamic hash-bound key injection, establishing a new state-of-the-art trade-off between security and clinical usability.

3 Encryption And Decryption Network

The proposed DDRN adopts an end-to-end symmetric reversible architecture, mapping the plaintext directly to the ciphertext without cumulative errors. As illustrated in Fig. 1, the framework consists of two complementary paths. In the encryption path, a Feature Encoder extracts deep semantic representations from the input image, followed by a Key Injection module that executes a content-aware feature transformation driven by dynamic keys. Subsequently, strict cryptographic confusion is achieved via four layers of Swin-fused Deep Reversible Transformation modules (SwinPosRevBlock), and a Feature Decoder generates the final visually random ciphertext.

Conversely, the decryption path guarantees mathematical invertibility. After dynamic key verification, a Position-aware Attention module (IPEAttentionBlock) is uniquely introduced to enhance spatial dependency modeling and selectively recover structural features. The features are then processed inversely through the reversible modules and accurately reconstructed by the decoder. This unified design seamlessly balances strict cryptographic security with high-fidelity medical data usability.

3.1 Feature Encoder Module

The feature encoder is responsible for mapping the input medical image into a dense semantic feature space. Although it adopts a symmetric encoder-decoder paradigm, its design philosophy significantly differs from the traditional U-Net

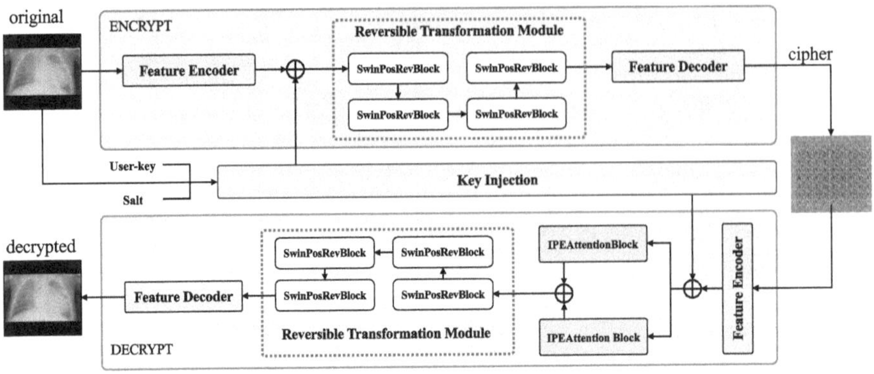

Fig. 1. The overall architecture of the proposed DDRN model.

architecture [21]. Due to rigorous cryptographic security requirements, no skip connections or feature concatenations are introduced between the encoder and decoder. This critical design choice prevents the residual leakage of plaintext statistical features, ensuring the ciphertext's robust resistance against cryptographic analysis.

As shown in Fig. 2, the encoder utilizes a five-stage hierarchical downsampling structure. The initial layer employs a 5×5 convolution to extract 32-channel shallow features while maintaining the original 256×256 spatial dimensions. The subsequent four stages perform spatial compression using 4×4 convolutions with a stride of 2, progressively doubling the channel capacity ($64 \rightarrow 128 \rightarrow 256 \rightarrow 512$). Residual blocks are strategically inserted at each stage to alleviate the vanishing gradient problem and enhance the representation of complex anatomical structures, ultimately yielding a compressed feature tensor of size $16 \times 16 \times 512$.

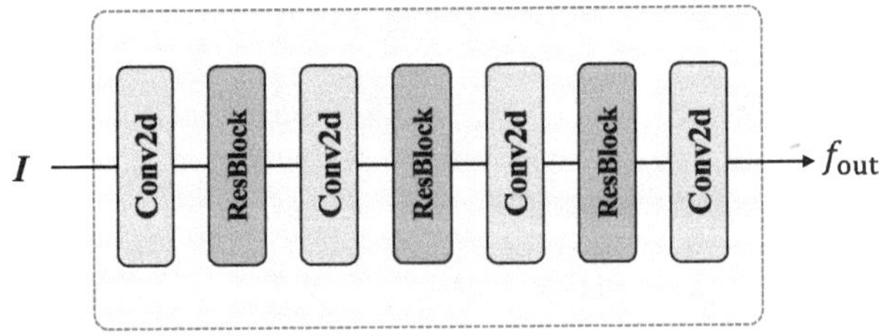

Fig. 2. Detailed structure of the Feature Encoder.

3.2 Dynamic Key Injection Module

To address the vulnerability of static weights in deep learningbased encryption, we propose a dynamic Key Injection scheme inspired by the security margins of PBKDF2 [25] and DeepKeyGen [8]. This module binds the network transformation parameters directly to both the user credentials and the input image, generating strictly dynamic keys.

Initially, a 256-bit master key (k_{master}) is derived from the user's passphrase via the PBKDF2-HMAC-SHA3-256 algorithm with 100,000 iterations. To bind the key to specific image content (resisting chosen-plaintext attacks), an image fingerprint (h_I) is computed using the SHA3-256 hash of the normalized input image I. The dynamic key κ_{dyn} is then derived securely:

$$
\begin{aligned}
k_{\text{master}} &= \text{HMAC}^{100{,}000}_{\text{SHA3-256}}(\text{passphrase}, \text{salt}), \\
h_I &= \text{SHA3-256}(\lfloor I \times 127.5 + 127.5 \rfloor), \\
\kappa_{\text{dyn}} &= \text{HMAC}_{\text{SHA3-256}}\left(k_{\text{master}}, h_I\right).
\end{aligned} \tag{1}
$$

Subsequently, κ_{dyn} is fed into a mapping function $\mathcal{M}$ (implemented via a three-layer Multilayer Perceptron with LeakyReLU and Tanh activations) to generate the transformation weights $\boldsymbol{w}$ for a 3×3 convolutional kernel:

$$
\boldsymbol{w} = \mathcal{M}(\kappa_{\text{dyn}}) : \mathbb{R}^{32} \xrightarrow{\text{LR}} \mathbb{R}^{256} \xrightarrow{\text{LR}} \mathbb{R}^{256} \xrightarrow{\tanh} \mathbb{R}^{9}. \tag{2}
$$

Finally, a depthwise group convolution applies these dynamic weights to the encoded features channel-by-channel (f_{in}), ensuring the ciphertext features (f_{out}) are strictly governed by the cryptographic key:

$$
f_{\text{out}}(c, i, j) = \sum_{m=-1}^{1} \sum_{n=-1}^{1} w_m \cdot f_{\text{in}}(c, i+m, j+n). \tag{3}
$$

3.3 Swin-Fused Deep Reversible Transformation

We construct a 4-layer bijective transformation chain (SwinPosRevBlock). As depicted in Fig. 3(a), the input features are evenly partitioned into two groups (x_1, x_2) along the channel dimension. Overall, the architecture follows the reversible design philosophy of i-RevNet [15], ensuring invertibility through structured channel splitting and coupling layers.

The core transformation function $\mathcal{F}$ comprises a PosSwinBlock and a Channel Attention mechanism. Building upon the Swin Transformer [17], we innovatively inject Positional Encoding (PED) via depthwise separable convolution into the input head to enhance position awareness:

$$
\text{PED}(z) = \mathcal{W}_{1\times1} \circ \text{SiLU} \circ \mathcal{W}^{\text{depthwise}}_{3\times3}(z). \tag{4}
$$

The strictly symmetric mathematical formulations for the forward (encryption) and inverse (decryption) transformations are defined as follows:

$$
\text{Forward:} \begin{cases} y_1 = x_1 + \mathcal{F}(x_2) \\ y_2 = x_2 + \mathcal{F}(y_1) \end{cases} \qquad \text{Inverse:} \begin{cases} x_2 = y_2 - \mathcal{F}(y_1) \\ x_1 = y_1 - \mathcal{F}(x_2) \end{cases} \tag{5}
$$

where $\mathcal{F}(\cdot)$ = PosSwinBlock(ChannelAttention($\cdot$)). This additive coupling design enables exact invertibility during inference while supporting full gradient backpropagation during training.

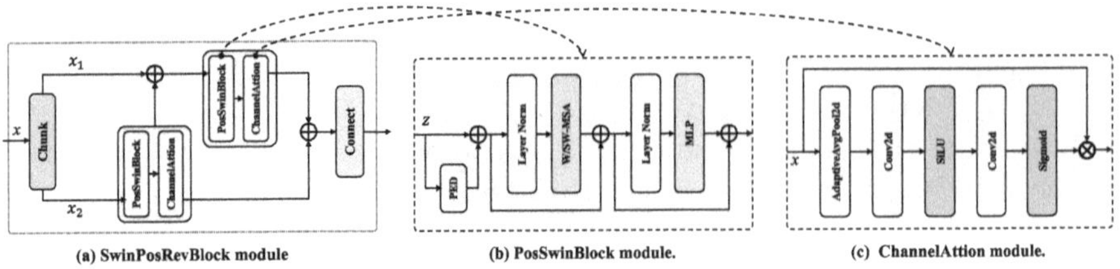

Fig. 3. Structure of the Swin-fused Deep Reversible Transformation Module.

3.4 Position-Aware Attention Module

To recover the delicate anatomical structures severely perturbed during the encryption phase, an Interactive Position-aware Enhanced Attention Block (IPEAttentionBlock) is integrated exclusively into the decryption path(as illustrated in Fig. 4). Inspired by the geometric capability of Geoformer [28], this module embeds a learnable spatial scaling factor to adaptively model global dependencies.

After projecting the input features x into Query (Q), Key (K), and Value (V) embeddings via standard 1×1 convolutions, the similarity matrix S is computed by incorporating a learnable interactive factor γ, which adaptively calibrates the attention intensity:

$$S = \mathrm{SiLU}\left(\gamma \cdot \frac{Q \cdot K^T}{\sqrt{d_k}}\right) \tag{6}$$

where d_k is the dimension of the key vector. The final feature representation is obtained by fusing the value features using softmax-normalized weights, followed by a 1×1 convolutional gate $\mathcal{W}_0$ and a residual connection:

$$\mathrm{Output} = x + \mathcal{W}_0 \left(\mathrm{Softmax}(S) \cdot V\right). \tag{7}$$

This asymmetric design mechanism explicitly restores the structural integrity and diagnostic value of the decrypted medical image.

3.5 Feature Decoder Module

The Feature Decoder employs a mirror-symmetric architecture corresponding to the encoder to achieve the reverse mapping from the latent space to the image domain, as shown in Fig. 5. Instead of mathematical redundancy, it utilizes five stages of 4×4 transposed convolutions (with a stride of 2) to progressively upsample the spatial resolution. Residual blocks are interwoven between upsampling layers to refine reconstruction details. Finally, a standard 3×3 convolution coupled with a Tanh activation function is applied to yield the normalized decoded image. This symmetrical inverse design ensures pixel-level anatomical accuracy.

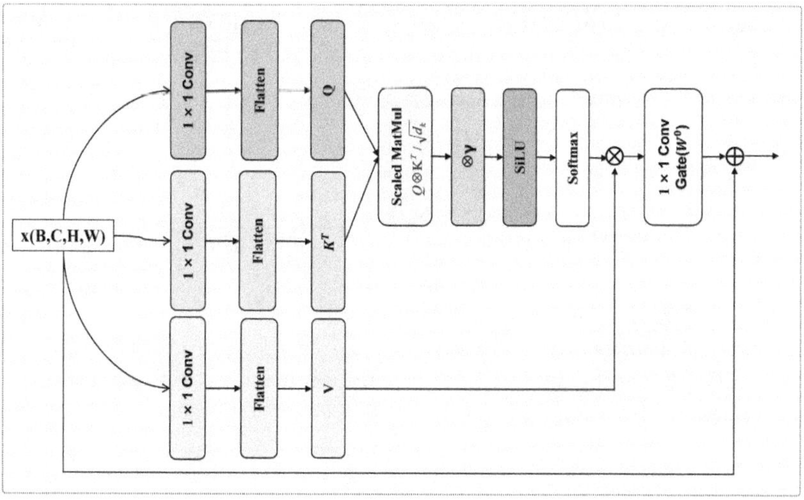

Fig. 4. Structure of the IPEAttentionBlock Module.

4 Loss Function Design and Model Training

4.1 Self-supervised Objective Functions

To simultaneously satisfy the dual constraints of cryptographic security and clinical decryption fidelity, we formulate an end-to-end self-supervised optimization framework. The total objective $\mathcal{L}_{\text{total}}$ comprises an encryption penalty $\mathcal{L}_{\text{enc}}$ (to enforce ciphertext randomness and diffusion) and a decryption penalty $\mathcal{L}_{\text{dec}}$ (to guarantee pixel-level diagnostic usability):

$$\mathcal{L}_{\text{total}} = \mathcal{L}_{\text{enc}} + \mathcal{L}_{\text{dec}}. \tag{8}$$

The loss weights are empirically calibrated to balance the magnitude of diverse constraints without requiring external paired labels. The encryption loss evaluates the statistical security of the ciphertext C:

$$\mathcal{L}_{\text{enc}} = 0.3\mathcal{L}_{\text{e}} + 0.3\mathcal{L}_{\text{h}} + 0.2\mathcal{L}_{\text{n}} + 0.2\mathcal{L}_{\text{c}}, \tag{9}$$

while the decryption loss ensures the structural integrity of the reconstructed image I':

$$\mathcal{L}_{\text{dec}} = 0.5\mathcal{L}_{\text{r}} + 0.5\mathcal{L}_{\text{s}}. \tag{10}$$

The mathematical definitions and rationales for each sub-objective are formalized as follows:

1) Information Entropy Loss ($\mathcal{L}_{\text{e}}$). To maximize ciphertext randomness and resist frequency analysis, we force the information entropy of C to approach the theoretical maximum of 8 (for 8-bit images):

$$\mathcal{L}_{\text{e}} = \left| 8 + \sum_{i=0}^{255} p_i \log_2 p_i \right|, \quad p_i = P\left(C \in \text{bin}_i\right). \tag{11}$$

2) Histogram Uniformity Loss ($\mathcal{L}_\mathrm{h}$) [2]. To defend against statistical attacks, this loss constraints the pixel intensity of C to follow a strictly uniform distribution. We employ a differentiable Gaussian kernel $\delta(x) \approx \frac{1}{\sigma\sqrt{2\pi}} e^{-\frac{(x-\mu_k)^2}{2\sigma^2}}$ to approximate the indicator function:

$$\mathcal{L}_\mathrm{h} = \left\| \frac{1}{HW} \sum_{i=1}^{H} \sum_{j=1}^{W} \delta\left(C_{i,j} - \mu_k\right) - \frac{1}{256} \right\|_2^2 \tag{12}$$

where $\sigma = 0.05$ and μ_k is the center of the k-th bin.

3) Pixel Change Rate Loss ($\mathcal{L}_\mathrm{n}$). To satisfy the cryptographic diffusion property (defending against known-plaintext attacks), this loss ensures that minute plaintext variations trigger global ciphertext divergence:

$$\mathcal{L}_\mathrm{n} = 1 - \frac{1}{HW} \sum_{i,j} \sigma_\mathrm{sig} \left(\frac{|C_{i,j} - I_{i,j}| - \tau}{T} \right) \tag{13}$$

where σ_sig is the sigmoid function, $\tau = 0.01$ is the change threshold, and $T = 0.001$ is the temperature parameter for differentiable approximation.

4) Local Correlation Loss ($\mathcal{L}_\mathrm{c}$) [16]. Medical images possess strong spatial correlations. This loss explicitly destructs the correlation coefficients of C across horizontal, vertical, and diagonal directions ($\Delta \in \{(0,1),(1,0),(1,1)\}$):

$$\mathcal{L}_\mathrm{c} = \frac{1}{3} \sum_{\Delta} \left| \frac{\mathbb{E}\left[(C - \mu_C)(C^{\Delta} - \mu_{C^{\Delta}})\right]}{\sigma_C \sigma_{C^{\Delta}}} \right|. \tag{14}$$

5) Reconstruction Loss ($\mathcal{L}_\mathrm{r}$). The L_1 norm is strictly employed over L_2 to preserve high-frequency edge information and subtle lesion details:

$$\mathcal{L}_\mathrm{r} = \frac{1}{HW} \sum_{i=1}^{H} \sum_{j=1}^{W} \left| I_{i,j} - I'_{i,j} \right|. \tag{15}$$

6) Structural Similarity Loss ($\mathcal{L}_\mathrm{s}$). To guarantee clinical diagnostic equivalence, we incorporate the SSIM index [3], which evaluates luminance, contrast, and structural fidelity holistically:

$$\mathcal{L}_\mathrm{s} = 1 - \mathrm{SSIM}(I, I'). \tag{16}$$

4.2 Model Training Scheme

The proposed DDRN was comprehensively evaluated using four diverse medical imaging datasets. To ensure a rigorous evaluation, each dataset was randomly partitioned into training (70%), validation (10%), and testing (20%) sets. Images were uniformly resized to 256×256, converted to single-channel grayscale, and normalized to $[-1, 1]$. The network was implemented in PyTorch and trained on

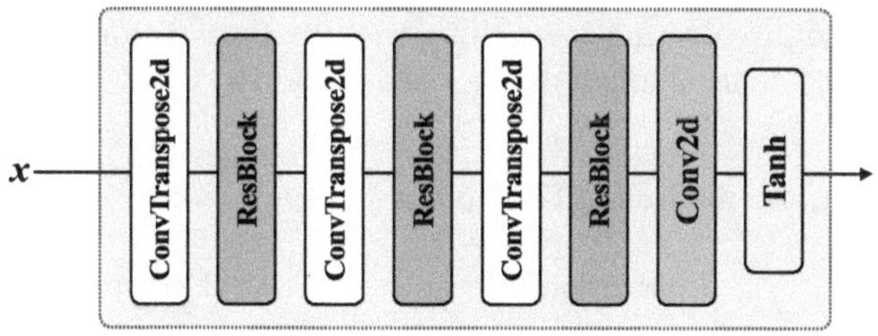

Fig. 5. Detailed structure of the Feature Decoder.

a single NVIDIA RTX 3090 GPU for 200 epochs. We optimized the parameters using the AdamW optimizer with an initial learning rate of 1×10^{-4} and a batch size of 8. During training, the batches were constructed by uniformly sampling from the mixed training pool or sampling from individual datasets per iteration. A ReduceLROnPlateau scheduler was adopted to dynamically decay the learning rate based on validation loss. To accelerate optimization and stabilize convergence, mixed-precision training (FP16) and gradient clipping were strictly applied. The model weights yielding the highest validation SSIM in each independent run were preserved, and subsequent independent test sets with unseen dynamic keys were utilized to rigorously verify cross-dataset generalization.

5 Experimental Results

5.1 Performance of Encryption and Decryption

We comprehensively evaluate the DDRN framework across four diverse medical imaging datasets: X-ray [4], HAM10000 [13], PANDA [19], and LungHist700 [10] (comprising 4000, 5000, 386, and 691 images, respectively).

Cryptographic Security. To assess ciphertext randomness and diffusion, we measure Information Entropy, Number of Pixels Change Rate (NPCR), and Correlation Coefficient (CORR). On the X-ray dataset, DDRN achieves an Information Entropy of 7.9933 bits/pixel (approaching the theoretical ideal of 8) and an NPCR of 99.87%, indicating optimal statistical randomness and extreme sensitivity to plaintext variations. Furthermore, the CORR plummets from 0.9877 (original plaintext) to 0.0007, confirming the complete destruction of anatomical textures.

Clinical Usability. To verify high-fidelity decryption, we calculate the Peak Signal-to-Noise Ratio (PSNR) and Structural Similarity Index (SSIM). DDRN achieves a PSNR of 37.89 dB and an SSIM of 0.9795 on X-ray images, significantly outperforming prevailing end-to-end architectures such as DeepEDN [9] and the framework by Long et al. [18]. As detailed in Table 1 and Table 2, this robust generalization is consistently maintained across all tested modalities.

These quantitative metrics are further corroborated by visual inspections. As shown in Fig. 6, the encrypted X-ray image manifests as unrecognizable white noise, successfully masking patient privacy. Upon decryption, critical diagnostic details (e.g., costophrenic angles and lung textures) are restored with pixel-level precision, fulfilling strict clinical diagnostic standards.

Table 1. Comparison of Encryption and Decryption Performance

Method	Encryption Metrics			Decryption Metrics	
	Entropy ↑	NPCR (%) ↑	CORR ↓	PSNR (dB) ↑	SSIM ↑
DeepEDN [9]	7.9695	94.21	0.0302	36.64	0.9130
Zhang et al. [29]	N/A	N/A	N/A	30.00	0.9306
FEDResNetSD [31]	7.9963	99.64	0.0180	31.20	0.9400
Zhou et al. [30]	N/A	N/A	N/A	32.40	0.9676
Long et al. [18]	7.9949	99.55	0.0010	30.99	0.9450
Chen et al. [7]	N/A	98.56	0.0018	34.46	0.9790
DDRN (Ours)	**7.9933**	**99.87**	**0.0007**	**37.89**	**0.9795**

Table 2. Performance of DDRN on Diverse Medical Datasets

Dataset	Encryption Metrics			Decryption Metrics	
	Entropy ↑	NPCR (%) ↑	CORR ↓	PSNR (dB) ↑	SSIM ↑
HAM10000	7.9933	98.91	0.0023	38.53	0.9798
PANDA	7.9942	99.34	0.0011	37.65	0.9711
LungHist700	7.9989	99.23	0.0008	40.43	0.9875

5.2 Computational Efficiency Analysis

Computational efficiency is crucial for real-time IoMT deployment. We benchmarked the processing throughput (Frames Per Second, FPS) of DDRN against state-of-the-art algorithms [9,14,24,30] for 256×256 and 512×512 resolutions. As depicted in Fig. 7, DDRN exhibits competitive speed at lower resolutions and achieves the fastest FPS on 512×512 images. Notably, when the spatial resolution quadruples, DDRN's throughput only halves, highlighting its significant efficiency advantage in high-resolution medical scenarios.

Furthermore, unlike block ciphers (e.g., DES, AES) that require padding, DDRN preserves the original data dimensions exactly, avoiding storage resource overhead. Tested on an Intel i7-13700K CPU without GPU acceleration, DDRN encrypts a 256×256 image in merely 0.067 s—faster than standard DES (0.205 s) and comparable to AES (0.051 s). In simulated clinical concurrency tests, processing 10 and 20 simultaneous decryption requests required less than 2 and 4 s respectively, perfectly satisfying real-time PACS access demands.

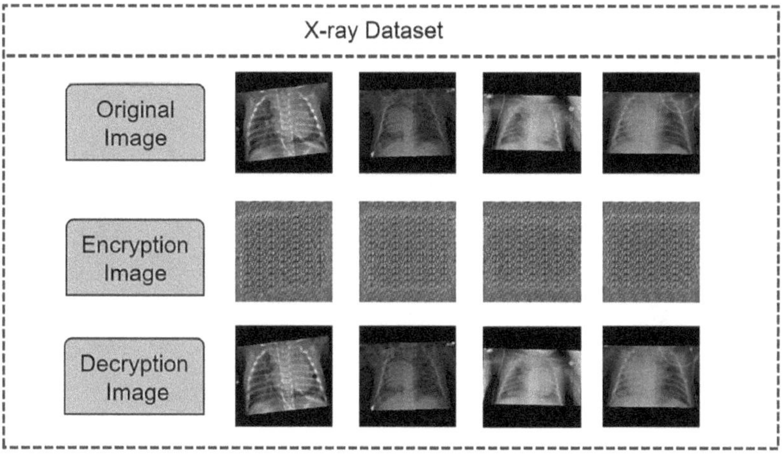

Fig. 6. Visualization of DDRN encryption and decryption on the X-ray dataset.

6 Security Analysis

6.1 Key Space and Sensitivity

DDRN employs a robust two-layer key generation mechanism comprising a static master key derived via PBKDF2-HMAC and an image-bound dynamic session key generated through HMAC-SHA3-256. Because both keys are 256 bits long, the system achieves a key space of 2^{256}, rendering exhaustive search attacks computationally infeasible. Furthermore, the key derivation mechanism exhibits profound sensitivity to initial conditions. As detailed in Table 3, introducing microscopic variations to either the plaintext or the user key yields completely divergent session keys, evidenced by an SSIM < 0.013 and an NPCR $> 99.6\%$. Finally, the Kolmogorov-Smirnov (KS) p-values consistently remain above 0.85, rigorously confirming that the generated key streams adhere to an ideal uniform distribution without predictable patterns.

Table 3. Key Randomness Test Results

Test Condition	SSIM	NPCR (%)	UACI (%)	KS p-value	Entropy
Same image, diff. user-key	0.0073	99.81	33.42	0.8562	7.976
Diff. images, same user-key	0.0128	99.72	33.28	0.9123	7.995
Same user-key, diff. salt	0.0091	99.68	33.51	0.8741	7.993

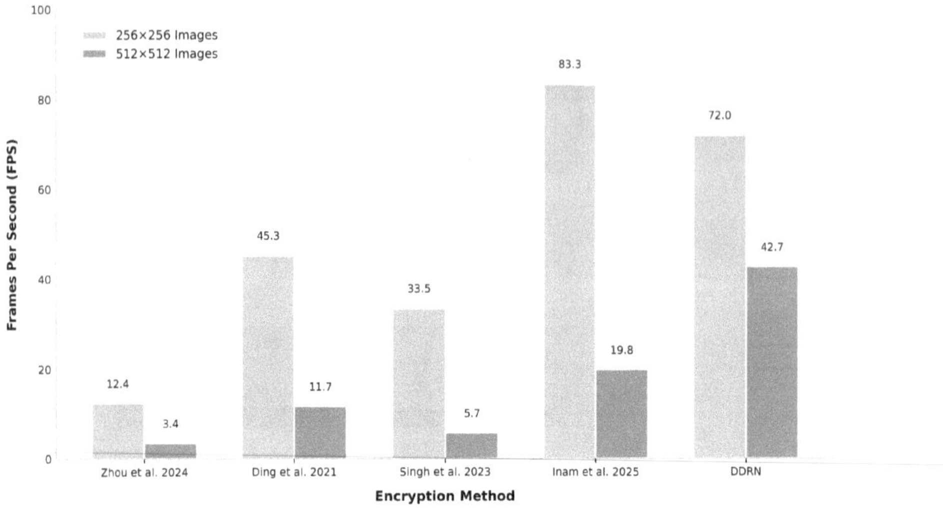

Fig. 7. Comparison of computational efficiency across different resolutions.

6.2 Cryptanalytic Resistance

Statistical and Ciphertext-Only Attacks (COA). As shown in Fig. 9, the original bimodal histogram of the X-ray image is flattened into a strict uniform distribution after encryption (88% of pixels fall within a ±10% tolerance). Additionally, the adjacent pixel correlation (Fig. 8) plummets to ≈ 0. The chi-square statistic is 14.04 (far below the critical $\chi^2_{0.05} = 293.25$), and the skewness is 0.007, definitively proving the ciphertext leaks no statistical patterns.

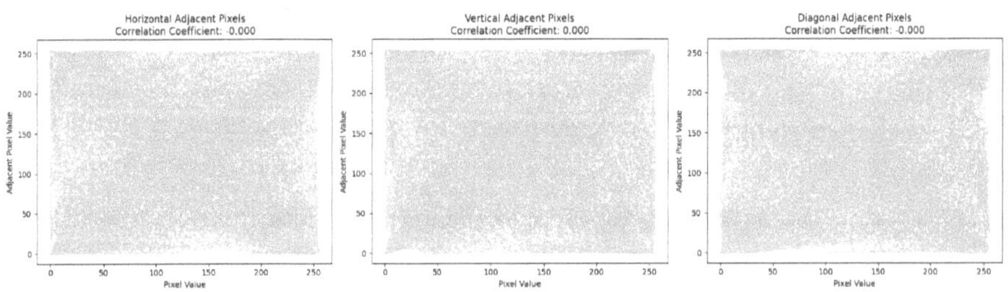

Fig. 8. Scatter plot demonstrating the complete decorrelation of adjacent pixels in the ciphertext.

Known/Chosen Plaintext Attacks (KPA/CPA). In the context of digital forensics, we assume an adversary may attempt to recover the secret key by analyzing potential pairs of original medical images and their corresponding ciphertexts. DDRN mitigates this threat by coupling the dynamic session key with the input image's unique fingerprint, effectively breaking the static

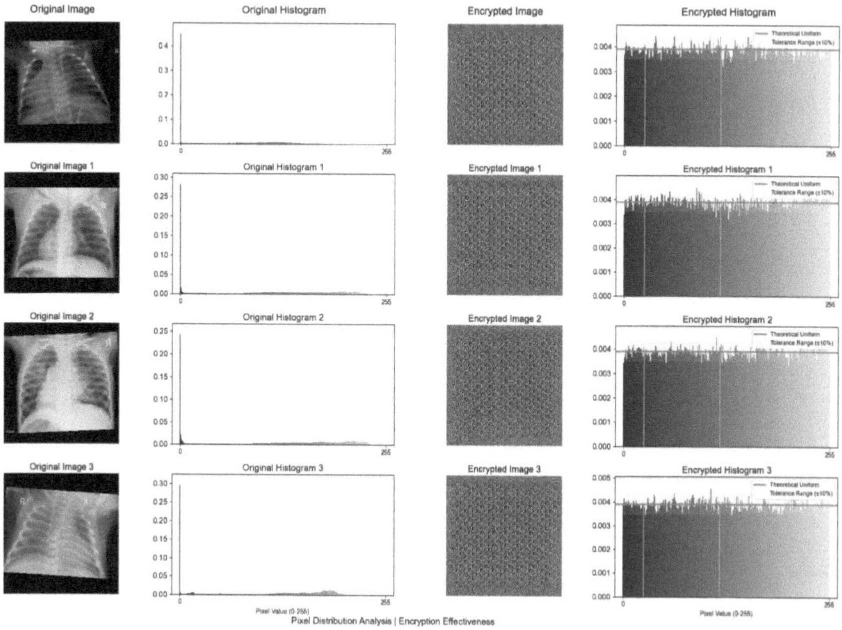

Fig. 9. Histogram distribution comparison between the original and encrypted X-ray images.

plaintext-ciphertext mapping. Our evaluation confirms that even with a single-pixel difference between two plaintexts, the encryption process yields an NPCR of 99.63% ($> 99\%$ ideal). This profound avalanche effect, combined with the image-specific key derivation, renders the system resistant to differential analysis (CPA) and ensures that the mapping remains mathematically intractable for KPA, thereby safeguarding the evidence against unauthorized reconstruction.

Model Inversion and Side-Channel Attacks. To verify resistance against intermediate feature leakage, we captured the encoder's latent tensors via forward hooks and applied t-SNE dimensionality reduction. As illustrated in Fig. 10, the high-dimensional features of 100 random samples exhibit zero semantic clustering and remain chaotically scattered in the 2D projection. Thus, even if network weights or intermediate activations are intercepted, attackers cannot reverse-engineer the anatomical structures.

7 Robustness Analysis

In IoMT environments, ciphertexts inevitably suffer from transmission interferences. An optimal medical encryption system must tolerate random noise (to preserve clinical utility) while remaining strictly sensitive to malicious modifications. To verify this trade-off, we evaluate DDRN against Salt-and-Pepper Noise (SPN, simulating bit errors), Gaussian Noise (GN, channel noise), Speckle Noise

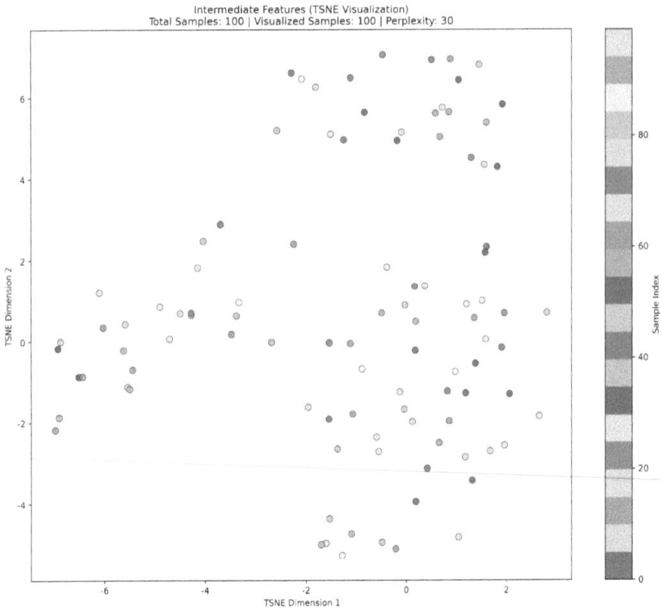

Fig. 10. t-SNE visualization of intermediate latent features, showing no semantic clustering.

(SN, equipment artifacts), and Cropping Attacks (CA, packet loss/occlusion attacks). As reported in Table 4, DDRN is benchmarked against recent state-of-the-art methods [5,7,27,32]. Although these baselines primarily belong to the visual security encryption paradigm—which traditionally boasts strong fault tolerance due to embedded data-hiding or compressive sensing mechanisms—DDRN still exhibits superior resilience without relying on carrier constraints. Under a 0.0005% noise intensity, our model achieves PSNRs of 37.43 dB (SPN), 37.10 dB (GN), and 36.55 dB (SN), outperforming the highly competitive baseline (Chen et al. [7]) by approximately 3.3 dB.

Regarding structural tampering, we simulate cropping attacks that remove contiguous ciphertext regions. Unlike random noise, such alterations may arise from packet loss or malicious tampering. As shown in Table 4, under 16×16, 32×32, and 48×48 pixel occlusions, DDRN yields PSNRs of merely 15.32 dB, 11.83 dB, and 9.60 dB, indicating catastrophic visual degradation and clinical uninterpretability. This contrasts sharply with random noise resilience and aligns with cryptographic expectations: DDRN fails to produce plausible plaintext under structural tampering. These results demonstrate a clear separation between usability under benign noise and strict sensitivity to malicious modifications.

Table 4. Robustness Comparison under Various Interferences

Interference	Intensity	PSNR (dB)				
		Zhu [32]	Wang [27]	Chai [5]	Chen [7]	**Ours**
SPN (Bit Error)	0.0001%	28.07	28.18	33.44	34.24	**37.89**
	0.0003%	28.07	28.18	33.44	34.24	**37.86**
	0.0005%	28.07	28.17	33.44	34.16	**37.43**
	0.005%	N/A	N/A	N/A	33.69	**36.54**
GN (Channel)	0.0001%	28.05	28.10	14.75	33.93	**37.89**
	0.0003%	28.00	28.02	9.35	33.87	**37.23**
	0.0005%	27.98	27.90	8.54	33.70	**37.10**
	0.005%	N/A	N/A	N/A	30.44	**36.23**
SN (Equipment)	0.0001%	28.70	28.18	33.44	33.94	**37.41**
	0.0003%	28.06	28.10	22.50	33.93	**36.69**
	0.0005%	28.06	28.09	17.30	33.92	**36.55**
	0.005%	N/A	N/A	N/A	33.07	**35.93**
CA (Cropping)	16×16	30.06	32.17	28.71	33.25	**15.32**
	32×32	28.65	30.18	27.21	31.66	**11.83**
	48×48	28.17	29.01	23.96	29.38	**9.60**

8 Conclusion

This paper proposes DDRN, an end-to-end, self-supervised medical image encryption framework designed for IoMT environments. By synergizing a dynamic, hash-bound key injection mechanism with a Swin-fused deep reversible architecture, DDRN successfully bridges the critical trade-off between strict cryptographic confusion and pixel-level diagnostic fidelity. Comprehensive evaluations across diverse modalities confirm that DDRN achieves state-of-the-art decryption quality and computational efficiency. Furthermore, the framework exhibits formidable resistance against statistical, differential, and model inversion attacks, alongside robust fault tolerance to transmission noise. DDRN provides secure encryption and forensic integrity, ensuring diagnostic evidence remains reliable throughout legal investigations. Future research will explore advanced local feature-recovery mechanisms, facilitating its widespread deployment in complex clinical networks.

9 Generative AI Use Disclosure

During the preparation of this work, the authors used Gemini 3.1 solely for language polishing and grammar refinement. No AI was used for scientific content, experimental design, data analysis, or code. All AI-suggested modifications were thoroughly reviewed by the authors to ensure accuracy and integrity.

References

1. Ahmed, F., et al.: A dna based colour image encryption scheme using a convolutional autoencoder. ACM Trans. Multimed. Comput. Commun. Appl. **19**(3s), 1–21 (2023)
2. Avi-Aharon, M., Arbelle, A., Raviv, T.R.: Differentiable histogram loss functions for intensity-based image-to-image translation. IEEE Trans. Pattern Anal. Mach. Intell. **45**(10), 11642–11653 (2023)
3. Bakurov, I., Buzzelli, M., Schettini, R., Castelli, M., Vanneschi, L.: Structural similarity index (SSIM) revisited: a data-driven approach. Expert Syst. Appl. **189**, 116087 (2022)
4. Candemir, S., et al.: Lung segmentation in chest radiographs using anatomical atlases with nonrigid registration. IEEE Trans. Med. Imaging **33**(2), 577–590 (2013)
5. Chai, X., Wu, H., Gan, Z., Zhang, Y., Chen, Y.: Hiding cipher-images generated by 2-D compressive sensing with a multi-embedding strategy. Signal Process. **171**, 107525 (2020)
6. Chai, X., Zheng, X., Gan, Z., Han, D., Chen, Y.: An image encryption algorithm based on chaotic system and compressive sensing. Signal Process. **148**, 124–144 (2018)
7. Chen, W., Ji, W., Wang, Y., Ren, J., Sheng, G., Hei, X.: Visually secure image encryption: exploring deep learning for enhanced robustness and flexibility. Expert Syst. Appl. **266**, 126027 (2025)
8. Ding, Y., Tan, F., Qin, Z., Cao, M., Choo, K.K.R., Qin, Z.: DeepKeyGen: a deep learning-based stream cipher generator for medical image encryption and decryption. IEEE Trans. Neural Netw. Learn. Syst. **33**(9), 4915–4929 (2021)
9. Ding, Y., et al.: DeepEDN: a deep-learning-based image encryption and decryption network for internet of medical things. IEEE Internet Things J. **8**(3), 1504–1518 (2020)
10. Diosdado, J., Gilabert, P., Seguí, S., Borrego, H.: Lunghist700: a dataset of histological images for deep learning in pulmonary pathology. Sci. Data **11**(1), 1088 (2024)
11. Feng, Q., et al.: Dhan: encrypted jpeg image retrieval via DCT histograms-based attention networks. Appl. Soft Comput. **133**, 109935 (2023)
12. Gao, X., Mou, J., Xiong, L., Sha, Y., Yan, H., Cao, Y.: A fast and efficient multiple images encryption based on single-channel encryption and chaotic system. Nonlinear Dyn. **108**(1), 613–636 (2022)
13. He, K., Zhang, X., Ren, S., Sun, J.: Deep residual learning for image recognition. In: Proceedings of the IEEE Conference on Computer Vision and Pattern Recognition, pp. 770–778 (2016)
14. Inam, S., Kanwal, S., Hajjej, F., Alluhaidan, A.S.: Secure breast cancer imaging: a novel advanced generative model encryption approach. Eng. Appl. Artif. Intell. **163**, 112747 (2026)
15. Jacobsen, J.H., Smeulders, A., Oyallon, E.: I-REVNET: deep invertible networks. arXiv preprint arXiv:1802.07088 (2018)
16. Li, X., Wu, J., Fang, H., Liao, Y., Wang, F., Qian, C.: Local correlation consistency for knowledge distillation. In: Vedaldi, A., Bischof, H., Brox, T., Frahm, JM. (eds.) European Conference on Computer Vision, pp. 18–33. Springer (2020). https://doi.org/10.1007/978-3-030-58610-2_2

17. Liu, Z., et al.: Swin transformer: hierarchical vision transformer using shifted windows. In: Proceedings of the IEEE/CVF International Conference on Computer Vision, pp. 10012–10022 (2021)
18. Long, B., Chen, Z., Liu, T., Wu, X., He, C., Wang, L.: A novel medical image encryption scheme based on deep learning feature encoding and decoding. IEEE Access **12**, 38382–38398 (2024)
19. Nir, G., et al.: Automatic grading of prostate cancer in digitized histopathology images: learning from multiple experts. Med. Image Anal. **50**, 167–180 (2018)
20. Raghuvanshi, K.K., Kumar, S., Kumar, S., Kumar, S.: Image encryption algorithm based on DNA encoding and CNN. Expert Syst. Appl. **252**, 124287 (2024)
21. Ronneberger, O., Fischer, P., Brox, T.: U-Net: convolutional networks for biomedical image segmentation. In: International Conference on Medical Image Computing and Computer-Assisted Intervention, pp. 234–241. Springer (2015). https://doi.org/10.1007/978-3-319-24574-4_28
22. Sang, Y., Sang, J., Alam, M.S.: Image encryption based on logistic chaotic systems and deep autoencoder. Pattern Recogn. Lett. **153**, 59–66 (2022)
23. Singh, K.N., Baranwal, N., Singh, O.P., Singh, A.K.: DeepENC: deep learning-based ROI selection for encryption of medical images through key generation with multimodal information fusion. IEEE Trans. Consum. Electron. **70**(3), 6149–6156 (2024)
24. Singh, M., Baranwal, N., Singh, K.N., Singh, A.K.: Using GAN-based encryption to secure digital images with reconstruction through customized super resolution network. IEEE Trans. Consum. Electron. **70**(1), 3977–3984 (2023)
25. Visconti, A., Mosnáček, O., Brož, M., Matyáš, V.: Examining PBKDF2 security margin–case study of LUKS. J. Inf. Secur. Appl. **46**, 296–306 (2019)
26. Wang, X., Li, Y., Jin, J.: A new one-dimensional chaotic system with applications in image encryption. Chaos, Solitons & Fractals **139**, 110102 (2020)
27. Wang, X., Liu, C., Jiang, D.: Visually meaningful image encryption scheme based on new-designed chaotic map and random scrambling diffusion strategy. Chaos, Solitons & Fractals **164**, 112625 (2022)
28. Wang, Y., Li, S., Wang, T., Shao, B., Zheng, N., Liu, T.Y.: Geometric transformer with interatomic positional encoding. Adv. Neural. Inf. Process. Syst. **36**, 55981–55994 (2023)
29. Zhang, Q., Li, J.: Single exposure phase-only optical image encryption and hiding method via deep learning. IEEE Photonics J. **14**(1), 1–8 (2022)
30. Zhou, Q., Wang, X., Jin, M., Zhang, L., Xu, B.: Optical image encryption based on two-channel detection and deep learning. Opt. Lasers Eng. **162**, 107415 (2023)
31. Zhu, L., Qu, W., Wen, X., Zhu, C.: FedresNet: a flexible image encryption and decryption scheme based on end-to-end image diffusion with dilated Resnet. Appl. Opt. **61**(31), 9124–9134 (2022)
32. Zhu, L., Jiang, D., Ni, J., Wang, X., Rong, X., Ahmad, M.: A visually secure image encryption scheme using adaptive-thresholding sparsification compression sensing model and newly-designed memristive chaotic map. Inf. Sci. **607**, 1001–1022 (2022)

AI-Assisted Steganography for Endpoint Protection in Adversarial Environments

Yi Anson Lam[1(✉)], Siu-Ming Yiu[1], and Raymond C.B. Chan[2]

[1] The University of Hong Kong, HKSAR, China
yiansonlam@connect.hku.hk, smyiu@cs.hku.hk
[2] Singapore Institute of Technology, Punggol, Singapore
raymond.chan@singaporetech.edu.sg

Abstract. Adversaries are increasingly employing artificial intelligence to enhance the sophistication and cost-effectiveness of cyberattacks targeting enterprise endpoint computers. This paper describes a technique employing an artificial-intelligence-based computer vision module involving optical character recognition and steganography as defense mechanisms to protect digital assets in enterprise endpoint systems. The technique recurses through files in system directories on corporate laptops and desktops, examining text as well as images to identify personally identifiable information, user credentials, and other sensitive information. This serves as a crucial first layer of protection against data breaches and exploits by flagging and quarantining high-risk files on endpoint computers. Next, steganography is employed to hide the existence of sensitive information in the form of innocuous random sentences or images, greatly decreasing the ability of adversaries to intercept the information from compromised endpoints. The technique holds promise because it integrates risk detection and risk mitigation to safeguard enterprise endpoint systems.

Keywords: Sensitive Information Protection · OCR · AI driven · Steganography · Risk Mitigation · Endpoint Protection · Enterprise Security

1 Introduction

Enterprise endpoint computers contain personally identifiable information, user credentials and other sensitive information that are frequently leveraged by adversaries to perpetrate insidious attacks. Sensitive information on corporate laptops and desktops is typically secured using encryption. The trouble with encryption is that it hides sensitive information but not the presence of that information. Since it is known that encrypted sensitive information exists on endpoint computers, the adversary can apply techniques to break encryption and recover the plaintext information.

© ICST Institute for Computer Sciences, Social Informatics and Telecommunications Engineering 2027
Published by Springer Nature Switzerland AG 2027. All Rights Reserved
H. Neukirchen et al. (Eds.): ICDF2C 2026, LNICST 720, pp. 246–262, 2027.
https://doi.org/10.1007/978-3-032-37274-1_15

To address this problem, we propose a technique that integrates an artificial-intelligence-based computer vision module involving optical character recognition (OCR) as a risk detection mechanism and steganography as a risk mitigation mechanism to protect digital assets in enterprise endpoint computers. The technique initiates by recursing through files in system directories, scrutinizing text as well as images to identify personally identifiable information, user credentials and other sensitive information on corporate endpoints. This crucial risk detection step identifies the sensitive information that could be leveraged by adversaries and proceeds to flag the information and containing files for protection. The risk mitigation step uses steganography to hide the existence of sensitive information in the form of innocuous random sentences or images, greatly decreasing the ability of adversaries to intercept the information from compromised endpoint systems.

2 Related Work

Research on optical character recognition (OCR) and steganography forms the foundation of our approach to enhancing endpoint data protection through intelligent document analysis and concealment.

Optical Character Recognition. OCR research has advanced from convolutional to transformer-based architectures. Shi et al. [1] introduced spatial transformer networks for robust scene-text recognition, while Baek et al. [2] proposed CRAFT for localizing arbitrarily shaped text using character-region awareness. Wang et al. [3] addressed low-resolution challenges via the TextZoom dataset and a super-resolution network (TSRN). Recent transformer models increasingly dominate document understanding: Han et al. [4] showed that Vision Transformer architectures can outperform conventional CNNs on many modern computer vision tasks, and Li et al. [5] developed TrOCR achieving state-of-the-art recognition on printed and handwritten text. Wang et al. [6] extended this direction with layout-aware OCR for structural document analysis. Madhusudhanan and Jose [7] further emphasized multi-method privacy preservation across data lifecycles, aligning with our security-oriented OCR use for PII detection and protection within endpoint workflows.

Steganography and Security. Classical work by Petitcolas et al. [8] and Fridrich [9] laid the theoretical basis for modern steganography and steganalysis. Deep learning now drives innovation: Telli et al. [10] designed a deep convolutional autoencoder-based multi-image steganography model that hides and reliably recovers several secret images within a single cover image by learning rich spatiotemporal features, and Apau et al. [11] provided a large-scale comparative study of adaptive and GAN-based approaches resilient to RS and chi-square attacks. Further, Mazurczyk and Caviglione [12] identified mobile threats and mitigation, while Zhang et al. [13] demonstrated protective network steganography for cyber-physical systems. Rahman et al. [14] surveyed evolving steganalysis tactics, reinforcing the need for adaptive concealment strategies under attack conditions.

Synergy of OCR and Steganography. Integrating OCR and steganography for endpoint defense remains underexplored. Our approach extracts sensitive text via OCR and embeds it into benign carriers, offering mitigation before an exfiltration occurs. Mishra et al. [15] explored rule-based and ML-driven PII anonymization in text workflows; our contribution extends such protection to document images and automated steganographic concealment rather than text masking. We also account for adversarial manipulation of ML models [16] and follow emerging research in detecting covert payloads within AI pipelines [17,18]. Real-world incidents like SolarWinds [19] emphasize the urgency of endpoint-aware protection.

Automation and SOAR Integration. SOAR automation enables orchestration between SIEM alerts, OCR-driven PII detection, and steganographic response. Low-code workflows such as those on the n8n platform [20] support rapid enrichment and response routing. Consistent with Kinyua and Awuah [21], our design adopts a human-on-the-loop model—automating post-alert protection while keeping analysts informed. Akbari Gurabi et al. [22] proposed a framework for machine-readable cybersecurity playbooks (BPMN, CACAO), and our workflow operationalizes these principles at the endpoint layer by encoding OCR–steganography actions as an executable playbook for automated, content-aware defense.

3 AI-Assisted Steganography Mechanism

Data exfiltration poses a significant threat to organizations as attackers increasingly employ sophisticated techniques to bypass traditional security measures protecting endpoint computers. The AI-assisted steganography mechanism is designed to prevent unauthorized data exfiltration and to protect sensitive information at rest on enterprise endpoints. Suspicious file transfers are monitored, and steganography is employed to conceal sensitive content within benign carriers so that, even if exfiltration from a compromised endpoint is successful, the sensitive information remains concealed.

Traditional security measures such as firewalls and intrusion detection systems primarily focus on preventing unauthorized access to enterprise endpoint computers. However, determined adversaries often circumvent these defenses, necessitating a more proactive and layered security approach. The strategic incorporation of steganography in the defense mechanisms not only leverages techniques commonly exploited by malicious actors but also transforms them into protective measures for endpoints. Even in ransomware-driven intrusions where attackers attempt both encryption and data theft, exfiltration can be detected and the content can be protected such that the attacker may believe the theft was successful while the sensitive plaintext remains concealed within innocuous carriers.

Figure 3 provides an overview of the AI-assisted steganography mechanism. The mechanism involves four key components:

- Triggering rules are set by the security administrator to execute the steganography mechanism or integrate it in an existing security information and event management (SIEM) system.
- Integrated optical character recognition tools are employed to scan various file types for sensitive information on endpoint computers.
- Appropriate carrier files that can discreetly conceal the sensitive information are selected.
- Robust steganographic techniques are employed to embed sensitive information to ensure it remains undetectable on enterprise endpoints (Fig. 1).

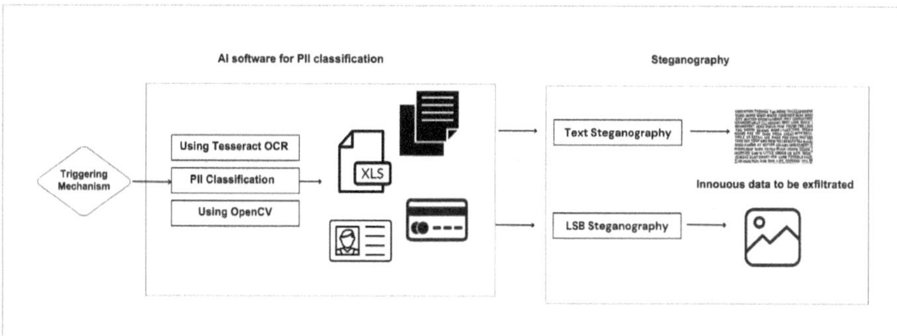

Fig. 1. Overview of the proposed AI and Steganography mechanism.

3.1 Triggering Rules

File transfers from endpoint computers are monitored continuously and triggering rules are used to raise alerts based on predefined anomaly criteria. A SIEM system could be used as an alert mechanism and a security administrator is expected to verify each alert. The window of response is an important consideration. It corresponds to the time gap between when an endpoint system or terminal is compromised and when a security administrator is notified. Even if the window is small, the opportunity for information to have been exfiltrated from the endpoint may already have occurred.

The triggering rules cover several characteristics of suspicious behavior from endpoint computers:

- **File Types**: Files commonly associated with data exfiltration from endpoints such as TXT, PDF, DOCX, XLSX and ZIP are potential targets of unauthorized access and are monitored accordingly.
- **Transfer Methods**: Transfers from enterprise endpoints leveraging unapproved cloud storage, personal email, file-sharing websites and unusual protocols constitute non-compliant behavior and should be flagged as potentially malicious.

- **Data Volume**: Transfers of unusually large files from endpoints and sudden increases in the number of files transferred are potentially signs of exfiltration and should raise alerts.
- **Recipients/Destinations**: Transfers from corporate computers to external domains, unknown email addresses and high-risk geographical regions are suspicious and should raise alerts.
- **Transfer Times**: Transfers occurring from endpoints outside normal business hours that deviate from typical user behavior should be flagged.
- **User Behavior**: Deviations from typical user file transfer patterns on endpoints indicating malicious insider activity and access to compromised accounts should raise alerts.
- **Protocol/Port Mismatch**: FTP traffic on non-standard ports from enterprise endpoints, especially SSH port 22, may constitute misuse of network protocols and should be flagged.

The rules are triggered by integrating within existing security solutions such as deep packet inspection, intrusion detection and prevention systems, endpoint detection and response systems monitoring corporate computers, and file integrity monitoring scripts. The proactive security mechanism hides sensitive information on endpoints immediately after a compromise is detected. The rapid response is essential to close the window of opportunity for an adversary. Reconnaissance and data sniffing by the adversary on compromised endpoints would not be of value because sensitive information, especially personally identifiable information, has already been embedded in innocuous content via steganography.

3.2 Automated Orchestration with N8n

To operationalize the triggering rules in an enterprise environment, we implement an event-driven automation workflow using an orchestration platform such as n8n. In this setup, security alerts emitted by the SIEM or EDR are delivered to an HTTP webhook node that acts as the entry point for the steganographic protection pipeline on endpoints. As an alternative to n8n, the same action can be implemented using SIEM-native automation (e.g., a custom script or playbook executed by the SIEM/SOAR layer) to trigger the endpoint laptop to run the protection workflow when compromise indicators or ransomware activity are detected.

The workflow first normalizes and enriches alert data (for example, endpoint identifier, file type, file name, and transfer context) and then routes events according to the file type of the suspected exfiltrated object. Separate branches handle common enterprise formats such as PDF, DOCX, XLSX and TXT, where dedicated extraction nodes are used to pull raw text content from the file. Image formats (e.g., PNG, JPEG, BMP, TIFF) are passed to an OCR branch, which applies an image preprocessing step followed by Tesseract-based recognition to obtain machine-readable text.

All textual content, whether extracted from documents or obtained via OCR, is then fed into an AI component responsible for PII detection. A language-model node, coupled with a structured output parser, identifies and returns

PII instances together with their type and position in the text. The results are forwarded to a steganographic processing node that applies text-based steganography for document content and least-significant-bit steganography for images, embedding sensitive fields into innocuous carrier files while preserving operational usability.

Finally, the workflow stores the protected artefacts in a secure storage service and notifies the security team (for example, via a collaboration platform such as Slack) that steganographic protection has been applied on a given endpoint and file. This automated orchestration closes the loop between detection and response: once a triggering rule fires, the endpoint protection logic is executed deterministically, without relying on manual intervention, thereby minimizing the exposure window for sensitive data. The proposed mechanism requires the SIEM to invoke the EDR through an API endpoint to execute the scripts on the target endpoint. Many enterprise-grade EDR platforms expose management and response APIs that can be invoked by SIEM or SOAR systems to automate endpoint actions; our design assumes such an API is available on the chosen EDR. Figure 2 shows the workflow starting from a SIEM alert, which instructs the endpoint detection and response (EDR) system to initiate the AI action, that is, the scripts wrapped as an executable on the endpoint computer. Subsequently, it extracts PII from documents and images, applying steganography to mitigate the adverse impact of exfiltration of sensitive digital assets from the corporation, and ends with a notification sent via the company's communication channel indicating that protection has been applied and specifying which data were classified as PII and redacted after exfiltration from a compromised endpoint. In our example, Slack can be used as the notification gateway, but this component is flexible and can be adapted to whichever communication medium an enterprise employs.

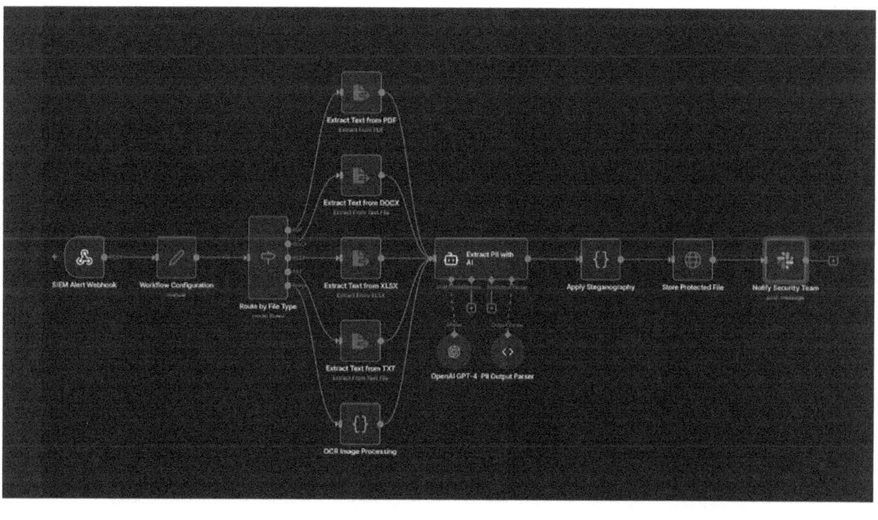

Fig. 2. Automation Workflow Orchestration with n8n tool.

4 AI-Powered Optical Character Recognition for Endpoint Protection

Integrating Tesseract OCR with OpenCV provides a comprehensive solution for extracting personally identifiable information from documents on enterprise endpoint computers. OpenCV, a popular computer vision library, can be used in conjunction with Tesseract to create a robust and efficient OCR pipeline for endpoint protection.

Once the security mechanism is triggered on an endpoint, an AI-based process identifies all the sensitive information embedded in all the documents using AI and personally identifiable information is hidden using standard steganography in the case of text content and least significant bit steganography in the case of images. Text processing employs the Tesseract open-source optical character recognition engine. Image processing leverages OpenCV, the world's largest computer vision library.

Figure 3 illustrates the AI computer vision modules and their respective defined logics in the proposed system for endpoint protection.

The following five key steps are involved:

- **Step 1: Image Preprocessing**: An image on the endpoint is transformed to grayscale following which image thresholding methods are used to enhance the text regions.
- **Step 2: Text Region Detection**: Text areas are detected in the preprocessed image using contours and dilation operations. The dilation operation clusters text blocks to facilitate more accurate detection. This step is implemented using OpenCV.
- **Step 3: Text Extraction**: Text content is extracted by cropping detected text regions from the image and processing it with Tesseract. Tesseract utilizes neural networks to recognize text with high accuracy.
- **Step 4: Sensitive Text Categorization**: The extracted text is scrutinized for personally identifiable information, password/credential-like content and other sensitive information. This step is crucial to identifying potential data leakage from endpoints.
- **Step 5: Steganography Triggering**: If suspicious non-application-level file transfer activity is detected from an endpoint, rules are triggered to hide sensitive information using steganography. The negative consequences of data exfiltration are mitigated by steganographically hiding sensitive information in the transferred files.

One of the key advantages of using OpenCV with Tesseract on endpoint computers is the ability to perform image preprocessing and text detection prior to passing the text regions to Tesseract for optical character recognition. OpenCV offers a variety of image processing functions, such as thresholding, de-skewing and contour detection, that significantly enhance optical character recognition accuracy on corporate laptops and desktops.

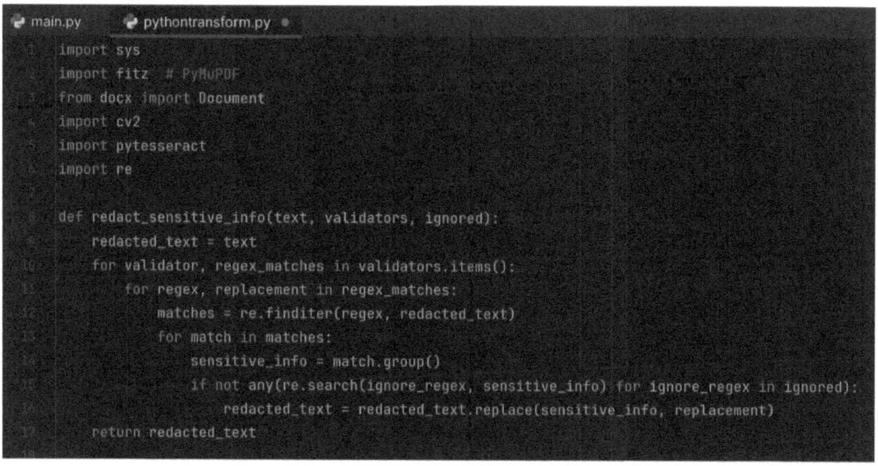

```
main.py    pythontransform.py
import sys
import fitz  # PyMuPDF
from docx import Document
import cv2
import pytesseract
import re

def redact_sensitive_info(text, validators, ignored):
    redacted_text = text
    for validator, regex_matches in validators.items():
        for regex, replacement in regex_matches:
            matches = re.finditer(regex, redacted_text)
            for match in matches:
                sensitive_info = match.group()
                if not any(re.search(ignore_regex, sensitive_info) for ignore_regex in ignored):
                    redacted_text = redacted_text.replace(sensitive_info, replacement)
    return redacted_text
```

Fig. 3. Modules and logic flow within the computer vision system.

Figure 4 shows the validators that define the data patterns associated with personally identifiable information to be selected for further processing on endpoint systems.

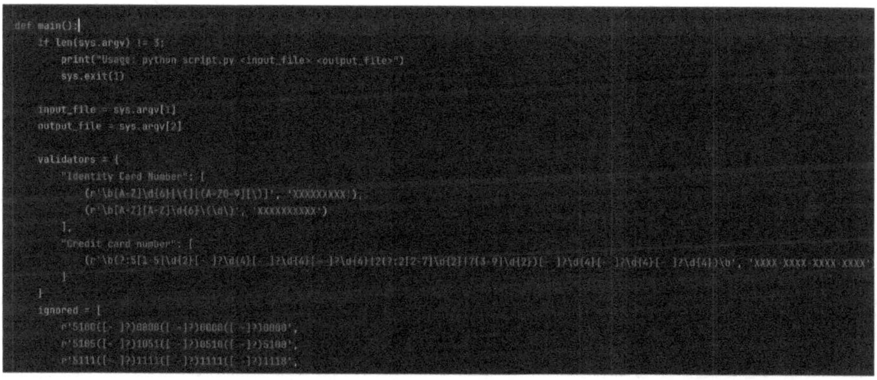

```
def main():
    if len(sys.argv) != 3:
        print("Usage: python script.py <input_file> <output_file>")
        sys.exit(1)

    input_file = sys.argv[1]
    output_file = sys.argv[2]

    validators = {
        "Identity Card Number": [
            (r'\b[A-Z]\d{6}\(][(A-Z0-9][\)]', 'XXXXXXXXX'),
            (r'\b[A-Z][A-Z]\d{6}\(\d\)', 'XXXXXXXXXX')
        ],
        "Credit card number": [
            (r'\b(?:5[1-5]\d{2}[- ]?\d{4}[- ]?\d{4}[- ]?\d{4}|2(?:2[2-7]\d{2}|7[3-9]\d{2})[- ]?\d{4}[- ]?\d{4}[- ]?\d{4})\b', 'XXXX-XXXX-XXXX-XXXX'
        ]
    }
    ignored = [
        r'5100([- ]?)0000([- ]?)0000([- ]?)0000',
        r'5105([- ]?)1051([- ]?)0510([- ]?)5100',
        r'5111([- ]?)1111([- ]?)1111([- ]?)1118',
```

Fig. 4. Validators for personally identifiable information parameters.

The validators contribute to the detection accuracy and integrity of the extracted personally identifiable information on endpoint computers. The algorithm is designed to detect and redact personally identifiable information, as well as to apply steganographic techniques to sensitive information using these validators. Steganography hides sensitive information within other information, rendering it imperceptible to adversaries who compromise endpoints.

Personally identifiable and other sensitive information are redacted by replacing them with placeholders or other representations. Figure 5 shows an example in which sensitive information is redacted based on the specified validators.

Confidential Document
Patient Information

Name: John Doe

Date of Birth: 01/01/1980

Hong Kong Identity Card Number: XXXXXXXXX
Medical Record Number: MRN123456

Insurance Information

Insurance ID: ABC123456
Policy Number: POL987654
Credit Card Number: XXXX-XXXX-XXXX-XXXX

Fig. 5. Example of identified and redacted PII within a text sample.

5 Text Steganography for Endpoint Protection

Text steganography offers distinct advantages over embedded techniques such as image or audio steganography for protecting enterprise endpoints. The advantages stem from the inherent properties of text-based data and the methods used to covertly embed information using normal text. The primary advantage of text steganography is its superior imperceptibility characteristic. Hiding information within the structure and content of regular text on endpoint computers conceals data without altering file type or format.

Text steganography is generally more reversible and less prone to detection compared with other steganographic methods. Examples of techniques include:

- **Whitespace Manipulation**: Spaces between words or sentences are used to encode information without altering the visible content.
- **Character Substitution**: Certain characters are replaced with similar-looking symbols or numbers to hide information without noticeable changes to the text.
- **Linguistic Structure**: Information is embedded within the syntax or semantics of text using sentence structures or phrases that carry additional meaning.

Figure 6 shows a text steganography example where the original text has been modified to include hidden information.

Fig. 6. Text Steganography.

These methods facilitate the restoration or extraction of hidden information on endpoint computers. An advantage of text steganography is its ability to carry large payloads. Text steganography can typically hide more data than image or audio methods that often face capacity restrictions on enterprise endpoints.

Additionally, text files are universal and ubiquitous on corporate laptops and desktops, making text steganography less detectable compared with embedding information in exotic file formats. Adversaries are less likely to suspect steganography embedded in plaintext on endpoints because it blends seamlessly with regular textual communication. Figure 7 shows Braille steganography as an alternative approach, though it is more easily detectable.

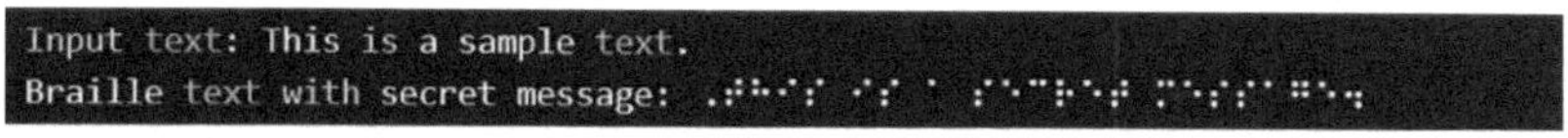

Fig. 7. Braille Steganography.

Combining encryption with steganography on endpoint computers provides multilayered protection. Steganography can conceal the presence of encrypted data on enterprise endpoints, making it less likely to be detected and targeted by adversaries. For instance, encrypted data could be hidden in innocuous image or audio files on corporate computers, significantly complicating the identification and extraction of sensitive information.

6 Image Steganography

Least significant bit (LSB) steganography leverages the ability of a digital image to covertly embed information while maintaining the visual integrity of the image on endpoint computers. The technique modifies the least significant bits of pixel values of an image to encode bits of secret information. Because only the least significant bits are altered, the image is not altered noticeably, making it difficult for an adversary who compromises an endpoint to detect the presence of hidden information.

The principal methods employed in LSB steganography include:

- **Pixel Modification**: The least significant bits of image pixel values are altered to embed hidden information. The alterations are typically imperceptible.

- **Color Channel Utilization**: Information is embedded in specific color channels (e.g., red, green or blue). The technique is flexible in that the embedding capacity and robustness can be optimized.
- **Pattern-Based Embedding**: Information is embedded based on specific patterns or at predefined locations within images on endpoints.

LSB steganography relies on a decoding algorithm that scrutinizes the modified bits in the steganographic image and reconstructs the hidden information. The main advantages of LSB steganography for endpoint protection include larger data embedding capacity compared with text steganography, and imperceptible embeddings. Additionally, LSB steganography is relatively easy to implement for various image formats on corporate computers, including BMP, PNG and JPEG.

7 Experiment

In our study, we set up the SIEM Syslog listener to receive Syslog messages from the EDR. We use Emsisoft as an example. Emsisoft EDR forwards detection events to the on-premises SIEM via Syslog, while a SIEM correlation rule triggers a local orchestration service, which in turn executes the AI-based PII redaction script on the affected endpoint.

Only high-severity EDR detection events and suspicious file-access behaviors are forwarded in CEF format to the SIEM. A SIEM correlation rule inspects these events (vendor, event type, severity, and affected file paths) and, when they match predefined conditions for sensitive data exposure, triggers a local orchestration service. This service locates the affected endpoint and executes an AI-based PII redaction script over the corresponding document set.

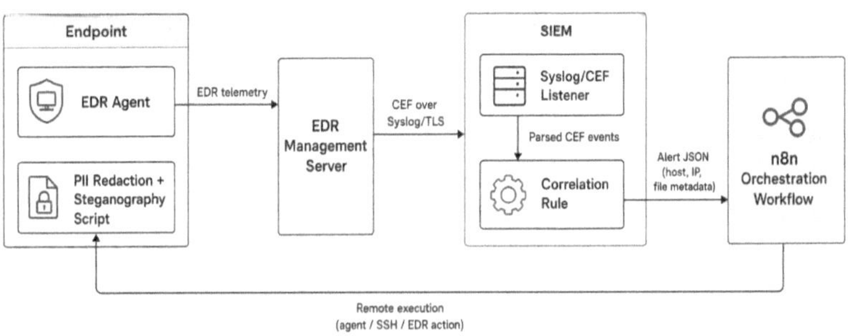

Fig. 8. Flowchart of SIEMEDR Interaction and Endpoint Script Execution.

Figure 8 shows the End-to-end orchestration workflow. The EDR agent on the endpoint continuously monitors local activity and sends detection telemetry to the EDR management server. The management server exports security-relevant events to the SIEM as CEF records transported over Syslog/TLS (CEF over Syslog/TLS). The SIEM's Syslog/CEF listener ingests these events and passes the parsed CEF fields to an internal correlation rule engine. When the correlation rule detects high-severity, document-centric behavior indicative of potential data exposure, the SIEM issues an HTTP POST to an on-premise n8n workflow (orchestration service), including the endpoint hostname, IP address, and document metadata in a JSON payload. The n8n workflow then automates the response by remotely invoking the endpoint-resident executable that wraps the Python-based PII redaction and steganography script, using the provided host and IP to connect to the correct machine over the enterprise's VPN network. This completes the chain from EDR detection through SIEM correlation to automated, endpoint-local PII protection.

Experimental Environment. The experiment tested a workflow to demonstrate the feasibility of correlating endpoint security events within a SIEM system to automatically protect sensitive documents. The setup included Emsisoft EDR, an on-premises SIEM, an orchestration service with an automation engine like n8n, and a protection component for endpoints developed as a Python script for PII redaction and steganography.

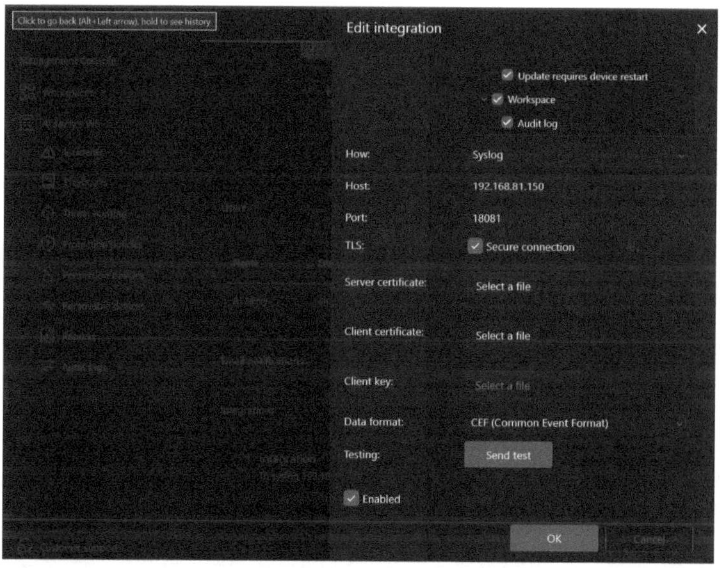

Fig. 9. EDR Configure to send CEF over Syslog using TLS.

Emsisoft was selected as it could export security events to external SIEMs. In this application, syslog was used to transport the events to and from the EDRs and the payload format was CEF (CEF over Syslog/TLS). In this example, we used the EDR management server to send the CEF-formatted events to the SIEM listener through a TLS-secured syslog connection (CEF over Syslog/TLS). Figure 9 shows the Emsisoft EDR configuration setting. The SIEM listener was set up by the syslog listener under Log Ingestion setting under data center category in which a new syslog log-ingestion service would then be set. In Emsisoft, the kinds of events were selected, the output was selected by selecting syslog, and the SIEM host and port were specified to ensure that all ingested events were converted into CEF-based endpoint security records.

Architectural Roles and Event Flow. With this design, the SIEM was both the ingestion and decision-making layer of the event process: the SIEM receives detections from the EDR, parses CEF fields, and applies correlation rules to determine whether an automated response is required. The correlation is performed entirely within the SIEM. A backend automation component, called orchestration, is connected to the SIEM via an HTTP webhook. Its task is to extract the alert context from the SIEM (i.e., hostname, source IP address, and document metadata) and remotely invoke the endpoint-side protection script on the affected endpoint in response to the EDR event.

The logic for PII redaction and steganography was at the endpoint where documents were stored. The Python script was written as a locally executable script which allows direct inspection, modification, and protection of files stored in the host file system. If suspicious behavior is detected by the EDR agent, the telemetry is sent to its management server and then exports the detections to the SIEM in CEF format using Syslog/TLS. All events had the usual CEF headers such as endpoint hostname, IP address, user information, event name, severity level, and file information (e.g. file name and type).

In the SIEM, we first developed a correlation rule that complements IP-based blocking rather than replaces it. The correlation rule did not consider the destination IP's reputation and instead looked for patterns that indicate high volumes or high-risk document activity (e.g., high-severity EDR detections for document types (PDFs or Word documents) and repeated document events from a single host in a short period of time). We were also able to determine that detections must come from Emsisoft with high severity to indicate suspicious or dangerous file behavior targeting document-type files and that triggers only occurred if multiple of these events were from one source. This approach enabled good responses even when exfiltration attempts were not successful at network boundaries and destination IPs were not categorized as malicious.

Endpoint-side Execution and Validation: Once correlation rules matched, alerts would be sent by the SIEM and structured payloads would be sent to orchestration services. These payloads would contain information about the affected endpoints like the hostname and IP addresses. They can then be sent back to a private or VPN address. The orchestration process then runs locally resident executables that wrap around the Python protection scripts using the right mechanisms such as endpoint actions or lightweight agents from remote management (SSH/WinRM).

When activated, these scripts scanned documents on endpoints for PII entities and applied protective measures locally. During redaction phases, sensitive entities found in text or image-based content were either removed or masked. During steganography phases, output was altered according to experimental designs in order to avoid leakage in the future. Because this logic worked on endpoints and not abstract log data sets, it was designed to apply to actual document collections.

The proof of concept was validated in an EDR-instrumented endpoint environment with SIEM integration by (1) confirming that Emsisoft events in CEF format were delivered to the SIEM listener via syslog, (2) verifying that CEF fields were parsed correctly and that correlation rules fired in controlled test scenarios, and (3) confirming that SIEM alerts invoked endpoint-local protection scripts through orchestration services. On execution, the redaction workflow was configured to overwrite the original files while simultaneously creating a protected backup copy stored in a designated database or cloud backup location. Overall, this demonstrated a complete end-to-end pipeline from EDR detection to SIEM correlation and orchestrated local response, which is critical in document-centric threat scenarios where destination filtering is delayed or improperly applied.

8 Advantages and Limitations

8.1 Advantages

A strong security posture combines multiple defensive layers (visibility, alerting, blocking, and data obfuscation). Integrating steganography with SIEM-driven workflows can enrich event context and enable faster, privacy-preserving responses. The advantages of the proposed solution include resilience to common threat scenarios, operational efficiency, reduced business impact, and protection of data at rest on enterprise endpoints.

Defense Against Common Threat Scenarios: In Man-In-The-Middle (MitM) and endpoint-compromise scenarios, steganography can conceal sensitive data within common carrier files, making it harder for adversaries and passive sniffers to discover or prioritize high-value content. This also helps disguise exfiltrated content sent to Command-and-Control (C2) infrastructure, increasing attacker effort and providing a deterrent effect.

Efficiency and Integration: The mechanism is designed for endpoint practicality by using trigger-only execution and focusing protection on detected PII rather than the entire dataset. It can integrate with existing SIEM solutions to automate response and provide actionable security intelligence while preserving data privacy.

Reduction of Business Impact: Automated, content-aware protection helps organizations maintain business continuity during security alerts. By applying protection locally and selectively, the approach can reduce disruption from false positives and avoid drawing attention to sensitive content.

Security and Usability: Steganography hides confidential information within innocuous carrier files or channels, reducing exposure even when files are intercepted. In many endpoint workflows, sensitive data can be protected in place without copying it to external or less trusted environments.

Sensitive Data Protected: Embedding sensitive content into benign carriers can reduce exposure for stored data on enterprise endpoints. When combined with SIEM triggers, the mechanism can narrow the time gap between detection and analyst intervention by applying immediate, automated protection.

8.2 Limitations

Vulnerability to Privileged Access: If an attacker gains administrative access, they may still view sensitive content locally. The approach primarily aims to make remote discovery and exfiltration more difficult by concealing high-value data within benign carriers.
Limited Steganographic Capacity: Payload capacity depends on carrier size and format, particularly for images. Large sensitive datasets may require multiple carriers, increasing operational complexity.
Performance Overhead: Embedding and extraction introduce computational overhead that can affect responsiveness on resource-constrained endpoints. A practical mitigation is to reserve processing capacity for security tasks or to apply protection only on high-severity triggers.
Dependence on Network Monitoring: Effectiveness depends on sufficient visibility to detect suspicious transfers and file-access patterns. Monitoring gaps can allow attackers to bypass triggers and reduce the opportunity for automated protection.

9 Conclusion

This research explores an endpoint-protection approach that combines AI-based computer vision with steganography to reduce the risk of sensitive-data exposure following endpoint compromise. The mechanism integrates a rule-based trigger with OCR-driven PII detection and steganographic concealment, operating under the premise that corporate endpoints will eventually be compromised.

By identifying personally identifiable information and embedding it within innocuous carriers, the system can mitigate the impact of data exfiltration even when perimeter controls fail. Key challenges include limited steganographic capacity, performance overhead, privileged-access scenarios, and the possibility of false negatives.

Future work will focus on (i) evaluating additional carrier formats and embedding algorithms suitable for enterprise endpoints, (ii) implementing and validating the approach in an enterprise-scale mock-up environment with more EDR-instrumented endpoints integrated with the SIEM, and (iii) extending fixed-pattern validators toward context-aware detection (e.g., via transformer-based classifiers or token-level named-entity recognition) for sensitive content that is implied rather than explicitly structured.

References

1. Shi, B., Wang, X., Lyu, P., Yao, C., Bai, X.: Robust scene text recognition with automatic rectification. In: Proceedings of the IEEE Conference on Computer Vision and Pattern Recognition, pp. 4168–4176 (2016)
2. Baek, Y., Lee, B., Han, D., Yun, S., Lee, H.: Character region awareness for text detection. In: Proceedings of the IEEE/CVF Conference on Computer Vision and Pattern Recognition, pp. 9357–9366 (2019)
3. Wang, W., et al.: Scene text image super-resolution in the wild. In: Vedaldi, A., Bischof, H., Brox, T., Frahm, J.M., (eds.) Computer Vision – ECCV 2020, pp. 650–666. Springer, Cham (2020). https://doi.org/10.1007/978-3-030-58607-2_38
4. Han, K., et al.: A survey on vision transformer. IEEE Trans. Pattern Anal. Mach. Intell. **45**(1), 87–110 (2023). https://doi.org/10.1109/TPAMI.2022.3152247
5. Li, M., et al.: TrOCR: transformer-based optical character recognition with pre-trained models. In: Proceedings of the Thirty-Seventh AAAI Conference on Artificial Intelligence (AAAI-23), pp. 4729–4737 (2023)
6. Wang, J., Hu, K., Huo, Q.: DLAFormer: an end-to-end transformer for document layout analysis. In: Proceedings of the International Conference on Document Analysis and Recognition (ICDAR 2024). arXiv:2405.11757 (2024). https://doi.org/10.48550/arXiv.2405.11757
7. Madhusudhanan, S., Jose, A.C.: Privacy preservation techniques through data lifecycle: a comprehensive literature survey. Comput. Secur. (2025)
8. Petitcolas, F., Anderson, R., Kuhn, M.: Information hiding - a survey. Proc. IEEE **87**(7), 1062–1078 (1999)
9. Fridrich, J.: Steganography in Digital Media: Principles. Cambridge University Press, Cambridge, United Kingdom, Algorithms and Applications (2010)
10. Telli, M., Othmani, M., Ltifi, H.: An Improved Multi-image Steganography Model Based on Deep Convolutional Neural Networks. In: Abraham, A., Pllana, S., Casalino, G., Ma, K., Bajaj, A. (eds.) Intelligent Systems Design and Applications, vol. 16, pp. 250–262. Springer, Cham (2023). https://doi.org/10.1007/978-3-031-35501-1_25
11. Apau, R., Asante, M., Twum, F., Ben Hayfron-Acquah, J., Peasah, K.: Image steganography techniques for resisting statistical steganalysis attacks: a systematic literature review. PLOS ONE **19**(9), e0308807 (2024)
12. Mazurczyk, W., Caviglione, L.: Steganography in modern smartphones and mitigation techniques. IEEE Commun. Surv. Tutorials **17**(1), 334–357 (2015)
13. Zhang, X., Yang, G., Ren, X.: Network steganography based security framework for cyber-physical systems. Inf. Sci. **609**, 963–983 (2022)
14. Rahman, S., et al.: A comprehensive study of digital image steganographic techniques. IEEE Access **11**, 6770–6791 (2023)
15. Mishra, K., Pagare, H., Sharma, K.: A hybrid rule-based NLP and machine learning approach for PII detection and anonymization in financial documents. Sci. Rep. **15**, 22729 (2025)
16. Macas, M., Wu, C., Fuertes, W.: Adversarial examples: a survey of attacks and defenses in deep learning-enabled cybersecurity systems. Expert Syst. Appl. **238**, 122223 (2024)
17. Crum, D.: Hidden threats in AI data: protecting against embedded steganography, Owl Cyber Defense Blog (2024)

18. Alhajeid, A.: Unlocking the secrets of steganography in cybersecurity. Blog, Wizard Cyber, London, United Kingdom (2024)
19. PDI Technologies: Steganography in cybersecurity: a growing attack vector. Blog, Alpharetta, Georgia (2025)
20. n8n, Automate SIEM alert enrichment with MITRE ATT&CK, Qdrant, and Zendesk in n8n, n8n Workflow Template Library (2025)
21. Kinyua, J., Awuah, L.: AI/ML in security orchestration, automation and response: future research directions. Intell. Autom. Soft Comput. **28**(2), 527–542 (2021)
22. Akbari Gurabi, M., et al.: Requirements for playbook-assisted cyber incident response, reporting and automation. Digit. Threats Res. Pract. **5**(3), 34, 1–11 (2024). https://doi.org/10.1145/3688810

Encrypted Traffic Analysis

DHGNN-MambaNet: Encrypted Traffic Analysis Based on Dual-Granularity Heterogeneous Graphs and Bidirectional Mamba

Xuan Yang, Zhiqiang Wang(✉), Ke Que, and Yaping Chi

Beijing Electronic Science and Technology Institute, Beijing 100070, China
wangzq@besti.edu.cn

Abstract. To address the forensic visibility challenges posed by the widespread adoption of robust encryption protocols, this paper proposes DHGNN-MambaNet, a novel encrypted traffic classification model that integrates Graph Neural Networks (GNNs) with State Space Models (SSMs). Through an innovative dual-granularity feature extraction and a bidirectional Mamba mechanism, the model enables fine-grained extraction of micro-level hidden fingerprints and macro-level temporal information. This effectively overcomes the bottlenecks in sequence feature learning inherent in traditional methods, thereby enhancing the model's attribution capability for encrypted traffic. DHGNN-MambaNet consists of four core components: dual-granularity parallel feature extraction, intra-packet spatial feature representation, inter-packet temporal aggregation, and a flow-level contrastive learning module. Extensive experiments on the ISCX-VPN benchmark dataset demonstrate that the model exhibits superior performance across key metrics, significantly outperforming baselines. Ablation studies further confirm the effectiveness of the bidirectional Mamba mechanism; its implementation yields a remarkable improvement of approximately 10% in F1-scores across various application scenarios compared to its unidirectional counterpart.

Keywords: Encrypted Traffic Classification · Traffic Fingerprinting · Digital Forensics · Graph Neural Networks · Mamba

1 Introduction

The widespread adoption of network encryption has revolutionized the modern digital landscape but simultaneously introduced the critical "Going Dark" phenomenon [2]. With protocols like TLS 1.3 and QUIC becoming ubiquitous [22], encryption effectively protects data privacy yet is increasingly weaponized by

X. Yang and Z. Wang contributed equally to this work. Supported by the Fundamental Research Funds for the Central Universities (Grant Number 3282024050).

© ICST Institute for Computer Sciences, Social Informatics and Telecommunications Engineering 2027
Published by Springer Nature Switzerland AG 2027. All Rights Reserved
H. Neukirchen et al. (Eds.): ICDF2C 2026, LNICST 720, pp. 265–281, 2027.
https://doi.org/10.1007/978-3-032-37274-1_16

cybercriminals. Recent reports indicate that nearly 70% of malware communications and Command and Control (C2) traffic are now hidden within legitimate encrypted channels [15], posing severe visibility challenges to digital forensics.

Traditional forensic systems based on Deep Packet Inspection (DPI) [3] are largely ineffective in this environment, as encrypted payloads are transformed into pseudo-random byte streams. To overcome the performance drop of DPI, the research community has shifted focus from content inspection to behavioral analysis [16]. By mining side-channel features unaffected by encryption such as packet lengths and inter-arrival times, these methods attempt to reconstruct traffic fingerprints non-intrusively.

Prior to Deep Learning (DL), most of the methods relied on rule matching and manual feature engineering. Research efforts mainly focused on classic machine learning (ML) models, such as Support Vector Machines (SVM) and Random Forests (RF). While literature [10,12] indicates that these models can achieve approximately 80% accuracy in specific scenarios by integrating port information with flow statistics (e.g., inter-arrival times and packet length distributions), reference [12] also exposes the inherent constraints of feature engineering. Traditional ML methods heavily depend on domain expertise for feature extraction, which not only constrains the efficiency, but also results in poor adaptability. In particular, when dealing with adversarial traffic, the robustness of hand-crafted features degrades significantly, failing to meet the strict requirements for real-time detection in high-speed networks.

Recently, DL has dominated encrypted traffic classification due to its end-to-end learning capabilities. Unlike traditional ML, DL models automatically extract high-dimensional abstract features from raw data. Early studies primarily used Convolutional Neural Networks (CNNs) to extract spatial features or Long Short-Term Memory (LSTM) networks for extracting temporal features. However, Shen et al. [14] exposed the limitations of these conventional DL approaches in their pioneering work on decentralized application (DApp) identification. They proposed that network traffic is not just sequence data but also contains complex topological interaction relationships. To address this, they introduced Graph Neural Networks (GNNs) to model traffic data as graph structures, demonstrating that mining non-Euclidean geometric relationships between bytes or packets significantly improves precision of traffic attribution. This discovery marks a paradigm shift in encrypted traffic classification, transitioning from sequence modeling to structured modeling.

In this paper, we propose DHGNN-MambaNet, a novel encrypted traffic classification model that integrates Graph Neural Networks with State Space Models (SSMs) to enhance forensic visibility in encrypted environments. Specifically, the model consists of four core modules: dual-granularity parallel feature extraction, intra-packet spatial feature representation, inter-packet temporal aggregation, and flow-level contrastive learning.

Our main contributions are summarized as follows:

- We propose a novel model named DHGNN-MambaNet, which employs a dual-view parallel processing architecture to construct dual-granularity heteroge-

neous graphs at both the 4-bit nibble and 8-bit byte levels, enabling the model to obtain deep representations of traffic features from both micro and macro perspectives.
- To further capture inter-packet temporal relationships, we incorporate a Bi-Mamba architecture that utilizes a bidirectional scanning mechanism to precisely model the global dependencies of traffic flows, ensuring no critical evidential context is overlooked during the session.
- We conduct extensive experiments on the widely-used ISCX-VPN dataset to validate the efficacy of DHGNN-MambaNet. The results confirm that our model achieves State-of-the-Art (SOTA) performance and exhibits superior robustness compared to existing baselines, demonstrating its potential as an efficient tool for identifying obfuscated communication channels in digital investigations.

2 Related Work

The evolution of network traffic analysis has progressed from rule-based methods to representation learning. Early port-based methods [9] and DPI techniques [3] fail against widespread encryption (e.g., TLS 1.3). While classic ML methods shifted focus to statistical features [13], they rely heavily on domain-specific manual feature engineering and lack robustness against protocol evolution. Recently, DL has become mainstream due to its powerful representation learning capabilities. Wang et al. [11] mined traffic patterns with an end-to-end 1D-CNN. Lopez-Martin et al. [19] further combined CNNs and LSTM networks to capture spatiotemporal features of traffic data. However, these methods merely treat traffic as flat 1D sequences, limiting complex attack attribution. Furthermore, recent literature [1,8] has highlighted the necessity of mining fine-grained payload representations to counter evolving obfuscation techniques; however, these methods still face challenges in combining temporal sequence modeling and spatial topological structures.

Given the significant advantages of GNNs in processing non-Euclidean data, researchers have introduced them into traffic analysis. Shen et al. [7] mapped network traffic sessions into graph structures, constructing a Traffic Interaction Graph (TIG) that accurately captures the complex bidirectional interaction topology between communication hosts. To address the widespread concurrent multi-flow patterns in mobile applications, Jiang et al. [6] proposed FG-Net, shifting the research focus from intra-flow packet interactions to macro-level inter-flow correlations. This method constructs a Flow Relationship Graph (FRG) where individual network flows serve as nodes, and edges are established based on spatiotemporal features such as concurrency timing and shared destination subnets. By learning these inter-flow correlations which remain stable under encryption, the model effectively tackles the challenges posed by concurrent traffic and the feature drift caused by application updates. To overcome the limitations of single-view approaches, Hua et al. [5] proposed the hierarchical

FTG-Net model. They designed a "Flow-to-Traffic" dual-layer graph architecture. Specifically, the bottom-layer flow graph captures micro-level temporal features of intra-flow packets and generates flow embeddings. Then, the embeddings serve as nodes for the top-layer traffic graph, realizing the modeling of macro-level topological correlations between flows. This hierarchical feature integration mechanism significantly enhances the model's capability to detect sophisticated network attacks, such as Distributed Denial of Service (DDoS).

Proposed by Gu and Dao [4] in 2023, the Mamba architecture realizes linear time sequence modeling by integrating the Selective Scan Mechanism with a hardware-aware algorithm. Traditional SSMs are typically based on Linear Time-Invariant (LTI) systems, where all dynamic parameters remain constant across time steps. Though these modules compute efficiently, they often fall short when processing discrete data. By introducing input-dependent selective parameters and a hardware-aware parallel scan algorithm, Mamba not only excels in long-sequence modeling but also simultaneously achieves high inference throughput and scalability when processing high-concurrency traffic tasks. Given its impressive sequence modeling capabilities, Mamba has been rapidly adapted to multi-modal domains. The Vision Mamba (Vim) architecture [21] employs bidirectional SSM scanning to capture the spatial context of 2D images, demonstrating superior performance over traditional CNNs in processing high-resolution images. Furthermore, reference [17] explored Mamba's application on graph data, demonstrating its potential to capture long-range dependencies within non-Euclidean structures. The success of Mamba in these domains provides a solid foundation for capturing complex temporal dependencies while ensuring real-time inference in network traffic classification.

In the field of encrypted traffic classification, Wang et al. [18] pioneered the NetMamba model. This work substitutes the conventional Transformer architecture with Mamba and designs a novel 1D strided traffic representation scheme, achieving significant improvements in both inference speed and classification accuracy. In contrast to NetMamba's approach of treating traffic as pure sequences, ET-Mamba [20] adopts a computer vision perspective. It converts packets into grayscale image patches and employs a Vim-like architecture to extract 2D features for traffic identification.

The aforementioned studies demonstrate that GNN and Mamba architectures have exhibited significant technical advantages in their respective domains, driving the efficient advancement of automated traffic analysis. On the one hand, existing research uses innovative graph structures, such as TIG and FRG, effectively compensating for the limitations of traditional sequence models in capturing traffic interaction topology. On the other hand, by using the linear computational complexity and Selective Scan Mechanism of the Mamba architecture, recent works have not only resolved the inefficiency of serial inference inherent in traditional Recurrent Neural Networks (RNNs) but also enabled the precise extraction of key protocol fingerprints from early handshake packets.

Motivated by these advancements, this paper aims to break the barriers of spatiotemporal modeling. By combining the deep topological representations of

GNNs with the sequence modeling capabilities of Mamba, we construct a novel classification architecture equipped with both spatial awareness and temporal analysis, thereby tackling the security challenges posed by the increasingly complex encrypted network environment.

3 Methodology

3.1 Architecture

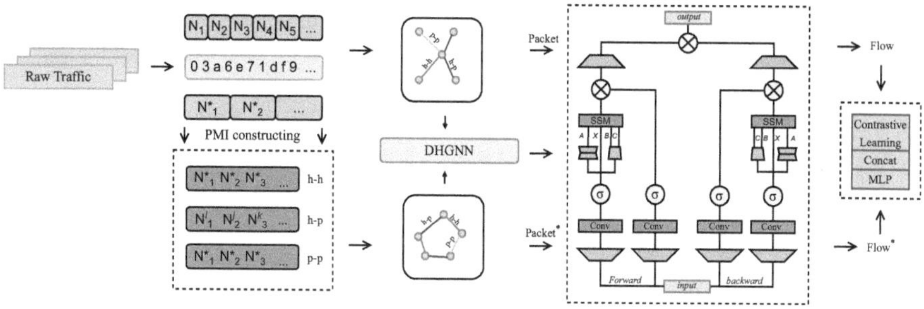

Fig. 1. The overall architecture of the proposed DHGNN-MambaNet.

The proposed DHGNN-MambaNet consists of four core components, as illustrated in Fig. 1. As an efficient end-to-end framework for encrypted traffic analysis, its core design aims to break the barriers of spatiotemporal modeling by deeply integrating micro-level feature mining with macro-level sequence modeling.

At the input stage, to overcome the limitations of traditional single-view byte stream analysis, we propose a novel dual-granularity parallel feature extraction mechanism. This mechanism uses 8-bit and 4-bit parallel windows to perform fine-grained analysis of raw network traffic. These multi-dimensional statistical windows effectively extract side-channel information across different granularities. By preserving the macro-level statistical distribution of payloads while capturing micro-level protocol header fingerprints, this mechanism establishes a solid foundation for subsequent feature learning.

Subsequently, the intra-packet spatial feature representation module defines traffic bit units as graph nodes and maps the three interaction relationships between traffic headers and payloads as edge types. Based on Pointwise Mutual Information (PMI), it constructs a heterogeneous topology graph reflecting the micro-level structure of traffic bits and uses an improved GraphSAGE algorithm for deep message passing. This graph construction process realizes a semantic transition from low-dimensional linear sequences to high-dimensional graph embeddings. It not only effectively preserves key statistical features within packets but also significantly enhances the representation capability of non-Euclidean spatial correlations between nodes, thereby precisely characterizing the complex mapping relationships between encrypted payloads and plaintext headers.

To address the challenge of capturing sequence features in encrypted traffic analysis, the architecture introduces an inter-packet temporal aggregation mechanism based on bidirectional Mamba. This module uses the linear computational advantage of SSMs to perform global modeling on the packet-level feature sequences output by the DHGNN via forward and backward Mamba scanning modules. This innovative design enables the processing of traffic session sequences while significantly reducing computational overhead. It ensures that the model captures both early handshake information and subsequent response patterns, thereby effectively overcoming the limitations of context preservation in traditional LSTM architectures.

At the final stage of the architecture, we construct a contrastive learning module for flow-level classification. This module concatenates the features from the dual-path processing and feeds them into a fully connected layer, while integrating a self-supervised contrastive learning branch based on random packet dropping. By pulling augmented views of the same flow together and pushing views of different flows apart in the feature space, this branch drives the model to focus on intrinsic features that remain invariant under network jitter and packet loss. This design not only improves classification accuracy but also significantly enhances the robustness and generalization of the model in real-world network environments.

3.2 Dual-Granularity Parallel Feature Extraction

In the task of encrypted traffic classification, the granularity of feature extraction directly determines the upper bound of the model's perception capability. Most existing DL methods adhere to computer storage standards, processing network traffic as 8-bit byte sequences consisting of decimal integers from 0 to 255. Although satisfying standard computer storage formats, this approach exposes inherent limitations when processing modern, complex encrypted protocols. In many protocols, the packet structure does not strictly conform to 8-bit boundaries. For instance, in the TLS Client Hello message, the high-order nibble (e.g., 0xC) of Cipher Suites typically indicates a specific family of key exchange algorithms, while the low-order nibble distinguishes specific encryption parameters. Similarly, the high-order 4 bits of the initial byte in the QUIC protocol strictly define the Header Form Bit and Fixed Bit, while the low-order 4 bits encode the packet type and packet number length. Relying solely on an 8-bit perspective would lead to the oversight of hidden information within these critical sub-byte structures.

Based on these observations, this paper proposes a dual-granularity parallel feature extraction mechanism. By constructing complementary 8-bit and 4-bit byte views, it achieves macro-level statistical analysis and micro-level feature mining. Specifically, the model processes raw traffic sequences through two parallel paths. At the macro level, the 8-bit view maintains the raw traffic sequence format, using 8-bit binary numbers as the basic nodes for graph construction.

Subsequently, it uses a sliding window to calculate byte co-occurrence frequency and compute PMI, thereby quantifying the macro-level correlations between bytes. Since encrypted payloads typically exhibit a high-entropy pseudo-random distribution, the 8-bit view effectively extracts statistical features such as byte frequency and entropy variations. This plays a foundational role in distinguishing application types with statistical patterns, such as large file downloads and streaming media transmission. At the micro level, the 4-bit view splits each original 8-bit node into two independent units: the high-order and low-order 4 bits, doubling the number of basic units. This perspective focuses on mining micro-level protocol fingerprints. Flag bits and control fields originally intermingled within the same byte are independently exposed, and subtle patterns implicit in encrypted packets are more easily observed.

3.3 Intra-packet Spatial Feature Representation

Following the dual-granularity feature extraction of raw traffic, the core challenge of the subsequent stage is to aggregate discrete feature primitives into packet-level features rich in semantic information. In fact, a network packet is a non-Euclidean topology composed of header and payload fields. Within this topology, tight control logic exists between the plaintext header and the encrypted payload, while specific encryption pattern correlations are hidden within the payload fields. In response to this characteristic, this paper designs an Intra-packet Spatial Feature Representation Module. This module aims to reconstruct this micro-topology using an improved GraphSAGE algorithm, achieving a paradigm shift from discrete bits to structured semantics.

Specifically, the model quantifies statistical dependencies between traffic units based on the previously calculated PMI results, and constructs dual-path heterogeneous graphs under both 8-bit and 4-bit views. In these graphs, nodes correspond to basic traffic units, while edge establishment strictly follows the principle of statistical significance—topological connections are established only when the PMI value between traffic units surpasses a predefined threshold. To precisely characterize the complex semantic interactions between headers and payloads, we classify edges into three heterogeneous types: h-h edges (header-header) connecting protocol control fields to capture protocol logic; p-p edges (payload-payload) connecting encrypted data payloads to mine pattern repetitions; and h-p edges (header-payload) connecting control information with content to establish deep mapping relationships between control fields and payload data.

3.4 Inter-packet Temporal Aggregation

Network traffic is inherently a combination of spatiotemporal data. Following the refined representation of intra-packet micro-spatial features, the critical task transitions to aggregating macro-level inter-packet sequential features from traffic interaction relationships. Traditional solutions typically rely on RNN architectures such as LSTM or GRU; however, their inherent serial computational nature constrains training efficiency and real-time inference capabilities. To address this limitation, this paper introduces the Mamba architecture based on SSMs. By using its hardware-aware parallel algorithms and linear computational complexity, the model achieves efficient inter-packet temporal aggregation.

Moreover, network traffic interaction is a bidirectional information exchange process, where each packet exhibits contextual dependency. This means that the semantics of the current packet are not only influenced by preceding packets but also require validation from succeeding packets; thus, relying solely on unidirectional modeling results in an information extraction limitation. In light of this, we design two independent SSM branches: the Forward SSM and the Backward SSM. The Forward SSM branch scans the sequence in chronological order. By using the core selective scan mechanism of Mamba, it dynamically adjusts state parameters based on the content of the current packet. This branch effectively bypasses redundant noise such as payload-free ACKs while significantly increasing the memory weight of key frames like handshake packets. This processing strategy simulates the real-time data processing flow of the interaction process, precisely captures traffic initialization behaviors and accumulates historical states. In contrast, the Backward SSM branch scans the sequence in reverse chronological order. This branch uses future information to complement the context; for instance, by backtracking the features of FIN packets during connection termination, it infers the duration and transmission intent of the entire session and generates backward state features. Finally, the bidirectional feature sequences are deeply fused via a linear gating unit.

3.5 Flow-Level Contrastive Learning for Classification

The final stage of the framework aims to output precise traffic classification results. However, real-world network environments are characterized by phenomena such as packet loss, out-of-order delivery, and retransmission. Although the preceding stages have acquired high-quality flow-level features, directly applying supervised classification faces the dual challenges of label scarcity and environmental noise. Given that the intrinsic semantics of traffic remain invariant even under partial packet loss, this paper introduces a contrastive learning auxiliary task based on random packet dropping into the flow-level classification task.

Specifically, for each original flow sample in the training batch, the model generates an augmented view by randomly dropping a portion of packets in the sequence with a specific probability. Unlike traditional self-supervised contrastive learning which solely regards same-source augmented views as positive samples, this paper uses label information to guide the calculation of the supervised contrastive loss. Consequently, traffic samples belonging to the same class are considered mutually positive pairs, while samples from different classes serve as negative pairs. Subsequently, both the original and augmented views are fed into a projection layer. By optimizing the Supervised Contrastive Loss (SupCon Loss) function, the model aims to minimize the distance between intra-class samples while maximizing the distance between inter-class samples within the feature space. By separately optimizing the loss functions of the dual branches, the model enforces that sequences derived from both 8-bit and 4-bit views can independently extract robust representations against packet loss interference.

4 Experimental Setup

4.1 Datasets

In this paper, we adopt the ISCX-VPN benchmark dataset as the validation platform. This dataset constructs obfuscated communication scenarios based on VPN tunneling technologies, effectively simulating real-world anti-forensic evasion. By wrapping original IP packets and encrypting payloads, it masks port features while simultaneously altering temporal statistical patterns. In terms of traffic composition, the dataset focuses on fine-grained fingerprinting of application-layer behaviors, covering six typical service categories: web browsing, email, voice chat, streaming media, file transfer, and P2P transmission. Each category is further divided into specific application instances (e.g., Skype and Hangouts), requiring the model to possess robust attribution capabilities across diverse scenarios. Furthermore, the dataset offers high-quality flow-based labels, such as traffic category and protocol type, laying a solid foundation for refined supervised training.

4.2 Data Preprocessing

During preprocessing, we employed the SplitCap tool to segment raw PCAP files into discrete bidirectional flows based on five-tuple information. To remove irrelevant noise, we filtered out payload-free packets and long flows exceeding 10,000 packets. Subsequently, we removed link-layer and network-layer identifiers (e.g., MAC and IP addresses) to prevent the model from overfitting on these redundant features.

For graph construction, the dataset was split into training and test sets with a $9:1$ ratio. We adopted a truncation strategy selecting the first 15 packets per flow. Protocol headers and payloads were separated with maximum lengths set to 54 and 784 bytes, respectively; insufficient segments were zero-padded. Traffic heterogeneous graphs were then constructed using the PMI algorithm with a threshold of 1.

Model training employed the Adam optimizer with a batch size of 16. The learning rate was initialized at 1×10^{-2} (warm-up ratio 0.1) and decayed smoothly to 1×10^{-4}. To prevent overfitting, the dropout rate was set to 0.2, and the sequence packet drop rate for contrastive learning was configured at 0.4. All experiments were conducted on an NVIDIA RTX 3080Ti GPU using PyTorch. To ensure statistical significance, each experiment was repeated 10 times, and the average values were reported.

5 Evaluation

5.1 Experimental Results

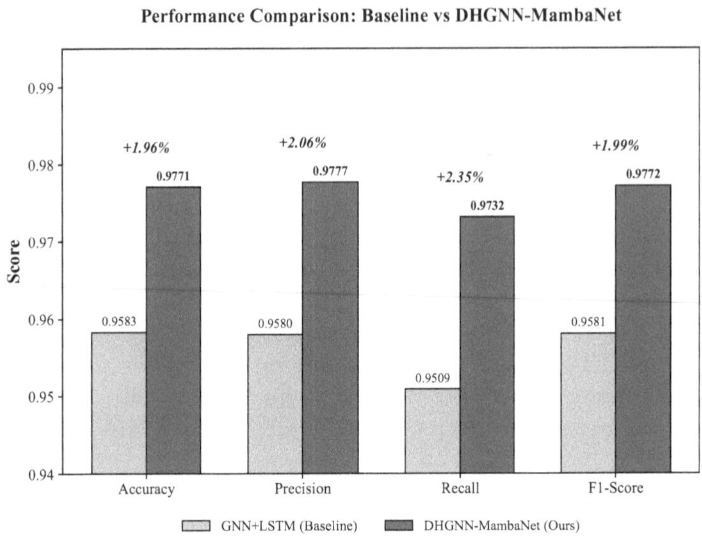

Fig. 2. The optimal test performance achieved by the DHGNN-MambaNet model on the ISCX-VPN dataset.

Figure 2 illustrates the optimal test performance achieved by the DHGNN-MambaNet model on the ISCX-VPN dataset, where Accuracy, Precision, Recall, and F1 Score reached 97.71%, 97.77%, 97.32%, and 97.72%, respectively. Simultaneously, we conducted a detailed comparative analysis in the encrypted traffic analysis experiments, using an existing advanced deep learning architecture to validate the performance advantages of the DHGNN-MambaNet architecture. Experimental results demonstrate that, compared to baseline models relying solely on single-granularity graph construction and LSTM methods, the proposed framework using dual-granularity feature extraction and the Mamba architecture achieved significant improvements across all evaluation metrics. Specifically, Accuracy increased by 1.96%, Precision improved by 2.06%, while Recall and F1 Score realized significant gains of 2.35% and 1.99%, respectively.

To further evaluate the balanced performance of the model across different classes, Fig. 3 presents the PR curves of DHGNN-MambaNet on the test set. The experimental data fully validates the complementary effectiveness of the bidirectional Mamba temporal modeling and dual-granularity feature extraction mechanisms. Through a comparative analysis of the PR curves for five models, it is observed that the baseline model employing traditional LSTM for temporal aggregation achieves an mAP value of 0.988, whereas the DHGNN-MambaNet

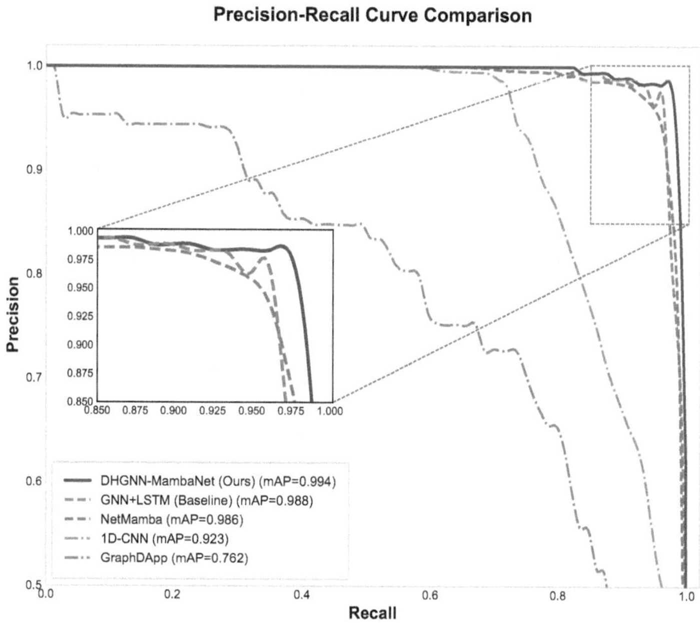

Fig. 3. Precision-Recall (PR) curves and Mean Average Precision (mAP) comparison on the test set.

model reaches 0.994, realizing an improvement in the high-performance range. At the same time, although the NetMamba model also employs the Mamba architecture, it attained a score of 0.986. Meanwhile, the mAP values of other comparative models (GraphDApp, 1D-CNN) are distributed in the lower range of 0.762–0.923, all of which are significantly inferior to the proposed model. In particular, the zoomed-in view reveals that when the Recall approaches the limit of 1.0, the Precision of both the baseline model and NetMamba exhibits a noticeable decline. In contrast, the proposed model maintains stability near a perfect score. These comparative results demonstrate the key role of the bidirectional Mamba architecture in capturing global contextual dependencies and enhancing model robustness.

Based on the experimental results, the primary advantages of the DHGNN-MambaNet architecture are manifested in three aspects. First, the 4-bit and 8-bit dual-view mechanism enhances feature representation by capturing micro-level protocol fingerprints, such as cipher suite identifiers and fixed bits, which are often obscured in standard 8-bit byte streams. Second, the Bi-Mamba module strengthens the modeling of traffic interaction logic. By employing a bidirectional selective scan, it overcomes the global context limitations of traditional temporal models, enabling efficient aggregation of session-level features. Finally, the integrated contrastive learning module based on random packet dropping enhances adaptability to real-world adversarial environments characterized by network jitter and packet loss.

Furthermore, the model employs an improved GraphSAGE algorithm during intra-packet spatial information aggregation. This algorithm accurately reflects the non-Euclidean topological correlations between header control fields and encrypted payloads. Experimental data confirms that this spatial awareness maintains stable performance in complex scenarios involving multi-layer encapsulation and covert channels like Skype.

In summary, by precisely using the dual-granularity heterogeneous graphs with bidirectional state space models, DHGNN-MambaNet provides an efficient pathway for traffic attribution in heavily obfuscated environments and offers a valuable template for integrating GNNs and SSMs in cybersecurity (Table 1).

Table 1. Performance comparison of encrypted traffic classification models on the ISCX-VPN dataset.

Model	Accuracy (%)	Precision (%)	Recall (%)	F1-Score (%)
GraphDApp	71.51	72.96	71.51	71.60
1D-CNN	91.73	91.25	91.50	91.37
NetMamba	95.38	95.46	95.38	95.34
GNN+LSTM	95.83	95.80	95.09	95.81
DHGNN-MambaNet (Ours)	**97.71**	**97.77**	**97.32**	**97.72**

5.2 Ablation Study

To validate the effectiveness of the key components within the DHGNN-MambaNet architecture and investigate the model's forensic reliability under different configurations, we designed comprehensive ablation studies adhering to the principle of controlled variables. Specifically, the experiments were conducted across three dimensions: feature extraction granularity, temporal modeling directionality, and input sequence length.

First, regarding the necessity verification of the dual-granularity parallel feature extraction mechanism, we compared models with only the 4-bit nibble view, only the 8-bit byte view, and the complete dual-granularity parallel architecture. The experimental results are illustrated in Fig. 4. The 4-bit nibble view showed unsatisfactory identification performance, achieving an accuracy of only 38.14%, indicating that high-frequency micro-slices lack sufficient contextual correlation to independently construct discriminative features. In contrast, the 8-bit view achieved 94.85%, confirming byte streams as the primary carrier of traffic patterns, though it still suffers from blind spots regarding fine-grained protocol details. Integrating dual granularities, DHGNN-MambaNet ultimately achieved a SOTA performance of 97.71%, an improvement of 2.86 percentage points over the single 8-bit model. This significant performance boost profoundly reveals the complementary mechanism of the dual views: 4-bit feature extraction is not

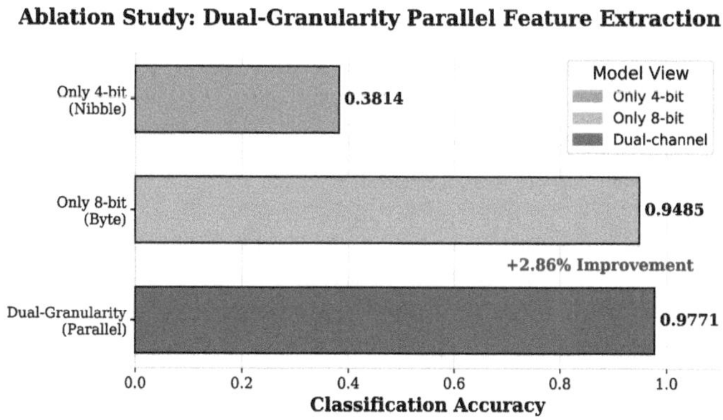

Fig. 4. Comparison of accuracy performance under different feature extraction granularities.

mere redundancy but plays a key role in fine-grained refinement. It effectively supplements the micro-level details lost during the smoothing process of the 8-bit view. Within the feature space, the former is responsible for constructing the macro-level global profile while the latter captures fine-grained local details. This dual-granularity parallel modeling strategy significantly enhances the model's interpretation capability and robustness against complex obfuscated protocol structures.

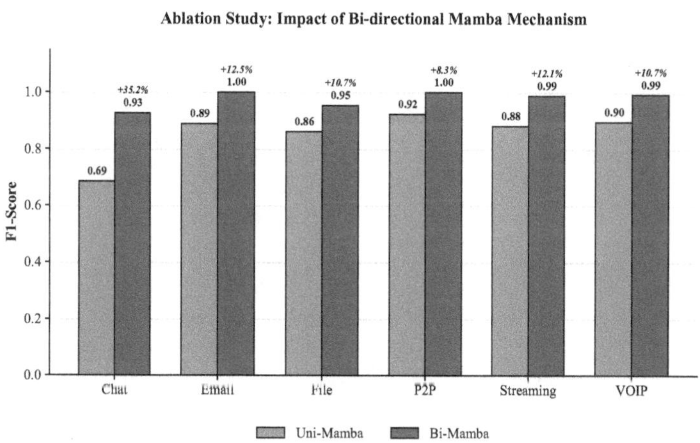

Fig. 5. F1 score performance comparison between Uni-Mamba and Bi-Mamba.

Beyond feature granularity, temporal modeling directionality serves as a decisive dimension determining the depth of the model's profiling of complex traffic patterns. To verify the necessity of introducing the backward state space, we conducted a detailed comparison of F1 score performance between Uni-Mamba and Bi-Mamba across six specific service scenarios. The experimental results illustrated in Fig. 5 show that the Bi-Mamba architecture achieved performance gains of nearly 10 percentage points across all categories. This confirms that network traffic interaction depends not only on the triggering by preceding packets but is also governed by the response patterns of subsequent packets.

Specifically, the most significant improvements in F1 scores were concentrated in the Chat and Email categories, where Bi-Mamba achieved substantial growth compared to the unidirectional model. This is attributed to the fact that these two types of traffic are typically characterized by short-term bursts and high-frequency interactions. Relying solely on preceding packets, the unidirectional model struggles to capture the required boundaries to distinguish between them, making it prone to misclassification. In contrast, the bidirectional scanning mechanism captures not only request patterns but also specific response patterns returned by the server. Such backward context information allows for retrospective analysis of forward information, effectively eliminating attribution ambiguity among similar protocols. Additionally, for the remaining four categories, the bidirectional mechanism similarly aggregates global context to effectively identify distributed transmission intents hidden within discrete packets, demonstrating that bidirectional modeling is a core component for enhancing the model's generalization performance.

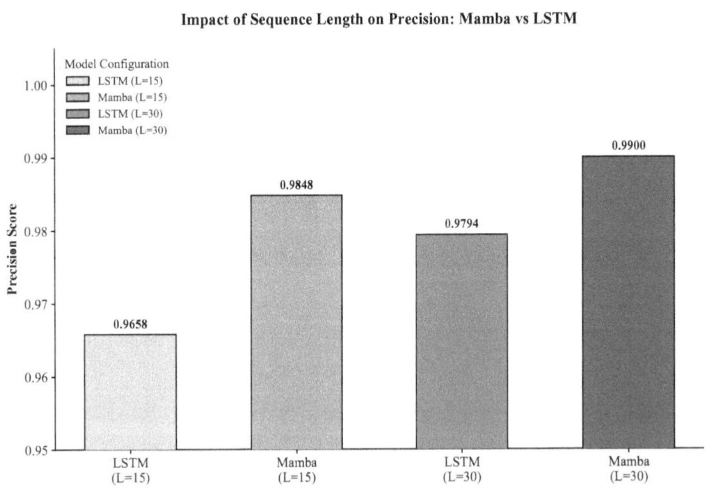

Fig. 6. Impact of input sequence length on model precision.

The truncation length of input sequences impacts the model's forensic discriminative ability. To investigate this impact and verify the adaptability of DHGNN-MambaNet when processing different traffic lengths, we conducted an ablation study on sequence length. We evaluated the precision performance of baseline models and the proposed model at sequence lengths $L = 15$ and $L = 30$, with results shown in Fig. 6. As the sequence length L increased from 15 to 30, both the baselines and our model exhibited an upward trend in precision. Notably, Mamba ($L = 30$) achieved a remarkable 99.00%. Although $L = 30$ yielded a marginal performance gain of 0.52%, it came at the cost of doubling both the input data volume and detection latency. In contrast, a comparative analysis reveals that our architecture at the short sequence length of $L = 15$ (98.48%) not only significantly outperforms baselines at the same length (96.58%) but even surpasses the LSTM model at the longer sequence of $L = 30$ (97.94%). This finding demonstrates that the Mamba architecture does not solely rely on long-range stacking for performance. Its core Selective Scan mechanism allows it to focus on critical fingerprints within a limited observation window. This enables it to surpass the feature extraction efficiency of traditional RNNs even in the early stages of a session, proving that the model possesses both long-sequence modeling potential and high data utilization efficiency. Considering that rapid identification is critical for time-sensitive investigations and blocking threats in real-world cybersecurity scenarios, we conclude that $L = 15$ strikes the optimal balance between detection efficiency and accuracy, which justifies our adoption of this configuration in the previous main experiments.

6 Conclusion

In this paper, we propose DHGNN-MambaNet, a unified end-to-end framework that integrates GNNs with SSMs to address the attribution challenges posed by robust encryption protocols. By coupling a dual-granularity heterogeneous graph with a bidirectional Mamba architecture, our model effectively captures both micro-level hidden byte fingerprints and macro-level temporal dependencies. This design successfully overcomes the bottlenecks regarding feature granularity and memory inherent in traditional deep learning approaches. Extensive experiments on the ISCX-VPN benchmark dataset demonstrate that DHGNN-MambaNet exhibits consistent and meaningful improvements over baseline methods. Furthermore, ablation studies validate that mining fine-grained correlations and leveraging linear-complexity global modeling provide valuable enhancements for robust traffic profiling.

While the ISCX-VPN dataset serves as a standard baseline, it may not fully reflect modern anti-analysis mechanisms, such as padding or Tor obfuscation. Consequently, our immediate future work will validate the model's generalization capabilities on recent datasets like CESNET-TLS22. Furthermore, we plan to develop lightweight architectures for resource-constrained IoT environments and explore the integration of Large Language Models (LLMs) to tackle unknown protocols. Overall, this research establishes a solid baseline for synergizing SSMs and GNNs in cybersecurity analysis.

References

1. Chen, Y., Wang, Y.: MPAF: Encrypted traffic classification with multi-phase attribute fingerprint. IEEE Trans. Inf. Forensics Secur. **19**, 7091–7105 (2024). https://doi.org/10.1109/tifs.2024.3428839
2. Comey, J.B.: Going Dark: are technology, privacy, and public safety on a collision course?, FBI Remarks at the Brookings Institution (2014)
3. Finsterbusch, M., et al.: A survey of payload-based traffic classification approaches. IEEE Commun. Surveys Tuts. **16**(2), 1135–1156 (2014)
4. Gu, A., Dao, T.: Mamba: linear-time sequence modeling with selective state spaces. In: ICML, vol. 235, pp. 16728–16783. PMLR (2024).https://doi.org/10.48550/arXiv.2312.00752
5. Hua, J., et al.: FTG-Net: Hierarchical flow-to-traffic graph neural network for DDoS attack detection. In: IEEE HPSR, pp. 173–178. IEEE (2023).https://doi.org/10.1109/HPSR57248.2023.10147929
6. Jiang, M., et al.: Accurate mobile-app fingerprinting using flow-level relationship with graph neural networks. Comput. Netw. **217**, 109309 (2022)
7. Lopez-Martin, M., et al.: Network traffic classifier with convolutional and recurrent neural networks for internet of things. IEEE Access **5**, 18042–18050 (2017)
8. Mei, H., Cheng, G., Yuan, Y.: High precision and efficient anonymous traffic classification in the real-world. IEEE/ACM Trans. Networking **33**(3), 966–981 (2025). https://doi.org/10.1109/ton.2024.3518976
9. Moore, A.W., Zuev, D.: Toward the accurate identification of network applications. In: PAM. LNCS, vol. 3431, pp. 41–54. Springer (2005)
10. Nguyen, T.T.T., Armitage, G.: A survey of techniques for internet traffic classification using machine learning. IEEE Commun. Surveys Tuts. **10**(4), 56–76 (2008)
11. Pacheco, F., et al.: Towards the deployment of machine learning solutions in network traffic classification: a systematic survey. IEEE Commun. Surveys Tuts. **21**(2), 1988–2014 (2019)
12. Rezaei, S., Liu, X.: Deep learning for encrypted traffic classification: an overview. IEEE Commun. Mag. **57**(5), 60–65 (2019)
13. Sen, S., Spatscheck, O., Wang, D.: Accurate, scalable in-network identification of P2P traffic using application signatures. In: WWW, pp. 512–521. ACM (2004)
14. Shen, M., et al.: Accurate decentralized application identification via encrypted traffic analysis. IEEE Trans. Inf. Forensics Secur. **16**, 3059–3074 (2021)
15. SonicWall: 2025 cyber threat report. Tech. rep., SonicWall, Milpitas, CA (2025)
16. Velan, P., et al.: A survey of methods for encrypted traffic classification and analysis. Int. J. Netw. Manag. **25**(5), 355–374 (2015)
17. Wang, C., et al.: Graph-Mamba: Towards long-range graph sequence modeling with selective state spaces. arXiv preprint arXiv:2402.00789 (2024).https://doi.org/10.48550/arXiv.2402.00789
18. Wang, T., et al.: NetMamba: efficient network traffic classification via pre-training unidirectional Mamba. In: IEEE ICNP, pp. 1–11. IEEE (2024). https://ieeexplore.ieee.org/document/10772274
19. Wang, W.: End-to-end encrypted traffic classification with one-dimensional convolution neural networks. In: IEEE ISI, pp. 43–48. IEEE (2017)

20. Xu, J., et al.: ET-Mamba: a Mamba model for encrypted traffic classification. Information **16**(4), 314 (2024). https://doi.org/10.3390/info16040314
21. Zhu, L., et al.: Vision Mamba: efficient visual representation learning with bidirectional state space model. In: ICML. vol. 235, pp. 61400–61416. PMLR (2024). https://doi.org/10.48550/arXiv.2401.09417
22. ThreatLabz, Z.: ThreatLabz 2024 encrypted attacks report. Tech. rep, Zscaler, San Jose, CA (December (2024)

Flash-Flood: A Low-Latency Generative Defense Against Website Fingerprinting Attacks

Yuanpeng Zhao[1,2], Zhong Guan[2(✉)], Junzheng Shi[1,2], Gang Xiong[1,2], and Gaopeng Gou[1,2]

[1] Institute of Information Engineering, Chinese Academy of Sciences, Beijing, China
{zhaoyuanpeng,shijunzheng,xionggang,gougaopeng,guanzhong}@iie.ac.cn

[2] School of Cyber Security, University of Chinese Academy of Sciences, Beijing, China

Abstract. In recent years, deep learning-based website fingerprinting (WF) attacks have posed significant threats to anonymous communication networks such as Tor. Existing defenses struggle to balance low overhead with strong protection. In this paper, we propose Flash-Flood, a generative WF defense framework based on Consistency Models and temporal manifold reconstruction. It compresses multi-step diffusion into one-step inference and generates high-fidelity adversarial traffic to mask real sequences. In addition, a best-fit parasitic fusion mechanism embeds real communication into pre-generated cover timelines, enabling global topology-level feature reshaping. Experimental results show that, with only 13.14 ms generation latency and approximately 34.81% bandwidth and 1.7% time overhead, Flash-Flood reduces attack accuracy to 12.2%–20.2% and lowers AP to 0.591 in the open-world setting, significantly outperforming existing defenses while achieving an effective balance between security and usability.

Keywords: Website Fingerprinting · Tor Network · Diffusion Models · Consistency Distillation · Traffic Obfuscation

1 Introduction

As a widely deployed low-latency anonymous communication system, Tor [2] provides basic privacy protection through multi-hop encryption. However, while encryption hides content, metadata such as timestamps, inter-arrival times (IAT), and packet directions still leak side-channel information. Website fingerprinting (WF) attacks exploit these features to infer user activity [7,8]. Recent studies show that local passive adversaries (LPA) equipped with deep learning can achieve high identification accuracy, as demonstrated by models such as DF [18] and Tik-Tok [14].

© ICST Institute for Computer Sciences, Social Informatics and Telecommunications Engineering 2027
Published by Springer Nature Switzerland AG 2027. All Rights Reserved
H. Neukirchen et al. (Eds.): ICDF2C 2026, LNICST 720, pp. 282–297, 2027.
https://doi.org/10.1007/978-3-032-37274-1_17

To counter these attacks, a series of defense mechanisms have been proposed.However, they struggle to simultaneously achieve indistinguishability, real-time performance, and low overhead.Heuristic link-padding methods (e.g., WTF-PAD [11] and FRONT [4]) inject dummy packets to obfuscate features but tend to introduce learnable patterns. Traffic clustering-based approaches (e.g., Palette [17]) improve defense by aligning traffic to cluster centers; however, strict alignment incurs significant queuing delays and leads to high time and bandwidth overhead under mismatch conditions.

To address the above limitations, we adopt a continuous manifold mimicry approach that maps protected traffic into a high-dimensional distribution consistent with real Tor statistics, thereby weakening the attacker's ability to form stable decision boundaries. Diffusion models [9] enable high-fidelity generation and are therefore suitable for traffic generation. However, due to their high inference cost, we propose Flash-Flood: an offline-trained diffusion teacher based on UNet1D learns the real traffic distribution, and a student model is obtained via consistency distillation [20] to compress the multi-step generation into a one-step mapping, reducing per-sample latency to within 20 ms. In the online deployment phase, Flash-Flood combines full-flow mimicry with a parasitic fusion mechanism. The system first selects an optimal cover flow via Best-Fit Retrieval, and then uses Adaptive Time Scaling and dummy-packet replacement to seamlessly constrain real traffic transmission within the feature structure of the cover flow, thereby balancing defense effectiveness against bandwidth and latency costs.

The main contributions of this paper are as follows:

- We propose a continuous manifold generation framework for website fingerprinting defense, extending the defense objective from rule-based perturbation or limited template matching to distribution-level mimicry.
- We introduce consistency distillation technology to compress diffusion generation into an extremely low-latency inference process, fully satisfying the latency constraints of online deployment.
- We design a parasitic fusion scheduling algorithm that combines best-fit retrieval and time scaling mechanisms to accomplish real traffic injection.
- We conduct system evaluations against models such as DF, Tik-Tok, and RF in both closed-world and open-world scenarios, validating the feasibility of this scheme in balancing defense effectiveness and overhead control.

The rest of this paper is organized as follows. Section 2 introduces the background and threat model. Section 3 details the architecture of Flash-Flood and its online fusion algorithm. Section 4 reports the evaluation results. Section 5 discusses potential improvements. Section 6 concludes the paper.

2 Background and Threat Model

This section introduces the evolution of website fingerprinting attacks and defense technologies, explains the theoretical foundations of diffusion generation and consistency distillation, and clarifies the threat model.

2.1 Website Fingerprinting Attacks and Defenses

Website Fingerprinting Attacks. Although Tor hides communication content via fixed-size cells and multi-hop routing, the underlying link still exposes side-channel features such as directional alternation, bursts, and inter-arrival times (IAT), forming the basis of website fingerprinting (WF) attacks [24]. Early approaches relied on high-dimensional features and statistical classifiers (e.g., Random Forest, TAM) [6,12]. With the rise of deep learning, DF [18] enables end-to-end modeling via 1D convolutions, while Tik-Tok [14] further jointly models packet direction and timing to capture fine-grained loading patterns, significantly enhancing attack effectiveness and driving WF toward nonlinear representations of raw traffic.

Website Fingerprinting Defenses. In response to increasingly powerful attacks, defense research has shifted from local heuristic perturbations to global traffic mimicry. Early methods (e.g., Tamaraw [1] and WTF-PAD [11]) either incur high latency or are easily detected by deep models. Subsequent approaches (e.g., Walkie-Talkie [25], Mockingbird [5,13], and Palette [17]) improve effectiveness through sequence reshaping or cluster alignment. However, these methods rely on a limited set of target mappings and struggle to match complex traffic dynamics in open networks. To address this, we propose mapping protected traffic to a broader "general traffic" distribution and leveraging generative models to produce diverse mimicry samples.

2.2 Diffusion Models and Consistency Distillation

To achieve distribution-level coverage and high-fidelity traffic generation, we adopt denoising diffusion probabilistic models (DDPMs) [9] to model traffic distributions, which can capture bursty patterns and silent intervals in a continuous latent space. However, multi-step reverse denoising process in diffusion models requires hundreds to thousands of iterations, resulting in second-level latency and making it unsuitable for online deployment. To address this, we introduce Consistency Models and consistency distillation [20]: a high-accuracy teacher model is first trained offline, and a lightweight student model is then distilled to compress multi-step generation into one-step inference, reducing latency to tens of milliseconds while preserving generation quality.

2.3 Threat Model

We adopt the Local Passive Adversary (LPA) model [21], assuming the attacker is positioned between the client and the Tor entry node, with access only to metadata such as timing and direction, and capable of launching attacks via offline-trained deep models,as shown in Fig. 1. The defense system is deployed at the client side to mitigate website fingerprinting attacks while balancing security, usability, and low overhead.

3 Methodology

This section presents the system architecture and methodology of Flash-Flood. Unlike heuristic defenses that rely on fixed delays or rule-based padding, Flash-Flood integrates generative modeling, retrieval, and online scheduling to build a generative full-stream mimicry framework.

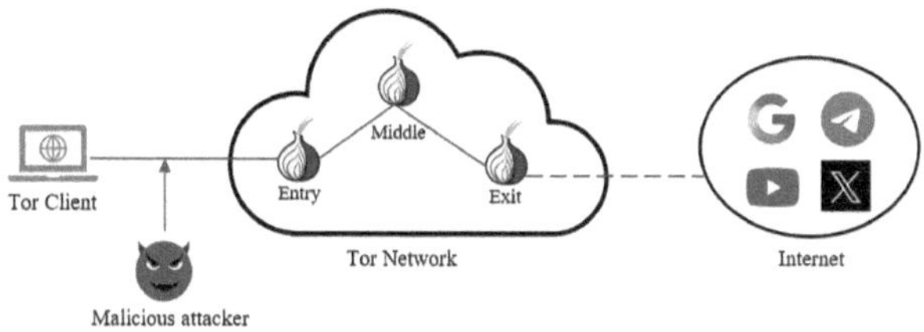

Fig. 1. Overview of the attacker model.

3.1 System Overview

Flash-Flood proposes a two-stage generative full-stream mimicry framework to resist deep learning-based WF attacks through low-latency scheduling. As shown in the Fig. 2, the architecture contains two components: offline training and distillation, and online parasitic defense. This shifts the defense objective from local feature perturbation to global distribution reshaping, achieving traffic obfuscation while preserving communication availability.

Offline Training and Distillation Stage. This module is responsible for generating high-quality virtual communication traces. Raw Tor traffic is processed into dual-channel tensors of inter-arrival times (IAT) and directions, and input to a DDPM teacher model to fit the real distribution. To eliminate the latency of multi-step denoising, a consistency student model is introduced via distillation, mapping noise to high-fidelity Tor-like traffic traces in a single step. These sequences are generated in batches and pre-stored in a Smart Cover Library, providing low-latency data support for online defense.

Online Parasitic Defense Stage. Traffic scheduling is performed based on a cover library under causality constraints. For real Tor traffic, the scheduler employs Best-Fit retrieval and adaptive time scaling to select a low-overhead timeline from the smart cover library and adjust its duration to meet QoS requirements. Subsequently, parasitic fusion embeds real packets into the timeline under causality constraints, while empty slots are filled with dummy packets. The resulting continuous stream closely matches the target distribution, effectively reducing the accuracy of WF attacks.

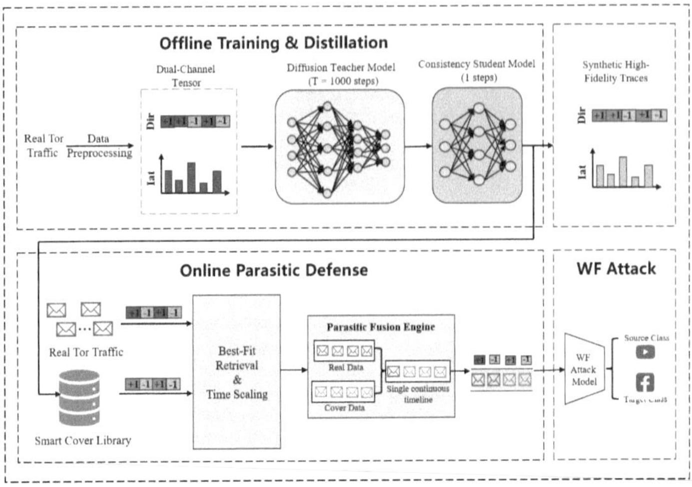

Fig. 2. The system framework of Flash-Flood.

3.2 High-Fidelity Traffic Generation

To improve the mimicry capability of defended traffic, generated traces must preserve both directional burst structure and temporal rhythm. Before model training, we first apply unified tensorization and normalization to raw traces, and then train both teacher and student models on the same model architecture.

Data Preprocessing. The raw Tor traffic is represented as a sequence of $\{\text{timestamp}, \text{direction}\}$. For effective model learning, it is transformed into a $\{\text{IAT}, \text{Direction}\}$ sequence. Due to the long-tailed distribution of IAT and its scale mismatch with the direction channel (taking values in $-1, 1$), training instability may arise. Therefore, logarithmic normalization is applied to IAT. Each traffic trace is finally represented as a fixed-length tensor $x \in \mathbb{R}^{2\times L}$ (with $L = 5000$), where the 0-th channel corresponds to the normalized IAT mapped to $[-1, 1]$, as defined in Eq. 1

$$\hat{x}_i = \frac{\ln(x_i + \epsilon) + \alpha}{\beta} \tag{1}$$

We set $\epsilon = 10^{-8}$ to avoid issues when $x_i = 0$. The parameters $\alpha = 12$ and $\beta = 16$ are determined from statistical analysis of the dataset to smooth the long-tailed IAT distribution and stabilize gradients. The second channel encodes packet direction ($+1$ for outgoing, -1 for incoming). Sequences shorter than L are zero-padded, while longer ones are truncated, resulting in batch tensors of shape $[B, 2, L]$, which provide a uniform and stable input for the model.

Model Architecture. To achieve high-fidelity traffic generation, both the teacher and student models adopt a 1D UNet architecture (F_θ) [15], consisting of four core components,as shown in Fig. 3.

1) Input and time embedding:The timestep t is encoded into a 128-dimensional vector via sinusoidal positional encoding and an MLP, and injected into each residual block. The input traffic x_0 is projected into a 32-channel feature space using an initial 1D convolution (kernel size 3, padding 1).
2) Encoder (downsampling):Composed of four DownBlocks, each including 1D Conv, GroupNorm [26], and SiLU [3]. Strided convolutions (stride 2) progressively downsample the sequence (halving length and doubling channels), while preserving skip connections.
3) Attention bottleneck:At the deepest layer, a self-attention module [23] is introduced to capture long-range temporal dependencies beyond the local receptive field of convolutions.
4) Decoder (upsampling):The decoder progressively upsamples the sequence via ConvTranspose and residual blocks, while fusing corresponding skip connections. A final convolution layer reconstructs the traffic sequence.

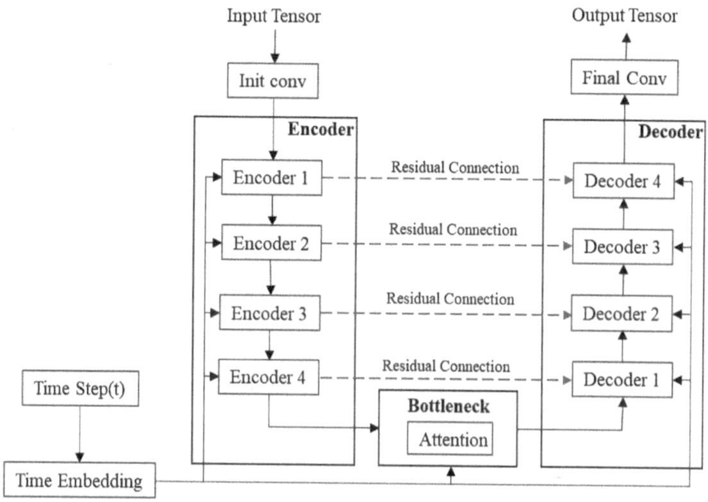

Fig. 3. UNet1D Architecture for Traffic Generation.

Teacher Diffusion Model and Student Consistency Distillation. The system first uses a DDPM teacher model as a high-fidelity generation reference for distillation. Let the clean trace be $x_0 \sim q(x_0)$ and Gaussian noise be $\epsilon \sim \mathcal{N}(0, \mathbf{I})$. To learn the data distribution, the forward diffusion process is modeled as a Markov chain, as given in Eq. 2

$$q(x_t|x_{t-1}) = \mathcal{N}(x_t; \sqrt{1-\beta_t}x_{t-1}, \beta_t\mathbf{I}), \quad x_t = \sqrt{\bar{\alpha}_t}x_0 + \sqrt{1-\bar{\alpha}_t}\epsilon \tag{2}$$

After $T = 1000$ diffusion steps, the teacher predicts the injected Gaussian noise $\hat{\epsilon} = \epsilon_\theta(x_t, t)$. The training objective minimizes the MSE between predicted and true noise, as defined in Eq. 3

$$\mathcal{L}_{Teacher} = \mathbb{E}_{x_0,\epsilon,t}\left[\|\epsilon - \epsilon_\theta(x_t,t)\|_2^2\right] \tag{3}$$

To remove the large latency of multi-step reverse sampling, we train an efficient single-step student via Consistency Distillation. The key objective is that for any noisy state at time t, the model can directly map it back to the clean state x_0. This consistency mapping is formulated in Eq. 4

$$f_\theta(x_t,t) = c_{skip}(t)x_t + c_{out}(t)F_\theta(x_t,t) \tag{4}$$

In Eq. 4, $c_{skip}(t) = \epsilon'/(t+\epsilon')$ and $c_{out}(t) = t/(t+\epsilon')$, with $\epsilon' = 0.002$. These terms stabilize boundary behavior and ensure smooth degradation to identity mapping as $t \to 0$. We discretize the continuous schedule into $N = 20$ nodes and use an exponential moving average (EMA) network [19,22] to provide stable targets. The student prediction and the distillation target are then computed according to Eqs. (5) and (6), respectively.

$$x_{\text{pred}} = c_{\text{skip}}(t_{\text{cur}})x_t + c_{\text{out}}(t_{\text{cur}})F_\theta(x_t, t_{\text{cur}}) \tag{5}$$

$$x_{\text{target}} = c_{\text{skip}}(t_{\text{next}})x^{\text{tea}}_{t_{\text{next}}} + c_{\text{out}}(t_{\text{next}})F_{\text{EMA}}(x^{\text{tea}}_{t_{\text{next}}}, t_{\text{next}}) \tag{6}$$

To improve robustness beyond a single norm, we optimize the student with a composite objective that combines MSE and L1, as shown in Eq. 7

$$\mathcal{L}_{Student} = 0.5 \cdot \text{MSE}(x_{pred}, x_{target}) + 0.5 \cdot \text{L1}(x_{pred}, x_{target}) \tag{7}$$

By combining mean squared error (MSE) to preserve overall trends and L1 loss to suppress over-smoothing, the method generates high-fidelity traffic traces under extremely low one-step computational cost.

3.3 Construction of the Smart Cover Library

To avoid high-latency online generation during real-time defense, Flash-Flood builds a rich candidate cover set offline using Algorithm 1. This design moves major computational cost to the offline stage and supports fast online retrieval through structured indexing.

As shown in Algorithm 1, once prefix-sum indices for C_{in}, C_{out}, and C_{dur} are stored for each candidate trace, the system can quickly locate feasible prefixes via binary-search-style logic. Compared with pointwise scanning, ordered prefix retrieval achieves near $O(\log L)$ query complexity. The smart cover library converts online generation into offline generation plus online retrieval, avoiding full sampling per session. It also provides explicit capacity constraints for fusion scheduling (inbound capacity, outbound capacity, cumulative duration), enabling stable control of bandwidth and delay overhead under availability constraints. Therefore, this module is not only a storage structure but also key infrastructure for deployable online defense.

Algorithm 1. Smart Cover Library Construction

Input: Student Generative Model M_{stu}, Library Size K (e.g., $K = 3000$), Batch Size B, Trace length constraint L
Output: Indexed Cover Library $\mathcal{D}$

Initialize List $\mathcal{D} \leftarrow []$
Compute $num\_batches \leftarrow \lceil K/B \rceil$
for $batch \leftarrow 1$ **to** $num\_batches$ **do**
  $X_{raw} \leftarrow \text{Model\_Generate}(M_{stu}, \text{batch\_size} = B)$
  for each $trace$ **in** X_{raw} **do**
    $iats \leftarrow \text{Inverse\_Log\_Normalize}(trace[0])$
    $dirs \leftarrow \text{Sign}(trace[1])$
    $C_{in}[0 \dots L], C_{out}[0 \dots L], C_{dur}[0 \dots L] \leftarrow 0$
    for $step\ k \leftarrow 1$ **to** L **do**
      $C_{in}[k] \leftarrow C_{in}[k-1] + \mathbb{I}(dirs[k] < 0)$
      $C_{out}[k] \leftarrow C_{out}[k-1] + \mathbb{I}(dirs[k] > 0)$
      $C_{dur}[k] \leftarrow C_{dur}[k-1] + iats[k]$
    end for
    $Cover \leftarrow \{iats, dirs, C_{in}, C_{out}, C_{dur}, n_{in}, n_{out}, total\_len\}$
    $\mathcal{D}.\text{append}(Cover)$
  end for
end for
Sort $\mathcal{D}$ ascending based on $total\_len$ and $C_{dur}[L]$
return $\mathcal{D}$

3.4 Retrieval and Full-Stream Mimicry

Optimal Retrieval and Adaptive Scaling To select the most suitable cover skeleton from a large offline candidate pool, we use a minimum-cost evaluation paradigm based on prefix truncation and multi-dimensional penalties. Given a target prefix C_{prefix} and real-session fingerprint features $\{N_{in}^{real}, N_{out}^{real}, D_{real}, L_{real}\}$, we define a joint penalty score as in Eq. 8

$$\text{Score} = \underbrace{\frac{L_{prefix} - L_{real}}{L_{real}}}_{(A)\ \text{Pkt\_OH}} + \alpha \underbrace{\left| \ln \left(\frac{D_{prefix}}{D_{real}} \right) \right|}_{(B)\ \text{Dur\_Pen}} + \beta \underbrace{\frac{\Delta_{in} + \Delta_{out}}{L_{real}}}_{(C)\ \text{Dir\_OH}} + \gamma \underbrace{\text{Bias}_{len}(L_{total}, L_{real})}_{(D)\ \text{Len\_Limit}} \tag{8}$$

Term (A) measures packet-overhead ratio; term (B) penalizes logarithmic duration mismatch between the selected prefix and real traffic; term (C) penalizes directional mismatch; and term (D) suppresses abnormally long sequences. Coefficients are set as $\alpha = 0.35$, $\beta = 0.25$, and $\gamma = 0.15$ based on empirical tuning. The prefix with the minimum score is selected as the cover flow.

Although the cover traffic matches the real flow in packet count and direction, their time spans are often misaligned. To address this, we introduce Adaptive Time Scaling, which adjusts the duration using a global factor S_t. Let D_{cover} and D_{real} denote the durations of the cover and real traffic, respectively. A tolerance range of $\pm 15\%$ with an additional 5% margin is applied, and S_t is computed as in Eq. 9(with $\epsilon = 10^{-3}$). All IATs are then uniformly scaled for alignment: if $D_{cover} > 1.15D_{real}$, compression is applied to avoid queue buildup; if $D_{cover} < 0.85D_{real}$, expansion is applied to reduce early exposure risk.

$$S_t = \begin{cases} 1.05 \cdot \frac{D_{real}}{D_{cover}}, & \text{if } D_{cover} > 1.15 \cdot D_{real} \text{ (Compress)} \\ 0.95 \cdot \frac{D_{real}}{\max(D_{cover}, \epsilon)}, & \text{if } D_{cover} < 0.85 \cdot D_{real} \text{ (Stretch)} \\ 1.0, & \text{otherwise} \end{cases} \quad (9)$$

After determining S_t, all IAT values in the selected cover prefix are multiplied by this factor to align physical time. This preserves communication quality and provides an accurate runtime timeline for subsequent parasitic fusion scheduling.

Causality-Driven Parasitic Fusion Engine. During the traffic fusion stage, scheduling is performed over the scaled cover timeline. The system maintains separate inbound and outbound queues, and at each timestep enforces direction matching and arrival constraints: a real packet is transmitted if available; otherwise, a dummy packet is inserted, as shown in Algorithm 2. This process is essentially a causality-constrained discrete event scheduler, where real packets are sent only if they have arrived and match the required direction. After the main loop, remaining packets are flushed to preserve semantic integrity. This mechanism ensures communication correctness while allowing the observable temporal patterns to be dominated by the cover traffic, achieving both statistical mimicry and semantic preservation. Overall, Flash-Flood adopts a two-stage pipeline–offline generation and distillation, followed by online retrieval and fusion—to enable distribution-level reshaping and balance security, usability, and overhead.

4 Evaluation

This section experimentally evaluates the security and usability of Flash-Flood, showing that it significantly reduces WF attack accuracy while maintaining low bandwidth and latency overhead.

4.1 Experimental Setup

Dataset. We use the widely adopted DS-19 dataset [4,18], which includes 100 sensitive websites (10,000 monitored samples in total) and 10,000 real background-noise samples (unmonitored). Experiments are conducted in both Closed-World and Open-World settings. In the closed-world setting, 10,000 monitored samples are used. In the open-world setting, an additional 10,000 non-monitored samples are introduced, which are treated as a single class. All data are strictly split into training, validation, and test sets with an 8:1:1 ratio. To ensure strict fairness, all defense baselines use the same data split, fully eliminating evaluation bias caused by data sampling differences.

Algorithm 2. Parasitic Fusion Dispatcher

Input: $\mathcal{T}_f = \{t_1, \ldots, t_m\}$, $\mathcal{D}_f = \{d_1, \ldots, d_m\}$, Q_{in}, Q_{out}
Output: Output Sequence *Seq*

$Seq \leftarrow []$, $added\_dummy \leftarrow 0$
for $j \leftarrow 1$ **to** m **do**
  $cur\_t \leftarrow \mathcal{T}_f[j]$, $tar\_dir \leftarrow \mathcal{D}_f[j]$, $sent \leftarrow$ False
  // Prioritize causality-constrained dispatch of real payload
  if $tar\_dir < 0$ **and** $Q_{in} \neq \emptyset$ **and** Q_{in}.time $\leq cur\_t$ **then**
    $p \leftarrow Q_{in}$.pop(), $sent \leftarrow$ True
  else if $tar\_dir > 0$ **and** $Q_{out} \neq \emptyset$ **and** Q_{out}.time $\leq cur\_t$ **then**
    $p \leftarrow Q_{out}$.pop(), $sent \leftarrow$ True
  end if
  // Fill every scheduled event regardless of availability
  Seq.append($\{cur\_t, tar\_dir\}$)
  if not *sent* **then**
    $added\_dummy \leftarrow added\_dummy + 1$
  end if
end for
// Flush remaining delayed real packets
while $Q_{in} \neq \emptyset$ **or** $Q_{out} \neq \emptyset$ **do**
  $p \leftarrow$ pop_earliest(Q_{in}, Q_{out})
  $last\_t \leftarrow \max(p.\text{time}, Seq.\text{last}().\text{time} + 0.001)$
  Seq.append($\{last\_t, p.\text{dir}\}$)
end while
return *Seq*

Attacker Models and Defense Baselines. To evaluate system security, we select three representative WF attack models:DF [18], Tik-Tok [14], and RF [16]. The baselines include WTF-PAD [11], FRONT [4], RegulaTor [10], and the SOTA method Palette [17]. All methods are faithfully reproduced with their recommended configurations, and key parameters are listed in Table 1 (the symbols are consistent with the definitions in the original papers).

Table 1. Experimental parameter settings of defense baselines

Defense Method	Parameters
WTF-PAD	`normal_rcv`
FRONT	$N_s = N_c = 2500, W_{\min} = 1, W_{\max} = 14$
RegulaTor	$R = 277, D = 0.94, T = 3.55, N = 1800, U = 4.5, C = 1.7$
Palette	$L = 1000, S = 30, R = 1, \alpha = 0.16, U = 45, B = 20$

4.2 Generation Quality and Inference Efficiency

To evaluate both distribution fitting quality and online deployment feasibility, we randomly sample 128 real traces (length 5000) from the test set, and then generate equal-sized samples independently using the Teacher and Student models for comparison.

Cumulative Direction Trajectory. We apply cumulative summation on direction sequences to evaluate macroscopic structural fitting, as shown in the Fig. 4. The trajectories generated by Flash-Flood (red dashed line) closely match the overall decreasing trend and local step-like patterns of real traffic, and smoothly transition to a flat line during idle periods, indicating effective learning of real transmission patterns.

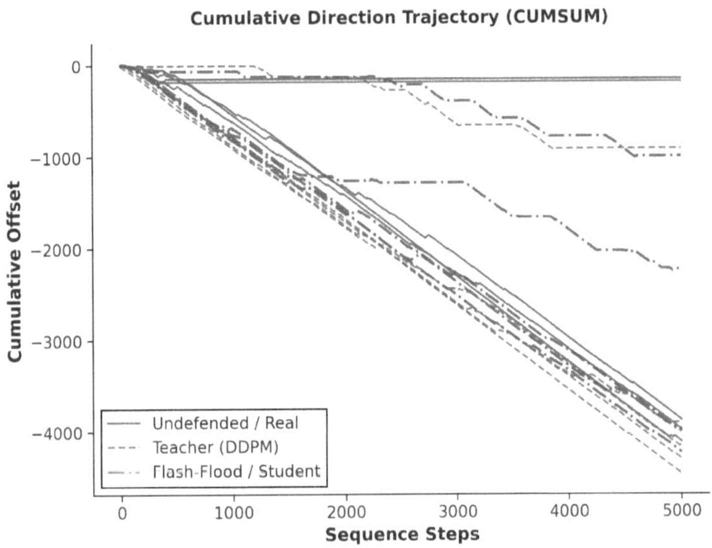

Fig. 4. Cumulative Direction Trajectory Comparison Between Real and Generated Traffic.

T-SNE Projection. As shown in the Fig. 5, in 2D projection, real data (blue), Teacher-generated data (purple), and Flash-Flood data (red) are fully fused into a unified topological manifold, without obvious isolated clusters. This statistical consistency in high-dimensional feature space prevents deep fingerprinting models (e.g., RF and DF) from constructing reliable decision boundaries, which explains from a feature-topology perspective why the defense is effective.

Inference Latency and Speedup. The experiment are conducted on a single NVIDIA Tesla V100 with a batch size of 1. Fig. 6.The diffusion-based teacher

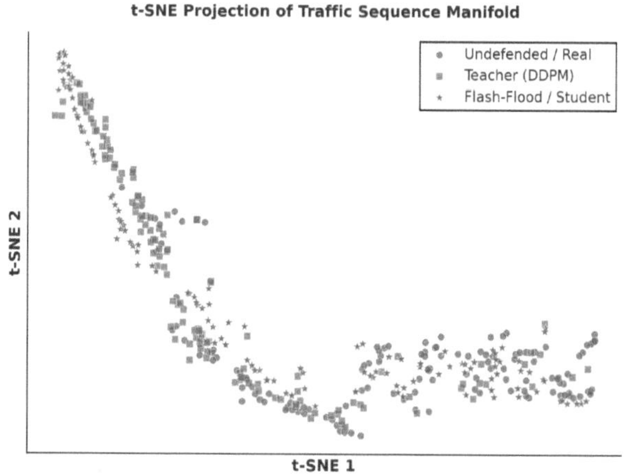

Fig. 5. t-SNE Manifold Projection Comparison of Real and Generated Traffic.

model requires nearly 1000 denoising steps, resulting in a per-sample latency of 14533.90 ms. In contrast, Flash-Flood compresses sampling into a single step, reducing latency to 13.14 ms and achieving a 1106× speedup, demonstrating its effectiveness in overcoming the diffusion bottleneck and enabling low-latency deployment.

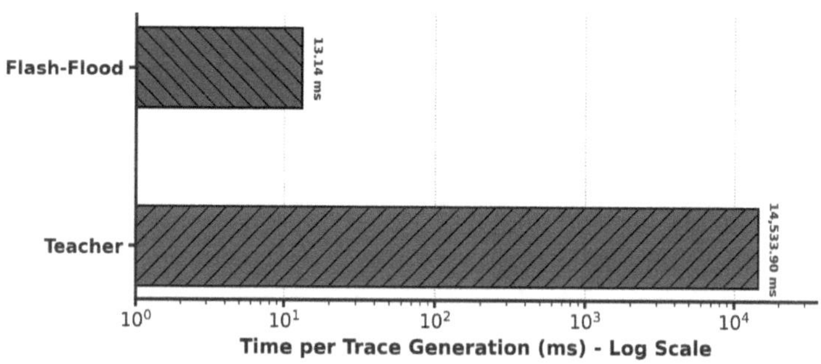

Fig. 6. Per-Trace Generation Latency Comparison.

4.3 Closed-World Defense Performance

Both closed-world and open-world evaluations adopt a white-box setting.Undefended traffic are first processed by each defense, then attacker models are retrained on defended traffic and evaluated on same-distribution test sets.

As shown in Table 2, all attacks achieve over 95% accuracy without defense. WTF-PAD and FRONT are ineffective against RF (94.4% and 93.8%), while

Table 2. Overhead and defense effectiveness comparison in closed-world scenario

Defenses	Overhead (%)		Accuracy (%)		
	Bandwidth	Time	DF	Tik-Tok	RF
Undefended	-	-	96.7	96.9	95.5
WTF-PAD	59.27	0	93.9	92.8	94.4
FRONT	63.42	0	54.2	55.6	93.8
RegulaTor	36.75	15.75	39.0	55.5	48.3
Palette	64.81	26.02	16.4	21.5	23.9
Flash-Flood	**34.81**	**1.70**	**12.2**	**14.9**	**20.2**

RegulaTor reduces accuracy to below 55%. Palette further lowers DF, Tik-Tok, and RF to 16.4%, 21.5%, and 23.9%, respectively. Flash-Flood achieves the strongest defense, reducing them to 12.2%, 14.9%, and 20.2%, with up to an 84.5-point drop. This indicates that Flash-Flood effectively disrupts traffic features relied upon by attackers through reshaping traffic patterns and micro-scale timing.

Moreover, Flash-Flood not only outperforms Palette in defense performance, but also introduces significantly lower bandwidth (34.81%) and time overhead (1.7%) than strong-intervention methods such as Palette (see Sect. 4.5). Results confirm that under white-box adaptive attacks, consistency-manifold-based defense design can effectively resist multiple advanced deep-learning fingerprinting attacks at low cost.

4.4 Open-World Defense Performance

The open-world setting evaluates the difficulty of identifying target websites under massive background noise. We use Precision Recall (PR) curves to measure performance. Greater shift toward the lower-left region indicates that classifiers under that threshold have greater difficulty simultaneously maintaining high precision and high recall.

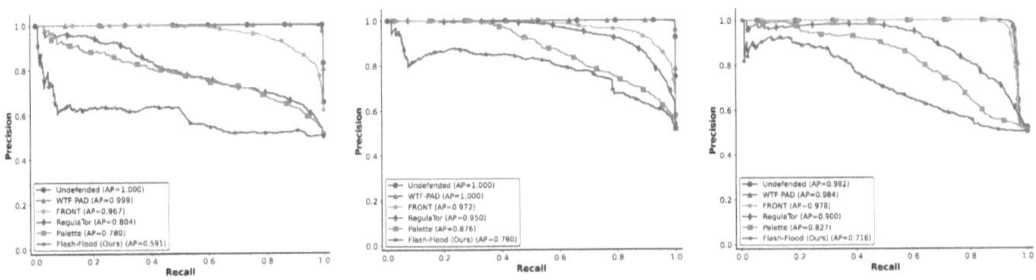

(a) DF (b) Tik-Tok (c) RF

Fig. 7. Precision-Recall curves of WF attacks in the open-world scenario.

As shown in the Fig. 7, without defense, all three models achieve near-saturated average precision (AP) (1.000 for DF and Tik-Tok, 0.982 for RF), with PR curves concentrated near the top-right corner. WTF-PAD and FRONT have limited impact due to their inability to obscure macroscopic traffic features (e.g., DF still reaches 0.967 under FRONT, and Tik-Tok remains 1.000 under WTF-PAD). RegulaTor reduces AP to 0.804, 0.950, and 0.900, while Palette further lowers them to 0.780, 0.876, and 0.827. In contrast, Flash-Flood achieves stronger obfuscation, shifting PR curves toward the lower-left and reducing AP to 0.591, 0.790, and 0.716. This is because the generated traffic exhibit high distributional and topological similarity, blurring decision boundaries: relaxing thresholds to maintain high recall introduces substantial false positives, whereas stricter thresholds lead to severe misses. As a result, the effective decision space is significantly compressed.

4.5 Overhead Analysis

In this subsection, we evaluate additional network resource consumption. Let the real packet count and defended packet count of trace i be $|P_i|$ and $|P_i'|$, and let total dataset size be N. The definition of bandwidth overhead is shown in Eq. 10

$$\text{BOH}_{dataset} = \frac{\sum_{i=1}^{N} |P_i'| - \sum_{i=1}^{N} |P_i|}{\sum_{i=1}^{N} |P_i|} \tag{10}$$

Similarly, let t_i^{real} and t_i^{def} denote the completion times of the last packet before and after defense scheduling, respectively. Dataset-level time overhead is defined in Eq. 11

$$\text{TOH}_{dataset} = \frac{\sum_{i=1}^{N} t_i^{def} - \sum_{i=1}^{N} t_i^{real}}{\sum_{i=1}^{N} t_i^{real}} \tag{11}$$

As shown in Table 2, defense methods such as Palette effectively reduce fingerprint features but incur 64.81% bandwidth overhead and 26.02% latency, significantly degrading QoS. In contrast, Flash-Flood improves defense performance while limiting bandwidth overhead to 34.81% and latency to only 1.7%. These results demonstrate its suitability for online deployment under low overhead.

5 Discussion

Although Flash-Flood achieves a favorable balance between defense effectiveness and overhead, its generative architecture still faces challenges in large-scale deployment. First, fixed-length traffic generation limits modeling of long-lived connections (e.g., WebSocket and streaming), potentially causing macro-level topological inconsistencies that can be captured by models with large receptive fields; this can be mitigated by adopting state space models or autoregressive methods for unbounded sequence generation. In addition, data-driven defenses must address concept drift: as protocols evolve (e.g., HTTP/3 replacing TCP), existing generated trajectories may gradually become outdated, motivating the use of federated continual learning to enhance long-term adaptability.

6 Conclusion

This paper proposes Flash-Flood, a generative WF defense based on Consistency Models and temporal manifold reconstruction. It compresses multi-step diffusion into one-step inference and generates high-fidelity padding traffic to mask real traffic patterns, breaking fixed-pattern fingerprints. In terms of overhead, an adaptive merging strategy limits bandwidth and latency to approximately 34% and 2%, respectively, enabling practical deployment in interactive settings. In terms of security, Flash-Flood reduces the accuracy of DF, Tik-Tok, and RF to 12.2%–20.2% in the closed-world setting and significantly lowers AP in the open-world scenario. These results demonstrate that effective traffic feature obfuscation can be achieved under controllable overhead.

Acknowledgments. We thank the reviewers for their valuable comments and suggestions. This work was supported by The Research Project NO.2024YFF1401301.

References

1. Cai, X., Nithyanand, R., Wang, T., Johnson, R., Goldberg, I.: A systematic approach to developing and evaluating website fingerprinting defenses. In: Proceedings of the 2014 ACM SIGSAC Conference on Computer and Communications Security, pp. 227–238 (2014)
2. Dingledine, R., Mathewson, N., Syverson, P.: Tor: the second-generation onion router. In: Proceedings of the 13th USENIX Security Symposium, San Diego, CA (2004)
3. Elfwing, S., Uchibe, E., Doya, K.: Sigmoid-weighted linear units for neural network function approximation in reinforcement learning. Neural Netw. **107**, 3–11 (2018)
4. Gong, J., Wang, T.: Zero-delay lightweight defenses against website fingerprinting. In: Proceedings of the 29th USENIX Security Symposium, pp. 717–734 (2020)
5. Goodfellow, I.: Generative adversarial nets. In: Advances in Neural Information Processing Systems (2014)
6. Hayes, J., Danezis, G.: k-fingerprinting: a robust scalable website fingerprinting technique. In: Proceedings of the 25th USENIX Security Symposium, pp. 1187–1203 (2016)
7. Herrmann, D., Wendolsky, R., Federrath, H.: Website fingerprinting: attacking popular privacy enhancing technologies with the multinomial Naïve-Bayes classifier. In: Proceedings of the 2009 ACM Workshop on Cloud Computing Security, pp. 31–42 (2009). https://doi.org/10.1145/1655008.1655013
8. Hintz, A.: Fingerprinting websites using traffic analysis. In: Proceedings of the Workshop on Privacy Enhancing Technologies. LNCS, vol. 2482, pp. 48–55. Springer (2002)
9. Ho, J., Jain, A., Abbeel, P.: Denoising diffusion probabilistic models. In: Advances in Neural Information Processing Systems, vol. 33, pp. 6840–6851 (2020)
10. Holland, J.K., Hopper, N.: RegulaTor: a straightforward website fingerprinting defense. Proc. Priv. Enhancing Technol. **2022**(2), 344–362 (2022). https://doi.org/10.2478/popets-2022-0049

11. Juarez, M., Imani, M., Perry, M., Diaz, C., Wright, M.: Toward an efficient website fingerprinting defense. In: Proceedings of the 21st European Symposium on Research in Computer Security, pp. 27–46 (2016). https://doi.org/10.1007/978-3-319-45744-4_2
12. Panchenko, A.: Website fingerprinting at internet scale. In: Proceedings of the Network and Distributed System Security Symposium (2016)
13. Rahman, M.S., Imani, M., Mathews, N., Wright, M.: Mockingbird: defending against deep-learning-based website fingerprinting attacks with adversarial traces. IEEE Trans. Inf. Forensics Secur. **16**, 4367–4382 (2021)
14. Rahman, M.S., Sirinam, P., Mathews, N., Gangwal, K.G., Wright, M.: Tik-Tok: the utility of packet timing in website fingerprinting attacks. Proc. Priv. Enhancing Technol. **2020**(3), 5–24 (2020). https://doi.org/10.2478/popets-2020-0043
15. Ronneberger, O., Fischer, P., Brox, T.: U-Net: convolutional networks for biomedical image segmentation. In: Proceedings of the International Conference on Medical Image Computing and Computer-Assisted Intervention, pp. 234–241 (2015)
16. Shen, M., Ji, K., Gao, Z., Li, Q., Zhu, L., Xu, K.: Subverting website fingerprinting defenses with robust traffic representation. In: 32nd USENIX Security Symposium, pp. 607–624 (2023)
17. Shen, M., et al.: Real-time website fingerprinting defense via traffic cluster anonymization. In: 2024 IEEE Symposium on Security and Privacy, pp. 3238–3256 (2024). https://doi.org/10.1109/SP54263.2024.00247
18. Sirinam, P., Imani, M., Juarez, M., Wright, M.: Deep Fingerprinting: undermining website fingerprinting defenses with deep learning. In: Proceedings of the 2018 ACM SIGSAC Conference on Computer and Communications Security, pp. 1928–1943 (2018). https://doi.org/10.1145/3243734.3243768
19. Song, J., Meng, C., Ermon, S.: Denoising diffusion implicit models. In: Proceedings of the International Conference on Learning Representations (2021)
20. Song, Y., Dhariwal, P., Chen, M., Sutskever, I.: Consistency models. In: Proceedings of the 40th International Conference on Machine Learning (2023)
21. Syverson, P., Tsudik, G., Reed, M., Landwehr, C.: Towards an analysis of onion routing security. In: Proceedings of the Workshop on Design Issues in Anonymity and Unobservability, pp. 96–114. Springer (2001)
22. Tarvainen, A., Valpola, H.: Mean teachers are better role models: weight-averaged consistency targets improve semi-supervised deep learning results. In: Advances in Neural Information Processing Systems (2017)
23. Vaswani, A.: Attention is all you need. In: Advances in Neural Information Processing Systems (2017)
24. Wang, T., Cai, X., Nithyanand, R., Johnson, R., Goldberg, I.: Effective attacks and provable defenses for website fingerprinting. In: Proceedings of the 23rd USENIX Security Symposium, pp. 143–157 (2014)
25. Wang, T., Goldberg, I.: Walkie-Talkie: an efficient defense against passive website fingerprinting attacks. In: Proceedings of the 26th USENIX Security Symposium, pp. 27–43 (2017)
26. Wu, Y., He, K.: Group normalization. In: Proceedings of the European Conference on Computer Vision (2018)

A Forensic Framework for Detecting Ransomware Evidence Using Burst-Based Network Analysis

Mohammed A. Makarem[1(✉)], Akram Algaolahi[2], Ashraf Mahmoud[2], and Mohammad Zulkernine[1]

[1] School of Computing, Queen's University, Kingston, ON, Canada
m.makarem@queensu.ca

[2] Computer Engineering Department, KFUPM, Dhahran, Saudi Arabia

Abstract. Ransomware continues to pose a major challenge to digital forensic investigations due to its rapid execution, encrypted communications, and evolving evasion strategies. Existing approaches largely emphasize host-based artifacts or conventional detection mechanisms, while providing limited support for post-attack forensic reconstruction using network-level evidence. This paper presents a forensic framework for identifying ransomware evidence through the analysis of short, intense outbound traffic bursts directed to suspicious IP addresses. The framework combines packet-level size-related feature extraction, burst detection, destination-based filtering, and machine-learning-based classification to generate evidence-rich forensic alerts containing destination, timing, and session-frequency information. Evaluation on the CICAndMal2017 dataset shows that Random Forest achieved the best performance, with 92.69% accuracy, 94.33% recall, 92.81% F1-score, and an AUC of 98.41%. End-to-end validation through controlled execution of real ransomware samples confirmed the framework's ability to identify actionable network evidence across multiple families for timeline reconstruction and incident investigation. These findings demonstrate that burst-based communication patterns provide a reliable forensic indicator that complements traditional host-based approaches.

Keywords: ransomware · digital forensics · network forensics · burst-based indicators · outbound traffic bursts · command-and-control (C2) · encrypted traffic analysis · anomaly detection

1 Introduction

Ransomware remains a major cybersecurity threat because it can rapidly disrupt operations, deny access to critical data, and cause substantial financial and organizational damage [1,18]. Although considerable progress has been made in ransomware detection using host, memory, and network-level indicators [1–3,18], post-attack digital forensic investigation remains comparatively less mature [8,22]. In particular, investigators still face challenges in extracting

© ICST Institute for Computer Sciences, Social Informatics and Telecommunications Engineering 2027
Published by Springer Nature Switzerland AG 2027. All Rights Reserved
H. Neukirchen et al. (Eds.): ICDF2C 2026, LNICST 720, pp. 298–317, 2027.
https://doi.org/10.1007/978-3-032-37274-1_18

interpretable evidence that supports attack reconstruction, correlates malicious behavior with external communication, and assists in tracing suspicious endpoints [8,22,24]. This limitation is especially important in ransomware incidents, where forensic value depends not only on detecting malicious activity, but also on reconstructing how the attack unfolded and identifying evidence that may support attribution and incident response [8,22].

In this paper, we propose a digital forensic investigation framework for ransomware analysis based on burst flows to suspicious IP addresses. The framework is designed to identify ransomware-related network evidence by combining packet-level feature extraction, burst detection, destination-based filtering, and machine-learning-based classification. In particular, it examines whether short, intense outbound traffic bursts can serve as a reliable forensic indicator for distinguishing ransomware-related communication from benign traffic. To validate the proposed approach, the work employs controlled experiments on the CICAndMal2017 dataset using multiple machine learning models, followed by end-to-end validation through the controlled execution of real ransomware samples. The framework generates forensic alerts containing suspicious destinations, burst timing, and session-frequency information. These alerts can support attack timeline reconstruction and incident investigation. The approach therefore extends beyond detection by emphasizing forensic interpretation and evidence generation.

The remainder of this paper is organized as follows. Section 2 reviews the relevant literature on ransomware detection and digital forensic analysis. Section 3 presents the proposed framework and the experimental methodology. Section 4 reports and discusses the experimental results, including end-to-end validation using real ransomware samples. Section 5 concludes the paper with the principal findings and contributions, and outlines the limitations of the present work together with directions for future research.

2 Literature Review

The escalating threat of ransomware has driven a critical need for advanced detection and forensic analysis techniques. While a substantial body of research has addressed ransomware detection and prevention using host-based, memory-based, and network-level indicators [2,3,6,18], post-attack digital forensic investigation remains comparatively less mature. Detection-oriented works have explored a wide range of approaches, including supervised machine learning on process memory features [3], behavioral models based on registry operations and file entropy [15], API call pattern analysis using NLP [21], network traffic classification through ensemble methods [13,20,31], hybrid anomaly detection with Isolation Forest and Gradient Boosting [11], GAN-based network anomaly detection [34], and encrypted traffic analysis targeting C2 communications [23,33]. Although these methods have achieved strong classification performance, they primarily focus on identifying or blocking ransomware in real time and do not address the forensic reconstruction that follows an attack.

In contrast, post-attack forensic investigation aims to recover evidence, reconstruct attack timelines, and support attribution and legal proceedings. This area has received far less attention despite its importance to incident response. On the memory forensics side, Joseph and Norman [16] conducted a practical implementation on memory dumps from a WannaCry-infected system, successfully tracing injected DLLs and identifying process hollowing through reverse engineering. Oh et al. [24] proposed volGPT, a novel ransomware triage method that leverages large language models in conjunction with the Volatility framework to identify ransomware-related processes within memory dumps from five different families, demonstrating higher accuracy and more comprehensive explanations than existing state-of-the-art triage methods. Lozano et al. [17] evaluated the maturity of live forensic techniques specifically for Linux ransomware, examining key recovery prospects across Icefire, Cl0p, and Blackbasta samples. Their findings revealed that while encryption key extraction during dynamic analysis was feasible for some families, others employed deliberate countermeasures that rendered memory-based forensic recovery ineffective, highlighting the fragility of relying on a single forensic data source.

For host-level forensic recovery, Rathod and Sharma [27] used open-source tools including FTK Imager, Autopsy, the Volatility Framework, and a Cuckoo sandbox to extract forensic artifacts from a WannaCry-infected Windows system, encompassing volatile memory analysis, registry examination, and disk artifact recovery. Singh et al. [28] confirmed the feasibility of using process memory as a forensic detection mechanism by analyzing access privileges across different memory regions using machine learning, achieving accuracy of up to 96.28%. Nguyen et al. [22] provided one of the most recent and comprehensive evaluations of digital forensics methodology for ransomware analysis on Windows-based desktops, spanning static and dynamic analysis, file system artifacts, and registry changes, and representing a significant step toward systematic forensic evaluation of ransomware behavior on modern Windows platforms.

Network-level forensic investigation of ransomware has received considerably less attention than host-based or memory-based approaches. Chimmanee and Jantavongso [8] conducted a digital forensic analysis of ransomware attacks targeting Virtual Private Networks in factory environments. Using the Microsoft ransomware attack framework and the MITRE ATT&CK knowledge base, they analyzed three real-world case studies and produced network diagrams, event logs, digital evidence summaries, and forensic timelines. While their work provides valuable case-specific forensic reconstruction, it focuses primarily on evidence compilation from specific incidents rather than proposing a generalizable network-level forensic framework applicable across different ransomware families and communication patterns. This gap is notable given that C2 infrastructure was involved in approximately 70% of ransomware intrusions in 2023 [14], and that adversaries are increasingly concealing C2 channels within legitimate cloud services and encrypted protocols [30], making network-level forensic evidence increasingly important for comprehensive incident investigation.

Table 1 summarizes the existing forensic-oriented ransomware works. From this analysis, several critical research gaps emerge. First, most forensic works rely on memory or host-level artifacts and do not systematically leverage network traffic as a primary evidence source. Second, the only network-level forensic work [8] focuses on case-specific VPN log analysis rather than proposing a generalizable framework for extracting forensic indicators from network communication patterns. Third, many proposed forensic methods lack validation against live ransomware execution in controlled environments, limiting confidence in their practical applicability. Fourth, no existing work has examined short, intense outbound traffic bursts to suspicious IP addresses as a forensic indicator, despite this pattern reflecting key exchange, encryption confirmation, and C2 beaconing behaviors common across ransomware families. The present work addresses these gaps through a network-centric forensic framework. The framework introduces burst-based communication as a new forensic indicator and generates structured forensic alerts containing destination IP, session frequency, and timing information. It is validated through both benchmark evaluation and controlled execution of real ransomware samples.

Table 1. Summary of ransomware forensic investigation work.

Reference	Forensic Level	Paradigm	Key Result	Deploy
Joseph rt al. [16]	Memory	Memory forensics	DLL injection traced	Yes
Rathod et al. [27]	Memory, registry, disk	Host forensics	Artifacts recovered	Yes
Singh et al. [28]	Memory	Supervised ML	Accuracy = 96.28%	No
Oh et al. [24]	Memory	LLM + Volatility	High triage accuracy	No
Chimmanee et al. [8]	Network, logs	Case study	Timeline produced	Yes
Lozano et al. [17]	Memory (Linux)	Live forensics	Key recovery (2/3)	Yes
Nguyen et al. [22]	Host (disk, registry)	Static + dynamic	Comprehensive	Yes
This work	**Network**	**Burst-based ML**	**Accuracy = 92.69%**	**Yes**

3 Methodology

This section outlines the end-to-end approach used in this work. First, a detailed description of the dataset and packet-level representation is provided, describing how PCAP files are parsed to materialize one row per packet, including header fields required for size-centric analysis. Then, the feature-extraction pipeline is presented, illustrating the packet-level and transport-layer features that are extracted and employed in the characterization of ransomware behavior. Subsequently, the model design is described, specifying the chosen classifier and the adopted training and validation procedures. After that, the system design and architecture are presented, detailing the Log Aggregator, External Database Server, Burst Detector, and ML-Based Classifier, as well as the interactions and data flow between these components. Finally, the experimental setup is also detailed, including the procedures for Specimen collection, the testing environment, data storage, and the investigation framework.

3.1 Dataset Acquisition

This work employs the CICAndMal2017 [19] PCAP files released by the Canadian Institute for Cybersecurity (CIC). The PCAP files contain a mixture of benign and malicious samples, including ransomware, scareware, SMS malware, and adware, captured under controlled conditions. The large number of ransomware and normal samples in these PCAP files makes CICAndMal2017 suitable for evaluating our burst-to-suspicious-IP indicator through comparative analysis between malicious and benign workloads. The ransomware PCAP files represent 10 different families, while the benign set includes traffic from more than 1,700 applications. Due to the much larger number of benign files compared with ransomware files, only benign-2017 PCAPs were used to derive the proposed dataset for training, validation, and offline testing. In this study, we regenerated a packet-based dataset from the original PCAP files instead of using the generated flow-based dataset, because our objective is to analyze and identify burst indicators at the packet level. Unlike the flow-based representation, which summarizes the entire communication flow, the packet-based representation preserves individual packet characteristics needed for burst analysis. To preserve evidentiary fidelity for forensic reconstruction and support small-burst analysis, we therefore materialized one record per packet. Operating at the packet level retains exact timestamps and header fields required by our size-centric indicator. The resulting dataset consists of 5,477,629 ransomware traffic records, of which 94.7% are TCP and 5.3% are UDP, along with 8,087,040 benign traffic records, providing a sufficient number of samples for subsequent analysis.

The derived dataset is moderately imbalanced, with approximately 40.4% ransomware records and 59.6% benign records (ratio $\approx$ 1:1.48). For model development, the dataset was partitioned using stratified random sampling into a training set (60%), a validation set (20%), and an independent test set (20%), preserving the original class proportions across all splits. To further mitigate the residual class imbalance, the Random Forest classifier was configured with the `balanced_subsample` class-weighting scheme, which reweights samples within each bootstrap subset inversely proportional to class frequency. This reduces bias toward the majority (benign) class while preserving the natural distribution of the underlying traffic.

CICAndMal2017 was retained as the primary benchmark because, despite predating several modern families, it remains one of the most recent publicly available labeled datasets that simultaneously provides (i) packet-level PCAP captures rather than pre-aggregated flow records, (ii) multiple ransomware families, and (iii) a large benign baseline drawn from over 1,700 applications—three properties that are jointly required for burst-level network analysis. More recent ransomware corpora released between 2022 and 2025 do not satisfy this combination: the *Ransomware Dataset 2024* [4] and the *Akira/LockBit Ransomware*

Dataset 2025 [5] are distributed as feature-extracted tabular data (CSV/XLSX) rather than packet captures; *CIC-MalMem-2022* [7] contains memory-dump features rather than network traffic; and *RanSAP* [12] captures storage-access patterns. Per-family repositories like the Stratosphere Facility [32] restrict ransomware coverage to just four legacy families that were captured and published between 2016 and 2017, offering no modern advantage over the same era in CICAndMal2017.

The framework is therefore designed around behaviors that are fundamental rather than family-specific. These behaviors include short, low-volume bursts toward external endpoints during key exchange, encryption-status signaling, and command-and-control beaconing. By focusing on these common network characteristics, the framework aims to remain effective across different ransomware families. Its applicability to recent families is further examined in Sect. 3.7 through controlled in-sandbox execution of live ransomware samples.

3.2 Feature Selection

To accurately detect the small, low-volume bursts that characterize ransomware communication, we selected a compact set of size and header-oriented features that directly reflect how ransomware typically exchanges small control messages (e.g., key material transfer, configuration retrieval, and encryption-status confirmation). The selected attributes emphasize packet and payload size, header structure, and fragmentation behavior, since these properties are stable indicators of bursty exchanges even when payload contents are encrypted.

The final feature set comprises packet-level [26] and transport-layer [10,25] fields: *packet length, header length, fragment identification, fragment offset, protocol type, transport PDU payload length, transport header length, transport window size.* The selected features were chosen to reflect burst size, structural characteristics, and fragmentation behavior commonly associated with ransomware communication:

- **Packet length and transport PDU payload length**: Capture the small message sizes commonly observed in brief ransomware signaling.
- **Header length, transport header length, and transport window size**: Provide structural context that helps distinguish benign short exchanges from repetitive burst patterns.
- **Fragment identification and fragment offset**: Model fragmentation-related behavior, which may occur when payloads are segmented or when attackers attempt to evade straightforward signature-based inspection.

All features are derived from observable metadata rather than application payloads, making the approach robust to encryption and suitable for continuous monitoring.

3.3 Size-Related Features Analysis

Packet-size distributions reveal characteristic transmission patterns in ransomware traffic. Across IP, TCP, and UDP, the density curves in Fig. 1

exhibit a consistent bimodal shape: (i) many small packets/datagrams (typically 0–200/300 B) and (ii) a second concentration near the Ethernet MTU (roughly 1,300–1,500 B, depending on headers). The small sizes reflect control-plane exchanges—handshakes, key negotiation, keep-alives, and short command-and-control (C2) messages—while near-MTU units indicate bulk transfers of encrypted payloads or exfiltrated data. This alternation between short control bursts and large contiguous payloads forms a distinctive size-based fingerprint of ransomware communications. This distinct separation reinforces the notion that ransomware communication alternates between short bursts of control exchanges and large, contiguous data transmissions.

The 300-byte boundary used by the burst detector was derived from the empirical bimodal structure observed in Fig. 1, where the lower mode terminates between approximately 280 and 320 bytes across the IP, TCP, and UDP distributions. To assess the sensitivity of this choice, the threshold was varied in 50-byte increments (200, 250, 300, 350, and 400 bytes) and the impact on burst extraction was examined on a held-out portion of the dataset. Smaller thresholds (200–250 B) excluded a measurable fraction of legitimate short control exchanges such as encryption-confirmation messages, increasing the rate of missed bursts. Larger thresholds (350–400 B) admitted more benign short-payload traffic—DNS responses, partial TLS handshake records, and HTTP/2 control frames—which increased the alert volume without improving detection coverage. The 300-byte threshold provided the most stable balance between alert volume and detection coverage and is also consistent with the typical size range of documented ransomware control-plane messages. We therefore retain 300 bytes as the operational threshold while acknowledging that, for deployments in atypical network environments, this parameter can be re-tuned from a short calibration phase on locally captured benign traffic.

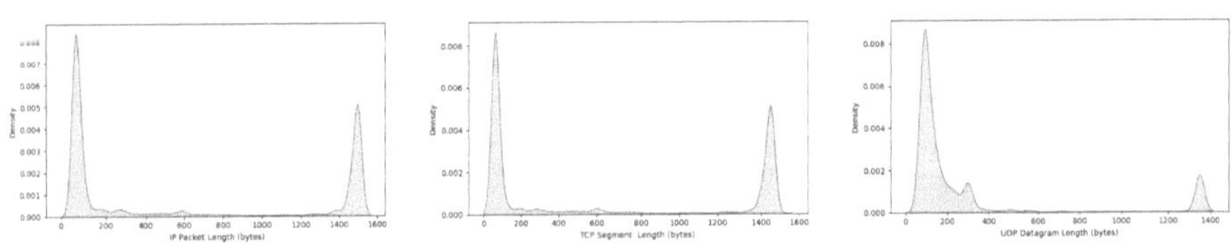

(a) IP packet length (b) TCP segment payload length (c) UDP datagram payload length

Fig. 1. Payload-size distributions observed in ransomware traffic.

3.4 System Design and Architecture

The proposed forensic investigation framework is designed to systematically identify network-level evidence indicative of ransomware activity. Figure 2 illustrates the overall architecture, which integrates four main components—*Log*

Aggregator, *External Database*, *Burst Detector*, and *ML-Based Classifier*—to facilitate the detection and forensic interpretation of small-burst communication patterns commonly associated with ransomware C2 behavior.

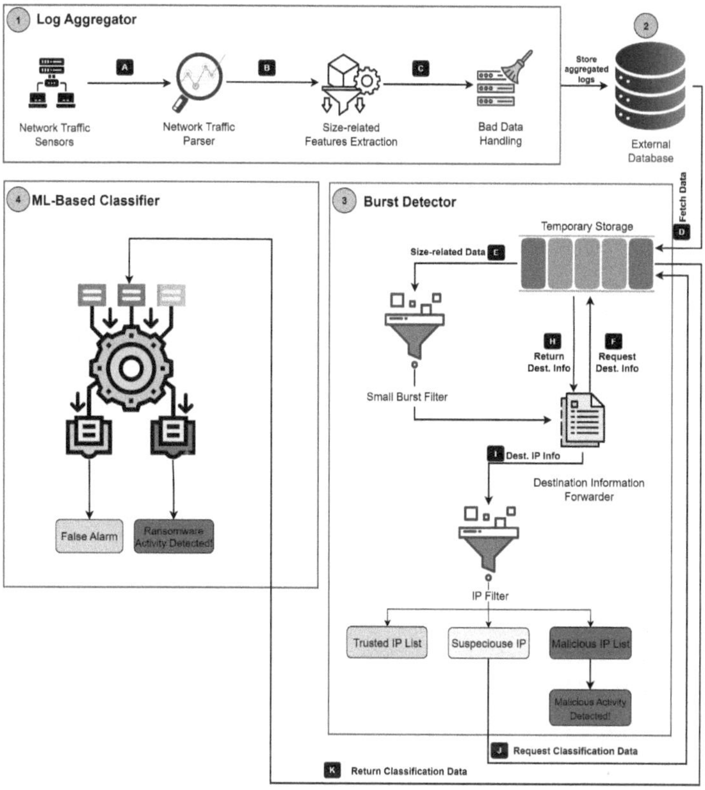

Fig. 2. Proposed Framework Architecture.

Log Aggregator serves as the foundational layer responsible for capturing, parsing, and preparing network data for future analysis.

- **Network Traffic Sensors:** These sensors continuously monitor and capture raw packet streams from network gateways or mirrors, ensuring that all inbound and outbound traffic is recorded for subsequent analysis. This approach guarantees the preservation of evidentiary integrity and temporal consistency, both critical for forensic reproducibility.
- **Network Traffic Parsers:** Captured network traffic is transformed from its native binary form into structured flow records. The parsing process extracts relevant metadata—such as IP addresses, ports, protocol types, and packet timestamps.

- **Size-related Features Extraction:** From each parsed flow, size-based attributes such as packet length and payload size are computed. These metrics are crucial for identifying short, high-frequency transmission bursts, which have been empirically associated with ransomware encryption key exchanges and beaconing patterns.
- **Bad Data Handling:** Incomplete or corrupted data samples are automatically detected and processed through imputation or exclusion mechanisms. This step mitigates analytical bias, ensuring data quality and consistency throughout the processing pipeline.

External Database functions as a centralized evidence repository for aggregated network logs. It ensures secure, persistent storage of the preprocessed data, enabling forensic analysts to reconstruct attack timelines or validate model inferences at any stage.
Burst Detector constitutes the analytical core of the proposed framework. It performs classification to identify network flows exhibiting burst-like characteristics indicative of ransomware activity.

- **Forensic Data Retrieval:** The classifier retrieves data batches from the external database using a sliding time window, enabling continuous analysis without compromising evidentiary continuity.
- **Burst Detector:** Detects short, low-volume bursts that are consistent with ransomware operations such as (exchanging encryption material and sending a compact "encryption complete / success" confirmation)
- **Destination Information Forwarder:** For each detected burst, it extracts the destination information and forwards this metadata to destination-based filtering to determine whether the IP belongs to one of three classes: Trusted, Malicious, or Suspicious.
- **IP Filter:** Classifies burst destinations into three categories: Trusted (resolved from the Cisco Umbrella Top 1 Million domains [9]), Malicious (compiled from the CICAndMal2017 dataset and Spamhaus [29]), or Suspicious (any IP not appearing in either list). Bursts to malicious IPs trigger immediate alerts, while those to suspicious IPs are escalated for final classification.

ML-Based Classifier receives the size-related data associated with the suspicious IPs identified by the IP Filter and performs the final decision-making stage. It uses a trained model to evaluate whether the observed small-burst behavior is consistent with ransomware communication patterns (e.g., key exchange or encryption-success confirmation) or represents benign bursty traffic, and then outputs either Ransomware Activity Detected or False Positive Alarm.

3.5 Operational Workflow

As shown in Fig. 2, the system workflow progresses sequentially from traffic capture to forensic inference. In log aggregator, network sensors feed raw data, where it is parsed, structured, and validated. The resulting records are stored in the External Database and periodically retrieved by the Burst Detector for small-burst detection. Once small bursts are identified, the associated destination information is forwarded to the IP Filter to determine whether the destination belongs to the Trusted, Malicious, or Suspicious categories. Bursts directed to malicious IPs may trigger an immediate alert, while bursts associated with suspicious IPs are escalated to the ML-Based classifier for final classification. When a suspicious burst event is confirmed as ransomware-related, the system generates an evidence alert containing the destination IP, session frequency, and timestamp, enabling timely incident response and post-attack reconstruction. In summary, the proposed architecture provides an end-to-end, evidence-centric forensic workflow that bridges data acquisition, automated classification, and contextual reasoning. This modular design enhances the accuracy, explainability, and forensic reproducibility of ransomware investigations, aligning with the work's objective of improving the identification and validation of burst-based forensic indicators.

3.6 Experimental Setup

The environment comprises four elements arranged along the data path: a Victim PC (sandbox), a Gateway that is the sole route to the Internet, a DB Server for durable evidence storage, and an ML-Based Forensic Server that performs feature extraction and classification. Figure 3 shows the controlled testbed used to generate, store, and analyze network evidence.

1. **Specimen collection and execution (sandbox).** Ransomware samples are obtained from a public malware repository VirusShare.com and staged to the Victim PC. Samples are executed only inside the sandboxed host. The sandbox's outbound connectivity is forced through the Gateway; no lateral movement or alternate egress paths are permitted. Benign background sessions (e.g., routine browsing or updates) may be generated on the same host to provide comparative traffic under identical capture conditions. Live ransomware execution is used here as a deliberate complement to the CICAndMal2017 evaluation rather than a replacement for it. CICAndMal2017 was recorded in a 2017 testbed and predates several modern C2 obfuscation techniques and TLS/HTTPS-encrypted endpoints; running recent samples in the sandbox allows the framework to be exercised against live key-exchange sequences, current external destinations, and present-day encryption practices that benchmark packet captures cannot reproduce. Four ransomware families were selected: WannaCry, Mamba, Petya, and Cerber. These families exhibit different communication models, including external C2 beaconing, SMB-based lateral movement, and hybrid behaviors. This diversity allows the framework to be evaluated across different burst profiles. Suspicious-destination matching succeeded for all four samples, confirming that the IP-filtering layer remained operative across families; the variation in detection ratios reported in Sect. 4.2 therefore reflects differences in burst behavior

rather than IP-filter failure. The testbed topology—a single sandboxed victim, a controlled gateway, and a centralized evidence store—was intentionally constrained to preserve evidentiary integrity and chain-of-custody, but this narrow scope necessarily limits exposure to enterprise factors such as proxies, NAT layers, and segmented internal networks. The live experiment is accordingly positioned as an operational feasibility study, with broader cross-dataset and multi-host validation identified as future work (Sect. 5).

2. **Packet capture and evidence storage.** The Gateway mirrors all ingress/egress traffic from the sandbox and records full PCAP traces. Captures are serialized to time-stamped files and transferred to the DB Server, which acts as the authoritative evidence repository. The repository preserves immutable snapshots to support auditability and chain-of-custody.
3. **Forensic analysis (DB → analysis server).** The ML-Based Forensic Server periodically retrieves logs from the DB Server for analysis. Using the extracted size-related features, the system detects small-burst episodes, extracts their destination IPs, and filters them so that only small bursts directed to suspicious IPs are escalated. Finally, the ML-Based classifier performs the final classification on the size-related data associated with those suspicious destinations to decide whether the activity indicates ransomware or a false positive, and raises a forensic alert when ransomware behavior is confirmed.

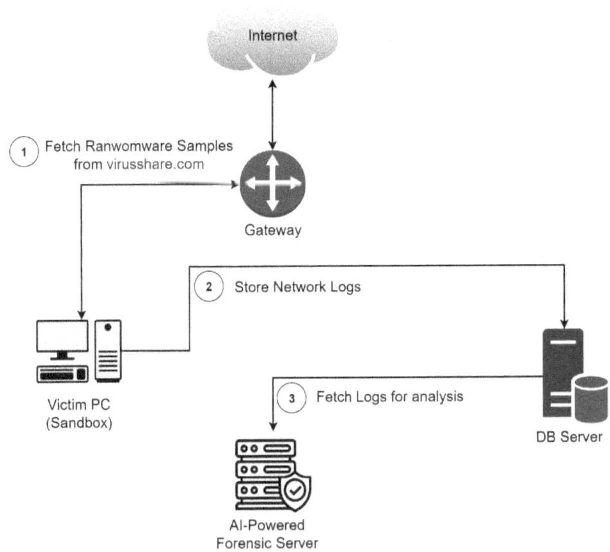

Fig. 3. Experimental Setup.

3.7 Experiment Execution

The sandbox experiment was designed to execute each ransomware sample in isolation and collect network evidence specific to that sample. In each run, a single ransomware file was launched inside the sandbox, and the developed Log Aggregator operated according to the proposed framework to monitor the resulting communication activity. The captured statistics were stored in a temporary datastore dedicated to each sample, ensuring that the recorded evidence could be attributed to the corresponding ransomware execution. The stored data were then processed to identify burst communications, defined as packets smaller than 300 bytes based on the previous analysis in Fig. 1, associated with suspicious IP addresses. These burst events were forwarded to the ML-Based Classifier, which analyzed the extracted features to determine whether the observed communication behavior is consistent with ransomware activity or not.

4 Results

The effectiveness of the proposed burst-based ransomware detection framework is evaluated through two complementary experiments. ML results quantify the ability of size-related traffic features to identify ransomware-like small-burst episodes. End-to-end validation is further provided by executing ransomware samples in a controlled environment, demonstrating reliable detection of burst communications directed to suspicious IPs and the generation of evidence-rich forensic alerts containing destination, frequency, and timing information.

4.1 Models Performance Evaluation

This subsection evaluates how well the proposed approach distinguishes ransomware bursts from benign traffic using size-related features. Performance is reported using accuracy, precision, recall, F1-score, and ROC–AUC, along with the false positive rate (FPR) given its direct impact on the operational usefulness of burst-based alerting. Four supervised classifiers were evaluated: Decision Tree (DT), Random Forest (RF), LightGBM (LGBM), and XGBoost, to assess the classification effectiveness of the burst-related features.

The observed values in Fig. 4 are consistent with how each model handles noisy, metadata-driven burst features and non-linear decision boundaries. Random Forest achieved the best overall performance. Aggregating multiple decorrelated trees reduces variance and limits overfitting, allowing the model to generalize more effectively to heterogeneous burst patterns. This behavior is reflected in its high recall and lower number of missed ransomware burst episodes. The Decision Tree baseline shows relatively balanced but slightly lower performance, which is typical for a single tree that can model non-linear splits but is more sensitive to small variations in the training data and therefore lacks the stability gained from ensembling. LGBM achieves strong sensitivity to ransomware-like burst events, reflected by its high recall, but its lower precision indicates that this sensitivity comes at the cost of more benign bursts being flagged as suspicious. This behavior is consistent with gradient-boosted models prioritizing detection of subtle positives when burst patterns overlap with legitimate short communications, which ultimately lowers the F1-score despite competitive recall. XGBoost yields the lowest scores across the reported metrics, suggesting that it is less effective at separating benign and ransomware-related burst episodes under the current feature set and training configuration. In practice, this can occur when boosted models are more sensitive to noise and parameter settings, leading to weaker generalization when the available size-related metadata provides limited discrimination for certain burst behaviors.

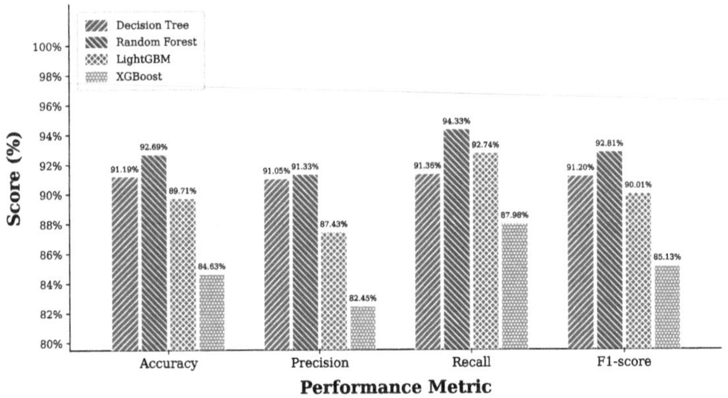

Fig. 4. Performance Comparison of the Evaluated Models.

Figure 5 presents the ROC curves and corresponding AUC scores for the evaluated models, illustrating their ability to separate ransomware-related burst episodes from benign traffic across all decision thresholds. All models achieve high AUC values, indicating strong overall discriminative power; however, Random Forest provides the best separability with an AUC of 0.9841, followed by LightGBM (0.9695), XGBoost (0.9373), and Decision Tree (0.9118). The Random Forest curve remains closest to the top-left corner, demonstrating a consistently higher true positive rate for a given false positive rate, which aligns with its superior performance in the metric-based comparison.

For the confusion matrix analysis, Fig. 6 reports the confusion matrices for the evaluated models; emphasis is placed on false negatives (FN), i.e., ransomware samples misclassified as benign, since these errors correspond to missed detections. The Random Forest model produces the lowest FN ratio (5.67%), indicating the strongest ability to capture ransomware-related burst events and the lowest risk of undetected activity. LightGBM shows a higher but still moderate FN ratio (7.26%), reflecting competitive sensitivity with a larger number of missed ransomware instances than Random Forest. The Decision Tree baseline further increases false negatives (8.64%), suggesting reduced robustness when

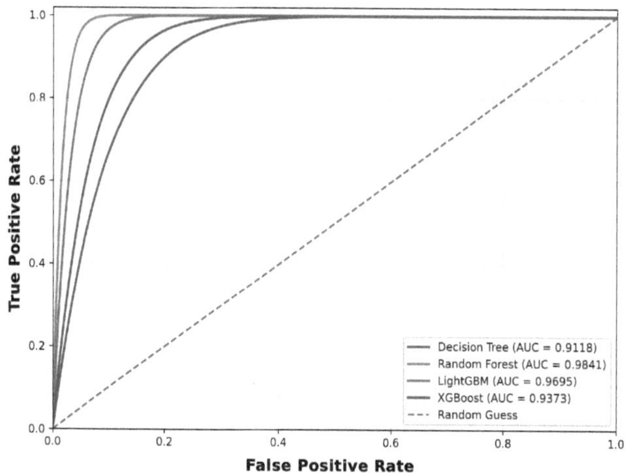

Fig. 5. ROC-AUC Curve Comparison of the Evaluated Models.

burst patterns overlap with benign behavior. XGBoost yields the highest FN ratio (12.02%), making it the least suitable option when minimizing missed ransomware detections is the primary requirement. Overall, the FN analysis reinforces the selection of Random Forest as the most reliable model for deployment in the proposed detection pipeline.

4.2 End-to-End Validation with Ransomware Samples

To assess the framework under live conditions, ransomware samples were executed in the sandbox and their network activity was analyzed using the proposed workflow. Figure 7 presents the traffic detection ratio observed for four tested ransomware samples: WannaCry, Mamba, Petya, and Cerber. Among these samples, Cerber produced the highest detection ratio at 48.2%, indicating that nearly half of its observed traffic was identified by the model as ransomware-related. Mamba and Petya showed moderate detection ratios of 28.3% and 24.5%, respectively, suggesting that their executions generated a noticeable but less dominant proportion of burst patterns matching the learned ransomware profile. In contrast, WannaCry exhibited the lowest detection ratio at 3.5%, which may indicate that, under the specific execution conditions of this experiment, its network behavior generated fewer traffic bursts that matched the model's learned discriminative features.

This low detection ratio is consistent with WannaCry's well-documented behavioral profile rather than a failure of the classifier. WannaCry is dominated by SMB-based lateral movement (notably the EternalBlue / MS17-010 exploit chain over TCP/445) and only contacts a small number of external endpoints, primarily its kill-switch domain and Tor-related addresses; it does not rely on continuous external C2 beaconing in the way that families such as Cerber do. As a result, the volume of short bursts directed to externally suspicious

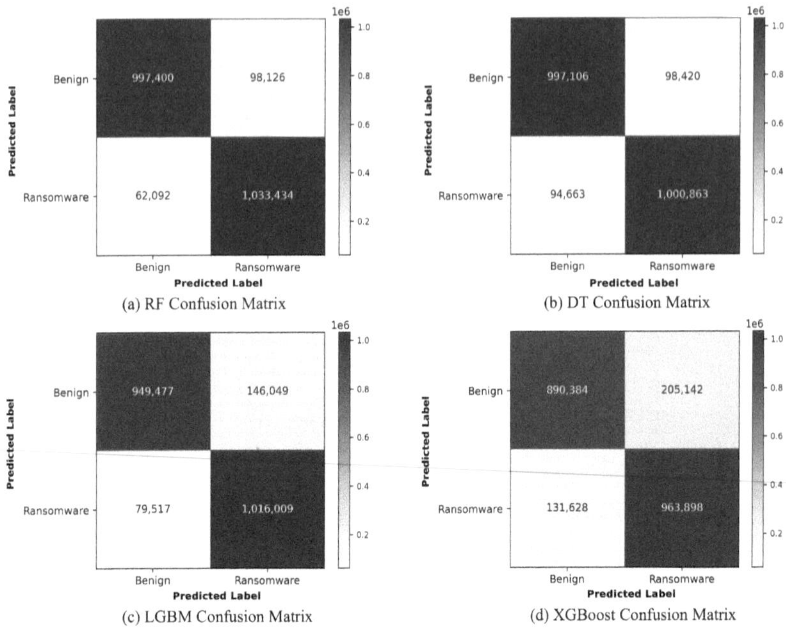

Fig. 6. Confusion Matrix of the Evaluated Models.

IPs is structurally low, leaving the burst-based indicator with comparatively few positive observations to act upon. More broadly, this finding highlights a systematic property of any externally-oriented network-burst framework: families whose malicious behavior occurs predominantly over internal protocols (e.g., SMB, RDP, internal RPC) or that embed encryption logic and keys locally generate fewer externally observable bursts and therefore yield lower detection ratios. Such cases are best addressed in combination with host- or memory-level forensic evidence and with internal east–west traffic monitoring, which we identify as a direction for future work in Sect. 5.

These results show that the proposed model can detect ransomware-related traffic across multiple families, although detection performance varies by sample. This variation is expected because ransomware families differ in communication behavior, timing, and dependence on external interactions. Since the framework focuses on short bursts toward suspicious IPs, families with clearer burst-based communication patterns are more likely to achieve higher detection rates.

From a forensic perspective, the value of this experiment lies not only in detection, but also in the generation of actionable evidence for reconstructing attacker activity. The results show that the framework can identify suspicious burst communications during ransomware execution and translate them into structured forensic signals. Even when the detection ratio is low, confirmed burst events remain valuable. They provide network-level evidence that can be corre-

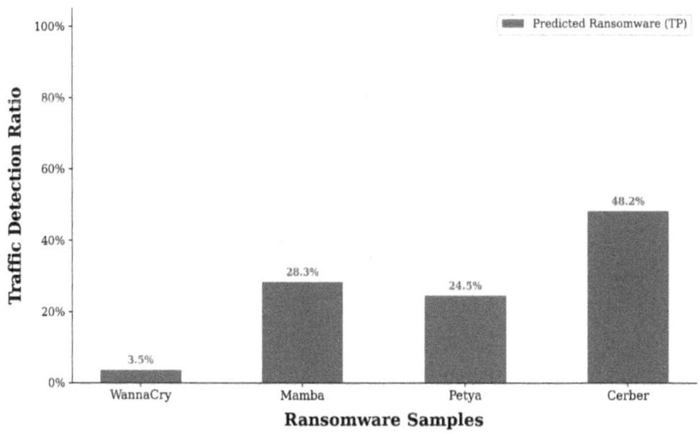

Fig. 7. Traffic Detection Ratio for the Evaluated Ransomware Samples

lated with timestamps, destination IPs, and event frequency during post-attack analysis.

4.3 Feature Importance Analysis

To further interpret the burst-based discriminative signal, mean decrease in impurity (MDI) feature importances were computed from the trained Random Forest model. The strongest contributions came from *transport PDU payload length* and *packet length*, followed by *transport window size* and *transport header length*; together these size- and structure-related features accounted for the dominant share of the total impurity reduction. Fragmentation-related fields (*fragment identification* and *fragment offset*) provided supplementary structural context but smaller individual contributions, while protocol type acted mainly as a gating feature separating TCP- and UDP-side bursts. This ranking aligns directly with the burst hypothesis: the size of the transport payload and the surrounding header structure are the strongest discriminators of short control-plane exchanges versus benign short flows. Equally important from a forensic standpoint, the dominance of metadata-only, size- and header-related features confirms that the framework's discrimination does not depend on payload content, and therefore remains effective under TLS- or otherwise encrypted C2 traffic.

4.4 Forensic Alert Example

To illustrate how the framework's output integrates into a forensic investigation, Table 2 shows a representative alert generated by the system during the controlled execution of a Cerber sample. Each alert is emitted as a structured JSON record and persisted alongside the corresponding PCAP slice, supporting both ingestion into SIEM and case-management tools and direct correlation with host-level evidence during timeline reconstruction. The fields capture the destination IP, the burst-window time range, the number of small bursts observed within that window (session frequency), the destination category produced by the IP-filtering layer (Trusted / Malicious / Suspicious), the ML classifier's family of origin and ransomware-class probability, the transport protocol, and a unique flow identifier together with a pointer to the underlying evidence file. This level of artifact-level detail, rather than a bare detection flag, is what enables the alerts to be consumed by an analyst as forensic evidence: each alert is timestamped, attributable to a specific destination, and reproducible from the persisted PCAP reference.

Table 2. Example forensic alert generated by the framework during Cerber execution.

Field	Example value
alert_id	alert-20250903-001142
timestamp_start	2025-09-03T11:42:08.214Z
timestamp_end	2025-09-03T11:42:11.058Z
src_ip	10.0.0.15 (sandboxed victim)
dst_ip	178.33.160.104
ip_filter_category	Suspicious (no match in Trusted/Malicious lists)
burst_count	8
avg_pkt_length_bytes	168
transport_protocol	UDP
classifier	RandomForest
ransomware_probability	0.94
session_frequency_per_min	6.0
flow_id	10.0.0.15:51723->178.33.160.104:6893:UDP
evidence_pcap_ref	evidence/cerber_run3_2025-09-03.pcap

4.5 Comparison with Existing Works

The proposed work differs from existing works in both purpose and practical outcome. As summarized in Table 1, most prior research focuses primarily on ransomware detection or prevention using memory, host, registry, disk, or general network features. In contrast, the present work emphasizes the forensic value of network traffic by using burst-based communication with suspicious IP addresses as an indicator for evidence generation and timeline reconstruction. From a performance perspective, some previous works report higher detection scores; however, these results are often obtained under different datasets, feature sets, and experimental conditions, which limits direct numerical comparison. The contribution of the present work therefore lies not only in classification performance, but also in the integration of detection with forensic interpretation. The achieved results, particularly with the RF model, show that burst-based traffic features can provide strong classification capability while remaining suitable for practical forensic use. In addition, unlike many existing works that stop at offline model evaluation, the proposed framework was further examined through controlled ransomware execution in a sandbox environment. This end-to-end validation demonstrates that the framework can detect suspicious burst communications during live execution and translate them into structured forensic alerts. Accordingly, the present work extends beyond conventional detection-oriented works by combining network-based machine learning with actionable evidence generation for ransomware investigation.

5 Conclusion

This paper presented a network-centric digital forensic framework for identifying ransomware evidence through burst-based communication patterns directed to suspicious IP addresses. The proposed approach integrates packet-level feature extraction, burst detection, IP filtering, and machine-learning-based classification into a unified workflow for post-attack analysis. Experimental results showed that Random Forest achieved the best overall performance, with the lowest false negative ratio among the evaluated models. Controlled execution of real ransomware samples further demonstrated the framework's ability to identify suspicious burst communications and generate forensic alerts containing destination, timing, and frequency information. Although detection performance varied across ransomware families, the results confirm that burst-to-suspicious-IP traffic can provide actionable and forensically meaningful evidence for timeline reconstruction and incident investigation.

6 Limitations and Future Work

A limitation of the framework is its reliance on observable burst-based network communication, which may reduce effectiveness for ransomware samples that operate with minimal external contact or embed their encryption logic locally, as illustrated by the lower detection ratio observed for WannaCry, whose behavior is dominated by SMB-based lateral movement rather than external C2 beaconing. In addition, the offline evaluation in this work was conducted on a single benchmark corpus (CICAndMal2017); cross-dataset validation on more recent ransomware traffic captures was not within the scope of the present submission, and the controlled sandbox topology likewise constrains exposure to enterprise-grade factors such as proxies, NAT, and segmented internal networks. Future work will therefore extend the evaluation to additional ransomware families and execution settings, perform cross-dataset validation against more recent network traffic corpora, compare the proposed pipeline against deep-learning baselines tailored to packet sequences, and investigate the integration of host-based evidence (memory, process, and file-system artifacts) together with internal east–west traffic monitoring to improve forensic completeness when externally observable network activity is limited.

References

1. Abdallah, L., et al.: Earlier decision on detection of ransomware identification: a comprehensive systematic literature review. Information **15**(8), 484 (2024)
2. Alhuwayshil, S., Ramachandran, S., Kim, K.: Enhancing ransomware threat detection: risk-aware classification via windows API call analysis and hybrid ML/DL models. J. Cybersecur. Privacy **5**(4), 96 (2025)
3. Aljabri, M., Alhaidari, F., Albuainain, A., et al.: Ransomware detection based on machine learning using memory features. Egypt. Inf. J. **25**, 100445 (2024)
4. Anonymous: Ransomware dataset 2024 (2024). https://zenodo.org/records/13890887. Accessed 5 Apr 2026
5. Anonymous: Ransomware dataset (Akira and LockBit) (2025). https://zenodo.org/records/14788965. Accessed 5 Apr 2026
6. Ashraf, J., et al.: A novel technique for ransomware detection using image-based dynamic features and transfer learning to address dataset limitations. Sci. Rep. **15**, 17647 (2025)
7. Canadian Institute for Cybersecurity: CIC-MalMem-2022: malware memory analysis dataset (2022). https://www.unb.ca/cic/datasets/malmem-2022.html. Accessed 5 Apr 2026
8. Chimmanee, K., Jantavongso, S.: Digital forensic of maze ransomware: a case of electricity distributor enterprise in Asean. Exp. Syst. Appl., 123652 (2024)
9. Cisco Developer: Get top most seen domains (legacy umbrella API). https://developer.cisco.com/docs/legacy-umbrella-api/get-top-most-seen-domains/. Accessed 5 Mar 2026
10. Eddy, W.: Transmission control protocol (TCP). RFC 9293 (2022)
11. Hagerty, J.: Ransomware detection via network traffic analysis using Isolation Forest and LSTM neural networks. Authorea Preprints (2024)
12. Hirano, M., Hodota, R., Kobayashi, R.: RanSAP: An open dataset of ransomware storage access patterns for training machine learning models (2022). https://www.sciencedirect.com/science/article/pii/S2666281721002390
13. Hossain, M.A.: Ensemble machine learning for proactive android ransomware detection using network traffic. Sci. Rep. (2026)
14. Hunt.io: Detect C2: Best practices for C&C traffic identification (2024). https://hunt.io/glossary/detect-c2
15. Jethva, B., Traoré, I., Ghaleb, A., Ganame, K., Ahmed, S.: Multilayer ransomware detection using grouped registry key operations, file entropy and file signature monitoring. J. Comput. Secur. **28**(3), 337–373 (2020)
16. Joseph, D.P., Norman, J.: A review and analysis of ransomware using memory forensics and its tools, pp. 505–514 (2020)
17. Korac, S., Moradpoor, N., Buchanan, B., Canberk, B., Maglaras, L., Kioskli, K.: Ransomware: analysis and evaluation of live forensic techniques and impact on Linux-based IoT systems. In: 2025 21st International Conference on Distributed Computing in Smart Systems and the Internet of Things (DCOSS-IoT), pp. 507–514. IEEE (2025)
18. Kritika: A comprehensive literature review on ransomware detection using deep learning. Cyber Secur. Appl. **3**, 100078 (2025)
19. Lashkari, A.H., Kadir, A.F.A., Taheri, L., Ghorbani, A.A.: Toward developing a systematic approach to generate benchmark android malware datasets and classification. In: 2018 International Carnahan Conference on Security Technology (ICCST), pp. 1–7. IEEE (2018)

20. Mehrban, S., Geransayeh, A.: Ransomware threat mitigation through network traffic analysis and machine learning techniques (2024). arXiv preprint arXiv:2401.15285
21. Molina, R.M.A., Torabi, S., Sarieddine, K., Bou-Harb, E., Bouguila, N., Assi, C.: On ransomware family attribution using pre-attack paranoia activities. IEEE Trans. Netw. Serv. Manage. **19**(1), 19–36 (2022)
22. Nguyen, H.A., Le, J., Baek, J., Susilo, W.: Digital forensics in ransomware analysis for windows-based computer systems. In: Data Security and Privacy Protection, Lecture Notes in Computer Science, vol. 16177, pp. 14–32. Springer (2026)
23. Novo, C.: Extending C2 traffic detection methodologies: From TLS 1.2 to TLS 1.3-enabled malware. In: Proceedings of the 27th International Symposium on Research in Attacks, Intrusions and Defenses (RAID) (2024)
24. Oh, D.B., Kim, D., Kim, D., Kim, H.K.: volGPT: evaluation on triaging ransomware process in memory forensics with large language model. Forensic Sci. Int. Digit. Invest. **49**, 301756 (2024)
25. Postel, J.: User datagram protocol. RFC 768 (1980)
26. Postel, J.: Internet protocol. RFC 791 (1981)
27. Rathod, D., Sharma, P.: Digital forensic analysis of ransomware infected Windows system. Int. J. Emerging Technol. Innov. Res. (JETIR) **6**(5) (2019)
28. Singh, A., Ikuesan, R.A., Venter, H.: Ransomware detection using process memory (2022). arXiv preprint arXiv:2203.16871
29. Spamhaus: Domain blocklist (DBL). https://www.spamhaus.org/blocklists/domain-blocklist/. Accessed 5 Mar 2026
30. Splunk: Modern C2 attacks: Detect & defend command-and-control (2025). https://www.splunk.com/en_us/blog/learn/c2-command-and-control.html
31. Srivastava, A., Handa, A., Kumar, N., Shukla, S.K.: Ransomware detection based on network behavior using machine learning and Hidden Markov Model with Gaussian emission. In: 2023 IEEE International Symposium on Smart Electronic Systems (iSES), pp. 1–6 (2023)
32. Stratosphere Laboratory: Malware capture facility project. https://www.stratosphereips.org/datasets-malware, per-family malware PCAP captures (including WannaCry and NotPetya); not a labeled multi-family ransomware benchmark with a paired benign baseline
33. Tambewagh, S.: Enhancing malware detection and classification in network traffic using deep learning techniques. J. Forensic Sci. (2026)
34. Wiles, A., Colombo, F., Mascorro, R.: Ransomware detection using network traffic analysis and generative adversarial networks. Authorea Preprints (2024)

Software Analysis and Forensics

Visualizing Differences in Versions of Software Files

Neil C. Rowe(✉)

U.S. Naval Postgraduate School, Monterey, CA 93943, USA
ncrowe@nps.edu

Abstract. Understanding differences between versions of the same file is important in digital forensics for analyzing update trends and recognizing anomalous activity. We examined a sample of 20,753 files with 582 distinct filenames having at least five different versions, drawn from a large corpus, with a focus on executable files for which version changes can have major implications. Most current file comparisons focus on block similarities, which are generally unhelpful with executables (unlike source code) for which updates are usually scattered throughout the file. This work first tested an alternative approach that sums weak evidence for offsets of matches between two files, then scanned the files to find matching sequences at the strongest offsets; the fraction of matches to the smaller file measured the similarity of the files. Several ways to make sequence matching more efficient were examined. This work then developed useful visualizations of the differences between two files and the evolution of software versions over time, often showing update patterns of every year or every two years. These methods provide a new tool independent of documentation and path names to identify normal updates, distinguish fraudulent (Trojan) software, and distinguish file near-copies and near-caches. This approach can provide new insights into processes of software updates.

Keywords: Software · Versions · Forensics · Comparison · Executables; Changes · Offsets · Visualization · Malware

1 Introduction

Digital forensics frequently must compare related files, most commonly different versions of the same file. Version comparison has been used to detect malicious code, predict code-maintenance problems [1], and suggest analogous updates [2]. However, it can also provide broader understanding of software development and use.

Versions of executable files are especially valuable to study, but versions of other software-related files can also provide insights. Versions of source code are easier to compare, but they are rarely found on digital systems since they are valuable intellectual property. Changes to executables are harder to find since registers and addresses can change significantly after recompilation for even a minor update. However, instruction codes ("opcodes") and constants change less with updates, and they should be matchable.

© ICST Institute for Computer Sciences, Social Informatics and Telecommunications Engineering 2027
Published by Springer Nature Switzerland AG 2027. All Rights Reserved
H. Neukirchen et al. (Eds.): ICDF2C 2026, LNICST 720, pp. 321–336, 2027.
https://doi.org/10.1007/978-3-032-37274-1_19

Matching enables seeing how much was added or subtracted from the executable with each version to get an idea of the magnitude of an update. Our research sponsor was particularly interested in recognizing unusual versions with substantial changes from any known version, which are potentially malicious, and versions with very few changes from previous versions, which are possible theft of intellectual property. These are concerns in software acquisition by organizations.

This paper first discusses previous work on comparing and visualizing software versions, then discusses how we assembled a test set from forensic images. We then discuss how we compared versions, which required a different technique from the standard hash-based file-comparison methods since important software-version differences are often spread through a file. Our technique incrementally builds matching sequences and can exploit several pruning methods for poor matches. We then discuss how file matches can be visualized using a novel branching plot, comment on detecting malware, and draw some conclusions.

2 Previous Work

Software development is complex, and many projects have tried to aid software engineers with tools to track changes between versions during design. Usually the tools focus on source code, and follow standard algorithms for comparing versions of text like the Linux "diff" command [3]. Changes can be abstracted by generalizations [4]. Most useful approaches focus on the changes to components [5].

Especially useful to software engineering is visualization of relationships in software [6]. Methods have developed visualizations of version clusters [7], tree diagrams of versions [8–12], diagrams using color and position to encode features [13–15], and diagrams of versions over time [16]. Work has graphed mappings between software components [17, 18], and parts of software [13, 19, 20], the last of which is closest to our approach. Some methods for comparing text documents also apply to software [21, 22].

Tracking versions of other files besides source code and text has been much less explored. Digital forensics often uses hash values to compare parts of storage media and files. Hashes can be compared on large segments of files, drive sectors, or whole drives to find large-block similarities that show patterns of copying [23]. This approach is unhelpful for versions of software-related files because they usually exhibit many non-contiguous similarities due to recompilation and re-encoding; recompilation changes many registers and addresses after even a minor update (though relative addressing reduces their number), and software-support files like configuration files often also change in scattered locations. Of three classic algorithms [24], block matching still needs significantly long byte sequences; rare-feature matching is only suited for very short features; and comparing blocks to a small set of prototype blocks only works well for data with similar patterns throughout. Matching using fuzzy hashes [24] only works when matching sequences longer than those found in executables, and is primarily useful for searching a drive, not for comparing files [25].

Classic algorithms for subsequence matching [26] are mostly ineffective in comparing software files because the subsequences sought cannot be enumerated in advance.

Edit distance could be a more useful concept [27] as it provides a flexible way to recognize fine-grain differences between two strings by computing the changes necessary to map one file to another. While computing it is exponential in complexity in the worst case, dynamic-programming and hierarchical algorithms [28] make it more efficient for strings that have few differences. However, most edit-distance algorithms try to completely explain the differences between two strings, and this level of detail requires considerable time on large files and is unnecessary for most digital-forensic needs. Decompiling executable files can approximate their source code for comparisons, but it is difficult, requires detailed knowledge of a specific machine language, and is inconsistent in its results.

Files can be quickly compared on simple statistics such as entropy and mean values for blocks, but preliminary experiments of ours found this was unhelpful for executables since many files with significantly different contents had similar statistics. A similar problem was observed with overall histograms of short sequences of byte values as compared using the classic technique of cosine similarity, where very little correlation was found between these similarities and the number of sequences matching between the files found using the methods to be described.

3 Test Data

We extracted a sample of 582 file families containing a total of 21,666 distinct files from the 2600 images in the full-image portion of the Real Drive Corpus, a collection of drive images obtained by purchase of used equipment around the world over 15 years from 2000 to 2015 [29], supplemented by a few versions of recent executables on our systems. Although the data is old, policies on updates to software have not changed much since then, while becoming more difficult to study with the increasing use of cloud storage for software, so our study could be valuable. Families were defined as all occurrences of a single file name (e.g., "mobsync.dll") ignoring its file path. The mean file size was 138,202 bytes with a standard deviation of 73,079. 290 families were of DLL format (7299 files), 84 were of EXE format (2683 files), and 50 were of the executable formats rpm, ocx, pyc, h, drv, pyo, class, obj, o, 8bf, pyd, cls, and scpt (2028 files). The remainder were a sampling of other software-related files including 54 families of document formats txt, rtf, pdf, doc, xls, ott, ppt, and pot (3471 files), 24 families of configuration-related files plist, ini, acm, tsp., zdct, cfg, properties, scp, and sys (1609 files), 10 families of source formats rb, js, vb, py, inc, and src (258 files), and 70 miscellaneous families with formats cab, zip, chm, hlp, htm, html, css, gif, and png (4318 files).

For each selected file name, all its occurrences in the Real Drive Corpus were identified using metadata. This metadata was calculated during initial forensic analysis. The Sleuth Kit "icat" command was used to extract one file for each distinct hash value from the images in EWF format (Expert Witness Format). Since many corpus files could not be retrieved because of faulty drive images (as many computers and devices we obtained were sold to the used-hardware market because they failed), retrievals were tried for each hash value until one provided a nonempty result. With so many drives, an undamaged copy for each hash value was usually found for common software families. All files were sanitized by storing modified versions inverting the bits to defang malware while not affecting file comparisons.

Families were excluded from our experiments if their files exceeded 50 MB in size, since comparing every pair within such families required too much time for our resources. Files marked for deletion by their operating system were excluded, as previous work showed that their file names were often wrong [30]. Nonetheless, some undeleted files could not be loaded either, as several things can go wrong is storing large amounts of data. Modification times were extracted for these files from metadata since modification time usually is set at the last change by the vendor and is independent of the installation. For this we used the earliest modification time of all the instances in the corpus of the hash value; around 5% of files had more than one modification time recorded for the same file contents, although this is poor software practice if the vendor is responsible.

The mean number of files in the families studied was 35.7 with a standard deviation of 54.7. There were a total of 1.3 million file pairs within families. In computing average file similarities for significance tests, using all the file pairs would unfairly bias the large file families against small file families as well as taking a long time. So tests were run on two samples of pairs, an intra-family sample and an inter-family sample, choosing a random 36 file pairs for each family, or all the pairs if they were less than 36; 36 was chosen because roughly half the families had fewer pairs. An intra-family experiment compared two randomly selected files in a file family, and an inter-family (control) experiment compared a file in a family with a file having the same file extension in a different family. 19,636 file pairs were compared in the intra-family experiment and 21,277 file pairs were compared in the inter-family experiment.

4 Efficient Sequence Comparison of Files

A typical update to a software-related file will insert, delete, or modify a few segments of code or data. Recompiled code of a mostly unmodified executable should have many identical instructions to the original compiled code though the address and register numbers may differ. We can count the fraction of unmatched segments of the smaller file as a metric of dissimilarity of two files.

Figure 1 plots two versions of an executable file soundman.exe where colors indicate sequences of identical code at least 24 bytes long found by our algorithm to be described in sect. 4, where white indicates unmatchable sequences. The top and earlier file came from a VAIO/Applications/Drivers/Audio/WDM directory on an Austrian machine, and bottom file came in a Program Files/Realtek/Audio/InstallShield directory on an Indian machine. Several insertions were made in the code section in the first half of the file, though much of the code was unchanged. By contrast, a single large red block of the data section towards the end is unchanged except for a few data differences in its second half. This is a typical pattern of changes during routine updates to an executable. Note that the matched pairs vary considerably in size, so an algorithm that picks a single block size for hash-based block comparison does poorly.

4.1 Finding Offsets of Matching Sequences

We defined in this work the degree of similarity between two files as the fraction of the bytes in the smaller file in byte sequences ("spans") that both files contain. An important

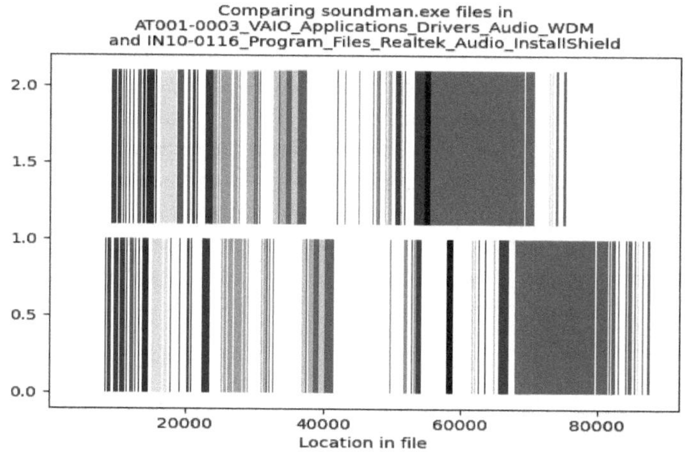

Fig. 1. Sequence matches between two versions of an executable file soundman.exe, with colors indicating matched sequences, and the earlier version on top

tuning parameter is the minimum length of a significant span. 24 bytes was chosen after experiments since it can include three 64-bit instructions, and nearly all spurious matches were found in spans less than 24.

To match files like executables where operands may change between versions but many operations will not, sequences should be considered where only one in every 2, 4, or 8 bytes need match; every 4th byte would be appropriate in matching 32-bit machine instructions, and every 8th byte in matching 64-bit instructions. This is called the "granularity" of the match in this work. For instance, the sequence of bytes with values 105, 107, 120, 115, 32, 68, 99, 102 matches a sequence of bytes of 105, 32, 120, 115, 32, 87, 99, 107 with granularities of 2, 4, and 8 but not 1.

Updates to executables found in our corpus almost always increased the size of the executable, as with Fig. 1. Hence updates more often insert than delete, and insertions shifted the positions of matches in the earlier version to later in the newer version. If changes between two versions of software were not extensive, we should be able to see consistent evidence of a few particular shifts or "offsets" between their two files. More precisely, an offset can be defined as the integer that must be added to a byte address in the first file to get the corresponding byte address in the second file. So rather than comparing each pair of bytes between files, one can look for the predominant offsets for particular byte values, and find contiguous sequences with those offsets.

Counting evidence for offsets can be done by first indexing the locations of each of the 256 possible byte values for each file. We can then count the number of possible occurrences of each offset by subtracting the pair of indexes for the same byte value in the two files, and keeping running counts in a hash table. On the average, this approach does 2 N retrievals to construct the indexes for files of N bytes, $256 * (\frac{N}{256}) * (\frac{N}{256}) = N^2/256$ increments by 1 to the offset counts if evenly distributed in the worst case; then it does $2Nlog_2(2N)$ comparisons to sort the 2 N possible offsets to find the K best, for

$2N + \frac{N^2}{256} + 2N\log_2(2N)$ comparisons total. For files of 50,000 bytes, this increases speed by an estimated factor of 210 over exhaustive comparison of bytes.

The offset counts show much noise in this weak evidence, much like the Hough transform in computer vision for finding broken lines. Byte values are not equally likely in real forensic data; Fig. 2 shows that the histogram of raw byte values in our full corpus, with big peaks for both 0 and 255. So it is important to exclude matches involving all-zero bytes and all-one bytes in sequence matching since they are common and create many spurious offsets. The figure shows that the remaining byte values vary significantly in occurrence rate, so their counts were weighted in rating possible offsets by $1/(n_{i1} + n_{i2})$ where n_{ij} is the count of byte value i found in file j, to provide fairer comparisons between sequences.

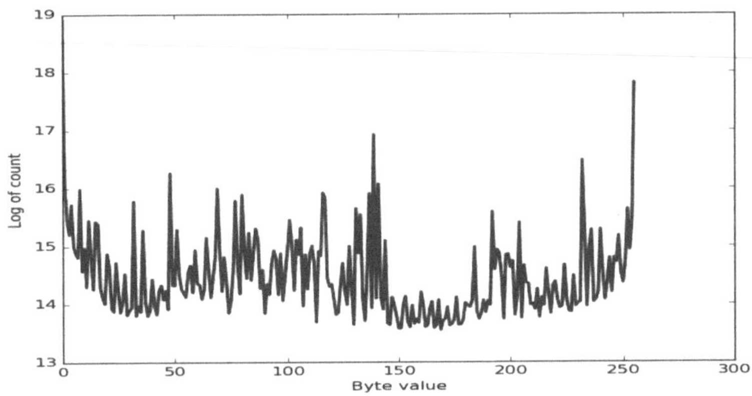

Fig. 2. Log histogram of integer byte values on a random sample of the corpus using raw bytes

4.2 Inference of Spans of Matching Bytes

Changes to an executable during an update usually cluster. Offsets with high weighted counts between two files must next be confirmed to predominantly occur in contiguous spans before they can be considered evidence of insertions or deletions. Comparison can be done by scanning the two files simultaneously at a particular offset value, counting consecutive matches. Now the occasional 0 and 255 byte values can be considered because we have eliminated most of their spurious matches. However, we found it desirable to require that spans contain at least one non-zero byte and have no zero-byte sequences of longer than half the minimum span length.

Because spans need not match every byte, spans found can conflict with one another about their offset recommendations for the same bytes. Three principles were used to exclude less-likely spans:

1. A longer span that overlaps a shorter span has priority in the area of their overlap, since the longer spans have more evidence. Length of a span was defined as the number of bytes it covered divided by its granularity, so it measured the number of actual bytes matched.

2. Spans than match with a smaller granularity (of 1, 2, 4, and 8) have priority over spans which map with a larger granularity in the area of their overlap, since their matches are more dense.
3. Shortened spans created by the first two principles that are less than the minimum span length (24 bytes) are eliminated.

For example in comparing two files, if one span with offset 100 covers locations 150 to 350 of a file on every byte (a granularity of 1), and another span with offset −50 covers locations 140 to 500 of a file on every second byte (a granularity of 2), then 150 to 350 of the second span should be eliminated as well as its too-short left side from 140 to 150. We get two spans with offset 100: 150 to 350 with a granularity of 1, and 350 to 500 with a granularity of 2.

It is important to find overlaps between spans in both directions of comparison. So for instance, for two spans with a granularity of 1 in a first file, one with an offset of 100 from 500 to 650 and one with an offset of −100 from 700 to 800, the two spans will overlap from 600 to 700 in the second file, and the shorter second span can be eliminated.

Table 1 shows statistics on the intra-family sample mentioned in sect. 3. Matches at granularities greater than 1 were uncommon, though they were important for some files and should not be ignored. The median number of spans found in an executable comparison was 68, and only 15.7% of the spans 24 bytes or longer found in all files were over 128 bytes. Nonetheless, the median length of the longest span for executables was 2373, suggesting that some longer sequences matched well despite considerable fragmentation in the matches. The last two rows were computed by finding the distance, for each span, of the nearest span in a comparison of two files that had at least two spans of at least 24 bytes; this method then averages the nearest distances over all spans in the comparison, and computes the median over all file comparisons. These numbers indicate significant gaps between matched parts of different versions of the same file, and suggest that block matching will likely do poorly with software files.

4.3 Other Criteria for Avoiding File and Sequence Comparisons

The methods of the last section still find many spurious matches between two files because of frequently reused programming constructs; this makes it hard to visualize the overall pattern of matching. The criterion that 5% of the smaller file's sequence were shared with the larger file was chosen as the minimum reasonable similarity of two files after experiments examining a sample of file pairs. In addition, many possible file pairs of a family collected over a long time are unlikely to be similar based on a large size disparity, and this eliminates the need to compare their bytes. Figure 3 plots the average similarity versus the log of the ratio of the larger file size to the smaller file size, and this justifies using a 5% size difference as a threshold for exclusion.

It is also desirable to avoid comparing files of high entropy since they are likely encoded or encrypted, and would lack clear insertions or deletions. Figure 4 shows the average similarity in the intra-family data as a function of the maximum of the 8-bit entropies of the two files; similar but less clear results were obtained from the minimum and average of the entropies. Very-high and very-low entropies fall below the 0.05 average similarity threshold, and we found maximum entropies <0.35 and > 5.25 were almost certain indicators of insufficient similarity.

Table 1. Statistics on the file comparisons in the intra-family sample

Statistic	Value
Mean file size in bytes	136,838
Mean number of bytes in spans of granularity 1	26,137
Mean number of bytes in spans of granularity 2	1,189
Mean number of bytes in spans of granularity 4	558
Mean number of bytes in spans of granularity 8	141
Mean maximum offset rating for file pair	19.89
Mean offset rating for file pair before filtering	0.108
Mean number of spans found per file-pair comparison	140.5
Mean fraction of bytes that match with spans of any granularity	0.2615
Mean 8-bit entropy	3.705
Number of executable pairs with at least one matching span	10,048
Number of non-executable pairs with at least one matching span	3257
Number of spans of 128 bytes or less in all files	25,954,000
Number of spans of more than 128 bytes in all files	483,000
Median number of spans in executable pairs, excluding pairs with 0	68
Median number of spans in non-executable pairs with at least one span	13
Median length in bytes of the longest span over all executable pairs	2,373
Median length in bytes of the longest span over all non-executable pairs	351
Median of mean nearest gap for each span over all executable pairs	50.5
Median of mean nearest gap for each span over all non-executable pairs	63.6

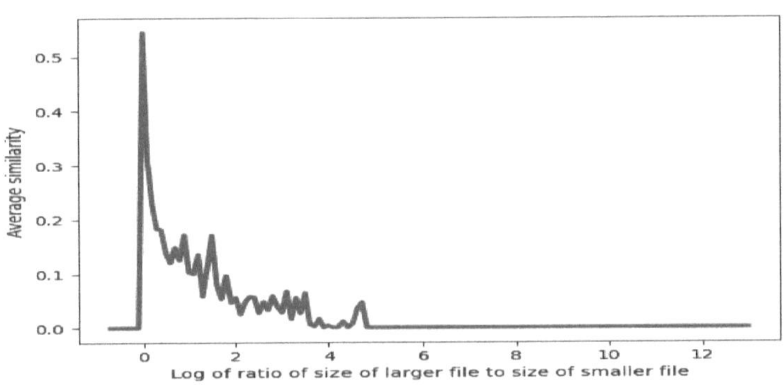

Fig. 3. Mean similarity versus ratio of compared file sizes for the intra-family sample

Another possible pruning criterion for file matching is when file modification times are far apart. When we compared epoch times (seconds since January 1, 1970) for every

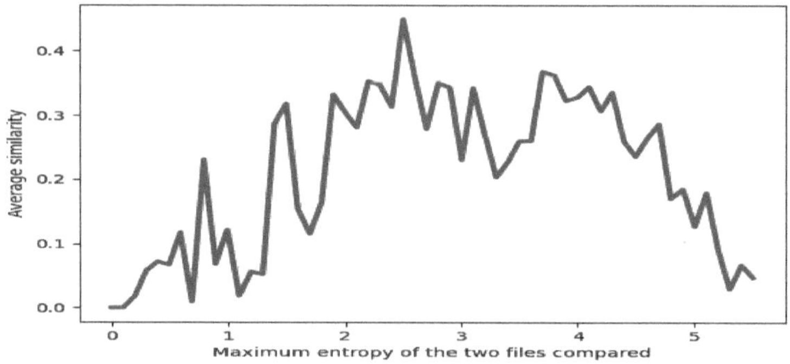

Fig. 4. Mean similarity versus the maximum of the entropies of the files compared in the intra-familiy sample

pair in every family in our corpus, only 14.1% of 18,130 closest-matching file pairs involved the most immediately previous files in terms of modification times. This means that file pairs in a family that are adjacent in time often have different operating systems and hardware, and have very different contents. As Fig. 5 shows for executables alone, similarities occur for files in a broad range from 0 to 15 on the graph (corresponding to a maximum of 37 years apart), and only then do similarities decrease significantly. This suggests that major updates occur no more than yearly (17.2 on the horizontal axis), but some software takes many years to get updated. Since file pairs in our corpus were rarely more than 15 years apart, modification timestamps did not provide useful pruning data.

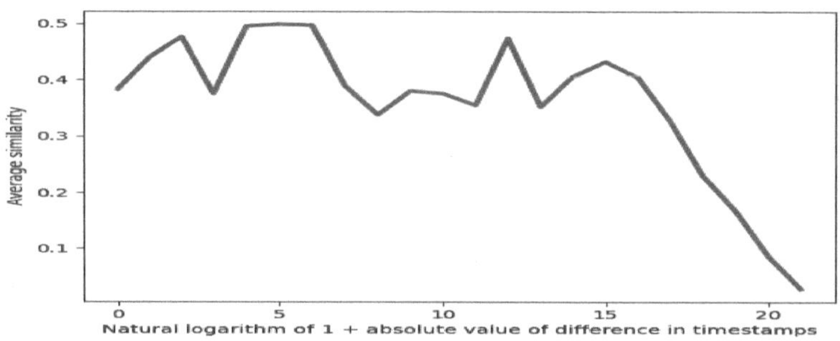

Fig. 5. Mean similarity of executable files in the intra-family sample versus the logarithm of one plus the absolute value of the difference of their timestamps

File-comparison speed can be further improved by excluding unlikely offsets below a rating. For rating, we used the similarity fractions (fraction of the smaller drive matching the larger drive). Figure 6 shows the distribution of the average logarithm of the ratio of intrafamily-similarity to the average interfamily-similarity for each family in the corpus; the horizontal axis is the logarithm of the intrafamily similarity. The instability on both left and right is due to small counts and is not statistically significant. As expected, high similarity values tend to occur within families, and low similarity values occur between families. Some intrafamily comparisons had low similarity values for major updates, and some interfamily comparisons had high similarity values for reused code. Nonetheless, a clear phase change occurs around −1 in the plot, and it is reasonable to say that no significant difference occurs in counts between the two experiments for offsets where the count ratio logarithm is greater than −1, which happens at −0.66 on the horizontal axis, corresponding to an offset rating greater than 0.52. This was used for pruning in subsequent experiments.

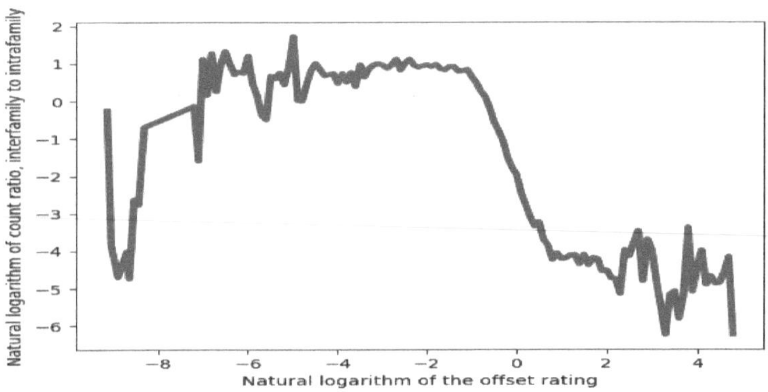

Fig. 6. Count ratio of spans bytes found versus offset rating for interfamily and intrafamily offset ratings

We also tested other pruning criteria for matches:

1. Exclude all but the K highest-ranking offsets for some value of K in comparing two files. This was excluded because it made too many errors, suggesting that small changes in updates are common.
2. Compute the mean offset weight for all the offsets found in comparing two unrelated (different-family) files, and only further consider offsets whose weight was more than three standard deviations greater than this mean. This was even worse that criterion 1.
3. Exclude parts of files unlikely to match. We found that code sections of an executable had a 5.9 byte entropy, text sects. 3.2, and encoded-data sects. 7.9. Executable formats like Microsoft PE [31] segregate executable files into code and data which could be exploited to rule out sequence matches. But this did not provide much pruning power in experiments.

5 File Family Visualization

The main goal of this work was to provide good visualization of the evolution of file versions (families). This can help learn the similarity patterns between versions in normal software schedules, suggest software-development anomalies, and find close copies of software, all without requiring hashes or signatures. It can also identify software components that could be fraudulent or a theft of intellectual property. The metric of dissimilarity of file sequences between two file versions introduced in sect. 4 is analogous to a distance in a plot of the space of file versions.

Related files can be visualized as connections in a graph. Earlier in this work, the Gephi software (https://gephi.org) for visualizing graphs was used, but we found it is mainly useful for graphs with thousands of nodes, more than in any of the families tested. It is also a non-metric visualization where edge lengths do not measure degree of similarity. Metric visualizations can better indicate important software updates, so we implemented one. In these plots, nodes represent files, the horizontal axis represents the modification time, and the vertical distances represent cumulative degree of dissimilarity for each file to its most-similar earlier file, plus 0.15 to prevent nodes from crowding vertically. Green dotted lines connect a file to its most-similar predecessor, except that files whose similarities to all other files in their family were less than 0.05 were assigned a vertical coordinate of 0.

Figure 7 shows the example visualization of the 45 members of the family of dunzip32.dll, an unzipping executable provided by Microsoft and used by a variety of software. One major line of development is clear, with a few outshoots, and six outliers are at the bottom. Updates were frequent at first, and then slowed, a typical pattern for the lifetime of software. Connecting lines become flatter (as 31–40, 31–43, and 31–44) as changes between versions became less extensive over time. Near-vertical alignments of nodes such as 2–3-4 and 16–18-19 suggest versions released at nearly the same time for different operating systems or hardware.

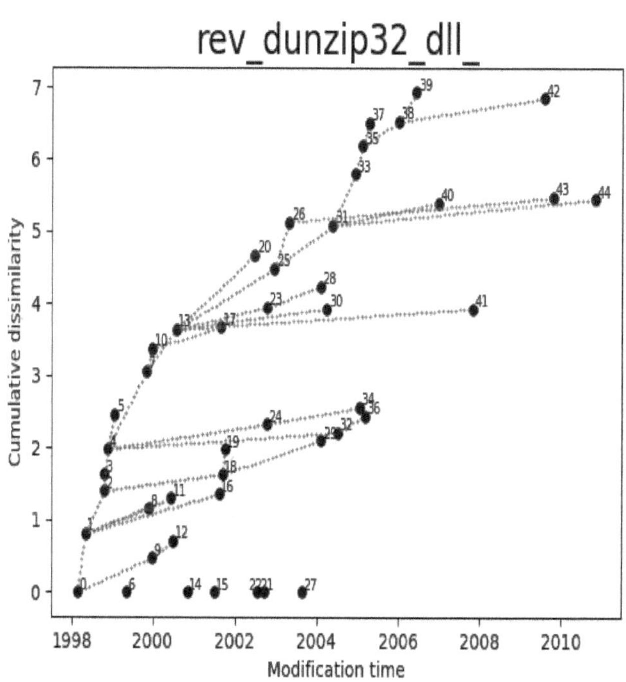

Fig. 7. Automatically generated graph visualization of the 45 versions of of dunzip32.dll in the corpus

Numbers in Fig. 7 represent the 45 distinct hash values of the 348 files with filename "dunzip32.dll"; the numbers are assigned in order of last modification time. The most common version was 44 at the furthest right in the figure, which occurred 142 times under Program Files/Real/RealPlayer in some of the last-collected drives. Other popular versions were 3 (fourth up on the left side) which occurred 30 times exclusively on Mexican drives under WINNT/system32, version 13 (eighth up on the left side) which occurred 7 times on a variety of drives under Corel Draw, version 29 (in 2004 at height 2) which occurred 25 times under Program Files/Real/RealPlayer, and version 33 (2006 at a height of 6) which occurred 12 times under Program Files/Auto CAD. Several versions (0, 2, 16, 32, 38, 42) related to anti-malware programs. It appears that many vendors use older versions of this executable for compatibility with the rest of their software; such executables are excellent sources for historical research even though drive imaging often gets only the latest version for each drive.

Figure 7 shows that the most-similar previous version of an executable is usually close in time, but not necessarily the closest. This was true for most of our file families, and is good support for our similarity algorithm. Earlier work of ours visualized simple statistics such as mean and standard deviation on blocks of files to indicate visual similarities, and made good pictures, but they correlated little with file matches.

Figure 8 shows a similar diagram for googlelicense.rtf, the Google license file, which has quite a few variants. It appears to have had simultaneous updates to variants in 2008, 2010, 2011 (twice), and 2012. This is typical of files intended for many systems.

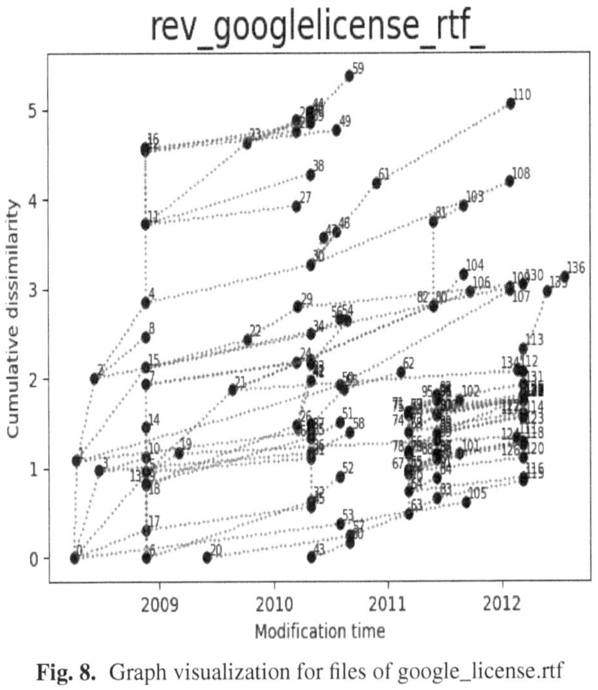

Fig. 8. Graph visualization for files of google_license.rtf

Figure 9 shows the histogram of the natural logarithm of modification-time gaps between the most-similar but different files found in each family. The horizontal axis is the logarithm of 0.0001 plus the time gap in years. A big peak occurs for minimal differences in the modification time for variants released simultaneously for different operating systems, a peak at two weeks (−3 on the horizontal axis) possibly for critical updates, and peaks at one (0.1) and two years (1.2) for routine updates.

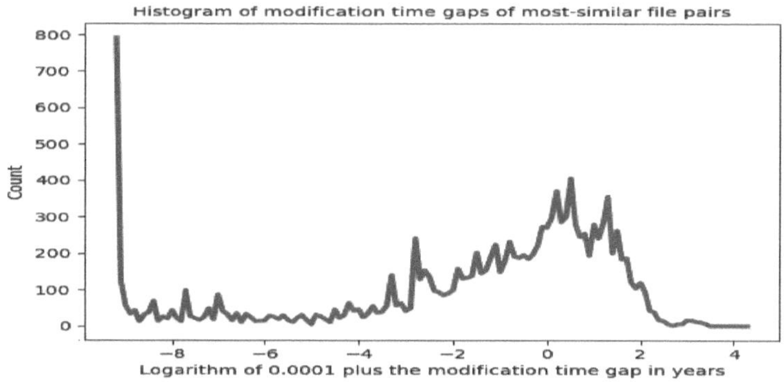

Fig. 9. Distribution of time gaps between most-similar file versions in the corpus

6 Identifying Potential Malware and Bug Fixes

Some files in the corpus were tagged as malware by one of five anti-malware tools in 2015: Bit9 (https://carbonblack.com), Open Malware (https://dannyquist.github.io/about/), VirusShare (https://virusshare.com), Symantec (https://broadcom.com), and Clam AV (https://www.clamav.net) [33]. We were curious if this malware had different time patterns than normal software. The corpus was purchased around the world and many drive owners were not diligent about cybersecurity, so there were around 350,000 instances (including duplicates) of malware in the full corpus from which the families were derived.

The visualizations in sect. 5 did provide a way to spot some kinds of anomalous software versions by marking nodes in red those that were tagged as malware by our tools. Figure 10 shows an example where malicious versions of webclnt.dll (a Web interaction tool) do form a separate vertical sequence of related variants from the legitimate variants in 2001–2005. We also discovered 7969 file pairs with identical hash values for the Counter Strike game where one member of the pair had "_xtreme_edition_" in its path and the other did not, suggesting illegal copies of a game. However, many software versions identified as malware by the five tools did not appear in any obvious patterns; as we noted in our previous work with this malware data, these five tools rarely identified the same files as malware, so many of those malware identifications may be spurious.

Current work is focusing on distinguishing the two major categories of updates, bug fixes and feature additions [34]. They are rarely distinguished in their file names, but can be distinguished by dissimilarity measure to the most recent version (bug fixes are more

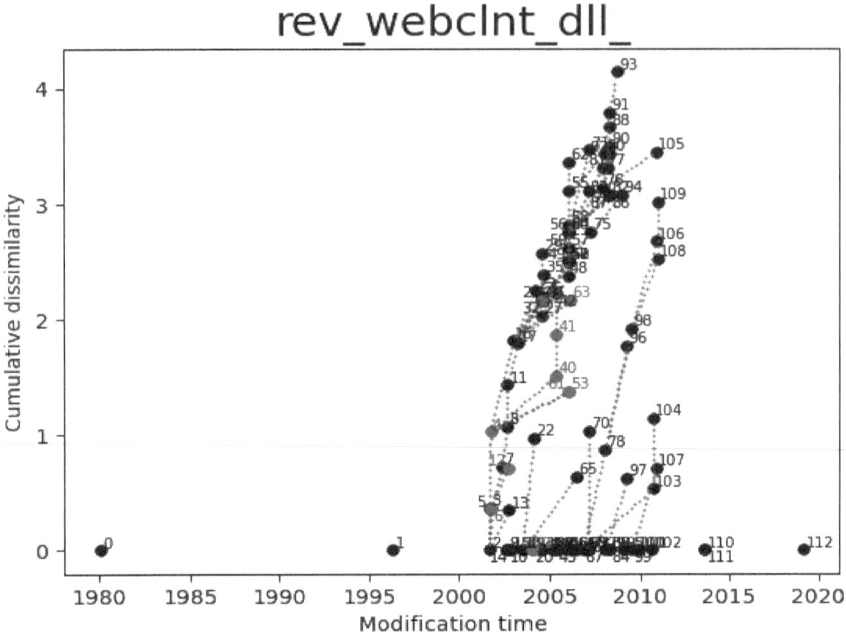

Fig. 10. Graph of versions of webclnt.dll showing malicious versions in red

similar) and time gap (bug fixes have shorter and more atypical gaps consistent with the left side of Fig. 10). We tested binary classification of updates based on applying a threshold to a weighted sum of those features, and got promising results.

7 Conclusions

This work developed a powerful tool for understanding patterns in the normal version history of software files. The software industry makes updates periodically, but until now we have not had a good tool to see what they have done and to distinguish normal from abnormal updates, nor detect distinctive characteristics of a particular vendor's update policy. A new algorithm was developed in this work for finding matching sequences between software files, a method that is made efficient by exploiting several kinds of pruning of spurious matches as shown by testing on a representative corpus. Tests on real executables also showed they could be usefully compared even with changes to addresses, registers, and constants between versions because enough clues are left to match the remaining bytes. This analysis yields dissimilarity measures which can be usefully visualized to see tree-like structures of updates. They also enable learning the directories used in normal patterns of updates, the relative frequency of insertions, deletions, and changes, and recognizing abnormal behaviors of several kinds that suggest bottlenecks, fraud, or malware. As software is increasingly distributed and assembled as needed, this study of already assembled software files will be increasingly difficult to duplicate, and its results will thus become increasingly valuable.

Acknowledgements. This work was supported by the Acquisition Research Program at the Naval Postgraduate School. Bruce Allen and Adam Montgomery helped with details. The data studied here can be obtained from the author.

References

1. Farago, C., Hegedus, P., Ladanyi, G., Ferenc, R.: Impact of version history metrics on maintainability. In: Proceedings of the 8th International Conference on Advanced Software Engineering and its Applications, pp. 30–35 (2015)
2. Zimmermann, T., Weissgerber, P., Diehl, S., Zeller, A.: Mining version histories to guide software changes. In: Proceedings of the 26th International Conference on Software Engineering (2004)
3. MacKenzie, D., Eggert, P., Stallman, R.: Comparing and Merging Files with Gnu Diff and Patch. Network Theory Ltd., Clifton, UK (2003)
4. Zeller, A., Snelting, G.: Unified versioning through feature logic. ACM Trans. Softw. Eng. Methodol. **6**(4), 398–441 (1997)
5. Gergic, J.: Towards a versioning model for component-based software assembly. In: Proceedings of the International Conference on Software Maintenance (2003)
6. Merino, L., Ghafari, M., Anslow, C., Neirstrsz, O.: A systematic literature review of software visualization evaluation. J. Syst. Softw. **144**, 165–180 (2018)
7. Beyer, D., Hassan, A.: Animated visualization of software history using evolution storyboards. In: Proceedings of the 13th Working Conference on Reverse Engineering (2006)
8. Arbuckle, T.: Visually summarising software change. In: 12th International Conference Information Visualization (2008)
9. Seemann, J., von Gudenberg, J.: Visualization of differences between versions of object-oriented software. In: Proceedings of the Euromicro Conference on Software Maintenance and Reengineering, Florence, Italy (1998)
10. Novais, R., Lima, C., Carneiro, G., Junior, P., Mendonca, M.: An Interactive Differential and Temporal Approach to Visually Analyze Software Evolution (2011).
11. Elsen, S.: VisGi: Visualizing Git branches. In: Proceedings of the IEEE Working Conference on Software Visualization (2013)
12. Novais, R., Santos, J., Mendonca, M.: Experimentally assessing the combination of multiple visualization strategies for software evolution analysis. J. Syst. Softw. **128**, 56–71 (2017)
13. Voinea, L., Telea, J., van Wijk, A.: Cvsscan: visualization of code evolution. In: Proceedings 2005 ACM Symposium on Software Visualization, pp. 47–56 (2005)
14. Kuhn, A., Stocker, M.: Code timeline: storytelling with versioning data. In: Proceedings of the ICSE, Zurich, SW (2012)
15. Hanjalic, A.: ClonEvol: visualizing software evolution with code clones. In: Proceedings of the IEEE Working Conference on Software Visualization, Eindhoven, NL (2013)
16. Aghajani, E., Mocci, A., Bavota, G., Lanza, M.: The code time machine. In: Proceedings of the IEEE 25th International Conference on Program Comprehension (ICPC) (2017)
17. Kim, M., Notkin, D.: Program element matching for multi-version program analyses. In: Proceedings of the MSR, pp. 58–64, Shanghai, CN (2006)
18. Kaur, P., Singh, H.: A model for versioning control mechanism in component-based systems. ACM SIGSOFT Softw. Eng. Notes. **36**(5) (2011)
19. Burch, M., Diehl, S., Weißgerber, P.: Visual data mining in software archives. In: Proceedings of the ACM Symposium on Software Visualization, pp. 37–46 (2005)
20. North, K., Sarma, A., Cohen, M.: Understanding git history: a multi-sense view. In: Proceedings of the SSE, Seattle, WA, US (2016)

21. See, A., Monnich, M., Fischer, M.: Enhancing binary code similarity analysis for software updates: a contextual diffing framework. In: Proceedings of the 20th ACM Asia Conference on Computer and Communications Security, pp. 1724–1740 (2025)
22. Shannon, R., Quigley, A., Nixon, P.: Deep diffs: visually exploring the history of a document. In: Proceedings of the AVI 20, Rome, IT (2010)
23. Young, J., Foster, K., Garfinkel, S., Fairbanks, K.: Distinct sector hashes for target file detection. Computer. **45**(12), 28–35 (2012)
24. Lee, A., Atkison, T.: A comparison of fuzzy hashes: evaluation, guidelines, and future suggestions. In: Proceedings of the ACM Southeast Conference, pp. 18–25, Kennesaw, GA, US (2017)
25. Drucker, S., Petschnigg, G., Agrawala, M.: Comparing and managing multiple versions of slide presentations. In: Proc. UIST, Montreux SU, pp. 47–56 (2006).
26. Bergroth, T., Hakonen, H.: A survey of longest common subsequence algorithms. In: Proceedings of the International Symposium on String Processing Information Retrieval, pp. 39–48 (2000)
27. Cormode, G., Muthukrishnan, S.: The string edit distance matching problem with moves. ACM Trans. Algorithms. **3**(1), 2 (2007)
28. Fluri, B., Wursch, M., Pinzger, M., Gall, H.: Change distilling: tree differencing for fine-grained source code change extraction. IEEE Trans. Softw. Eng. **33**(11) (2007)
29. Garfinkel, S., Farrell, P., Roussev, V., Dinolt, G.: Bringing science to digital forensics with standardized forensic corpora. Digit. Investig. **6**, S2–S11 (2009)
30. Rowe, N.: Identifying forensically uninteresting files in a large corpus. EAI Endorsed Trans. Secur. Saf. **16**(7), e2 (2016)
31. Microsoft: PE Format. Accessed at. https://docs.microsoft.com/en-us/windows/win32/debug/pe-format. (August 11, 2020).
32. Rowe, N.: Efficiently comparing versions of software files. Technical Report, NPS. https://nps.edu/web/research/calhoun/. in preparation.
33. Rowe, N.: Finding contextual clues to malware using a large corpus. In: ISCC-SFCS Third International Workshop on Security and Forensics in Communications Systems, Larnaca, Cyprus (2015)
34. Mockus, A., Votta, L.: Identifying reasons for software changes using historic databases. In: Proceedings of the International Conference Software Maintenance (ICSM), pp. 120–130 (2000). https://doi.org/10.1109/ICSM.2000.883028

SOMIA: Disassembling ARM Binaries by Knowledge-Aware Transfer Learning

Ke Zhang[1], Shuaike Dong[2], Fan Yang[1], Yutong Zhou[1], Zirui Song[1], and Kehuan Zhang[1](✉)

[1] The Chinese University of Hong Kong, Hong Kong, China
zk019@ie.cuhk.edu.hk, yf020@ie.cuhk.edu.hk, zy319@ie.cuhk.edu.hk, sz019@ie.cuhk.edu.hk, khzhang@ie.cuhk.edu.hk

[2] Ant Group, Hangzhou, China
dongshuaike.dsk@antgroup.com

Abstract. ARM disassembly plays a crucial role in ARM security area. However, due to the unique properties of ARM architecture, like implicit ISA switching, prevalent inline data and implicit function calls, ARM disassembly has always been a challenging task. Existing techniques are limited in achieving high accuracy, especially when dealing with complex real-world ARM binaries.

To address these limitations, we propose a novel knowledge-aware transfer learning based ARM binary disassembly framework, SOMIA. Unlike previous transfer-learning-based approaches like XDA, which focuses on x86/x64 and relies solely on the original masked language model capturing general relationships between bytes, SOMIA employs a multi-level masking strategy, which not only integrates domain knowledge about ARM architecture into the model but also captures deeper connections among basic units, fields, and instructions. We evaluate SOMIA against several state-of-the-art disassemblers using a comprehensive dataset containing 3693 binaries generated from SPEC benchmarks and real-world operating systems projects. Our evaluation demonstrates that SOMIA consistently outperforms all baseline techniques across various compilation settings.

Keyword: Digital Forensics, Reverse Engineering, Binary Analysis, Disassembly, Deep Learning

1 Introduction

The ARM architecture has emerged as the predominant standard for mobile and embedded systems, spanning smartphones, tablets, IoT devices, robotic vehicles, and more. However, the firmware software powering these platforms often remains closed-source. Because of this sad fact, static binary analysis is still a dominating methodology used by the community [16,34].

Existing binary analysis works usually leverage off-the-shelf tools to disassemble stripped ARM binaries, assuming that reliable disassembling binaries and function

© ICST Institute for Computer Sciences, Social Informatics and Telecommunications Engineering 2027
Published by Springer Nature Switzerland AG 2027. All Rights Reserved
H. Neukirchen et al. (Eds.): ICDF2C 2026, LNICST 720, pp. 337–356, 2027.
https://doi.org/10.1007/978-3-032-37274-1_20

recognition are well-solved problems. Unfortunately, this assumption has been proven to be inaccurate most of the time [16].

A fundamental challenge in ARM binary analysis is ARM disassembly, which is mostly the first step of any further binary analysis. Previous work [16] has shown that the classical disassembling techniques used for x86 architecture are not fully suitable for disassembling ARM binaries, especially 32-bit AArch32 binaries.

In contrast to x86/x64, current off-the-shelf tools, including linear sweeping disassemblers (e.g., objdump [11]) and recursive traversal-based disassemblers (e.g., IDA-Pro [14] and Ghidra [1]) cannot handle 32-bit ARM binaries well due to some special properties adopted by the ARM instruction set architecture (ISA).

Property 1: Runtime Instruction Set Switching. 32-bit ARM architecture provides two instruction sets, ARM and Thumb/Thumb-2. These two instruction sets are usually interleaved in real-world binaries. Instruction set switching may occur either explicitly or implicitly at runtime, posing great challenges to static-analysis-based dissemblers.

Property 2: Inline Data. Inline data is more prevalent in AArch32 or AArch64 than in x86/x64. It is possible that a static analysis-based disassembler depending heavily on predefined rules and heuristics, incorrectly recognizes a piece of inline data as a valid instruction, then misleads the disassembly of the followed after machine code.

Property 3: Implicit Function Call. Unlike `call` instruction in x86/x64, Thumb instruction set lacks the explicit function call instructions. For example, `BL` instruction can represent either a direct jump or a function call.

Recently, to overcome the limitation of linear sweep and recursive traversal, superset disassembly paradigm has been proposed [4]. It first constructs an overapproximate instruction superset at each address, then prunes false positives using predefined heuristics. P-Disasm [22] considers using a probabilistic method to compute the posterior probabilities of addresses denoting proper instructions. The probabilities are computed based on several predefined hints and heuristics, such as the number of definition-use relations encountered. Ddisasm [10] follows the superset disassembly strategy and integrates all predefined heuristics into the false positive (FP) reduction stage by Datalog [17]. Unlike P-Diasm and Diasm, a recent work, D-ARM [35], adopts abstract interpretation and graph theory analysis instead of probabilistic inference. A key limitation of the preceding static program analysis-based disassembly techniques is that all these techniques depend heavily on handcrafted rules and hints to reduce false recognition. However, heuristics and rules are usually incomplete, and their predictive weights are hard to determine, which may distort the true distribution and sacrifice precision.

Besides the traditional program analysis-based techniques, a series of machine learning based disassemblers like XDA [28] and DeepDi [36] are proposed. XDA learns how to disassemble x86/x64 binaries by training on a massive set of binary samples following the pretraining-finetuning scheme proposed by BERT [9]. However, another recent research [35] shows that XDA largely depends on general syntactic patterns and cannot be applied to ARM disassembly directly. XDA treats all tokens equally in its pretraining stage without considering the actual distribution in ARM binaries. We argue that fusing domain knowledge into the pretraining stage could facilitate the performance of the machine-learning-based model. Some other neural disassembly works leveraging instruction structural relations and memory modeling focus solely on x86-x64 like Tady [29] and Dias [33].

In this paper, we propose SOMIA, a knowledge-aware transfer learning-based ARM executable disassembler, to address challenges brought by special properties of ARM. Our big idea is to embed ARM domain knowledge into model pretraining before fine-tuning downstream tasks. We implement this idea by designing a multi-level masking strategy and adding another pretraining objective, span boundary object (SBO), tailored to ARM characteristics during the pretraining stage. We design a multi-level masking strategy for ARM so that the masked areas can represent the *common and possible* variations among instruction fields in real ARM instructions. The input ARM binary is randomly masked by multi-level masking, including unit, field, and span levels. Then, we use the preprocessed data to unsupervised pretrain a knowledge-aware masked language model (MLM) consisting of a basic MLM and a span MLM that are jointly optimized during the pretraining stage. MLM_{basic} can understand variations among fields inside an instruction, and MLM_{span} aims to capture the implicit relation between consecutive instructions. The contributions in this paper are summarized as follows:

- We propose a knowledge-aware transfer learning disassembly for ARM. Multi-level masking and tailored pretraining integrate factual ARM architecture knowledge into the model. Subsequent finetuning then specializes the model to disassembly tasks.
- We demonstrate that the knowledge-aware masked language model pretraining effectively compels the model to learn general contextual information from machine code with consideration of factual knowledge, which provides a strong foundation for downstream disassembly.
- We implement a prototype SOMIA and evaluate it on more than 3,000 binaries, including those compiled from SPEC CPU 2000, SPEC CPU 2006, SPEC CPU 2017, MbedOS, FreeRTOS, AOSP, and OpenWRT with different compilation options, architecture, and instruction set configurations. We also compare it with IDA-Pro, Ghidra, and XDA. The results show that in most cases, SOMIA is the best-performing tool, with the highest F1 score.

2 Background

ARM Architecture and Properties. Modern 32-bit ARM binaries predominantly utilize the 32-bit Arm (A32), 16-bit Thumb (T16), and 32-bit Thumb (T32) instruction sets. Developers can select the targeted CPU architecture of their programs through compiling options (`-march`). As both encodings occupy 32 bits in length, it poses a challenge for disassemblers to accurately differentiate between the two without additional context. Note that while the AArch64 is popular in high-end mobile devices and the server-level CPU market, AArch32 still dominates the microcontroller and resource-constrained embedded device market segment, and there are innumerable deployed AArch32 devices in the real world. **1) ISA Switching** Switching between ARM and Thumb states may occur explicitly or implicitly. For example, Branch with Link and Exchange (`blx`) always change the instruction set, In contrast, the behavior of Branch and Exchange (`bx`) instruction is dependent on the target address it branches to. For example, `blx #0x8eff8` at Line 9 of Fig. 1a switches from Thumb (`$t`) to ARM instruction set (`$a`), while from Line 9 `$t: blx #0x8eff8` to Line 10 `$a : b #0xcabd8` in Fig. 1a, the control transfer from Thumb (`$t`) to ARM (`$a`). Differently, the `bx Rm` derives the target instruction set from `bit[0]` of the operand register `Rm`. If the `bit[0]` is 0, then the target instruction set is ARM. Otherwise, it is Thumb. Apart from `blx` and `bx`, the target instruction set of some other instructions, e.g., `pop {pc, Rm ...}`, may switch its instruction set according to the last bit of the address popped into `pc` register. Since the value of `Rm` can only be obtained precisely at runtime, therefore it poses challenges to static ARM disassembly. **2) Inline Data in ARM Code Section** Inline data may cause a lot of false positives and false negatives in ARM disassembly compared to x86/x64 disassembly. In x86/x64, inline data is believed to be rare [2] and therefore easy to handle. However, due to the compact encoding of RISC, inline data becomes more prevalent for ARM binaries. As previous research [16] shows, around 4%–5% of code inside an ARM binary is inline data whereas the rate drops to 0%-1% in x86. For example, at line 16 and line 26 in Fig. 2a, two 32-bit inline data, `$d: 0x000f2af4` and `$d: 0x000ede5e` , are inserted into the code section. In Fig. 2a, Lines 3, 4, 6, and 8 indicate inline data misidentified as code by IDA-Pro and XDA. **3) Implicit Function Call** Different from x86/x64, there is no explicit instruction like `call` in ARM, multiple instructions could indicate an invocation to a function, like `b` (branch to target), `push{< reglist >,lr}` (push the value of a register list and link register into stack), `ldr` (load data from memory to register), etc. For example, in Fig. 1a, line 1, `push {r4, lr }`, line 8, `b #0xcabd8`, and line 9 `ldr r3, [pc, #0x14]` are all function entry points. The first mnemonic `push` is a 16-bit Thumb instruction, and the latter two are 32-bit ARM instructions. However, line 17, `push {r7, lr }`, and line 27 `push {r4, lr }` are wrongly identified as function entry points by IDA-Pro. Note that line 1 and line 27 hold the same machine code (`0xb510`) while only the former is a true function entry point.

Disassembly Strategies. Disassembly mainly refers to the process of recovering the lost high-level program constructs from binary code, such as assembly instruction, function boundary, function signature, control flow graph, and call graph [20,25]. Most disassembly tools recover these constructs via static analysis, because dynamic analysis has large runtime overheads and struggles to achieve high completeness in complex modern programs [2,16,26] compiled with high-level optimization.

1) Traditional Disassembly Strategies Recursive traversal starts the disassembly from the entry point of a program and follows along branches (e.g. `objdump` [11], `IDA-Pro` [14] and `Ghidra` [1]). Due to the unawareness of control flow information, linear sweep is prone to inline code and instruction set switching in ARM binaries. Recursive traversal, on the other hand, handles inline data better but risks missing indirect branches determined at runtime and can suffer from low code coverage. Another advanced strategy is superset disassembly [4] that decouples elimination of false positive from false negative by disassembling all possible instructions and then reducing redundant instructions. P-disasm [22] adopts superset disassembly and optimizes the FP reduction procedure by using a probabilistic analysis to achieve better performance on x86/64. D-ARM [35] is a recent research work focusing on ARM disassembly also using superset disassembly but adopting abstract interpretation to transform the ARM

```
1  /* Motivated Case 1: Start */
2  /* Address: Bytes, Mapping Symbol, Instruction*/
3  0x8160: 0xb510,     $t: push {r4, lr}        //f.s ✓
4  0x8162: 0x4604,     $t: mov r4, r0
5  0x8164: 0xfe52f091, $t: bl  #0x99e0c
6  0x8168: 0x2000,     $t: movs r0, #0
7  0x816a: 0xfef1f091, $t: bl  #0x99f50
8  0x816e: 0x4620,     $t: mov r0, r4
9  0x8170: 0xef42f086, $t: blx  #0x8eff8        //f.e ✓
10 0x8174: 0xea030a97, $a: b  #0xcabd8          //f.s ✓
11 0x8178: 0xe59f3014, $a: ldr r3, [pc, #0x14]//f.s ✓
12 0x817c: 0xe08f3003, $a: add r3, pc, r3
13 0x8180: 0xe5932008, $a: ldr r2, [r3, #8]
14 0x8184: 0xe3520000, $a: cmp r2,  #0
15 0x8188: 0x12fff1e,  $a: bxeq lr
16 0x818c: 0xe5930004, $a: ldr r0, [r3,  #4]
17 0x8190: 0xeafffff7, $a: b  #0x8174
18 0x8194: 0x000f2af4, $d: 0x000f2af4           //f.e ✓
```

(a) Motivated Case 1: Part 1

```
19 /* Motivated Case 1: (Con't)*/
20 /* Address: Bytes, Mapping Symbol, Instruction*/
21 0x8198: 0xb580,     $t: push {r7, lr}        //f.s ✗
22 0x819a: 0x2004,     $t: movs r0,  #4
23 0x819c: 0xfdf0f053, $t: bl  #0x5bd80
24 0x81a0: 0x4902,     $t: ldr r1, [pc,  #8]
25 0x81a2: 0x2200,     $t: movs r2,  #0
26 0x81a4: 0x6002,     $t: str r2, [r0]
27 0x81a6: 0x4479,     $t: add r1, PC
28 0x81a8: 0x6008,     $t: str r0, [r1]
29 0x81aa: 0xbd80,     $t: pop {r7, pc}
30 0x81ac: 0x000ede5e, $d: 0x000ede5e
31 0x81b0: 0xb510,     $t: push {r4, lr}        //f.s ✗
32 0x81b2: 0x2004,     $t: movs r0,#4
33 0x81b4: 0xfde4f053, $t: bl #0x5bd80
34 0x81b8: 0x4907,     $t: ldr r1, [pc,#0x1c]
35 /* ...... */
36 /* Motivated Case 1: End */
```

(b) Motivated Case 1: Part 2

Fig. 1. Motivated Case 1. Function Boundary Detection. An assembly code piece in AOSP [12]. (`$a`, `$t`, and `$d` are mapping symbols representing ARM, Thumb, and inline data, respectively.) Line 18 and Line 30 are inline data. IDA-Pro (v7.6) can detect function start (f.s ✓): at Line 3: `push {r4, lr}`, Line 10: `b #0xcabd8`, and Line 11: `ldr r3, [pc, #0x14]`, but misidentified (f.s ✗) Line 21: `push {r7, lr}` and Line 31: `push {r4, lr}` as function starts.

```
/* Address: Raw Bytes, Ground Truth; IDA-Pro */
0x551f2: 0x88ccef66, $t: vadd.i32 q12, q11, q6;
   ↪          $t: vadd.i32 q12, q11, q6  ✓
0x551f6: 0xe38cffba, $d: 0xe38cffba;
   ↪          $t: shalsul.32 q7, q6  ✗
0x551fe: 0x0c6aef16, $d: 0x0c6aef16;
   ↪          $t: shalp.32 q0, q3, q13  ✗
0x55202: 0xa8ceef66, $t: vadd.i32 q13, q11, q7;
   ↪          $t: vadd.i32 q13, q11, q7  ✓
0x55206: 0x62c0ffb9, $d: 0x62c0ffb9;
   ↪          $t: shalh.32 q3, q0  ✗
0x55010: 0x0000bf00, $t: nop; $t: nop  ✓
0x55212: 0x0c68ef14, $d: 0x0c68ef14;
   ↪          $t: shalp.32 q0, q3, q13  ✗
0x55216: 0x2844ef22, $t: vadd.i32 q1, q1, q2;
   ↪          $t: vadd.i32 q1, q1, q2  ✓
0x5521a: 0x086cef20, $t: vadd.i32 q0, q0, q14;
   ↪          $t: vadd.i32 q0, q0, q14  ✓
```

(a) Motivated Case 2

Three-Address Code:
(Opcode, $Oprnd_{dest}$, $Oprnd_{src1}$, $Oprnd_{src2}$))

A32 Instruction:
(Cond, Special, [Opcode], [$Oprnd_{dest}$], $Oprnd_{src1}$, [$Oprnd_{src2}$])
(Cond, Special, Reg_{dest}, Reg_{src1}, Reg_{src2})
(Cond, Special, Reg_{dest}, Reg_{src}, Imm)
(Cond, Special, Reg_{src1})
(Cond, Special, Imm)

T16 Instruction:
(Special, [Cond], [Opcode], $Oprnd_{src1}$, [$Oprnd_{src2}$], [$Oprnd_{dest}$])

T32 Instruction:
($Special_1$, [Opcode], [$Oprnd_{src1}$]), ($Special_2$, [$Oprnd_{src2}$], [$Oprnd_{dest}$])

(b) ARM ISA Encoding Rules

Fig. 2. (a) Motivated Case 2. Both IDA-Pro and XDA misclassified these inline data as code. (b) ARM ISA Encoding Mechanism.

instruction disassembly problem into a graph analysis problem that existing graph analysis algorithms can solve. The authors do not claim D-ARM can recover function boundary.

2) Machine learning-based disassembly Researchers also proposed many machine-learning-based solutions. XDA [28] is a transfer learning-based disassembly framework consisting of pretraining and fine-tuning. However, XDA only focuses on x86/x64 architecture and takes plain bytes as the only masking units to capture general relations between each pair of bytes, which is insufficient in ARM. Meanwhile, XDA largely depends on the syntactic patterns and captures only general semantics in these samples without consideration of factual knowledge of the target binaries architecture. DeepDi [36] is another graph neural network-based disassembly research work primarily focusing on x86/x64 architecture. Some other neural disassbly works leveraging customized attention mechanism or instruction structural relations and memory modeling focus solely on x86-x64 like Tady [29] and Disa [33].

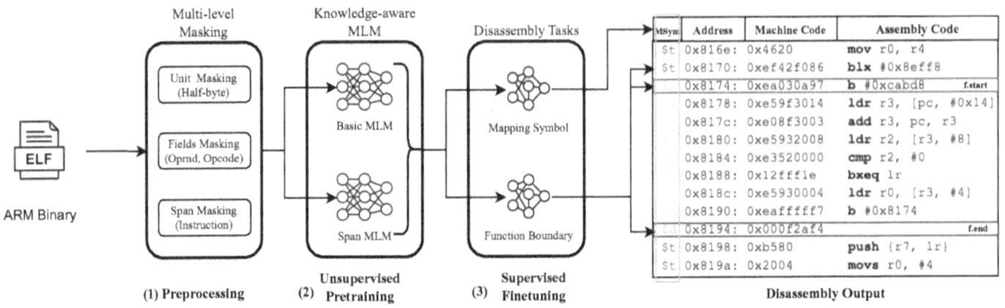

Fig. 3. § 3: The diagram of SOMIA. *Stage (1) Preprocessing.* Multi-level masking for unit, field, and span. *Stage (2) Pretraining.* Knowledge-aware MLM training in unsupervised manner. *Stage (3) Finetuning.* Mapping symbol identification and function boundary detection. In the disassembly output, the purple box: identified mapping symbol ($a, $t , or $d) for each instruction or inline data, the red box and brown box: each detected function start (f.start) and function end (f.end).

3 Design of SOMIA

Motivation. Previous work like XDA adopts the same strategy as BERT [9] to pretrain a general unsupervised model and finetune it with smaller models on disassembly tasks (instruction recovery and function boundary detection). However, some recent research like [35] shows that XDA is prone to be erroneous when multiple ISAs are mixed, due to that it relies on general-purpose byte-level patterns and may only capture "shallow" semantics between instructions. More analysis is given in § 4.2. We argue that fusing domain knowledge into the pretraining stage could facilitate the performance of the machine-learning-based model. For example, XDA takes one byte as a unit, which is unsuitable for ARM architecture due to its compact instruction encoding mechanism. Apart from that, XDA using vanilla BERT treats all tokens equally in its pretraining stage without considering the actual distribution in ARM binaries (e.g., prevalent inline data), making it fail to capture the "really-mattered" intra-instruction and inter-instruction relations.

Our Techniques. To overcome this limitation of vanilla BERT, we propose SOMIA, a knowledge-aware transfer learning-based framework. The overall pipeline is shown in Fig. 3. First, we apply a multi-level masking strategy to preprocess the input ARM binary, so that the masked areas can represent the *common and possible* variations among fields in real ARM instructions. Then we use the preprocessed data to unsupervised pretrain a knowledge-aware masked language model ($KMLM$). $KMLM$ consists of a basic MLM (MLM_{basic}) and a span MLM (MLM_{span}). MLM_{basic} can understand variations among fields inside an instruction, and MLM_{span} aims to capture the implicit relation between consecutive instructions. MLM_{basic} and MLM_{span}

are jointly optimized during the pretraining stage. Finally, we fine-tune the $KMLM$ on two downstream disassembly tasks, 1) mapping symbol identification, and 2) function boundary detection. The former aims to identify the mapping symbol of each aligned binary code snippet, and the latter aims to detect the function start and end.

3.1 Preprocessing: Multi-level Masking

As discussed in § 2, the RISC design of ARM enables a compact yet flexible encoding scheme for its instruction set. Figure 2bshows the formats of ARM and Thumb encodings. ARM instruction set (A32) holds a 32-bit fixed-length encoding. Each instruction starts with a 4-bit conditional field {`Cond`} indicating which condition will be checked by it. For example, `0000` (mnemonic `EQ`), indicates that the zero flag must be set. The subsequent 4-8 bit {`Opcode`} field encodes the instruction class, including data processing, branching and other operations. The remaining part of an instruction is {`Operand`}, specifying the instruction's operands, with flexible combinations of immediate, registers, and addressing modes. On the other hand, the Thumb instruction set (T16) uses a more compact 16-bit encoding. It omits the conditional execution field and reduces the {`Opcode`} to 6 bits with the remaining 10 bits for {`Operand`}, which restricts available operations and addressing mode. To expand the capabilities, Thumb-2 (T32) supplements 16-bit Thumb encodings with a new 32-bit format for more complex behaviors while retaining 16-bit Thumb. Each T32 instruction can be divided into high 16 bits and low 16 bits with different field compositions as shown in Fig. 2b. Following are two examples of ARM and Thumb instructions and their machine code encodings shown in Fig. 4.

Example 1: Line 12 in Fig. 1a demonstrates a representative data processing instruction: `add r3, pc, r3`. This performs addition of the `pc` and register `r3` values, storing the result back into `r3`. The half-byte encoding of this `add` instruction with six fields is shown in Fig. 4a. The 4-bit conditional field {`Cond`} contains "`1110`", meaning unconditional execution. The 8-bit {`Opcode`} field encodes the ADD operation as "`00000100`". The operand registers are specified in 4-bit fields as {`Rn`} = `r15`, {`Rd`} = `r3` encoding the `pc`, and {`Rm`} = `r3`. Note that there is no equivalent Thumb instruction due to the complex addressing mode. ***Example 2:*** Different from the data processing instructions mentioned above, a branch instruction (i.e., at line 10 of Fig. 1a), `b 0xcabd8` is encoded with only three fields: 1) 4-bit condition code `1110` meaning the instruction is always unconditional. 2) 4-bit {`special`} function bits being `1010`, including reserved bits (101) and function bit L being 0, indicating it is a branch (`b`) without saving the return address. 3) 24-bit immediate value `imm32`, which is used to calculate the offset from current program counter (`pc`).

Our Approach. Based on the above observation, we choose 4-bit as the masked unit length L_{min} and then apply a series of transformations on L_{min} so that masked units fulfill both ARM and Thumb encoding. In contrast to instructions, we realize that each inline data could represent an arbitrary 32-bit value without inherent structure, making it meaningless to mask its value. Considering this, we encode the positions of inline data instead of its value. Unit-level masking enables the model to understand the fundamental structure of instructions. Building on unit-level masking, we then apply a

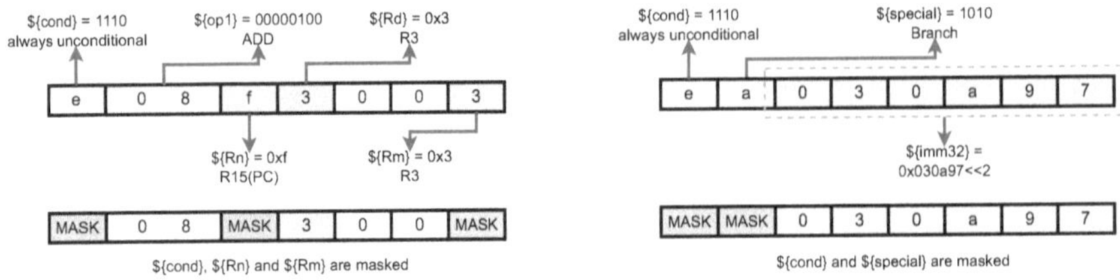

(a) The encoding of A32 instruction `add r3,pc,r3`

(b) The encoding of A32 instruction `b #0xcabd8`

Fig. 4. § 3: Field-level masking examples.

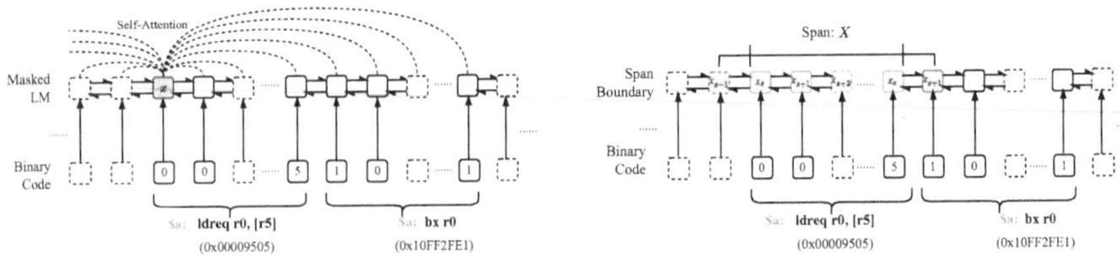

(a) The MLM_{basic} architecture. For each unit $x \in X$, the self-attention mechanism will compute the attention score between each pair of units $\{(x, x')|\forall\ x' \in X\}$ where X is the sequence.

(b) The MLM_{span} architecture. The MLM_{span} will predict the contents of each masked instruction span $(x_s, ..., x_e)$ based on corresponding span embedding stored at external boundary x_{s-1} and x_{e+1}.

Fig. 5. The architecture of MLM_{basic} and MLM_{span}.

more advanced masking strategy, field-level masking, which targets the semantic components inside an instruction based on its encoding scheme. For example, masking conditional codes, opcodes, and operands emphasizes the elements that give meaning to an instruction. Finally, to capture a higher-level context, we apply span-level masking across consecutive instructions. This enables the model to learn implicit relationships in instruction sequences. Different aspects of information among instructions can be captured and embedded into the masked areas through the multi-level masking strategy, which can be used to pretrain the model more comprehensively.

1) Unit-level Masking We denote each input as a unit sequence of size n, $\mathbf{x} = (x_1, ..., x_n)$, where each x_i, $i \in \mathbb{N}$ is a 4-bit unit. Each input unit $x_i \in x$ is mapped to a one-hot encoded vector with 16 digits. For example, an input unit `b` is encoded as "0000100000000000". An input byte `b5` is encoded as two 16-bit vectors. The first vector is the same as the one of `b`, and the second vector has fifteen "`0`" bits and one "`1`" at position 5. In total, we define 18 words in the vocabulary. Apart from "`0-15`" representing a hexadecimal, we append `[MASK]` on behalf of masked basic units. We mask some percentage of units in each sequence randomly. The $\texttt{MASK}(x_i)$ function denotes the output of masking the i-th unit in a given binary $\mathbf{x}$. The P_{unit} is a set of masked unit positions in $\mathbf{x}$. Given an ARM binary code dataset $\mathcal{D}$, where

$|\mathcal{D}| = N$, the basic MLM (MLM_{basic}) is trained with masked unit sequences in $\mathcal{D}$. $\mathcal{D} = \{\mathbf{x}_{m\_unit} \mid (x_1, ..., \text{MASK}_{unit}(x_i), ..., x_n),\ i \in P_{unit}\}$, where $\mathbf{x}_{m\_unit}$ is the units sequence after masking. To predict the values of the masked units, a Softmax layer with 18 dimensions is stacked to MLM_{basic} to get the prediction result. $\{\hat{x}_i|\ i \in P_{unit}\} = Softmax(MLM_{basic}(\mathbf{x}_{m\_unit}))$, where $\hat{x}_i$ is the predicted value of corresponding masked unit x_i. We adopt the same strategy of XDA [28] using the learned positional embedding E_{pos} to capture the positional information of each unit,

2) Field-level Masking The second masking strategy we take is field-level masking. It aims to emphasize the fields of ARM/Thumb instructions in the pretraining stage to learn facts and knowledge about the ARM ISA and real binaries. Every field inside each instruction can be masked by one or multiple `[MASK]` units. Considering the different properties of the three types of instructions (A32, T16, and T32), we define a series of field masking rules. For ARM Instructions, *Rule (1):* For each 32-bit instruction, the 4-bit condition code field {`Cond`} is consistently masked. *Rule (2):* For data processing instructions shown in Fig. 2b*Rule (3):* For instructions containing three register operands, all three 4-bit {`Operand`} fields can be masked. *Rule (4):* For instructions with two register operands and one immediate operand, both registers are masked, excluding any immediate value. *Rule (5):* For branch instructions with an immediate value as the target, the condition code {`Cond`} and {`Special`}bit fields are masked while preserving the offset.

Thumb (T16) instruction encoding is much more compact than A32. For example, most of the `Opcode` fields are 2-bit (4-bit in A32), and all register fields are encoded into 3 bits. Different from A32 in which condition code `Cond` is the beginning of each instruction, only conditional branch instruction contains `Cond`. To reuse the 4-bit mask `[MASK]`, we add padding to the field for alignment. For T16, Masking rules are as below: *Rule (1):* all {`Special`} bits can be masked. *Rule (2):* for register {$\texttt{Oprnd}_{\texttt{src1}}$}, it could be masked with one-bit padding at the least significant bit. *Rule (3):* immediate values (i.e., offset for operands shift or as the branching target) are never masked. *Rule (4):* the opcode filed {`Opcode`} in a conditional branch is masked. *Rule (5):* for `push` and `pop` operations, register list as {$\texttt{Opnd}_{\texttt{src1}}$} is masked. Note that for T32, the masking rules are quite similar to A32, so they are omitted here.

We reuse the two examples mentioned above in § 3.1 to show the process of field-level masking. In ***Example 1*** (Fig. 4a), `$a: add r3, pc, r3` has five candidate fields: `cond`, `op1`, `Rn`, `Rm` and `Rd`. Following our defined rules, one viable masking generates a conditional code mask and randomly selects register operands to mask, as shown in the bottom part of Fig. 4a. In Fig. 4b, ***Example 2*** applies similar principles to branch instructions, in which `cond` is always masked and `special` bits are optionally masked. After field-level masking, the structural and syntactic knowledge inside each instruction is integrated into the data for pretraining.

3) Span-level Masking Many binary analysis tasks involve reasoning about inter-instruction relationships. For example, in ISA and inline data identification tasks, the order in the `ldreq r0, [r5]` precedes a `bx r0;` informs the mapping symbol type, `$a` of the `ldreq` instruction. For self-supervised learning, modeling such dependencies is more challenging under unit-level masking, as the original MLM only captures relationships at the unit level. To represent full instructions better, we employ a third span-level masking strategy, where each masked unit encompasses an entire 32-bit instruction sequence. Rather than masking the 32 bits directly as eight `[MASK]` and expecting the model to infer their values, we introduce a customized Span Boundary Object (SBO) to explicitly train the pretrained model to predict complete instruction spans given contextual instructions. The SBO depicts instruction boundaries, compelling the model to learn holistic multi-unit patterns. This enables richer modeling of inter-instruction dependencies compared to individual unit prediction.

In AArch32, one 32-bit binary sequence can represent various elements, including one ARM instruction, two 16-bit Thumb instructions, one 32-bit Thumb-2 instruction (for ARMv6 and higher version ARM binaries), or one inline data. All the units in a span are replaced by `[MASK]`. The MLM_{span} model to be pretrained will take the sequence $\mathbf{x}_{m\_span}$ with random 32-bit (8 units) aligned span masked as input: $\mathbf{x}_{m\_span} = (x_1, \cdots, \texttt{MASK}(x_{4i}, ..., x_{4i+7}), \cdots, x_n)$

, where $i \in \mathbb{N}$, the index i is the position of span $(x_{4i}, ..., x_{4i+7})$ in the input binary $\mathbf{x}_{m\_span}$. We follow the masking rate 15% mentioned in previous section but perform this replacement at the instruction span rather than each unit. MLM_{span} predicts the values of the masked units inside each span in a set of position P_{span}: $\{\hat{x}_i | \ i \in P_{span}\} = Softmax(MLM_{span}(\mathbf{x}_{m\_span}))$, where $\hat{x}_i$ is the prediction of each masked unit in each span.

3.2 Pretraining: Knowledge-Aware Masked-LM

The Knowledge-aware Masked Language Model ($KMLM$) in `SOMIA` consists of basic MLM (MLM_{basic}) and span MLM (MLM_{span}). In this section, we introduce how to pretrain the $KMLM$.

Basic MLM Pretraining. After preprocessing by multi-level masking strategy, we get a unit sequence of each input program with some units and fields randomly masked by `[MASK]`. As shown in Fig. 5a, MLM_{basic} pretraining process can be divided into the following steps. ***Step 1.*** Each input basic unit is encoded as a one-hot vector concatenated with its positional embedding. ***Step 2.*** The output embeddings of *Step 1* are then fed into the MLM_{basic}. The updated embedding here is usually described as context-aware embedding as it considers the information of other units within the binary sequence. ***Step 3.*** Transformer units of MLM_{basic} dynamically update the embeddings from the first layer to the last layer using a multi-head self-attention mechanism. ***Step 4.*** The final output of MLM_{basic} is then fed to a stacked Multi-Layer Perceptron (MLP). The output of the stacked MLP has the same dimension as the input vocabulary set, which is then used to calculate the cross-entropy loss.

Span MLM Pretraining. To solve the above challenges, inspired by SpanBERT [18], we adopt a fancy learning object, span boundary object (SBO), to compel the model to learn instruction prediction based on contextual information. Figure 5b illustrates a span encoding example of an ARM instruction `$a : ldreq r0, [r5]`. Given a masked span of units $\texttt{MASK}(x_s, ..., x_e)$, where (s, e) indicates its start and end positions, we represent each unit x_i in the span using the output encoding of the external boundary units, as well as the position embedding of the target span P_{i-s+1}: $y^{(j)} = f(x_{s-1}, x_{e+1}, P_{i-s+1})$, where position embeddings $p_1, p_2, \cdots$ mark relative positions of the masked tokens concerning the left boundary token x_{s-1}. As in SpanBERT [18], we implement the representation function $\mathbf{y}^{(j)}$ as a 2-layer feed-forward network with GeLU activations and layer normalization $h_0 = [x_{s-1}; x_{e+1}; P_{i-s+1}]$, $h_1 = \text{LayerNorm}(\text{GeLU}(\text{W}_1\text{h}_0))$, $\mathbf{y}^{(i)} = \text{LayerNorm}(\text{GeLU}(\text{W}_2\text{h}_1))$ We then use the vector representation $y^{(i)}$ to predict the unit x_i and compute the cross-entropy loss exactly like the objective of MLM_{basic}. $\mathcal{L}_{MLM_{span}}(x_i) = -logP(y_i|\mathbf{y}_i)$, where $P(y_i|\mathbf{y}_i)$ is the condition probability of y_i based on the span boundary representation $\mathbf{y}_i$. To jointly optimize MLM_{basic} and MLM_{span}, SOMIA sums the loss from both the span boundary and the regular masked language model objectives for each token x_i in the masked span $(x_s, ..., x_e)$, while reusing the input embedding for the target tokens in both MLM_{basic} and MLM_{span}: $\mathcal{L}_{pre}(x_i) = \mathcal{L}_{MLM_{basic}}(x_i) + \mathcal{L}_{MLM_{Span}}(x_i)$, $= -logP(x_i|\mathbf{x}_i) - logP(x_i|\mathbf{y}_i)$, where $\mathcal{L}_{pre}(x_i)$ is the overall loss of *K-MLM*, which is optimized by gradient descent.

3.3 **Finetuning:** ARM Disassembly Tasks

Instruction identification and function boundary recovery are the two most fundamental tasks in disassembly. Other disassembly primitives like control flow graph and call graph generation are based on the qualified result of instruction and function recovery. As a result, We design two fine-tuning tasks, mapping symbol classification and function boundary detection, to assist in disassembling ARM binaries.

Given a sequence of embedding vectors produced by the pre-trained model f_{pre}: $E_l^{(j)} = (E_{l,1}, E_{l,2}, ..., E_{l,n})$, The corresponding ground truth $\mathbf{y}$ in each finetuning task is a sequence of labels of the same length n: $\mathbf{y} = \{y^{(j)}|y^{(j)} \in C_y\}^n$, where C_y denotes the set of all possible class labels of y. Each embedding $E_{l,i}$ will be mapped to a label $y^{(j)}$ after the process of f_{pre}. The symbol f_{task} denotes the model to be fine-tuned, which takes each embedding $E_{l,i}$ as input, and predicts the corresponding label $y^{(j)}$, where $y_i = f_{task}(E_{l,i})$. Let f_{task} be parameterized by Θ_{task} : $f_{task}(E_{l,i}; \Theta_{task})$, the objective of training the fine-tuning model f_{task} is thus to search for Θ_{task} that minimizes the cross entropy between the predicted labels of all inputs and their actual labels: $\hat{y}^{(j)} = f_{task}(f_{pre}(\mathbf{x}^{(j)}; \Theta_{pre}); \Theta_{task})$, $\mathcal{L}_{task} = \arg\min_{\Theta_{task}} \sum_{j=1}^{N} -y^{(j)} \log(\hat{y}^{(j)})$

Mapping Symbol Identification. Due to the nature of RISC architecture, it is easy to know the boundary of each ARM instruction but hard to differentiate code v.s. data at certain addresses. To disambiguate, ARM utilizes `mapping symbols`. The mapping symbol is an architecture-specific extension of the ARM ELF file generated by compilers to identify transitions between instructions (A32, T16 and T32) and inline data. For instance, the mapping symbol `$t: 0x0001043c` denotes that the offset `0x0001043c` contains Thumb code. There are three types of mapping symbols: (1) `$a` : The start address of a ARM code region. (2) `$t` : The start address of a Thumb code region (3) `$d` : The start address of a data region.

Inline data is prevalent in ARM binaries. To distinguish the inline data (`inc. data`) from the data section (`$d.realdata`), we combine inline data detection and instruction set identification together by merging their labels. Specifically, we add a new label for inline data, `D` (`$d`), in $|\mathbf{y}|$, which represents inline data. Finally, the possible class label for each 32-bit aligned binary code snippet: $|\mathbf{y}| = \{\mathtt{A}, \mathtt{T}, \mathtt{D}\}$ denotes the ARM (`A`) instruction, the Thumb (`T`) instruction, or inline data (`D`).

Function Boundary Detection. Similar to XDA, we also define an end-to-end function boundary detection task, where all units are divided into three categories: $|C_y|$ = $\{$S, E, N$\}$, denoting the function start (S), function end (E), and neither function start nor function end (N), respectively. The function boundaries are computed based on the probability distributions of the three possible labels, where the predicted label is the one with the highest probability.

4 Evaluation

The evaluation of SOMIA addresses the following research questions:

- **RQ1:** How does SOMIA compare to existing works on instruction recovery and function boundary detection? (§ 4.1)
- **RQ2:** How does the multi-level masking strategy improve the performance? (§ 4.2)
- **RQ3:** Can downstream security applications benefit from SOMIA? (§ 4.3)

Experimental Setup. We build SOMIA using PyTorch [27] with CUDA 11.8 [23]. We employ fairseq [24] to implement the self-attention mechanism over GPU computation. We run the training and prediction procedures on a Linux server running Ubuntu'22 with 128 cores AMD EPYC CPU, 1.5T RAM, and 1 NVIDIA A100 40GB GPU.

1) Dataset Settings Considering the diversity of binaries used in the real world, we construct a comprehensive dataset containing two sources. *1) SPEC benchmarks.* SPEC is an authoritative testing benchmark for performance measurements on computation-intensive tasks, which are widely used by previous works [28]. We select the latest three versions, SPEC CPU 2017 [8], SPEC CPU 2006 [32], and SPEC CPU 2000 [7], and build ARM binaries with different levels of optimizations in GCC and Clang. *2) Real-world Operating Systems.* We select FreeRTOS (v10.1) [31], the most popular real-time operating system, and MbedOS (v6.0) [21], an open-source embedded operating system designed for ARM-based IoT devices. We also select AOSP (v9) [12] and OpenWRT (v18.0) [6], which are leading operating systems used by mobile devices and IoT devices.

2) Compilers and options. We use GCC and Clang compilers to build ARM binary executable files. Specifically, we use GCC v12.0 and Clang v10.0 , which cover the major compilers used in the wild nowadays. We also apply different compilation options (i.e., with or without `-mthumb`) and different optimization flags (i.e., `O1`, `O2`, `O3`). According to GCC documents, we believe `-mthumb` remains the most representative setting, and other supplementary options like `-mthumb-interwork` and `-mflip-thumb` are unlikely to impact SOMIA's disassembly accuracy significantly. Unlike the SPEC benchmarks, four operating systems have complex dependencies among frameworks, libraries, and binary utilities, and, therefore, we only follow the default compilation configurations instead of applying all optimization options. To evaluate SOMIA under real-world settings, the ARM binaries in our dataset are generated with each software package's original scripts and configurations.

3) Ground-truth Generation. We refer to the ground truth collection guidance provided by previous work [16]. We employ pyelftools [5] and Capstone [30] to extract the mapping symbol [19] and the offset of each instruction and inline data in ARM

Table 1. RQ1: The F1 score of each baseline on each dataset.

Dataset	Arch.	Mapping Symbol Identification - F1 Score (%)						Function Boundary Detection - F1 Score (%)					
		IDA-Pro	Ghidra	XDA	DeepDi	D-ARM	SOMIA	IDA-Pro	Ghidra	XDA	DeepDi	D-ARM	SOMIA
SPEC CPU 2017	ARMv5t	99.55	95.41	98.85	93.75	99.14	**99.77**	84.99	71.59	93.56	75.48	N/A	**96.73**
	ARMv7a	98.77	97.41	98.26	98.24	99.23	**99.75**	85.58	72.52	93.57	85.75	N/A	**96.79**
SPEC CPU 2006	ARMv5t	94.89	91.56	98.98	94.68	98.99	**99.40**	80.15	75.98	94.46	78.85	N/A	**98.78**
	ARMv7a	94.87	91.55	99.18	98.85	98.78	**99.46**	80.13	75.97	94.45	95.83	N/A	**98.74**
SPEC CPU 2000	ARMv5t	99.18	93.66	99.45	97.94	98.69	**99.99**	87.78	78.90	95.16	92.58	N/A	**98.24**
	ARMv7a	99.16	93.64	99.48	98.90	99.20	**99.89**	87.75	78.92	95.14	96.25	N/A	**98.24**
AOSP	AOSP_ARM	96.53	95.88	99.20	85.47	99.10	**99.95**	78.99	75.45	90.78	72.45	N/A	**96.59**
MbedOS	ARMv4t	99.31	96.44	99.13	96.78	99.00	**99.58**	82.77	73.32	94.44	85.75	N/A	**98.75**
FreeRTOS	ARMv4t	97.14	94.10	99.80	91.80	99.82	**99.86**	83.66	74.64	93.30	85.78	N/A	**97.88**
OpenWRT	ARMv4t	99.15	94.13	99.26	95.80	98.78	**99.45**	82.56	68.29	93.66	85.80	N/A	**97.79**

binaries. Additionally, we leverage DWARF [13], a debugging file format, to retrieve the function boundaries in each ARM binary.

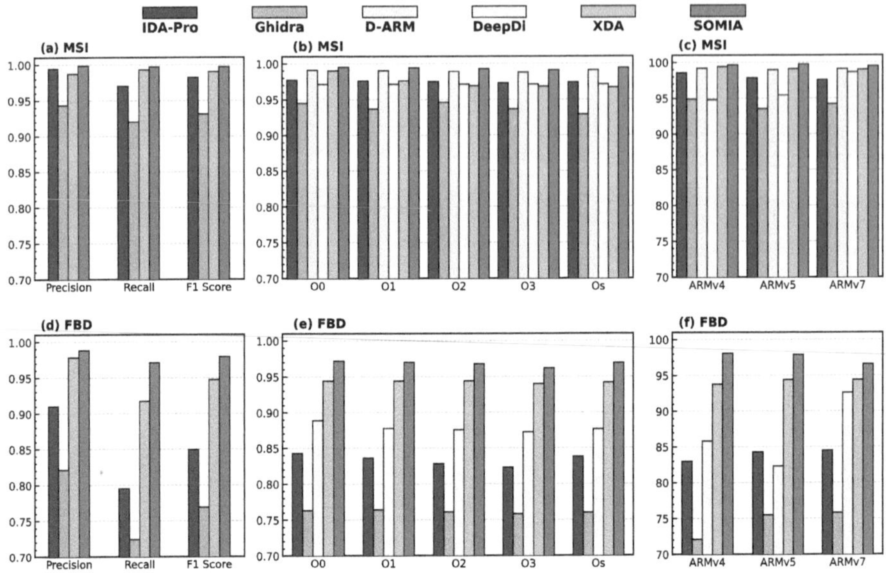

Fig. 6. RQ1: The Precision, Recall, and F1 score of de-factor disassemblers (IDA-Pro and Ghidra), XDA, and SOMIA on two disassembly primitives. (1) Mapping symbol identification ($a, $t, or $d) and (2) Function boundary detection (f.start, f.end) of each tool against Precision, Recall and F1 Score, optimization levels, and ARM architecture versions.

4) Baselines. Specially, we select IDA-Pro (v7.6) [14], Ghidra (v9.1) [1], DeepDi [36], D-ARM [35], and XDA [28] as baselines. Note that the pretrained model provided by the author of XDA is trained on x86/x64 binaries. To make it work for ARM, we retrain XDA, strictly following the guidance in their paper and codebase. DeepDi [36] is another recent machine learning-based disassembly research work primarily focusing on x86/x64 and ARMv7 architecture. D-ARM [35] is a static analysis-based technique focusing on ARM disassembly.

5) Metrics. We use precision ($P = \frac{TP}{TP+FP}$), recall ($R = \frac{TP}{TP+FN}$), and F1 score ($F1 = \frac{2 \cdot P \cdot R}{P+R}$) to measure the actual performance of SOMIA and all other tools. Following conventions in language model pretraining for NLP, we utilize perplexity (PPL) [15] to evaluate pertaining quality. PPL ($PPL = 2^{-\frac{1}{N}\sum \log(p(x))}$) intuitively gauges the model's uncertainty about its predicted distribution matching the targets. $p(x)$ refers to the probability produced by the pretrained model that the masked units match ground truth values. During pertaining, the pretrained model achieving high confidence on masked units will exhibit *lower* perplexity, indicating high-quality pretraining and will probably benefit the fine-tuning disassembly tasks.

6) Training and Evaluation Settings. We pretrain on the other six subsets for each subset and leave the selected subset as the fine-tuning dataset for performance evaluation. We also define the train-test overlap rate as the percentage of overlapping byte sequences between testing and training following XDA [28] and monitoring PPL [15]. *1) Pretraining.* To strictly separate the binaries used for pretraining, finetuning, and testing, we select one subset of binaries in Table 1 as the fine-tuning dataset and leave the other six subsets as the pertaining dataset without any labels for fine-tuning tasks. The strict dataset-splitting strategy ensures that no testing binaries in fine-tuning appear in the training dataset. *2) Finetuning.* In the fine-tuning stage, for each subset shown as each row in Table 1, we randomly choose only 10% of the dataset as our fine-tuning set and treat the remaining binaries as the testing set.

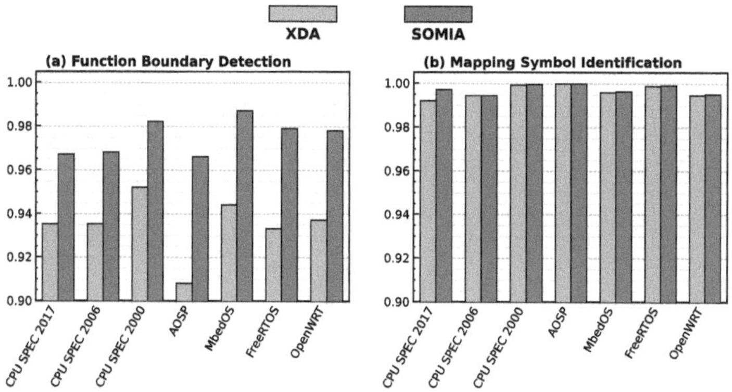

Fig. 7. RQ2: The F1 score of XDA and SOMIA on function boundary detection task over each dataset.

4.1 RQ1: Performance Comparison

We evaluate the performance of SOMIA on two disassembly tasks - mapping symbol identification and function boundary detection. 1) For mapping symbol identification, Table 1 displays the F1 scores across tools and settings. SOMIA consistently achieves the highest F1 score, outperforming other baselines in all configurations. Figure 6a provides additional precision-recall insights, revealing an obvious recall drop for IDA-Pro (v7.6) and Ghidra (v9.1), which means they do well in identifying valid instructions, however, suffer from a low analysis coverage, leading to a large portion of unrecognized instructions. 2) Function boundary identification proves even more challenging, with results in Table 1, which makes recovering higher-level constructs (e.g., intra-procedural control flow graph) much harder. Figure 6d shows that IDA-Pro and Ghidra have higher precision than recall, indicating their failure in robustly identifying many true function boundaries. IDA-Pro maintains a large database of manually crafted rules and queries the database to search for matched patterns in disassembly. However, for ARM binaries, the control flow patterns are often broken by inline data and non-fixed function call sites, which makes the function boundary hard to determine. 3) For different compiler optimization levels, SOMIA constantly outperforms other approaches on both two ARM disassembly primitives (Fig. 6b, Fig. 6e). Besides, SOMIA also shows better performance stability on all three ARM architectures (Fig. 6c, Fig. 6f).

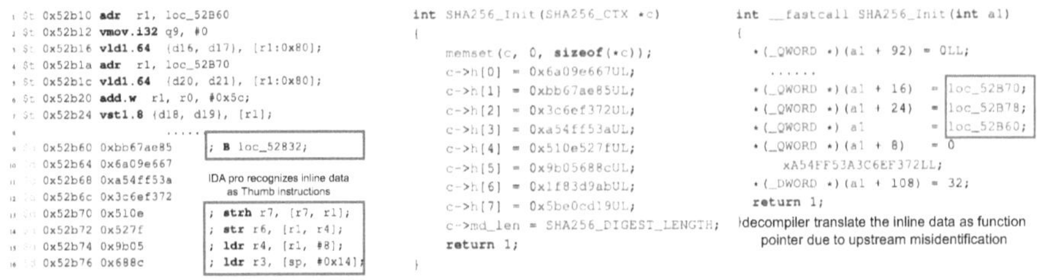

(a) The disassembly of SHA256_Init

(b) The source code and decompilation of function SHA256_Init

Fig. 8. Case1: IDA-Pro misidentifies inline data as Thumb instructions, leading to inaccurate decompilation output.

4.2 RQ2: Ablation Study

To measure the effectiveness of our multi-level masking technique, we conduct an ablation study to show the effect of multi-level masking. We compare the performance of SOMIA with XDA to show the benefit of knowledge-aware MLM. XDA represents vanilla-MLM, and SOMIA is equipped with our multi-level masking techniques. Compared with XDA using vanilla-MLM, SOMIA can achieve better results on both two disassembly tasks (Table 1). Figure 7a and Fig. 7b show the F1 score of SOMIA and XDA on mapping symbol identification and function boundary detection. We observe that with the supplementary knowledge provided by multi-level masking, SOMIA can further reduce the erroneous disassembly classifications and improve the precision and recall metrics on each dataset. Multi-level masking can improve the performance of SOMIA compared to vanilla MLM on both mapping symbol identification and function boundary detection over each dataset.

4.3 RQ3: Downstream Applications Case Study

As a primitive of binary security analysis, the accuracy of disassembly heavily impacts downstream tasks. Decompilation plays a crucial role in reverse engineering and vulnerability discovery, and it heavily relies on the quality of upper-stream output quality and, in our case, the disassembly results. To evaluate how ARM disassembly output influences the correctness of decompilation results, we integrate SOMIA into a widely-used open-source decompiler RetDec [3] by replacing RetDec's default disassembler Capstone [30] with SOMIA. We then manually check the decompilation results to determine which version is more close to the original semantics of the source code. We highlight two representative examples where off-the-shelf disassemblers produce incorrect results, leading to incorrect decompilation results, while SOMIA successfully recovers the authentic semantics and shows how the wrong results exacerbate the subsequent analysis.

```
$t 0x85586 pop {r4,r5,pc}
$t 0x85588 str.w r2, [r0],#4
$t 0x8558c strh.w r3, [r0],#2
$t 0x85590 mov.w r3, r3,lsr#16
$t 0x85594 strb r3, [r0]
$t 0x85596 pop {r4,r5,pc}
$t 0x85598 tbb.w [pc,r3]
$d 0x8559c 0x4c300400
$d 0x855a0 0xd2b48c72
$t 0x855a4 ldr r2, [r1], #4
$t 0x855a8 sub.w ip, r2, #0x1010101
$t 0x855ac bic.w ip, ip, r2
                ......
$t 0x85634 ldr r2, [r1], #4
                ......
$t 0x85680 ldr r2, [r1], #4
                ......
```

(a) The disassembly of stpcpy.

```
LABEL_22:
  _R3 = (unsigned __int8) v17 & 7;
  if ( ((unsigned __int8) v17 & 7) != 0 )
  __asm
  {
    TBB.W  [PC, R3]          IDA pro decompiler fails to
                             recover switch-case structure
  }
  while ( 1 )
  {
    v33 = *(_QWORD *) v17;
    v17 += 8;
    v32 = v33;
    __pld(v17 + 64);
    v34 = (v33 - 16843009) & ~(_DWORD) v33
    ↪ & 0x80808080;
    if ( v34 )
      break;
    ......
  }
```

(b) The incomplete decompilation result of stpcpy by IDA-Pro.

Fig. 9. Case2: The incomplete decompilation result of function `stpcpy` by IDA-Pro.

Case 1: As depicted in Fig. 8a, IDA-Pro (v7.6) recognizes the byte sequence at `0x52b60` as a thumb instruction (`B loc_52832`) instead of inline data, which disrupts the contiguous disassembly, leading to cascading misinterpretations from `0x52b70` to `0x52b76`. The misclassification then leads to the wrong decompilation result, in which constant data is regarded as function pointers and original semantics are disrupted. Figure 8b shows the corresponding source and decompiled pseudo codes. We assume the error occurs because the byte sequence at `0x52b60` can be decoded as a valid instruction, and IDA-Pro (v7.6) prefers instruction recognition more than inline data identification. In contrast, `SOMIA` learns the dependencies between SIMD instructions like `vld` and `vst` with subsequent inline data through their relative positioning and successfully obtains the disassembly results.

Case 2: Figure 9a shows the disassembly of function `stpcpy`, which is used for string copy utility. The function itself is well-optimized for the speed using a `switch-case` structure to handle unaligned bytes. However, IDA-Pro (v7.6) fails to recognize the `switch-case` structure by misclassifying all 478 bytes after `tbb [pc, r3]` as inline data rather than valid thumb instructions, which subsequently impedes the decompilation phase, producing highly incomplete pseudocode without the switch-case logic. The incomplete decompiled code is shown in Fig. 9b. Unlike IDA-Pro's failure, `SOMIA` can recover all bytes missed by IDA-Pro.

5 Conclusion

In this paper, to overcome the difficulties of disassembly brought by special ARM properties, we propose a novel knowledge-aware transfer learning-based ARM binary disassembly technique to address these challenges for 32-bit ARM binaries. We adopt a multi-level masking method to integrate rich factual knowledge about ARM architecture into our system. Unlike previous works, SOMIA leverage knowledge-aware deep learning model equipped with embedded facts that are very helpful in subsequent downstream disassembly tasks. Our evaluation with a number of state-of-the-art disassemblers on 3693 binaries generated from SPEC benchmarks and real-world operating systems projects with various compilation settings, show that our technique, SOMIA, can achieve 98+% F1 scores on both instruction and function boundary recovery, and outperforms all baselines.

Acknowledgement. We thank anonymous reviewers for their insightful comments. This work was supported in part by Hong Kong S.A.R. Research Grants Council (RGC) General Research Fund No. 14205625.

References

1. Agency, N.S.: Ghidra (2019). https://ghidra-sre.org/
2. Andriesse, D., Chen, X., Van Der Veen, V., Slowinska, A., Bos, H.: An in-depth analysis of disassembly on full-scale x86/x64 binaries. In: USENIX Security Symposium, pp. 583–600., USENIX, Austin, TX (2016)
3. Avast software: RetDec: a retargetable machine-code decompiler. https://retdec.com/
4. Bauman, E.: Superset disassembly: statically rewriting x86 binaries without heuristics. NDSS (2018)
5. Bendersky, E.: Parsing elf and dwarf in Python (2023). https://github.com/eliben/pyelftools
6. OpenWrt Community: OpenWrt (2018). https://openwrt.org/releases/18.06/notes-18.06.0
7. SPE Corporation: Spec CPU2000 (2000). https://www.spec.org/cpu2000/
8. SPEC Corporation: Spec CPU2017 (2017). https://www.spec.org/cpu2017/
9. Devlin, J., Chang, M., Lee, K., Toutanova, K.: BERT: pre-training of deep bidirectional transformers for language understanding. In: Burstein, J., Doran, C., Solorio, T. (eds.) Proceedings of the 2019 Conference of the North American Chapter of the Association for Computational Linguistics: Human Language Technologies, NAACL-HLT 2019, Minneapolis, MN, USA, June 2-7, 2019, Volume 1 (Long and Short Papers), pp. 4171–4186. Association for Computational Linguistics (2019)
10. Flores-Montoya, A., Schulte, E.: DataLog disassembly. In: Proceedings of the 29th USENIX Security Symposium, pp. 1075–1092 (2020)
11. GNU: OBJDUMP. GNU Binutils (2023). https://sourceware.org/binutils/docs/binutils/objdump.html
12. Google: Android open source project (2018). https://source.android.com/
13. DW Group: Dwarf (1992). http://www.dwarfstd.org/
14. Hex-Rays: IDA pro. https://www.hex-rays.com/products/ida/. Accessed 2 June 2023
15. Jelinek, F.: Perplexity - a measure of the difficulty of speech recognition tasks. ICASSP. IEEE (1977)
16. Jiang, M., Zhou, Y., Luo, X., Wang, R., Liu, Y., Ren, K.: An empirical study on ARM disassembly tools. ISSTA 2020 - Proceedings of the 29th ACM SIGSOFT International Symposium on Software Testing and Analysis, pp. 401–414 (2020). https://doi.org/10.1145/3395363.3397377
17. Jordan, H., Scholz, B., Subotić, P.: Soufflé: On synthesis of program analyzers. In: Chaudhuri, S., Farzan, A. (eds.) Computer Aided Verification, pp. 422–430. Springer International Publishing, Cham (2016). https://doi.org/10.1007/978-3-319-41540-6_23

18. Joshi, M., Chen, D., Liu, Y., Weld, D.S., Zettlemoyer, L., Levy, O.: SpanBert: improving pre-training by representing and predicting spans. Trans. Assoc. Comput. Linguistics **8**, 64–77 (2020)
19. Kim, T., Saltaformaggio, B.: ReARM: a platform-agnostic ARM binary rewriter for security applications. In: Proceedings of the 33rd Annual Computer Security Applications Conference, pp. 412–424. ACM (2017)
20. Kruegel, C., Robertson, W., Valeur, F., Vigna, G.: Static disassembly of obfuscated binaries. In: Proceedings of the 13th USENIX Security Symposium, pp. 1–23 (2004)
21. ARM Limited: MBED-OS-6.0.0 (2023). https://os.mbed.com/mbed-os/releases/
22. Miller, K.A., Kwon, Y., Sun, Y., Zhang, Z., Zhang, X., Lin, Z.: Probabilistic disassembly. In: Atlee, J.M., Bultan, T., Whittle, J. (eds.) Proceedings of the 41st International Conference on Software Engineering, ICSE 2019, Montreal, QC, Canada, May 25-31, 2019, pp. 1187–1198. IEEE / ACM, Montréal, QC, Canada (2019)
23. NVIDIA, Vingelmann, P., Fitzek, F.H.: Cuda, release: 12.1 (2023). https://developer.nvidia.com/cuda-toolkit
24. Ott, M., et al.: FAIRSEQ: a fast, extensible toolkit for sequence modeling. In: Proceedings of NAACL-HLT 2019: Demonstrations (2019)
25. Paleari, R., Martignoni, L., Roqlia, G.F., Bruschi, D.: N-version disassembly: differential testing of x86 disassemblers. ISSTA 2010 - Proceedings of the 2010 International Symposium on Software Testing and Analysis, pp. 265–274 (2010). https://doi.org/10.1145/1831708.1831741
26. Pang, C., et al.: SOK: all you ever wanted to know about x86/x64 binary disassembly but were afraid to ask. arXiv (2020). http://arxiv.org/abs/2007.14266
27. Paszke, A., et al.: PyTorch: an imperative style, high-performance deep learning library. In: Wallach, H.M., Larochelle, H., Beygelzimer, A., d'Alché-Buc, F., Fox, E.B., Garnett, R. (eds.) Advances in Neural Information Processing Systems 32: Annual Conference on Neural Information Processing Systems 2019, NeurIPS 2019, December 8-14, 2019, Vancouver, BC, Canada, pp. 8024–8035 (2019)
28. Pei, K., Guan, J., Williams-King, D., Yang, J., Jana, S.: XDA: accurate, robust disassembly with transfer learning. In: 28th Annual Network and Distributed System Security Symposium, NDSS 2021, virtually, February 21-25, 2021. The Internet Society (2021). https://www.ndss-symposium.org/ndss-paper/xda-accurate-robust-disassembly-with-transfer-learning/
29. Qin, Z.: TADY: a neural disassembler without structural constraint violations. In: 34th USENIX Security Symposium (USENIX Security, vol. 25 (2025)
30. Quynh, N.A.: Capstone (2013). https://www.capstone-engine.org/
31. Amazon Web Services (AWS): Freertos version 10 (2023). https://www.freertos.org/FreeRTOS-V10.html
32. Standard-performance-evaluation-corporation: Spec CPU2006 (2006). https://www.spec.org/cpu2006/
33. Wang, Y., et al.: DISA: accurate learning-based static disassembly with attentions. In: ACM SIGSAC Conference on Computer and Communications Security (CCS 25) (2025)
34. Wartell, R., Mohan, V., Hamlen, K.W., Lin, Z.: Binary stirring: self-randomizing instruction addresses of legacy x86 binary code. In: Proceedings of the ACM Conference on Computer and Communications Security, pp. 157–168 (2012). https://doi.org/10.1145/2382196.2382216
35. Ye, Y., Zhang, Z., Shi, Q., Aafer, Y., Zhang, X.: D-ARM: disassembling arm binaries by lightweight superset instruction interpretation and graph modeling. In: 2023 IEEE Symposium on Security and Privacy (SP), pp. 728–745. IEEE Computer Society, IEEE, SAN FRANCISCO, CA (2022)

36. Yu, S., Qu, Y., Hu, X., Yin, H.: DeepDI: learning a relational graph convolutional network model on instructions for fast and accurate disassembly. In: Butler, K.R.B., Thomas, K. (eds.) 31st USENIX Security Symposium, USENIX Security 2022, Boston, MA, USA, August 10–12, 2022, pp. 2709–2725. USENIX Association, BOSTON, MA, USA (2022)

Role-Driven Comparative Forensic Analysis of an Android Marketplace Mobile Application

Mark Daniels and Murat Gunestas(✉)

University of New Haven, West Haven, CT 06515, USA
mdani7@unh.newhaven.edu, mgunestas@newhaven.edu

Abstract. This study examined the digital artifacts generated by the eBay mobile application on Android devices to assess their forensic significance and implications for user privacy. Using a controlled experimental setup with emulated Android environments, three user profiles—seller, buyer, and guest—were created to replicate realistic app interactions. The results revealed that the eBay app retains measurable data across all user modes. The findings confirm that meaningful forensic evidence can be obtained from the eBay app using only open-source tools, supporting their value for transparent and accessible investigations. The research establishes a reproducible methodology for future digital forensic analyses of mobile marketplace applications and contributes to ongoing discussions on balancing forensic accessibility with data privacy.

Keywords: Mobile forensics · Android · eBay · Digital Forensics · Autopsy · Digital artifact

1 Introduction

As mobile applications increasingly change the way people communicate, shop, and conduct business, they also generate vast amounts of data that remain on the devices used to access them. These lingering pieces of data, often referred to as digital artifacts, can take many forms including chat logs, browsing history, cached images, and deleted records. While invisible to the average user, these artifacts are of great interest to forensic investigators and consumer privacy advocates; digital artifacts can serve as evidence in criminal investigations, highlight vulnerabilities in data management practices, and reveal how applications manage and store user behaviors.

Digital forensics, the practice of recovery and analysis of digital artifacts, has grown increasingly relevant as mobile applications are used for a wider range of purposes, yet forensic analysis of mobile applications is not always

© ICST Institute for Computer Sciences, Social Informatics and Telecommunications Engineering 2027
Published by Springer Nature Switzerland AG 2027. All Rights Reserved
H. Neukirchen et al. (Eds.): ICDF2C 2026, LNICST 720, pp. 357–373, 2027.
https://doi.org/10.1007/978-3-032-37274-1_21

a straightforward process. Each application handles data in its own way and storage methods used can vary significantly between devices, app versions, and operating systems. This presents a challenge for forensic investigators who rely on commercial tools that may not offer full support for every app. At the same time, many widely used applications, especially those that involve sensitive transactions or user interactions, lack publicly available research that details what artifacts they leave behind or how those artifacts can be recovered. The eBay mobile application is a frequently used platform for online buying, selling, and communication. Its popularity and transactional nature suggest that it has the potential to store a rich set of data locally on user devices. This data could include important data such as user activity, communication logs, or transaction records. However, to date, there is no dedicated open-source forensic tool designed specifically to extract and analyze data from the eBay app on Android devices. Moreover, existing literature does not offer a clear, replicable method for examining this app in a controlled or investigative setting.

This study addresses the lack of research on the forensic analysis of marketplace mobile applications from a multi role perspective specifically addressing digital artifacts left behind by the eBay app on Android devices and what those artifacts mean for digital forensic investigations and user privacy. Using only open-source tools, this research will identify recoverable data from the app, document the structure and location of those artifacts, and propose a repeatable methodology that others can follow in their own investigations and research involving the eBay app on Android devices. A proof-of-concept for an eBay forensic analysis tool will also be outlined to demonstrate how such artifacts could be recovered automatically, offering a resource for investigators who rely on accessible and transparent forensic tools. The results aim to inform both forensic investigators and consumer privacy advocates by highlighting where sensitive data may remain and how it can be responsibly examined or secured.

2 Related Work

This review begins with a section on digital forensic tools and methodologies, examining how investigators extract, analyze, and preserve data from Android devices. This foundation is important for understanding the capabilities and limitations of the tools that will be used to examine the eBay app. The second section focuses on case studies involving different Android applications, which demonstrate how forensic techniques have been applied to real apps and what types of data can typically be recovered. These examples help shape realistic expectations for what might be found within the eBay app. The final section addresses anti-forensic techniques, including app behaviors that are designed to hide or delete data. This is especially relevant when considering user privacy and the potential challenges in recovering meaningful artifacts during forensic investigations.

2.1 Digital Forensic Tools and Methodology

Roy et al. [1] performed a comparative evaluation of multiple Android forensic tools, focusing on factors such as the categories of data extracted and whether each tool was open-source or proprietary. Their findings indicated that commercial solutions typically provide more refined reporting features and user-friendly interfaces, whereas open-source alternatives remain versatile and can be customized for advanced use cases. Similarly, Raji et al. [2] compared the proprietary tool Paraben E3:DS with the open-source platform Autopsy to assess their effectiveness in retrieving artifacts from an Android device. Their results showed that while the commercial tool successfully recovered nearly all recorded activities with associated timestamps, the open-source tool achieved partial recovery, lacking temporal metadata in many instances. Collectively, these studies emphasize that the choice of forensic tool can substantially influence the completeness and quality of recovered data, underscoring the importance of appropriate tool selection when examining applications such as eBay.

2.2 Case Studies on Android Applications

Zhang et al. [3] performed a structured forensic investigation of four Android instant messaging applications, following the standard phases of identification, preservation, analysis, and reporting. Their work revealed that although many communication records were encrypted, locally stored databases on rooted devices often remained accessible in plaintext, enabling the recovery of chat artifacts and user-related information. This demonstrates that encryption provides partial protection, but valuable evidence may still persist within local storage, particularly on devices with elevated privileges. Similarly, Mahendra and Khairunnisa [4] examined data recovery from two online dating platforms, Tantan and Omi, using the commercial MOBILedit Forensic suite. Their findings indicated that artifact recovery outcomes varied significantly depending on the application and user activity context, emphasizing the importance of app-specific factors and controlled testing conditions when assessing data recoverability. Hong Khoa et al. [5] investigated the TikTok application on Android devices to identify locations of stored user activity such as search queries, private messages, and follower interactions. Their results confirmed that notable user information could still be retrieved even after users deleted certain actions, reinforcing the need for tailored examination strategies that account for the unique data structures and behaviors of each app. This insight is particularly relevant to forensic analysis of eBay's mobile application, where user engagement data may persist in unconventional locations. Barghouthy et al. [6] explored the forensic recovery of private browsing sessions within the Orweb browser and discovered that meaningful data could only be extracted when the device was rooted. In follow-up work, Al Barghouthy and Marrington [7] evaluated alternative acquisition approaches for Android devices, comparing methods such as reflashing the recovery partition and rooting the device. Their findings suggested that both techniques enabled session reconstruction, though the recovery-mode approach was preferable because it preserved the integrity of the system and user partitions. This consideration is directly relevant to the eBay app investigation, where acquiring digital artifacts must be balanced with maintaining forensic soundness.

2.3 Challenges of Anti-Forensics

Mehrotra and Mehtre [8] performed a forensic investigation of the Wickr messaging platform across both rooted and non-rooted Android devices. Their analysis yielded no recoverable traces of Wickr activity, indicating that the application likely implements anti-forensic mechanisms to erase message content and associated metadata. This finding underscores the difficulties investigators face when analyzing applications engineered with privacy-preserving or data-sanitization features. Mirza et al. [9] examined the anti-forensic obstacles associated with WhatsApp on Android devices, particularly those introduced by its functionality that enables users to delete messages from both sender and recipient accounts, even after blocking. Although the feature enhances user control and privacy, it complicates the reconstruction of complete communication histories during forensic analysis. Their research highlights how privacy centric design choices in modern messaging apps can impede the acquisition of reliable digital evidence. Hermawan et al. [10] carried out a comparative evaluation of the Universal Forensic Extraction Device (UFED) and MOBILedit tools to assess their effectiveness in recovering unsent message artifacts from instant messaging applications. The study found that UFED achieved higher recovery rates for unsent messages across a variety of applications but was still unable to extract artifacts from all tested platforms. These results reinforce the importance of employing multiple forensic tools when examining privacy oriented applications, as no single solution guarantees comprehensive artifact recovery.

3 Problem Definition and Research Questions

The reviewed literature highlights several important considerations for conducting a forensic analysis an application on Android devices. Foundational studies on forensic tools demonstrate that both commercial and open-source platforms vary in effectiveness and that tool selection significantly impacts the quality and completeness of recovered data. Case studies on various mobile applications confirm that meaningful digital artifacts can be recovered, especially when testing is conducted under controlled conditions, and that app-specific behaviors heavily influence forensic outcomes. Finally, research on anti-forensic techniques shows the challenge of analyzing applications that intentionally obscure or delete user data. Together, these studies support the need for a structured, multi-tool and role-driven methodology to examine the eBay app and establish whether valuable user artifacts can be recovered in a forensically sound manner.

This study addresses this gap by asking the following research questions:

Research Questions

- **RQ1 (Identification):** What kinds of digital artifacts does the eBay Android application generate and where are they stored?
- **RQ2 (Effects of roles):** How do different user modes (seller, buyer, or guest) and authentication status affect the volume and type of artifacts retained?
- **RQ3 (Privacy):** Does the eBay app securely protect sensitive information (such as login credentials or personal identifiers), or can any such data be recovered from the device?
- **RQ4 (Tools and techniques):** What open-source forensic tools and procedures can be combined into a systematic methodology for analyzing the eBay app?

By answering these questions, this research examines whether role-driven forensic analysis can expose a broader range of artifacts and ultimately enable more accurate reconstruction of e-commerce mobile app activities performed by different user types. The outcomes of this work establish a concrete foundation for developing open-source tools or plugins that support reliable extraction and interpretation of eBay-related artifacts.

4 Methodology

This research was conducted using a controlled and reproducible digital forensic environment designed to simulate typical user interactions with the eBay mobile application on Android. The experiment utilized emulated Android devices, test user accounts, and open-source forensic tools to ensure transparency and repeatability. All steps were documented to maintain a clear chain of custody for data acquisition and analysis. To prevent accidental purchases during testing, all seller listings were configured with the pickup-only method and assigned artificially high prices. No sales occurred during the experiment, and all listings were removed from the platform after testing to maintain safety and prevent interference with actual users.

4.1 Experimental Environment Setup

The Android emulator provided by Android Studio was used to simulate a physical Android device. Three virtual devices were created using identical configurations to represent different user scenarios (buyer, seller, and guest). Each emulator was configured as a Google Pixel 5 running Android 13.0 (Tiramisu). Using emulators offered a consistent and controllable environment that avoided hardware-level variations while accurately replicating Android filesystem behavior. The APKMirror Installer (Official) version 1.11.0 (36dccaefd) [11] was used to sideload the official eBay app (version 6.167.0.3) from APKMirror [12]. This ensured that the same app version and signing certificate were used across all devices. The APKs were verified using SHA-1 and SHA-256 hash values to confirm integrity prior to installation. Each virtual device was configured with a dedicated Google account and test eBay account:

- Guest account: continued without sign-in
- Buyer account: testbuyer374@gmail.com
- Seller account: testseller74@gmail.com

All accounts were created using consistent parameters, including a shared password and a fixed date of birth, to minimize extraneous variability between tests. The tools used through our experiments are listed in Table 1 below.

4.2 User Activity Simulation

To replicate realistic user behavior within the eBay app, separate virtual devices were used for the buyer, seller, and guest accounts. Each account performed a structured sequence of actions designed to simulate typical interactions within the app. All steps were documented to ensure reproducibility.

Guest Account Activity: The guest account simulated interactions by a user who did not log in or register. This account was used to perform keyword searches for products such as "Gameboy" and "Gameboy games" and to view several item listings. No account-based actions, such as saving items or adding to a watchlist, were possible. The guest account workflow focused solely on browsing activity without requiring authentication or creating persistent account data.

Buyer Account Activity: The buyer account, test- buyer374@gmail.com, was used to replicate common shopping behavior within the eBay app. The user performed searches for products, saved the Veldspar item created by the seller, and performed searches for items such as the Nintendo Switch. Items were added to the watchlist, and item details were viewed to simulate typical browsing interactions. All actions were conducted while logged into the buyer account to maintain the distinction between registered user behavior and guest activity.

Seller Account Activity: The seller account, testseller74@gmail.com, was used to simulate the creation and management of product listings. Two items, "Scorodite" and "Veldspar," were prepared for listing. For each item, the first image retrieved from Google Images with a public domain license was downloaded and transferred to the device's Downloads folder. The Scorodite listing was drafted with the condition marked as "Used," a description detailing the mineral sample, a location set to Alaska (ZIP 99555), the pickup method set to "Pickup Only," payment handled by eBay, and the return policy marked as "Not accepted." The Veldspar listing was prepared with the same attributes but was publicly posted to simulate an active listing. All images were pushed to the emulator using the Android Debug Bridge to ensure they were available during listing creation.

Summary of Activity: By separating activities into seller, buyer, and guest workflows, the study established a controlled framework for simulating distinct user interactions. Each account followed a structured sequence of actions, including the use of public domain images for listings, performing searches, viewing items, and adding content to watchlists where applicable. All listings created during the experiment used pickup-only methods and artificially high prices to prevent accidental purchases, and were removed after testing to ensure safety. This

Table 1. Tools and Components Used in the Study

Tool / Component	Version	Purpose / Notes
Android Studio Emulator	2023.1.1	Simulated Pixel running Android 13 (Tiramisu)
Autopsy	4.21.0	Forensic analysis of extracted logical files
ADB (Android Debug Bridge)	1.0.41	Used to access emulator shell and extract /data/data directory
APKMirror Installer	1.11.0 (36-dccaefd)	Sideloaded verified eBay APK from trusted source
EBay Mobile Application (APK)	6.167.0.3	Target app under examination

methodological approach allowed for reproducible user behavior simulations while maintaining the integrity of the experimental environment.

4.3 Forensic Imaging Procedure

After completing the structured user activity simulations, a logical acquisition of each device's eBay application data was performed to capture all relevant files. The acquisition process began by creating a TAR archive of the /data/-data/com.ebay.mobile directory, which contains the private files of the eBay mobile application. Using the Android Debug Bridge (ADB) shell, root access was obtained and the tar utility was executed to compress only the eBay application folder into a single archive, ebay_data.tar, stored on the device's SD card. The archive was created by executing commands shown in Listing 1 below.

```
adb shell
su
cd /data/data
tar -cvf /sdcard/ebay_data.tar com.ebay.mobile
exit
```

Listing 1. ADB shell commands for extracting eBay application data

The compressed archive was then transferred from the emulator to the host Windows system using adb pull, ensuring that all app data was preserved in a single location on the local filesystem.

Once the archive was transferred, it was safely extracted on the host system using tar, which preserved file permissions, directory structure, and timestamps exactly as they existed on the device.

This procedure ensured that all data from the emulator, including app-specific directories, databases, cache, and preferences, was captured in a forensically sound manner. The resulting files were then prepared for analysis using Autopsy, providing a controlled and reproducible environment for subsequent forensic investigation.

4.4 Forensic Analysis Workflow

Following the creation of the forensic images, each directory containing the logical files of the application was examined as a separate case using Autopsy, an open-source digital forensic platform. This approach allowed independent and reproducible analysis of each virtual device's data. Each directory was added to Autopsy through the "Add Data Source" option by selecting Logical Files, providing full access to each directory and its contents while preserving the original file metadata. Within Autopsy, analysis focused exclusively on the eBay application's subdirectories, including databases, cache, shared preferences, and temporary files. Standard forensic procedures were followed to ensure the integrity of the data during examination, including mounting the directory in read-only mode to prevent any inadvertent modification of timestamps, permissions, or file contents. All examination steps were systematically documented, including the paths navigated, the types of files inspected, and the tools and features used within Autopsy. Both user-level and system-level components relevant to the eBay application were reviewed to provide a comprehensive understanding of how data was stored across different scenarios. Special attention was given to maintaining reproducibility, with all commands, file paths, and configuration settings noted for future replication. This workflow allowed for a controlled and methodical exploration of the eBay application's logical files. By adhering to forensic principles such as data integrity, reproducibility, and thorough documentation, the analysis was conducted in a manner suitable for academic research and potential application in investigative contexts.

5 Findings

During the forensic examination of the buyer, seller, and guest devices, several directories and file types were consistently recovered across the sessions. These artifacts provide insight into application behavior, user authentication state, and cached content, regardless of the specific user role. Table 2 summarizes the artifact categories observed and their general forensic relevance across devices. These artifact categories were observed across the examined devices, although the content and completeness varied depending on whether the device was used in a Guest, Buyer, or Seller session. High-value artifacts, such as those in shared_prefs, reliably indicated authentication state and configuration, while low-value artifacts, such as cached images, primarily reflected app activity and stored UI data in binary form without containing directly viewable images.

5.1 Findings for Guest User

The forensic image of the guest account device revealed artifacts characteristic of unauthenticated browsing activity within the com.ebay.mobile directory. The cache and cacheManager subdirectories contained numerous binary .dat and .dat-slack files, all consistent in format with the image cache artifacts observed in the buyer and seller devices. These files exhibited three identifiable data regions—header, payload, and trailing slack—suggesting they store compressed media or serialized network responses. While the main data segments were not human-readable, several cache entries contained structured metadata fields defining attributes such as expirationTime, itemSize, and is_ai_generated. These values indicate that each cached object maintains descriptive properties for lifecycle management and cache indexing, confirming that the application retains partial contextual information even in guest mode. The code_cache directory was empty, indicating that the app did not retain optimized bytecode or compiled execution traces during guest use. Within the databases directory, several SQLite databases were present, including transport_events.db and google_app_measurement_local.db, both structurally valid but devoid of meaningful records. The nautilus.db contained a populated recent_search_entity table, recording the queries "gameboy" and "gameboy games" with associated timestamps and category identifiers. The suggestions.db contained a corresponding record of the same search terms under the columns display1, query, and date, confirming that search suggestions and recent query history are stored locally, even for unauthenticated users. These findings demonstrate that while item interactions are limited in guest mode, transient search related data is still cached to improve user experience upon subsequent app launches.

Table 2. App Directories and Files Unrelated to User Activity

Directory	File Type	Forensic Value	Notes
shared_prefs	XML preference files	High	Contains authentication state, configuration flags, identifiers, and sometimes token-based authorization.
databases	SQLite databases	Moderate	Contains app analytics (e.g., measurement data) and user search suggestions. Some databases exist only as placeholders with no records.
cache/ cacheManager	.dat image cache blobs	Low	Contains cached thumbnails of previously viewed items or UI elements, but no embedded user identifiers.
files	JSON state files, installation IDs, rollout flags	Medium	Can reveal installation identifiers and feature roll out status associated with the device.
no_backup	WorkManager DB files	Low	Contains job scheduling metadata, but no user identity or activity data.
code_cache	Compiled/dex-optimized code	None	No forensic value for user identification. Contains execution artifacts only.

The files directory contained configuration and identification files similar in structure to those found on the authenticated devices. Keys stored in a JSON-formatted file referenced default system attributes such as carrier ID, locale, timezone, and network type, but did not include user-specific identifiers. The device remained unregistered with any eBay account, as evidenced by the field "userId":"<not-signed-in>". Additional JSON and XML files recorded Crashlytics configuration, session identifiers, and Firebase installation metadata. A Crashlytics report object confirmed the app's build version and environment, while the Firebase configuration included device-specific tokens and installation UUIDs.

The shared_prefs directory preserved several XML preference files defining the app's internal state and telemetry configuration. Files such as com.ebay.dataservice.prefs.xml and forter_sdk_prefs.xml reflected that the onboarding screen had been shown and telemetry frameworks initialized. The com.ebay.dataservice.prefs.xml file also recorded the last search keyword, "gameboy games," under the key com.ebay.dataservice.prefs.searchLast Keywords. Several preference files stored long cryptographic values, device registration tokens, and analytics identifiers, including entries for ThreatMetrix, Firebase, and Google Measurement services. The presence of a valid eBay app authentication token (com.ebay.nautilus.domain.app_auth_access_token) suggests the app provisions a device-level token for session management even in guest mode, potentially used for anonymous tracking or pre-login network operations.

Overall, the guest device's forensic footprint demonstrated that the eBay app retains limited but meaningful session metadata, including cached search queries, locally stored preference files, and analytic tokens. No personal user data or transaction history was present, confirming that unregistered sessions maintain a constrained data scope while still generating identifiable telemetry and device-level keys that could be of forensic interest in future session correlation analysis.

To provide a visual overview of artifact distribution across the three user roles, Table 3 presents a Matrix table chart comparing Guest, Buyer, and Seller devices. The diagram highlights which artifacts are common to all devices, which are shared between specific roles, and which are unique to a particular device. This representation allows for immediate comparison of baseline Guest activity against the additional artifacts introduced by authenticated Buyer and Seller interactions.

5.2 Findings for Buyer User

The analysis of the buyer device's filesystem, specifically the /data/data/-com.ebay.mobile directory, revealed several subdirectories and files corresponding to cache storage, web data, application databases, and preference files. These artifacts reflect the app's local storage behavior after typical buyer interactions such as searching for products and adding items to a watchlist.

The app_webview directory contained Chromium based WebView artifacts under Default, including Cookies, Web Data, and Local Storage. The LevelDB files found under Local Storage/leveldb (for example, 000003.log and MANIFEST-000001) represented low-level browser storage and were not readily interpretable as plaintext application content. The WebView Cookies and Web Data SQLite files were present but, in this controlled experiment, did not contain active session credentials. The WebView cache and GPU/Dawn cache files were present as binary artifacts consistent with browser caching layers.

Within the cache/cacheManager directory a large number of binary .dat files were present; these files appear to serve as image and resource caches for listing thumbnails and item previews. A separate cache file associated with the shopping cart (ShopExShoppingCartCache.disk) contained a single JSON-like record representing cart metadata (for example, "shoppingCartId":"16088422226" and related module metadata), indicating that UI/cart state was persisted to disk in a serialized form.

The databases directory contained multiple SQLite databases including nautilus_db, suggestions.db, and google_app_measurement_local.db. Of these, suggestions.db stored explicit search suggestion records; table rows include an identifier, the displayed text, the underlying query string, and a timestamp. Example rows recovered from suggestions.db included entries for scordite, veldspar, and nintendo switch with epoch timestamps corresponding to the experiment session as shown in Listing 2 below.

```
_id | display         | query           | date
3   | scordite        | scordite        | 1759110xxxx
5   | veldspar        | veldspar        | 1759110xxxx
6   | nintendo switch | nintendo switch | 1759110xxxx
```

Listing 2. Search history data from Chrome database

The nautilus_db schema included tables such as recent_search_entity, share_entity (which included a userId column), and a key_value table storing assorted app metadata and lifecycle values (for example, app rating prompt snooze timers and buyable item counts). The google_app_measurement_local.db and related measurement files contained telemetry and session metadata consistent with Firebase/Google Analytics instrumentation. The files directory included JSON-formatted installation records such as the PersistedInstallation...json file, which contained Firebase installation identifiers and token material (fields such as Fid, AuthToken, and RefreshToken). Several other files related to rollout and profile installation timestamps were present but empty or minimally populated in this controlled environment. The Crashlytics folder contained a settings JSON and session related JSON files describing a single app session and associated exception traces; these artifacts captured app runtime metadata and diagnostic logs. The no_backup area held Android WorkManager state (for example, androidx.work.workdb and its WAL/SHM counterparts), which stored work specification entries and scheduling metadata rather than direct user content. The shared_prefs directory contained multiple XML preference files (for example, com.ebay.dataservice.prefs.xml, PushService.prefs.xml, and ThreatMetrixMobileSDK.xml). These XML files included configuration values, installation and session timestamps, internal user identifiers (for example, the public user id string txrazoumtlm), cached tokens and device-registration metadata, and saved search keywords (for example, the key com.ebay.dataservice.prefs.searchLastKeywords contained nintendo switch). A short illustrative snippet of the SharedPreferences format is shown in Listing 3 below.

```
<map>
  <string name="com.ebay.dataservice.prefs.searchLastKeywords">
    nintendo switch
  </string>
```

```
  <string name="com.ebay.identity.user.auth.activePublicUserId">
    txrazoumtlm
  </string>
</map>
```

Listing 3. eBay application preferences XML data

Collectively, the buyer device image contained a mix of binary caches, structured SQLite databases with explicit search queries and timestamps, serialized JSON installation records, and XML preference files that preserved app configuration and internal identifiers. These artifacts document the types of contextual metadata the eBay Android application persisted locally in the controlled experiment.

5.3 Findings for Seller User

The forensic image of the seller device revealed a distinct pattern of data persistence compared to the buyer and guest configurations. Within the com.ebay.mobile directory, several subdirectories contained artifacts indicative of authenticated account usage, cached network content, and diagnostic telemetry generated during listing setup and general app interaction. While no records were recovered showing specific items listed for sale or user-entered text, the available artifacts clearly confirmed that the device had been logged into the test seller account and actively interacted with eBay's network services. Sensitive information such as passwords or personal identifiers was not found in plaintext, but the structure and metadata of the recovered files demonstrated normal app operation within a logged-in context.

The app_webview directory stored browser-related metadata generated by the in-app WebView component. While the browser_metrics file was empty, the pref_store file contained structured JSON entries preserving internal metrics such as the last package name logging rule update, an uninstall timestamp, and a user entropy source value. The file confirmed that eBay's embedded web framework maintains app-specific telemetry across sessions, even when no explicit browsing activity occurs. A populated Cookies SQLite database was also recovered under app_webview/Default, containing numerous entries associated with the domain .ebay.com. Each record preserved host keys, cookie names, and timestamp values. Although the encrypted_value fields were stored as BLOBs and therefore unreadable without the device's encryption keys, the recovered names, expiration dates, and domain fields verified the presence of authenticated session cookies and tracking identifiers. Common fields such as ebaysid, __ssds, and __uzmaj2 were identified, reflecting that the seller account remained logged in at the time of imaging.

Other WebView-related data structures, including browsing history and form data, were empty. Several LevelDB and IndexedDB logs within the Default folder further corroborated this activity. These logs recorded database creation events for multiple eBay service domains such as signup.ebay.com, devicebind.ebay.com, onboardweb.ebay.com, and h.onlinemetrix.net. Each entry noted

Table 3. Presence of forensic artifacts across Guest, Buyer, and Seller accounts

Artifact / Data	**Guest**	**Buyer**	**Seller**	**Notes**
shared_prefs basic telemetry				Basic telemetry across devices
cache/cacheManager UI blobs				UI binary blobs
databases minimal search history				Simple history, minimal entries
files JSON IDs, Crashlytics/Firebase config				Installation and crash logs
code_cache				Low forensic value
Expanded search history				Buyer history more detailed than Guest
recent_search_entity table				
Local SQLite analytics				Minimal telemetry, local storage
Serialized shopping cart metadata				Includes cart info
WebView data (Cookies, Local Storage, LevelDB)				Session and storage data
quota_manager entries				Web storage quotas per device
Device-level session tokens				Tokens for authenticated sessions
Partially populated session metadata				
Installation/profile timestamps				
Authenticated session cookies (.ebay.com)				
Listing-related prefs				
Full telemetry entries				
Databases for network/analytics				

database initialization, compaction, and manifest reuse timestamps, indicating background service communication during account onboarding and session verification. The quota_manager database contained a populated buckets table referencing the same subdomains, confirming that these sites were registered within the app's isolated web storage environment. These records collectively demonstrate that the eBay app leverages its embedded browser for user authentication and persistent session management through web storage mechanisms.

Beyond the WebView layer, additional cached data were found under the http_cache and image_cache directories. The HTTP cache contained several .dat files embedding binary image content, along with HTTP response headers referencing eBay's content delivery infrastructure. Entries included assets from domains such as ir.ebaystatic.com and i.e.bayimg.com, accompanied by

SSL certificate metadata issued by "Sectigo Public Server Authentication CA OV R3" and "USERTrust RSA Certification Authority." These cache entries confirm that the app locally stored web assets—including images and interface components—retrieved from eBay's servers during normal browsing. The image_cache directory also contained small JSON fragments specifying fields like itemSize and expirationTime, reflecting the app's use of time-based cache expiration. One notable file, shopping_cart.dat, preserved a serialized JSON object describing an empty shopping cart. It included attributes such as "shoppingCartId":"16092275193" and "selectedShippingCountry":"US", along with textual elements stating "You don't have any items in your cart." These data suggest that although the seller account accessed cart-related functionality, no items were stored or purchased during testing.

The databases directory contained several SQLite databases, transport_events.db, measurement.db, and nautilus.db, all of which were structurally intact but contained no meaningful records. Their presence implies that the app maintains these databases as placeholders for network or analytic data but defers actual content storage to remote APIs. This supports the conclusion that listing creation and management operations occur via server-side processes rather than local persistence. Multiple preference and configuration files were also recovered under shared_prefs, providing insight into the app's internal configuration and linked services. Files such as firebase_app_id.xml, google_app_measurement.xml, and appsflyer-data.xml stored keys and unique identifiers related to Firebase, Google Analytics, and AppsFlyer telemetry frameworks. Additionally, XML entries under io.fabric.sdk.android.fabric.xml revealed tokenized configuration values associated with Crashlytics crash reporting. None of these files included explicit user credentials, but they did confirm the activation of analytic and diagnostic services tied to the seller device instance.

6 Conclusion and Future Work

This study successfully identified and documented the digital artifacts produced by the eBay mobile application on Android devices under different user scenarios. By employing an entirely open-source and reproducible forensic workflow, the research demonstrated that the eBay app retains measurable amounts of locally stored data, even when limited user interaction occurs. Across all test configurations—seller, buyer, and guest—distinct categories of forensic evidence were recovered, confirming that the app maintains session-related and analytic data as part of its normal operation.

The forensic images revealed that authenticated sessions (buyer and seller) generated a more substantial and diverse set of artifacts than guest interactions. Authenticated devices retained persistent identifiers, search histories, preference files, and web session cookies, many of which could serve as evidentiary markers of user activity. In contrast, guest sessions produced only transient cache and search suggestion artifacts, reflecting a more privacy-conscious behavior but still leaving identifiable traces of device-level telemetry. Across all cases, sensitive information such as plaintext credentials or personal identifiers was not recovered, suggesting that the app employs appropriate security controls to prevent direct data exposure. Nevertheless, the persistence of search keywords, identifiers, and analytics metadata presents potential privacy implications, as these artifacts could allow partial reconstruction of user behavior if device access were obtained.

The findings reinforce several broader insights for mobile forensic practitioners. First, the study demonstrates that meaningful forensic artifacts can be extracted from common consumer applications using only open-source tools, validating their utility for investigative and academic purposes. Second, it underscores the necessity of examining app-specific behaviors, as each mode of interaction within eBay—authenticated or guest—produces unique forensic signatures. Finally, it highlights the importance of balancing forensic recoverability with user privacy: applications may not expose sensitive data, yet their operational telemetry can still yield investigative value.

While this research manually performed each stage of data extraction and analysis, future development could automate the process into a dedicated tool or module for e-commerce application investigations. Such a tool could parse known databases, extract relevant tables, and generate investigator-ready summaries of search and account activity. Implementing the proposed framework would streamline forensic workflows, enhance repeatability, and contribute toward the standardization of mobile e-commerce artifact analysis.

References

1. Roy, N.R., Khanna, A.K., Aneja, L.: Android phone forensic: Tools and techniques. In: 2016 International Conference on Computing, Communication and Automation (ICCCA), pp. 605–610 (2016). https://doi.org/10.1109/CCAA.2016.7813792.
2. Raji, M., Wimmer, H., Haddad, R.J.: Analyzing data from an Android smartphone while comparing between two forensic tools. In: SoutheastCon 2018, pp. 1–6 (2018). https://doi.org/10.1109/SECON.2018.8478851.
3. Zhang, H., Chen, L., Liu, : Digital forensic analysis of instant messaging applications on Android smartphones. In: 2018 International Conference on Computing, Networking and Communications (ICNC), pp. 647–651 (2018). https://doi.org/10.1109/ICCNC.2018.8390330.
4. Mahendra, N.F., Khairunnisa, R.: Digital forensic analysis of online dating applications on android using the digital forensic research workshop 2001 investigation model. In: 2023 IEEE International Conference on Cryptography, Informatics, and Cybersecurity (ICoCICs), pp. 218–223 (2023). https://doi.org/10.1109/ICoCICs58778.2023.10276752.
5. Hoang Khoa, N., The Duy, P., Do Hoang, H., Thi Thu Hien, D., Pham, V.-H.: Forensic analysis of TikTok application to seek digital artifacts on Android smartphone. In: 2020 RIVF International Conference on Computing and Communication Technologies (RIVF), pp. 1–5 (2020). https://doi.org/10.1109/RIVF48685.2020.9140739.
6. Barghouthy, N.A., Marrington, A., Baggili, I.: The forensic investigation of Android private browsing sessions using Orweb. In: 2013 5th International Confer-

ence on Computer Science and Information Technology, pp. 33–37 (2013). https://doi.org/10.1109/CSIT.2013.6588754.

7. Al Barghouthy, N., Marrington, A.: A comparison of forensic acquisition techniques for Android devices: a case study investigation of Orweb browsing sessions. In: 2014 6th International Conference on New Technologies, Mobility and Security (NTMS), pp. 1–4 (2014). https://doi.org/10.1109/NTMS.2014.6813993.
8. Mehrotra, T., Mehtre, B.M.: Forensic analysis of Wickr application on Android devices. In: 2013 IEEE International Conference on Computational Intelligence and Computing Research, pp. 1–6 (2013). https://doi.org/10.1109/ICCIC.2013.6724230.
9. Mirza, M.M., Salamh, F.E., Karabiyik, U.: An android case study on technical anti-forensic challenges of WhatsApp application. In: 2020 8th International Symposium on Digital Forensics and Security (ISDFS), pp. 1–6 (2020). https://doi.org/10.1109/ISDFS49300.2020.9116192.
10. Hermawan, T., Suryanto, Y., Alief, F., Roselina, L.: Android forensic tools analysis for unsend chat on social media. In: 2020 3rd International Seminar on Research of Information Technology and Intelligent Systems (ISRITI), pp. 233–238 (2020). https://doi.org/10.1109/ISRITI51436.2020.9315364.
11. APKMirror: APKMirror installer (official) 2024. https://www.apkmirror.com/apk/apkmirror/apkmirror-installer-official/. Accessed 19 Jan 2026
12. APKMirror: eBay 6.167.0.3 APK (2024). https://www.apkmirror.com/apk/ebay-mobile/ebay/ebay-6-167-0-3-release/. Accessed 19 Jan 2026

Evidence Triage and Threat Detection Tools

Risk-Based Digital Evidence Triage: A Framework for Artifact, Device, and Case Prioritization in Child Sexual Offense Investigations

Lukas Jaeckel[1,2](✉) and Dirk Labudde[1,2]

[1] Technische Universität Bergakademie Freiberg, Akademiestraße 6, 09599 Freiberg, Germany

[2] University of Applied Sciences Mittweida, Technikumplatz 17, 09648 Mittweida, Germany

{jaeckel1,labudde}@hs-mittweida.de

Abstract. Digital forensic investigators face increasingly large data volumes, resulting in significant delays in case processing. In the context of child sexual offense investigations, these delays are especially critical due to heightened social urgency and increased risks to victims. Although validated criminal psychological risk assessment instruments for sexual offenses are available, they are not yet integrated into digital evidence triage workflows. This paper introduces a conceptual framework for risk-based digital evidence triage in child sexual offense investigations. The framework systematically maps selected risk factors, such as indications of pedophilic interests and contact sexual offense history, to digital proxies derived from forensic artifacts and generates an explainable prioritization score. The framework enables both artifact- and device-level prioritization, allowing investigators to focus on the most relevant evidence first. Furthermore, the framework supports case-level prioritization by partially pre-filling instruments such as the Child Pornography Offender Risk Tool (CPORT). Finally, this paper discusses the strengths, limitations, and directions for future research of the presented approach.

Keywords: Digital Evidence Triage · Risk-Based Prioritization · Case Prioritization · Device Prioritization · Forensic Scoring Framework · Risk Assessment System · Explainable Digital Forensics

1 Introduction

Investigations of child sexual offenses are characterized by a high degree of urgency. On the one hand, investigators must check whether unknown victims need to be identified. On the other hand, experts must assess whether the accused

© ICST Institute for Computer Sciences, Social Informatics and Telecommunications Engineering 2027
Published by Springer Nature Switzerland AG 2027. All Rights Reserved
H. Neukirchen et al. (Eds.): ICDF2C 2026, LNICST 720, pp. 377–394, 2027.
https://doi.org/10.1007/978-3-032-37274-1_22

poses a high risk of committing further offenses. Many child sexual offense investigations concern not only the analogue world but also the digital space. In particular, child sexual abuse material (CSAM) is produced, acquired, possessed, and distributed [18]. In addition, initiating sexual contact with minors via the internet, known as cybergrooming, is an emerging problem [15]. The corresponding investigations involve a wide range of data storage devices, including computers, smartphones, cameras, and USB sticks, among others. As devices increase in number and capacity, investigators face large amounts of data that cannot be examined manually within reasonable time frames. This overload already causes significant case delays, highlighting the need for effective triage and prioritization in digital forensics [17]. Without systematic triage, critical evidence may be missed for extended periods, slowing victim identification and risk assessment. Efficient prioritization is necessary to allocate limited resources to the most relevant artifacts, devices, and cases. Current triage approaches in digital forensics primarily focus on search strategies, hash value comparisons, metadata-based filtering, or the use of artificial intelligence (AI) [17]. Furthermore, validated criminal psychological instruments can assess the risk of an offender committing further sexual offenses [13,14,22]. However, the instruments used in criminal psychology are disconnected from digital forensic workflows.

This work proposes a novel integration of criminal psychological risk assessment instruments and AI-assisted digital forensics triage. We introduce a conceptual framework for risk-based digital evidence triage tailored to child sexual offense investigations. The framework operationalizes selected criminal psychological risk factors as digital proxies and integrates them into a scoring engine that prioritizes individual artifacts. By aggregating these scores across seized devices, the framework enables device-level prioritization. It thus supports and relieves investigators in deciding which devices and artifacts should be analyzed first. In contrast to conventional triage, the proposed framework directly connects triage outputs to established risk assessment systems, facilitating partial pre-filling and case-level prioritization. The hybrid workflow combines automated proxy detection with expert validation. This approach aims to enhance investigative efficiency, sharpen focus on relevant evidence, and increase transparency.

Section 2 presents and discusses current digital forensic triage approaches and risk assessment instruments in criminal psychology. The research gap is identified and the need for a risk-based prioritization framework is highlighted. Section 3 introduces a conceptual framework for artifact and device prioritization. Risk factors from criminal psychology are mapped using digital proxies and integrated into a scoring engine. Section 4 shows how the framework could be implemented in practice and which existing methods could be used. Section 5 discusses the possibility of integrating the framework with risk assessment systems for prioritizing cases. Section 6 compares the strengths and weaknesses of the proposed system and includes legal and ethical considerations. Section 7 summarizes this work and provides an outlook for future work.

2 Related Work

Casey et al. [6] describe triage as the first level of a forensic examination. In this process, a targeted review is conducted to determine which sources of evidence are most useful and should be further processed. Casey et al. advocate moving away from the standard practice of examining everything, instead favoring a tiered, risk-based forensic strategy. This is the only known way for digital forensics laboratories to meet increasing demands without delaying investigations or compromising evidence.

Triage in digital forensics can pursue different objectives. Relevant devices can be detected from a large number of others [11, 19]. In multimedia forensics, triage can accelerate the analysis of images and videos [12, 21]. Furthermore, triage can detect the software that was executed on a compromised system [1, 26]. This paper introduces a framework that uses a scoring system based on criminal psychological risk factors to identify the most relevant artifacts and devices for a given case. It also incorporates methods from multimedia forensics and AI.

Jusas et al. [17] critically reviewed a significant number of studies on digital triage and categorized the various approaches into two forms. The live digital triage is conducted on the live system, where the main goal is to obtain information rapidly. However, this form of triage carries the risk of system manipulation. In contrast, the postmortem triage is conducted on digital images in the laboratory. It focuses on ranking devices based on potentially relevant evidence. Both forms have similar relevance and employ a wide variety of methods, including keyword searches, hash value comparisons, and metadata filtering. Jusas et al. identify intelligent technologies as a research direction for the future. None of the presented studies pursues an interdisciplinary approach, such as combining digital triage with criminal psychological risk assessment approaches.

Horsman [16] created a risk-based hierarchy with 16 priority levels for prioritizing cases, using 'risk of harm' as a principal prioritization metric. Case backlogs can be addressed by managing time and resources more effectively through the hierarchy. The digital forensic laboratories are responsible for assigning cases to specific levels. However, the author does not provide a detailed description of how the assignment should be made for each individual case. Possible support through intelligent automation is not discussed.

Hanson and Thornton [14] developed Static-99 in the field of criminal psychology to assess the risks of further sexual offenses being committed. The instrument is intended exclusively for use with males aged 18 years or older who are known to have committed at least one sexual offense against a child or adult. The authors of Static-99 derived ten statistical risk factors from previous studies. The respective assessments of the risk factors result in a scale with four risk levels: low (0-1), medium-low (2-3), medium-high (4-5), and high (6+) [14]. Each factor was rated as 0 (not applicable) or 1 (applicable). Only the factor 'previous sexual offenses' was scored between 0 and 3, depending on the number of offenses. Due to statistical factors, the Static-99 is practical and easy to use, but it does not account for dynamic changes. Furthermore, the instrument does not include any specific evidence in the digital space. Consequently, a combination with triage approaches would only be possible through extensive expansion by experts from both fields of research.

The Stable-2007 [13] was developed to assess the risk of recidivism in sexual offenses and takes stable-dynamic risk factors into account. The instrument is used for adult male offenders and was derived from a study involving 997 sex offenders from 16 regions. The authors of Stable-2007 describe 13 risk factors, which are rated 0 (no problem), 1 (minor problem), or 2 (definite problem). The determined total value is used to categorize the risks into three groups: low (0-3), medium (4-11), and high (12+) [13]. Trained experts are required, and digital evidence is explicitly not considered. For these reasons, linking Stable-2007 with triage methods from digital forensics appears unsuitable.

CPORT [24] is a risk assessment instrument for CSAM offenses to estimate the likelihood of future sexual crimes within the next five years. It is based on an initial study of 301 Canadian case files over a five-year observation period and focuses specifically on adult male sex offenders. The authors of CPORT described seven risk factors, whereby each applicable factor is rated 1:

1. Offender is aged 35 or younger.
2. Any prior criminal history.
3. Any prior or index failure on conditions.
4. Any prior or index contact sexual offense history.
5. Indications of pedophilic interests.
6. More boy than girl content ($\geq 51\%$) in CSAM.
7. More boy than girl content ($\geq 51\%$) in child nudity and other child content.

The sum of all factors results in a risk score that can be compared with CPORT scores from other cases [24]. Since determining the fifth factor is not trivial, the authors developed the Correlates of Admission of Sexual Interest in Children Scale (CASIC) [25]. CASIC contains six items, at least three of which must apply for the fifth risk factor of CPORT to be satisfied:

1. Never married.
2. Child pornography videos.
3. Child pornography stories.
4. Evidence interest in child pornography ($\geq$ two years).
5. Volunteering in a role with high access to children.
6. Engaging in online sexual communications with a minor.

In addition to CPORT, the Estimated Risk for Internet Sexual Offending (ERISCO) and the Kent Internet Risk Assessment Tool Version 2 (KIRAT-2) are also discussed in the literature on online CSAM offending [22]. However, Reichel et al. [22] note that ERISCO, which comprises almost 40 items, has not yet been empirically evaluated, while KIRAT-2, with 9 items, focuses almost exclusively on criminal history. Against this background, CPORT is currently the most suitable instrument for prioritizing artifacts, devices, and cases.

Despite a wide range of triage and risk assessment approaches, none of the existing methods integrates the two strategies. Triage is typically conducted as the initial step in a forensic investigation, whereas risk assessment instruments are applied to estimate the recidivism risk of offenders after case processing. In contrast to other risk assessment tools, digital evidence could already be used to answer selected CPORT and CASIC items, while the remaining questionnaire items would continue to be completed manually by investigators or other experts. Accordingly, this work focuses on linking CPORT and CASIC with digital evidence triage to develop a risk-based prioritization framework for artifacts, devices, and cases. This approach is designed to help investigators prioritize cases of CSAM offenses and quickly identify relevant artifacts and devices. Since CPORT was originally developed for adult male offenders, the scope of this study is likewise limited to this offender group. To the best of our knowledge, no prior work has systematically combined digital evidence triage with established risk assessment instruments. Our study addresses this gap by proposing a conceptual framework that operationalizes selected CPORT and CASIC items through digital proxies.

3 Framework for Artifact and Device Prioritization

This section presents a conceptual framework for postmortem triage, which can be used to prioritize artifacts and devices. The prerequisite is that the defendant's devices have been seized. Section 2 showed that CPORT and CASIC are currently the most suitable risk assessment instruments in criminal psychology for transferring them to triage approaches in the digital space. Table 1 summarizes the possible proxy mapping of risk factors to digital artifacts.

Some of the corresponding risk factors relate to objective biographical data on the accused and information about his criminally relevant history. In the case of CPORT, such factors include the defendant's age, criminal history, and failure on conditions. The easiest way to make a corresponding assessment is through the investigator's knowledge. For this purpose, no analysis of the seized devices is required. Accordingly, these factors should not influence the prioritization of artifacts and devices. CPORT item 4, the contact sexual offense history, can also be answered by the investigators. However, the seized devices might also hold evidence of related contact sexual offenses that are not yet identified. CSAM could be found in the media files on the devices, created by the accused himself, and showing his own offense. The face, body, clothing, and voice can be analyzed in the CSAM files to identify the accused. Further indications about the accused may be provided by the background of the relevant media or the metadata from the used camera.

The indications of pedophilic interests can be determined by a forensic psychologist or by using CASIC. Two of the CASIC items do not require an analysis of the devices and should be irrelevant for artifact and device prioritization. Whether the accused was never married and whether he had volunteered in a role with high access to children can be answered by the knowledge of the investigators. The remaining four CASIC items can be analyzed using the data on the seized devices. The devices can be examined for the presence of CSAM

Table 1. Proxy mapping of criminal psychological risk factors to digital artifacts.

Risk Factors	Digital Artifacts
CPORT item 1	–
CPORT item 2	–
CPORT item 3	–
CPORT item 4	CSAM in media files depicting offenses committed by the accused
CPORT item 5	Three or more CASIC items are applicable
CPORT item 6	Most of CSAM in media files is of boys
CPORT item 7	Most of child nudity and other child content in media files is of boys
CASIC item 1	–
CASIC item 2	CSAM videos in media files
CASIC item 3	CSAM stories in text and document files
CASIC item 4	Metadata of CSAM and its thumbnails; timestamps in log files, caches and databases; browser and search history; networking in CSAM groups
CASIC item 5	–
CASIC item 6	Cybergrooming in social networks and instant messaging services

videos. Finding CSAM stories in the text and document files of the devices also increases the CASIC score. Various data sources on the devices are suitable for proving interest in CSAM over a period of more than two years. The browser and search history provide indications of such interest. For example, the defendant may have frequently searched for CSAM or related terms. He may also have regularly visited websites that enable the consumption and exchange of CSAM. In addition, metadata from CSAM files, directories, and thumbnails on the devices can provide information on when the defendant downloaded, created, or last viewed the files. Depending on the operating system, log files, caches, and databases may contain further timestamps relating to activities involving CSAM files. Networking in groups on internet forums, social networks, or instant messengers to exchange CSAM is also evidence of interest in CSAM. All of the described indicators can be placed in a time series to examine whether the accused has had an interest in CSAM for two or more years. To prove that the accused was engaging in online sexual communications with a minor, social network and instant messenger chats on the seized devices can be examined for cybergrooming.

CPORT item 6 is satisfied if more boy than girl content is depicted in CSAM. This risk factor can be investigated by analyzing the CSAM contained within the media files of seized devices. Similarly, child nudity and other child content in media files can also be checked concerning the boy-to-girl ratio. If at least 51% of the relevant files depict boys, CPORT item 7 was coded positively.

Applying criminal psychological risk assessment instruments, such as CPORT and CASIC, is traditionally a manual and time-consuming task, as experts must first analyze seized devices before coding the respective items. Automation can accelerate this process by extracting and processing relevant information directly from digital artifacts. In particular, CPORT items 4, 5, 6, and 7, as well as CASIC items 2, 3, 4, and 6, can be partially pre-filled using digital proxies. This enables investigators to rely on prioritization from an early phase of case processing, rather than only after a full manual examination. The automated prioritization of artifacts and devices reduces backlog and directs attention to potentially high-risk material.

A scoring engine is required to automatically prioritize artifacts and devices based on the analyzed risk factors. To ensure a transparent and mathematically rigorous prioritization process, the scoring model distinguishes explicitly between proxies originating from CPORT and those derived from CASIC. In particular, CPORT proxies contribute directly to the device score. In contrast, CASIC proxies only increase the device score by 1 if at least three of them are satisfied, according to CPORT item 5. Let P_{CPORT} and P_{CASIC} denote the disjoint sets of CPORT- and CASIC-based proxies. The full proxy set P is then defined as:

$$P = P_{CPORT} \cup P_{CASIC}. \tag{1}$$

For each artifact a and each proxy $p \in P$, the relevance indicator $x_{a,p}$ is defined as:

$$x_{a,p} = \begin{cases} 1, \text{ if artifact } a \text{ satisfies proxy } p, \\ 0, \text{ otherwise.} \end{cases} \tag{2}$$

where applicable, proxies may also be assigned a confidence score $c_{a,p} \in [0,1]$, that reflects the uncertainty inherent in machine-generated classifications (e.g., grooming detection, gender estimation). In this context, $c_{a,p} = 1$ represents the highest level of confidence. In addition, each proxy has an investigator-defined weight $w_p > 0$. This allows investigators' experience to be incorporated as domain-specific prior knowledge within a controlled parameterization of the scoring model. By default, $w_p = 1$. Weight assignments are transparently documented to ensure reproducibility and traceability. Through discussion within the investigative team and with recorded justification, w_p can be adjusted to reflect case-specific investigative priorities. This multidimensional scoring reflects not only relevance, but also urgency, complexity, and probative value. The artifact-level score $s(a)$ is then defined as:

$$s(a) = \sum_{p \in P} w_p \cdot x_{a,p} \cdot c_{a,p}. \tag{3}$$

The automated analysis of a device may return a prioritized list of artifacts with a score greater than 0. Investigators can review the list and the attached documentation to quickly examine and manually evaluate artifacts that are likely to be relevant. Device-level scoring is derived from the artifact-level proxies. For a device d, the CPORT and CASIC items are modeled as binary indicator variables:

$$\begin{aligned} X_{d,i}^{CPORT} &\in \{0,1\}, \quad i \in \{4,5,6,7\}, \\ X_{d,j}^{CASIC} &\in \{0,1\}, \quad j \in \{2,3,4,6\}. \end{aligned} \tag{4}$$

An indicator variable is set to 1 if the device's artifacts satisfy the proxy for the specific item. The device-level CPORT and CASIC scores are obtained by summing all corresponding indicator variables:

$$S_{CPORT}(d) = \sum_{i=4}^{7} X_{d,i}^{CPORT}, \quad S_{CASIC}(d) = \sum_{j \in \{2,3,4,6\}} X_{d,j}^{CASIC}. \tag{5}$$

The CPORT item 5 is satisfied if the CASIC score is at least 3. The described metric aligns with the conceptual logic of CPORT and CASIC, where risk is determined by the number of positively coded items. Based on Table 1, CPORT items 13 are excluded because they require background information unavailable through digital artifacts. The resulting device scores therefore range from 0 to 4, producing five distinct prioritization levels.

CPORT assumes the presence of CSAM on seized devices but does not integrate CSAM quantity into its scoring. As a result, devices that contain CSAM but do not fulfill any CPORT item may receive a risk score of 0. To prevent such cases from being deprioritized, we introduce the quantity of CSAM files $Q_{CSAM}(d)$ as a second, independent scoring dimension. The complete device-level risk score is thus expressed as a two-dimensional vector:

$$S_{risk}(d) = (S_{CPORT}(d), Q_{CSAM}(d)) \tag{6}$$

Devices with higher CPORT score $S_{CPORT}(d)$ take precedence. If two devices have the same CPORT score, the one with higher CSAM quantity $Q_{CSAM}(d)$ is prioritized. This extension preserves the primacy of validated psychological risk factors while ensuring that devices containing CSAM are not overlooked.

4 Proposed Workflow for Artifact and Device Prioritization

Building on the proxy mapping in Table 1 and scoring principles from the previous part, this section describes a structured forensic workflow that operationalizes artifact- and device-level prioritization (Fig. 1). The workflow is designed to process input from seized devices, extract relevant artifacts, map them to proxy definitions, and route the results through the scoring engine. The outputs are ranked artifact lists and aggregated device scores, accompanied by transparent documentation to support investigator validation. By distinguishing modular components, the workflow ensures flexibility and extensibility, for example, to support weighted or multidimensional scoring models.

Before the data from the seized devices can be analyzed, it must first be extracted and preprocessed. As this work focuses on scoring and prioritization, addressing acquisition challenges is beyond its scope. It is therefore assumed that relevant artifacts are already available in semi-structured formats, such as those produced by forensic tools (e.g., XML or JSON exports). Alternatively, the acquired data can be represented in an ontology, which enables artifacts to be

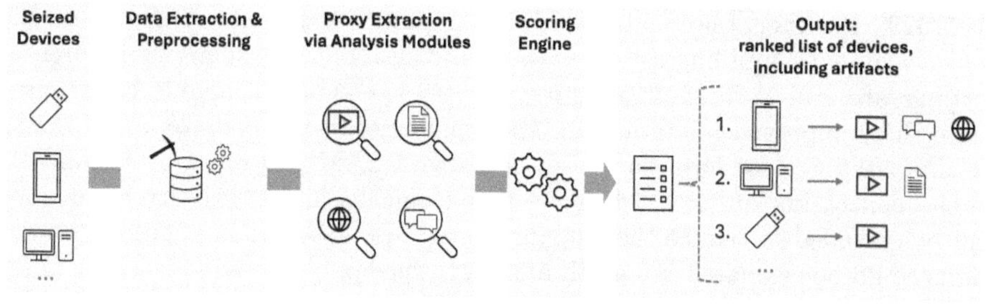

Fig. 1. Proposed workflow for prioritizing artifacts and devices, consisting of data extraction and preparation, proxy analysis modules, scoring engine, and output.

linked across sources and supports pattern recognition, reasoning, and visualization. A promising basis in this context is the Cyber-investigation Analysis Standard Expression (CASE) [5], an ontology-driven standard specifically developed to support cyber investigations.

Following data acquisition, each proxy from Table 1 is extracted by a dedicated analysis module. A module for the automatic detection of CSAM plays a central role in proxy extraction, since several criminal psychological items depend on its outcome. Specifically, CPORT items 4 and 6, as well as CASIC items 2, 3, and 4, require the detection of CSAM. Beyond coding these items, the quantity of CSAM files per device should also be incorporated into the scoring model, as discussed in Sect. 3. The module takes the media files of each device as input and outputs a list of files that are likely to constitute CSAM. Different approaches can be employed to implement this functionality. One established method is the comparison of hash values against known CSAM hash databases, with PhotoDNA being a particularly robust and widely used perceptual hashing technique [27]. Pereira et al. [20] proposed an alternative approach that leverages only file path information: rather than analyzing file content, they apply machine learning (ML) models to path strings and achieve promising results with character-based convolutional neural networks (CNNs). More advanced frameworks combine image and video content analysis with deep learning. For example, Gangwar et al. [10] developed a two-stage CNN architecture. In the first stage, images are classified as pornographic or non-pornographic. In the second stage, detected faces are analyzed to determine whether they belong to minors or adults. An image is classified as CSAM if it contains pornographic content and at least one minor is identified. While results are promising, such systems are vulnerable to errors in face detection. Beyond image and video files, textual artifacts also provide important evidence. Here, techniques from natural language processing (NLP) and ML can be employed to detect erotic or abusive content in documents and text files [3]. These methods can be complemented by keyword-based searches targeting CSAM-related terminology to identify CSAM stories. Suitable keywords (e.g., child, teen, preteen, or lolita) can be chosen by investigators or identified in studies, such as those by Westlake et al. [29]. However, the reliability of such approaches depends strongly on context, vocabulary, and linguistic variation, and systematic evaluations in forensic settings are still lacking. In practice, the CSAM analysis module could integrate these approaches into a multi-stage pipeline. In the first step, files would be compared against hash databases of known CSAM and non-CSAM content. Consequently, known CSAM files are found quickly, and clearly irrelevant files can be excluded to reduce the amount of data. In a second step, suspicious file paths could be evaluated using ML models trained on path string features. Only files that remain unresolved after these steps would undergo content-based analysis with ML models and NLP methods. This cascading strategy ensures that computationally intensive image and text classification is applied only where necessary, thereby combining efficiency with high detection accuracy. As a result, the module forwards the artifacts identified as CSAM to the scoring engine.

CPORT item 4 can be addressed by a dedicated module that builds upon the outputs of the CSAM analysis module. While this module detects and classifies potential CSAM, the module for CPORT item 4 extends this functionality by assessing whether the accused is depicted in the detected material. This requires that reference images or videos of the accused be available for comparison. As a first step, metadata can be automatically examined to identify whether the recording device matches one of the seized devices. Additionally, CSAM can be subjected to person identification and face recognition methods to determine whether the accused is depicted. Amirgaliyev et al. [2] provide a comprehensive review of approaches in this field, demonstrating that CNNs currently achieve state-of-the-art performance, while classical computer vision methods, such as Support Vector Machines (SVMs) or Eigenfaces, remain viable options for resource-constrained settings. The module for CPORT item 4 can be extended beyond facial recognition to include additional modalities. One promising approach is speaker verification in videos, which requires reference voice recordings of the accused. Brydinskyi et al. [4] demonstrate that deep learning models achieve strong results in this domain, with embedding-based methods proving particularly robust for voice matching. Another complementary extension is place recognition, where images and videos are analyzed to determine whether they depict a known environment. If reference images of the accused's premises are available, CSAM can be examined for background similarities that may identify a premise as the crime scene. Schubert et al. [23] provide an overview of this emerging research field and outline potential techniques.

CPORT item 5 is coded as positive if at least three of the CASIC items 2, 3, 4, and 6 are satisfied for a device. CASIC item 2 can be evidenced if the CSAM module classifies videos from a seized device as relevant. Video detection can rely on filtering by file type or signature. The CASIC item 3 can be determined by filtering the text and document files from the CSAM module output.

For CASIC item 4, a dedicated module can analyze temporal aspects of relevant artifacts. First, metadata of files and directories identified by the CSAM module can be examined, with a focus on timestamps. The creation and modification dates, as well as the date of last access, are usually included and can be associated with timeline events [7]. However, creation and modification dates are often unreliable, as they may be influenced by system processes. In contrast, the last access date can provide a stronger indication of user activity and may therefore be prioritized in an initial implementation. Second, browser and search histories can be screened for CSAM-related terms, provided such data are available on the seized devices. Suitable keyword lists can be derived from investigative practice or previous studies such as those by Westlake et al. [29]. As a result, the dates of relevant queries or page visits can be included in the time series. Third, the accused's participation in CSAM-related groups on social networks and instant messenger services can be considered. An initial approach could filter groups in which detected CSAM has been exchanged and record the timestamps of joining, first interaction, and last activity. As an extension, ML techniques could be explored to automatically identify CSAM-related groups from communication data. Together, these approaches would enable a time series that reflects the persistence of CSAM-related behavior and interest.

CASIC item 6 can be addressed by a module that analyzes communication data from seized devices. Its purpose is to identify grooming conversations in which the accused deliberately targets minors via social networks or instant messaging platforms. Felser et al. [9] noted that existing research has explored a variety of ML approaches, with SVM, Random Forest, and deep learning methods showing promising results. However, the authors emphasize that no single algorithm achieves the best results in all circumstances. Moreover, almost all studies are based on English-language datasets and largely neglect multimodal communication features, such as voice messages or shared media files. Since grooming detection is inherently complex and highly context-dependent, systematic evaluations are required to establish which methods are both reliable and efficient for integration into a triage framework, where rapid identification of suspect communications can directly influence investigative priorities.

A dedicated module for CPORT item 6 must first detect minors in the material and subsequently determine their gender. The relevant artifacts identified by the CSAM module serve as input for this process. In the first stage, similar to the CSAM pipeline, CNNs can be applied to recognize minors in images or videos. In the second stage, gender classification can be performed, for example, by extracting facial features with a deep CNN and processing them through a stacking classifier that combines multiple ML models [28]. For child-specific gender determination, separate datasets are available, including either real or synthetically generated facial images [8].

For CPORT item 7, the corresponding analysis module must determine whether boys or girls are more frequently depicted in non-CSAM images or videos that contain child-related content. The detection of minors and subsequent gender classification can be performed using approaches similar to those described for the CPORT item 6 module.

An overview of applicable candidate methods per analysis module is provided in Table 2. While the modules address specific criminal psychological proxies, their efficient integration into a prioritization system requires careful design and implementation. Several strategies can be employed to achieve scalability. First, modules can be executed in parallel since they typically operate on distinct artifact types (e.g., images, text, communication logs). Second, a cascading strategy can be applied, in which general filters or the CSAM module provide preprocessed artifacts that are only forwarded to specialized modules if they are relevant. Third, shared preprocessing steps such as face detection should be centralized and their results distributed across modules to avoid redundant computation. Finally, prioritization can be made adaptive. Intermediate findings from one module may influence the execution order or weighting of others. Such design principles ensure that the system remains both efficient and flexible, which is critical in the triage context where rapid results are essential. However, the relative benefits and practical feasibility of these integration strategies in real-world forensic settings remain to be systematically evaluated.

Table 2. Practical implementation of the analysis modules. Each module addresses a specific criminal psychological risk factor proxy.

Analysis Module	Methods
CSAM module	Hash database comparison; suspicious file paths detection; combination of pornography & minor detection; detection of erotic texts with content involving minors
CPORT item 4 module	CSAM module results + recording device detection; person identification; face recognition; speaker verification; place recognition
CPORT item 5 module	Aggregation of the module results for CASIC 2, 3, 4, 6
CPORT item 6 module	CSAM module results + minor detection & gender determination
CPORT item 7 module	Minor detection & gender determination
CASIC item 2 module	CSAM module results + video filtering
CASIC item 3 module	CSAM module results + text & document filtering
CASIC item 4 module	Time series analysis using metadata analysis of CSAM module results; browser & search history analysis; CSAM group detection
CASIC item 6 module	Cybergrooming detection

For documentation, a JSON-based implementation could record for each device which artifacts are relevant, which items they satisfy, and the relevant content of complex artifacts. A higher-level file can record the satisfied items and the overall score, and reference the corresponding artifacts. Alternatively, in an ontology, scoring results and documentation could be linked directly to the artifacts themselves. Ultimately, a user interface would provide investigators with a prioritized list of devices, displaying each score together with the relevant artifacts and documentation. This documented and transparent scoring ensures that prioritization results remain verifiable and actionable in forensic practice.

5 Integration with Risk Assessment Systems for Case Prioritization

This work follows a semi-automated approach to prioritize cases. On the one hand, information automatically extracted and processed during artifact- and device-level prioritization provides partial input to risk assessment instruments. On the other hand, investigators contribute their domain expertise to answer the remaining questions that cannot be resolved solely through digital evidence. Figure 2 illustrates the integrated system, where artifact and device prioritization inform the case-level risk assessment workflow. This approach aims to ensure that high-risk cases can be addressed more rapidly, while maintaining the transparency and expert oversight required in forensic practice.

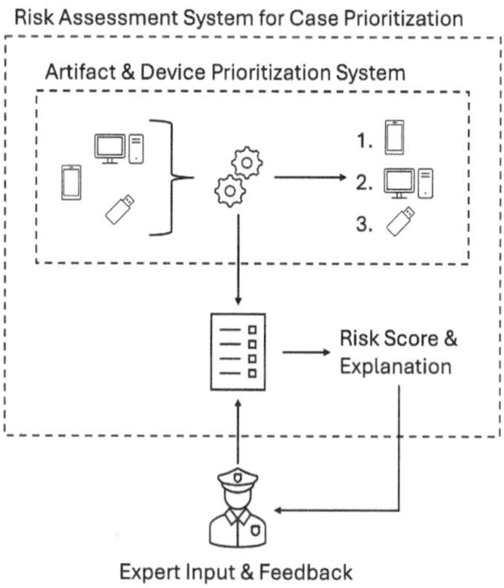

Fig. 2. Schematic design of a risk assessment system for case prioritization, including an integrated system for artifact and device prioritization.

We propose a risk assessment system in which investigators complete a digital questionnaire to provide case-specific information about the accused. This includes CPORT items 14 and CASIC items 1 and 5. Alternatively, such information could be represented in an ontology where relevant data are already stored. The remaining CPORT and CASIC items are automatically pre-filled by the prioritization system, using the ranked list of devices and associated documentation. If CPORT items 4 or 5, or CASIC items 2, 3, or 6 are met at the artifact- or device-level, they are considered satisfied for the entire case. For

CPORT items 6 and 7, statistics from all devices must be aggregated to calculate the global ratio across CSAM and other child-related content. To determine CASIC item 4 at the case-level, the duration of interest in CSAM across all devices is taken into account. These aggregations ensure that CPORT items 6 and 7, and CASIC item 4 are determined consistently at the case-level rather than per device. Finally, all satisfied CPORT items are aggregated into a score from 0 to 7, which represents the total number of CPORT items that can be positively coded for a given case.

To formalize case-level prioritization, let c denote a case consisting of a set of devices D_c. CPORT and CASIC items are derived from the investigator input and from the results of the proxies of each device. For case c, the CPORT and CASIC items are modeled as binary indicator variables:

$$\begin{aligned} X_{c,i}^{CPORT} &\in \{0,1\}, \quad i \in \{1,2,3,4,5,6,7\}, \\ X_{c,j}^{CASIC} &\in \{0,1\}, \quad j \in \{1,2,3,4,5,6\}. \end{aligned} \tag{7}$$

An indicator variable is set to 1 if the case's artifacts and devices satisfy the proxy for the specific item. The case-level CPORT and CASIC scores are obtained by summing all indicator variables:

$$S_{CPORT}(c) = \sum_{i=1}^{7} X_{c,i}^{CPORT}, \quad S_{CASIC}(c) = \sum_{j=1}^{6} X_{c,j}^{CASIC}. \tag{8}$$

The CASIC score must be at least 3 to fulfill CPORT item 5. As a second dimension for the case-level prioritization, the total CSAM volume across all devices is aggregated as:

$$Q_{CSAM}(c) = \sum_{d \in D_c} Q_{CSAM}(d). \tag{9}$$

The final case-level risk score is represented as a two-dimensional vector:

$$S_{risk}(c) = \big(S_{CPORT}(c), Q_{CSAM}(c)\big), \tag{10}$$

where cases are prioritized first by $S_{CPORT}(c)$, and in the event of a tie, by $Q_{CSAM}(c)$. This score provides investigators with a transparent and comparable measure to prioritize cases, supporting real-world decisions about which require immediate action. By focusing resources on cases with more risk factors, this system improves resource allocation and potentially enhances victim protection.

Since false positives are possible with the artifact- and device-level prioritization system, human verification remains essential. Investigators can view the ranked list of devices and their documentation at any time and are empowered to override system assessments. A user interface should present a prioritized list of devices, including scores, relevant artifacts, and associated CPORT or CASIC items. From this overview, investigators can drill down to artifact-level details, confirm or revoke relevance, adjust item weights, and add annotations. Transparency is supported by linking each score to the underlying artifacts and by displaying how investigator input affects prioritization results in real-time. Reports are generated only after all artifacts have been manually reviewed, ensuring that the final output provides a complete audit trail with investigator-confirmed artifacts, calculated scores, generated explanations, and annotations. This design combines efficiency with forensic soundness, traceability, and legal admissibility.

6 Discussion

The proposed framework offers several notable strengths. It introduces a structured and explainable method for prioritizing artifacts, devices, and cases, which enables investigators to identify the most relevant evidence at an early stage. By mapping criminal psychological risk factors from validated instruments such as CPORT and CASIC to digital proxies, the system bases triage on established criminal psychological knowledge rather than on ad hoc heuristics. Structured documentation and investigator validation ensure transparency, making prioritization outcomes interpretable and auditable. The modular design enables the addition, adaptation, or replacement of analysis modules without requiring the restructuring of the entire system, thereby supporting adaptability to evolving forensic methods and investigative requirements. The semi-automated approach reduces investigator workload while maintaining expert oversight, achieving a balance between efficiency and forensic accuracy.

Several limitations of the framework should be recognized. The framework remains conceptual and has not yet been implemented or empirically evaluated in operational investigations. For triage purposes and the proxy analysis modules, the optimal balance between reliability, computational efficiency, and robustness against adversarial conditions remains an open research question. The accuracy of the system is contingent on the reliability of its component modules. For example, false positives or negatives in CSAM detection or cybergrooming classification can influence prioritization outcomes. While false positives can often be identified and corrected during investigator review, false negatives may leave relevant artifacts remaining undetected, thereby diminishing the completeness of the results. The framework also assumes that digital artifacts are available in semi-structured formats. In practice, data acquisition and preprocessing are complex and resource-intensive. Furthermore, the framework inherits the limitations of CPORT, which was developed for adult male offenders, restricting the system's applicability to this population and limiting its generalizability to broader investigative contexts.

The integration of automated prioritization with risk assessment tools also raises important legal and ethical considerations. Forensic outputs must remain auditable and subject to investigator correction to ensure their admissibility in court. It is essential to note that CPORT should only be used for risk assessment if no more than one CPORT item is missing [24]. Consequently, verification and supplementation by the investigators are indispensable. The framework should provide comprehensive traceability, including documentation of both automated results and subsequent investigator actions. Ethically, it is essential to prevent over-reliance on automated scores, as the system is designed to support, not replace, professional judgment. The use of sensitive data, such as CSAM, necessitates strict adherence to legal safeguards and data protection requirements. As a result, any practical implementation of the framework must prioritize privacy, accountability, and proportionality.

7 Conclusion and Future Work

This paper introduced a conceptual framework for risk-based digital evidence triage in child sexual offense investigations. In view of the increasing amount of data, the presented framework is intended to support and relieve investigators. Selected items from validated risk assessment instruments, including CPORT and CASIC, are mapped to digital proxies derived from forensic artifacts. The framework enables multi-level prioritization at the artifact, device, and case levels. The proposed scoring engine, combined with structured documentation and investigator validation, provides a transparent and explainable basis for prioritization while maintaining forensic soundness. This approach addresses the gap between digital triage and criminal risk assessment and offers a novel decision-support tool for time-critical CSAM investigations.

Although the framework is promising, it remains conceptual and has yet to be implemented. Subsequent research will develop a prototype that integrates the analysis modules and scoring engine into existing forensic workflows. Planned evaluation will examine scalability, accuracy, and investigator usability in real case environments. Computational performance, including processing time and potential time savings relative to traditional methods, will also be evaluated. Obtaining real-world case data for evaluation remains a significant challenge. Collaboration with law enforcement agencies is therefore essential. Legal and ethical considerations, such as data protection, automation bias, and the admissibility of semi-automated assessments, require systematic review. Expanding the framework to include offender groups beyond the CPORT focus is also identified as a future research direction. The primary objective is to transition from a conceptual framework to an operational system that has been validated in practice. This progression will enable empirical evaluation of the effectiveness and efficiency of risk-based prioritization in investigations, thereby supporting forensic decision-making and facilitating adoption within law enforcement.

Acknowledgments. This work was made possible through funding from the ESF Plus program, which is co-financed by the European Union and the Free State of Saxony. The company FZ forensic.zone GmbH supported this work financially.

References

1. Al-Sharif, Z., Al-Saleh, M., Jararweh, Y., Alawneh, L., Shatnawi, A.: The effects of platforms and languages on the memory footprint of the executable program: a memory forensic approach. J. Univ. Comput. Sci. **25**, 1174–1198 (2019). https://doi.org/10.3217/jucs-025-09-1174

2. Amirgaliyev, B., Mussabek, M., Rakhimzhanova, T., Zhumadillayeva, A.: A review of machine learning and deep learning methods for person detection, tracking and identification, and face recognition with applications. Sensors **25**(5) (2025). https://doi.org/10.3390/s25051410
3. Barrientos, G.M., Alaiz-Rodríguez, R., González-Castro, V., Parnell, A.C.: Machine learning techniques for the detection of inappropriate erotic content in text. Int. J. Comput. Intell. Syst. **13**, 591–603 (2020). https://doi.org/10.2991/ijcis.d.200519.003
4. Brydinskyi, V., et al.: Comparison of modern deep learning models for speaker verification. Appl. Sci.**14**(4) (2024). https://doi.org/10.3390/app14041329
5. Casey, E., Barnum, S., Griffith, R., Snyder, J., van Beek, H., Nelson, A.: Advancing coordinated cyber-investigations and tool interoperability using a community developed specification language. Digit. Investig. **22**, 14–45 (2017). https://doi.org/10.1016/j.diin.2017.08.002
6. Casey, E., Ferraro, M., Nguyen, L.: Investigation delayed is justice denied: proposals for expediting forensic examinations of digital evidence. J. Forensic Sci. **54**(6), 1353–1364 (2009). https://doi.org/10.1111/j.1556-4029.2009.01150.x
7. Du, X., Le, Q., Scanlon, M.: Automated artefact relevancy determination from artefact metadata and associated timeline events. In: 2020 International Conference on Cyber Security and Protection of Digital Services (Cyber Security), pp. 1–8 (2020). https://doi.org/10.1109/CyberSecurity49315.2020.9138874
8. Farooq, M.A., Yao, W., Costache, G., Corcoran, P.: ChildGAN: large scale synthetic child facial data using domain adaptation in StyleGAN. IEEE Access **11**, 108775–108791 (2023). https://doi.org/10.1109/ACCESS.2023.3321149
9. Felser, J., Preuß, S., Labudde, D., Spranger, M.: Technical Perspectives of Sexual Online Grooming. In: Kuhle, L.F., Stelzmann, D. (eds.) Sexual Online Grooming of Children, Sexuality, Health and Society, vol. 2, chap. 4.4, pp. 263–296. Nomos, Baden-Baden, 1 edn. (2025)
10. Gangwar, A., González-Castro, V., Alegre, E., Fidalgo, E.: AttM-CNN: attention and metric learning based CNN for pornography, age and child sexual abuse (CSA) detection in images. Neurocomputing **445**, 81–104 (2021). https://doi.org/10.1016/j.neucom.2021.02.056
11. Gentry, E., McIntyre, R., Soltys, M., Lyu, F.: SEAKER: A Tool for Fast Digital Forensic Triage. In: Arai, K., Bhatia, R. (eds.) Advances in Information and Communication. 2019 Future of Information and Communication Conference (FICC), vol. 2, pp. 1227–1243. Springer International Publishing, Cham (2020). https://doi.org/10.1007/978-3-030-12385-7_87
12. Hales, G., Bayne, E.: Investigating Visualisation Techniques for Rapid Triage of Digital Forensic Evidence. In: Moallem, A. (ed.) HCI for Cybersecurity, Privacy and Trust, pp. 277–293. HCII 2019, Springer International Publishing, Cham (2019). https://doi.org/10.1007/978-3-030-22351-9_19
13. Hanson, R.K., Harris, A.J.R., Scott, T.L., Helmus, L.: Assessing the risk of sexual offenders on community supervision: The dynamic supervision project. User Report 2007-05, Public Safety Canada, Ottawa, Ontario (2007)
14. Hanson, R.K., Thornton, D.: Static 99: Improving Actuarial Risk Assessments for Sex Offenders. Solicitor General of Canada, Ottawa (1999)
15. Hille, Z., Stelzmann, D., Kuhle, L.F.: Definition and Characteristics of the Phenomenon of Sexual Online Grooming. In: Kuhle, L.F., Stelzmann, D. (eds.) Sexual Online Grooming of Children, Sexuality, Health and Society, vol. 2, chap. 1.1, pp. 17–38. Nomos, Baden-Baden, 1 edn. (2025)

16. Horsman, G.: The hierarchy of case priority (HiCaP):- a proposed method for case prioritisation in digital forensic laboratories. Sci. Justice **62**(5), 594–601 (2022). https://doi.org/10.1016/j.scijus.2022.08.008
17. Jusas, V., Birvinskas, D., Gahramanov, E.: Methods and tools of digital triage in forensic context: survey and future directions. Symmetry **9**(4) (2017). https://doi.org/10.3390/sym9040049
18. Lee, H.E., Ermakova, T., Ververis, V., Fabian, B.: Detecting child sexual abuse material: a comprehensive survey. Forensic Sci. Int.: Digit. Investig.**34** (2020). https://doi.org/10.1016/j.fsidi.2020.301022
19. Lim, M., Jones, J.: A Digital Media Similarity Measure for Triage of Digital Forensic Evidence. In: Peterson, G., Shenoi, S. (eds.) Advances in Digital Forensics XVI. pp. 111–135. DigitalForensics 2020, Springer International Publishing, Cham (2020). https://doi.org/10.1007/978-3-030-56223-6_7
20. Pereira, M., Dodhia, R., Anderson, H., Brown, R.: Metadata-based detection of child sexual abuse material. IEEE Trans. Dependable Secure Comput. **21**(4), 3153–3164 (2024). https://doi.org/10.1109/TDSC.2023.3324275
21. Quick, D., Choo, K.K.R.: Big forensic data management in heterogeneous distributed systems: quick analysis of multimedia forensic data. Softw.: Pract. Experience **47**(8), 1095–1109 (2017). https://doi.org/10.1002/spe.2429
22. Reichel, R., Daser, A., Gnielka, F., Schmidt, A., Blokland, A., Lehmann, R.: A review of risk factors for online and mixed child sexual abuse material offending: what is being researched?. J. Sex. Aggression, pp. 1–44 (2024). https://doi.org/10.1080/13552600.2024.2418100
23. Schubert, S., Neubert, P., Garg, S., Milford, M., Fischer, T.: Visual place recognition: a tutorial [tutorial]. IEEE Robot. Autom. Mag. **31**(3), 139–153 (2024). https://doi.org/10.1109/MRA.2023.3310859
24. Seto, M., Eke, A.: Predicting Recidivism Among Adult Male Child Pornography Offenders: Development of the Child Pornography Offender Risk Tool (CPORT). Law and human behavior **39** (2015). https://doi.org/10.1037/lhb0000128
25. Seto, M., Eke, A.: Correlates of Admitted Sexual Interest in Children Among Individuals Convicted of Child Pornography Offenses. Law Hum. Behav.**41** (2017). https://doi.org/10.1037/lhb0000240
26. Soltani, S., Hosseini Seno, S.A.: Detecting the software usage on a compromised system: a triage solution for digital forensics. Forensic Sci. Int.: Digit. Investig.**44** (2023). https://doi.org/10.1016/j.fsidi.2022.301484
27. Steinebach, M.: An analysis of PhotoDNA. In: Proceedings of the 18th International Conference on Availability, Reliability and Security, pp. 1–8. ARES '23, Association for Computing Machinery, New York, NY, USA (2023). https://doi.org/10.1145/3600160.3605048
28. waris, F., Da, F., Liu, S.: Stacked ensemble learning for facial gender classification using deep learning based features extraction. Cluster Comput. **27**, 11491–11513 (2024). https://doi.org/10.1007/s10586-024-04340-7
29. Westlake, B., Bouchard, M., Frank, R.: Comparing methods for detecting child exploitation content online. In: 2012 European Intelligence and Security Informatics Conference, pp. 156–163 (2012). https://doi.org/10.1109/EISIC.2012.25

Hate Speech Detection in Digital Forensics: Autopsy Hate Speech Detector Plugin

Svetlana Tomić(✉), Miroslav Tomić, and Stevan Gostojić

Faculty of Technical Sciences, University of Novi Sad, Trg Dositeja Obradovića 6, 21000 Novi Sad, Serbia
{svetlanaantesevic,tmiroslav,gostojic}@uns.ac.rs

Abstract. Digital forensic investigations increasingly face an imbalance between the volume of digital evidence and the time and resources available for its examination. This challenge is particularly evident in hate speech cases, where investigators may need to review large volumes of messages whose harmful meaning depends on linguistic variation, implicit wording, and context. Traditional keyword-based searches are often insufficient, especially in multilingual and informal communication environments. This paper proposes the design of Hate Speech Detector, a forensic-support solution implemented as an Autopsy ingest module for hate speech detection within the digital forensic workflow. English binary hate speech classification was evaluated across multiple datasets to support model comparison and integration into the proposed tool. The evaluation revealed noticeable differences among the compared models, with the strongest overall results observed for the model that best balanced the adopted measures, especially recall, which was important in the forensic context, while the selected models also satisfied key forensic integration requirements, including local execution, reproducibility, and evidence linkage. The proposed solution supports the examination and analysis phases by prioritizing potentially relevant messages, supporting a more efficient review large volumes of communication evidence, while preserving confidentiality, repeatability, traceability, and evidential integrity.

Keywords: Hate Speech · Digital Forensics · NLP · Autopsy

1 Introduction

In the contemporary digital environment, the importance of the timely identification and processing of hate speech is further underscored by the attention it has received from the United Nations (UN), which emphasizes the seriousness of this phenomenon and defines it as: *"any kind of communication in speech, writing or behaviour, that attacks or uses pejorative or discriminatory language with reference to a person or a group on the basis of who they are, in other words, based on their religion, ethnicity, nationality, race, colour, descent, gender or other identity factor."* [1]. At the same time, the UN emphasizes that the dissemination of such content, particularly in the online space, represents a serious social problem. In response, the UN Strategy and

© ICST Institute for Computer Sciences, Social Informatics and Telecommunications Engineering 2027
Published by Springer Nature Switzerland AG 2027. All Rights Reserved
H. Neukirchen et al. (Eds.): ICDF2C 2026, LNICST 720, pp. 395–413, 2027.
https://doi.org/10.1007/978-3-032-37274-1_23

Plan of Action on Hate Speech [2] was adopted in 2019 to strengthen a coordinated response at both the global and national levels, while the General Assembly proclaimed 18 June as the International Day for Countering Hate Speech. Such normative and institutional measures indicate that hate speech should no longer be viewed solely as a social and communicative problem, but also as an important subject of Digital Forensic (DF) analysis, in which tools for its automatic detection and processing can significantly contribute to the more efficient identification of relevant content and provide support for investigative procedures. This need becomes particularly evident in contemporary DF practice, where laboratories increasingly face a mismatch between the growing volume of digital evidence and their limited capacity to process it in a timely manner. Mobile devices, computers, and messaging applications generate large quantities of artifacts that may contain indicators of harassment, threats, hate speech, and other hate-motivated incidents.

Due to growing volume of digital evidence, a need for automation to improve both speed and accuracy is evident which could be addressed with application of Machine Learning (ML) in DF. However, existing ML applications are unevenly distributed across DF domains and are predominantly concentrated in multimedia forensics, particularly image forensics. This disparity, in turn, highlights an opportunity for targeted advances in text-oriented analysis, especially for messages and communication artifacts that are central to hate speech detection. A typical DF investigation follows the DFRWS roadmap [3]: identification of potential sources of evidence (P1), collection of digital artifacts (P2), preservation of acquired forensic images (P3), examination of forensic images (P4), analysis of forensic images (P5), and presentation of findings and expert opinion (P6). Consequently, the greatest opportunity for improving efficiency lies in phases P4–P6, where ML and Artificial Intelligence (AI) methods can be applied while preserving the core forensic principles, including integrity, repeatability, and reproducibility, in line with ISO/IEC 27042:2015 [4] and while maintaining human-in-the-loop decision-making.

In the context of hate speech, manual review of message histories is often infeasible within realistic investigative timelines, while keyword-based searches yield limited results. Linguistic variability, morphological changes, implicit forms of hate, obfuscated language, slang, and irony make reliable detection based solely on lexical cues difficult. Research on automated hate speech detection indicates that distinguishing hate speech from general offensive language is methodologically and empirically challenging, and that models often fail in borderline cases [5]. Consequently, in forensic applications of ML, the emphasis is primarily on triage (prioritization) and organization of potentially relevant messages, rather than on autonomous decision-making. Although hate speech detection has been intensively studied within the Natural Language Processing (NLP) community, its systematic adoption in DF remains relatively limited, particularly with respect to integration into existing forensic workflows while simultaneously meeting the above-mentioned forensic principles.

The aim of this research is to develop a DF tool, named Hate Speech Detector (HSD), that integrates NLP methods for hate speech detection into a DF workflow in order to reduce investigative processing time. Such integration is intended to support automated triage of digital artifacts while increasing transparency, improving the repeatability of the investigative process, and enabling evidence-linked reporting, without removing the central role of the forensic examiner in making the final expert assessment.

The rest of the paper is structured as follows. Following the introduction, Sect. 2 provides the related work, Sect. 3 presents the research methodology, Sect. 4 describes the proposed solution, Sect. 5 provides the discussion, Sect. 6 presents the conclusion, outlines the limitations of the study, and discusses future directions.

2 Related Work

ML is increasingly used in DF as a decision-support capability to cope with the growing volume and heterogeneity of digital artifacts, which makes manual examination and analysis increasingly time-consuming, often spanning phases P4–P6, particularly P5. Text analysis represents key area because everyday user activities generate abundant textual traces, authors [6] illustrate how ML can assist investigators in triaging chat logs, for example, by flagging conversations likely to contain sexually inappropriate topics. From a tooling perspective, Baroto [7] discusses ML integration in Autopsy 4.15.0, arguing that ML can enhance evidence handling through tasks such as classification, clustering, and link analysis, while emphasizing that results still require careful expert interpretation, thereby positioning ML as an enabler of efficiency and prioritization rather than a replacement for the forensic examiner.

Recent DF research explores Large Language Models (LLMs) and AI agents as decision-support tools for examination, analysis, and reporting [8], but consistently highlights limitations: hallucinations, poor explainability, bias, and domain knowledge gaps [9], as well as operational risks such as data leakage through external services and low reproducibility due to prompt sensitivity [10]. Empirical studies indicate LLMs can help with summarization and reporting when outputs are carefully reviewed [11], and that semantic retrieval is often more effective than keyword search for investigative chat analysis, with local or Retrieval-Augmented Generation (RAG) designs preferred for sensitive contexts [12]. However, fine-tuning local LLMs remains costly and data-limited due to confidentiality and licensing constraints [13], motivating a cautious, auditable integration aligned with legally defensible AI-supported DF practice [14].

In parallel, hate speech and offensive language research within the NLP community has advanced considerably through standardized shared-task benchmarks and evaluation protocols, particularly through SemEval shared tasks [15]. Representative examples include OffensEval (SemEval-2019 Task 6) on identifying and categorizing offensive language in social media [16], HatEval (SemEval-2019 Task 5) on multilingual hate speech targeting immigrants and women on Twitter [17], and OffensEval 2020 (SemEval-2020 Task 12) on multilingual offensive language identification [18]. Such shared tasks have helped establish common datasets, label schemas, and metrics, enabling more comparable and reproducible experimental results across studies. However, broader reviews of hate speech detection emphasize that important open challenges remain, including cultural variation, data sparsity, class imbalance, dataset availability, and the need to account for country or region-specific characteristics of hate speech [19]. Beyond shared-task settings, the NLP literature has explored several complementary modeling directions. One line of work investigates hybrid text representations, as illustrated authors in [20], who report improved results by combining multiple embedding-based features for social-media content classification. Another influential direction is the adaptation of pretrained transformer models to abusive-language detection, as illustrated by HateBERT, a BERT-based model retrained specifically for English abusive language detection, showing that domain-adapted transformer models can improve performance on this task [21]. At the same time, multilingual hate speech detection has received increasing attention through transformer-based approaches. Roy et al. [22] demonstrate the use of multilingual transformer models such as XLM-RoBERTa for both binary and fine-grained hate speech classification across English, German, and Hindi. Glazkova et al. [23] further show that transformer-based methods can be applied not only to binary hate speech detection in English but also to fine-grained classification of hate, offensive, and profane content, while additionally exploring multilingual fine-tuning and cross-lingual settings in the Marathi language. Collectively, these NLP benchmarks and model families provide the methodological foundations and pretrained architectures that can be integrated into forensic workflows for scalable triage and prioritization of potentially harmful textual evidence.

Hate speech detection has also been explored in DF-adjacent settings, though with differing levels of alignment to case-based forensic workflows. Wafula [24] discusses hate speech identification from a forensic perspective, but the proposed approach is methodologically closer to Open-Source INTelligence (OSINT)-style monitoring than to post-acquisition forensic analysis: the system primarily crawls public web forums, stores the collected content, and applies lexicon and keyword-based filtering to flag potentially relevant posts, without leveraging contemporary NLP/ML classification methods. As a result, the contribution functions mainly as a data collection and initial triage pipeline rather than an evidence-driven, case-centric DF workflow. More recently, authors [25] propose a hate speech classifier explicitly framed for social media forensics and focus on a key operational issue: the ambiguity between "hate" and "offensive" language. Their method models this uncertainty using neutrosophic logic. Evaluated on the Davidson dataset [5], the authors report improved performance for the hate class ($F1 = 0.54$) compared to their baselines. This is important for forensic use, since the approach produces an explicit uncertainty signal that could be surfaced in investigative triage and reporting tools.

Overall, while hate speech detection has matured substantially in the NLP literature, systematic, end-to-end integration into DF workflows remains limited, either because approaches resemble OSINT monitoring [24] or because they focus on model design without being embedded into repeatable investigative pipelines [25]. This gap indicates a clear opportunity to automate and accelerate text-based triage, especially in phases P4–P5, provided that validation, repeatability, and forensic defensibility are adequately addressed.

3 Research Methodology

To address the stated problem, this research follows the Design Science Research (DSR) methodology proposed by Peffers et al. [26]. Design Science creates and evaluates IT artifacts intended to solve identified problems [27]. In addition, practice rules are provided for conducting this research. One of them is that research must produce an artifact created to address a problem, which should be relevant to the solution, and its utility, quality, and efficacy must be rigorously evaluated. Because our research aims to produce an artifact, this methodology fits our needs. The methodology comprises six iterative activities: (i) problem identification and motivation, (ii) definition of solution objectives, (iii) artifact design and development, (iv) demonstration, (v) evaluation, and (vi) communication. The problem, its motivation, and the objectives of the proposed solution are outlined in Sect. 1. HSD is developed as an Autopsy ingest module intended to integrate hate speech detection into the DF workflow. The design and development activity is structured into two sub-steps: (1) the identification, selection, and comparative assessment of ML models for hate speech detection in the English language, and (2) the design and implementation of the ingest module itself, including a Graphical User Interface (GUI) within Autopsy. The developed artifact is demonstrated in Sect. 4 and further discussed in Sect. 5. In the evaluation step, the developed solution is assessed from both a ML and a forensic perspective. This includes comparative testing of the selected models using standard classification metrics, as well as consideration of repeatability, practical usability, and selected NIST-oriented principles [28] relevant to forensic tool testing, with reference to the relevant phases of the DF workflow. Particular emphasis is placed on the recall measure, due to the forensic importance of minimizing missed potentially relevant messages, as well as on stable and repeatable execution within a controlled processing environment. Practical usability is further considered through realistic scenario. As a case study, the proposed approach is evaluated on English-language communication artifacts extracted from messaging applications. Finally, the results of the research are communicated through the presentation of the developed artifact, implementation, and role within the DF workflow, together with a discussion of its practical relevance, current limitations, and directions for further improvement.

4 Solution

4.1 Model Selection and Comparative Assessment

The first step in the development of the proposed solution involved the identification and comparative assessment of suitable ML models for hate speech detection in the English language. The objective of this phase was not to identify the single best hate speech detection model in absolute terms, but rather to select models that were publicly available, sufficiently documented, feasible to execute in a controlled local environment, and suitable for integration into the proposed DF tool. In addition, preference was given to transformer-based models, as such architecture represents the dominant state-of-the-art paradigm in contemporary text classification, and priority was assigned to models already fine-tuned specifically for hate speech detection tasks, making them relevant to the intended application. This choice is further supported by recent survey evidence indicating that transformer-based models are highly effective for sentiment analysis and hate speech detection due to their contextual understanding, bidirectional context, large-scale pretraining, transfer-learning capability, and attention mechanisms [29]. To ensure that the selection was both practically relevant and grounded in existing research, the search for candidate models was conducted through two complementary sources. First, publicly available pretrained models were explored on the Hugging Face platform

[30], which provides access to models together with accompanying documentation. These candidate models were further examined in the scientific literature on hate speech detection, toxic language detection, and related text classification tasks to confirm their research relevance and contextualize their use within existing work. This search resulted in a broader set of potentially relevant models. However, for this study for further analysis and integration, a subset of four models was selected:

- **TehranNLP-org/electra-base-hateXplain (M1),** a hate speech classifier obtained by fine-tuning *google/electra-base-discriminator* on the HateXplain dataset [31];
- **facebook/roberta-hate-speech-dynabench-r4-target (M2),** a model released by Facebook in the context of dynamically generated datasets for improving online hate detection, based on the R4 target setting [32];
- **cardiffnlp/twitter-roberta-base-hate-latest (M3),** a binary hate speech classifier obtained by fine-tuning *cardiffnlp/twitter-roberta-base-2022-154 m* on a combination of 13 English hate speech datasets. This model is a RoBERTa-base model trained on 154 M tweets [33];
- **Hate-speech-CNERG/bert-base-uncased-hatexplain (M4),** a classifier based on *bert-base-uncased* and trained on the HateXplain dataset originating from Gab and Twitter, with human rationales incorporated during training [34].

Although the selected models differ in their training data and task formulation, they belong to closely related transformer-based model families, which makes their usage sufficiently similar to support abstraction within the proposed integration pipeline. The selected models are trained and fine-tuned on English-language data, but there is also the possibility of extending such architectures to multilingual settings. The procedure for model usage consists of: (i) text preprocessing (normalization), (ii) tokenizing the text using the native pretrained tokenizer of each model, (iii) running model inference on the tokenized text, and (iv) output postprocessing. Since the selected models were trained and fine-tuned under different data conditions and preprocessing assumptions, preprocessing is not treated as a uniform step applied identically across all models. Instead, the preprocessing strategy was aligned with the preprocessing specific to each model. For some selected models, the exact task-specific preprocessing pipeline was not explicitly documented in the model card. In such cases, preprocessing assumptions were derived conservatively from the corresponding base model, tokenizer behavior, and model family characteristics, while avoiding aggressive text transformations that could distort the original training conditions.

Accordingly, the preprocessing pipeline was designed so that the original extracted text was preserved for forensic traceability, whereas a separate normalized version was used exclusively for model inference across all selected models (M1, M2, M3, M4). To improve input consistency, Unicode normalization, removal of control characters, and whitespace normalization were applied. For the ELECTRA-based and BERT-based models (M1, M4), preprocessing was kept compatible with uncased architectures. For the RoBERTa-based M2 model, the text was retained in a form close to the raw input, as no explicit task-specific social media normalization was documented for that model. By contrast, in the M3 model, user mentions and URLs were normalized into common placeholders, such as @user and http. In all cases, tokenization was performed using the native pretrained tokenizer of the corresponding selected model (M1, M2, M3, M4). At the same time, stemming, lemmatization, and other aggressive linguistic transformations were intentionally avoided to minimize semantic distortion and preserve the evidential value of the original content.

In the final step of the model usage procedure, the selected models differed slightly in their prediction logic, since some of them were inherently designed for binary classification, whereas others were formulated as multiclass classifiers. For multiclass models, the original output labels were mapped to a binary decision space consisting of hate and non-hate classes. For instance, M1 and M4 produce the classes *offensive*, *hatespeech*, and *normal*. Their output was therefore adapted using the argmax decision, such that the classes *offensive* and *hatespeech* were merged into a single positive class, while normal was retained as the negative class. This adaptation was motivated by the forensic objective of the proposed tool. Although distinctions between hate speech, offensive language, racism, sexism, and related categories are important from a linguistic and annotation perspective, in the forensic context, the primary goal is to identify as much potentially relevant harmful content as possible for subsequent expert review. For this reason, the binary mapping was intentionally designed to favor broader retrieval of suspicious content. For binary and multilabel models, the decision was threshold-based, with the positive class assigned when the hate-related score exceeded a defined threshold. This design made it possible to incorporate different pretrained models into a common inference pipeline while preserving compatibility with their original output structure.

Once the model outputs had been harmonized into a shared binary decision space, the selected models could be compared under a unified evaluation setting. In this context, baseline performance on the task of English binary hate speech classification was evaluated for subsequent model comparison and integration into the proposed forensic tool. To obtain a more realistic estimate of the generalization capability of the selected models, the evaluation was not performed on the datasets used for their original training or development. Using such datasets could lead to an overly optimistic assessment of model performance and would not adequately reflect their behavior on previously unseen data. Instead, additional benchmark datasets were identified and collected from publicly available repositories. For this purpose, datasets were selected from the Hate Speech Data catalog [35] and the OffensEval shared-task resources [36]. Through this process, four English-language datasets were chosen for comparative testing:

- **DS1** - The SemEval-2020 Task 12: Multilingual Offensive Language Identification in Social Media [18] dataset was included because it represents a widely used benchmark for offensive and hateful language detection in social media content and provides a standardized evaluation setting.
- **DS2** - The dataset by Davidson et al. [5] was selected because it is one of the most frequently used benchmark datasets in the hate speech detection literature and enables comparison with a large body of prior work.
- **DS3** - The Gab dataset [37] was included because it provides conversational threads annotated for binary hate speech classification, together with candidate intervention responses. It was selected as a complementary benchmark for evaluating hate speech detection in a richer conversational setting and on a platform characterized by a relatively high prevalence of hateful content.

- **DS4** - The Reddit dataset [37] was also included because, like DS3, it was created by the same authors using a comparable methodology, while representing a different online platform. It was selected to support comparative evaluation across distinct online environments.

Each of the selected models was then executed on all selected datasets under a unified evaluation procedure. The comparative results are summarized in Table 1, which presents the obtained performance measures across all evaluated datasets. The comparison considered standard classification measures such as accuracy, precision, recall, and F1-score, with particular attention to recall due to the forensic importance of minimizing missed potentially relevant messages.

Table 1. Comparative performance of the selected hate speech detection models

Dataset	Metrics / Models	M1	M2	M3	M4
DS1	Accuracy	0.6117	**0.7791**	0.5793	0.5859
	Precision	0.9389	0.9233	**0.9564**	0.9407
	Recall	0.2405	**0.6096**	0.1679	0.1849
	F1-score	0.3829	**0.7343**	0.2856	0.3090
DS2	Accuracy	0.5955	**0.9319**	0.7484	0.6866
	Precision	0.9579	0.9762	**0.9907**	0.9569
	Recall	0.5375	**0.9411**	0.7043	0.6527
	F1-score	0.6886	**0.9583**	0.8233	0.7761
DS3	Accuracy	0.8386	**0.8520**	0.8511	0.8444
	Precision	0.7470	0.7959	**0.8358**	0.7574
	Recall	**0.9481**	0.8850	0.8163	0.9422
	F1-score	0.8356	0.8381	0.8259	**0.8397**
DS4	Accuracy	0.8377	0.8383	**0.8471**	0.8405
	Precision	0.6178	0.6367	**0.7070**	0.6239
	Recall	**0.8162**	0.7308	0.5996	0.8138
	F1-score	0.7033	0.6805	0.6489	**0.7063**

The results indicate that model performance is strongly dataset-dependent, suggesting that differences in training data, annotation schemes, and communication style have a substantial influence on effectiveness under the adopted binary evaluation setting. As shown in Table 1, while M2 achieved the best overall balance of performance on DS1 and DS2, this advantage did not necessarily transfer to the conversational datasets, where the structure and linguistic variability of the content are different. In contrast, M1 achieved the highest recall on DS3 and DS4, while M3 consistently obtained the highest precision across all evaluated datasets. From a forensic perspective, recall was treated as the most important measure, since the practical value of a model depends primarily on its ability to minimize missed potentially relevant harmful content during triage. Overall, the results support the need for context-aware model selection rather than assuming that a single pretrained model will be equally suitable across all types of communication evidence.

4.2 Design and Implementation

To automate and accelerate the P4 and P5 phases of a DF investigation focused on hate speech detection, we propose HSD,[1] a modular Autopsy ingest plugin that integrates this functionality into an established DF environment rather than introducing a separate standalone tool. HSD is implemented in Java as a data-source-level ingest module [38], since it analyzes textual artifacts already extracted during the standard Autopsy ingest workflow. This design reuses Autopsy's case-processing infrastructure, including access to data sources, extracted artifacts, and ingest results, while detected hate speech results are stored as Blackboard Artifacts [39] under the Analysis Result category, preserving traceability between each result and its source artifact. The architecture separates the Autopsy integration layer from the ML inference layer. The Java module manages case interaction, configuration, artifact retrieval, and result storage, while hate speech classification is performed by a standalone Python CLI component. This separation was adopted because transformer-based models and preprocessing pipelines are typically supported by the Python ML ecosystem, while the CLI component can also be tested independently outside Autopsy [40]. It also avoids relying on Autopsy's Jython-based Python modules, which are limited to Python 2.7, cannot use libraries with native code, and are less suitable for user-interface development [41]. The architecture of the HSD is shown in Fig. 1, while its main components are described below.

Module Configuration. The GUI of the HSD module is designed to allow the examiner to configure the analysis before execution within the Autopsy workflow. At the configuration level, the examiner can choose whether to execute the module for the current ingest job. Once enabled, the interface provides a set of options for defining the scope of hate speech detection. In particular, the examiner can select which categories of previously extracted communication artifacts should be included in the analysis. These sources may include e-mail messages, SMS/MMS messages, and message artifacts originating from supported communication applications such as WhatsApp, Viber, Telegram, as well as other previously uncategorized message artifacts available in the case. Thus, the module operates over a configurable subset of communication-related artifacts rather than over the entire data source, which also helps reduce execution time. In addition to selecting the message sources, the examiner can choose the ML model to be used for hate speech detection. The interface provides supporting information for each available model, including the model alias, model identifier, original classification setting, a short description of its expected characteristics, such as whether the model is more suitable when higher accuracy or higher recall is desired, and the type of data on which it was originally trained. This helps the examiner select a model better aligned with the investigated data source. The configuration interface also provides execution-management controls. The examiner may enable a time limit for model execution and define the timeout value in seconds, helping to ensure predictable runtime behavior and to reduce the

[1] https://github.com/SvetlanaAnt/Hate-Speech-Detector

risk of excessively long processing. The interface also supports downloading selected models and storing them locally, which enables subsequent execution in offline mode. In addition, the interface exposes the location of the generated log file, thereby supporting traceability, troubleshooting, and later review of the module's execution behavior.

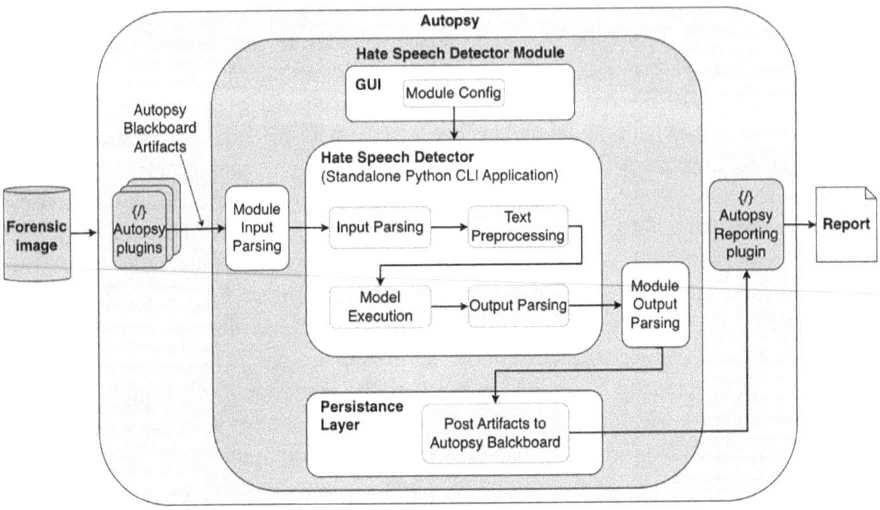

Fig. 1. Hate Speech Module Architecture

Module Input Parsing. The module input parsing component is responsible for identifying and retrieving the communication artifacts that should be analyzed, based on the configuration previously defined by the examiner through the GUI. More specifically, the module queries Autopsy's Blackboard storage and selects only those artifacts that correspond to the user-selected message sources. In the current implementation, communication-related blackboard artifacts of types TSK_EMAIL_MSG and TSK_MESSAGE are retrieved, which represent extracted e-mail and message content made available through the standard ingest workflow. The selection process is driven by two complementary criteria: the examiner's configuration choices and the artifact information available in the Blackboard. First, the module determines which categories of communication sources have been enabled in the GUI. It then searches the Blackboard for artifacts of the relevant types and filters them according to the available metadata and source-related attributes, so that only artifacts belonging to the selected scope of analysis are retained. After retrieval, the selected artifacts are grouped and transformed into a structured input representation that is passed to the standalone Python Command-Line Interface (CLI) application.

Standalone Python CLI Application. The core hate speech detection logic is executed outside the Java-based Autopsy layer through a standalone Python CLI application. The Java-based ingest module invokes this application after artifact retrieval and structuring, using the selected configuration. Its role is to receive the prepared input, parse the forwarded data and parameters, perform text preprocessing, execute the selected ML model, and transform the obtained predictions into a structured output format suitable for reintegration into the Autopsy workflow.

Input parsing. Within the Python layer, the received input is first parsed into a consistent internal representation that preserves the linkage between each processed text item and its associated forensic context. This step ensures that the downstream analysis can be applied systematically, while also enabling the prediction results to remain traceable to the original artifact from which the text was obtained.

Text preprocessing. Before inference, model-dependent text preprocessing is applied to improve input consistency while preserving the evidential value of the original content, as described in Sect. 4.1.

Model execution. Model execution. After preprocessing, the selected model is applied to the prepared textual input, producing a binary hate speech classification result, as described in Sect. 4.1.

Output parsing. Once inference is completed, the raw model outputs are parsed into a structured result representation that can be returned to the Autopsy ingest module. In addition to the final binary decision, the output includes supporting information such as classification scores, label mappings, and the normalized text used during inference, while preserving the original text linked to the forensic artifact for transparency. Thus, the Python CLI layer not only performs classification but also prepares the results for subsequent persistence, interpretation, and reporting within the forensic environment.

Persistence Layer - Posting Artifacts to Autopsy Blackboard. After model execution and output parsing, the obtained results are persisted within Autopsy by posting new blackboard artifacts that represent the analytical findings of the module. When a potentially hateful message is identified, the module creates a new TSK_HATE_SPEECH_HIT artifact under the ANALYSIS_RESULT category on the Autopsy Blackboard. The module output is thus recorded as an analysis result derived from an existing evidential artifact rather than as a modification of the original evidence itself. Each analysis result is explicitly linked to the corresponding source artifact, thereby preserving traceability to the original evidential context. The recorded result also includes relevant supporting information, such as model-related metadata and references needed for later review and reporting. The generated result is not treated as a final verdict, but as a prioritized indicator for expert examination, allowing the forensic examiner to review the flagged content in context and make the final professional assessment. This preserves a human-in-the-loop decision-making regime while supporting transparency, traceability, and repeatability. These analysis results can also be used within Autopsy's standard reporting workflow, enabling the forensic examiner to incorporate the flagged artifacts into the final case report together with their evidential references and contextual interpretation.

Logging and Traceability. To further support transparency, repeatability, and troubleshooting, the systematic logging is performed at both the Autopsy wrapper layer and the standalone Python CLI layer. The Python CLI writes its execution logs within the case-specific *Case/ModuleOutput/HateSpeech/* directory, while the Autopsy-side wrapper logs are written within *Case/Log/*. The recorded information includes the start and end of each run, execution timestamp, selected model and runtime arguments, software and package versions, platform information, input and output file locations, number of parsed items, model configuration metadata, and summary statistics on the number of flagged messages. At the Autopsy layer, logging additionally captures wrapper-side execution steps, including artifact retrieval, input preparation, invocation of the external CLI process, and result persistence. Together, these logs provide an auditable record of how the analysis was performed and under which technical conditions.

4.3 Forensic Use Case Evaluation

To evaluate the HSD plugin in a realistic forensic workflow, a formal time-and-motion study was conducted using an Android 11 forensic image obtained from the Digital Corpora cell-phone image repository [42]. The image was analyzed in Autopsy with the Android Analyzer ingest module [43], which extracted 119 TSK_MESSAGE artifacts from several messaging and social media applications. Since neither manual review nor HSD plugin-based review identified hate speech content in the original artifacts, the image was extended with annotated messages to create a controlled evaluation scenario. Therefore, the SMS/MMS, WhatsApp, and Viber databases were selected for modification, as they produced relevant TSK_MESSAGE artifacts during the initial Android Analyzer extraction. To create a controlled evaluation case with known ground truth, an annotated subset was prepared from the DS2 dataset. The original DS2 dataset contains 24,783 messages in three classes: 1,430 *hate-speech* messages, 19,190 *offensive-language* messages, and 4,163 messages labeled as *neither*. For this evaluation, the original three-class scheme was mapped to a binary task, where *hate_speech* and *offensive_language* were treated as the positive class, while *neither* was treated as the negative class. From this binary-mapped dataset, 600 messages were selected, including 100 hate/offensive and 500 normal messages, resulting in a controlled 1:5 positive-to-negative ratio. This distribution was chosen to keep the evaluation case manageable while maintaining the realistic assumption that harmful content represents a smaller portion of the overall communication. The selected messages were shuffled using a fixed random seed, ensuring that hate/offensive messages were distributed throughout the sample rather than grouped together, while also making the sampling process reproducible. The resulting JSON file contained the message identifier, text, and binary ground-truth label for each selected item. The 600 messages were then inserted sequentially into the selected application databases: 200 into SMS/MMS, the next 200 into WhatsApp, and the final 200 into Viber. Since each application uses a different SQLite database structure, the insertion process adapted the messages to the required tables, column values, identifiers, timestamps, and conversation or thread references of each target database. To preserve a realistic communication context, the messages were inserted into existing conversations or threads, with sender/receiver direction information and timestamps generated close to the time range of the existing messages. After the modified databases were placed back into the working forensic image or extracted file set, a new Autopsy case was created and analyzed again with Android Analyzer enabled. The number of extracted TSK_MESSAGE artifacts increased from 119 to 719.

Three investigators, denoted as I1, I2, and I3 independently manually reviewed the TSK_MESSAGE artifacts extracted by Android Analyzer in Autopsy and, for each message, recorded the review time and assigned a binary label indicating whether the message contained hate/offensive content. Since English was not the native language of the investigators, the review also reflected a realistic scenario in which examiners assess English-language communication as non-native speakers. During annotation, the investigators followed the hate speech definition introduced in Sect. 1. The collected annotations and message-level review times provided a human baseline for comparison with the HSD plugin results and with the known ground-truth labels from the extracted DS2 subset. The HSD plugin was executed using the M2 model, which achieved the best overall performance in Sect. 4.1. The evaluation was performed in a virtualized environment using a Windows 10 workstation with 8 GB of RAM, 4 CPU (AMD Ryzen 7 3700 U), Autopsy 4.22.1, Java 17.0.12 LTS, and the locally packaged Python runtime. All models were downloaded and stored locally before execution, enabling offline processing. During execution, the plugin generated a Comma Separated Value evaluation log in the case module directory, containing item-level records for each processed message and summary records for the complete run. The log captured the total runtime for all 719 messages, as well as the minimum, maximum, and average processing time per message. Since batch inference was used, with a default batch size of 32 and a maximum sequence length of 512 tokens, per-message time was estimated by dividing each batch runtime by the number of messages in that batch. This preserved the plugin's normal batch-based execution while still enabling message-level runtime reporting. When ground-truth labels were available for the inserted messages, the same log was also used to calculate the confusion matrix and compare the plugin results with the known DS2 annotations from the extracted subset. The results of the manual review and HSD processing are summarized in Table 2, which reports total review/processing time, average, minimum, and maximum time per message, and the number of messages identified as hate/offensive for each investigator and the plugin. Table 3 further compares manual annotations and HSD predictions with the DS2 ground truth. For each investigator and the M2-based plugin execution, the confusion matrix was calculated, including True Positive (TP), False Positive (FP), False Negative (FN), and True Negative (TN). Based on these values, precision, recall, F1-score, and accuracy are calculated. This enables comparison of both processing efficiency and classification correctness in the controlled forensic case.

In addition to classification performance, the developed module was considered from the perspective of forensic applicability, with emphasis on repeatability, practical usability, and traceability of results within the Autopsy environment. Repeatability was supported through controlled execution settings, model-specific preprocessing rules, systematic logging, and the preservation of evidence-linked analytical results on the Autopsy Blackboard. The plugin was also executed multiple times on the same case under identical configuration settings, and all executions produced the same output, thereby indicating stable behavior under controlled conditions. The module was designed so that its outputs remain explicitly connected to the original artifacts from which the processed text was obtained, allowing the examiner to review flagged content in its evidential context. Practical usability was addressed through integration into the existing Autopsy ingest workflow, where the examiner can configure the relevant message sources, select the detection model, and review the generated results without

Table 2. Time-and-motion results for manual review and HSD processing

Method	Average time / Message	Min. time / Message	Max. time / Message	Total time	Hate message detected
Manual – I1	2.53 s	0.19 s	12.73 s	1756.43 s	160
Manual – I2	4.84 s	0.1 s	30.2 s	2755.35 s	284
Manual – I3	3.88 s	0.2 s	17.61 s	2693.17 s	132
Manual – Mean	3.75 s	0.16 s	20.18 s	2401.65 s	192
HSD – M2	0.37 s	0 s	1.11 s	268.12 s	150

Table 3. Confusion matrix and classification metrics compared with DS2 ground truth

Method	TP	TN	FP	FN	Precision	Recall	F1-score	Accuracy
Manual – I1	90	549	70	10	56.25%	90%	69.23%	88.87%
Manual – I2	92	427	192	8	32.39%	92%	47.92%	72.18%
Manual – I3	69	556	63	31	52.27%	69%	59.48%	86.93%
HSD – M2	91	560	59	9	60.67%	91%	72.8%	90.54%

leaving the forensic environment. Although the selected models remain largely black-box in terms of their internal decision-making process, a degree of forensic transparency is achieved through configuration visibility, logging, model metadata, and explicit linkage between predictions and source artifacts. In this sense, the module output is not intended to represent a final forensic conclusion, but rather a prioritized analytical aid that supports subsequent expert review.

5 Discussion

This study shows that integrating hate speech detection models into a DF setting involves more than achieving high predictive performance. In addition to classification quality, it is equally important that the selected models can be executed locally, are sufficiently documented, produce reproducible results, remain linked to the original evidence, and can be integrated into the forensic environment without disrupting the established workflow. For this reason, the models were considered not only as benchmark candidates, but also as practical analytical components that had to function reliably within a controlled forensic process. In this context, the proposed solution demonstrates that NLP-based hate speech detection can be meaningfully integrated into an existing DF workflow through an Autopsy ingest module. Rather than functioning as a standalone analytical tool, the developed approach embeds automated text analysis directly into the environment already used by forensic examiners, thereby supporting continuity of workflow and reducing the need for additional tool familiarization. To the best of our knowledge, there are no directly comparable, publicly available forensic tools for hate speech detection, making a quantitative benchmark against similar systems infeasible. Compared with the related approaches discussed in Sect. 2, the proposed solution focuses on post-acquisition analysis of communication artifacts within an existing forensic case. Unlike Wafula [24], which is oriented toward OSINT-style collection and keyword-based triage, and [25], which focuses on hate speech model evaluation, our solution integrates ML-based detection into a repeatable Autopsy workflow with evidence-linked results, local execution, traceability, and human-in-the-loop review.

The proposed solution's value lies primarily in assisting the P4 and P5 phases of the forensic process, where large volumes of communication artifacts make manual review increasingly difficult. The formal time-and-motion study indicates that the HSD can accelerate these phases by automatically filtering and prioritizing potentially relevant messages, thereby reducing the number of artifacts that require immediate manual inspection. In this setting, the module does not replace expert judgment but instead supports forensic triage by highlighting potentially relevant messages for subsequent examination. In addition, the decision to map model outputs to a binary classification reflects a forensic rather than purely linguistic objective, since the main goal is to retrieve as much potentially relevant harmful content as possible for subsequent expert review, even when the original model categories differ in their annotation schema or semantic specificity. Although this study does not directly examine the effect of training data composition, a likely reason for the stronger performance of M2 is that the data on which it was originally trained may be more compatible with the evaluation datasets used here, especially in terms of class definitions, linguistic patterns, and the types of hate-related content included.

6 Conclusion

This paper contributes to addressing the problem of integrating hate speech detection into the DF workflow and presents HSD as an Autopsy ingest module developed for that purpose. The study combines the comparative assessment of selected English-language hate speech detection models, the design and implementation of a modular forensic plugin for analyzing previously extracted communication artifacts, applying model-specific preprocessing, and posting evidence-linked analytical results to the Autopsy Blackboard, and a formal time-and-motion study on a realistic Android forensic case. In this way, the proposed module supports the prioritization of potentially relevant messages while preserving traceability, repeatability, and the central role of the forensic examiner in the final interpretation of findings. Overall, the results indicate that NLP-based hate speech detection can provide valuable support in DF investigations involving large volumes of textual communication data and can contribute to more scalable, evidence-aware, and analytically assisted examination and analysis.

The proposed solution has several limitations. The current implementation is restricted to English-language hate speech detection and cannot be directly generalized to other languages without additional model selection, adaptation, and validation. It also relies on binary classification, which is useful for forensic triage but does not preserve finer distinctions between different categories of harmful content. Detection performance depends on the selected pretrained model, its original training data, and the alignment between the applied preprocessing and the model's original assumptions. In addition, the current implementation primarily analyzes message text and does not yet incorporate richer conversational context, related messages, or metadata, which may be important for interpreting ambiguous or implicit harmful content. The module output is not intended to represent a final forensic conclusion, but rather an analytical aid for prioritizing potentially relevant content for expert review. Finally, the solution inherits limitations of the underlying pretrained models, including possible dataset bias, annotation inconsistencies, and reduced generalizability across domains and communication platforms.

Future work may extend the flexibility and analytical scope of the module through multilabel classification, multilingual processing, automatic language detection, and model recommendation based on the selected data source and language. Additional improvements could include support for user-imported models, ensemble voting, and the incorporation of message metadata, artifact-level information, and neighboring messages to improve context-aware interpretation. Beyond these technical improvements, future research could explore multimodal harmful-content detection by extending the analysis to images, video recordings, and voice messages. Another important direction is the evaluation of LLMs for hate speech detection in forensic settings, with particular attention to repeatability, reproducibility, determinism, explainability, and output stability under controlled conditions. The development of DF-oriented models also remains an important challenge, particularly due to the limited availability of publicly accessible DF datasets for training and evaluation.

Acknowledgements. This research has been supported by the Ministry of Science, Technological Development and Innovation (Contract No. 451-03-34/2026-03/200156) and the Faculty of Technical Sciences, University of Novi Sad through project "Scientific and Artistic Research Work of Researchers in Teaching and Associate Positions at the Faculty of Technical Sciences, University of Novi Sad 2026" (No. 01-3609/1).

References

1. Nations, U.: What is hate speech? https://www.un.org/en/hate-speech/understanding-hate-speech/what-is-hate-speech. Accessed 25 Mar. 2026
2. Nations, U.: The UN Strategy and Plan of Action. https://www.un.org/en/hate-speech/un-strategy-and-plan-of-action-on-hate-speech. Accessed 25 Mar. 2026
3. A Road Map for Digital Forensic Research - DFRWS. (2001).
4. ISO/IEC 27042:2015. https://www.iso.org/standard/44406.html. Accessed 20 Mar 2026
5. Davidson, T., Warmsley, D., Macy, M., Weber, I.: Automated hate speech detection and the problem of offensive language. Proc. Int. AAAI Conf. Web Soc. Media. **11**, 512–515 (2017). https://doi.org/10.1609/icwsm.v11i1.14955

6. Ngejane, C.H., Eloff, J.H.P., Sefara, T.J., Marivate, V.N.: Digital forensics supported by machine learning for the detection of online sexual predatory chats. Forensic Sci. Int. Digit. Invest. **36**, 301109 (2021). https://doi.org/10.1016/j.fsidi.2021.301109
7. Baroto, W.: Advancing digital forensic through machine learning: an integrated framework for fraud investigation. Asia Pac. Fraud J. **9**, 1–16 (2024). https://doi.org/10.21532/apfjournal.v9i1.346
8. Wickramasekara, A., Scanlon, M.: A Framework for Integrated Digital Forensic Investigation Employing Auto Gen AI Agents (2024). doi:https://doi.org/10.1109/ISDFS60797.2024.10527235.
9. Yin, Z., et al.: Digital forensics in the age of large language models. In: Iyengar, S.S., Furton, K.G., Mohanty, P., Chaudhary, N.K. (eds.) Artificial Intelligence Driven Forensics, pp. 55–82. Springer Nature, Switzerland, Cham (2026). https://doi.org/10.1007/978-3-031-98036-7_3
10. Scanlon, M., Breitinger, F., Hargreaves, C., Hilgert, J.-N., Sheppard, J.: ChatGPT for digital forensic investigation: the good, the bad, and the unknown. Forensic Sci. Int. Digit. Invest. **46**, 301609 (2023). https://doi.org/10.1016/j.fsidi.2023.301609
11. Michelet, G., Breitinger, F.: ChatGPT, llama, can you write my report? An experiment on assisted digital forensics reports written using (local) large language models. Forensic Sci. Int. Digit. Invest. **48**, 301683 (2024). https://doi.org/10.1016/j.fsidi.2023.301683
12. Kim, K.J., Lee, C.H., Bae, S.E., Choi, J.H., Kang, W.: Digital forensics in law enforcement: a case study of LLM-driven evidence analysis. Forensic Sci. Int. Digit. Invest. **54**, 301939 (2025). https://doi.org/10.1016/j.fsidi.2025.301939
13. Michelet, G., Henseler, H., van Beek, H., Scanlon, M., Breitinger, F.: Fine-tuning large language models for digital forensics: case study and general recommendations. Digit. Threats. (2025). https://doi.org/10.1145/3748264
14. Baggili, I., Behzadan, V.: Founding the domain of AI forensics. In: Proceedings of the AAAI Workshop on Artificial Intelligence Safety (SafeAI 2020), pp. 31–35 (2020)
15. SemEval: https://semeval.github.io/. Accessed 27 Jan. 2026
16. Zampieri, M., Malmasi, S., Nakov, P., Rosenthal, S., Farra, N., Kumar, R.: SemEval-2019 task 6: identifying and categorizing offensive language in social media (OffensEval). In: May, J., Shutova, E., Herbelot, A., Zhu, X., Apidianaki, M., Mohammad, S.M. (eds.) Proceedings of the 13th International Workshop on Semantic Evaluation, pp. 75–86. Association for Computational Linguistics, Minneapolis, Minnesota, USA (2019). https://doi.org/10.18653/v1/S19-2010
17. Basile, V., et al.: SemEval-2019 task 5: multilingual detection of hate speech against immigrants and women in twitter. In: May, J., Shutova, E., Herbelot, A., Zhu, X., Apidianaki, M., Mohammad, S.M. (eds.) Proceedings of the 13th International Workshop on Semantic Evaluation, pp. 54–63. Association for Computational Linguistics, Minneapolis, Minnesota, USA (2019) https://doi.org/10.18653/v1/S19-2007
18. Zampieri, M., et al.: SemEval-2020 task 12: multilingual offensive language identification in social media (OffensEval 2020). In: Herbelot, A., Zhu, X., Palmer, A., Schneider, N., May, J., Shutova, E. (eds.) Proceedings of the Fourteenth Workshop on Semantic Evaluation, pp. 1425–1447. International Committee for Computational Linguistics, Barcelona (2020). https://doi.org/10.18653/v1/2020.semeval-1.188
19. Mullah, N.S., Zainon, W.M.N.W.: Advances in machine learning algorithms for hate speech detection in social media: a review. IEEE Access. **9**, 88364–88376 (2021). https://doi.org/10.1109/ACCESS.2021.3089515
20. Badri, N., Kboubi, F., Chaibi, A.H.: Combining FastText and glove word embedding for offensive and hate speech text detection. Procedia Comput. Sci. **207**, 769–778 (2022). https://doi.org/10.1016/j.procs.2022.09.132

21. Caselli, T., Basile, V., Mitrović, J., Granitzer, M.: HateBERT: retraining BERT for abusive language detection in English. In: Mostafazadeh Davani, A., Kiela, D., Lambert, M., Vidgen, B., Prabhakaran, V., Waseem, Z. (eds.) Proceedings of the 5th Workshop on Online Abuse and Harms (WOAH 2021), pp. 17–25. Association for Computational Linguistics, Online (2021) https://doi.org/10.18653/v1/2021.woah-1.3
22. Roy, S.G., Narayan, U., Raha, T., Abid, Z., Varma, V.: Leveraging multilingual transformers for hate speech detection. In: Mehta, P., Mandl, T., Majumder, P., Mitra, M. (eds.) Working Notes of FIRE 2020 - Forum for Information Retrieval Evaluation, Hyderabad, India, December 16–20, 2020, pp. 128–138 (2020) CEUR-WS.org
23. Glazkova, A., Kadantsev, M., Glazkov, M.: Fine-tuning of Pre-trained Transformers for Hate Offensive and Profane Content Detection in English and Marathi. Presented at the Working Notes of FIRE 2021 - Forum for Information Retrieval Evaluation, Gandhinagar, India, December 13–17, 2021 (2021).
24. Wafula, G.W.: Social Media Forensics For Hate Speech Opinion Mining. http://erepository.uonbi.ac.ke/handle/11295/97833 (2016).
25. Ibrahim, Y.M., Essameldin, R., Darwish, S.M.: An adaptive hate speech detection approach using Neutrosophic neural networks for social media forensics. Comput. Mater. Continua. **79**, 243–262 (2024). https://doi.org/10.32604/cmc.2024.047840
26. Peffers, K., Tuunanen, T., Rothenberger, M., Chatterjee, S.: A design science research methodology for information systems research. J. Manag. Inf. Syst. **24**, 45–77 (2007). https://doi.org/10.2753/MIS0742-1222240302
27. Hevner, A.R., March, S.T., Park, J., Ram, S.: Design science in information systems Research1. MIS Q. **28**, 75–106 (2004). https://doi.org/10.2307/25148625
28. Computer Forensics Tool Testing Program (CFTT). NIST (2017).
29. Subramanian, M., Easwaramoorthy Sathiskumar, V., Deepalakshmi, G., Cho, J., Manikandan, G.: A survey on hate speech detection and sentiment analysis using machine learning and deep learning models. Alex. Eng. J. **80**, 110–121 (2023). https://doi.org/10.1016/j.aej.2023.08.038
30. Models – Hugging Face. https://huggingface.co/models. Accessed 25 Mar. 2026
31. hate-alert/HateXplain (2026). https://github.com/hate-alert/HateXplain
32. Vidgen, B., Thrush, T., Waseem, Z., Kiela, D.: Learning from the worst: dynamically generated datasets to improve online hate detection. In: Zong, C., Xia, F., Li, W., Navigli, R. (eds.) Proceedings of the 59th Annual Meeting of the Association for Computational Linguistics and the 11th International Joint Conference on Natural Language Processing (Volume 1: Long Papers), pp. 1667–1682. Association for Computational Linguistics, Online (2021). https://doi.org/10.18653/v1/2021.acl-long.132
33. Antypas, D., Camacho-Collados, J.: Robust hate speech detection in social media: a cross-dataset empirical evaluation. In: Chung, Y., R{\textbackslash"ottger}, P., Nozza, D., Talat, Z., and Mostafazadeh Davani, A. (eds.) The 7th Workshop on Online Abuse and Harms (WOAH). pp. 231–242. Association for Computational Linguistics, Toronto, Canada (2023). https://doi.org/10.18653/v1/2023.woah-1.25.
34. Mathew, B., Saha, P., Yimam, S.M., Biemann, C., Goyal, P., Mukherjee, A.: HateXplain: a benchmark dataset for explainable hate speech detection. Proc. AAAI Conf. Artif. Intell. **35**, 14867–14875 (2021). https://doi.org/10.1609/aaai.v35i17.17745
35. Hate Speech Dataset Catalogue. https://hatespeechdata.com/. Accessed 25 Mar. 2026
36. OffensEval Shared Task. https://sites.google.com/site/offensevalsharedtask/. Accessed 25 Mar. 2026

37. Qian, J., Bethke, A., Liu, Y., Belding, E., Wang, W.Y.: A benchmark dataset for learning to intervene in online hate speech. In: Inui, K., Jiang, J., Ng, V., Wan, X. (eds.) Proceedings of the 2019 Conference on Empirical Methods in Natural Language Processing and the 9th International Joint Conference on Natural Language Processing (EMNLP-IJCNLP), pp. 4755–4764. Association for Computational Linguistics, Hong Kong, China (2019). https://doi.org/10.18653/v1/D19-1482
38. Autopsy: Developing Ingest Modules. https://sleuthkit.org/autopsy/docs/api-docs/4.22.0/mod_ingest_page.html. Accessed 21 Mar. 2026
39. Sleuth Kit Java Bindings (JNI): Standard Artifacts Catalog. https://sleuthkit.org/sleuthkit/docs/jni-docs/4.13.0/artifact_catalog_page.html. Accessed 21 Mar. 2026
40. Pipelines Hugging Face. https://huggingface.co/docs/transformers/en/main_classes/pipelines. Accessed 26 May 2026
41. Autopsy: Python Development Setup. https://sleuthkit.org/autopsy/docs/api-docs/4.22.0/mod_dev_py_page.html. Accessed 26 May 2026
42. New Android 11 and 12 Images! – Digital Corpora. https://digitalcorpora.org/2022/09/06/new-android-10-and-11-images/. Accessed 29 May 2026
43. Autopsy User Documentation: Android Analyzer (aLEAPP). https://sleuthkit.org/autopsy/docs/user-docs/4.22.0/aleapp_page.html. Accessed 29 May 2026

X4SFF-ITD: An Extensible and Explainable Plugin-Based Framework for Insider Threat Detection

Federica Ferrara, Arcangelo Castiglione(✉), Raffaele Pizzolante, and Francesco Palmieri

University of Salerno, via Giovanni Paolo II n. 132, 84084 Fisciano, Italy
{arcastiglione,rpizzolante,fpalmieri}@unisa.it

Abstract. Insider threat detection remains a challenging problem due to heterogeneous data sources, ambiguous user behavior, and the limited transparency of many existing detection approaches. This paper presents X4SFF-ITD, an extensible and explainable plugin-based framework designed to support insider threat detection through a unified and reproducible processing pipeline.

The framework normalizes heterogeneous telemetry into a common event schema and introduces an idempotent ingestion mechanism based on stable event hashing and cursor-based state management. Detection logic is implemented through modular plugins that generate evidence-linked findings, while a transparent risk scoring model records the contribution of contextual factors to the final severity.

A proof-of-concept prototype is evaluated using SEI-CERT logs and Falco events. The evaluation focuses on framework-level properties, including ingestion correctness, resume and deduplication behavior, explainability of generated findings, and processing overhead. The results show that X4SFF-ITD provides a reproducible foundation for studying explainable and extensible insider threat detection pipelines, while highlighting the need for broader quantitative assessment of detection effectiveness in future work.

Keywords: Insider Threat Detection · Explainable Security · Risk Scoring · Security Analytics · Plugin-Based Architecture

1 Introduction

Insider threat detection represents a persistent challenge in cybersecurity due to the intrinsic complexity of human behavior, the heterogeneity of data sources, and the contextual nature of malicious or anomalous activities [1–3]. Unlike external attacks, insider threats often manifest through sequences of seemingly legitimate actions that become suspicious only when correlated across time, users, and systems. This makes detection difficult when relying on isolated logs, static rules, or tools that do not preserve sufficient investigative context.

© ICST Institute for Computer Sciences, Social Informatics and Telecommunications Engineering 2027
Published by Springer Nature Switzerland AG 2027. All Rights Reserved
H. Neukirchen et al. (Eds.): ICDF2C 2026, LNICST 720, pp. 414–425, 2027.
https://doi.org/10.1007/978-3-032-37274-1_24

Existing approaches include rule-based systems, anomaly detection models, graph-based methods, and user behavior analytics (UEBA) [10–12]. Although these techniques provide valuable capabilities, many solutions remain tightly coupled to specific data sources or platforms, provide limited transparency in their detection or scoring logic, and do not always support reproducible experimentation or easy extension to new detection scenarios [4–6]. These limitations make it difficult for analysts and researchers to understand why an alert was generated, validate the underlying evidence, or adapt detection logic to new telemetry sources and behavioral patterns.

To address these issues, this paper presents X4SFF-ITD, an extensible and explainable plugin-based framework for insider threat detection. The framework supports heterogeneous telemetry ingestion, normalization into a common event schema, plugin-based detection, evidence-linked findings, and transparent risk scoring. A central design objective is to improve robustness and reproducibility through idempotent ingestion based on stable event hashing and cursor-based state management.

A proof-of-concept prototype has been developed using SEI-CERT logs as the primary dataset [13] and Falco-generated events as an additional telemetry source [7]. The evaluation focuses on framework-level properties: ingestion correctness under duplication and resume scenarios, explainability of generated findings, and the processing overhead introduced by plugin-based detection.

The main contributions are: (i) a normalized and extensible plugin-based framework for insider threat detection; (ii) an idempotent ingestion model based on event hashing and cursor-based state management; (iii) an explainable finding and scoring model linking alerts to supporting evidence; and (iv) a proof-of-concept evaluation focused on ingestion robustness, traceability, and processing overhead.

This work does not claim to outperform state-of-the-art machine learning or graph-based insider threat detection systems in terms of detection accuracy. Rather, it focuses on the design and validation of a reproducible and inspectable framework that can support future integration of more advanced behavioral models.

The remainder of the paper is organized as follows. Section 2 reviews related work, Sect. 3 presents the framework design, Sect. 4 describes the prototype, Sect. 5 reports the evaluation, and Sects. 6–7 discuss limitations and conclusions.

2 Related Work and Research Gap

Insider threat detection has been widely studied through rule-based systems, anomaly detection, graph-based analytics, and behavior-driven models [2]. Anomaly-based approaches model normal user behavior and identify deviations as potential threats [10,11]. These methods are useful for detecting previously unseen behaviors, but they often suffer from false positives, behavior drift, cold-start issues, and limited interpretability when alerts are not directly connected to human-readable evidence.

Graph-based and context-aware approaches model relationships between users, hosts, resources, and actions [2,12]. They are particularly relevant for insider threat scenarios, where suspicious behavior may emerge as a sequence of weak signals rather than a single decisive event. However, these approaches may require complex feature engineering, semantic modeling, and tuning before their outputs can be transformed into actionable and explainable findings.

Operational security platforms such as SIEM, UEBA, EDR, runtime security tools, and insider risk management systems provide log aggregation, correlation, alerting, and workflow support [7,14–16]. Enterprise platforms offer mature operational features, while open-source tools such as Wazuh and Falco provide transparency and rule-level control. Nevertheless, these systems frequently cover only part of the pipeline required for research-oriented insider threat detection, especially when reproducible experimentation, stateful ingestion, evidence-linked findings, and transparent scoring are required.

Explainability has become increasingly important in security analytics, particularly because black-box models may provide risk scores or alerts without exposing the evidence and reasoning behind them [4–6]. In insider threat detection, explainability is especially relevant because anomalous behavior does not necessarily imply malicious intent. Analysts need to inspect the events, contextual factors, and scoring rationale that led to a finding.

Despite these advances, several gaps remain. Many approaches do not provide a unified and reproducible pipeline that integrates heterogeneous telemetry, normalizes it into a common representation, preserves evidence links, and supports robust ingestion through duplicate handling and recovery. In addition, explainability is often added after detection rather than being embedded into the generation of findings and scores. X4SFF-ITD addresses these limitations by combining normalized multi-source ingestion, idempotent processing, plugin-based detection, evidence-linked findings, and transparent risk scoring within a reproducible proof-of-concept framework.

3 X4SFF-ITD Design

X4SFF-ITD is designed as a modular and explainable framework for insider threat detection. Its main objectives are extensibility, explainability, robustness, and reproducibility. Extensibility allows new telemetry sources and detection plugins to be added without modifying the core engine; explainability requires findings to be linked to evidence and scoring details; robustness is addressed through duplicate handling and recovery; and reproducibility is supported through deterministic normalization and persisted ingestion metadata.

3.1 Threat Model and Assumptions

X4SFF-ITD focuses on technical and operational indicators of insider threat activity observable through logs and security telemetry. The considered actor may be a malicious insider, a negligent user, or a legitimate account compromised by an external attacker. In all cases, the activity may appear legitimate when observed in isolation, such as authentication, file access, process execution, or interaction with organizational resources.

The framework assumes that relevant activities are at least partially observable through available telemetry sources. It does not infer psychological intent and does not treat an anomaly as proof of malicious behavior. Instead, it produces explainable findings that require analyst validation and contextual interpretation. The current prototype focuses on rule-based and window-based indicators, while more advanced UEBA, graph-based, or machine learning models are considered future extensions.

3.2 Architecture and Normalized Event Schema

X4SFF-ITD follows a pipeline composed of ingestion, normalization, plugin-based detection, risk scoring, and persistence, as shown in Fig. 1. Raw telemetry from heterogeneous sources is first mapped into a normalized event representation. Detection plugins operate only on normalized events, while findings, evidence links, scoring details, and ingestion metadata are persisted for later inspection.

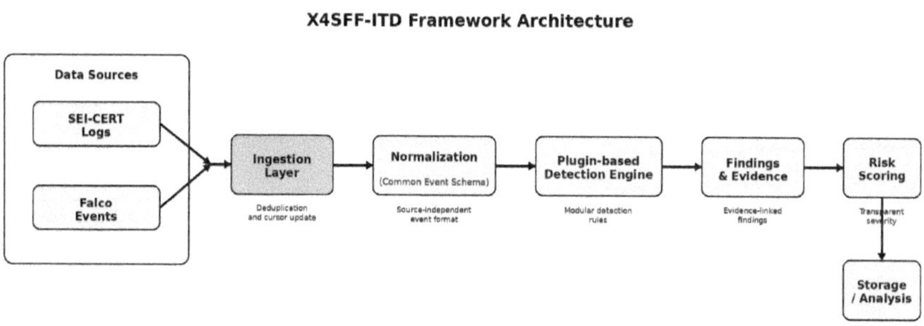

Fig. 1. Architecture of the X4SFF-ITD framework.

The normalized event schema acts as a lightweight contract between data sources and detection plugins, inspired by standardized security event representations such as ECS and OCSF [8,9]. Table 1 summarizes the core fields.

This schema enables detection logic to be written independently of the original source format. For example, a plugin can reason about logon activity, file access, or process execution without depending on whether the input was originally a CSV row, a JSON event, or a runtime security alert.

3.3 Idempotent Ingestion and State Management

A key design element of X4SFF-ITD is the combination of stable event hashing and cursor-based state management. These mechanisms address different aspects

Table 1. Core fields of the normalized event schema

Field	Description
`source`	Origin of the event, e.g., SEI-CERT or Falco
`event_type`	Normalized event category
`ts`	Event timestamp
`actor`	User, account, or process identity
`host`	Hostname or system identifier
`process`	Process name, when available
`command_line`	Executed command line, when available
`resource`	File, URL, object, or asset involved
`action`	Observed action, e.g., read, write, execute, or modify
`outcome`	Result of the action, e.g., success, failure, or unknown
`event_hash`	Stable fingerprint used for deduplication

of robust ingestion. The cursor tracks the last consumed position in a source, while the event hash prevents duplicate persistence.

Let S be a data source and c_S its cursor. The cursor represents the last processed position in the source. In a CSV dataset, it may correspond to the number of consumed rows; in a JSON lines stream, it may correspond to a byte offset. Each raw record r is normalized into an event e, and a deterministic fingerprint $h(e)$ is computed over a canonical representation of the normalized event. In the prototype, this fingerprint is stored as `event_hash` and constrained to be unique.

Algorithm 1. Idempotent ingestion with cursor-based recovery

```
Require: Data source S, batch size b
offset ← ReadCursor(S)
run ← StartIngestRun(S, offset)
while HasRecords(S, offset) do
    R ← ReadBatch(S, offset, b)
    for all r ∈ R do
        e ← Normalize(r)
        h ← Hash(e)
        if Exists(h) is false then
            InsertEvent(e, h)
            inserted ← inserted + 1
            EvaluatePlugins(e)
        else
            skipped ← skipped + 1
        end if
        processed ← processed + 1
    end for
    offset ← CurrentPosition(S)
    UpdateCursor(S, offset)
end while
CloseIngestRun(run, processed, inserted, skipped, offset)
```

Algorithm 1 separates progress tracking from duplicate prevention. Cursor state determines where the importer resumes, while the uniqueness of `event_hash` guarantees that replayed records are not persisted twice. This distinction is important because recovery may require re-reading part of the input source, but correctness is preserved at the persistence layer.

If ingestion is interrupted before the cursor is updated, some records may be replayed during recovery. However, already persisted events are skipped because their `event_hash` already exists. Therefore, failures may introduce bounded reprocessing, but not duplicate records. Each ingestion execution is also recorded as an ingestion run containing counters such as `processed`, `inserted`, `skipped`, and cursor values before and after execution.

3.4 Plugin-Based Detection and Explainable Scoring

Detection logic is implemented through modular plugins. A plugin encapsulates a specific rule or behavioral pattern and operates on normalized events. Event-centric plugins evaluate individual events, such as suspicious shell execution or after-hours logons, while window-based plugins aggregate recent events associated with the same actor or host, such as bursts of file operations.

At runtime, the engine iterates over registered plugins, invokes the matching function on each normalized event, extracts plugin-specific signals, computes the score, creates the finding, and links it to the supporting evidence. This lifecycle preserves traceability without coupling detection logic to source-specific input formats.

X4SFF-ITD uses a transparent scoring model. Each plugin is associated with a base score, adjusted through contextual modifiers derived from observed signals. The raw score is:

$$S_{\text{raw}}(p, \text{signals}) = base_p + \sum_i \Delta_i(p, \text{signals})$$

where $base_p$ is the base score associated with plugin p, and each Δ_i is a contextual contribution derived from observed signals. The final score is bounded to $[0, 100]$:

$$S(p, \text{signals}) = \min\left(100, \max\left(0, \text{round}(S_{\text{raw}})\right)\right)$$

The resulting score is mapped to a severity level such as low, medium, high, or critical. The scoring details, including base score, applied modifiers, observed signals, and configuration metadata, are stored with the finding, allowing analysts to inspect why a finding received a specific severity.

4 Prototype Implementation

A proof-of-concept prototype of X4SFF-ITD was implemented to validate the design choices described in Sect. 3. The prototype focuses on heterogeneous ingestion, normalization, idempotent persistence, plugin-based detection, evidence-linked findings, and configurable risk scoring. It is intended as a reproducible experimental implementation rather than as a production-grade deployment.

4.1 Implementation Stack and Data Model

The prototype is implemented as a Python web application based on Django, with SQLite as the storage backend. Django provides a structured data model, deterministic management commands for command-line execution, and an administrative interface for inspecting persisted objects. SQLite was adopted to simplify deployment in a single-node proof-of-concept environment; production-oriented deployments would require a transactional database such as PostgreSQL.

The core data entities are `NormalizedEvent`, `IngestCursor`, `IngestRun`, `Finding`, and `FindingEvidence`. `NormalizedEvent` stores source-independent events and their `event_hash`; `IngestCursor` stores the last processed position for each source; `IngestRun` records execution metadata such as `processed`, `inserted`, `skipped`, and cursor values; `Finding` stores the generated alert, score, severity, and explanation; and `FindingEvidence` links each finding to the supporting normalized events.

4.2 Data Sources and Ingestion Workflow

The prototype integrates SEI-CERT logs and Falco events. SEI-CERT records are consumed from CSV files and include event kinds such as logon, email, HTTP, file, and device activity where available. Falco events are consumed in JSON lines format and mapped to the same normalized schema. For SEI-CERT, the cursor represents the number of consumed rows; for Falco, it represents a byte offset in the JSONL stream.

The ingestion workflow is source-specific only before normalization. After normalization, all records follow the same processing path: event hash computation, duplicate check, persistence of new events, optional plugin evaluation, and ingestion-run update. The detection engine is invoked only on newly inserted events, avoiding duplicate findings when records are replayed during recovery or deduplication tests.

4.3 Detection Plugins and Evidence Linking

The prototype includes representative rule-based plugins covering both event-centric and window-based detection. Event-centric plugins evaluate individual events, such as after-hours logons or suspicious shell execution. Window-based plugins aggregate recent events associated with the same actor or host, such as bursts of file-system operations or email activity.

When a plugin detects a suspicious pattern, the prototype creates a `Finding` and links it to the triggering event or event window through `FindingEvidence`. Each finding stores the plugin identifier, actor, host, timestamp, severity, numerical score, and structured explanation. The explanation includes observed signals, threshold values, scoring contributions, and configuration metadata.

The risk scoring model is implemented through an external configuration file defining severity thresholds and plugin-specific parameters such as base scores, modifiers, and caps. At runtime, plugins extract signals, the scoring module computes the bounded score and severity, and the resulting details are persisted with the finding. Django Admin and a lightweight reporting interface are used only to inspect events, cursors, runs, findings, and linked evidence.

5 Experimental Evaluation

This section evaluates X4SFF-ITD with respect to framework-level properties: ingestion correctness, resume and deduplication behavior, explainability of generated findings, and processing overhead. The evaluation does not aim to demonstrate detection superiority over machine learning or graph-based insider threat detection systems.

5.1 Setup and Metrics

The evaluation uses SEI-CERT user activity logs as the primary dataset [13], considering event categories such as logon, email, HTTP, and file/device activity where applicable. Falco events are used as an additional JSONL telemetry source [7] to validate ingestion and normalization of runtime security events. Experiments are executed through deterministic Django management commands, using parameters such as `limit`, `batch-size`, `reset-cursor`, and `run-engine`.

Each execution produces an `IngestRun` record containing the source, event kind, execution status, input limit, batch size, processed records, inserted records, skipped records, and cursor values before and after execution. These metadata make the experiments inspectable and allow the reported results to be reproduced from persisted run-level evidence.

The evaluation uses the following metrics: `processed`, `inserted`, and `skipped` records to validate ingestion behavior; cursor values before and after execution to validate resume; and throughput in events per second to measure processing overhead. Precision, recall, and F1-score are not used as primary metrics because the implemented plugins validate framework-level properties rather than covering the complete insider threat labeling space. This limitation is discussed in Sect. 6.

5.2 Ingestion Robustness

To validate resume and deduplication, three controlled runs are executed over the same SEI-CERT email input with fixed `limit` and `batch-size`. Run #1 resets the cursor and ingests the first input window. Run #2 executes the same import without resetting the cursor, validating resume from the previous offset. Run #3 resets the cursor and replays the first window, validating hash-based deduplication.

As shown in Table 2, Run #2 advances the cursor from the previous position, confirming cursor-based resume. Run #3 replays records already persisted during

Table 2. Resume and deduplication validation on SEI-CERT email logs

Run	Reset	Processed	Inserted	Skipped	Cursor after
Run #1	true	5000	4900	100	5000
Run #2	false	5000	5000	0	10000
Run #3	true	5000	0	5000	5000

Run #1, and all events are skipped because their `event_hash` values already exist. These results confirm that cursor tracking improves recovery efficiency, while event hashing prevents duplicate persistence during replay.

5.3 Explainability and Performance

The explainability of the framework is evaluated by inspecting the structure of generated findings. Each finding stores the plugin identifier, actor, host, timestamp, numerical score, severity level, structured explanation, and evidence links to the normalized events that triggered the detection. For example, the after-hours logon plugin records the temporal conditions and contextual modifiers contributing to the final score, while window-based plugins record the aggregated event counts and thresholds that caused the finding.

This structure allows analysts to distinguish between the detection condition, the supporting evidence, and the scoring rationale. Therefore, the output is intended for triage and investigation rather than for automatic attribution of malicious intent.

Performance is evaluated by comparing ingestion-only execution with execution where the plugin engine is enabled. Throughput is computed as:

$$\text{throughput}_{eps} = \frac{N_{processed}}{T_{seconds}}$$

where $N_{processed}$ is the number of processed records and $T_{seconds}$ is the execution time in seconds. Table 3 reports representative results.

The results show a clear overhead when the detection engine is enabled, as expected. This overhead is caused by plugin evaluation, possible window-based queries, finding creation, evidence linking, and scoring. These results should not be interpreted as proof of production-grade scalability; rather, they quantify the cost of explainable detection relative to ingestion-only processing in the proof-of-concept.

Compared with operational platforms such as Wazuh, Falco, Splunk UBA, and Microsoft Purview IRM, X4SFF-ITD does not aim to provide broader operational coverage or higher detection accuracy. Instead, its contribution is the explicit combination of normalized multi-source ingestion, idempotent processing, evidence-linked findings, and explainable scoring in a reproducible proof-of-concept framework. This qualitative positioning is intended to clarify the architectural focus of X4SFF-ITD, not to claim superiority over existing systems.

Table 3. Throughput comparison with and without detection engine

Kind	Records	Engine	Throughput (eps)
email	50k	on	143.0
email	50k	off	5893.7
email	100k	on	201.3
email	100k	off	6140.3
logon	100k	on	554.4
logon	100k	off	6819.1
http	200k	on	476.3
http	200k	off	5710.4

6 Discussion and Limitations

The evaluation shows that X4SFF-ITD supports a reproducible proof-of-concept pipeline for insider threat detection, validating framework-level properties such as normalized ingestion, duplicate handling, cursor-based resume, evidence-linked findings, and explainable scoring. However, the current prototype should be interpreted as an architectural and experimental validation rather than as a production-ready insider threat detection system.

Several limitations remain. First, the framework focuses on technical telemetry represented as normalized events, such as logons, file operations, process execution, and runtime events. It does not infer user intent, incorporate HR or organizational signals, or automatically distinguish malicious insiders from negligent users or compromised accounts. Generated findings must therefore be treated as investigatory signals requiring analyst validation.

Second, the implemented plugins are primarily rule-based. This improves transparency and auditability, but may not capture subtle behavioral deviations, long-term low-and-slow strategies, or complex multi-step attack chains. The current evaluation also does not provide a full quantitative assessment of detection effectiveness in terms of precision, recall, or F1-score, because the implemented plugins validate selected framework capabilities rather than the complete insider threat labeling space.

Finally, scalability and usability require further evaluation. The performance results quantify the overhead introduced by the detection engine under controlled input sizes, but they do not demonstrate production-grade scalability under concurrent ingestion, distributed deployment, or real-time high-volume streaming. Future evaluations should also assess analyst workload, false-positive management, triage time, and explanation usefulness.

7 Conclusion

This paper presented X4SFF-ITD, an extensible and explainable plugin-based framework for insider threat detection. The framework combines heterogeneous telemetry ingestion, normalization into a common event schema, cursor-based state management, event-hash deduplication, plugin-based detection, evidence-linked findings, and transparent risk scoring.

The proof-of-concept evaluation validated framework-level properties rather than detection superiority. In particular, the ingestion pipeline correctly handled resume and deduplication scenarios, generated audit metadata through ingestion runs, produced explainable findings linked to supporting evidence, and exposed the processing overhead introduced by plugin-based detection. Future work will focus on richer behavioral models, temporal and graph-based correlation, broader datasets, quantitative detection metrics, false-positive analysis, and scalability evaluation under more realistic operational conditions.

References

1. European Union Agency for Cybersecurity (ENISA): ENISA Threat Landscape 2020: Insider Threat. ENISA Technical Report (2020). https://www.enisa.europa.eu/publications/enisa-threat-landscape-2020-insider-threat
2. Liu, L., De Vel, O., Han, Q.-L., Zhang, J., Xiang, Y.: Detecting and preventing cyber insider threats: a survey. IEEE Commun. Surv. Tutorials **20**(2), 1397–1417 (2018)
3. Cybersecurity and Infrastructure Security Agency (CISA): Insider Threats (2024). https://www.cisa.gov/topics/physical-security/insider-threat-mitigation/insider-threats, Accessed 17 Dec 2025
4. National Institute of Standards and Technology: Artificial Intelligence Risk Management Framework (AI RMF 1.0) (2023). https://nvlpubs.nist.gov/nistpubs/ai/NIST.AI.100-1.pdf
5. Molnar, C.: Interpretable Machine Learning (2025). https://christophm.github.io/interpretable-ml-book/
6. Gunning, D., Aha, D.: DARPA's Explainable Artificial Intelligence (XAI) Program (2019). https://arxiv.org/abs/1902.01876
7. The Falco Authors (CNCF): Falco Documentation (2025). https://falco.org/docs/, Accessed 17 Dec 2025
8. Amazon Web Services: Open Cybersecurity Schema Framework (OCSF) Integration with Amazon Security Lake (2024). https://docs.aws.amazon.com/security-lake/latest/userguide/open-cybersecurity-schema-framework.html Accessed 17 Dec 2025
9. Elastic: Elastic Common Schema (ECS) Reference (2025). https://www.elastic.co/guide/en/ecs/current/ecs-reference.html Accessed 17 Dec 2025
10. Chandola, V., Banerjee, A., Kumar, V.: Anomaly detection: a survey. ACM Comput. Surv. **41**(3) (2009). https://doi.org/10.1145/1541880.1541882
11. Tuor, A., Kaplan, S., Hutchinson, B., Nichols, N., Robinson, S.: Deep Learning for Unsupervised Insider Threat Detection in Structured Cybersecurity Data Streams (2017). https://arxiv.org/abs/1710.00811
12. Eberle, W., Holder, L.: Insider threat detection using graph-based anomaly detection. In: Proceedings of the 2009 Cybersecurity Applications & Technology Conference for Homeland Security (CATCH), pp. 237–241 (2009). https://doi.org/10.1109/CATCH.2009.47

13. Software Engineering Institute (SEI), Carnegie Mellon University: Insider Threat Test Dataset (2024). https://www.sei.cmu.edu/library/insider-threat-test-dataset/ Accessed 17 Dec 2025
14. Microsoft: Microsoft Purview Insider Risk Management Documentation (2025). https://learn.microsoft.com/en-us/purview/insider-risk-management Accessed 17 Dec 2025
15. Wazuh: Wazuh Documentation (2025). https://documentation.wazuh.com/ Accessed 17 Dec 2025
16. Security Onion Solutions: Security Onion Documentation (2025). https://docs.securityonion.net/ Accessed 17 Dec 2025

Ensuring Trust

Leveraging Device Motion Events to Track Fraud in Remote Identity Verification

Luís Rosário(✉), Sérgio Boer, Pedro Madeira, Arthur Pajot, Adam Wozniak, and Daniel Serrano

Entrust Identity Verification Biometrics Team, 1187 Park Place, Minneapolis, MN 55379, USA
{luis.rosario,sergio.boer,pedro.madeira,arthur.pajot, adam.wozniak,daniel.serrano}@entrust.com
https://www.entrust.com/

Abstract. With an increase in the adoption of Identity Verification (IDV) for online services, and an ever-increasing rate of sophisticated identity fraud attempts in part due to the prevalence of deepfake usage, this paper introduces a novel approach to perform fraud detection in remote identity verification systems by leveraging device motion events collected during user sessions. Specifically, this work contributes a feature engineering and modeling strategy that exploits physical constraints of gravitational acceleration and signal patterns captured via the browser DeviceMotionEvent API. By engineering features from both observed fraud behaviours and frequency analysis, a Gradient Boosted Tree classifier was trained on an expert-reviewed labelled dataset. The proposed method achieved strong performance, with a test *precision* of 0.918 ± 0.032, *recall* of 0.949 ± 0.021, *F1* of 0.933 ± 0.020, and *PR_AUC* of 0.979 ± 0.011, effectively distinguishing fraudulent from genuine sessions. These results demonstrate that the engineered features enable lightweight, near real time detection of injected or synthetic motion data, showing promise in the usage of behavioural biometric data as an additional evaluation signal to increase the overall security of identity verification systems.

Keywords: Identity Verification · Deepfakes · Signal processing · Identity Fraud · Gradient boosting · Behavioral biometric data

1 Introduction

1.1 Identity Verification and Fraud

For the past few years, the landscape of Identity Verification (IDV) has been brought to the foreground, as major legislative shifts have transitioned digital authentication from a convenience to a regulatory mandate.

Supported by Entrust.

© ICST Institute for Computer Sciences, Social Informatics and Telecommunications Engineering 2027
Published by Springer Nature Switzerland AG 2027. All Rights Reserved
H. Neukirchen et al. (Eds.): ICDF2C 2026, LNICST 720, pp. 429–440, 2027.
https://doi.org/10.1007/978-3-032-37274-1_25

In the European Union, the adoption of Regulation (EU) 2024/1183 has institutionalized the European Digital Identity Wallet, requiring member states to provide a secure digital identity that is recognized across borders and private services [4]. In parallel, the United Kingdom has intensified requirements for age-restricted digital environments through the Online Safety Act 2023. This legislation mandates the implementation of age verification or age estimation technologies to prevent minors from accessing age-inappropriate content online [17].

With the widespread adoption of online verification services and the rapid advancement of technologies that enable identity fraud such as highly realistic GenAI video generation systems (e.g., Google Veo, OpenAI Sora, Runway Gen-3), the prevalence of sophisticated fraud attempts has reached unprecedented levels and continues to grow more difficult to detect over time [3].

Given this, there is a case to be made to keep on improving existing IDV solutions, making them more resilient to fraud, either by using more cutting-edge detection methods or making the authentication flow harder to spoof (e.g., requiring the applicant to perform a randomized task).

1.2 Behavioral Biometric Data - Device Motion Events

The use of behavioral biometric data has evolved significantly, transitioning from foundational research on areas such as human motion tracking [5,18] into being incorporated in complex fraud detection systems [12] or as part of an authentication method [6,7,9,13] such as the analysis of touchscreen interaction patterns [8].

Following this trend, the use of behavioral biometric data, such as Device Motion data, could be a natural progression to enhance the fraud-detection capabilities of existing biometric authentication services by introducing new layers of defense against potential fraud vectors, such as the injection of Deepfakes or the use of stolen media posing as real users.

By collecting *DeviceMotionEvents* data from browser Web APIs [11], which retrieve information from a device's accelerometer and gyroscope sensors, it enables the analysis of several data modalities, including device acceleration (with and without the gravitational component) and rotation rate of all three axis. The individual axis measurements obtained from these events are defined according to the device coordinate frame specified by the World Wide Web Consortium (W3C), as illustrated in Fig. 1. This data then allows for the identification of unique movement profiles similar to those established in multi-modal behavioral studies [16].

Considering this, this work contributes a feature engineering strategy grounded in the physical constraints of gravitational acceleration exploiting invariants such as magnitude stability and patterns captured through the browser based DeviceMotionEvent API and demonstrates that these features enable lightweight, near real time detection of injected or synthetic motion data in remote identity verification sessions.

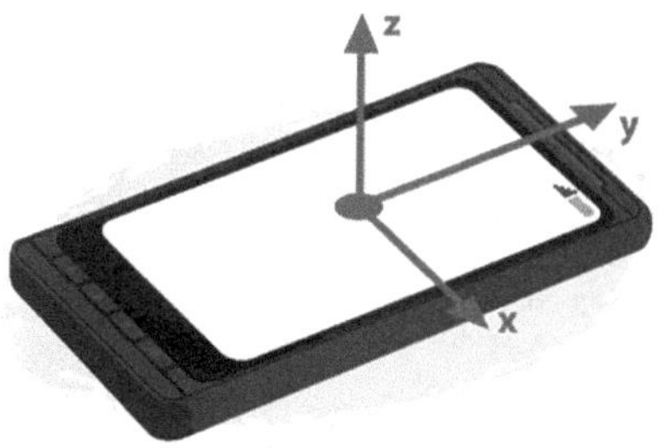

Fig. 1. W3C proposed device coordinate frame for motion and device orientation. Image source: [10].

2 Device Motion Features

During the initial stages of this research, for sake of simplicity it was decided to narrow the scope of device motion data analysis to the most informative signal available from the *DeviceMotionEvents*. For this purpose, the gravitational acceleration data was selected as the best candidate, as it encodes the gravity vector projected onto each device axis, reflecting device orientation and tilt relative to Earth's gravitational field.

During feature development, it was considered not only to treat each axis individually but also to aggregate them, since the gravitational acceleration should adhere to the laws of physics regardless of device positioning over time. For instance, the magnitude of the gravitational acceleration vector should remain approximately $9.8\,\mathrm{m/s^2}$, as dictated by Earth's gravity. This physical constraint provides a useful reference for detecting anomalies in the recorded motion data by its resulting features.

With these principles in mind, two complementary sets of features were engineered to capture distinct aspects of fraudulent behaviour (51 features in total): **observed fraud behaviour features** and **frequency analysis features**.

2.1 Observed Fraud Behaviour Features

As the name implies, this first set of features was derived primarily from empirical observation of gravitational acceleration data in known fraud cases found in live traffic. In collaboration with domain experts in fraud, data generated using commercially available injection tools was also analyzed to better understand the characteristic behaviour of synthetically generated device motion. This approach provided insight into what could be considered fraudulent data behavior, whether originating from synthetic data injected with commercial tools or from genuine data exhibiting patterns indicative of fraud (e.g. motion patterns inconsistent with the uploaded media).

With these observations in mind, this feature set development centered on two main areas: identifying patterns indicative of fraudulent behavior, such as a lack of device movement throughout a remote identity verification session (e.g.

by examining the standard deviation of individual and aggregated axes), and detecting nonsensical, injected gravitational acceleration data, which could be achieved by checking core physical heuristics that the data must comply with, such as:

- The magnitude of the gravitational acceleration being close to 9.8 m/s^2 at all times;
- Individual axis pairs should exhibit the expected value correlation, given the device coordinate frame described in Fig. 1.

The resulting feature set from these observations consists of 19 distinct features.

2.2 Frequency Analysis Features

Besides solely relying on known data patterns or abnormal behaviour that could be inferred by the feature set detailed above, this feature set is intended to better reflect the underlying spectral characteristics of device motion gravitation acceleration data. To achieve this, a spectral analysis of the signal on each axis is performed using the Fast Fourier Transform (*FFT*). The rationale is that genuine device motion exhibits a characteristic frequency profile shaped by natural hand tremors and postural sway which would fall under a set low frequency generally below 12 Hz [15,18], whereas injected signals could be prone to concentrate energy in narrow or atypical frequency bands.

While the *FFT* provides a global frequency representation of the entire session, it discards temporal information that may be relevant for fraud detection. To address this, spectrogram-based features were also derived, which divide the signal into overlapping time windows and apply the *FFT* to each one, yielding a time-frequency representation which reflects how the frequency content of the signal evolves throughout the session.

From the combination of *FFT*-based and spectrogram-based analysis a total of 32 frequency analysis features were derived.

3 Modeling

3.1 Data

For the purpose of this work, two distinct manually curated device motion datasets were developed from several thousand data points obtained from live traffic of remote identity verification sessions in the wild, which have been labelled by domain experts. The raw data used to engineer these feature datasets consists of three distinct time series, corresponding to each gravitational acceleration axis, collected during the applicant's IDV session. Both datasets underwent identical pre-processing steps prior to feature extraction. Specifically, the data was capped to the last 30 s of each session to mitigate session duration skewness and to focus on the time interval most likely to coincide with a short live selfie recording, as the vast majority of sessions do not exceed 20 s. Additionally, sessions presenting data issues (e.g. missing values) were excluded. The remaining data was then used for feature engineering.

The first dataset consists of features obtained from **660 confirmed fraudulent applicant session** which contains a diverse set of different fraud types (e.g. deepfakes, injections of genuine videos). The second dataset was constructed from a selection of **6204 genuine applicant sessions**. Both these datasets were then appropriately labelled and combined for use in training.

The combined dataset is made up of capture sessions from **4936 unique applicants**. Gender and geographic data are derived from associated document uploads. Gender metadata was available for 4247 applicants (86.0%), yielding a total dataset split of **33.9% female, 52.1% male, and 14.0% unknown/missing**. Geography metadata and mappable regional assignment was available for 4,643 applicants (94.1%). Using a UN M49-inspired, ISO 3166-based grouping adapted to the reporting bins used here, the **regional distribution was 31.6% North America, 18.2% Eastern Europe, 18.0% Western Europe, 15.2% East Asia, 5.6% South America, 2.7% Africa, 1.9% West Asia, 0.8% India, and 5.9% unknown/missing/unmapped region**. These missing data rates are reported explicitly to contextualise representativeness.

3.2 Training

For training, a Gradient Boosted Trees classifier was selected, as it tends to perform well on structured tabular data. Additionally, its support for *SHAP (SHapley Additive exPlanations)* based feature importance analysis [1] which provides valuable interpretability, enabling a deeper understanding of the features driving the fraud detection decisions.

The combined dataset mentioned in Sect. 3.1 was split into training (80%) and test (20%) sets ensuring that the proportion of fraud and legitimate samples was preserved across both sets and that all sessions belonging to a given applicant are assigned exclusively to either set. Due to the imbalanced nature of the data, balanced per-sample weights were computed using *scikit-learn's compute_sample_weight* utility and applied during training, thus reducing model bias towards the majority genuine class.

Hyperparameter optimization was performed by using a grid search (Table 1) approach with 5-fold cross-validation scored on *Average Precision* (*PR-AUC*) as it provides a more robust evaluation of model performance under significant class imbalance by focusing on the detection of the minority fraud class [14]. The same approach was used for the baseline models mentioned in Sect. 4, with the respective grid search parameter spaces being in Tables 2 and 3.

Early stopping was also used to prevent overfitting when no tangible improvement is seen during training

Model performance was assessed on both training and test sets using the following metrics: *Precision*, *Recall*, *Accuracy*, *F1 Score*, *PR_AUC*, and *ROC_AUC*.

Table 1. Gradient Boosted Trees hyperparameter grid search space.

Hyperparameter	Values
Number of estimators	{100, 200}
Learning rate	{0.05, 0.1}
Maximum tree depth	{3, 5}
Subsample ratio	{0.8}
Minimum samples per split	{20, 50}
Minimum samples per leaf	{10, 20}

Table 2. Logistic Regression hyperparameter grid search space.

Hyperparameter	Values
C	{0.01, 0.1, 1.0, 10.0}
Solver	{lbfgs}
Maximum iterations	{1000}

Table 3. Shallow Decision Tree hyperparameter grid search space.

Hyperparameter	Values
Maximum tree depth	{2, 3, 5}
Minimum samples per split	{10, 20, 50}
Minimum samples per leaf	{5, 10, 20}

All the results in the following result Sect. 4 were obtained across 10 independent training runs, each using a distinct user-disjoint train/test partition.

4 Results and Discussion

Starting with Table 4, which reports per feature group performance, it can be seen that the observed fraud behaviour feature group outperforms the Frequency Analysis one, on every test metric except recall where it is marginally surpassed (0.920 ± 0.026 vs 0.932 ± 0.015). This suggests that while spectral features are slightly better at catching fraud cases, the observed behaviour features produce fewer false positives and achieve stronger overall discrimination (PR_AUC 0.967 ± 0.011 vs 0.941 ± 0.019). Combining both feature groups yields substantial gains across all metrics. Precision increases by over 4 percentage points compared to either group alone, and PR_AUC rises from 0.967 ± 0.011 to 0.979 ± 0.011. This confirms the complementary nature of both feature groups which seem to target different aspects of what is considered fraudulent behaviour.

Since the entire feature space is of high dimensionality (51 total features), a top k feature dimensionality analysis was performed to identify the minimal feature set with negligible performance loss 5. The features were ranked by mean

Table 4. Feature group performance analysis: test-set metrics (mean ± std) over 10 training runs.

Feature Group	Precision	Recall	F1	PR_AUC	ROC_AUC	Accuracy
Frequency Analysis	0.844 ± 0.039	0.932 ± 0.015	0.885 ± 0.019	0.941 ± 0.019	0.989 ± 0.006	0.976 ± 0.005
Observed Fraud Behaviour	0.876 ± 0.040	0.920 ± 0.026	0.897 ± 0.021	0.967 ± 0.011	0.991 ± 0.005	0.980 ± 0.003
All	**0.918 ± 0.032**	**0.949 ± 0.021**	**0.933 ± 0.020**	**0.979 ± 0.011**	**0.994 ± 0.005**	**0.987 ± 0.004**

absolute SHAP value from a full-feature training run, and for each value of k, the model was retrained over 10 runs under the same configuration described above, using only the top k ranked features.

Table 5. Top k feature analysis: test-set metrics (mean ± std) over 10 training runs.

top k	Precision	Recall	F1	PR_AUC	ROC_AUC	Accuracy
5	0.809 ± 0.021	0.939 ± 0.024	0.869 ± 0.016	0.953 ± 0.013	0.991 ± 0.003	0.973 ± 0.003
10	0.854 ± 0.043	0.942 ± 0.023	0.895 ± 0.027	0.970 ± 0.012	0.994 ± 0.003	0.979 ± 0.006
15	0.881 ± 0.038	0.945 ± 0.023	0.912 ± 0.027	0.974 ± 0.012	0.994 ± 0.004	0.982 ± 0.006
20	0.875 ± 0.043	0.953 ± 0.026	0.912 ± 0.027	0.975 ± 0.012	0.994 ± 0.004	0.982 ± 0.006
25	0.885 ± 0.029	0.952 ± 0.023	0.917 ± 0.020	0.975 ± 0.012	0.994 ± 0.004	0.983 ± 0.004
30	0.878 ± 0.025	0.946 ± 0.025	0.911 ± 0.018	0.974 ± 0.012	0.994 ± 0.004	0.982 ± 0.004
All	**0.918 ± 0.032**	**0.949 ± 0.021**	**0.933 ± 0.020**	**0.979 ± 0.011**	**0.994 ± 0.005**	**0.987 ± 0.004**

Table 5 shows that at k=15 the top 15 features already achieve close to the maximum F1 score (0.912±0.027 vs 0.933±0.020) and PR-AUC (0.974±0.012 vs 0.979±0.011). The performance gains between k=5 and k=15 highlight that features ranked 6 to 15 still provide substantial discriminative power, while beyond k=15 all metrics plateau, with less important features only aiding disambiguation in borderline samples and increasing F1 up to a maximum of 0.933 ± 0.020 when the full feature set is used.

Table 6. Baseline comparison: test-set metrics (mean ± std) over 10 user-disjoint splits. Also includes baseline and proposed model runs using top 15 features

Model	Precision	Recall	F1	PR_AUC	ROC_AUC	Accuracy
Majority Class	0.000	0.000	0.000	0.096	0.500	0.904
Gravitational Threshold	0.309 ± 0.018	0.589 ± 0.038	0.405 ± 0.022	0.199 ± 0.016	0.729 ± 0.016	0.834 ± 0.009
Shallow Tree (k=15)	0.692 ± 0.036	0.939 ± 0.018	0.796 ± 0.024	0.904 ± 0.021	0.965 ± 0.007	0.954 ± 0.007
Shallow Tree	0.737 ± 0.053	0.943 ± 0.026	0.826 ± 0.034	0.892 ± 0.039	0.968 ± 0.012	0.962 ± 0.009
Logistic Regression (k=15)	0.781 ± 0.041	0.943 ± 0.022	0.854 ± 0.023	0.951 ± 0.014	0.988 ± 0.006	0.969 ± 0.006
Logistic Regression	0.840 ± 0.025	0.960 ± 0.018	0.895 ± 0.010	0.957 ± 0.017	0.991 ± 0.004	0.978 ± 0.002
Proposed model (k=15)	**0.881 ± 0.038**	**0.945 ± 0.023**	**0.912 ± 0.027**	**0.974 ± 0.012**	**0.994 ± 0.004**	**0.982 ± 0.006**
Proposed model	**0.918 ± 0.032**	**0.949 ± 0.021**	**0.933 ± 0.020**	**0.979 ± 0.011**	**0.994 ± 0.005**	**0.987 ± 0.004**

Finally, Table 6 compares the proposed model trained on both the top 15 features and the full feature set against several baselines: a majority-class classifier, a gravitational-threshold heuristic, shallow decision trees, and logistic regression. All models were evaluated over 10 independent user-disjoint splits and as mentioned in 3.2 hyperparameter tuning for the logistic regression and shallow tree baselines was done via 5-fold cross-validation on each training partition.

The majority-class baseline, which always predicts the dominant (genuine) class, achieves 0.904 accuracy but zero precision, recall, and F1, confirming that accuracy alone is misleading under class imbalance. The gravitational threshold heuristic, which flags sessions based on whether the mean accelerometer magnitude deviates from 9.8 m/s^2, reaches an F1 of only 0.405 ± 0.022, demonstrating that this single heuristic is also unreliable. Shallow decision trees improve substantially, with the top 15 variant reaching an F1 of 0.796 ± 0.024 and the full-feature variant 0.826 ± 0.034; however, the shallow tree with all features shows a slight drop in PR-AUC (0.892 ± 0.039 vs 0.904 ± 0.021). Logistic regression closes part of the gap, where the top 15 variant achieves an F1 of 0.854 ± 0.023 and a PR-AUC of 0.951 ± 0.014, and the full-feature variant further improves to an F1 of 0.895 ± 0.010 and a PR-AUC of 0.957 ± 0.017, benefiting from access to the complete feature space.

The proposed Gradient Boosted Trees model outperforms all baselines across every metric in both configurations. When limited to the top 15 features, it achieves an F1 of 0.912 ± 0.027 and a PR-AUC of 0.974 ± 0.012, already surpassing the best baseline (logistic regression on all features). With the full feature set, performance improves further to an F1 of 0.933 ± 0.020 and a PR-AUC of 0.979 ± 0.011, confirming that the combination of gradient boosting with the complete engineered feature set provides the best results for fraud detection.

4.1 Feature Importance Analysis

Figure 2 presents the *SHAP* beeswarm plot for the top 15 most relevant features, ordered by mean absolute *SHAP* value, with the most important features at the top. In this plot, each point represents a single prediction, and its color indicates the actual value of the feature relative to its range. The horizontal axis shows the *SHAP* value, which reflects the extent to which each feature value influenced the prediction toward being classified as fraud (positive *SHAP*) or as genuine (negative *SHAP*).

Among the top 5 most influential features, 4 belong to the observed fraud behaviour feature set. These are strong examples of informative features, largely due to the clean polarization between high/low values and their corresponding positive and negative *SHAP* values. Specifically, low values for both the z and y standard deviations, which indicate little to no variation in the device signal along these axes, tend to be a strong indicator of fraud (positive *SHAP*), while high standard deviation values are more characteristic of genuine sessions. Since std_x does not appear in the plot, it proves itself to be considerably less influential than its counterparts. This is expected, as most device movement during a session occurs along the y and z axes with std_x only yielding meaningful non-zero values when the device is tilted sideways or held in landscape orientation.

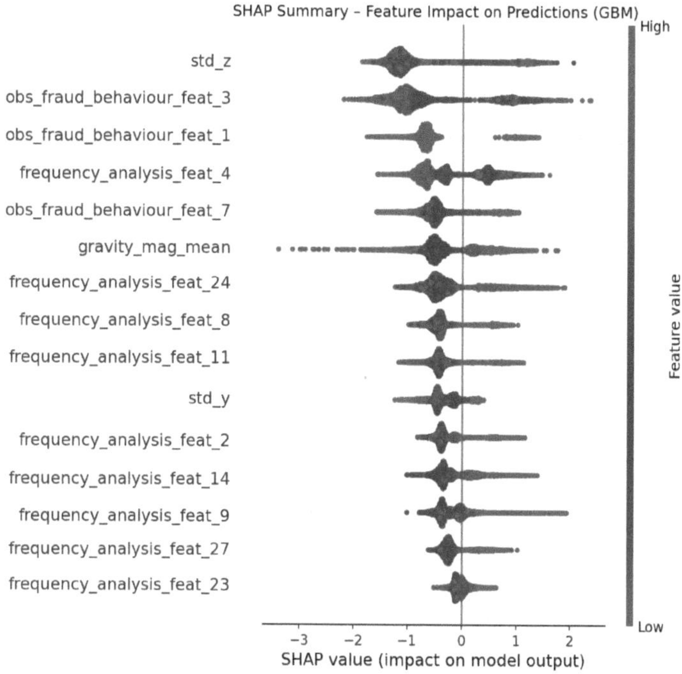

Fig. 2. SHAP value feature importance beeswarm plot from training (Top 15 features - 9 features belong to the frequency analysis group while 6 to the observed fraud behaviour group.)

Another feature worth discussing is the *gravity_mag_mean*, which stands out due to its long negative *SHAP* value tail, making it a clear outlier among the other features. While high feature values still have some marginal influence in identifying fraud, the pronounced negative tail suggests a threshold-dependent exclusionary logic: a "low" gravitational acceleration magnitude is interpreted by the model as a strong indicator that the sample is genuine, regardless of other feature values. This is supported by the feature's distribution shown in Fig. 3, where the vast majority of fraud samples exhibit a magnitude greater than $9.8\,m/s^2$. It is important to note, however, that this low-value exclusion could have been skewed by the range of feature values present in the fraud dataset used. One could argue that any value drifting away from $9.8\ m/s^2$, in any direction, might be indicative of fraud, even if this was not observed in the obtained fraud sample.

4.2 Real-World Validation

Beyond the experimental results presented above, positive validation has been obtained for several observed fraud behaviour features that have since been periodically applied to independently sourced, expert-labelled datasets reflect-

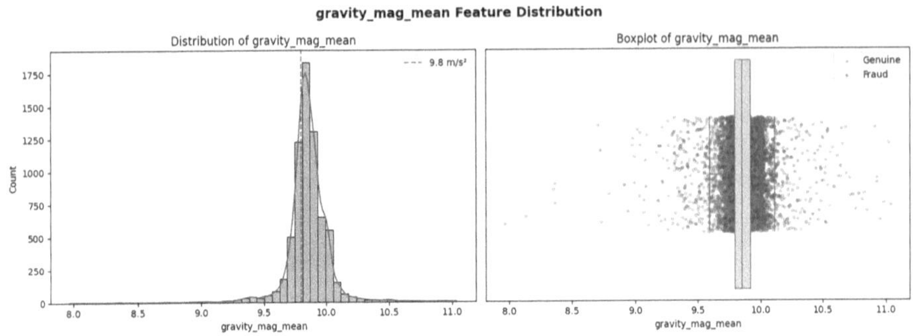

Fig. 3. Gravity magnitude mean feature value distribution.

ing recent fraud activity. These datasets are compiled at regular intervals from operational traffic distinct from the training data. This exercise has proved valuable, as these features have consistently uncovered previously unseen fraudulent sessions.

5 Limitations

Understandably, regardless of the positive results presented a motion only system is not sufficient to guarantee robustness against a fully adaptive attacker. Our method aims to capture legitimate human like device motion and flag out of distribution behaviour, but it may be blind to injected genuine pre recorded traces or sufficiently realistic synthetic signals. We therefore frame it as one layer in a defense in depth (*"Swiss cheese"*) architecture for remote identity verification, alongside PAD (presentation attack detection), IAD (injection attack detection), other behavioural signals, active or passive randomization, and cross-checks between biometric and document capture. Its role is to increase attacker effort, not to serve as the sole defense.

6 Future Work

Continued development of solutions that leverage these or similar signals is planned, including efforts to incorporate additional device motion and orientation signals, such as rotation rate, to derive new features. Ultimately, the creation of a multimodal model capable of interpreting subtle background movements in video media and cross-checking them with recorded device motion data represents the natural end goal, one that could prove to be a compelling answer to the persistent challenge of detecting fraud perpetrated through the injection of genuine, often stolen, videos.

Additionally, we plan to explore integrating device motion features with complementary device intelligence signals, such as mobile fingerprinting and metadata, into a unified fraud scoring framework. The motion-based features proposed here capture physical behavioural anomalies, while device intelligence signals target environmental inconsistencies (e.g., emulated hardware). We hypothesize that combining these orthogonal signals can further improve the detection of fraud attempts that rely on exploiting a single modality, reinforcing the case for a holistic, multi-signal approach to fraud detection.

7 Conclusion

This work demonstrates that browser based DeviceMotionEvents can be effectively leveraged to enhance fraud detection in remote identity verification services. By engineering a comprehensive set of features around gravitational acceleration data, spanning both empirically observed fraud behaviours and frequency based signal characteristics, and using them in conjunction with a Gradient Boosted Trees classifier, the proposed approach achieved strong performance, with test precision of 0.918 ± 0.032, recall of 0.949 ± 0.021, F1 of 0.933 ± 0.020, and PR_AUC of 0.979 ± 0.011, beating all tested baseline models in the process.

Additionally, using the complete feature set was shown to contribute to higher performance overall, with a more impactful improvement in F1 (0.933 ± 0.020 vs 0.912 ± 0.027 for $k = 15$) and precision (0.918 ± 0.032 vs 0.881 ± 0.038 for $k = 15$).

The feature analysis provided interpretability, confirming the relevance of the engineered features. These results highlight the potential value of device motion analysis as a robust, practical layer for improving the security of existing digital identity verification systems.

References

1. Shap documentation. https://shap.readthedocs.io/en/latest/, Accessed 20 March 2026
2. (Feb 2025). https://www.w3.org/TR/2025/CRD-orientation-event-20250212/, Accessed 20 March 2026
3. Cloud, K., Severyukhin, A., Brovin, I.: How identity fraud is changing in the age of AI (Dec 2025). https://www.weforum.org/stories/2025/12/how-identity-fraud-is-increasing-in-the-age-of-ai/, Accessed 26 March 2026
4. Council of European Union: Council regulation (EU) no 2024/1183 (2024). https://eur-lex.europa.eu/eli/reg/2024/1183/oj
5. Dapeng, Q., Pang, G.K., Mui, M.K., Lam, D.C.: A new pcb-based low-cost accelerometer for human motion sensing. In: 2008 IEEE International Conference on Automation and Logistics (Sep 2008). https://doi.org/10.1109/ical.2008.4636119
6. Feng, T., Zhao, X., Shi, W.: Investigating mobile device picking-up motion as a novel biometric modality. In: 2013 IEEE Sixth International Conference on Biometrics: Theory, Applications and Systems (BTAS), pp. 1–6 (Sep 2013). https://doi.org/10.1109/btas.2013.6712701
7. Finnegan, O.L., et al.: The utility of behavioral biometrics in user authentication and demographic characteristic detection: a scoping review. Systematic Rev. **13**(1) (2024). https://doi.org/10.1186/s13643-024-02451-1

8. Frank, M., Biedert, R., Ma, E., Martinovic, I., Song, D.: Touchalytics: on the applicability of touchscreen input as a behavioral biometric for continuous authentication. IEEE Trans. Inform. Forensics Sec. **8** (2012). https://doi.org/10.1109/TIFS.2012.2225048
9. K., Y.: Behavioral biometrics for continuous authentication. Inter. J. Sci. Res. Eng. Mana. **09**(05), 1–9 (2025). https://doi.org/10.55041/ijsrem47231
10. LePage, P.: Device orientation & motion (Jun 2014). https://web.dev/articles/device-orientation, Accessed 20 March 2026
11. MozDevNet: WebAPI: devicemotion event. https://developer.mozilla.org/en-US/docs/Web/API/Window/devicemotion_event, Accessed 25 March 2026
12. Onesi-Ozigagun, O., James Ololade, Y., Louis Eyo-Udo, N., Oluwaseun Ogundipe, D.: Ai-driven biometrics for secure fintech: pioneering safety and trust. Inter. J. Eng. Res. Updates **6**(2), 001–012 (2024). https://doi.org/10.53430/ijeru.2024.6.2.0023
13. Oğuz, A.: Ömer Faruk Ertuğrul: human identification based on accelerometer sensors obtained by mobile phone data. Biomed. Signal Process. Control **77**, 103847 (2022). https://doi.org/10.1016/j.bspc.2022.103847. https://www.sciencedirect.com/science/article/pii/S174680942200369X
14. Saito, T., Rehmsmeier, M.: The precision-recall plot is more informative than the roc plot when evaluating binary classifiers on imbalanced datasets. PLOS ONE **10**(3) (2015). https://doi.org/10.1371/journal.pone.0118432
15. Santos, P., Set al.: .: The hand tremor spectrum is modified by the inertial sensor mass during lightweight wearable and smartphone-based assessment in healthy young subjects. Sci. Rep. **12**(1) (2022). https://doi.org/10.1038/s41598-022-21310-4
16. Sitová, Z., Sedenka, J., Yang, Q., Peng, G., Zhou, G., Gasti, P., Balagani, K.: Hmog: a new biometric modality for continuous authentication of smartphone users (Jan 2015)
17. United Kingdom Parliament: Online safety act 2023 (2023). https://www.legislation.gov.uk/ukpga/2023/50/contents
18. Verplaetse, C.: Inertial proproceptive devices: self-motion-sensing toys and tools. IBM Systems Journal **35**(3.4), 639–650 (1996). https://doi.org/10.1147/sj.353.0639

FL-Forensics: A Blockchain-Enabled Framework for Forensic Accountability and Auditability in Federated Learning

Safiia Mohammed(✉) and Alioune Ngom

University of Windsor, Windsor, ON N9B 3P4, Canada
{mohamm7d,angom}@uwindsor.ca

Abstract. Federated Learning (FL) enables collaborative model training without sharing raw data, but most defenses emphasize attack prevention and provide limited support for post-incident accountability. We present FL-Forensics, a forensic-ready FL framework that combines a local hash-chained ledger with digital signatures and periodic blockchain anchoring of ledger digests to create externally verifiable audit trails. We introduce a composite Forensic Quality Index (FQI), together with complementary auditability and traceability metrics, to evaluate integrity, attribution quality, and evidence availability in FL settings. We implement FL-Forensics in controlled simulations and as an end-to-end extension of Flower. Experiments involving data poisoning, backdoor injection, and model-update manipulation show improved integrity verification, attack attribution, and event reconstruction with low runtime overhead. Overall, FL-Forensics strengthens accountability and auditability in federated learning, supporting more trustworthy and legally defensible collaborative AI deployments. The framework preserves evidence provenance across rounds and enables chain-of-custody checks for investigators, auditors, and compliance teams in regulated environments.

Keywords: Federated Learning · Blockchain · Forensic Accountability

1 Introduction

Federated Learning (FL) enables collaborative model training without sharing raw data, making it valuable in privacy-sensitive domains. However, FL remains vulnerable to poisoning, backdoor insertion, and model-update manipulation, and current defenses are mostly prevention-focused [1,3,14,27].

In many practical deployments, post-incident needs are still weakly supported: investigators often cannot reliably reconstruct event order, verify evidence integrity, or attribute malicious behavior to specific participants. This limitation is critical in regulated settings where auditability and legal defensibility are required.

We address this gap through FL-Forensics, a forensic-ready extension of Flower that combines signed updates, hash-chained logging, and periodic

© ICST Institute for Computer Sciences, Social Informatics and Telecommunications Engineering 2027
Published by Springer Nature Switzerland AG 2027. All Rights Reserved
H. Neukirchen et al. (Eds.): ICDF2C 2026, LNICST 720, pp. 441–456, 2027.
https://doi.org/10.1007/978-3-032-37274-1_26

blockchain anchoring. The framework is designed to provide verifiable evidence provenance, timeline reconstruction, and accountable attribution while preserving FL's privacy-preserving training paradigm.

Contributions. The main contributions of this work are:

1. **Forensic-ready FL architecture.** We embed evidence-aware logging into federated training to support reliable post-incident reconstruction and accountability.
2. **Blockchain-anchored evidence pipeline.** We combine local hash-chained ledgers, digital signatures, and periodic on-chain digest anchoring to provide tamper-evident, externally verifiable audit trails.
3. **Forensic quality evaluation metrics.** We introduce a *Forensic Quality Index* (FQI) with complementary auditability, traceability, and evidence-readiness measures for FL environments.
4. **Implementation and empirical validation.** We implement FL-Forensics in simulation and as a Flower extension, showing improved integrity verification, attribution support, and event reconstruction under poisoning, backdoor, and model-manipulation scenarios with low runtime overhead.

2 Background and Related Work

Federated Learning (FL) lets distributed clients train a shared model without centralizing raw data, making it valuable in domains such as healthcare, finance, and edge systems. By exchanging model updates instead of datasets, FL reduces local-data exposure and enables cross-organization collaboration. However, decentralization lowers observability and introduces mixed trust assumptions: clients vary in data quality, compute capacity, and reliability, and some may be adversarial. Deployments must balance privacy, robustness, communication efficiency, and utility under non-IID data and intermittent participation [7,14]. Although existing defenses improve resilience, support for post-incident accountability, evidence preservation, and verifiable reconstruction remains limited. This section reviews FL foundations, threats, and blockchain-based trust mechanisms to motivate a forensic-ready design [11,19,22].

2.1 Federated Learning

In canonical FL, a server broadcasts the global model, selected clients train locally, and updates are aggregated into the next global model, typically with Federated Averaging (FedAvg) [20]. This process keeps data local and eases collaboration [7,14,16]. Because only a subset of clients joins each round and clients differ in bandwidth, compute capacity, and data distributions, convergence, fairness, and stability vary [4,13]. FL therefore improves privacy but still faces a trust-and-coordination challenge when aggregating updates from partially trusted participants.

Figure 1 shows this workflow. While decentralization protects raw data, it also limits observability, making incident attribution harder and motivating stronger traceability and accountability.

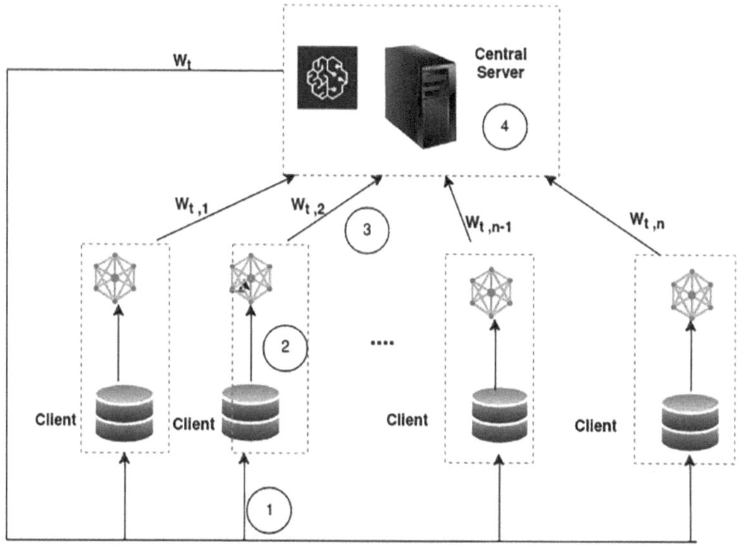

Fig. 1. Standard federated learning workflow showing interactions between a central server and distributed clients.

2.2 Threats and Vulnerabilities in Federated Learning

Although FL keeps raw data local, its distributed and collaborative design introduces vulnerabilities across confidentiality, integrity, and availability [1,3,14,22,27]. Because training occurs across partially trusted clients under central coordination, the attack surface spans the full pipeline. Main threat categories include:

- **Data poisoning attacks:** Adversaries manipulate local training data to bias learning and corrupt the global model, reducing accuracy or steering predictions toward attacker-chosen outcomes [9].
- **Model poisoning attacks:** Malicious clients tamper with model updates before submission, degrading performance or implanting stealthy backdoors triggered under specific conditions [3,35].
- **Inference attacks:** Even without raw-data sharing, exchanged gradients or parameters can leak sensitive information; attackers may reconstruct samples, infer labels, or recover private attributes [12,18,25,38].
- **Evasion attacks:** At inference time, crafted inputs can force misclassification without changing training, undermining deployed-model reliability [37].
- **Server-side attacks:** Since the server controls orchestration and aggregation, a compromised server can manipulate aggregation, drop updates, leak information, or bias the global model [32].

To mitigate these risks, prior work applies differential privacy to reduce leakage [10,28], secure aggregation and homomorphic encryption to protect updates in transit [8,21], robust aggregation methods such as Krum and

Trimmed Mean to tolerate malicious updates [5,34], and anomaly detection to flag suspicious clients [26].

Despite this progress, most defenses remain prevention-focused and offer limited support for post-incident investigation, forensic evidence preservation, and accountability. Consequently, many FL systems still cannot reliably reconstruct incidents, verify tampering, or attribute attacks to specific participants. This gap motivates forensic-ready architectures with verifiable audit trails.

2.3 Blockchain for Transparency and Accountability in FL

Blockchain offers tamper-evident records, decentralized verification, and immutable audit trails, improving transparency in partially trusted FL settings [17,31,36].

Most blockchain-FL studies emphasize coordination, incentives, or monitoring: Lo et al. [19] log training events; Goh et al. [11] use consistency checks for backdoor detection; Li et al. [15] design incentive mechanisms; Xu et al. [33] study decentralized edge orchestration; and Ramanan et al. [23] build immutable audit trails.

Yet these approaches are not fully forensic-ready. They often lack structured evidence capture, local hash-chained logs, reliable malicious-client attribution, and systematic post-attack reconstruction. As Qammar et al. [22] also note, blockchain alone is insufficient for admissible investigations.

2.4 Comparative Analysis with Related Frameworks

To position FL-Forensics against representative systems, we compare each framework's primary objective and evaluation focus. VeSAFL targets secure-aggregation correctness and efficiency, TrustFLow targets trust governance and revocation, Blockchain-Audited FL targets detection latency and blockchain cost, and Atlas targets provenance completeness and replayability [2,6,29, 30]. These are important contributions, but none primarily targets end-to-end forensic accountability.

FL-Forensics addresses this gap by adding explicit forensic-readiness metrics: evidence completeness (LCR), hash-chain integrity (HCIR), evidence availability (EAS), attribution quality (Attribution Accuracy and FAR), reconstruction capability (RSR), and overhead (FCO). Architecturally, many blockchain-FL systems use blockchain for coordination or monitoring, whereas FL-Forensics uses it as an immutable notarization layer for forensic evidence.

2.5 Research Gaps

Despite progress, post-incident accountability in FL remains constrained by prevention-centric defenses, under-specified evidence lifecycle practices, weak attribution support, and limited reconstruction-focused evaluation. These gaps motivate FL-Forensics as a forensic-ready architecture for auditable federated learning.

3 Forensic-Ready Federated Learning (FR-FL)

FL-Forensics, referred to in this section as FR-FL, complements attack detection with forensic accountability. It assumes malicious clients, potentially compromised servers, and external network adversaries, and is designed to preserve evidence integrity, non-repudiation, and chain of custody throughout training and post-incident analysis.

3.1 Tamper-Evident Forensic Logging Framework

A core FR-FL component is a tamper-evident logging framework. For each round, the system records client submissions, anomaly decisions, and aggregation summaries as signed, hash-linked forensic records.

Hash Chaining for Immutability. To protect evidentiary integrity, FR-FL links ledger entries through a cryptographic hash chain. Each entry stores the previous digest, creating an append-only tamper-evident sequence. Let E_t denote the entry at time t; its hash is

$$H(E_t) = \mathrm{SHA256}(E_t \parallel H(E_{t-1})). \tag{1}$$

Any deletion, modification, or reordering propagates forward and breaks consistency. This structure provides a verifiable chain of custody for FL evidence.

Digital Signatures for Non-repudiation. FR-FL uses digital signatures to bind updates and critical actions to originators. Each client signs its model update and metadata with its private key, and the server signs aggregation outputs, enabling attribution and non-repudiation [24]. For client i with update U_i, the signature is

$$\sigma_i = \mathrm{Sign}_{sk_i}(H(U_i \parallel \mathrm{metadata}))\,. \tag{2}$$

Signature artifacts and key references are logged for independent verification.

Trusted Timestamping. Each ledger entry receives a secure timestamp at creation time. Timestamping supports event ordering and replay detection.

Secure Retention and Evidence Preservation. FR-FL preserves forensic artifacts through append-only ledgers and exported reports, protected by hash chaining, digital signatures, and optional blockchain anchoring.

3.2 Blockchain Anchoring Layer

Blockchain anchoring provides tamper-evident assurance without storing raw updates on-chain. FR-FL anchors compact commitments—hashes, signatures, and round references—to support independent integrity and provenance checks while preserving privacy.

Anchoring occurs after client-update intake and round aggregation. Blockchain therefore stores cryptographic references rather than raw updates, binding off-chain evidence to an immutable audit trail.

Blockchain Data Schema. Each anchoring transaction stores a compact commitment to round-level forensic state:

$$T_t = \langle \text{round\_id}, H(\text{entry}_t), \text{timestamp}_t, \text{signature}_{\text{server}}, \text{prev\_block\_hash} \rangle. \quad (3)$$

This schema supports provenance checks and tamper detection: modifying any included record changes entry hashes and breaks verification.

3.3 Blockchain Deployment and Consensus Assumptions

FR-FL uses a lightweight forensic blockchain only for anchoring, not model coordination. It relies on hash-linked signed records for tamper evidence; deployment-specific consensus is implementation dependent.

4 Implementation

This section summarizes the Flower-based FL-Forensics implementation; the results are presented in Sect. 5.

4.1 Integration with the Flower Framework

FL-Forensics extends Flower [4] with client/server forensic modules. The main components are:

- **Forensic ledger:** the server keeps hash-chained JSONL entries for client updates and round summaries.
- **Digital signing:** clients sign updates before transmission.
- **Tamper-evident aggregation workflow:** the server verifies signatures, computes votes, and logs screening before FedAvg.
- **Blockchain anchoring hooks:** the system anchors signed hash-linked references for client updates and round summaries.

These changes enable continuous forensic capture.

4.2 System Architecture and Components

The system comprises one server and twenty clients ($N = 20$). Figure 2 summarizes the architecture used in FL-Forensics.

The architecture has three FL layers: client-side evidence generation, server-side verification and aggregation, and blockchain anchoring of commitments. Together, they maintain a continuous trail from local training to global updates. The core components are:

- **Client Forensic Layer:** logs local events, builds SHA-256 chains, signs records, and captures forensic metrics.
- **Server Forensic Layer:** verifies signatures, computes anomaly indicators, and stores hash-linked round summaries.

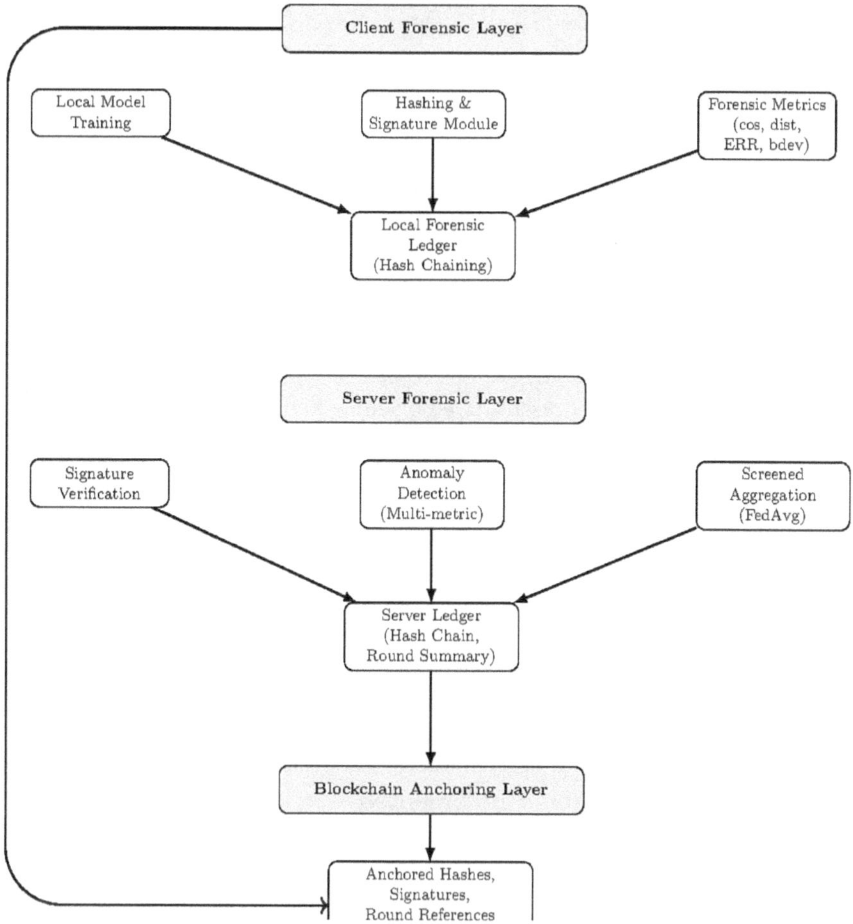

Fig. 2. Compact forensic-ready federated learning architecture.

- **Blockchain Anchoring Layer:** anchors signed client-update and round-summary references for decentralized existence proof.
- **Screened Aggregation Module:** filters suspicious client updates before FedAvg.

The implementation uses Python and Flower together with NumPy, `hashlib`, and PyNaCl for Ed25519 signing and verification.

4.3 Dataset Preparation and IID Split

Experiments use IID client partitions for each evaluated dataset (MNIST, Fashion-MNIST, CIFAR-10, and SVHN) to isolate forensic behavior from data-distribution effects.

Each client receives an equal data share drawn from the same distribution in each dataset run. This setup keeps evaluation focused on detection and attribution rather than statistical heterogeneity. Non-IID settings are left for future work.

4.4 Poisoning Attack Configuration

To evaluate forensic readiness, three malicious clients are designated ($\{3, 5, 8\}$). The attack behavior includes:

- label flipping on selected classes,
- trigger-based backdoor injection to a target class, and
- manipulated model updates (e.g., scaled, sign-flipped, or noisy variants).

These settings reflect representative poisoning and backdoor scenarios widely studied in federated learning security [3].

4.5 Model Architecture

Experiments use a LeNet-5-style CNN with:

- two convolution plus max-pooling layers,
- fully connected representation and classification layers, and
- input-channel handling for grayscale and RGB datasets.

The model is feasible for clients and reveals poisoning effects for forensic evaluation.

4.6 Forensic Mechanisms Implemented

Multi-metric Anomaly Detection. Client updates are scored by four indicators each round. Let $\Delta_i^{(t)}$ be client i's flattened update at round t, $\ell_i^{(t)}$ its loss, $b_i^{(t)}$ a bias statistic, and K the participant count:

$$\cos_i^{(t)} = \frac{\langle \Delta_i^{(t)}, \bar{\Delta}^{(t)} \rangle}{\|\Delta_i^{(t)}\|_2 \, \|\bar{\Delta}^{(t)}\|_2}, \qquad \bar{\Delta}^{(t)} = \frac{1}{K}\sum_{j=1}^{K} \Delta_j^{(t)}, \tag{4}$$

$$\mathrm{ERR}_i^{(t)} = \left| \ell_i^{(t)} - \mathrm{median}_j\left(\ell_j^{(t)}\right) \right|, \tag{5}$$

$$\mathrm{dist}_i^{(t)} = \left\| \Delta_i^{(t)} - \tilde{\Delta}^{(t)} \right\|_2, \qquad \tilde{\Delta}^{(t)} = \text{coord-median}_j\left(\Delta_j^{(t)}\right), \tag{6}$$

$$\mathrm{bdev}_i^{(t)} = \left| b_i^{(t)} - \mathrm{median}_j\left(b_j^{(t)}\right) \right|. \tag{7}$$

Adaptive thresholds are set per metric using a median–MAD rule:

$$\tau_m^{(t)} = \mathrm{median}_j\left(m_j^{(t)}\right) + \lambda_m \, \mathrm{MAD}_j\left(m_j^{(t)}\right), \quad m \in \{\mathrm{ERR}, \mathrm{dist}, \mathrm{bdev}, 1 - \cos\}. \tag{8}$$

Here, cos denotes directional similarity to the mean update, whereas ERR, dist, and bdev represent loss, update-distance, and bias deviations from robust client medians. A client is flagged when any transformed score exceeds its corresponding threshold; bias-deviation checks begin after the warm-up period.

Screened Aggregation. Screening outcomes are logged with FedAvg; the server ledger stores per-round metrics, votes, flagged clients, and hashes.

Forensic Bundle Creation. After training, forensic artifacts include:

- the event ledger,
- hash-linked round summaries and update references,
- anomaly decisions, and
- precision, recall, and F1-score.

These artifacts are validated through hash-chain verification and cross-checked against anchored blockchain records. Together, they provide end-to-end auditability and traceability.

4.7 Security Analysis

FL-Forensics improves assurance with limited exposure. Only hashes and signatures are anchored on-chain; raw data stays local. Signed updates and hash-chained ledgers provide integrity and non-repudiation, while anchoring adds tamper evidence. JSON records support reconstruction.

5 Experimental Evaluation

FL-Forensics is evaluated on MNIST, Fashion-MNIST, CIFAR-10, and SVHN using 20 clients over 10 rounds. Three malicious clients ($\{3, 5, 8\}$) perform label-flipping and backdoor attacks. We report utility, detection quality, evidence integrity, and cost.

5.1 Experimental Setup

Clients train locally with batch sizes ranging from 64 to 128. Server-side FedAvg includes round-level screening and forensic logging. This setup isolates the effect of forensic controls on quality, attribution, and auditability.

5.2 Evaluation Metrics

We report utility (Accuracy and ASR), detection (Precision, Recall, and F1), and forensic metrics (HCIR, BCS, ERUT, EAS, ART, and FCO):

$$\text{Accuracy} = \frac{TP + TN}{TP + TN + FP + FN}, \tag{9}$$

$$\text{ASR} = \frac{N_{\text{succ}}}{N_{\text{trig}}}, \tag{10}$$

$$\text{Precision} = \frac{TP}{TP + FP}, \tag{11}$$

$$\text{Recall} = \frac{TP}{TP + FN}, \tag{12}$$

$$F1 = \frac{2 \cdot \text{Precision} \cdot \text{Recall}}{\text{Precision} + \text{Recall}}. \tag{13}$$

Forensic metrics are:

$$\mathrm{HCIR} = \frac{V_h}{L}, \tag{14}$$

$$\mathrm{BCS} = \frac{V_b}{B}, \tag{15}$$

$$\mathrm{ERUT} = \frac{E_r}{E}, \tag{16}$$

$$\mathrm{EAS} = \frac{E_a}{E}, \tag{17}$$

$$\mathrm{ART} = \frac{1}{Q}\sum_{q=1}^{Q} T_q. \tag{18}$$

Runtime overhead is:

$$\mathrm{FCO} = \frac{T_{\mathrm{forensic}} - T_{\mathrm{baseline}}}{T_{\mathrm{baseline}}}. \tag{19}$$

In Eq. (19), T_{baseline} and T_{forensic} are average per-round times without and with forensic instrumentation.

For attribution in FQI:

$$\mathrm{AA} = \frac{N_{\mathrm{ca}}}{N_{\mathrm{ad}}}, \qquad \mathrm{FAR} = \frac{N_{\mathrm{fa}}}{N_{\mathrm{benign}}}. \tag{20}$$

Overall forensic readiness is:

$$\mathrm{FQI} = 0.25 \cdot \frac{\mathrm{EAS} + \mathrm{HCIR} + \mathrm{BCS}}{3} + 0.25 \cdot \frac{\mathrm{AA} + (1 - \mathrm{FAR})}{2} + 0.50 \cdot F1. \tag{21}$$

In Eq. (21), term 1 measures evidence quality (EAS, HCIR, and BCS), term 2 measures attribution quality (high AA and low FAR), and term 3 measures detection quality (F1). Higher FQI indicates better forensic readiness.

6 Results

FL-Forensics preserves utility while adding tamper-evident evidence and enabling post-incident attribution and reconstruction beyond baseline and detector-only FL.

6.1 Model Performance

Table 1 summarizes accuracy and ASR.

MNIST and SVHN maintain high accuracy, whereas CIFAR-10 is lower, as expected. ASR values (10.63%–16.22%) indicate a partial attack effect without major utility degradation (Table 2).

Table 1. Accuracy and ASR under FL-Forensics.

Dataset	Accuracy (%)	Attack Success Rate (%)
MNIST	98.58	10.63
Fashion-MNIST	87.26	15.15
CIFAR-10	57.40	13.73
SVHN	87.62	16.22

Table 2. Detection quality by dataset.

Dataset	Precision	Recall	F1
MNIST	0.75	1.00	0.857
Fashion-MNIST	0.60	1.00	0.750
CIFAR-10	0.286	0.667	0.400
SVHN	0.75	1.00	0.857

6.2 Attack Detection Performance

Recall reaches 1.00 on MNIST, Fashion-MNIST, and SVHN. CIFAR-10 is more challenging ($F1 = 0.400$), likely because of noisier gradients. FL-Forensics detects most malicious clients, although false positives remain.

6.3 Detection Timeline

Table 3 shows when malicious clients become detectable in SVHN. All malicious clients are detected by Round 4 and remain flagged through Round 10, supporting clear temporal reconstruction of attack progression.

Table 3. Detection timeline for malicious clients (SVHN).

Round	Detected Clients
1	5
2	3
3	3
4–10	3, 5, 8

6.4 Forensic Auditability

Table 4 reports auditability metrics (HCIR, BCS, ERUT, ART).

HCIR, BCS, and ERUT are 1.000 for all datasets, indicating intact hash chains, blockchain consistency, and complete reconstruction. ART remains low (0.029–0.072 ms), showing that verification is practical at runtime.

Table 4. Auditability metrics by dataset.

Dataset	HCIR	BCS	ERUT	ART (ms)
MNIST	1.000	1.000	1.000	0.045
Fashion-MNIST	1.000	1.000	1.000	0.029
CIFAR-10	1.000	1.000	1.000	0.072
SVHN	1.000	1.000	1.000	0.037

6.5 Forensic Quality Index

Table 5 reports FQI from Eq. (21) on a $[0, 1]$ scale.

Table 5. FQI by dataset.

Dataset	FQI
MNIST	0.811
Fashion-MNIST	0.762
CIFAR-10	0.435
SVHN	0.755

MNIST achieves the highest FQI (0.811), followed by Fashion-MNIST and SVHN (0.762 and 0.755), whereas CIFAR-10 records the lowest value (0.435).

6.6 Forensic Cost Overhead

Table 6 reports FCO from Eq. (19); FCO $= 0.10$ means the forensic run is 10% slower than baseline.

Table 6. FCO by dataset.

Dataset	FCO
MNIST	0.115
Fashion-MNIST	0.102
CIFAR-10	0.127
SVHN	0.092

FCO ranges from 0.092 to 0.127 (mean ≈ 0.11), indicating low overhead for hashing, signing, and anchoring.

6.7 Per-client Forensic Attribution

Table 7 shows flag rates for selected SVHN clients:

$$\text{FlagRate}_i = \frac{1}{R_i} \sum_{r=1}^{R_i} \mathbb{1}[\text{client } i \text{ is flagged in round } r] \times 100\%. \quad (22)$$

Here, R_i denotes the number of evaluated rounds for client i. In this study, $R_i = 10$, so the rate equals the number of flagged rounds out of 10 (e.g., $90\% = 9/10$).

Table 7. Per-client attribution example (SVHN).

Client ID	Flag Rate	Ground Truth
3	90%	Malicious
5	60%	Malicious
8	50%	Malicious
16	10%	Benign

Malicious clients have higher flag rates (90%, 60%, and 50%) than the benign client (10%), supporting reliable attribution.

7 Discussion

Across baseline FL, detector-only FL, and FR-FL, detection and forensic accountability are related but distinct. Detector-only FL flags suspicious updates during training but does not preserve verifiable evidence for later review. As a result, its alerts support real-time mitigation but remain weak for retrospective analysis, third-party audit, and formal dispute resolution.

FR-FL addresses this limitation by combining anomaly screening with signed hash-chained records and periodic blockchain anchoring. This closes the gap between online detection and forensic accountability: detector-only FL can raise alerts, but it does not retain verifiable, attribution-ready evidence for post-incident reconstruction and audit. The design separates local, high-frequency evidence capture from external immutable ledger commitments, enabling verification of submitter identity, timing, and record tampering. The low runtime overhead (about 0.11) indicates that forensic readiness can be integrated without materially disrupting training workflows.

The results also clarify dataset-level variation in forensic quality. CIFAR-10 scores lower because complex features and noisier gradients make malicious and benign updates harder for anomaly detectors to distinguish. Crucially, this drop reflects attribution difficulty rather than evidence-integrity failure: signed, hash-chained records remain intact even when classifier confidence declines. Operationally, this points improvement efforts toward detector calibration rather than ledger redesign.

From a deployment perspective, FR-FL provides a practical accountability layer for high-stakes domains such as healthcare and finance, where organizations need both privacy-preserving learning and defensible incident narratives. The framework supports chain-of-custody-style reasoning over FL events while remaining compatible with existing FL training loops. In addition, periodic anchoring allows operators to tune cost and throughput by adjusting the anchoring frequency, providing a configurable balance between the immediacy of external verification and blockchain transaction overhead.

Despite these strengths, several limitations remain. First, the evaluation assumes a controlled network and does not fully capture prolonged partitions or adversaries that adapt to detector thresholds. Second, attribution quality depends on threshold choice and client heterogeneity, requiring local calibration. Third, although anchoring strengthens tamper evidence, legal admissibility still depends on governance, key management, and organizational policy. These limitations motivate future work on adaptive adversaries, larger-scale deployments, and operational integration.

8 Conclusion

FR-FL adds forensic accountability to federated learning through signed updates, hash-chained logs, and blockchain anchoring. Across four benchmarks and 20 clients, it preserves utility while producing verifiable evidence.

The results show low overhead (≈ 0.11), strong auditability, and practical client attribution. CIFAR-10 mainly challenges detector separability rather than evidence integrity.

9 Future Work

Future work includes scaling to larger models and cross-silo settings, strengthening robustness against adaptive adversaries, and evaluating higher-throughput anchoring strategies for deployment-scale verification.

References

1. Almutairi, S., Barnawi, A.: Federated learning vulnerabilities, threats and defenses: A systematic review and future directions. Internet of Things, p. 100947 (2023)
2. Atlas (ML provenance framework): Framework summary (2024), comparison resource provided by the authors for this study
3. Bagdasaryan, E., Veit, A., Hua, Y., Estrin, D., Shmatikov, V.: How to backdoor federated learning. In: International Conference on Artificial Intelligence and Statistics, pp. 2938–2948 (2020)
4. Beutel, D.J.: Flower: a friendly federated learning research framework, arXiv preprint arXiv:2007.14390 (2020)
5. Blanchard, P.: Machine learning with adversaries: Byzantine tolerant gradient descent. In: NeurIPS (2017)

6. Blockchain-Audited: Federated Learning: Framework summary (2025), comparison resource provided by the authors for this study
7. Bonawitz, K., et al.: Towards federated learning at scale: system design. In: Proceedings of Machine Learning and Systems (MLSys), vol. 1, pp. 374–388 (2019)
8. Bonawitz, K.: Practical secure aggregation for federated learning. ACM CCS (2017)
9. Fang, M.: Local model poisoning attacks to federated learning. USENIX Security (2020)
10. Geyer, R.: Differentially private federated learning: a client-level perspective. In: Privacy Enhancing Technologies Symposium (2017)
11. Goh, E., Liyanage, D., Mishra, R., Thompson, M.: Blockchain-enabled federated learning: a reference architecture design, implementation, and verification. IEEE Access **11**, 145749–145776 (2023)
12. Hitaj, B., Ateniese, G., Perez-Cruz, F.: Deep models under the GAN: information leakage from collaborative deep learning. In: Proceedings of the 2017 ACM SIGSAC Conference on Computer and Communications Security (CCS), pp. 603–618. Association for Computing Machinery, Dallas, TX, USA (2017). https://doi.org/10.1145/3133956.3134012
13. Hsieh, K.H.: Non-IID data in federated learning: A survey, arXiv preprint arXiv:2006.12085 (2020)
14. Kairouz, P., McMahan, H.B., Avent, B., Bellet, A., Bennis, M., Bhagoji, A.N., et al.: Advances and open problems in federated learning. Foundat. Trends Mach. Learn. **14**(1–2), 1–210 (2021)
15. Li, J., Sun, J., Li, F., Yang, X., Wang, Y.: BIFLC: a blockchain and IPFS-based multi-consensus federated learning framework. In: Proceedings of the IEEE International Conference on Computer Supported Cooperative Work in Design (CSCWD), pp. 1330–1335 (2023)
16. Li, L., Fan, Y., Tse, M., Lin, K.Y.: A review of applications in federated learning. Comput. Indust. Eng. **149**, 106854 (2020)
17. Li, Q.: Blockchain for federated learning: a comprehensive survey. IEEE Intell. Syst. (2021)
18. Liu, P., Xu, X., Wang, W.: Threats, attacks and defenses to federated learning: issues, taxonomy and perspectives. Cybersecurity **5**(1), 4 (2022). https://doi.org/10.1186/s42400-021-00086-2
19. Lo, S.K., et al.: Toward trustworthy AI: blockchain-based architecture design for accountability and fairness of federated learning systems. IEEE Internet Things J. **10**(4), 3276–3284 (2023)
20. McMahan, B., Moore, E., et al.: Communication-efficient learning of deep networks from decentralized data. In: AISTATS (2017)
21. Mohassel, P., et al.: SecureML: a system for secure machine learning. In: IEEE S&P (2017)
22. Qammar, A., Abdelaziz, A., Barnawi, S.: Securing federated learning with blockchain: a systematic literature review. Artif. Intell. Rev. **56**(5), 3951–3985 (2023)
23. Ramanan, D.K.: Blockchain-based audit trails for trustworthy machine learning. In: ACM CODASPY (2020)
24. Schneider, J., Breitinger, F.: Towards AI forensics: did the artificial intelligence system do it? J. Inform. Sec. Appli. **76**, 103517 (2023)
25. Song, M., et al.: Analyzing user-level privacy attack against federated learning. IEEE J. Sel. Areas Commun. **38**(10), 2430–2444 (2020). https://doi.org/10.1109/JSAC.2020.3007061

26. Sun, J.: Can we detect malicious updates in federated learning? arXiv preprint arXiv:2106.03778 (2021)
27. Tian, Z., et al.: A comprehensive survey on poisoning attacks and countermeasures in machine learning. ACM Comput. Surv. **55**(8), 1–35 (2022)
28. Truex, S.: Hybrid differential privacy for federated learning. In: ACM AISec (2019)
29. TrustFLow: Framework summary (2025), comparison resource provided by the authors for this study
30. VeSAFL (Verifiable Secure Aggregation): Framework summary (2023), comparison resource provided by the authors for this study
31. Wang, S.: Blockchain-enabled machine learning: a survey. ACM Comput. Surv. (2022)
32. Wu, Y.: Malicious server behavior in federated learning systems. In: IEEE INFOCOM (2023)
33. Xu, R.: BEAS: blockchain-enabled asynchronous federated learning for edge AI. IEEE Internet Things J. (2021)
34. Yin, D.: Byzantine-robust distributed learning: towards optimal statistical rates. In: ICML (2018)
35. Zhao, X.: On the vulnerability of backdoor attacks in FL. In: IEEE TDSC (2022)
36. Zheng, W., Zheng, Z., Chen, X., Dai, K., Li, P., Chen, R.: NutBaaS: a blockchain-as-a-service platform. IEEE Access **7**, 134422–134433 (2019)
37. Zhou, X., Xu, M., Wu, Y., Zheng, N.: Deep model poisoning attack on federated learning. Future Internet **13**(3), 73 (2021). https://doi.org/10.3390/fi13030073
38. Zhu, L.: Deep leakage from gradients. NeurIPS (2019)

Chain-Resilience: A Blockchain-Based Federated Continual Learning Framework for Defending Against Forgetting and Distrust

Xinyu Zhang, Wenyuan Wang, Kejia Zhang, and Gang Du(✉)

School of Computer and Big Data (School of Cyber Security), Heilongjiang University, Harbin 150080, China
{2242766,2242098}@s.hlju.edu.cn, {zhangkejia,dugang}@hlju.edu.cn

Abstract. As encrypted protocols like DNS over HTTPS (DoH) complicate network intrusion detection, Federated Learning (FL) offers a privacy-preserving solution but struggles with catastrophic forgetting and adversarial vulnerabilities. To address these challenges, we propose Chain-Resilience, a blockchain-enhanced federated continual learning framework. It leverages a knowledge anchoring mechanism, referencing historical on-chain checkpoints to constrain parameter drift and mitigate forgetting. Simultaneously, a smart contract-based reputation protocol evaluates participant contributions to neutralize low-quality or malicious updates. Extensive experiments on CIRA-CIC-DoHBrw-2020 and UNSW-NB15 confirm the framework's efficacy. In decentralized settings, Chain-Resilience achieves F1-scores up to 0.978 with positive backward transfer, ensuring strong knowledge retention. Furthermore, under severe 25% poisoning scenarios, it robustly recovers model performance from a degraded F1-score of 0.422 to over 0.95. These results demonstrate that integrating blockchain with federated continual learning provides a highly robust and adaptive solution for evolving network environments.

Keywords: Federated Learning · Continual Learning · Blockchain · Network Intrusion Detection

1 Introduction

In recent years, the growing prevalence of the DNS over HTTPS (DoH) [9] protocol has increasingly demonstrated its dual nature: while enhancing user privacy, it also provides convenience for attackers. Attackers can encapsulate malicious Command and Control (C2) traffic or data within encrypted DoH tunnels, thereby bypassing traditional Intrusion Detection Systems (IDS) that rely on traffic analysis [2]. Research indicates that machine learning models can effectively identify malicious activities hidden within encrypted traffic. However, their training requires vast amounts of data. Due to data privacy constraints, sharing such sensitive data directly is impractical. The advent of FL has broken

© ICST Institute for Computer Sciences, Social Informatics and Telecommunications Engineering 2027
Published by Springer Nature Switzerland AG 2027. All Rights Reserved
H. Neukirchen et al. (Eds.): ICDF2C 2026, LNICST 720, pp. 457–473, 2027.
https://doi.org/10.1007/978-3-032-37274-1_27

this limitation [23]. It allows individual nodes to train their own models locally without sharing their raw data. Upon completion of training, they share the models with a central server, which then aggregates them to compute a global model [19]. Subsequently, the proposal of decentralized Federated Learning eliminated this central server. Users share models in a peer-to-peer fashion after training, thereby enhancing the system's robustness and scalability [16,21,22].

Despite the significant success of FL and decentralized Federated Learning (DFL) in privacy preservation, they still face two critical challenges owing to the dynamic and complex nature of real-world network environments:

Catastrophic Forgetting: As attack patterns evolve, federated models adapting to novel threats often forget previously learned knowledge [13]. While Co-DEFEND [4] introduced continual learning, it lacked a dedicated mechanism to mitigate this catastrophic forgetting.

Trust and Robustness Deficit: Verifying node integrity is difficult against strategic adversaries who exploit decentralized aggregation via stealthy backdoors, "ReLU Death" illusions, or evasion attacks. Conventional frameworks relying on simple moving averages are fundamentally ill-equipped to counter such deceptive behaviors [29].

Existing decentralized paradigms fail to simultaneously resolve this trust-adaptation conflict. To bridge this critical gap, we propose **Chain-Resilience**, a unified blockchain-driven federated continual learning architecture.

Rather than a simple modular combination, our framework achieves deep synergy: the blockchain provides verifiable historical anchors such as "collective memory", while a smart contract acts as a feedback controller. This closed-loop design balances stability (anti-forgetting) and plasticity (new task adaptation), ensuring trust directly drives safe knowledge evolution without preserving poisoned parameters.

The core contributions are summarized as follows:

- We propose **Chain-Resilience**, explicitly coupling blockchain immutability with decentralized continual learning to guarantee both long-term memory retention and Byzantine-resilient collaboration.
- We design a **Blockchain-driven Knowledge Anchoring** mechanism. By constraining local optimization trajectories to historical on-chain checkpoints via an adaptive L2-penalty, it physically preserves critical structural memory and mitigates catastrophic interference.
- We develop a **Smart Contract-based Reputation Federation** protocol featuring **Proof of Evaluation (PoE)** and **Zero-Tolerance Slashing**. Surpassing standard Exponential Moving Average (EMA), this hard-cutoff mechanism permanently blacklists evasive or severely poisoned nodes, providing a strictly verifiable trust oracle.
- Extensive evaluations on intrusion detection benchmarks (e.g., CIRA-CIC-DoHBrw-2020 [20]) demonstrate that Chain-Resilience robustly restores global model performance from 0.422 to over 0.95 F1-score under severe 25% poisoning scenarios.

2 Related Work

Catastrophic forgetting, systematically described by McCloskey and Cohen [18], remains a pivotal challenge where new knowledge overwrites previously learned information during sequential training. To address this, the academic community has developed three primary strategies:

(1) **Regularization-based methods**, such as EWC [13], SI [32], and CEL [1], which add penalty terms to the loss function to constrain the updates of parameters crucial for old tasks;
(2) **Replay-based methods**, including iCaRL [24], LwF [15], and L2P [26], which consolidate knowledge by replaying representative data or soft labels from previous tasks;
(3) **Parameter-isolation methods**, such as Progressive Networks [25] and LoRA [10], which allocate independent model parameters or sub-networks to different tasks to prevent structural interference.

Concurrently, blockchain technology has been integrated into Federated Learning (BCFL) to enhance trust and security [7,31]. Early efforts introduced reputation schemes for incentive mechanisms [11] and worker selection [12], while smart contracts, known for their immutable logic and decentralized execution [3,5,28], were employed to automate identity management [17]. Frameworks like DeepChain [27] and BAFFLE [14] leverage blockchain for public auditing and consensus-based model aggregation. Recent advancements further incorporate zero-knowledge proofs for verifiable off-chain computation [8] and ZKPoT consensus mechanisms [6].

Table 1. Comparison of Chain-Resilience with State-of-the-Art Frameworks

Framework	Core Tech	Anti-Forgetting	Trust/Robustness	Continual Learning	Decentralized
DeepChain [27]	Incentive Mechanism, Audit	×	✓	×	✓
BAFFLE [14]	Committee-based Consensus	×	✓	×	✓
Co-DEFEND [4]	Federated Continual Learning	✓	×	✓	✓
ZKPoT [6]	Zero-Knowledge Proof	×	✓	×	✓
Fed-EWC [13]/ LwF [15]	Regularization/Distillation	✓	×	✓	×
Chain-Resilience	**KA + RF Mechanisms**	✓	✓	✓	✓

As summarized in Table 1, while existing BCFL frameworks [6,14,27] enhance robustness, they largely overlook catastrophic forgetting. Conversely, FCL frameworks like Co-DEFEND [4,30,33] address continual learning but lack proactive defense against both forgetting and distrust. **Chain-Resilience achieves a unique synergy between these domains**, being the first unified framework to simultaneously resolve forgetting (via Knowledge Anchoring) and collaborative distrust (via Reputation Federation) within a decentralized architecture.

3 Framework Design

Chain-Resilience is a decentralized, blockchain-based framework designed to address the intertwined challenges of catastrophic forgetting and trust deficiency. Unlike prior modular approaches, our design is rooted in the principle of **functional synergy**, where blockchain immutability and reputation dynamics are deeply coupled with the model optimization process.

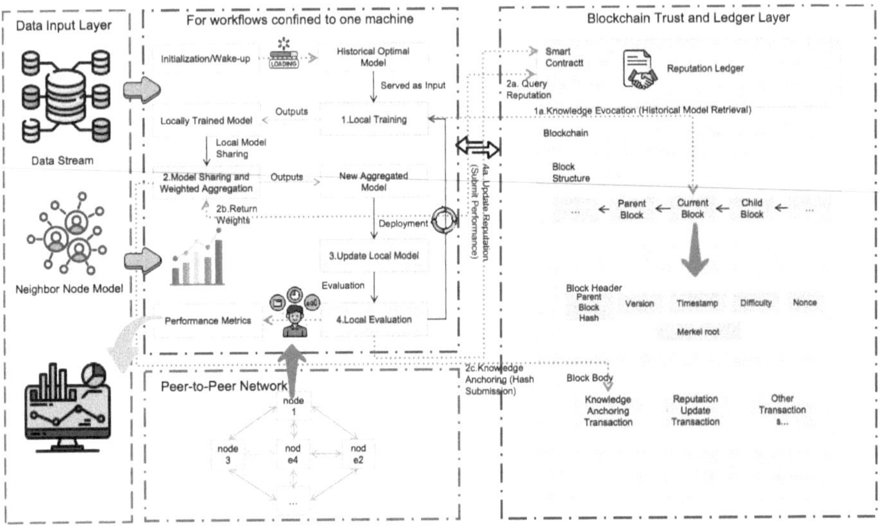

Fig. 1. System Architecture of Chain-Resilience.

As illustrated in Fig. 1, the framework consists of two synergistic layers: the P2P Network Layer, which executes collaborative optimization, and the *Blockchain Trust and Memory Layer*, which provides a verifiable foundation for historical knowledge.

Mechanism Synergy: The synergy within Chain-Resilience is manifested through a closed-loop feedback mechanism: the Blockchain provides cryptographically verified historical "anchors" that constrain local learning (preventing forgetting); meanwhile, the Smart Contract evaluates the quality of this learning via Proof of Evaluation (PoE), updating reputation scores that dictate each node's influence in the collective memory. This integration ensures that the anti-forgetting mechanism is not merely an optimizer constraint, but a trust-driven evolution process where only benign and high-quality knowledge is allowed to persist in the "collective memory" of the blockchain.

Every node independently runs the workflow (detailed in Algorithm 1), forming an adaptive closed loop for continual learning. The specific steps are as follows:

1. **Local Training:** At the beginning of each learning round (except for the first), the node initiates a 'Knowledge Evocation' process. This involves retrieving the historical optimal model from the blockchain to initialize the local model, M_{new}. Once the model is initialized, the node proceeds to train it using its incoming local data stream.
2. **Model Sharing and Weighted Aggregation:** Upon completion of the training, the node shares its model parameters with neighboring nodes in a P2P fashion and, in turn, receives models from them. Subsequently, the node executes a 'Reputation Federation' mechanism. This involves querying a smart contract to obtain the reputation values of its neighbors, which are then used as weights for a weighted aggregation process, resulting in the generation of a new, higher-performing model.
3. **Knowledge Anchoring:** The node packages the hash of the newly aggregated model, along with the metadata of the current round, into a "knowledge anchoring transaction". This transaction is then submitted to the blockchain for permanent storage, thereby facilitating the subsequent retrieval of historical models.
4. **Model Update and Local Evaluation:** The node updates its current local model with the newly aggregated model and subsequently evaluates its performance on a local test set. This process generates key metrics, such as Backward Transfer (BWT).
5. **Reputation Update and Continual Learning:** The node submits the performance metrics generated during the evaluation to the smart contract, which in turn dynamically updates the node's reputation value. Following this, the system advances to the next iteration, thereby completing a full, continual learning closed-loop.

3.1 Blockchain-Based Knowledge Anchoring

To counteract the phenomenon of catastrophic forgetting that occurs during model training, we have designed a lightweight blockchain to serve as a distributed, immutable, and traceable knowledge base for the models.

Block Structure: As shown in Fig. 1, the blockchain links blocks chronologically, each with a header containing the Merkle root and a body storing transactions such as knowledge anchoring and reputation updates, ensuring immutability and verifiability.

Anchoring and Retrieval

Anchoring: After each aggregation, nodes compute a hash H for the new local model M_{new}. Model parameters are stored off-chain (Key: H, Value: $M_{new.params}$), while H and metadata are recorded on-chain in a knowledge anchoring transaction.

Recall and Initialization: For new tasks, nodes query the blockchain to obtain H_{hist} of past models, retrieve the full parameters off-chain, and initialize the

Algorithm 1. The Chain-Resilience Framework with PoE and Slashing

Require: Clients $C = \{c_1, ..., c_N\}$, Tasks $S = \{S_1, ..., S_T\}$, Rounds R
Require: EMA rate α, Hard cutoff threshold τ_{slash}
Ensure: The final global model θ_T
Init global model θ_0, Blacklist $\mathcal{B} \leftarrow \emptyset$. Set $Rep_i \leftarrow 1.0, \forall c_i \in C$ on Contract $\mathcal{SC}$
for each task $S_t \in S$ **do**
  $H_{\text{hist},t} \leftarrow$ QueryBlockchainAnchor() **if** $t > 1$ **else** null ▷ Get anchor
  for each round $r = 1, ..., R$ **do**
    — **Phase 1: Local Update & Evaluation** —
    for each client $c_i \in C \setminus \mathcal{B}$ **in parallel do**
      Train $\theta_i^r \leftarrow$ **ClientUpdate**$(\theta^{r-1}, H_{\text{hist},t}, D_i)$ and eval proof M_i
    end for
    — **Phase 2: Smart Contract (PoE & Slashing)** —
    for each client $c_i \in C \setminus \mathcal{B}$ **do**
      if M_i is missing **or** $M_i < \tau_{slash}$ **then** ▷ Evasion or severe poisoning
        $Rep_i \leftarrow 0, \mathcal{B} \leftarrow \mathcal{B} \cup \{c_i\}$ ▷ Zero-tolerance slashing
      else
        $Rep_i \leftarrow (1 - \alpha) Rep_i + \alpha M_i$ ▷ Benign EMA update
      end if
    end for
    — **Phase 3: Aggregation & Anchoring** —
    $\theta^r \leftarrow \sum_{i \notin \mathcal{B}} (Rep_i \cdot \theta_i^r) / \sum_{i \notin \mathcal{B}} Rep_i$ ▷ Reputation-weighted agg.
    Submit $H^r \leftarrow \text{Hash}(\theta^r)$ to blockchain as Knowledge Anchor
  end for
end for
return θ_T

model via `set_params()`, allowing retrospective access to prior knowledge and mitigating forgetting.

Mathematical Formulation: The composite loss function $\mathcal{L}_{total}$ optimized by clients balances current task learning ($\mathcal{L}_{task}$) and historical knowledge retention ($\mathcal{L}_{anchor}$). Specifically, we employ standard cross-entropy for task learning:

$$\mathcal{L}_{task}(\theta) = \frac{1}{B} \sum_{(x,y) \in B} \text{CrossEntropy}(f(x;\theta), y) \tag{1}$$

To counteract parameter drift from the historically validated optimal model θ_{anchor}, the knowledge-anchoring loss is constrained via a squared L_2 penalty:

$$\mathcal{L}_{anchor}(\theta, \theta_{anchor}) = \|\theta - \theta_{anchor}\|_2^2 = \sum_j (\theta_j - \theta_{anchor,j})^2 \tag{2}$$

The final objective function balances these two components via an anchoring strength coefficient λ:

$$\mathcal{L}_{total}(\theta, \theta_{anchor}) = \mathcal{L}_{task}(\theta) + \lambda \cdot \mathcal{L}_{anchor}(\theta, \theta_{anchor}) \tag{3}$$

3.2 Smart Contract-Based Reputation Federation

To ensure robustness and efficiency in federated collaboration and to address the issue of mutual distrust among nodes, we have designed a dynamic reputation system based on smart contracts.

The core of this system is a blockchain-deployed smart contract comprising two primary components:

Internal State and Logic: The contract internally maintains a critical state variable—a reputation ledger. This is a mapping table that records the IDs of all participating nodes and their corresponding reputation scores (e.g., Node1: 0.95). Concurrently, the contract also contains the logic to "verify and execute an update algorithm", which is designed to update reputation scores while avoiding drastic fluctuations based on a single instance of model performance.

Externally Callable Functions: The contract provides two core interfaces for external nodes:

1. `updateReputation(nodeID, score)`: After a node completes its local model evaluation, it calls this function, submitting its ID and the performance score from the current round as parameters to the smart contract to request an update to its reputation.
2. `getReputation(nodeID)`: Before model aggregation, a node (acting as the aggregator) calls this function to query the current reputation values of its neighboring nodes, which are then used as weights for the weighted aggregation.

Mathematical Formulation: The contract internally evaluates node i's performance in round r as its F1-Score on local validation data D_{val}:

$$M_i^{(r)} = \text{F1-Score}(\theta_i^{(r)}, D_{val}) \tag{4}$$

To prevent catastrophic poisoning and penalize strategic evasion, the smart contract updates the reputation $R_i^{(r)}$ using a piecewise function enforcing a Proof of Evaluation (PoE) and a zero-tolerance slashing protocol:

$$R_i^{(r)} = \begin{cases} 0, & \text{if } R_i^{(r-1)} \leq 0 \quad \text{(Immutable Blacklist)} \\ 0, & \text{if } M_i^{(r)} \text{ is missing} \quad \text{(PoE Slashing)} \\ 0, & \text{if } M_i^{(r)} < \tau_{slash} \quad \text{(Hard Cutoff)} \\ \alpha \cdot R_i^{(r-1)} + (1-\alpha) \cdot M_i^{(r)}, & \text{otherwise} \quad \text{(Benign EMA)} \end{cases} \tag{5}$$

Finally, the global model $\theta_{global}^{(r)}$ is aggregated proportionally to active reputations. Nodes that triggered the slashing conditions will have a weight of zero, effectively excising their poisoned parameters from the global knowledge base:

$$\theta_{global}^{(r)} = \frac{\sum_{i=1}^{N} R_i^{(r)} \cdot \theta_i^{(r)}}{\max\left(\epsilon, \sum_{i=1}^{N} R_i^{(r)}\right)} \tag{6}$$

This rigorous closed-loop defense mechanism incentivizes high-quality collaboration while inherently guaranteeing Byzantine robustness.

4 Experimental Evaluation

4.1 Experimental Setup

To evaluate Chain-Resilience's efficacy in mitigating catastrophic forgetting and resisting Byzantine attacks, we utilize two primary quantitative metrics: F1-Score and Backward Transfer (BWT). The F1-Score provides a balanced evaluation critical for class-imbalanced network traffic data. BWT measures catastrophic forgetting by calculating the average performance change on previous tasks after learning a new task; a near-zero or positive BWT indicates effective retention of historical knowledge.

Datasets and Configuration: Experiments are conducted on two primary datasets: **CIRA-CIC-DoHBrw-2020 (DoH-2020)** (focusing on encrypted malicious tunneling) and **UNSW-NB15** (a comprehensive intrusion detection dataset). To simulate the continuous evolution of attack patterns, both datasets are partitioned into five consecutive learning tasks based on attack categories.

In our federated continual learning setup, all base models (LR, SVM, DT, RF, MLP) are distributed across 10 clients and trained over 10 FL rounds. Locally, models are trained for 1 epoch using the Adam optimizer with a learning rate of 0.001 and a batch size of 10. For our core defense mechanisms, both the anchoring strength coefficient λ and the reputation EMA smoothing factor α are set to 0.5. The hard cutoff threshold τ_{slash} is set to 0.1. This value was empirically determined through sensitivity analysis on the validation set, providing an optimal balance between isolating catastrophic adversarial anomalies and preserving benign, sub-optimal learning updates.

Comparative Frameworks

To evaluate Chain-Resilience, we compare it against several baselines. The **Baseline Model** employs standard Federated Averaging (FedAvg) without our mechanisms, representing the original Co-DEFEND architecture. We also compare against two state-of-the-art FCL methods: **Fed-EWC** [13], which uses the Fisher Information Matrix to regularize critical parameters, and **Fed-LwF** [15], which utilizes knowledge distillation to preserve old knowledge. Finally, to isolate our contributions, we evaluate two ablation variants: **KA-Only** (activating only Knowledge Anchoring with standard FedAvg) and **RF-Only** (activating only Reputation Federation without historical recall). The **Full Version** integrates both mechanisms for synergistic defense.

4.2 Comprehensive SOTA Performance Comparison

We compared Chain-Resilience with Fed-EWC and Fed-LwF using MLP models in centralized and decentralized settings (Table 2). Traditional methods showed negative transfer (BWT: -0.013, -0.024), whereas Chain-Resilience achieved positive BWT (0.013), demonstrating that 'Knowledge Anchor' better mitigates forgetting in federated environments. It also attained the highest average F1-score (0.975) in decentralized scenarios, surpassing Fed-EWC (0.963) and Fed-LwF (0.964), confirming improved stability and plasticity.

Table 2. Performance comparison between Chain-Resilience and SOTA continual learning methods.

Model	Framework	CFL (Centralized)		DFL (Decentralized)	
		BWT	F1-Score	BWT	F1-Score
LR (Traditional Representative)	FedAvg (Baseline)	−0.03	0.93	−0.029	0.93
	Fed-EWC (SOTA)	N/A	N/A	N/A	N/A
	Fed-LWF (SOTA)	N/A	N/A	N/A	N/A
	KA-Only	0.013	0.97	0.001	0.983
	RF-Only	0.013	0.97	-0.002	0.984
	Chain-Resilience (Full)	**0.015**	**0.971**	**0.002**	**0.985**
MLP (Neural Network Representative)	FedAvg (Baseline)	0	0.97	0.002	0.975
	Fed-EWC (SOTA)	-0.013	0.965	0	0.963
	Fed-LWF (SOTA)	-0.024	0.94	0.001	0.964
	KA-Only	0.008	0.972	0.003	0.973
	RF-Only	0.007	0.972	0.004	0.974
	Chain-Resilience (Full)	**0.013**	**0.975**	**0.005**	**0.978**

Note: Fed-EWC and Fed-LwF are continual learning algorithms based on loss function modifications. Consequently, they are applicable only to our PyTorch-based MLP models and are incompatible with traditional LR models implemented in Scikit-learn (denoted as N/A)

4.3 Ablation Study on Core Mechanisms

Through extensive experiments on the CIRA-CIC-DoH Brw2020 and UNSW-NB15 datasets, we validated the effectiveness of the proposed system in mitigating catastrophic forgetting. As shown in Table 3, our method significantly outperforms baseline approaches in terms of key performance metrics such as F1-score and BWT. This section provides an in-depth analysis of these results and discusses their profound academic implications.

Evaluating the Anti-Forgetting Effectiveness of the Knowledge Anchoring Mechanism

To evaluate the effectiveness of the Knowledge Anchoring mechanism in mitigating catastrophic forgetting, we conducted an ablation study comparing models with and without this mechanism. The evaluation metric is Backward Transfer (BWT), which measures how well a model retains knowledge of previous tasks after learning new ones.

Results on the CIRA-CIC-DoHBrw2020 dataset confirm the effectiveness of the mechanism. As shown in Fig. 2a, the baseline model exhibits consistently

Table 3. Comprehensive performance evaluation of Chain-Resilience and its ablation variants across different datasets and federated scenarios

		Metric	BWT				F1			
		Federated Scenario	**CFL**	**NFL**	**DFL**	**DFL-Gossip**	**CFL**	**NFL**	**DFL**	**DFL-Gossip**
CIRA-CIC-DoHBrw2020	LR	Baseline	-0.03	-0.003	-0.029	-0.029	0.93	0.87	0.93	0.896
		Chain-Resilience	**0.015**	**0.002**	**0.002**	**0**	**0.971**	**0.982**	**0.985**	**0.983**
		KA-Only	0.013	0.001	0.001	0	0.97	0.978	0.983	0.982
		RF-Only	0.013	0.001	-0.002	0	0.97	0.976	0.984	0.983
	SVM	Baseline	-0.001	-0.015	-0.015	-0.015	0.969	0.929	0.969	0.967
		Chain-Resilience	**0.012**	**0.004**	**0.008**	**0.005**	**0.977**	**0.984**	**0.98**	**0.981**
		KA-Only	0.009	0.003	0.006	0.004	0.977	0.979	0.982	0.981
		RF-Only	0.011	0.003	0.007	0.005	0.977	0.976	0.982	0.983
	DT	Baseline	-0.003	-0.016	-0.032	-0.032	0.961	0.844	0.967	0.981
		Chain-Resilience	**0.019**	**0.001**	**0.009**	**0.014**	**0.982**	**0.965**	**0.968**	**0.983**
		KA-Only	0.013	0.004	0.009	0.003	0.976	0.963	0.967	0.963
		RF-Only	0.002	0.004	0.006	0.005	0.961	0.963	0.964	0.964
	RFI	Baseline	0	-0.032	0.002	-0.032	0.985	0.758	0.98	0.982
		Chain-Resilience	**0.025**	**0.005**	**0.019**	**0.013**	**0.982**	**0.956**	**0.973**	**0.967**
		KA-Only	0.012	0	0.018	0.009	0.972	0.955	0.97	0.976
		RF-Only	0.015	0	0.001	0.005	0.973	0.955	0.955	0.964
	MLP	Baseline	0	-0.05	0.002	0	0.97	0.96	0.975	0.964
		Chain-Resilience	**0.013**	**0.027**	**0.005**	**0.003**	**0.975**	**0.965**	**0.978**	**0.968**
		KA-Only	0.008	0.003	0.003	0.002	0.972	0.961	0.973	0.966
		RF-Only	0.007	0.006	0.004	0.002	0.972	0.962	0.974	0.965
UNSW-NB15	LR	Baseline	0	0.5	0.589	0.586	0.82	0.83	0.825	0.846
		Chain-Resilience	**0.003**	**0.56**	**0.597**	**0.585**	**0.823**	**0.833**	**0.848**	**0.826**
		KA-Only	0.004	0.553	0.601	0.588	0.823	0.831	0.855	0.825
		RF-Only	0.004	0.536	0.598	0.588	0.848	0.831	0.837	0.809
	SVM	Baseline	0.003	0.416	0.636	0.555	0.87	0.59	0.892	0.723
		Chain-Resilience	**0.006**	**0.425**	**0.634**	**0.562**	**0.882**	**0.6**	**0.892**	**0.735**
		KA-Only	0.005	0.422	0.634	0.549	0.877	0.598	0.881	0.732
		RF-Only	0.006	0.415	0.625	0.554	0.873	0.595	0.872	0.734
	DT	Baseline	0	0.314	0.675	0.665	0.926	0.62	0.93	0.901
		Chain-Resilience	**0.012**	**0.422**	**0.678**	**0.645**	**0.932**	**0.623**	**0.931**	**0.929**
		KA-Only	0.003	0.314	0.678	0.664	0.93	0.623	0.929	0.922
		RF-Only	0.007	0.372	0.676	0.661	0.927	0.616	0.929	0.924
	RFI	Baseline	0.416	0.432	0.683	0.589	0.779	0.595	0.932	0.929
		Chain-Resilience	**0.639**	**0.316**	**0.689**	**0.657**	**0.837**	**0.637**	**0.932**	**0.93**
		KA-Only	0.439	0.327	0.691	0.66	0.79	0.63	0.936	0.928
		RF-Only	0.437	0.334	0.687	0.662	0.789	0.629	0.936	0.931
	MLP	Baseline	0.025	-0.299	-0.098	-0.147	0.834	0.908	0.687	0.921
		Chain-Resilience	**0.063**	**0.005**	**0.057**	**0.054**	**0.865**	**0.913**	**0.836**	**0.949**
		KA-Only	0.055	0.003	-0.01	0.021	0.848	0.913	0.798	0.917
		RF-Only	0.023	0.002	-0.08	0.013	0.856	0.91	0.769	0.887

negative BWT values across scenarios, indicating severe forgetting. In contrast, with Knowledge Anchoring enabled, BWT values are stabilized near or above zero. For example, in the CFL scenario, the LR model improves its BWT from -0.03 to 0.013. This result demonstrates that retrieving historical model parameters from the blockchain before learning new tasks effectively reinforces prior knowledge and mitigates forgetting.

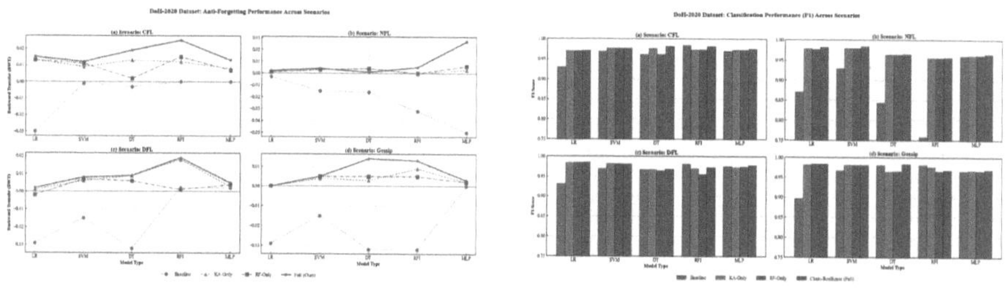

(a) Impact of Knowledge Anchoring (b) Impact of Reputation Federation

Fig. 2. Ablation Study: Effectiveness of individual core mechanisms (evaluated on CIRA-CIC-DoHBrw2020 dataset).

On the UNSW-NB15 dataset (as detailed in Table 3), BWT values were generally high, indicating positive knowledge transfer between attack tasks. The 'Knowledge Anchor' mechanism consistently outperformed or matched baselines across decentralized scenarios, with the RFI model achieving a BWT of 0.69, showing that new task learning reinforced previous attack recognition. Overall, results from both datasets confirm that 'Knowledge Anchoring' effectively prevents forgetting while enabling positive transfer in correlated tasks.

Evaluating the Performance Enhancement of the Reputation Federation Mechanism

The 'Reputation Federation' mechanism mitigates decentralized trust deficiencies by rewarding high-quality contributions. Evaluated via the F1-Score, it significantly boosts model performance on the CIRA-CIC-DoHBrw-2020 dataset (Fig. 2b). For instance, the baseline RFI model's F1-Score in the NFL scenario improves from 0.758 to 0.955. By weighting contributions via smart contracts, the system prioritizes benign models and suppresses malicious updates, ensuring robust global accuracy.

Similarly, on the more complex UNSW-NB15 dataset (Table 3), the mechanism maintains a consistent upward trend. For example, the DFL-Gossip DT model's F1-Score increases from 0.901 to 0.924. This confirms that quantifying historical node contributions provides a reliable trust foundation, successfully enhancing overall detection reliability across both localized DoH and comprehensive network attack scenarios.

Comprehensive Performance Evaluation of the Full Chain-Resilience Framework

The full Chain-Resilience framework integrates two core mechanisms, Knowledge Anchoring and Reputation-based Federated learning, to address catastrophic forgetting and trust deficits in Federated Continual Learning. Figure 3 presents the overall performance of the framework across different datasets, models, and network scenarios.

Performance on the CIRA-CIC-DoHBrw2020 Dataset: As shown in Fig. 3a, Chain-Resilience achieves stable performance in encrypted traffic detection. The framework maintains consistently high F1-scores across all scenarios and significantly improves simple models in decentralized settings; for example, the F1-score of Logistic Regression increases from 0.93 to 0.985. In terms of catastrophic forgetting, the Backward Transfer (BWT) values remain consistently above zero, indicating positive knowledge transfer. For instance, the MLP model in the CFL scenario improves its BWT from 0.00 to 0.013, demonstrating that Knowledge Anchoring effectively preserves historical malicious traffic patterns while adapting to new attacks.

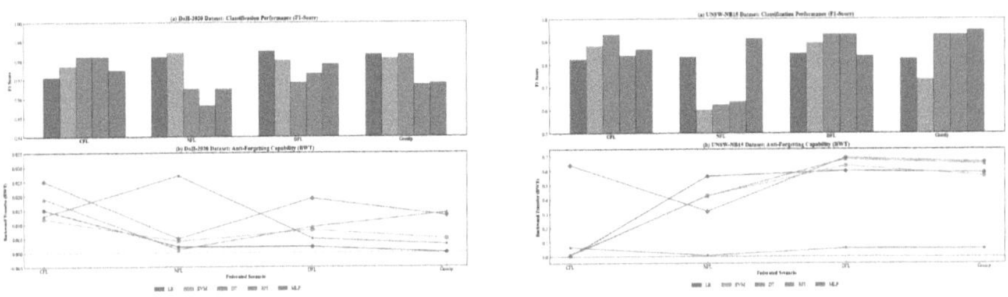

(a) CIRA-CIC-DoHBrw2020 Dataset (b) UNSW-NB15 Dataset

Fig. 3. Comprehensive performance evaluation of the complete Chain-Resilience framework.

Performance on the UNSW-NB15 Dataset: Figure 3b illustrates the framework's robustness in handling more complex network intrusion detection tasks, where the advantages of 'synergistic defense' become particularly pronounced. For the Neural Network model (MLP), the introduction of Chain-Resilience enabled the BWT curve to successfully rebound to the positive domain, effectively reversing the trend of catastrophic forgetting. Simultaneously, as shown in the F1 bar chart, the complete framework significantly elevated the detection performance of the MLP from 0.687 to 0.836 in the Decentralized (DFL) scenario. This provides compelling evidence that the combination of the Reputation Federated mechanism and the Knowledge Anchor mechanism ensures the model's capability for continuous evolution, even in adverse environments characterized by data heterogeneity and the absence of central supervision.

4.4 Robustness Evaluation Against Poisoning Attacks

To further validate the effectiveness of the Reputation Federation mechanism in defending against malicious actors (i.e., the "distrust" challenge), we simulated various data and model poisoning scenarios. In these experiments, 25% of the participating clients were compromised. We evaluated the system's resilience under Centralized Federated Learning (CFL) across three classic attack vectors: Label-Flipping, Sign-Flipping, and Backdoor attacks.

Table 4. Comprehensive performance comparison of continuous learning frameworks under various poisoning attacks (25% malicious nodes) across CFL and DFL scenarios.

Model	Scenario	Framework	0% Attack		Label-Flipping		Sign-Flipping		Backdoor	
			F1	BWT	F1	BWT	F1	BWT	F1	BWT
LR	CFL	FedAvg (Baseline)	0.930	–0.030	0.472	–0.017	0.511	–0.020	0.917	-0.042
		Fed-EWC (SOTA)	N/A	N/A	N/A	N/A	N/A	N/A	N/A	N/A
		Fed-LWF (SOTA)	N/A	N/A	N/A	N/A	N/A	N/A	N/A	N/A
		KA-Only	0.970	0.013	0.536	0.000	0.510	0.000	0.952	0.002
		RF-Only	0.970	0.013	0.943	0.002	0.941	0.003	0.948	0.002
		Chain-Resilience (Full)	**0.971**	**0.015**	**0.944**	**0.003**	**0.943**	**0.002**	**0.962**	**0.003**
	DFL	FedAvg (Baseline)	0.930	–0.029	0.248	–0.110	0.258	–0.040	0.914	–0.060
		Fed-EWC (SOTA)	N/A	N/A	N/A	N/A	N/A	N/A	N/A	N/A
		Fed-LWF (SOTA)	N/A	N/A	N/A	N/A	N/A	N/A	N/A	N/A
		KA-Only	0.983	0.001	0.482	0.001	0.502	–0.003	0.964	0.000
		RF-Only	0.984	–0.002	0.473	-0.003	0.495	–0.001	0.950	0.000
		Chain-Resilience (Full)	**0.985**	**0.002**	**0.849**	**0.000**	**0.850**	**0.000**	**0.974**	**0.001**
MLP	CFL	FedAvg (Baseline)	0.970	0.000	0.728	0.000	0.970*	–0.003	0.970*	–0.004
		Fed-EWC (SOTA)	0.965	–0.013	0.601	–0.032	0.952*	0.000	0.952*	0.000
		Fed-LWF (SOTA)	0.940	–0.024	0.814	0.000	0.962*	–0.006	0.960*	–0.006
		KA-Only	0.972	0.008	0.717	–0.002	0.970*	0.000	0.965*	–0.008
		RF-Only	0.972	0.007	0.960	0.000	0.970	–0.002	0.962	–0.001
		Chain-Resilience (Full)	**0.975**	**0.013**	**0.966**	**0.002**	**0.976**	**0.003**	**0.962**	**–0.002**
	DFL	FedAvg (Baseline)	0.975	0.002	0.422	-0.015	0.884*	0.040	0.953*	0.013
		Fed-EWC (SOTA)	0.963	0.000	0.496	0.000	0.956*	0.057	0.947*	0.010
		Fed-LWF (SOTA)	0.964	0.001	0.293	–0.095	0.930*	0.014	0.947*	–0.010
		KA-Only	0.973	0.003	0.588	–0.014	0.919*	0.003	0.913*	0.004
		RF-Only	0.974	0.004	0.683	–0.024	0.905	0.003	0.939	0.014
		Chain-Resilience (Full)	**0.978**	**0.005**	**0.958**	**0.003**	**0.946**	**0.015**	**0.962**	**0.019**

Note: Fed-EWC and Fed-LwF are loss-remapping-based continual learning algorithms implemented via PyTorch, making them structurally incompatible with the Scikit-learn-based LR models, denoted as N/A. * Indicates the statistical illusion of high F1 due to ReLU death (Sign-Flipping) or stealthiness (Backdoor) on highly imbalanced datasets, which our system successfully detects and neutralizes

As shown in Table 4, under a severe 25% Label-Flipping attack, traditional FedAvg suffers catastrophic degradation (e.g., MLP F1 drops to 0.728 in CFL and 0.422 in DFL), which conventional methods (Fed-EWC, Fed-LWF) fail to prevent. In contrast, our **Full framework** effectively isolates poisoned updates via the τ_{slash} cutoff, restoring global MLP F1-scores to 0.966 (CFL) and 0.958 (DFL). Similar robust recoveries are observed for LR models (restoring F1 from 0.472 to 0.944).

Furthermore, our framework demonstrates exceptional resilience against other complex vectors. Under Sign-Flipping attacks, the deceptively high FedAvg MLP F1 (0.970) is merely a statistical illusion caused by **"ReLU Death"** and severe class imbalance, which degenerates the model into a useless majority-class classifier. Chain-Resilience proactively slashes these corrupted parameters to maintain genuine representation capability (e.g., restoring LR F1 from 0.511 to 0.943). Finally, against stealthy Backdoor attacks, malicious nodes attempting **Evasion Attacks** by withholding validation scores are instantly thwarted by our **Proof of Evaluation (PoE)** mechanism. The smart contract strictly slashes these unresponsive nodes, securely isolating backdoored weights and preserving global network integrity.

4.5 System Overhead Analysis

To evaluate the practical feasibility of Chain-Resilience, we measured its system overhead using the CIRA-CIC-DoHBrw-2020 dataset under a decentralized (DFL) scenario with frequent communication. The RFI model was trained for 100 rounds.

The analysis focuses on the blockchain mining overhead introduced by the Knowledge Anchoring mechanism and the smart contract invocation overhead from the Reputation Federation mechanism. As shown in Fig. 4a, even in communication-intensive scenarios, the average latency remains at the millisecond level (0.94 ms for mining and 4.13 ms for contract calls). Given that federated learning tasks typically operate on cycles of hours or days, this overhead is negligible. In terms of storage, as shown in Fig. 4b, the system's storage overhead exhibits a very clear and predictable linear growth trend, with an increase of approximately 0.14 MB for every 10 learning rounds. Based on this, we can infer that even if the system operates over a long term, its total storage requirement would be entirely manageable for modern servers or edge nodes. In conclusion, the Chain-Resilience framework successfully achieves its core functionalities

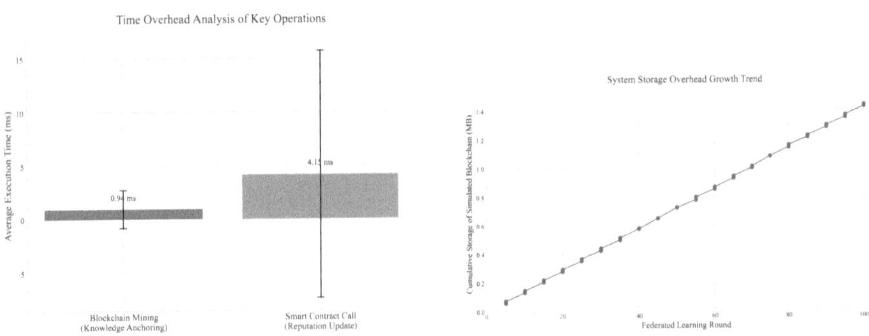

(a) Time Overhead Analysis (b) Storage Overhead Analysis

Fig. 4. System Overhead Analysis in DFL Scenario.

while introducing additional system overhead that is both lightweight and controllable.

5 Conclusion and Future Work

In conclusion, we proposed Chain-Resilience, a decentralized federated continual learning architecture designed to tackle the intertwined challenges of catastrophic forgetting and Byzantine trust deficits in NIDS. By integrating a Blockchain-driven Knowledge Anchoring mechanism, we effectively bounded parameter drift, ensuring the robust retention of historical task knowledge. Crucially, our Smart Contract-based Reputation Federation, fortified with a Proof of Evaluation (PoE) and Zero-Tolerance Slashing protocol, proved highly effective in neutralizing both direct parameter poisoning and strategic evasion attacks.

Extensive empirical evaluations on the CIRA-CIC-DoHBrw-2020 and UNSW-NB15 datasets confirmed that even under a severe 25% poisoning rate across various attack vectors, our framework robustly restored the global F1-score to over 0.96. Notably, it successfully exposed the "ReLU Death" data illusions and backdoor stealthiness present in traditional baselines, while maintaining near-zero or positive Backward Transfer (BWT). In addition, the blockchain-related overhead grows linearly and remains at the millisecond level, indicating an acceptable performance trade-off for security-sensitive applications.

Despite these promising results, several challenges remain. In future work, we plan to explore more advanced knowledge transfer strategies, such as combining Knowledge Anchoring with knowledge distillation to further balance knowledge retention and new learning. We will also investigate methods for handling extreme data heterogeneity, including personalized federated learning approaches to improve model robustness under highly non-IID conditions.

References

1. Aslam, S., Rasool, A., Wu, H., Li, X.: Cel: A continual learning model for disease outbreak prediction. arXiv preprint arXiv:2401.08940 (2024). https://doi.org/10.48550/arXiv.2401.08940
2. Bumanglag, K., Kettani, H.: On the impact of dns over https paradigm on cyber systems. In: 3rd International Conference on Information and Computer Technologies. pp. 494–499. IEEE (2020). https://doi.org/10.1109/ICICT50521.2020.00085
3. Buterin, V.: A next-generation smart contract and decentralized application platform (2014). ethereum White Paper
4. Cajaraville-Aboy, D., et al.: Co-defend: continuous decentralized federated learning for secure doh-based threat detection. arXiv preprint arXiv:2504.01882 (2025). https://doi.org/10.48550/arXiv.2504.01882
5. Christidis, K., Devetsikiotis, M.: Blockchains and smart contracts for the internet of things. IEEE Access **4**, 2292–2303 (2016). https://doi.org/10.1109/ACCESS.2016.2566339
6. Fu, T., Hu, J., Min, G., Wang, Z.: Zero-knowledge proof-based consensus for blockchain-secured federated learning. arXiv preprint arXiv:2503.13255 (2025). https://doi.org/10.48550/arXiv.2503.13255

7. Guo, S., Li, L., Du, J., Lin, H.: A survey of blockchain-based federated learning system schemes. Comput. Eng. Appl. (2025). https://doi.org/10.3778/j.issn.1002-8331.2410-0227
8. Heiss, J., Grunewald, E., Tai, S., Haimerl, N., Schulte, S.: Advancing blockchain-based federated learning through verifiable off-chain computations. In: IEEE International Conference on Blockchain, pp. 194–201. IEEE (2022). https://doi.org/10.1109/BLOCKCHAIN55522.2022.00034
9. Hoffman, P.E., McManus, P.: Dns queries over https (doh). RFC 8484 (2018). https://doi.org/10.17487/RFC8484
10. Hu, E.J., et al.: Lora: low-rank adaptation of large language models, arXiv preprint arXiv:2106.09685 (2021)
11. Huang, C., et al.: Repchain: a reputation based secure, fast and high incentive blockchain system via sharding. arXiv preprint arXiv:1901.05741 (2019)
12. Kang, J., Xiong, Z., Niyato, D., Xie, S., Zhang, J.: Incentive mechanism for reliable federated learning. IEEE Internet Things J. **6**, 10700–10714 (2019). https://doi.org/10.1109/JIOT.2019.2940820
13. Kirkpatrick, J., et al.: Overcoming catastrophic forgetting in neural networks, arXiv preprint arXiv:1612.00796 (2016)
14. Li, Y., Chen, C., Liu, N., Huang, H., Zheng, Z., Yan, Q.: A blockchain-based decentralized federated learning framework with committee consensus. IEEE Netw. **35**, 234–241 (2021). https://doi.org/10.1109/MNET.011.2000263
15. Li, Z., Hoiem, D.: Learning without forgetting. IEEE Trans. Pattern Anal. Mach. Intell. **40**, 2935–2947 (2017)
16. Lian, X., Zhang, C., Zhang, H., Hsieh, C.J., Zhang, W., Liu, J.: Can decentralized algorithms outperform centralized algorithms? a case study for decentralized parallel stochastic gradient descent. In: Advances in Neural Information Processing Systems.,pp. 5330–5340 (2017)
17. Lu, Y., Huang, X., Dai, Y., Maharjan, S., Zhang, Y.: Blockchain and federated learning for privacy-preserved data sharing in industrial iot. IEEE Trans. Industr. Inf. **16**, 4177–4186 (2020). https://doi.org/10.1109/TII.2019.2942190
18. McCloskey, M., Cohen, N.J.: Catastrophic interference in connectionist networks: the sequential learning problem. In: Psychology of Learning and Motivation, vol. 24, pp. 109–165. Elsevier (1989)
19. McMahan, B., Moore, E., Ramage, D., Hampson, S., y Arcas, B.A.: Communication-efficient learning of deep networks from decentralized data. In: Proceedings of the 20th International Conference on Artificial Intelligence and Statistics, vol. 54, pp. 1273–1282. PMLR (2017)
20. MontazeriShatoori, M., Davidson, L., Kaur, G., Lashkari, A.H.: Detection of doh tunnels using time-series classification of encrypted traffic. In: IEEE International Conference on Dependable, Autonomic and Secure Computing, pp. 63–70. IEEE (2020). https://doi.org/10.1109/DASC-PICOM-CBDCOMCYBERSCITECH49142.2020.00026
21. Nakamoto, S.: Bitcoin: A peer-to-peer electronic cash system (2008)
22. Narayanan, A., Bonneau, J., Felten, E.W., Miller, A., Goldfeder, S.: Bitcoin and Cryptocurrency Technologies: A Comprehensive Introduction. Princeton University Press (2016)
23. Quyen, N.H., Duy, P.T., Nguyen, N.T., Khoa, N.H., Pham, V.H.: Fedkd-ids: a robust intrusion detection system using knowledge distillation-based semi-supervised federated learning and anti-poisoning attack mechanism. Inform. Fusion **117**, 102807 (2025). https://doi.org/10.1016/j.inffus.2024.102807

24. Rebuffi, S.A., Kolesnikov, A., Sperl, G., Lampert, C.H.: icarl: incremental classifier and representation learning. In: IEEE Conference on Computer Vision and Pattern Recognition, pp. 5533–5542. IEEE (2017). https://doi.org/10.1109/CVPR.2017.587
25. Rusu, A.A., et al.: Progressive neural networks, arXiv preprint arXiv:1606.04671 (2016)
26. Wang, Z., et al.: Learning to prompt for continual learning. In: IEEE/CVF Conference on Computer Vision and Pattern Recognition, pp. 139–149. IEEE (2022). https://doi.org/10.1109/CVPR52688.2022.00024
27. Weng, J., Weng, J., Zhang, J., Li, M., Zhang, Y., Luo, W.: Deepchain: auditable and privacy-preserving deep learning with blockchain-based incentive. IEEE Trans. Dependable Sec. Comput. **18**, 2438–2455 (2021). https://doi.org/10.1109/TDSC.2019.2952332
28. Xu, G., et al.: A model value transfer incentive mechanism for federated learning with smart contracts in aiot. IEEE Internet Things J. **12**, 2530–2544 (2025). https://doi.org/10.1109/JIOT.2024.3468443
29. Xu, G., Lei, L., Mao, Y., Li, Z., Chen, X.B., Zhang, K.: Cbrfl: a framework for committee-based byzantine-resilient federated learning. J. Netw. Comput. Appl. **238**, 104165 (2025). https://doi.org/10.1016/j.jnca.2025.104165
30. Yoon, J., Jeong, W., Lee, G., Yang, E., Hwang, S.J.: Federated continual learning with weighted inter-client transfer. In: Proceedings of the International Conference on Machine Learning, vol. 139, pp. 12073–12086. PMLR (2021)
31. Yuan, Y., Wang, F.Y.: Blockchain and cryptocurrencies: model, techniques, and applications. IEEE Trans. Syst. Man Cybernet. Syst. **48**, 1421–1428 (2018). https://doi.org/10.1109/TSMC.2018.2854904
32. Zenke, F., Poole, B., Ganguli, S.: Continual learning through synaptic intelligence. In: Proceedings of the International Conference on Machine Learning, vol. 70, pp. 3987–3995. PMLR (2017)
33. Zhao, Y., Li, M., Lai, L., Suda, N., Civin, D., Chandra, V.: Federated learning with non-iid data, arXiv preprint arXiv:1806.00582 (2018)

Human Factors

Human Factors in Cybersecurity in Icelandic Small and Medium-Sized Enterprises

Goda Cicėnaitė(✉), Thomas Welsh, and Helmut Neukirchen

University of Iceland, Reykjavik, Iceland
goc1@hi.is, tomwelsh@hi.is, helmut@hi.is

Abstract. Cybersecurity threats are increasing in all aspects of society due to the integration of digital systems into modern-day life and a volatile geopolitical landscape. Technical factors are an ongoing arms race; however, the threat surface from human and social factors is still present, often providing malicious actors the means to bypass complex technical security controls. Understanding human factors in light of technical evolution is essential to ensure security controls remain effective. This study presents the results of a survey on cybersecurity challenges within public and private sector organisations, including critical infrastructure providers, in Iceland ($N = 130$). From the management perspective, human factors were strongly noted as challenges and barriers to their organisations' security. These challenges include a lack of adequate training or awareness, hiring issues, poor cybersecurity culture, and time and/or financial resource constraints. Based on these findings, recommendations for mitigating threats from human factors are derived. These include: prioritising targeted over generic training to reduce employee fatigue, external government support for financially constrained organisations, and building a strong cybersecurity culture through constructive communication around shared responsibilities.

Keywords: Cybersecurity · Survey · Human factors · Iceland

1 Introduction

Cybersecurity is not merely a technical matter; it is also impacted by human factors [16]. Decision-making processes, human interaction, and organisational culture can affect the safety performance of digital security systems [25]. Human factors are well studied for their ability to both enhance and degrade cybersecurity.

Social engineering attacks, whereby an attacker manipulates psychosocial phenomena to deceive a legitimate user into granting access to a system, are pervasive. In a cybersecurity context, they date back to the 1960 s phone 'phreakers' [19] and continue to this day. There is now a diverse array of social engineering techniques [6], further evidencing the effectiveness of attacking the

© ICST Institute for Computer Sciences, Social Informatics and Telecommunications Engineering 2027
Published by Springer Nature Switzerland AG 2027. All Rights Reserved
H. Neukirchen et al. (Eds.): ICDF2C 2026, LNICST 720, pp. 477–497, 2027.
https://doi.org/10.1007/978-3-032-37274-1_28

human factor and highlighting the variety of prevention approaches necessary for each attack vector. Such approaches largely consist of training and awareness programmes. Yet, technical countermeasures such as machine learning-based phishing detection and browser-based defences are also present. However, some authors argue that to be successful, these approaches must be informed by the users' psychological factors or organisational context, as cybersecurity is an inherently social phenomenon [29]. Human-centric cybersecurity frameworks can integrate psychological resilience, socio-technical approaches, adaptive training, and diverse practical strategies to improve organisational compliance, decrease vulnerabilities, and enhance cybersecurity awareness [25]. Even so, for such approaches to be successful, it is first important to understand the context, as society and culture may impact cybersecurity maturity at a nationwide level [14].

This paper focuses on the nation of Iceland and seeks to address the principal research question: What are the main cybersecurity challenges of Icelandic small and medium enterprises (SMEs) and public organisations?

As an island nation, Iceland is a geographically isolated country with a relatively small (around 400,000 inhabitants [40]), traditionally homogeneous population with a high level of interpersonal trust and a high level of digital literacy [22]. This high level of trust was identified as not conflicting with cybersecurity practices among the general population who accept a national electronic ID as a two-factor digital security solution [41]. However, complicating factors include the potential impact of increased migration on cultural norms and ongoing geopolitical security threats. These factors make understanding how Iceland's public and private sector organisations are positioned in terms of cybersecurity increasingly important, yet heavily understudied. To close this research gap, this study investigates the current state of cybersecurity in Iceland by surveying 130 SMEs via a questionnaire focused on the challenges and barriers they face. This paper presents a subset of these results, focusing upon the human factors.

The remainder of this paper is structured as follows: Related work is reviewed in Sect. 2. The survey methodology is detailed in Sect. 3. The survey results are provided in Sect. 4 and subsequently discussed in Sect. 5. Finally, Sect. 6 concludes this paper. Data on statistical significance is provided in an appendix.

2 Related Work

This section positions our work by presenting and discussing selected related studies that focus on cybersecurity in SMEs across different nations.

Colabianchi et al. conducted a Delphi study, consisting of 30 participants, to identify managerial actions that can improve cybersecurity [12]. Their panel consisted of academics with interests in human factors in cybersecurity, in addition to participants from a wide spectrum of industrial roles who have been involved in cybersecurity in some capacity. The participants agreed upon 16 actions, including training/awareness campaigns, proper role management, and appropriate incident response. They also highlighted atypical factors such as ensuring a good workload balance, developing a cybersecurity culture, and encouraging personal responsibility, which indicates the direct impact of the general work culture on cybersecurity in organisations.

Other works explicitly focus on SMEs, which lack the resources of larger organisations to effectively deal with cyber threats. Chidukwani et al. conducted a literature survey on studies which focus on cybersecurity challenges in SMEs, highlighting that SMEs are often overlooked. Furthermore, they note that the bias in most studies is towards the United States of America. In addition, the studies themselves are biased towards strategies and policies, yet are biased against implementation, detection, response, and recovery. Consequently, they conducted a survey of SMEs' cybersecurity preparedness across Western Australia [9]. Despite contacting all 235,060 SMEs in Western Australia, they received only 36 responses, with 29% of respondents abandoning the survey, likely because of its length. The three main challenges observed were a lack of funds, of cybersecurity knowledge, and of general understanding of cybersecurity standards.

Khan et al. [27] take a different perspective by performing semi-structured interviews with 12 organisations that provide cybersecurity support to SMEs in the UK. A key issue they identified was related to communication that was deemed ineffective due to misunderstood technical language and negative messaging associated with the topic of cybersecurity. In addition, the authors note a general lack of resources (financial, human) to provide adequate support. They also note issues with being able to support the wide range of tools and technologies used by the SMEs. In a related study, the authors conducted semi-structured interviews with 12 SMEs and 12 cybersecurity providers to investigate specifically how cybersecurity guidance material (e.g. online resources) can impact their cybersecurity adoption [26]. The findings highlight that a lack of knowledge, and, as in the previous work, comprehension due to the technical language used, was a common barrier to receiving cybersecurity guidance.

Kappe et al. [24] also conducted semi-structured interviews ($N = 154$) with SMEs in Germany with a focus on the relationship between cybersecurity and cybercrime. A key finding related to human factors was that 40% provided cybersecurity awareness training yearly, 37% monthly, 7% weekly, and 17% only once; indicating wide variation in cybersecurity awareness policy. They also highlight that time and the ability to comprehend cybersecurity information are key barriers to receiving assistance from third parties.

Kabanda et al. studied SME cybersecurity perspectives in South Africa [23]. They performed semi-structured interviews with employees in varying roles of three SMEs. Key challenges to cybersecurity they identified internal to the organisations were: budget constraints, management issues, and a lack of employee support or commitment to cybersecurity in general. In addition, the authors highlight external challenges, such as the need to adhere to government policy and regulation or professional standards. They note that SMEs feel less concerned with professional standards or training methods than larger organisations which typically feel coerced as part of professional groups. Conversely, these SMEs are more likely to adopt cost-effective open source solutions which have a weaker element of influencing behaviour towards professional standards.

Rawindaran et al. study how cybersecurity for SMEs is impacted by government support [36]. They conducted a survey of $N = 34$ SMEs from diverse industries in Wales. Their findings for how the government can support SMEs include: providing general guidance and practices, delivering training and offering financial support, performing audits, providing certification, and providing partnerships with cybersecurity firms to tailor offerings towards the SMEs.

This reviewed literature highlights several key findings related to human factors and cybersecurity for SMEs; these include resource constraints related to people, cost and time, as well as a general lack of cybersecurity knowledge preventing information from being understood and consumed. Moreover, organisational and management culture was highlighted as a barrier. Considering that employee awareness was also an issue, yet training was lacking or inconsistently applied across organisations, this might indicate a rift between employees and managers regarding who should take responsibility. The work in this paper contributes to this literature by providing a study of challenges and barriers to cybersecurity for SMEs in Iceland, aiming to understand how these issues manifest in this specific national context.

3 Methodology

The data used in this study were collected via an online survey based on closed-ended and open-ended questions designed by the Computer Science Department of the University of Iceland. The survey aimed to assess cybersecurity challenges and practices of SMEs and critical infrastructure providers in Iceland as a part of an initiative by the National Coordination Centre for Cybersecurity Iceland (NCC-IS) to address national cybersecurity challenges.

The survey comprised 14 questions and 8 subquestions distributed across 6 sections: Organisational background, Challenges, General, Skills and training, Recruitment, Incidents. Data collection for the survey was conducted by the Social Science Research Institute of the University of Iceland from August 13 to September 10, 2025. 641 SMEs were randomly selected, stratified by sector to ensure proportional representation of the Icelandic business landscape. To ensure a sufficient representation of critical infrastructure, the sample was subsequently supplemented with 52 critical infrastructure organisations.

A two-step approach was then used for data collection. The first step included telephone inquiries to the selected organisations, to identify lead staff members responsible for cybersecurity within those organisations. In the second step, the identified lead staff received an email containing the URL of the survey.

The survey findings demonstrate statistical significance, based on a Chi-Square Goodness-of-Fit test [2] (see Appendix A for details). This indicates a statistically significant, meaningful preference among the respondents, rather than a random distribution of opinions.

Since the survey included closed-ended and open-ended questions, the RStudio [34] software was used for the statistical analysis of the data and the creation of figures and tables - the visual representation of data that allowed identification of patterns and comparisons. The data from the surveyâĂŹs open-ended questions were thematically analysed using Atlas.ti [5] software. First, the answers were inductively coded by one person using the bottom-up approach; the codes were organised by patterns and themes. Subsequently, the patterns were observed between these established themes. The themes were then checked against the data and codes, a step that was necessary to identify the defining patterns of meaning that are the most important for the study. Thematic analysis provides flexibility and supports the researcher's active role in the process of data analysis through the development of codes and themes [11].

4 Survey Results

A total of 693 Icelandic organisations were contacted, yielding 130 survey participants (19% response rate). Among these respondents, 109 completed the survey in its entirety, 4 completed at least half, but not all, of the questions, and 17 completed fewer than half. Notably, the initial pool of 693 contacted organisations, and the 130 final respondents include the subset of 52 critical infrastructure organisations, which yielded 20 responses (39% response rate).

Fig. 1. Organisation size (Q1 How many people work in your organisation?)

Figure 1 shows the distribution of organisation size (Q1): As the focus was on SMEs, the largest share (41%) of organisations had 10 to 49 employees, next was an organisation size of 9 employees or fewer (28%). In the responses, the following sectors (Q2) had the largest share: 10% hotels/accommodation/restaurants, 10% specialist and scientific activities. Two-thirds (66%) of the survey respondents

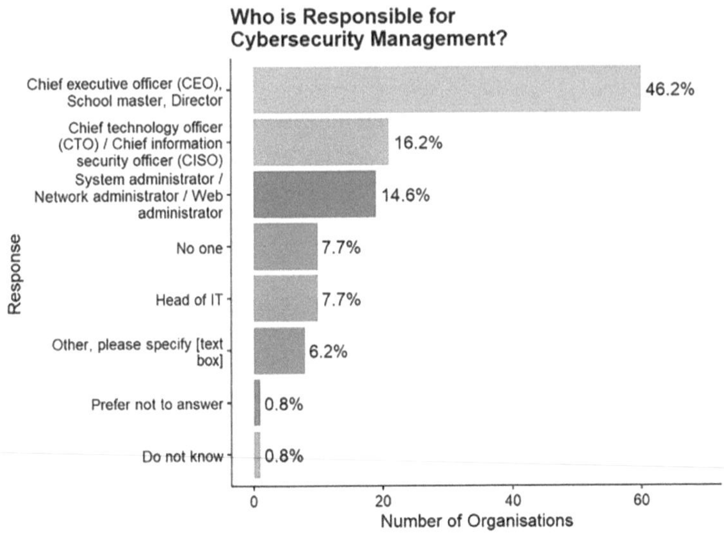

Fig. 2. Responsibilities (Q4 Who is responsible for cybersecurity management in your organisation?).

work in IT-specific roles (Q3.1), and 83% of the respondents answered that they are in a senior or leadership position within their organisations (Q3.2). A thematic analysis of the open-ended questions (see Sect. 3) helped to cluster the data into the following themes: cybersecurity management roles, challenges and barriers, perceived protection and incidents, training, and hiring.

4.1 Cybersecurity Management Role

Figure 2 shows which role holds responsibility for cybersecurity management (Q4): the largest share (46%) of the respondents said that the CEO, school master, or director is responsible.

4.2 Cybersecurity Challenges and Barriers

The main goal of the survey was to identify the main cybersecurity challenges respondents' organisations face. Therefore, Question Q5.1 asked "*What are the main challenges when it comes to cybersecurity within your organisation?*", followed by "*Please explain why it is a challenge, list the barriers.*" (Q5.2). A word cloud of the given answers is shown in Fig. 3. Note that "*employees*" was the most common word, emphasising managerial perspectives on employee responsibility.

Both of these questions were open-ended allowing study participants to write down their answers in a text box. In the responses to Q5.1, the most commonly typed-in challenge was about "*phishing*" and "*emails*", i.e., "*careless employees*" clicking on scam emails. Other often-mentioned challenges include "*ineffective*" or "*unfocused*" employee training and the challenge of ensuring that

Fig. 3. Word cloud for answers to Q5.1 (cybersecurity challenges) and Q5.2 (barriers).

employees have digital security knowledge. Further, the written answers to Q5.1 included challenges such as "*keeping software up-to-date*", password management and multi-factor authentication considered annoying by staff, "*high load of attacks*", "*DoS*" (Denial of Service attacks), challenges caused by the "*need to assure that external service providers have their cybersecurity in place*", and the challenges caused by "*credit card or payment frauds*".

The survey's open-ended answers on barriers to cybersecurity (Q5.2) included "*fragmented/too complex IT ecosystems*", i.e., too many different software and hardware systems to manage. As the two questions, Q5.1 and Q5.2 are related, some respondents mentioned as barriers what others had mentioned as a challenge: "*human errors*", "*lack of employees' knowledge*", reluctance to follow efficient cybersecurity practices, unwillingness to spend time on training or updates. Further barriers listed by the respondents were economic barriers in the form of "*lack of money and/or time*"; these can also be classified as both challenges and barriers. These economic barriers also hint at conflicts around responsibilities and organisational culture in general, such as: "*Owners and managers generally want everything to be secure, but are not necessarily willing to bear the cost of having the staff required to ensure that this is the case*".

Some of the survey respondents also mentioned the linguistic factors that might affect non-Icelandic employees, pointing out that numerous scam emails received are written in the Icelandic language, and thus some respondents perceive it to be more challenging for their employees with a foreign background to identify scams before clicking on them.

4.3 Perceived Protection, Real Incidents and Protection Measures

In question Q6.1 "*Do you feel your organisation is adequately protected against the following attacks?*", survey respondents were asked to select, on a Likert scale, to what extent they feel their organisations are protected against the

Table 1. Perceived Protection Against Cybersecurity Attacks (Q6.1)

Attack	To a great extent	To some extent	To a small extent	Not at all	Do not know	Prefer not to answer
Attacks against network equipment	31.0%	38.1%	11.5%	3.5%	15.9%	0.0%
Attacks against web-based services	23.9%	45.1%	12.4%	5.3%	13.3%	0.0%
Authentication-related attacks	29.1%	40.9%	10.9%	3.6%	15.5%	0.0%
Denial-of-service attacks	27.6%	34.5%	13.8%	6.0%	17.2%	0.9%
Hardware/software supply chain attacks	14.7%	43.1%	10.1%	3.7%	26.6%	1.8%
Ransomware attacks	23.5%	47.8%	7.8%	7.8%	12.2%	0.9%
Social engineering attacks (phishing, scams)	28.7%	40.9%	20.0%	3.5%	6.1%	0.9%

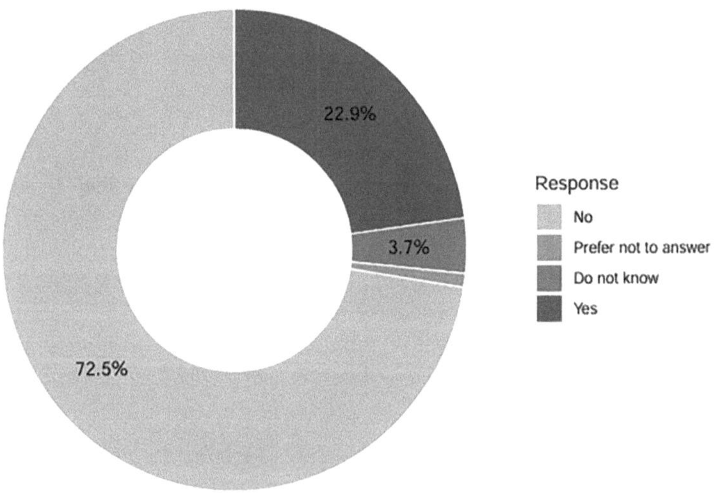

Fig. 4. Incidents (Q14.1 Has your organisation experienced any cybersecurity incidents in the past year?)

listed attacks. Table 1 shows that a large majority perceives that they are either to a great extent or to some extent protected against the listed attacks.

However, in another question (Q14.1, see Fig. 4) almost a quarter, 23%, responded that their organisation experienced a cybersecurity incident in the past year (i.e. 2024/2025). These real incidents contradict the perceived feel-

Table 2. Perceived Protection Against Threats (Q6.2)

Threat	To a great extent	To some extent	To a small extent	Not at all	Do not know	Prefer not to answer
Insufficient backup of data	33.3%	31.4%	14.3%	14.3%	6.7%	0.0%
Lack of keeping IT systems up to date	28.7%	34.3%	13.0%	14.8%	9.3%	0.0%
Loss of laptops, access cards, door keys	19.8%	40.6%	16.0%	17.0%	6.6%	0.0%
Shadow IT use by employees	12.4%	30.5%	24.8%	19.0%	13.3%	0.0%
Users not adhering to security policies	15.2%	41.0%	23.8%	11.4%	7.6%	1.0%
Weak passwords	25.5%	32.1%	22.6%	14.2%	5.7%	0.0%

ing of protection. When asked about the attack vector used for the reported attack (Q14.3), social engineering (e.g. phishing) was the most commonly (36%) selected attack vector by the survey respondents, underlining the relevance of investigating human factors in cybersecurity in Iceland.

Another indicator of overestimating their own protection is the results of question Q8 that asked "*How often do you have any kind of security audits? Examples: penetration testing, code review, compliance audit.*" 37% selected a response option identifying that security audits in their organisations never take place. On the other hand, at almost half (49%) of Q8 respondents' organisations, security audits are performed at least once a year or less often than once a year.

Question Q6.2 "*Do you feel your organisation is adequately protected against the following threats?*" was about internal threats to cybersecurity. Table 2 shows that a large majority perceives that they are either to a great extent or to some extent protected against the listed threats. However, with respect to 'shadow IT' use by employees, the respondents were not as confident that they would be protected as for the other threats.

4.4 Training Employees

Figure 5 demonstrates the answers to the question Q9.1 "*Has your organisation offered any sort of mandatory cybersecurity awareness training for employees in the past year? (Examples: phishing simulations, educational seminars)*". The data indicate low levels of cybersecurity awareness training in SMEs in Iceland. Only 27% of the respondents stated that their organisations offered cybersecurity awareness training for employees in the "*past year*" (2024/2025). More than two-thirds of the respondents, 68%, answered that such training was not offered.

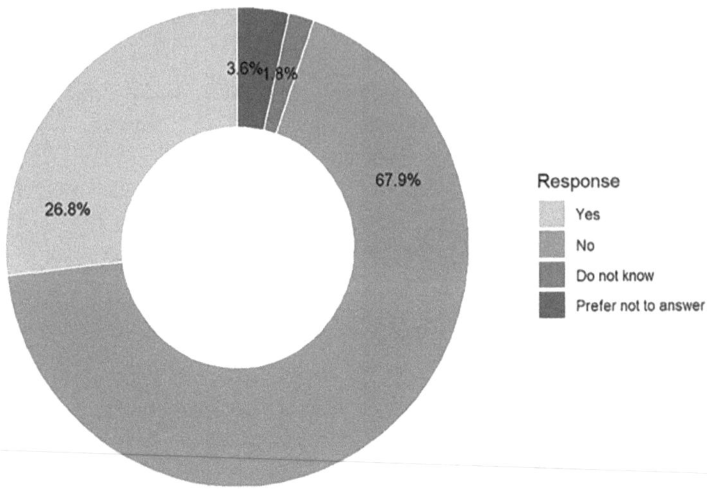

Fig. 5. Training (Q9.1 Has your organisation offered any sort of mandatory cybersecurity awareness training for employees in the past year?)

This confirms what was mentioned as one of the main challenges (Q5.1) and barriers (Q5.2) in Sect. 4.2, namely insufficient digital security practices and employee knowledge. Ironically, employee training is among the most frequently mentioned issues survey respondents listed as challenges and barriers when answering Q5.1 and Q5.2. Some of the survey respondents expressed uncertainty about whether the training provided is "*sufficient*", as well as disappointment that "*training employees in cybersecurity is time-consuming, costly, and results are uncertain.*"

The open-ended survey responses to Q9.2 about the type of awareness training gave insights into the types of courses, tools and platforms used for cybersecurity awareness training. The responses included simulated cyberattacks, training with the focus on phishing, courses on secure coding, use of password managers, and general cybersecurity awareness courses for all employees, yet emphasising training provided to new employees by local or foreign providers. Some of the written responses to Q9.2 suggest that SMEs in Iceland use various providers of cybersecurity courses, either local or foreign. Moreover, in the written answers, a clear recurring emphasis is placed on the requirement for all employees to take courses; in some answers, the emphasis is placed more on the training of *new* employees. The answers to the survey also suggest that training in hypothetical cybersecurity incidents could be improved.

4.5 Hiring Cybersecurity Experts

The answers to question Q12.1 "*Has your organisation hired or attempted to hire professionals with cybersecurity skills in the past year?*" are depicted in Fig. 6. 83% of the survey respondents expressed that their organisations have

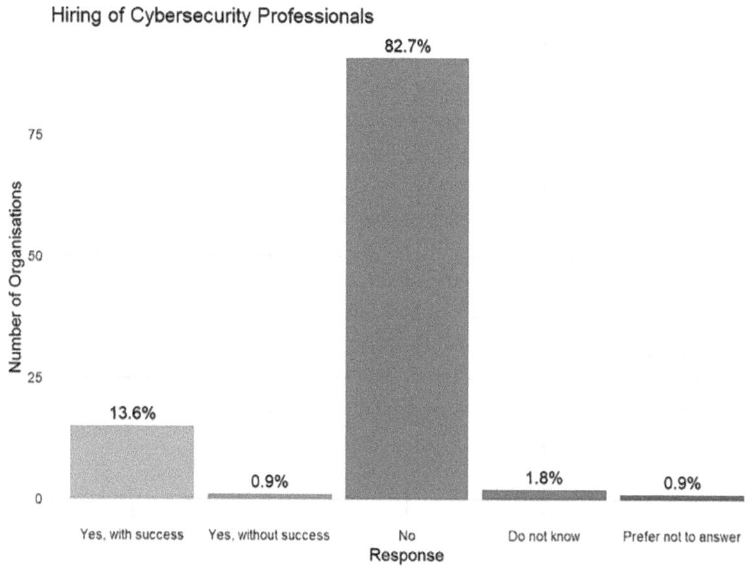

Fig. 6. Hiring (Q12.1 Has your organisation hired or attempted to hire professionals with cybersecurity skills in the past year?)

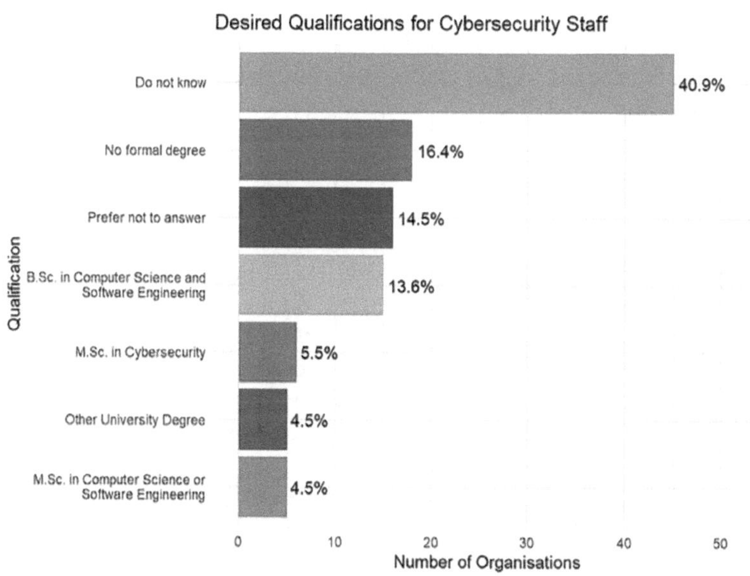

Fig. 7. Hiring (Q13 If you hire, what qualification would your staff member responsible for cybersecurity need?)

not hired or attempted to hire professionals with cybersecurity skills in the "past year" (2024/2025), while 14% hired with success, and only less than 1% attempted to hire without success.

When asked (if applicable) the open-ended question, "*What challenges has your organisation faced when recruiting talent for cybersecurity positions?*" (Q12.2), respondents most frequently pointed to difficulties in finding staff with sufficient knowledge and experience. Other commonly mentioned challenges included high costs and finding candidates who fit into the organisation's workplace culture.

Question Q13 asked, "*If you hire, what qualification would your staff member responsible for cybersecurity need?*". The largest share (41%) indicated that they did not know what qualification would be required. 15% preferred not to answer. 16% expressed that no formal degree is needed, while 28% were in favour of some university degree to qualify for cybersecurity positions in their organisations. For a further breakdown, see Fig. 7.

5 Discussion

This section analyses the survey answers and puts them into context with other work. The survey data, particularly the results from the open-ended answers (Sects. 4.2, 4.4, and 4.5), show the presence of human behaviour-related factors contributing to cybersecurity difficulties across most of the identified cybersecurity challenges and barriers in Icelandic SMEs.

Notably, when comparing these results with the related work in Sect. 2, similarities include: a general lack of staff expertise, a false sense of security, managerial overconfidence, as well as ineffective training policies, time and financial resources constraints, and organisational culture.

5.1 Roles and Expertise

Reflecting on the study participants' organisational background, it is important to note that the invitation to participate in the survey was sent to the person in charge of the organisation's cybersecurity. While 66% of the survey participants reported having IT-specific roles at their organisation (second paragraph of Sect. 4), when asked who is responsible for cybersecurity in their organisations (Q4), 46% selected the roles of Chief Executive Officer (CEO), School master, Director. This suggests that cybersecurity in a large part of respondents' organisations is not the responsibility of professionals who can devote their entire time to cybersecurity. It also indicates that many respondents have multiple roles within their organisations (e.g. for a very small SME, the CEO is simultaneously in charge of IT) which might negatively affect their cybersecurity qualification. Other studies show that IT professionals' cybersecurity awareness levels in SMEs are low because of conflicting priorities and due to lack of appropriate education [8].

Furthermore, the responses related to hiring (Sect. 4.5) suggest that there is not a lot of in-house cybersecurity expertise. On the other hand, SMEs in general often hire external companies to take care of their systems [20]; hence, recruitment of in-house talent for cybersecurity positions is often not needed. It is important to acknowledge the presence of employees with a foreign background in Icelandic SMEs, especially due to the present need to attach foreign labour in the country arising from the ageing of the Icelandic labour force. Some of the existing literature shows that expatriates easily adjust to Icelandic culture due to quick establishment of trust, and almost non-existent language barriers as the majority of locals speak English [17]. The survey data indicate, however, that language factors can still introduce additional layers of challenges for employees with a foreign background when identifying scam emails received in the Icelandic language (Sect. 4.2).

The above findings show that SMEs in Iceland are not different from SMEs in other countries with respect to cybersecurity roles and hiring. However, one aspect stands out when compared to other countries, even in comparison to other Nordic countries that are often used as a benchmark for Iceland: the Icelandic SMEs show a low preference for university degrees as a qualification for hired cybersecurity staff (Sect. 4.5). Moreover, it has to be noted that the largest share of responses was "*Do not know*". In contrast, international research indicates that employers globally frequently rely on formal university degrees as a primary filtering mechanism and baseline requirement for cybersecurity positions [35]. However, these results are confirmed by other non-cybersecurity labour market research: the Icelandic labour market is characterised by high flexibility and a pragmatic 'just do it' work culture [32]. In addition, there is a persistent skills mismatch [31], meaning employers frequently hire based on demonstrated skills and experience rather than relying on formal university degrees.

In fact, this 'skills-first' approach utilised by Icelandic SMEs is exactly what the World Economic Forum advocates [43], noting that organisations worldwide (specifically including SMEs) struggle to fill cybersecurity positions precisely because they over-rely on traditional educational degrees.

5.2 False Sense of Security

For the surveyed SMEs, there is a clear discrepancy between perceived protection and the reality of their incidents, and security audits (Sect. 4.3): the organisations feel far better protected than the actual incidents and the lack of protection measures would indicate. This suggests that many respondents may be operating under a false sense of security regarding their cybersecurity posture.

This aligns with existing literature indicating that SME decision-makers frequently exhibit optimism bias and managerial overconfidence, believing their organisations are adequately protected despite lacking empirical evidence [3]. Furthermore, organisations often confuse the implementation of basic IT controls with actual security but without aggressively measuring the effectiveness of these defences (such as through regular penetration testing), SMEs remain unaware of their true vulnerability until a successful cyberattack occurs [15,42].

However, respondents were notably more realistic regarding the threat posed by 'shadow IT' (Table 2). As recent academic literature emphasises, shadow IT creates critical blind spots for organisations, representing a significant insider threat that increases susceptibility to data breaches, compliance violations, and cyberattacks [1,18].

To address this false sense of security, SMEs must bridge the gap between perceived and actual protection by elevating the organisation's overall cybersecurity expertise – for example, through targeted employee training programmes, the strategic hiring of dedicated staff, or, particularly for resource-constrained SMEs, the use of external cybersecurity service providers.

5.3 Ineffective Training Policies

Employee training was among the most frequently listed challenges (Sect. 4.2). However, when respondents were asked whether their organisations offered cybersecurity awareness training (Sect. 4.4), more than two-thirds answered in the negative. The responses to the challenges and barriers (Sect. 4.2) suggest a reason why training is not offered: namely, costs associated with training and expressed uncertainty about whether training is effective. That data also made clear that training is a challenge due to a lack of interest of employees, which is partly due to inconveniences associated with training, a lack of time, or a lack of a sense of responsibility towards the organisation's cybersecurity.

A number of studies show the need for organisations' risk management plans to include cybersecurity awareness training to keep organisations secure [8,33]. On the other hand, while security awareness programmes frequently rely on simulated phishing campaigns, recent empirical research indicates that such approaches are often ineffective at producing long-term behavioural change [21] and can even be counterproductive [28]. Rather than fostering a culture of security, poorly implemented phishing simulations frequently annoy staff, contribute to 'cybersecurity fatigue' and organisational mistrust [7]. Furthermore, the nature of these campaigns has been shown to induce unnecessary workplace stress and lower employees' self-efficacy regarding threat detection [38]. Therefore, organisations should aim to target training toward their specific needs as opposed to generic solutions which increase stress [13].

5.4 Time, Staff and Financial Resource Constraints

In contrast to large organisations, SMEs often experience difficulties in managing workplace stress because of their limited resources [20,30]. The survey data on challenges and barriers (Sect. 4.2) show three intersecting resource challenges of SMEs in Iceland that are heavily affected by human factors.

The first resource challenge is the shortage of time; a significant share of the survey respondents mentioned a lack of time to, for example, ensure that employees attend trainings to obtain cybersecurity knowledge or to ensure that the systems are up-to-date. Considering that the biggest challenge (Sect. 4.2) is social engineering, such as phishing emails, ensuring that employees have enough cybersecurity awareness/knowledge is a crucial task. According to Chowdhury et al., time pressure is among the main factors impacting human behaviour and decision-making and it plays a crucial role behind non-secure behaviour [10]. However, employees' lack of a sense of responsibility towards their organisation's cybersecurity as well as time pressure affecting managerial practices, such as unwillingness to spend money on up-to-date systems or to hire more staff (Sect. 4.2) can be seen as organisational culture challenges.

The second resources-related challenge of Icelandic SMEs is a shortage of staff with expertise in cybersecurity (Sects. 4.2 and 4.5). Modern organisations characterised by hyper-connectivity face challenges in supporting their cyber programmes due to a shortage of qualified cybersecurity professionals [39]. The hiring situation (Sect. 4.5) suggests that not only is the availability of such professionals in the labour market an issue for Icelandic SMEs, but the lack of funding for hiring additional staff represents an equally significant barrier.

The third resource-related challenge identified based on the survey data is exactly that lack of funding for cybersecurity (Sect. 4.2). Hiring limitations imposed by the lack of financial resources in SMEs are a known challenge, as compared to large organisations, SMEs are less likely to hire dedicated general IT staff, without even considering cybersecurity specialists [8].

According to Sapiński et al., there is a need to shift the perception of cybersecurity from purely technological to one that takes into consideration not only technology but also psychology [37]. This idea aligns with KhadkaâĂŹs and UllahâĂŹs encouragement to integrate psychological resilience and a socio-technical approach to bridge the gap between technical and human factors [25]. Psychological factors can impact cybersecurity decision-making affecting resilience and vulnerability, for instance, stress and cognitive fatigue increase the likelihood of errors [25]. Singh et al. point out that cybersecurity professionals experience stress related to unpredictability in job tasks due to ever-changing and advancing security threats [39].

Although the survey was completed by a broad range of professionals responsible for digital security within their respective SMEs – rather than exclusively by dedicated cybersecurity personnel (see Sect. 4.1) – the data clearly highlighted the challenge of staying up-to-date with newly emerging threats. Thus, while the survey respondents have not explicitly named the stress factor, the challenge of unpredictability, the need for "*staying on their toes for a new threat*", and lack of resources (time, IT staff, and funding) were listed among cybersecurity challenges – a list of challenges that have the potential to cause stress.

In summary, staff responsible for cybersecurity in Icelandic SMEs experience some level of stress due to unpredictability and ever-developing security threats. This stress is often heightened by a lack of time and/or funding, outdated systems, but most significantly by a shortage of IT staff – essential conditions required to address newly emerging cybersecurity threats effectively.

One approach for SMEs who lack the resources may be external government support [36]. The European Cybersecurity Competence Centre's network of National Coordination Centres across Europe is therefore a step in the correct direction.

5.5 Organisational Culture

It is evident from the survey data that some SMEs in Iceland face persisting organisational culture challenges that are resulting not only from employees' reluctance to follow successful cybersecurity practices (Sect. 4.2) but also as a consequence of managerial practices. For instance, a significant share of written responses included the issue of being understaffed without elaborating too much on why this issue exists; others have noted that it is due to high cost; only a small share of the written answers included more detailed explanations. The fact that the most common word in the open answers for challenges and barriers is "*employees*" indicates that, from the managerial perspective, employee behaviour is at fault.

However, managerial responsibilities were identified as key barriers to effective cybersecurity, such as low rates of mandatory cybersecurity awareness training (Sect. 4.4, question Q9.1), low rates of hiring (Sect. 4.5) and a lack of understanding of which qualifications matter. This suggests that changes in managerial culture are key to lowering these barriers. Although it should be reiterated that cybersecurity degrees are not always advised (see the discussion in Sect. 5.1) and that the efficacy of some training (e.g., phishing) has recently been cast into doubt [7,21,28], requiring more targeted approaches. Regardless, these conflicts between employee and employer responsibilities for cybersecurity within the organisations suggest room for improvement in cybersecurity culture; for example, constructive communication (such as a dedicated cybersecurity communication champion [4]) could support defining shared and collaborative responsibilities [13].

6 Summary and Conclusions

This study of 130 Icelandic SMEs investigates the influence of human factors on cybersecurity of these organisations from a management perspective. The findings show that in Icelandic SMEs, human factors were indeed influential challenges and barriers to cybersecurity.

An analysis of these results identified five themes, many of which are aligned with studies in other countries, see related work in Sect. 2: (i) Inadequate capacity of cybersecurity roles and expertise. However, one reason could be related to Iceland's perspective on hiring for skills over formal qualifications, an approach that is also in line with World Economic Forum guidelines. (ii) Organisations having a false sense of security, in that they felt they were adequately protected yet lacked the expertise to be accurately aware of threats to their organisation. Such issues can only be solved by increasing cybersecurity expertise either internally or externally. (iii) The use of ineffective training policies. In line with related literature, cybersecurity training was inconsistently applied, which is concerning given the lack of general cybersecurity expertise. However, we recommend that education policies should be applied in a targeted fashion to prevent employee fatigue. (iv) Resource constraints including time, finances, and staff. These were common for SMEs with limited resources and can be mitigated through external government support. (v) A general lack of cybersecurity culture creating ambiguity around cybersecurity roles and responsibilities. To mitigate this, we recommend the implementation of a dedicated cybersecurity champion to promote constructive communication within the organisation. In future work, we aim to extend this study through a deeper multivariate analysis of this data to understand the relationship between the studied factors and incident occurrence. We will also conduct new studies focusing upon the employee (rather than managerial) perspective.

Acknowledgments.. This project has received co-funding from the European Union's Digital Europe Programme under grant agreements no. 101127453 (NCC-IS) and 101226821 (EYVOR NCC-IS), managed by the European Cybersecurity Competence Centre (ECCC). Views and opinions expressed are however those of the authors only and do not necessarily reflect those of the European Union or the ECCC. Neither the European Union nor the granting authority can be held responsible for them.

A Statistical Significance Based on Chi-Square Analysis of Survey Data

This appendix provides details on the statistical significance of the survey data by applying the Chi-Square Goodness-of-Fit test [2] to the relevant survey questions covered in this paper.

Table 3 presents the analytical parameters for each non-demographic question with mutually exclusive answer categories. For each item, it provides the number of valid responses (N), the degrees of freedom (*df*, derived from the number of answer categories), the calculated χ^2 value, and the applicable critical value at a significance level of $\alpha = 0.05$.

As an example, consider the first sub-question of Q6.1 (see Table 1 in Sect. 4.3) that has four discrete answer categories where 19 "*Do not know*" and "*Prefer not to answer*" responses are excluded from the total sample of 118 respondents. With the remaining $N = 99$ valid responses distributed across observed frequencies of 37, 45, 13, and 4, this question yields a χ^2 value of 45.61. In this case, the null hypothesis – which assumes random answers leading to an equal distribution of responses across all four answer categories – can be rejected because the χ^2 value substantially exceeds the critical value of 7.81 that is applicable for four answer categories, i.e. 3°C of freedom at a significance level of $\alpha = 0.05$ (i.e. a 5% chance that a result is a false positive). This indicates a statistically significant meaningful preference among the respondents, rather than a random distribution of opinions.

As can be seen in Table 3, χ^2 is typically above the critical value. The only exception is question Q14.3 "*If yes, what was the attack vector used?*" which had rather few responses (the total number of responses was only 25) because it was only presented to those survey participants who had before answered that their organisation experienced a cybersecurity incident in the past year (Q14.1).

Table 3. Chi-Square Goodness-of-Fit Analysis of Survey Data ($\alpha = 0.05$)

Survey Question	N	df	χ^2	Critical Value
Q6.1.1	99	3	45.61	7.81
Q6.1.2	102	3	49.14	7.81
Q6.1.3	100	3	48.56	7.81
Q6.1.4	97	3	29.8	7.81
Q6.1.5	84	3	61.24	7.81
Q6.1.6	102	3	58.08	7.81
Q6.1.7	109	3	37.97	7.81
Q6.2.1	105	3	16.18	7.81
Q6.2.2	103	3	15.80	7.81
Q6.2.3	100	3	48.56	7.81
Q6.2.4	98	3	10.00	7.81
Q6.2.5	103	3	25.27	7.81
Q6.2.6	106	3	7.89	7.81
Q8	97	2	6.21	5.99
Q9.1	106	1	19.96	3.84
Q12.1	107	2	131.51	5.99
Q13	49	4	15.80	9.49
Q14.1	104	1	28.04	3.84
Q14.3	22	4	8.00	9.49

References

1. van Acken, J.P., Jansen, F., Jansen, S., Labunets, K.: Who is the IT department anyway: an evaluative case study of shadow IT mindsets among corporate employees. In: Twentieth Symposium on Usable Privacy and Security (SOUPS 2024). USENIX Association (2024)
2. Agresti, A.: An Introduction to Categorical Data Analysis, 3rd edn. John Wiley & Sons, Hoboken, NJ (2018)
3. Alahmari, A.A., Duncan, R.A.: Investigating potential barriers to cybersecurity risk management investment in SMEs. In: 2021 13th International Conference on Electronics, Computers and Artificial Intelligence (ECAI) (2021)
4. Alshaikh, M.: Developing cybersecurity culture to influence employee behavior: a practice perspective. Comput. Sec. **98**, 102003 (2020)
5. ATLAS.ti Scientific Software Development GmbH: ATLAS.ti (2026). https://atlasti.com
6. Birthriya, S.K., Ahlawat, P., Jain, A.K.: A comprehensive survey of social engineering attacks: taxonomy of attacks, prevention, and mitigation strategies. J. Appli. Sec. Res. **20**(2), 244–292 (2025)
7. Brunken, L., Buckmann, A., Hielscher, J., Sasse, M.A.: "To do this properly, you need more resources": the hidden costs of introducing simulated phishing campaigns. In: 32nd USENIX Security Symposium (USENIX Security 2023). USENIX Association (2023)
8. Chidukwani, A., Zander, S., Koutsakis, P.: A survey on the cyber security of small-to-medium businesses: challenges, research focus and recommendations. IEEE Access **10**, 85701–85719 (2022)
9. Chidukwani, A., Zander, S., Koutsakis, P.: Cybersecurity preparedness of small-to-medium businesses: a Western Australia study with broader implications. Comput. Sec. **145**, 104026 (2024)
10. Chowdhury, N.H., Adam, M.T., Teubner, T.: Time pressure in human cybersecurity behavior: theoretical framework and countermeasures. Comput. Sec. **97**, 101963 (2020)
11. Clarke, V., Braun, V.: Thematic analysis. J. Posit. Psychol. **12**(3), 297–298 (2017)
12. Colabianchi, S., Costantino, F., Nonino, F., Palombi, G.: Transforming threats into opportunities: the role of human factors in enhancing cybersecurity. J. Innovat. Knowl. **10**(3), 100695 (2025)
13. Corradini, I.: Building a cybersecurity culture. In: Building a cybersecurity culture in organizations: how to bridge the gap between people and digital technology, pp. 63–86. Springer (2020)
14. Creese, S., Dutton, W.H., Esteve-González, P.: The social and cultural shaping of cybersecurity capacity building: a comparative study of nations and regions. Pers. Ubiquit. Comput. **25**(5), 941–955 (2021)
15. ENISA: Cybersecurity for SMEs: Challenges and recommendations. Tech. rep., European Union Agency for Cybersecurity, Athens, Greece (2021). https://www.enisa.europa.eu/publications/enisa-report-cybersecurity-for-smes
16. Furnell, S., Vasileiou, I.: Security education and awareness: just let them burn? Netw. Secur. **2017**(12), 5–9 (2017)
17. Guðmundsdóttir, S., Guðmundsdóttir, Á.E., Ísleifsdóttir, A.I.: An expatriate in Iceland: adjusting to the new culture. In: Loftsdóttir, K., Hafsteinsson, S.B., Skaptadóttir, U.D. (eds.) Mobility and Transnational Iceland: Current Transformations and Global Entanglements, pp. 83–95. Háskólaútgáfan, Reykjavik, Iceland (2020)

18. Haag, S., Eckhardt, A.: Dealing effectively with shadow IT by managing both cybersecurity and user needs. MIS Q. Exec. **23**(4), 5 (2024)
19. Hatfield, J.M.: Social engineering in cybersecurity: the evolution of a concept. Comput. Sec. **73**, 102–113 (2018)
20. Heidt, M., Gerlach, J.P., Buxmann, P.: Investigating the security divide between SME and large companies: how SME characteristics influence organizational IT security investments. Inf. Syst. Front. **21**(6), 1285–1305 (2019)
21. Ho, G., et al.: Understanding the efficacy of phishing training in practice. In: 2025 IEEE Symposium on Security and Privacy (SP), pp. 37–54 (2025)
22. International Telecommunication Union: Measuring digital development: ICT development index 2024. Tech. rep., International Telecommunication Union (ITU), Geneva (2024). https://www.itu.int/hub/publication/d-ind-ict_mdd-2024-3/
23. Kabanda, S., Tanner, M., Kent, C.: Exploring sme cybersecurity practices in developing countries. J. Organ. Comput. Electron. Commer. **28**(3), 269–282 (2018)
24. Kappe, M., Härting, R.C., Karg, C., Deffner, D.: Cybersecurity in smes-drivers of cybercrime, insufficient equipment and prevention. Proc. Comput. Sci. **225**, 3631–3640 (2023)
25. Khadka, K., Ullah, A.B.: Human factors in cybersecurity: an interdisciplinary review and framework proposal. Int. J. Inf. Secur. **24**(3), 119 (2025)
26. Khan, N., Furnell, S., Bada, M., Nurse, J.R., Rand, M.: The hidden barriers to cyber security adoption amongst small and medium-sized enterprises. Inform. Comput. Sec. (2025)
27. Khan, N., Furnell, S., Bada, M., Rand, M., Nurse, J.R.: Investigating the experiences of providing cyber security support to small-and medium-sized enterprises. Comput. Sec. **154**, 104448 (2025)
28. Lain, D., Kostiainen, K., Čapkun, S.: Phishing in organizations: findings from a large-scale and long-term study. In: 2022 IEEE Symposium on Security and Privacy (SP). IEEE (2022)
29. McAlaney, J., Benson, V.: Cybersecurity as a social phenomenon. In: Benson, V., McAlaney, J. (eds.) Cyber Influence and Cognitive Threats, pp. 1–8. Elsevier (2020)
30. Molek-Winiarska, D., Drzewiecki, J., Juhász, Á.: What is the current state of stress management in small and medium-sized enterprises? a review of practices, approaches, and impact. J. Workplace Behav. Health 1–26 (2026)
31. OECD: Fostering strong and relevant skills in Iceland. OECD Economics Department Working Papers 1582, OECD Publishing, Paris (2019)
32. Óladóttir, Á.D., Aðalsteinsson, G.D.: Nordic management: icelandic managers in Nordic comparison. Inter. J. Bus. Res. **17**(1), 17–29 (2017)
33. Parkar, S., Mishra, D.K.: Cybersecurity workforce development and training: a comprehensive review on the significance, strategies, opportunities and challenges. In: 2024 International Conference on Intelligent Systems for Cybersecurity (ISCS). IEEE (2024)
34. Posit Team: RStudio: Integrated Development Environment for R. Posit Software, PBC (2026). https://posit.co/
35. Ramezan, C.A.: Examining the cyber skills gap: an analysis of cybersecurity positions by sub-field. J. Inf. Syst. Educ. **34**(1), 94–105 (2023)
36. Rawindaran, N., Jayal, A., Prakash, E., Hewage, C.: Perspective of small and medium enterprise (SME's) and their relationship with government in overcoming cybersecurity challenges and barriers in Wales. Inter. J. Inform. Manag. Data Insights **3**(2), 100191 (2023)

37. Sapiński, A., Hlynskyy, N., Binda, J., Lisun, Y.: Cyber stress management among employees as part of cybersecurity and psychological resilience in organisations. Sci. J. Bielsko-Biala School Finance and Law **29**(4) (2025)
38. Schöps, M., Gutfleisch, M., Wolter, E., Sasse, M.A.: Simulated stress: a case study of the effects of a simulated phishing campaign on employees' perception, stress and self-efficacy. In: 33rd USENIX Security Symposium (USENIX Security 2024). USENIX Association (2024)
39. Singh, T., Johnston, A.C., D'Arcy, J., Harms, P.D.: Stress in the cybersecurity profession: a systematic review of related literature and opportunities for future research. Organizat. Cybersec. J. Pract. Process People **3**(2), 100–126 (2023)
40. Statistics Iceland: Iceland's population was 394,324 at the beginning of 2026 (2025). https://www.statice.is/publications/news-archive/inhabitants/population-1-january-2026/ Accessed 28 March 2026
41. Stefánsson, B., Helgadóttir, A.G., Nizon-Deladoeuille, M., Neukirchen, H., Welsh, T.: Understanding trust in authentication methods for Icelandic digital public services. In: 2024 11th International Conference on Social Networks Analysis, Management and Security (SNAMS). IEEE (2024)
42. Vuggumudi, S.R.: A False Sense of Security: Organizations Need a Paradigm Shift on Protecting Themselves against APTs. Doctoral dissertation, Dakota State University (2022). https://scholar.dsu.edu/theses/374
43. World Economic Forum: Strategic cybersecurity talent framework. Tech. rep., World Economic Forum (WEF), Geneva, Switzerland (2024). https://www.weforum.org/publications/strategic-cybersecurity-talent-framework/

Archetypical Modelling for Cybersecurity and Personal Data Protection for SMEs

Sofia Almpani[1,2](✉), Pericles Loucopoulos[1], and Yannis Skourtis[1]

[1] Institute of Digital Innovation & Research (IDIR), Naas, Ireland
{sofia,peri,yannis}@idir.eu

[2] National Technical University of Athens (NTUA), Athens, Greece

Abstract. Data breaches cause massive losses to organisations. Smaller enterprises often do not possess advanced solutions to cope with an evolving threat landscape whereby sophisticated cyberattacks can bypass traditional security systems. Cloud-based services, despite their profound value-for-money proposition, come with opaque and pre-packaged provisions, making adoption difficult for these smaller enterprises. It is, therefore, desirable to offer these enterprises solutions that are easy and inexpensive to deploy. To this end, this paper presents an approach for empowering small enterprises to identify their vulnerabilities, and to design solutions for automated support to ameliorate any threats. The approach is generic so that is applicable across different enterprises and domains. This is achieved by *archetypical conceptual frameworks* that offer targeted solutions to recurring problems of cybersecurity and privacy, especially relevant to small enterprises. The paper introduces such frameworks whose semantics are based on well-founded conceptual modelling principles. The utility of these frameworks is exhibited using a design case for an automated system to support requirements for cybersecurity and privacy for small enterprises.

Keywords: cybersecurity · personal data protection · archetypes · conceptual modelling

1 Introduction

The twin challenge of Cyber Security (CS) and Personal Data Protection (PDP) is greatly magnified for Small and Medium-sized Enterprises (SMEs), over and above that which is faced by large enterprises, due to lack of resources and of relevant in-house expertise [1]. According to Accenture, 43% percent of cyberattacks are aimed at small businesses, but only 14% are prepared to defend themselves, leading to losses of $200,000 on average [2]. To mitigate against these threats, SMEs have tended to migrate their operations to the Cloud, in dramatically increasing numbers. Today, this infrastructure is being challenged by cyber threats, such as viruses, trojans, phishing attacks, malware, APTs, and sophisticated attacks such as zero-day threats. The need is apparent, therefore, to simplify security technology procurement by removing expensive consulting and middlemen from the process, and to offer SMEs compliance intelligence to assist them in the choices of solutions to adopt.

© ICST Institute for Computer Sciences, Social Informatics and Telecommunications Engineering 2027
Published by Springer Nature Switzerland AG 2027. All Rights Reserved
H. Neukirchen et al. (Eds.): ICDF2C 2026, LNICST 720, pp. 498–515, 2027.
https://doi.org/10.1007/978-3-032-37274-1_29

The multifarious challenges faced by SMEs in relation to CS and PDP are the *context* of the work presented in this paper. This work is *motivated* by the desire to empower SMEs to address the question of how best to utilise automated services that require neither detailed technological knowledge nor the use of expensive consultancy assistance. To this end, the main *contribution* of this paper is demonstrating a systematic approach by which CS and PDP challenges can be identified, specified, and analysed and based upon the analyses to develop supporting digital services in an effective and efficient manner with a minimum of effort and costs.

In the context of a system development process the paper focuses on the modelling of early requirements with emphasis on the engagement of end users. To this end, the modelling being proposed is intended to serve as the basis for (a) capturing requirements, (b) validating the information by end users and (c) defining the essential system elements for implementation.

The background to the work presented herein is two projects which have provided both the opportunity for theoretical advancements and the backdrop against which these advances have been applied. The ambition of the SENTINEL[1] project [3] was to provide tangible benefits for SMEs looking to improve their security situational awareness and adopt measures towards the protection of personal data for their customers, employees, partners, beneficiaries, having in mind that, security and data breaches are a risk not just to the SME's assets and reputation but, more critically, to the fundamental rights and freedoms of individuals. This project involved two SMEs, an investment group (TIG) made up of many companies dealing with providing social care and a company (CG) dealing with Genomic solutions. The ambition of the AVALANCHE[2] project [4–6] has been to enhance the ability of Law Enforcement Agencies (LEAs) to detect, analyse, track, investigate and prevent criminal activity, focusing on malicious synthetic media use, coordinated influence campaigns and online incitement.

Overall, users from SMEs were involved, resulting in a voluminous, diverse and relevant information. This had the following benefits to the approach discussed in this paper: (a) end users were deeply involved in the articulation, modelling and validation of requirements (examples of which are found in Sect. 6); (b) real world data was used for the development of the archetypes (see Sect. 5), which is an important consideration for the validity and applicability of archetypes; and (c) evaluation of the engineering approach, in which requirements were a very important part, was achieved through the delivery of working platforms and the satisfiability of key performance indicators (see Sect. 6).

The paper is organised as follows. Section 2 gives a short exposition to the challenges faced by SMEs in dealing with CS and PDP. Section 3 presents the conceptual frameworks upon which the semantics of the models for requirements specification and analysis are established. A baseline meta-model is defined which is application-agnostic and one which can be used in many different problem situations. Two conceptual modelling frameworks are defined, one for CS and one for PDP, building on this baseline meta-model. Section 4 provides details of the way that these conceptual frameworks can be used for defining the archetypical models. Section 5 shows the instantiation of these

[1] https://www.sentinel-project.eu

[2] https://avalancheproject.eu

models onto a mapping of a support system architecture that meets the requirements presented in the models. Section 6 introduces the process of using the approach and related to this the way that the results were evaluated by end users. Finally, Sect. 7 concludes the paper with a summary and reflective discussion.

2 CS and PDP Challenges to SMEs

SMEs face interconnected cybersecurity and personal data protection challenges that span technological risks, legal obligations, and risk-management requirements.

2.1 Operational and Technical Challenges

SMEs are key drivers of innovation, economic growth, and digital transformation [7]. However, their limited personnel and resources make it difficult to manage risks arising from the development and use of digital technologies. A major risk concerns the exposure of users' data, which may undermine customer trust and organisational reliability. ENISA reports that over 80% of surveyed SMEs process "critical" information which, if exposed, could place both the SME and its owners under significant risk [7].

Cybersecurity (CS) and personal data protection (PDP) concerns arise from the vulnerability of **assets**. An asset is any entity under the company's responsibility that has value, including infrastructure such as servers, networks, Cloud and SaaS services, hardware such as workstations, laptops and mobile devices, software systems and applications, and, most importantly, information such as personal or financial data. Risks to these assets may originate from internal or external threats [8]. The Cloud Security Alliance identifies 13 critical Cloud Computing areas relating to security and privacy, summarised in [9] as governance and operations concerns.

2.2 Legal Challenges

SMEs must also address legal obligations related to PDP, particularly those arising from the EU General Data Protection Regulation (GDPR) [10]. Compliance is not only a regulatory requirement but also a strategic factor, as businesses that demonstrate transparency are more likely to gain customer trust. The GDPR applies fully to SMEs and establishes a harmonised framework for processing personal data. It aims to protect the fundamental rights and freedoms of natural persons while ensuring legal certainty for businesses operating in the internal market.

Central to the GDPR is the broad concept of "personal data", including information relating to an identifiable person and special categories of sensitive data, such as health, biometric, genetic, political, or religious information. The GDPR is founded on principles including lawfulness, fairness, transparency, data minimisation, integrity, and confidentiality. It also requires controllers to apply privacy by design and default, notify breaches, conduct DPIAs for high-risk processing, appoint a Data Protection Officer where required, and demonstrate compliance through documentation and organisational measures.

2.3 Requirements in Dealing with the Threat of CS and PDP

SME-related requirements for CS and PDP, including confidentiality, integrity and availability, have been reported in [11]. Fragmented or ad-hoc cybersecurity and GDPR measures often produce complex and ineffective outcomes. CS should therefore follow a risk-management approach, prioritising confidentiality, integrity and availability according to assets and processing activities. While standards such as [12] may be burdensome for SMEs, ENISA's risk-based methodology offers a more proportionate approach. According to ENISA [7, 13], SMEs should adopt four phases: i) define the processing operation and context; ii) evaluate impact; iii) assess threat likelihood; and iv) mitigate risk.

The breadth and interdependence of these requirements highlight the need for an overarching *conceptual framework* on which a digital platform can be systematically designed and implemented. Such a framework should translate complex CS and PDP requirements into structured, actionable and proportionate steps aligned with SME realities. Without this abstraction layer, digital tools risk becoming overly technical, inaccessible, fragmented, or ineffective. These requirements motivate the development of the conceptual framework detailed in Sect. 3, which forms the basis for a structured and systematic approach to specifying requirements for a digital platform supporting SMEs in addressing CS and PDP challenges.

3 Modelling CS and PDP Requirements Based on Archetypes

There is a close association between the notion of *archetype*, used extensively in System Dynamics c.f [14–16]., and the notion of *pattern*, used primarily in Computer Science [17, 18]. Archetypes focus on understanding the problem whereas patterns focus on the solution. They both share important conceptual facets: (i) capture *repeated phenomena* across contexts (recurrence); (ii) generalise beyond specific instances (abstraction); (iii) enable transfer of expertise (knowledge reuse); (iv) guide reasoning under complexity (heuristic value); (v) derived from empirical observation and practice (experience). All these characteristics were relevant to the work reported in this paper. Given that in the area of requirements one is attempting to understand the problem in hand and reason about it, rather than the solution, the term 'archetype' is preferred and used throughout this paper. The archetypical models presented in this paper are built using a baseline conceptual framework, known as e-CORE [19] that has a clear semantic foundation based on three well established modelling paradigms.

3.1 The e-CORE Framework

Central to the e-CORE framework is the confluence of three modelling paradigms namely those of (a) **capability modelling** as advocated within the strategic management field [20–23], (b) **intentional modelling** [24–26], and (c) **sociotechnical modelling** [27, 28].

The confluence of these three modelling viewpoints is depicted in the meta-model shown in Fig. 1. This meta-model is referred to as the *baseline framework*. It is application-agnostic with the intention of being the foundation upon which other application-specific frameworks can be constructed. Primary classes are denoted in blue, while classes in white refer to concepts already represented, in order to avoid graphical complexity through relationships. The key concepts of the baseline framework are visualised in models using appropriate notation, as shown in Sect. 4.

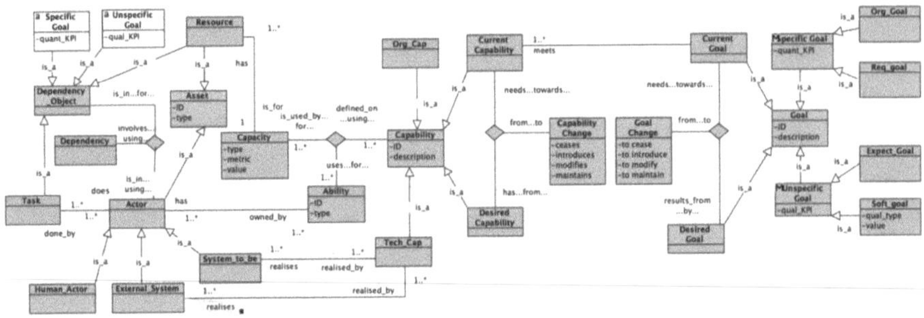

Fig. 1. The baseline conceptual framework

A Capability is the confluence of Capacities and Abilities owned or being accessed by an organisation. A Capability may be Organisational or Technical depending on the modelling view being considered. An Organisational Capability is defined as being of strategic importance to meeting Organisational Goals whereas a Technical Capability refers to a supporting role executed by a System to be or by an External System. An Actor can be Human, or a System_to_be or an External_System any of which has the Ability which together with some Capacity of some Resource defines a Capability. Actors may collaborate, establishing a Dependency between them by using some Resource or by working on some Task. Furthermore, a Dependency between Actors may also be defined on the satisfaction of some goal which may be either a measurable Specific Goal or some other Unspecific Goal concerning a quality intention. Capabilities and Goals are represented in Current and Desired states, with their evolution captured through defined Change relationships, represented by Desired Capabilities and Desired Goals respectively. This offers the opportunity to a Requirements Engineer to model the as-is status and what is required for change.

3.2 Conceptual Models for CS and PDP for SMEs

The meta-model of the baseline conceptual framework acts as the backdrop against which more specific meta-models can be defined. Two such specific meta-models are introduced in this section, one for CS and another for PDP. Both of these are considered for developing archetypical models using the three modelling dimensions (intentional, capability and sociotechnical) as shown in Sect. 4.

The meta-model for the CS case, is shown in Fig. 2. It builds upon the baseline meta-model (see Fig. 1) appending the basic concepts with those (shown in yellow) that are specific to CS cases. The baseline meta-model guides the CS meta-model so that this would conform to any instantiation for any problem domain within SMEs. The CS specific concepts, found in the CS meta-model, emerged from those found in international standards [7, 29–31], as well as consulting Systematic Literature Review reports [32, 33], design efforts [34, 35] and development concerns [36].

These additional concepts involve CS_GOALs for CAPABILITIEs that the SME should establish, as well as defining the ASSETs thus enabling the identification of intentions for CAPABILITIEs, for THREATENED_ASSETs, the most noteworthy of which will be those of INFRASTUCTURE together with the CS_RISCs on these ASSETs. As part of appropriate CAPABILITIEs is the ACTORs (human as well as technical) which will have the ABILITY and CAPACITY to execute PROCESSEs corresponding to Organisational and Technical Measures (OTM).

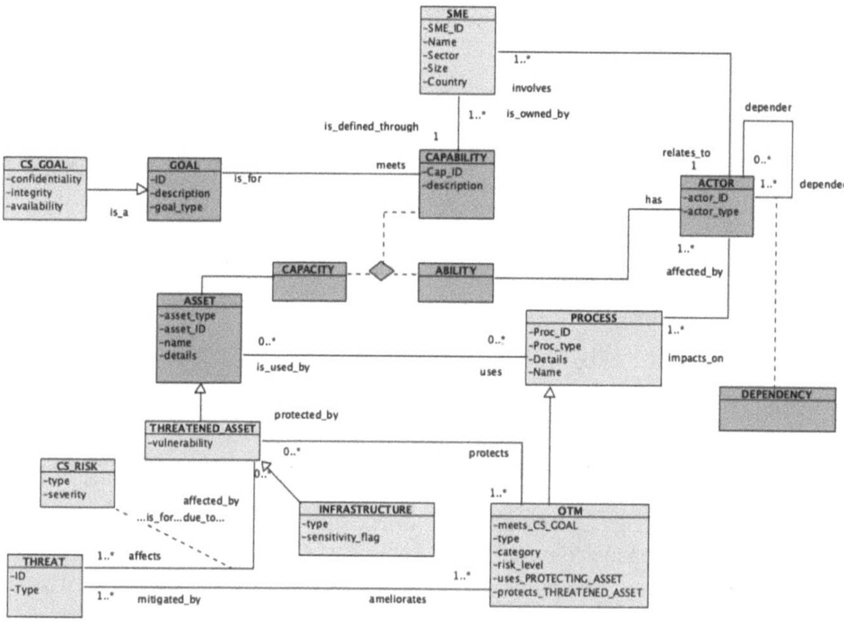

Fig. 2. The CS conceptual framework

The meta-model for the PDP case, is shown in Fig. 3. It builds upon the baseline meta-model (see Fig. 1) appending the basic concepts with concepts that are specific to PDP cases. The baseline meta-model guides the PDP meta-model so that this would conform to any instantiation for any problem domain within SMEs. The PDP specific concepts emerged from standards [10, 37, 38], as well as from reviews and analysis of studies in the legal domain [39], design strategies [40–42], personal data collection [43] and visual analytics [44].

The PDP meta-model, building on the e-CORE meta-model, introduces PDP_GOALs for CAPABILITIEs that the SME should establish.

A key difference of the PDP case from that of the CS is that the main ASSET at risk is that of DATA and specifically PD_RISK that concerns DATA_SUBJECTs affected by some PD_PROCESSING_ACTIVITY. There are a number of potential ACTORs involved, a RECIPIENT (could be a local or remote ACTOR), a PROCESSOR, or a CONTROLLER who are likely to be involved in the processing of the DATA_SUBJECTs. The THREATENED_ASSET will be protected by PROCESSEs corresponding to Organisational and Technical Measures (OTM).

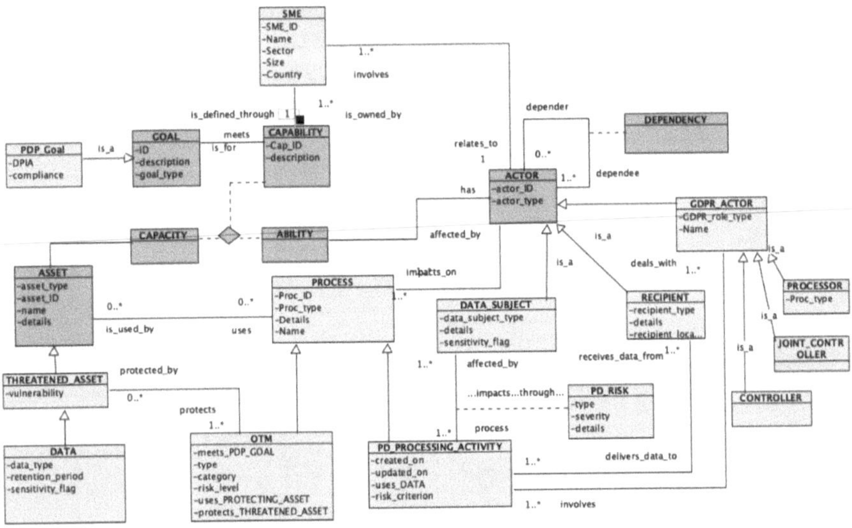

Fig. 3. The PDP conceptual framework

4 Archetypical Models for CS and PDP Digital Support

Based on the CS and PDP conceptual frameworks introduced in Sect. 3, a set of archetypical models are developed and presented in Sects. 4.1, 4.2, and 4.3, along the three axes of intentional modelling, capability modelling, and sociotechnical modelling. They are presented using appropriate visualisation means that facilitate ease of understanding and offer the means by which stakeholders can review and agree on the concepts to be included in a problem application.

These archetypical models were built using empirical evidence from the involvement of end users from the SMEs introduced in Sect. 1. To facilitate effective dialogue between modellers and end users, models are expressed through visual notations for each one of the three perspectives (intentional, capability and socio-technical), using the extension of a software tool [45]. The semantics of these notations are based on the meta-models presented in Sect. 3.

4.1 Intentional Archetypical Model for CS and PDP

The intentional archetypical model in Fig. 4 describes how the overarching objective of "G0. To ensure CS and PDP for SMEs" is realized through a structured decomposition of interrelated goals, tasks, and capabilities.

At the top level, the model decomposes this objective into four major goals: "G1. To ensure a safe and reliable digital ecosystem", "G2. To ensure accredited staff and services", "G3. To achieve GDPR compliance", and "G4. To ensure monitoring of service impacts and incidents". These goals are further refined into more specific concerns such as "G1.1 To ensure secure data handling" and "G1.2 To ensure secure operational lifecycle management", which address secure processing, sharing, and lifecycle management of data. Human and organizational aspects are captured through "G2.1 To ensure high staff CS competence", "G2.2 To assess cybersecurity risks", and "G2.3 To ensure privacy awareness". Regulatory and oversight dimensions are addressed through G3.1, G3.2 and G4.1, G4.2 respectively. All goals and tasks are assigned to enabling capabilities – "C1. Digital Service Providing", "C2. Data Protecting", "C3. Regulations Complying", and "C4. External Security Control Integration" - showing how coordinated technical and organizational capabilities collectively support secure, compliant, and trustworthy digital services for SMEs.

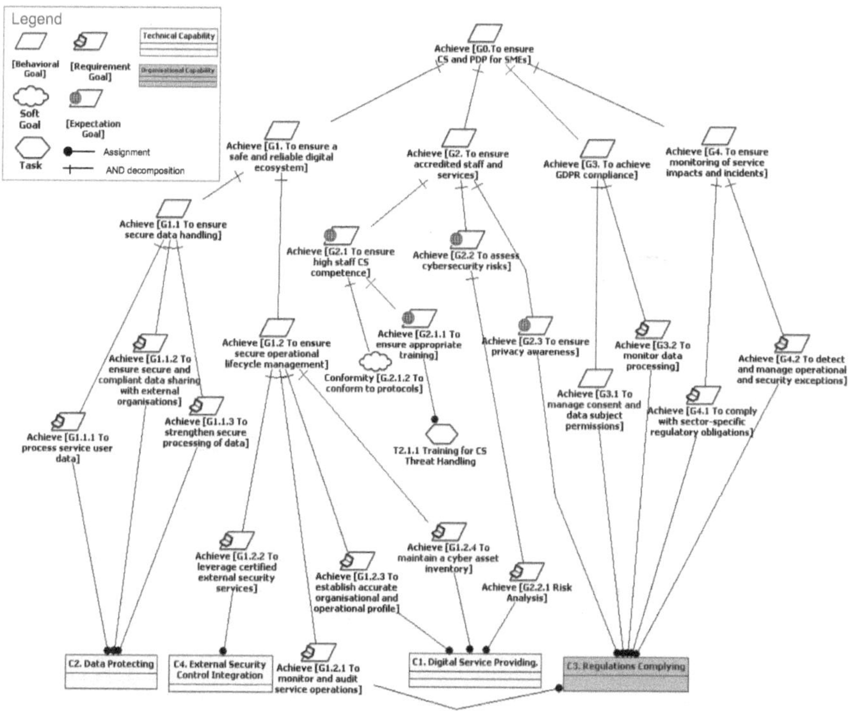

Fig. 4. The *intentional* archetypical model

4.2 Capability Archetypical Model for CS and PDP

The capability archetypical model in Fig. 5 shows how CS and PDP protection is supported through a small set of tightly integrated organisational and technical capabilities.

At the centre, "C1. Digital Service Providing" delivers core services. It is realized through "C1.1 Workforce and Role Managing", "C1.2 User Service Executing", "C1.3 Organisation profiling", and "C1.4 Receiving security notifications", covering staff management, service execution, risk analysis, identity management, and organisational context awareness. Data security is reinforced by "C2. Data Protecting", which supports secure data processing and sharing, while "C4. External Security Control Integration" connects the platform with external security sources and controls. Governance and oversight are provided by "C3. Regulations complying", composed of auditing, cyber incident reporting and handling, policy recommendations, enforcement monitoring, and observatory information exchange.

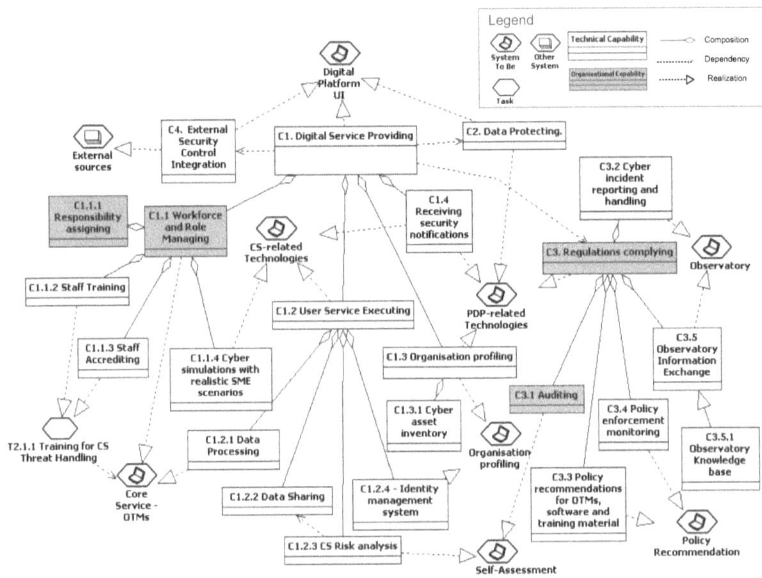

Fig. 5. The *capability* archetypical model

Together, these capabilities illustrate how operational service delivery, protection mechanisms, external integration, and regulatory compliance collectively enable secure and compliant digital services for SMEs.

4.3 Sociotechnical Archetypical Model for CS and PDP

The sociotechnical archetypical model in Fig. 6 illustrates how "SME Staff" is involved in delivering secure and compliant services by interacting with multiple internal and external actors and systems.

"SME Staff" depends on "External sources", "CS-related technologies", "PDP-related technologies", and the "Cloud" to upload, collect, assess, and monitor service user data, while also supporting activities such as incident monitoring and external security control. Compliance and oversight are achieved through dependencies on the "DPO", "Regulators", and the "Observatory", as well as processes like "Self-Assessment" and obtaining service user consent. Internally, coordination with the "HR Team", "Management", and the "Internal ICT system" enables staff accreditation, responsibility assignment, and staff data management, ensuring that operational, technical, and regulatory responsibilities are clearly aligned.

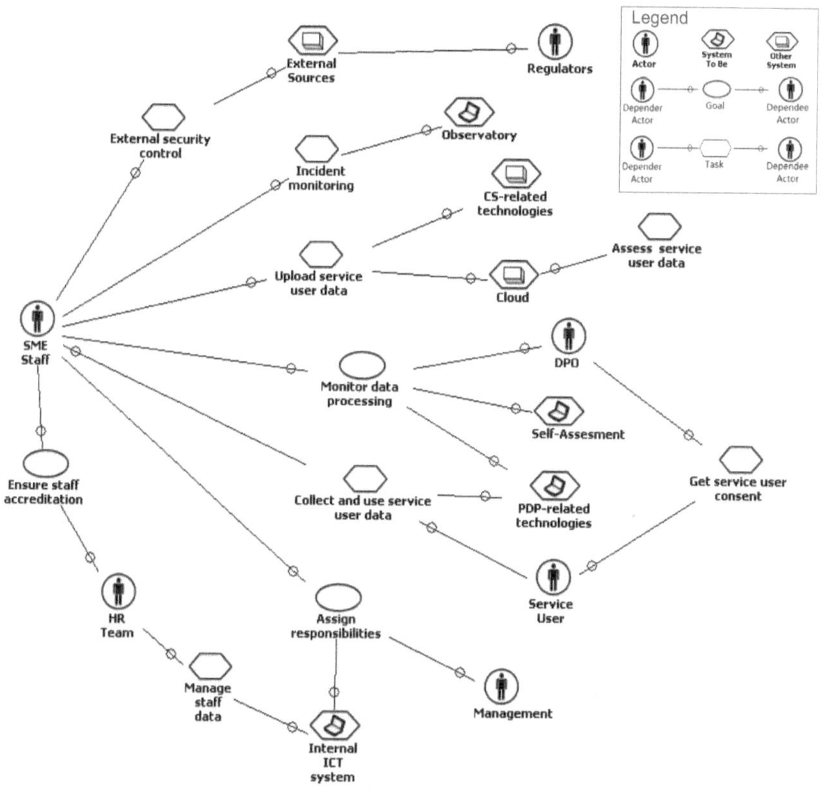

Fig. 6. The *sociotechnical* archetypical model

4.4 Risk Analysis through Intertwining of Models

By using the models in an interrelated manner, as illustrated by the fragments shown in Fig. 7 it is possible to trace how operational activities and assets contribute to the satisfaction of security and data protection goals. Fig. 7 illustrates how elements from the Sociotechnical, Intentional, and Capabilities Model are semantically linked to assess whether data protection goals are achieved. The intertwining of the models and the analysis based on these provides strong evidence that the captured information in the models is *necessary* and *sufficient*. Thus, there is evidence that the models are verifiable and complete. If during the reviewing of the models by end users it is discovered that some elements are superfluous or some are missing, that would be the trigger for revising the models.

In the example shown in Fig. 7, the red dashed circles highlight selected example elements and mappings across the models, while the blue dashed lines show traceability links across models. In particular, the activity "`Monitor data processing`" in the sociotechnical model satisfies the goal "`G1.1.1 To process service user data`", while the capability "`C2. Data Protecting`" supports the related secure data handling goals "`G1.1.1-G1.1.3`". Furthermore, the "`PDP-related technologies`" appear consistently across models, represented as an asset in the capabilities model and as a supporting element in the sociotechnical model, enabling traceability between technical assets, operational behaviour, and goal satisfaction.

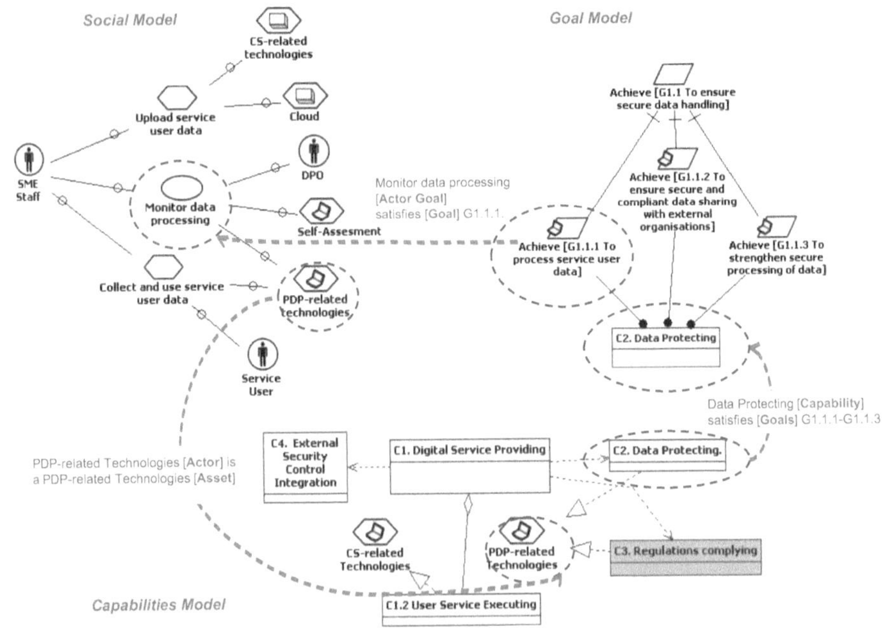

Fig. 7. Inter-model relationships between archetypical models

Risk analysis aims to ascertain the current CS- and privacy-related risk, based on the identified threats noted in the capability model. In particular, the analysis is based on: (a) the occurrence probability of each threat which is calculated based on relevant vulnerabilities pertaining to related assets and their collaboration (described in the sociotechnical model), as well as the sensitivity of relevant data; and (b) the level of impact of the threat (high, medium, low) on the affected capability (described in the capability model).

Using the models, fragments of which are shown in Fig. 7, it is possible to evaluate to what degree the goals may be satisfied. It involves the assessment of the type and level of mitigation for the perceived threat of the desired capability to satisfy the goal. This type of analysis is guided by the semantic relationships between the different e-CORE modelling concepts.

5 From Generic Archetypical to Specific Models – an Example

The utility of archetypes, in the context of requirements modelling, lies in their provision of generic frameworks that constitute ontologically relevant descriptions applicable to many situations. The meta-models presented in Sect. 4 are such generic frameworks. In practice, these archetypes provide a clear path for developing specific models, a subject matter of this section in which the archetypes are applied to a specific use case.

Consider the case of CG, introduced in Sect. 1. CG is an SME whose aim is to advance patient care and support through the development and provision of state-of-the-art decision-support and cutting-edge solutions in Genomic Medicine for physicians and patients. The types of data dealt by CG include: Human DNA sequence variants; simple anonymous pro-band demographic data; technical/experimental data.

The analysis of the CG business environment involved the modelling of existing capabilities, goals and actors as well as the requirements for change that resulted in new capabilities. Space limitations prevent the description of the full process and associated results but nevertheless, the models shown in Fig. 8, Fig. 9 and Fig. 10 show the resultant customised models derived from the generic ones (shown in Sect. 4) as they apply to the new capabilities.

The goal model in Fig. 8 captures how the overarching objective `"G0. To deliver reliable services"` is refined into security, efficiency, and legal compliance concerns within the genomic data context. Sub-goals related to secure processing of genomic and customer data, map directly to generic goals on secure data handling and lifecycle management, GDPR-oriented goals align with the generic compliance and monitoring objectives, while the introduction of soft goals such as `"Security [G1.3 Ensure data integrity]"` and improvement goals (e.g., assurance of genomic data) mirrors the generic model's use of soft and expectation goals.

The capability model in Fig. 9 refines the goal structure into concrete capabilities and explicitly introduces security and privacy threats. Capabilities such as `"C1. Service Providing"`, `"C1.1 Genome Data Processing"`, `"C1.2 Customer Data Managing"`, and `"C2 Regulations Complying"` align with the archetypical capability model's `"Digital Service Providing"`, `"Data Protecting"`, and `"Regulations Complying"` capabilities. Threats like `"Data Breach"` and `"Privacy Breach"` provide an explicit risk perspective that complements the archetype models' implicit risk and monitoring goals.

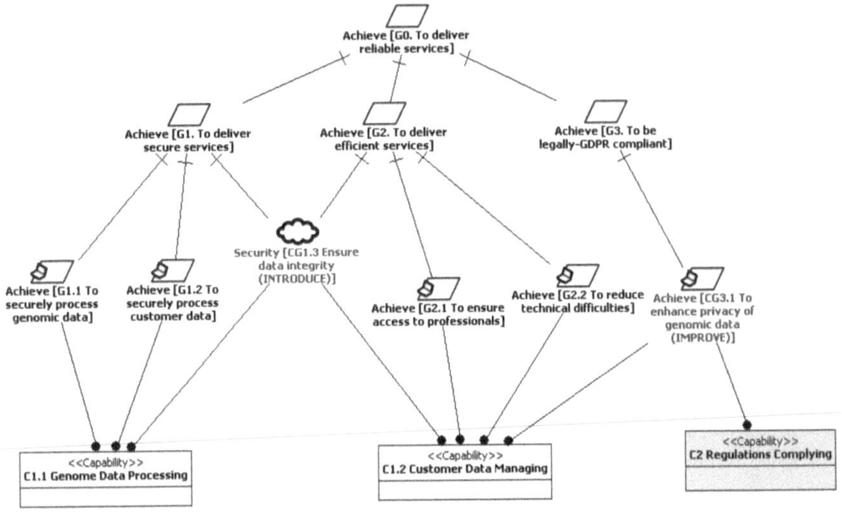

Fig. 8. The intentional model for CG

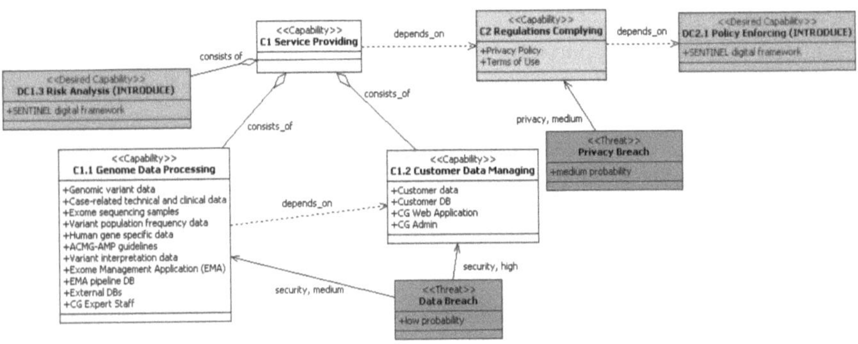

Fig. 9. The capability model for CG

The sociotechnical model for CG in Fig. 10 details the operational realization by showing how actors (e.g., `"Genetics Professional"`, `"CG Expert Staff"`, `"CG Admin"`) interact with systems and perform tasks such as uploading genomic data, filtering variants, managing users, and delivering results.

These tasks correspond to the operational tasks identified in the generic sociotechnical and capability realization models. Vulnerabilities such as `"Presence of PII Data"` and `"Inadequate security awareness"` directly relate to generic concerns around data protection, staff competence, and privacy risks.

Overall, the three CG use case models are consistently aligned with the generic archetype framework in terms of goals, capabilities, actors, and tasks. The goal model provides a clear refinement from high-level service objectives to security, efficiency, and compliance concerns, which are systematically realized by the capability model

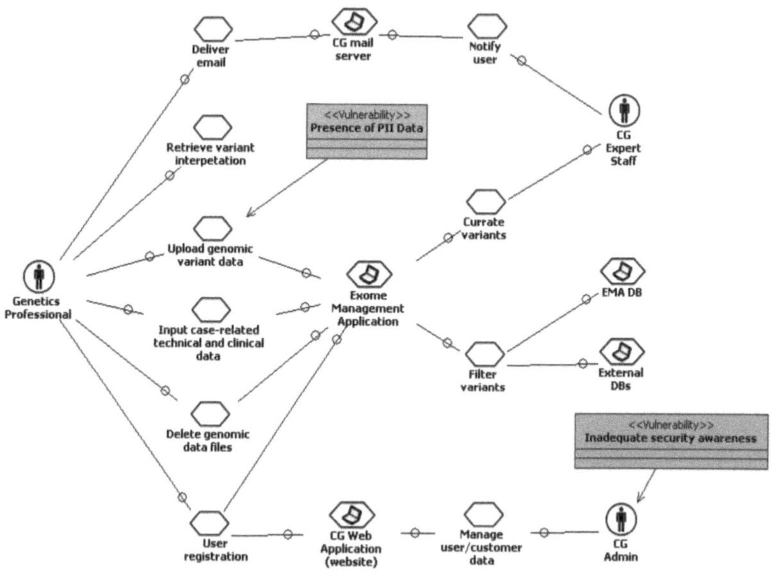

Fig. 10. The sociotechnical model for CG

and operationalized through actor–task interactions. This alignment enables a coherent end-to-end trace from strategic goals to concrete capabilities and runtime activities.

6 Applying and Evaluating the Approach

The manner in which the approach is used for eliciting, and modelling end user requirements, and mapping these onto system requirements involves 3 key phases each of which involves a set of distinct steps. These are shown in Fig. 11.

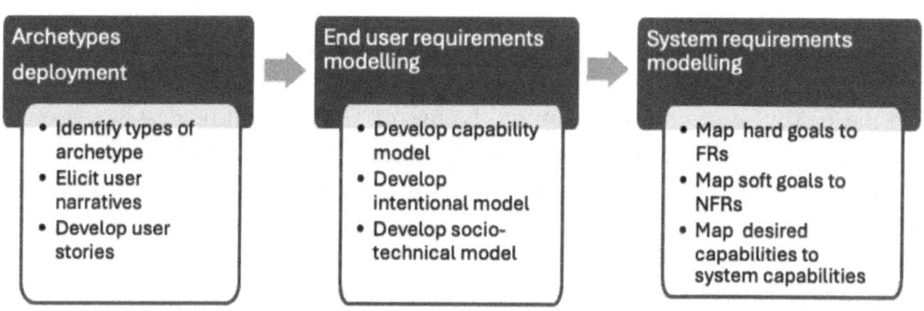

Fig. 11. The requirements process from archetypes to system requirements

In practice, once it is understood that a case requires modelling and analysis of CS and PDP for the SME, end-users become involved in informing Requirements Engineers about their business and technical capabilities and their requirements for improving their approach to handling CS and PDP threats. With reference to the use case described in Sect. 5, this involved the use of questionnaires, guided by the meta-models (see Sect. 3) to elicit information regarding intentions, capabilities and sociotechnical components. Questionnaires were complemented by interviews, to uncover any limitations or challenges encountered, to explore desired improvements, and to determine how these may enhance their work. The responses of end-users were subsequently analysed through the development of user stories [46]. These were analysed and translated into the three types of models, each one being guided by the archetype models as shown in Sect. 4, resulting in the specific models for CG detailed in Sect. 5.

The specific details of these models are used as input to define the system requirements and specifically the functional requirements (FRs) and non-functional requirements (NFs). Associated with these are key performance indicators (KPIs) that are *evaluation* measures for both the system functionality and for its quality characteristics. Therefore, the approach supports the gradual, systematic and formal transformation from fuzzy user-expressed narratives to specific system components that are subject to evaluation by end users as to whether the developed system is aligned with their requirements. This is most effectively done in structured workshops whereby many stakeholders with a variety of knowledge and experience, use the system, evaluate it against the established evaluation criteria and provide feedback. An example of such a workshop is reported here.

7 Conclusions and Discussion

Commercial enterprise IT security solutions, feature comprehensive CS and PDP assurance but, they are often beyond the financial capability of SMEs. On the other hand, free security options provide rudimentary protection at the endpoint level but leave exposed sensitive personal data residing in web apps and other infrastructures.

The overarching aim of the work detailed in this paper is to facilitate SMEs' *self-assessment* and raising awareness of internal or external services for boosting their CS and PDP capabilities. Towards this aim, the approach being put forward is one of exploiting archetypical models which, because of their generality and abstraction, enable system developers to build customised specifications efficiently and effectively for the problem domain in hand.

In the field of conceptual modelling the use of archetypical models has been formally investigated [17]. Somewhat similarly to the way that archetypical conceptual models are discussed in this paper is the definition of analysis patterns as conceptual models capturing generic domain structures, and discussing methods for increased reuse, description, and specification of such conceptual patterns [47]. In [48] the authors report on their experiences in using archetypical conceptual modelling stating that these models significantly enhanced both the understanding and improvement of the modelling process. The idea of exploiting archetypical models for the purpose of CS and PDP has been investigated in related works [49–52].

The knowledge contained within the 3 archetypical models presented in Sect. 4 has been specifically developed to support CS and PDP for SMEs. This knowledge has been historically discovered, reviewed, revised and validated in different problem areas by a number of stakeholders to the extent that the models represent accumulated expertise in the analysis of problems in the field [5, 19, 23].

The modelling paradigm presented in this paper has been instrumental in the development of software platforms that can assist SMEs in their quest to deal with CS and PDP challenges.

Acknowledgments. The authors wish to express their gratitude to colleagues for exchanges of scientific views and experiences within two related projects, the SENTINEL project (grant agreement n° 101021659) and the AVALANCHE project (grant agreement n°101168393) both of which have been funded by the European Union's Horizon 2020 Work Programme for research and innovation.

References

1. Benz, M., Chatterjee, D.: Calculated risk? A cybersecurity evaluation tool for SMEs. Bus. Horiz. **63**(4), 531–540 (2020)
2. Accenture: Cyberattacks now cost companies $200,000 on average, putting many out of business (2019). Retrieved, 2020. https://www.cnbc.com/2019/10/13/cyberattacks-cost-small-companies-200k-putting-many-out-of-business.html.
3. Trantidou, T., et al.: SENTINEL - approachable, tailor-made cybersecurity and data protection for small enterprises. In: IEEE International Conference on Cyber Security and Resilience (CSR), Rhodes, Greece (2022)
4. Vladuta, V.A.: Building trust: a conceptual architecture to detect disinformation and reduce its influence in contemporary society. In: 6th International Conference in Electronic Engineering & Information Technology (EEITE) (2025)
5. Almpani, S., Kavakli, E., Loucopoulos, P., Valari, E.: Requirements modelling for hate speech detection and analysis. In: 14th World Conference on Information Systems and Technologies (WorldCIST'26), Madeira Island, Portugal Lecture Notes in Networks and Systems, Springer (2026)
6. Konidi, M., Karagiorgou, S., Veroni, E., Nikolopoulos, C.: Addressing disinformation and deep fakes spread through AI-fuelled international collaboration. In: 6th International Conference in Electronic Engineering & Information Technology (EEITE), Chania, Greece, pp. 1–5 (2025)
7. ENISA (2021). Cybersecurity for SMEs: Challenges and Recommendation.
8. Jouini, M., Rabai, L.B.A., Aissa, A.B.: Classification of security threats in information systems. In: 5th International Conference on Ambient Systems, Networks and Technologies (ANT-2014), Procedia Computer Science 32, pp. 489–496 (2014)
9. Cloud Security Alliance (CSA): Security Guidance for Critical Areas of Focus in Cloud Computing v4.0 (2017). Retrieved 30 July 2021. https://cloudsecurityalliance.org/artifacts/security-guidance-v4/
10. European Parliament and of the Council: On the protection of natural persons with regard to the processing of personal data and on the free movement of such data (GDPR) (2016).
11. Kavakli, E., Loucopoulos, P., Skourtis, Y.: The SENTINEL baseline (2022).
12. ISO/IEC: Information technology — Security techniques — Information security management systems — Requirements (2013).
13. ENISA: Guideline on Security Measures under the EECC (2021).
14. Oosthuizen, R.: Application pf system archetypes to improve system dynamics modelling. In: 9th Annual South African System Dynamics Conferences, pp. 13–21 (2021)

15. Špicar, R.: System dynamics archetypes in Capacity planning. Proceedia Eng. **69**, 1350–1355 (2014)
16. Sánchez, M.A.: Exploring the landscape of system dynamics archetypes: a systematic review. Syst. Res. Behav. Sci. **42**(27), 1–15 (2024)
17. Guizzardi, G.: Ontological patterns, anti-patterns and pattern languages for next-generation conceptual Modeling. In: Invited Companion Paper to the Keynote Speech Delivered at the 33rd International Conference on Conceptual Modeling (ER 2014), Atlanta, U.S.A (2014)
18. Hruby, P.: Model-Driven Design Using Business Patterns. Springer, New York (2006)
19. Loucopoulos, P., Kavakli, E., Mascolo, J.: Requirements engineering for cyber physical production systems: the e-CORE approach and its application. Inf. Syst. **104**(2022), 1–17 (2022)
20. Helfat, C.E., Peteraf, M.A.: Understanding dynamic capabilities: Progress along a developmental path. Strateg. Organ. **7**(1), 91–102 (2009)
21. Teece, D.J.: Dynamic Capabilities: A guide for Managers. Ivey Bus. J. (2011)
22. Danesh, M.H., Yu, E.: Modeling Dynamic Capabilities to Reason about Information Systems Flexibility. CAiSE 2014 (Submitted) (2014).
23. Kavakli, E., Loucopoulos, P., Skourtis, Y.: Capability oriented RE for cybersecurity and personal data protection: meeting the challenges of SMEs. In: 9th International Workshop on "Evolving Security & Privacy Requirements Engineering", pp. 244–249. IEEE, Melbourne, Australia (2022)
24. Dalpiaz, F., X. Franch, J. Horkoff: iStar 2.0 Language Guide. pp. 1–15 (2016).
25. Kavakli, E., Loucopoulos, P.: Experiences with goal-oriented modelling of organisational change. IEEE Trans. Syst. Man Cybern. Part C. **36**(2), 221–235 (2006)
26. Lamsweerde, A.V.: Goal-oriented requirements engineering: a guided tour. In: Proceedings of the Fifth IEEE International Symposium on Requirements Engineering, pp. 249–262, Toronto, Ontario, Canada (2001)
27. Yu, E., Giorgini, P., Maiden, N., Mylopoulos, J., (Eds): Social Modeling for Requirements Engineering. Yu, E., P. Giorgini, N. Maiden, and J. Mylopoulos (ed.). MIT Press. 752 pages (2010).
28. Yu, E.S.K., Mylopoulos, J.: Towards modelling strategic actor relationships for information systems development - with examples from business process reengineering. In: 4th Workshop on Information Technologies and Systems (WITS'94), Vancouver, B.C., Canada (1994)
29. ENISA: Cloud Security Guide for SMEs: Cloud computing security risks and opportunities for SMEs (2015).
30. ENISA: ENISA Threat Landscape Report 2016–15 Top Cyber-Threats and Trends (2017).
31. ENISA: Cybersecurity Guide for SMEs (2022).
32. Jafari, A.J., Rasoolzadegan, A.: Security patterns: a systematic mapping study. J. Comput. Lang. **56**(2020) (2020)
33. Washizaki, H., et al.: Systematic Literature Review of Security Pattern Research. Information 12 (1) (2021).
34. Dantas, Y.G., Nigam, V.: Automating safety and security co-design through semantically rich architecture patterns. ACM Trans. Cyber Phys. Syst. **7**(1), 1–28 (2023)
35. Sabau, A.R., Lammers, D., Lichter, H.: SecuRe - an approach to recommending security design patterns. In: 2025 IEEE 22nd International Conference on Software Architecture Companion (ICSA-C), pp. 186–189. IEEE XPlore, Odense, Denmark (2025)
36. Ryan, I., Roedig, U., Stol, K.J.: Understanding developer security archetypes. In: IEEE/ACM 2nd International Workshop on Engineering and Cybersecurity of Critical Systems (EnCyCriS). IEEE, Madrid, Spain (2021)
37. ENISA: Information security and privacy standards for SMEs: Recommendations to improve the adoption of information security and privacy standards in small and medium enterprises (2015).

38. Jasmontaite-Zanieewicz, L., A. Calvi, R. Nagy, D. Barnard-Wills, (Eds.): The GDPR Made Simple(r) for SMEs. Jasmontaite-Zanieewicz, L., A. Calvi, R. Nagy, and D. Barnard-Wills (ed.). VUBPress: Brussels, Belgium (2021).
39. Haapio, H., Hagan, M., Palmirani, M., Rossi, A.: Legal Design Patterns for Privacy. 21st International Legal Informatics Symposium IRIS 2018 (2018).
40. Colesky, M., J.H. Hoepman, C. Hillen: A Critical Analysis of Privacy Design Strategies. IEEE Security and Privacy Workshops (2016).
41. Rest, J.V., Boonstra, D., Everts, M., Rijn, M.V., Paassen, R.V.: Designing privacy-by-design. In: Lecture Notes in Computer Science, vol. 8319, pp. 55–72. Springer (2014)
42. Maloku, A., A. Klymenko, S. Meisenbacher, F. Matthes: Privacy Starts with UI: Privacy Patterns and Designer Perspectives in UI/UX Practice. Symposium on Usable Security and Privacy (USEC) 2026. (ed.). San Diego, CA, USA (2026).
43. Jarovsky, L.: Dark patterns in personal data collection: definition, taxonomy, and lawfulness. SSRN Electron. J. (2022)
44. Zhou, J., et al.: DPVisCreator: incorporating pattern constraints to privacy-preserving visualizations via differential privacy. IEEE Trans. Vis. Comput. Graph. **29**, 809–819 (2023)
45. Supakkul, S., L. Chung: RE-Tools: A Multi-notational Modelling Toolkit (2009–2012). Retrieved 1 July 2021. http://www.utdallas.edu/~supakkul/tools/RE-Tools/index.html
46. Dalpiaz, F., Brinkkemper, S.: Agile requirements engineering with user stories. In: IEEE 26th International Requirements Engineering Conference (RE), pp. 506–507. IEEE, Banff, AB, Canada (2018)
47. Purao, S., Storey, V.C., Han, T.: Improving analysis pattern reuse in conceptual design: augmenting automated processes with supervised learning. Inf. Syst. Res. **14**(3), 269–290 (2003)
48. Fumagalli, M., et al.: Mining frequent structures in conceptual models. Softw. Syst. Model. (2025)
49. Washizaki, H.: Security patterns: research direction, metamodel, application and verification. In: 2017 International Workshop on Big Data and Information Security (IWBIS), pp. 1–4, Jakarta, Indonesia (2017)
50. Papoutsakis, M., Fysarakis, K., Spanoudakis, G., Ioannidis, S., Koloutsou, K.: Towards a collection of security and privacy patterns. Appl. Sci. (11) (2021)
51. Rajmohan, T., Nguyen, P.H., Ferry, N.: A decade of research on patterns and architectures for IoT security. Cybersecurity. **5**(1) (2022)
52. Diamantopoulou, V., Kalloniatis, C., Gritzalis, S., Mouratidis, H.: Supporting privacy by design using privacy process patterns. In: 32th IFIP International Conference on ICT Systems Security and Privacy Protection (SEC), pp. 491–505, Rome, Italy (2017)

Temporal Evolution and Conceptual Fragmentation of Research on Human Behavior in Social Engineering Cybersecurity

Rahmat Hidayat[1], Zalik Nuryana[2](✉), Erdisna[3], Aldo Erianda[1], Alde Alanda[1], and Andri Pranolo[2]

[1] Politeknik Negeri Padang, Padang, Indonesia
{rahmat,aldo,alde}@pnp.ac.id
[2] Universitas Ahmad Dahlan, Yogyakarta, Indonesia
zalik@ascee.org, andri.pranolo@tif.uad.ac.id
[3] Universitas Negeri Padang, Padang, Indonesia
erdisna@unp.ac.id

Abstract. The increasing sophistication of social engineering attacks highlights a key limitation in cybersecurity research: the inadequate integration of human behavioral factors into technology-centered approaches. This study examines the evolution, conceptual structure, and human-centric integration of social engineering research through a bibliometric analysis of 1,009 Scopus-indexed publications using VOSviewer and Biblioplot. The results show significant growth in research output, driven largely by advances in artificial intelligence and machine learning. However, behavioral and psychological perspectives have not progressed at the same pace. Keyword co-occurrence analysis identifies three main themes: human factors and security awareness, information security and user behavior, and AI-driven cybersecurity approaches. Thematic mapping reveals that technology-focused topics are well developed and central to the field, whereas decision-making, cognitive factors, and psychological vulnerability remain underexplored. These findings indicate a fragmented knowledge structure in which technological and human-centered perspectives evolve separately. Future research should prioritize behavior-aware cybersecurity frameworks that integrate cognitive and psychological insights to improve the effectiveness of social engineering defense strategies.

Keywords: Artificial intelligence · cybersecurity · human · behavior · machine learning · phishing · social engineering

1 Introduction

In the era of rapid digital transformation, cybersecurity threats are growing not only from the technical side, but also through the exploitation of the human aspect as the weakest point in the security system. Attacks such as phishing and social engineering

© ICST Institute for Computer Sciences, Social Informatics and Telecommunications Engineering 2027
Published by Springer Nature Switzerland AG 2027. All Rights Reserved
H. Neukirchen et al. (Eds.): ICDF2C 2026, LNICST 720, pp. 516–530, 2027.
https://doi.org/10.1007/978-3-032-37274-1_30

take advantage of users' behavioral, psychological, and cognitive weaknesses to gain unauthorized access to sensitive information [5, 31]. In contrast to traditional technical attacks, this approach directly targets the human factor, making it more difficult to detect and prevent [26]. A number of studies have shown that the success of social engineering attacks is strongly influenced by user behavioral characteristics, such as trust levels, impulsivity, and lack of security awareness [12, 21]. In addition, cognitive biases such as trust bias, urgency effect, and decision fatigue also contribute significantly to an individual's vulnerability to such attacks [27]. These factors suggest that cybersecurity can no longer be viewed as just a technical problem, but also as a human behavior problem.

Furthermore, literature studies show that demographic and psychological variables, such as age, experience, and digital literacy level, have an influence on the level of vulnerability to phishing [15]. Other research also highlights that the organizational environment and social factors, such as work culture and social influence, contribute to shaping user safety behaviors [18, 32]. This reinforces the view that a multidisciplinary approach that combines psychology, behavior, and technology is indispensable in understanding cybersecurity comprehensively. On the other hand, various studies have also shown that security awareness and training have an important role in reducing the risk of human-based attacks [16, 25]. However, most of the approaches that exist are still general and have not taken into account the variation in individual behavior in depth [34]. In addition, many security solutions still focus on technology without strong integration with aspects of user behavior [20].

Recent developments also show the integration of artificial intelligence-based approaches and behavioral analysis to detect and prevent social engineering attacks [4, 30]. In addition, new approaches such as cyber linguistics are also beginning to be used to understand how language is used to manipulate victims in digital attacks [24]. This shows a shift in research trends towards a more human-centric and interdisciplinary approach. However, there is still a significant research gap. Most studies focus on the analysis of individual factors or specific case studies, while studies that systematically map the development of research related to human behavior in social engineering are still limited [3, 23]. In addition, there have not been many studies that integrate bibliometric analysis to comprehensively identify trends, patterns of collaboration, and the evolution of topics in this domain.

To address the identified research gaps and provide a comprehensive understanding of the domain, this study formulates several research questions focusing on the evolution, structure, and perspective of human behavior in social engineering within cybersecurity. Specifically, this research aims to explore the temporal development of the field, identify the underlying conceptual structure through bibliometric analysis, and examine the extent to which human-centric approaches have been incorporated into cybersecurity research. Accordingly, the following research questions are proposed.

RQ1:How has research on human behavior in social engineering within cybersecurity evolved over time?

RQ2:What are the main conceptual structures and research themes identified through keyword co-occurrence analysis in this domain?

RQ3: To what extent has the human-centric cybersecurity perspective been integrated into existing research, and what gaps remain?

2 Methods

Investigating the evolution of human behavior research in social engineering requires more than a conventional literature review due to the rapid growth and multidisciplinary nature of the field. Existing studies are dispersed across cybersecurity, psychology, information security, and artificial intelligence, making it difficult to obtain a comprehensive understanding of how the domain has developed over time. Therefore, a bibliometric approach was employed to systematically examine the intellectual structure of the field, identify dominant and emerging research themes, and evaluate the extent to which human-centric perspectives have been incorporated into cybersecurity research. By combining temporal analysis, keyword co-occurrence mapping, and thematic evaluation, this study provides a data-driven assessment of the evolution, conceptual organization, and future research directions of human behavior research in social engineering.

2.1 Data Collection

As shown in Fig. 1, the research begins with topic identification, focusing on the intersection of social engineering, human behavior, and cybersecurity. The search strategy was then developed and applied to the Scopus database (https://scopus.com/) to ensure comprehensive coverage of peer-reviewed academic publications. Data were collected on March 30, 2026, using the following query:

TITLE-ABS-KEY ("social engineering" OR phishing OR "human factor") AND TITLE-ABS-KEY (behavior OR behaviour OR "human behavior" OR psychology) AND TITLE-ABS-KEY (cybersecurity OR "information security").

The retrieved records included bibliographic metadata such as titles, abstracts, authors, keywords, source titles, and citation information. These data were used to support bibliometric mapping and thematic analysis of research on human behavior in social engineering within cybersecurity.

The data collection procedure began with identifying relevant publications through a structured search query using predefined keywords related to social engineering, human behavior, and cybersecurity. The search was performed on March 30, 2026, resulting in an initial dataset, which was subsequently refined based on document types and relevance criteria, leading to a final dataset of 1,009 documents. Following data retrieval, the dataset was exported and further processed using bibliometric tools, namely VOSviewer. These tools were utilized to perform network visualization and bibliometric mapping, including keyword co-occurrence, collaboration networks, and thematic evolution analysis [6]. In addition, the analysis was strengthened using thematic mapping approaches such as enhanced strategic diagrams to better interpret research trends and thematic development [29, 36].

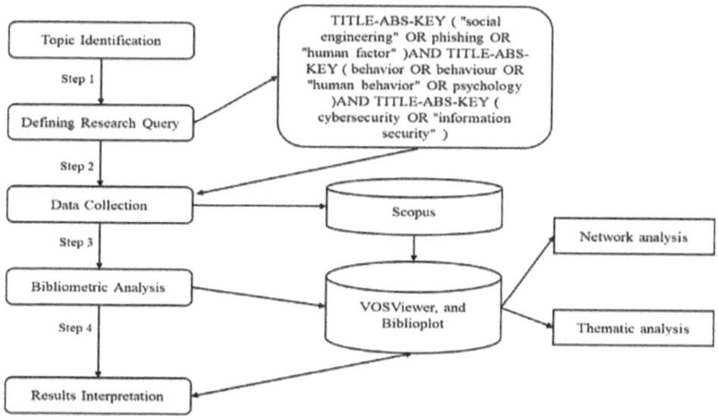

Fig. 1. Research framework for bibliometric analysis of human behavior in social engineering

2.2 Data Identification

Following the data collection stage, the data identification process was conducted to ensure the quality, consistency, and reliability of the dataset prior to analysis. The process began with screening and filtering the retrieved documents to ensure their relevance to the research topic, namely human behavior in social engineering within cybersecurity. Documents that were not aligned with the research scope were excluded. Subsequently, data cleaning was performed by removing duplicate entries and incomplete records to maintain dataset integrity. In addition, a keyword standardization process was applied to unify variations in terminology, such as "behavior" and "behaviour," as well as synonymous terms like "cybersecurity" and "information security." This step is essential to prevent the dispersion of similar concepts across different labels, which can negatively affect co-occurrence and clustering results.

To further enhance consistency, a thesaurus file was developed and applied within VOSviewer. The thesaurus was used to merge equivalent terms, eliminate irrelevant keywords, and harmonize frequently used variations in author keywords and index keywords. For example, terms such as "human behaviour," "user behavior," and "human behavior" were consolidated under a unified term, while general or non-informative terms were excluded. This approach improves the accuracy of network visualization and ensures that the resulting clusters more accurately represent the underlying knowledge structure.

2.3 Data Analysis

To examine the evolution of research trends (RQ1), Biblioplot was utilized to perform temporal analysis of the dataset. This includes evaluating annual scientific production and analyzing thematic evolution. Through this approach, it is possible to detect shifts in research focus, such as the transition from security awareness to cognitive bias and more recent developments in AI-driven cybersecurity approaches. Furthermore, to explore the conceptual structure of the domain (RQ2), a co-occurrence network analysis was conducted using VOSviewer, supported by Biblioplot. This analysis focuses on identifying key research themes, mapping relationships among keywords, and detecting clusters that represent major research areas within the field. In addition, to analyze the integration of the human-centric cybersecurity perspective (RQ3), this study applies a thematic analysis approach. This analysis is based on thematic mapping, particularly using centrality and density measures to classify themes into categories such as motor themes, basic themes, emerging themes, and niche themes.

3 Results and Discussion

The increasing complexity of social engineering attacks has stimulated the development of a multidisciplinary body of knowledge that integrates cybersecurity, psychology, behavioral science, and artificial intelligence. Mapping this evolving landscape is crucial for understanding the dominant themes that shape the field, the relationships among key concepts, and the extent to which human-centric perspectives have been incorporated into contemporary cybersecurity research.

3.1 Temporal Evolution of Research on Human Behavior in Social Engineering

Understanding the temporal evolution of research is essential to capture how scholarly attention and thematic priorities have developed within the domain of human behavior in social engineering. Bibliometric approaches enable the identification of publication growth patterns and thematic shifts, providing insights into how a research field matures over time [7]. In this context, the increasing complexity of cyber threats has driven a transition from traditional security-focused studies toward more behavior-oriented investigations, reflecting the growing recognition of human factors as a critical component in cybersecurity.

The results of the temporal analysis Fig. 2 reveal a clear and continuous growth in research on human behavior in social engineering within cybersecurity over the observed period (2007–2026). In the early phase (2007–2012), the number of publications remained relatively low and stable, indicating that this research area was still emerging and had not yet gained significant academic attention.

Figure 2 presents four complementary indicators of the temporal development of the research field. The blue bars represent annual research productivity, defined as the number of publications produced each year. The orange bars indicate cited documents, referring to the number of publications that have received at least one citation rather than the total citation count. The percentage values above the orange bars show the proportion of published documents that have been cited. In addition, the horizontal green dashed line represents the dataset H-index threshold ($H = 57$), indicating that at least 57 publications in the dataset have received 57 or more citations. The green star highlights the publication with the highest citation impact within the dataset, providing an indication of particularly influential contributions in the field.

Starting from around 2013, a gradual increase in research productivity can be observed, followed by a more pronounced growth after 2018. This trend suggests that the topic began to attract wider interest, likely driven by the increasing prevalence of cyber threats targeting human vulnerabilities. The most significant growth occurs in the period 2021–2025, where the number of publications rises sharply, reaching its peak

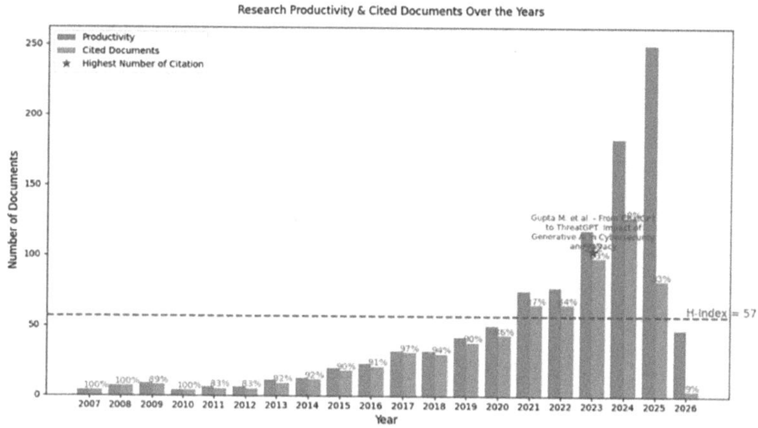

Fig. 2. Annual research productivity (number of publications) cited documents (publications receiving at least one citation), citation ratio, and H-index trend in human behavior and social engineering research (2007–2026)

in 2025. This surge reflects the rapid expansion of research in response to the growing complexity of social engineering attacks and the recognition of human behavior as a critical factor in cybersecurity.

In terms of citation patterns, earlier publications (2007–2016) show relatively high citation ratios compared to their productivity, indicating that foundational studies during this period had a strong influence on subsequent research. As the number of publications increases in later years, the proportion of cited documents becomes more varied, which is typical in rapidly expanding research fields where newer publications have had less time to accumulate citations.

Notably, the data also highlight a peak in citation impact in recent years, particularly around 2023–2024, suggesting the emergence of highly influential studies. This is further supported by the presence of highly cited works related to generative AI and cybersecurity, indicating a shift toward integrating advanced technologies into human-centric cybersecurity research.

In addition to publication and citation trends, Fig. 3 provides deeper insights into the evolution of key research themes over time through keyword occurrence analysis. Figure 3 illustrates the temporal dynamics of the most frequently occurring keywords, where bubble size reflects annual occurrence frequency and larger bubbles indicate periods of increased research attention. During the early phase (2007–2012), keywords such as information security and human factor appear with relatively low and stable frequencies, indicating that research was still centered on foundational security concepts with limited emphasis on behavioral dimensions. This aligns with the initial stage of the field, where technical perspectives dominated and human aspects were only beginning to be explored.

From 2013 onwards, there is a noticeable increase in keywords such as phishing, social engineering, and security awareness, suggesting a transition toward understanding human vulnerabilities and user-related risks. This shift reflects the growing recognition

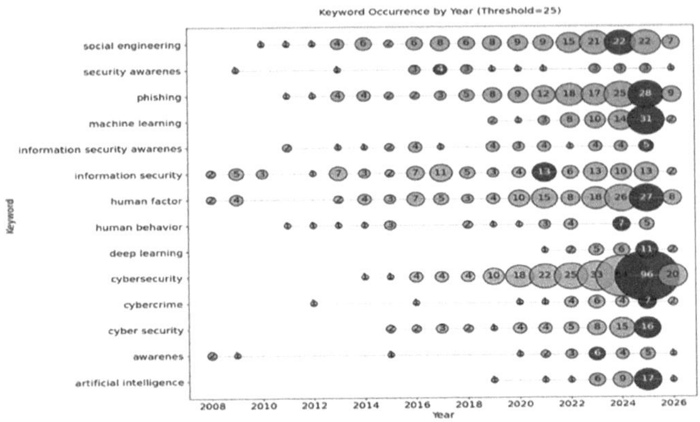

Fig. 3. Temporal evolution of high-frequency keywords in human behavior and social engineering research (threshold = 25 occurrences). Bubble size represents annual keyword frequency, while the horizontal trajectory indicates the persistence of keywords over time

that attackers increasingly exploit human behavior rather than purely technical weaknesses. A more significant transformation occurs after 2018, where keywords such as cybersecurity show a sharp rise in occurrence, becoming one of the most dominant terms in the dataset. At the same time, behavioral-related terms such as human behavior and awareness continue to grow, indicating the strengthening integration of human-centric perspectives within cybersecurity research. Notably, in recent years (2021–2025), there is a clear emergence of technology-driven keywords such as machine learning, deep learning, and artificial intelligence. The rapid increase in these terms suggests a shift toward data-driven and automated approaches in addressing social engineering threats.

3.2 Conceptual Structure and Thematic Clustering Based on Keyword Co-Occurrence

Understanding the conceptual structure of research on human behavior in social engineering is essential to reveal how key themes are interconnected within cybersecurity studies. Previous research has consistently shown that social engineering attacks are strongly rooted in human vulnerabilities, particularly behavioral and psychological factors, which makes this domain inherently multidisciplinary [13, 22]. The keyword co-occurrence analysis reveals a structured and interconnected research landscape composed of three major thematic clusters, each representing a distinct yet related dimension of the domain. As illustrated in Fig. 4, the network is centered around key terms such as cybersecurity and phishing, which act as bridging nodes connecting multiple thematic areas. This indicates that the field is not fragmented but rather integrated through shared concepts across behavioral and technical perspectives.

The red cluster emphasizes human-related aspects, particularly human factors, security awareness, and decision-making. This finding aligns with previous studies that identify human behavior as a primary vulnerability exploited in social engineering attacks [8, 35]. The presence of terms such as phishing susceptibility and protection motivation theory further suggests that this cluster is grounded in psychological and behavioral theories used to explain user responses to cyber threats.

The blue cluster reflects the intersection between information security and user behavior, where concepts such as training, cyber hygiene, and privacy are prominent. This indicates that research in this area focuses on how user practices and awareness can influence security outcomes. Studies have shown that behavioral patterns and individual characteristics significantly affect users' ability to recognize and respond to phishing attempts [1, 9]. The strong linkage between this cluster and the central nodes suggests that user behavior plays a mediating role between awareness and actual security practices.

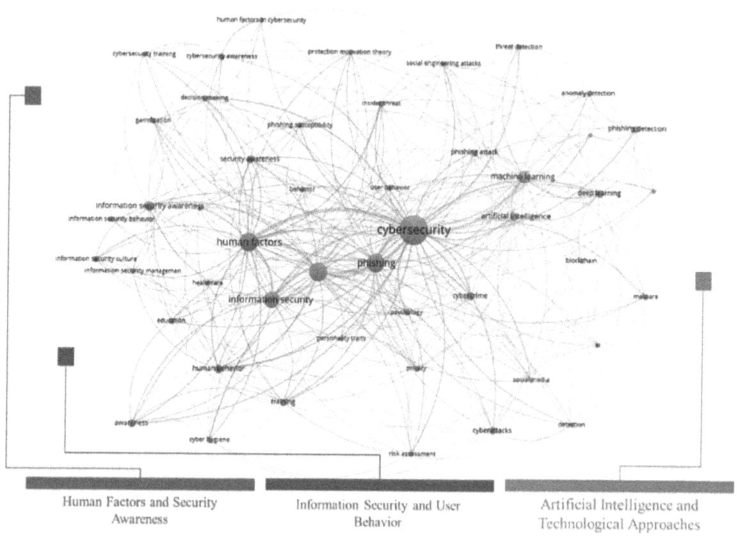

Fig. 4. Keyword co-occurrence network of human behavior in social engineering within cybersecurity

Meanwhile, the green cluster represents the technological dimension, characterized by keywords such as machine learning, artificial intelligence, deep learning, and phishing detection. This cluster highlights the increasing adoption of data-driven and automated approaches to address cybersecurity challenges. Recent research emphasizes that integrating AI with behavioral insights can significantly enhance the detection and prevention of social engineering attacks [30].

Figure 4 primarily focuses on identifying the conceptual structure of the research domain by grouping related keywords into thematic clusters. The visualization reveals how the field is organized into major knowledge areas and serves as the basis for interpreting the dominant research themes. The interconnections among these clusters demonstrate that the domain is inherently multidisciplinary, combining human-centered perspectives with technological solutions. For example, the linkage between user behavior (blue cluster) and AI-based detection (green cluster) suggests an emerging trend toward behavior-aware security systems. Similarly, the connection between human factors (red cluster) and information security practices (blue cluster) indicates that awareness alone is insufficient without practical behavioral implementation.

3.3 Integration of Human-Centric Cybersecurity Perspective and Research Gaps

The increasing complexity of cybersecurity threats has led to a growing recognition that technical solutions alone are insufficient to address modern attack vectors, particularly those exploiting human vulnerabilities. As a result, the concept of human-centric cybersecurity has emerged as a critical approach that emphasizes the role of human behavior, cognition, and decision-making in shaping security outcomes. This perspective highlights the need to integrate psychological and behavioral insights into cybersecurity frameworks to better understand and mitigate risks associated with social engineering attacks [20].

In the context of social engineering, human-centric approaches are particularly relevant, as attackers often rely on manipulation techniques that exploit trust, emotions, and cognitive biases rather than technical system weaknesses. Previous studies have emphasized that user behavior, awareness, and psychological traits significantly influence susceptibility to such attacks, reinforcing the importance of incorporating human factors into cybersecurity strategies [17, 19]. This has encouraged researchers to move beyond purely technical defenses and consider interdisciplinary approaches that combine behavioral science with information security.

Figure 5 presents the overlay visualization of keywords based on their average publication year. The color gradient ranges from earlier topics (blue-green) to more recent topics (yellow), allowing the identification of thematic shifts within the research domain. Established themes such as information security, psychology, personality traits, security awareness, and human factors are associated with earlier publication periods, indicating that initial studies primarily focused on understanding user vulnerabilities, security awareness, and behavioral aspects of cybersecurity. These topics form the intellectual foundation of the field and reflect the early recognition that human behavior represents a critical component of cybersecurity risk.

In contrast, more recent themes are concentrated around artificial intelligence, machine learning, natural language processing, phishing detection, and cybersecurity awareness. The emergence of these topics suggests a gradual transition from awareness-oriented research toward technology-assisted and predictive approaches. Rather than focusing solely on user education and behavioral responses, recent studies increasingly employ computational methods to detect, predict, and mitigate social engineering attacks. This temporal shift indicates the growing influence of data-driven cybersecurity strategies and highlights the expanding role of AI-based technologies in addressing human-centered security challenges.

Meanwhile, Fig. 6 illustrates the keyword co-occurrence network based on occurrence frequency. Unlike Fig. 5, which emphasizes temporal development, Fig. 6 focuses on the structural relationships among research themes and the relative prominence of keywords within the field. The network retains the same cluster composition identified in Fig. 4, enabling direct comparison between the conceptual structure and the prominence of individual topics. The blue cluster is centered on cybersecurity, phishing, and social engineering; the red cluster represents human-centric and behavioral dimensions; while

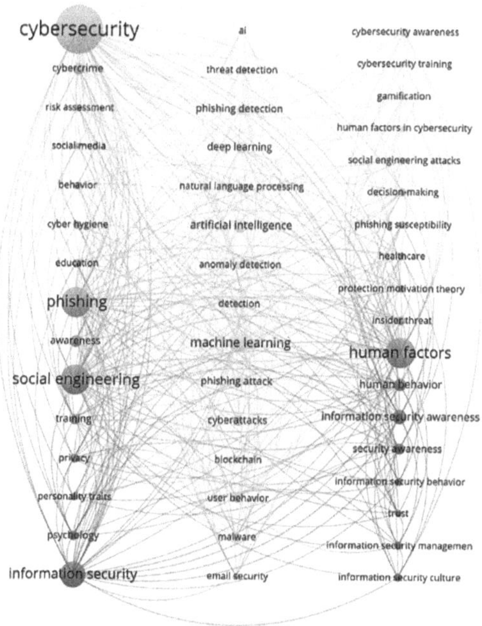

Fig. 5. Temporal evolution of research themes based on average publication year within the human behavior and social engineering domain

the green cluster reflects technology-driven approaches including artificial intelligence, machine learning, and phishing detection.

The visualization reveals that cybersecurity-related topics remain the dominant research focus, as indicated by the larger node sizes and stronger interconnections surrounding cybersecurity, phishing, and social engineering. Human-centric concepts such as human factors, human behavior, and decision-making are also well represented but remain largely concentrated within their own cluster. Similarly, technology-oriented themes form a separate cluster centered on AI and machine learning applications. The persistence of these relatively distinct clusters suggests that behavioral and technological perspectives continue to evolve alongside one another rather than as a fully integrated research paradigm.

Although Fig. 6 retains the same cluster composition identified in Fig. 4, its analytical purpose differs. Figure 4 was used to establish the conceptual structure of the field by identifying major thematic clusters. In contrast, Fig. 6 focuses on the relationships among these clusters, allowing the assessment of whether behavioral, technological, and cybersecurity-oriented themes have evolved as an integrated body of knowledge or as relatively independent research streams.

Meanwhile, Fig. 7 presents a thematic mapping analysis that categorizes research topics based on their centrality (relevance) and density (development level), distinguishing between novel (recent) and established (older) research themes. This visualization enables a deeper understanding of how human-centric cybersecurity topics are positioned within the research landscape and provides a strong basis for identifying research

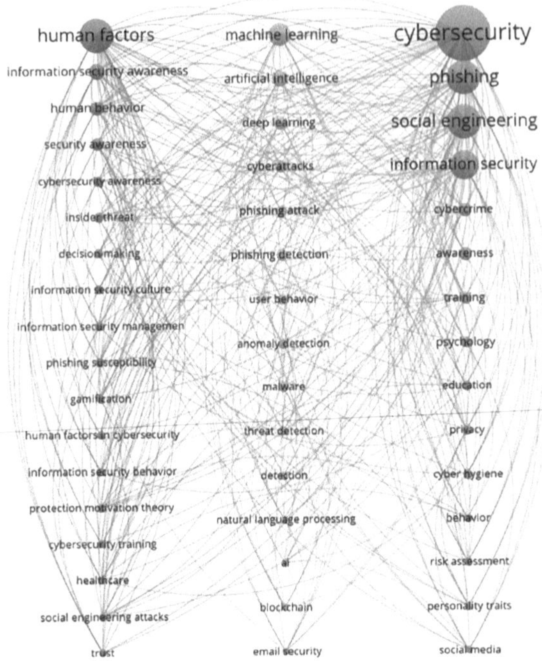

Fig. 6. Cross-cluster integration of behavioral, technological, and cybersecurity themes in human-centric cybersecurity research

gaps and potential future directions. In the novel publication year perspective (Fig. 7a), cybersecurity appears as a core theme (Q1) with high centrality and density, indicating that it is both highly relevant and well-developed in recent research. In contrast, topics such as machine learning, artificial intelligence, and deep learning are positioned near the core but slightly less dense, suggesting that they are rapidly developing and becoming increasingly central to the field. Meanwhile, themes such as phishing attack, detection, and user behavior fall into the emerging quadrants (Q2–Q3), indicating that these areas are gaining attention but are not yet fully mature.

Notably, behavioral-related themes such as decision-making and cyber hygiene are in lower-density regions, suggesting that although these topics are recognized, they remain underdeveloped compared to technical domains. This highlights a critical imbalance where technological advancements are progressing faster than the theoretical and empirical understanding of human behavior in cybersecurity contexts. In the older publication perspective (Fig. 7b), topics such as phishing, social engineering, and human factors are positioned within the mature quadrant (Q5), indicating that these areas have been extensively studied and are well-established in literature. However, themes such as privacy, training, education, and psychology appear in isolated or declining quadrants (Q6–Q8), suggesting that although they were previously explored, they have not evolved at the same pace as emerging technological topics.

These findings align with previous studies that highlight the need to bridge the gap between human factors and technological solutions in cybersecurity. For instance,

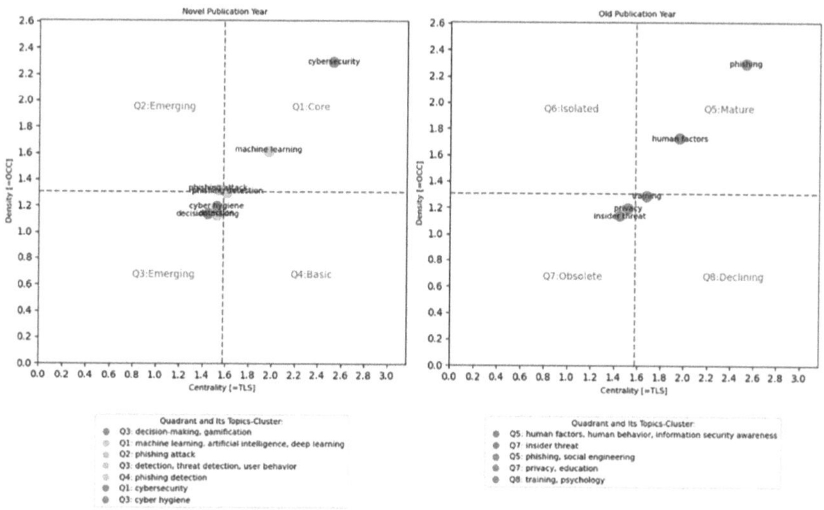

Fig. 7. Thematic evolution of research topics based on centrality and density in human behavior and social engineering

research has emphasized that human behavior remains one of the most critical vulnerabilities in cybersecurity systems and requires deeper integration with technical defenses [2]. Similarly, studies have shown that phishing susceptibility is strongly influenced by psychological and behavioral traits, reinforcing the importance of human-centered approaches [33, 37].

Furthermore, recent research highlights that while machine learning and AI have significantly improved threat detection, their effectiveness is limited without incorporating user behavior and contextual understanding [28]. Other studies also emphasize the role of cognitive biases and decision-making processes in shaping user responses to cyber threats, suggesting that purely technical solutions are insufficient [14]. In addition, the growing complexity of cyber threats has led to calls for integrated frameworks that combine behavioral science with cybersecurity technologies to develop more adaptive and resilient systems [10, 11].

4 Conclusion

This study demonstrates that the research landscape of human behavior in social engineering is not merely evolving, but undergoing a directional transformation dominated by technological acceleration. While the volume and complexity of research have increased significantly, this growth is disproportionately driven by advances in AI and machine learning, rather than by a deeper understanding of human behavior itself. The findings expose a fundamental misalignment within the field. Human factors despite being widely acknowledged as the primary attack surface in social engineering remain conceptually underdeveloped and weakly embedded within dominant cybersecurity models. Instead of being treated as a core analytical component, human behavior is still frequently positioned as a peripheral variable, resulting in a fragmented research structure where behavioral insights and technological solutions coexist but rarely converge. More critically, the current trajectory of research suggests that the field is advancing toward increasingly sophisticated detection mechanisms without adequately addressing the cognitive and behavioral mechanisms that enable attacks in the first place. This creates a paradox: as cybersecurity systems become more intelligent, they remain structurally limited by an incomplete understanding of the human element they are designed to protect. Future progress in this domain depends not on further technological refinement alone, but on the development of integrated, behavior-aware cybersecurity models that explicitly incorporate cognitive processes, decision dynamics, and psychological vulnerabilities as fundamental design components rather than secondary considerations.

References

1. Abroshan, H., et al.: Phishing happens beyond technology: the effects of human Behaviors and demographics on each step of a phishing process. IEEE Access. **9**, 44928–44949 (2021). https://doi.org/10.1109/ACCESS.2021.3066383
2. Albladi, S.M., Weir, G.R.S.: A Semi-automated Security Advisory System to Resist Cyber-Attack in Social Networks. Presented at the (2018). doi:https://doi.org/10.1007/978-3-319-98443-8_14.
3. AlNusif, M.: Emerging threats in cybersecurity: a comprehensive analysis of DDoS and social engineering attacks. Int. J. Eng. Comput. Sci. **14**(07), 27473–27487 (2025). https://doi.org/10.18535/ijecs.v14i07.5185
4. Asfour, M., Murillo, J.C.: Harnessing large language models to simulate realistic human responses to social engineering attacks: a case study. Int. J. Cybersecurity Intell. Cybercrime. **6**(2), 21–49 (2023). https://doi.org/10.52306/2578-3289.1172
5. Chowdhury, A., et al.: A comprehensive review of phishing in cybersecurity: risks, impacts, and defence strategies. Int. J. Sci. Res. Eng. Manag. **08**(10), 1–7 (2024). https://doi.org/10.55041/IJSREM38040
6. van Eck, N.J., Waltman, L.: Software survey: VOSviewer, a computer program for bibliometric mapping. Scientometrics. **84**(2), 523–538 (2010). https://doi.org/10.1007/s11192-009-0146-3
7. van Eck, N.J., Waltman, L.: Visualizing bibliometric networks. In: Measuring Scholarly Impact, pp. 285–320. Springer International Publishing, Cham (2014). https://doi.org/10.1007/978-3-319-10377-8_13
8. Fan, W., et al.: Social engineering: I-E based model of human weakness for attack and Defense investigations. Int. J. Comput. Netw. Inf. Secur. **9**(1), 1–11 (2017). https://doi.org/10.5815/ijcnis.2017.01.01
9. Gallo, L., et al.: The human factor in phishing: collecting and analyzing user behavior when reading emails. Comput. Secur. **139**, 103671 (2024). https://doi.org/10.1016/j.cose.2023.103671
10. Hadlington, L.: Employees attitude towards cyber security and risky online behaviours: an empirical assessment in the United Kingdom. Int. J. Cyber Criminol. **12**(1), 269–281 (2018)
11. Hadlington, L.: Human factors in cybersecurity; examining the link between internet addiction, impulsivity, attitudes towards cybersecurity, and risky cybersecurity behaviours. Heliyon. **3**(7), e00346 (2017). https://doi.org/10.1016/j.heliyon.2017.e00346

12. Hussain, F., et al.: Understanding human behavior in phishing attacks across diverse user groups: an ethical hacking analysis. In: 2024 IEEE 1st Karachi Section Humanitarian Technology Conference (KHI-HTC), pp. 1–7. IEEE (2024). https://doi.org/10.1109/KHI-HTC60760.2024.10482040
13. Jeong, J., et al.: Towards an improved understanding of human factors in cybersecurity. In: 2019 IEEE 5th International Conference on Collaboration and Internet Computing (CIC), pp. 338–345. IEEE (2019). https://doi.org/10.1109/CIC48465.2019.00047
14. Junger, M., et al.: Priming and warnings are not effective to prevent social engineering attacks. Comput. Human Behav. **66**, 75–87 (2017). https://doi.org/10.1016/j.chb.2016.09.012
15. Kavvadias, A., Kotsilieris, T.: Understanding the role of demographic and psychological factors in users' susceptibility to phishing emails: a review. Appl. Sci. **15**(4), 2236 (2025). https://doi.org/10.3390/app15042236
16. Kudalkar, M. et al.: Exploring phishing awareness and user behavior: a survey-based investigation. Int. J. Res. Appl. Sci. Eng. Technol. 12, 4, 4713–4718 (2024). 10.22214/ijraset.2024.61106.
17. Marble, J.L. et al.: The Human Factor in Cybersecurity: Robust & Intelligent Defense BT - Cyber Warfare: Building the Scientific Foundation. Presented at the (2015). doi:https://doi.org/10.1007/978-3-319-14039-1_9.
18. Mashiane, T., Kritzinger, E.: Identifying behavioral constructs in relation to user cybersecurity behavior Eurasian J. Soc. Sci. 9, 2, 98–122 (2021). https://doi.org/10.15604/ejss.2021.09.02.004.
19. Masmoudi, S.: Unveiling the Human Factor in Cybercrime and Cybersecurity: Motivations, Behaviors, Vulnerabilities, Mitigation Strategies, and Research Methods BT - Cybercrime Unveiled: Technologies for Analysing Legal Complexity. Presented at the (2025). doi:https://doi.org/10.1007/978-3-031-80557-8_3.
20. Moustafa, A.A., et al.: The role of user behaviour in improving cyber security management. Front. Psychol. **12** (2021). https://doi.org/10.3389/fpsyg.2021.561011
21. Pasupuleti, M.K.: Human-centric cybersecurity: evaluating phishing susceptibility using Behavioral metrics. Int. J. Acad. Ind. Res. Innov. **05**(06), 412–424 (2025). https://doi.org/10.62311/nesx/rphcrcscrcp4
22. Rahman, T., et al.: Human factors in cybersecurity: a scoping review. In: The 12th International Conference on Advances in Information Technology, pp. 1–11. ACM, New York, NY, USA (2021). https://doi.org/10.1145/3468784.3468789
23. Rajalim, S.: Understanding human vulnerabilities: a study on social engineering techniques in cybersecurity. Int. J. Res. Appl. Sci. Eng. Technol. **13**(6), 1660–1666 (2025). https://doi.org/10.22214/ijraset.2025.72502
24. Ramchandra, B.S., Dond, V.T.: Cyber linguistics: an exploration of methodologies use by hackers to tap the English language for social engineering and phishing schemes. Int. J. Sci. Res. Eng. Manag. **09**(04), 1–9 (2025). https://doi.org/10.55041/IJSREM44361
25. Reddy Pothu, A.: Behavioural analysis of end-users for enhancing cybersecurity awareness and prevention. AVE Trends Intell. Comput. Lett. **1**(1), 31–40 (2025). https://doi.org/10.64091/ATICL.2025.000094
26. Rohini, D.S.G.A., et al.: Social engineering attacks in cybersecurity. Int. J. Res. Appl. Sci. Eng. Technol. **13**(5), 7590–7594 (2025). https://doi.org/10.22214/ijraset.2025.72253
27. Sahni, M., Kalra, R.: The science of social engineering – a legal and Behavioral perspective on cybersecurity awareness. In: Izazovi međunarodnog krivičnog prava i krivičnog prava: tom II, pp. 75–84. Udruženje za međunarodno krivično pravo (2025). https://doi.org/10.51204/Zbornik_UMKP_25134A
28. Sarker, I.H., et al.: Effectiveness analysis of machine learning classification models for predicting personalized context-aware smartphone usage. J. Big Data. **6**(1), 57 (2019). https://doi.org/10.1186/s40537-019-0219-y

29. Shafin, N., et al.: Thematic analysis of multiple sclerosis research by enhanced strategic diagram. Mult. Scler. J. **28**(14), 2160–2170 (2022). https://doi.org/10.1177/13524585221075542
30. Sridhar, A.P.: Analyzing social engineering attack patterns using Behavioral psychology and AI-driven Defense mechanisms. J. Internet Serv. Inf. Secur. **15**(1), 502–519 (2025). https://doi.org/10.58346/JISIS.2025.I1.033
31. Pujari, S.R., Hussain, M.A.: Human factor in cybersecurity: Behavioral insights into phishing and social engineering attacks. Nanotechnol. Perceptions., 630, 10.62441/nano-ntp.vi.3556–642 (2024)
32. Taib, R. et al.: Social Engineering and Organisational Dependencies in Phishing Attacks. Presented at the (2019). doi:https://doi.org/10.1007/978-3-030-29381-9_35.
33. Troublefield, T.C.: Human-centric artificial intelligence in cybersecurity: integrating Cyberpsychology for the next generation Defense mechanisms. Int. J. Secur. **16**(1), 1–25 (2025)
34. Tsauri, M.S.: Human vulnerabilities to social engineering attacks: a systematic literature review for building a human firewall. J. Appl. Inform. Comput. **9**(4), 1127–1136 (2025). https://doi.org/10.30871/jaic.v9i4.9585
35. Wang, Z., et al.: Social engineering in cybersecurity: effect mechanisms, human vulnerabilities and attack methods. IEEE Access. **9**, 11895–11910 (2021). https://doi.org/10.1109/ACCESS.2021.3051633
36. Wijaya, A., Hermawan, B.: BiblioPlot: Enhanced Data Visualization for Bibliometric Analysis (2025). https://biblioplot. metlit.net/
37. Zhuo, S., et al.: SoK: human-centered phishing susceptibility. ACM Trans. Priv. Secur. **26**(3), 1–27 (2023). https://doi.org/10.1145/3575797

Posters

Enhanced Security Operations Center for Cyber Threat Detection and Mitigation Using Agentic AI

Alde Alanda[1,2](✉) and Nurul Hidayah Ab Rahman[2]

[1] Department of Information Technology, Politeknik Negeri Padang, Padang, Indonesia
alde@pnp.ac.id

[2] Faculty of Computer Science and Information Technology, Universiti Tun Hussein Onn Malaysia, Parit Raja, Malaysia
hidayahar@uthm.edu.my

Abstract. Cyber threats are increasing rapidly in both scale and sophistication, creating significant challenges for organizations responsible for monitoring and protecting digital infrastructures. However, traditional SOC environments often rely heavily on rule-based detection mechanisms and manual analysis, resulting in alert fatigue, high false positive rates, and delayed incident response. This research pro-poses an Agentic AI–Enhanced Security Operations Center framework that integrates autonomous AI agents into an open-source SOC architecture. The proposed system aims to improve cyber threat detection, automate operational tasks, and enhance incident response efficiency. The study adopts the Design Science Research (DSR) methodology to design, implement, and evaluate the proposed artifact. The evaluation is conducted using simulated cyber-attack scenarios and benchmark datasets, including CSE-CIC-IDS2018 and Loghub-2.0. System performance is measured using SOC operational metrics such as Mean Time to Detect (MTTD), Mean Time to Respond (MTTR), Detection Rate, False Positive Rate (FPR), and MITRE ATT&CK coverage, along with agentic AI metrics such as Automation Rate and Autonomous Action Accuracy. The results are expected to demonstrate that integrating agentic AI into SOC workflows can significantly enhance operational efficiency and reduce analyst workload.

Keywords: Security Operations Center · Agentic AI · Cyber Threat Detection · SOC Automation · Cybersecurity

1 Introduction

Cyber-attacks are becoming more prevalent as evidenced by Reports of ransomware, malware, intrusion, cryptographic threats and other attacks are on the rise. As an example, a report by SonicWall has shown the increased of intrusion attempts from 11% to 5.3 trillion and ransomware attacks are increasing from 105% to 623 million attacks [1, 2]. It indicates that Protection against cyberattacks is an ongoing endeavour that requires a comprehensive approach and cooperation across technology, people, and processes. The

© The Author(s), under exclusive license to Springer Nature Switzerland AG 2027
Published by Springer Nature Switzerland AG 2027. All Rights Reserved
H. Neukirchen et al. (Eds.): ICDF2C 2026, LNICST 720, pp. 533–539, 2027.
https://doi.org/10.1007/978-3-032-37274-1

adoption of the strategy would enable organizations to be better prepared in addressing the ever-evolving threats in the inter-connected digital world.

At the same time, the global Artificial Intelligence (AI) market in the field of cybersecurity was valued at $24.8 billion in 2024. It is anticipated that the market will expand to $29.6 billion by 2025 and surpass $146.5 billion by 2034 [3]. The third wave of AI, known as Agentic AI, is poised to garner a substantial portion of this market. Agentic AI has been demonstrated to enhance the functionality of (SOCs) through the analysis of substantial datasets comprising threat intelligence, thereby facilitating the identification of authentic threats while minimizing the occurrence of false positives.

Therefore, this research aims to design, implement, and evaluate an Agentic AI–enhanced open-source SOC framework to improve cyber threat detection, analytical efficiency, and response capabilities.

2 Material and Method

2.1 Security Operation Center (SOC)

Security Operations Centers (SOCs) have evolved significantly in response to the increasing sophistication and frequency of cyber threats. Initially, SOCs primarily focused on monitoring security events, detecting incidents, and coordinating reactive responses. As cyberattacks became more advanced and persistent, SOCs expanded their capabilities to include proactive defense strategies such as predictive analytics, cyber threat intelligence, and AI-enabled automation. Modern SOCs integrate a wide range of security technologies and operational processes to support continuous log monitoring, threat detection, incident investigation, response orchestration, and regulatory compliance. This evolution reflects a transition from traditional reactive security operations to adaptive, intelligence-driven defense models that continuously anticipate and mitigate emerging cyber risks [4].

2.2 Agentic AI in SOC

Agentic AI is transforming the SOC landscape through automation of decision-making processes and adaptation to dynamic threats [5]. Agentic AI has been demonstrated to enhance workflow efficiency by automating tasks such as alert triage and incident response. In the context of cybersecurity, the application of this technology has been shown to facilitate autonomous threat detection and response. It has been reported that organisations which have adopted agentic AI for the purposes of security and governance have experienced significant benefits, including faster decision-making and improved risk management [6].

AI systems have been developed to facilitate dynamic access management by adjusting user access based on behavioural and risk factors, thereby aligning with zero trust principles. Furthermore, agentic AI perpetually observes activities, thereby identifying anomalous patterns with a view to detecting and mitigating insider threats prior to their escalation. Moreover, it has been demonstrated to assist in the reduction of financial losses incurred as a result of cyber security incidents that have been caused by applications that are not connected to one another. These incidents have been identified as a primary cause of breaches. The integration of these applications into existing identity and governance platforms has been demonstrated to enhance overall security and minimise financial losses from such incidents [6].

3 Results and Discussion

3.1 Proposed Agentic SOC Framework

The proposed architecture adopt from [4] for the baseline SOC based on the SOC lifecycle (Fig. 1).

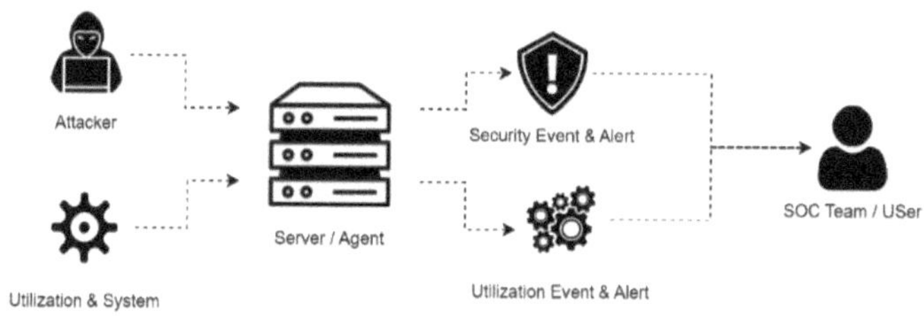

Fig. 1. SOC Architecture Baseline

The illustrated architecture represents a basic Security Operations Center (SOC) monitoring workflow in which both attacker-driven activities and normal system utilization generate events that are collected by a centralized server or agent. These events are processed and classified into security events and alerts, which indicate potential threats, and utilization events and alerts, which reflect system performance or operational conditions. The resulting alerts are then forwarded to the SOC team or end users for review and action. This architecture emphasizes centralized data collection, event categorization, and human-driven analysis, forming a foundational SOC model that provides visibility into both security incidents and system behavior but relies on manual interpretation and response rather than autonomous decision-making (Fig. 2).

The proposed framework introduces a five-layer Multi-Agent Agentic AI Security Operations Center (SOC) that enables autonomous cybersecurity operations across the entire incident lifecycle. The framework starts with the Data Collection and Monitoring Layer, where open-source tools such as Wazuh, Suricata, Zeek, and Filebeat collect security data from endpoints, networks, cloud services, and applications. The Data Processing and Detection Layer then normalizes and enriches the data before applying an XGBoost-based threat detection engine to identify anomalies and generate security alerts.

The core of the framework is the Multi-Agent Agentic AI Coordination Layer, where specialized AI agents collaboratively perform log analysis, alert triage, threat investigation, threat intelligence enrichment, response planning, and ticket management under the supervision of a Coordinator Agent. The Response and Automation Layer executes automated playbooks through SOAR platforms (TheHive and Cortex) to perform containment, mitigation, and recovery while integrating with external security systems.

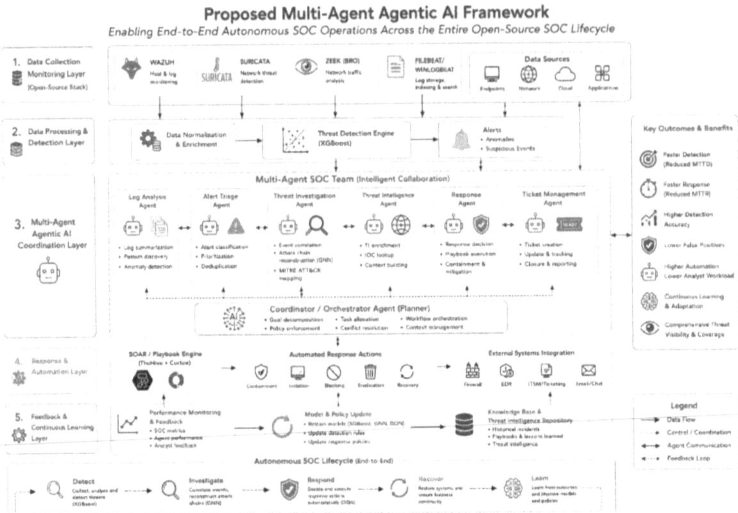

Fig. 2. Enhanced SOC with Agentic AI

Finally, the Feedback and Continuous Learning Layer continuously improves detection models, response policies, and the knowledge base using operational feedback. This architecture enables faster detection and response, higher automation, improved detection accuracy, reduced analyst workload, and continuous adaptation to evolving cyber threats.

Table 1. Metrics and Algorithms

SOC Phase	Metric	Algorithm	Reference
Detection	Detection Rate, FPR, F1	**XGBoost**	[9, 10]
Correlation	MITRE ATT&CK Coverage	**GNN**	[11]
Response	MTTD, MTTR, Automation Rate, Autonomous Accuracy	**Deep Q-Network (RL)**	[12, 13]

3.2 Evaluation Metric

The evaluation aims to compare a Baseline SOC with the proposed SOC integrated with Agentic AI capabilities, focusing on detection effectiveness, operational efficiency, and autonomous intelligence reliability.

No	Metric	Definition	Formula	Definition	Ref
1	**Detection Rate (Recall/TPR)**	Proportion of actual attacks correctly detected	TP/(TP + FN)	Measures SOC detection effectiveness	Forsberg & Frantti (2023), *Computers & Security*
2	**False Positive Rate (FPR)**	Proportion of benign events incorrectly classified as threats	FP/(FP + TN)	Direct indicator of alert fatigue and operational precision	Forsberg & Frantti (2023)
3	**F1-Score**	Harmonic mean of precision and recall	2PR/(P + R)	Balances detection performance and false alarms	Srinivas et al. 2025
4	**Mean Time To Detect (MTTD)**	Average time between attack occurrence and detection	Σ(Detection − Attack Time)/N	Global standard metric for SOC responsiveness	Srinivas et al. 2025
5	**Mean Time To Respond (MTTR)**	Average time between detection and mitigation	Σ(Response − Detection Time)/N	Key indicator of operational efficiency	Srinivas et al. 2025
6	**MITRE ATT&CK Coverage (%)**	Percentage of ATT&CK techniques successfully detected	(Detected Techniques/Total Tested) × 100%	Measures tactical detection depth and coverage	Chamkar et al. (2024)
7	**Automation Rate (%)**	Percentage ofincidents handled autonomously	Automated Incidents/Total Incidents	Quantifies AgenticAI contribution	Srinivas et al. 2025
8	**Autonomous Action Accuracy**	Proportion of automated mitigation actions that are correct	Correct Automated Actions/Total Automated Actions	Validates reliabilityof AI-driven decisions	Srinivas et al. 2025

4 Conclusion

This study presents an Agentic AI–Enhanced Security Operations Center (SOC) framework designed to address key limitations SOC environments, By integrating autonomous AI agents into an open-source SOC architecture, the proposed framework enables intelligent automation of threat detection, analysis, and response processes.

Using the Design Science Research (DSR) methodology, the framework was systematically designed and evaluated through simulated cyber-attack scenarios and benchmark datasets such as CSE-CIC-IDS2018 and Loghub-2.0. The evaluation based on SOC operational metrics including Mean Time to Detect (MTTD), Mean Time to Respond (MTTR), Detection Rate, and False Positive Rate (FPR) demonstrates the potential of agentic AI to significantly improve detection accuracy, reduce response time, and enhance overall SOC efficiency.

Furthermore, the incorporation of agentic AI metrics such as Automation Rate and Autonomous Action Accuracy highlights the system's capability to reduce human workload while maintaining reliable decision-making. Overall, this research confirms that agentic AI can play a transformative role in modern SOC operations, enabling more adaptive, scalable, and efficient cybersecurity defense mechanisms.

Future work may focus on real-world deployment, integration with advanced threat intelligence platforms, and further enhancement of agent collaboration and explainability.

References

1. VanKirk, B.: Sonicwall cyber threat report (2024). https://www.sonicwall.com/medialibrary/en/white-paper/2024-cyber-threat-report.pdf
2. Sonicwall, "2021 SonicWall Cyber Threat Report," 2021 SonicWall, pp. 1–38 (2021). https://www.sonicwall.com/resources/2020-cyber-threat-report-pdf/
3. Precedence Research, "Artificial intelligence (AI) in cybersecurity market size, share, and trends 2024 to 2034." Accessed 13 Jan 2025. https://www.precedenceresearch.com/artificial-intelligence-in-cybersecurity-market
4. Perera, A., Rathnayaka, S., Perera, N.D., Madushanka, W.W., Senarathne, A.N.: The next gen security operation center. In: 2021 6th International Conference for Convergence in Technology, I2CT 2021. Institute of Electrical and Electronics Engineers Inc., April 2021. https://doi.org/10.1109/I2CT51068.2021.9418136
5. Columbus, L.: "Cybersecurity at AI speed: How agentic AI is supercharging SOC teams in 2025," VentureBeat. Accessed 13 Jan 2026. https://venture-beat.com/ai/cybersecurity-at-ai-speed-agentic-ai-supercharging-soc/
6. Chiodi, M.: "Agentic AI in cybersecurity: Closing the last mile in identity security." Cerby. Accessed 13 Jan 2026. https://www.cerby.com/resources/blog/agentic-ai-in-cybersecurity
7. Muntean, M., Militaru, F.D.: Design science research framework for performance analysis using machine learning techniques. Electronics (Switzerland), **11**(16) (2022). https://doi.org/10.3390/electronics11162504
8. Peffers, K., Tuunanen, T., Rothenberger, M.A., Chatterjee, S.: A design science re-search methodology for information systems research. J. Manage. Inf. Syst. **24**(3) (2007) https://doi.org/10.2753/MIS0742-1222240302
9. Hu, Y., Xiao, K., Luo, L., Chen, L.: An XGBoost-based intrusion detection frame-work with interpretability analysis for IoT networks. Appl. Sci. **16**(2), 980 (2026). https://doi.org/10.3390/app16020980
10. Hosain, Y., Çakmak, M.: XAI-XGBoost: an innovative explainable intrusion detection approach for securing internet of medical things systems. Sci. Rep. **15**(1), 22278 (2025). https://doi.org/10.1038/s41598-025-07790-0
11. Zhong, M., Lin, M., Zhang, C., Xu, Z.: A survey on graph neural networks for intrusion detection systems: methods, trends and challenges. Comput. Secur. **141**, 103821 (2024). https://doi.org/10.1016/j.cose.2024.103821

12. Janardhanan, H.: A reinforcement learning approach to cybersecurity: deep Q-Net-works for threat modeling. In: 2025 International Conference on Machine Learning and Autonomous Systems (ICMLAS), pp. 265–270. IEEE, March 2025. https://doi.org/10.1109/ICMLAS64557.2025.10968270
13. Mpoporo, L.J., Owolawi, P.A., Tu, C.: Deep reinforcement learning algorithms for intrusion detection: a bibliometric analysis and systematic review. Appl. Sci. **16**(2), 1048 (2026). https://doi.org/10.3390/app16021048

Author Index

© ICST Institute for Computer Sciences, Social Informatics and Telecommunications Engineering 2027
Published by Springer Nature Switzerland AG 2027. All Rights Reserved

H. Neukirchen et al. (Eds.): ICDF2C 2026, LNICST 720, pp. 541–542, 2027.
https://doi.org/10.1007/978-3-032-37274-1

FSC
www.fsc.org
MIX
Papier | Fördert gute Waldnutzung
FSC® C083411

Kolibri 360 GmbH
Ferdinand-Jühlke-Straße 7
99095 Erfurt, Deutschland
produktsicherheit@kolibri360.de